Software Architect and .NET 8

Fourth Edition

Build enterprise applications using microservices, DevOps, EF Core, and design patterns for Azure

Gabriel Baptista

Francesco Abbruzzese

BIRMINGHAM—MUMBAI

Software Architecture with C# 12 and .NET 8

Fourth Edition

Publishing Product Manager: Lucy Wan

Acquisition Editor – Peer Reviews: Tejas Mhasvekar

Project Editor: Parvathy Nair

Content Development Editors: Ruksar Malik, Shazeen Iqbal, Lucy Wan

Copy Editor: Safis Editing

Technical Editor: Kushal Sharma

Proofreader: Safis Editing

Indexer: Rekha Nair

Presentation Designer: Ganesh Bhadwalkar

Senior Developer Relations Marketing Executive: Priyadarshini Sharma

First published: November 2019

Second edition: December 2020

Third edition: March 2022

Fourth edition: February 2024

Production reference: 1260224

Published by Packt Publishing Ltd.

Grosvenor House

11 St Paul's Square

Birmingham

B3 1RB, UK.

ISBN 978-1-80512-765-9

`www.packt.com`

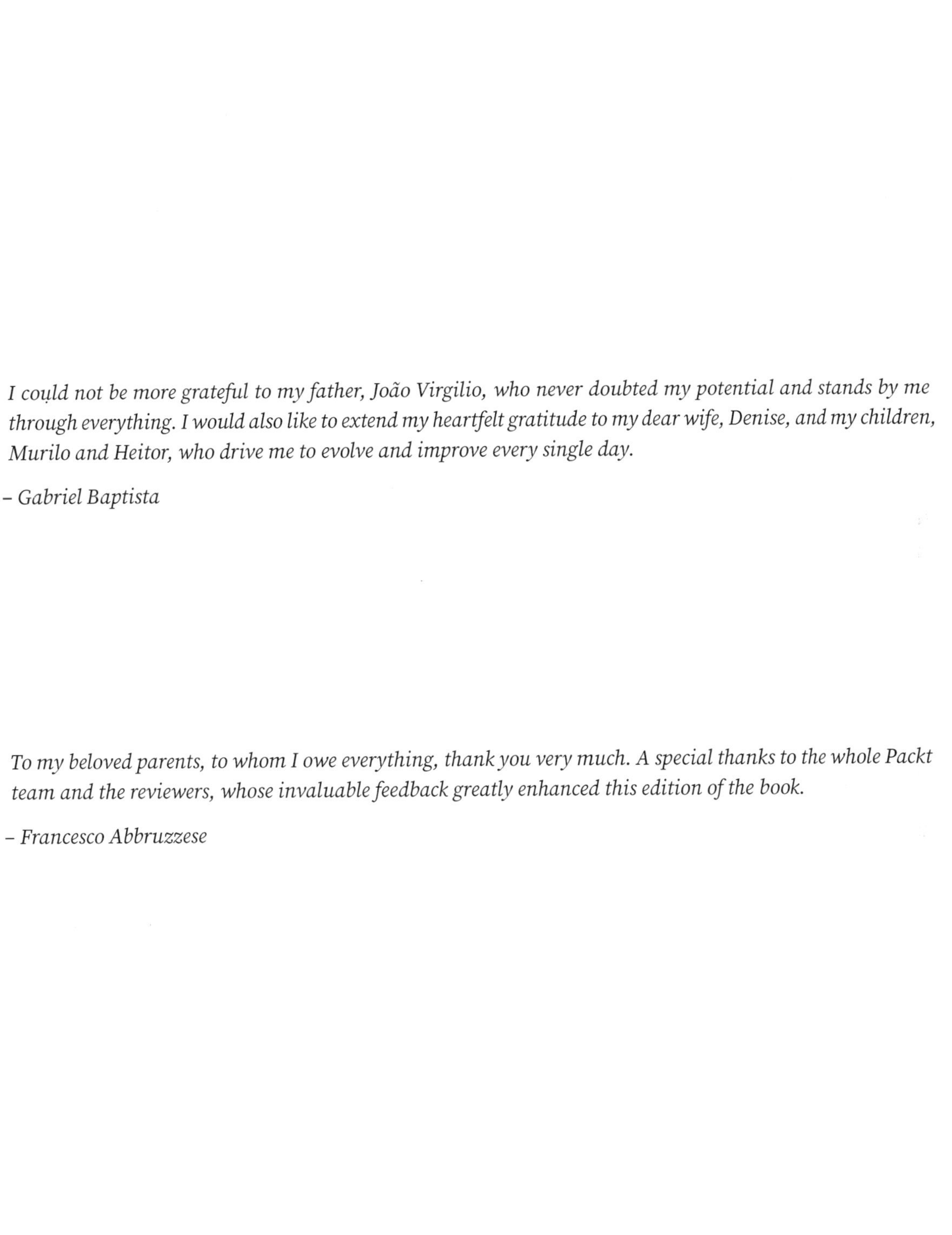

I could not be more grateful to my father, João Virgilio, who never doubted my potential and stands by me through everything. I would also like to extend my heartfelt gratitude to my dear wife, Denise, and my children, Murilo and Heitor, who drive me to evolve and improve every single day.

– Gabriel Baptista

To my beloved parents, to whom I owe everything, thank you very much. A special thanks to the whole Packt team and the reviewers, whose invaluable feedback greatly enhanced this edition of the book.

– Francesco Abbruzzese

Contributors

About the authors

Gabriel Baptista is a tech manager who leads various teams across a diverse range of projects using the Microsoft platform for industry and retail. Also an Azure specialist, he is responsible for designing a SaaS platform in partnership with Microsoft. In addition, he is a computing professor, has published many papers, and taught subjects such as software engineering, development, and architecture. He has also spoken at many global tech conferences over the past few years and co-founded SMIT, a software development company, and SmartLoad, the first cargo mobility insurtech in Brazil.

Francesco Abbruzzese has dedicated his entire life to his two great passions: software and powerlifting. He is the author of the Blazor Controls Toolkit library and contributed to the diffusion and evangelization of the Microsoft web stack since the first .NET version. His company, Mvcct Team, offers web applications, tools, and services for web technologies. His last product, SimpleProcess, is sophisticated Blazor and .NET microservices-based process management software. He has moved from working on AI systems for financial institutions to top-10 video game titles such as *Puma Street Soccer*.

About the reviewers

Kieran Foot is the lead software developer at ConnX Business Solutions Ltd, a small company based in the UK specializing in stock control and bespoke system integrations.

Having always had a thirst for knowledge, Kieran embarked on his software development journey in his early teens. He started with QBASIC and navigated through ASM, C, C++, and VB before finding his niche in C#.

He's passionate about delving into the .NET framework and sharing his discoveries, notably with the Packt Discord community. Kieran has also contributed to the book *Apps and Services with .NET 8* published by Packt, showcasing his commitment to both learning and teaching in the tech world.

I would like to thank the team at Packt for their kindness, guidance, and encouragement whilst on my journey as a new book reviewer.

Alexander Christov brings over 35 years of experience as a programmer and IT specialist, with a specific focus on desktop and web applications. His career began in 1984 at Infos, where he programmed on one of the initial four IBM PCs imported during the communist regime.

In his pursuit of excellence, Alexander has consistently pushed the boundaries of .NET technology, with a particular emphasis on the C# language. He transitioned from WebForms to MVC, then to .NET Core MVC, and is currently focused on .NET 8.

In a significant shift, he has chosen Blazor over JavaScript for front-end development.

Alexander's drive to develop versatile web applications has led him to work on extendable systems, culminating in the creation of CoreXF.

Currently, he manages his own consulting company, Code Solidi, and has been working closely with 100Programmers, a consulting agency and software development company based in London.

Learn more on Discord

To join the Discord community for this book – where you can share feedback, ask questions to the authors, and learn about new releases – follow the QR code below:

`https://packt.link/SoftwareArchitectureCSharp12Dotnet8`

Table of Contents

Chapter 2: Non-Functional Requirements 25

Chapter 3: Managing Requirements 55

Chapter 4: Best Practices in Coding C# 12 75

Chapter 5: Implementing Code Reusability in C# 12 105

Chapter 6: Design Patterns and .NET 8 Implementation 119

Chapter 7: Understanding the Different Domains in Software Solutions 139

Chapter 9: Testing Your Enterprise Application 205

Chapter 10: Deciding on the Best Cloud-Based Solution 233

Chapter 11: Applying a Microservice Architecture to Your Enterprise Application 251

Chapter 12: Choosing Your Data Storage in the Cloud 287

Chapter 13: Interacting with Data in C# – Entity Framework Core 309

Chapter 20: Kubernetes 535

Chapter 21: Case Study 573

Chapter 22: Case Study Extension: Developing .NET Microservices for Kubernetes 671

Answers 695

Other Books You May Enjoy 709

Index 713

Preface

This book covers the most common design patterns and frameworks involved in modern cloud-based and distributed software architectures. It discusses when and how to use each pattern by providing you with practical, real-world scenarios.

This book also presents techniques and processes such as DevOps, microservices, Kubernetes, continuous integration, and cloud computing so that you can have a best-in-class software solution developed and delivered to your customers.

This book will help you to understand the product that your customer wants from you. It will guide you to deliver and solve the biggest problems you may face during development. It also covers the dos and don'ts that you need to follow when you manage your application in a cloud-based environment. You will learn about different architectural approaches, such as layered architectures, onion architecture, service-oriented architecture, microservices, single-page applications, and cloud architecture, and understand how to apply them to specific business requirements.

Finally, you will deploy code in remote environments or on the cloud using Azure.

All the concepts in this book will be explained with the help of a real-world practical use case where design principles make a world of difference when creating safe and robust applications. By the end of the book, you will be able to develop and deliver highly scalable and secure enterprise-ready applications that meet your end customers' business needs.

It is also worth mentioning that this book will not only cover the best practices that a software architect should follow for developing C# and .NET Core solutions, but it will also discuss all the environments that you need to master in order to develop a software product based on the latest trends, such as Kubernetes, ASP .NET Core, and Blazor.

This fourth edition has seen improvement in terms of code, level of detail, and explanations and was adapted to the new opportunities offered by C# 12 and .NET 8.

Moreover, we have also added a lot of completely new content, such as a chapter dedicated to the book case study and a chapter dedicated to .NET development for Kubernetes as an extension to the case study, since we use insights from the case study to build on this chapter.

Who this book is for

This book is for engineers and senior developers who are aspiring to become architects or wish to build enterprise applications with the .NET stacks. It is also for any software architect who wishes to improve their knowledge related to enterprise solutions based on .NET and C#. Notably, experience with C# and .NET is required.

What this book covers

Chapter 1, Understanding the Importance of Software Architecture, explains the basics of software architecture. This chapter will help you develop the right mindset to face customer requirements and then select the right tools, patterns, and frameworks.

Chapter 2, Non-Functional Requirements, guides you in an important stage of application development, that is, collecting and accounting for all constraints and goals that the application must fulfill, such as scalability, availability, resiliency, performance, multithreading, interoperability, and security.

Chapter 3, Managing Requirements, describes techniques for managing requirements, bugs, and other information about your applications. While most of the concepts are general, the chapter focuses on the usage of Azure DevOps and GitHub.

Chapter 4, Best Practices in Coding C# 12, describes best practices to be followed when developing .NET 8 applications with C# 12, including metrics that evaluate the quality of your software and how to measure them with the help of all the tools included in Visual Studio.

Chapter 5, Implementing Code Reusability in C# 12, describes patterns and best practices to maximize code reusability in your .NET 8 applications with C# 12. It also discusses the importance of code refactoring.

Chapter 6, Design Patterns and .NET 8 Implementation, describes common software patterns with .NET 8 examples. Here, you will learn the importance of patterns and best practices for using them.

Chapter 7, Understanding the Different Domains in Software Solutions, describes the modern domain-driven design software production methodology and related design patterns and architectures. Here, you will also learn how to use it to face complex applications that require several knowledge domains and how to use it to take advantage of cloud and microservices-based architectures.

Chapter 8, Understanding DevOps Principles and CI/CD, describes the DevOps basis for software development and evolution. Here, you will learn how to organize your application's continuous integration/continuous delivery cycle, discussing the opportunities and difficulties in reaching this scenario. It also describes how to automate the whole deployment process, from the creation of a new release in your source repository through various testing and approval steps to the final deployment of the application in the actual production environment. Here, you will learn how to use Azure Pipelines and GitHub Actions to automate the whole deployment process.

Chapter 9, Testing Your Enterprise Application, describes how to test your applications, including the various kinds of tests that must be included in the development lifecycle and the test-driven development methodology. Here, you will also learn how to test .NET Core applications with xUnit and see how easily you can develop and maintain code that satisfies your specifications with the help of test-driven design.

Here, you will also learn how to use functional tests to verify automatically whether a version of a whole application conforms to the agreed functional specifications.

Chapter 10, Deciding on the Best Cloud-Based Solution, gives you a wide overview of the tools and resources available in the cloud, and more specifically on Microsoft Azure. Here, you will learn how to search for the right tools and resources and how to configure them to fulfill your needs.

Chapter 11, Applying a Microservice Architecture to Your Enterprise Application, offers a broad overview of microservices and Docker containers. Here, you will learn how the microservices-based architecture takes advantage of all the opportunities offered by the cloud, and you will see how to use microservices to achieve flexibility, high throughput, and reliability in the cloud. You will learn how to use containers and Docker to mix different technologies in your architecture as well as make your software platform independent.

Chapter 12, Choosing Your Data Storage in the Cloud, describes the main storage engines available in the cloud and in Microsoft Azure. Here, you will learn how to choose the best storage engines to achieve the read/write parallelism you need, how to configure them, and how to interact with them from your C# code.

Chapter 13, Interacting with Data in C# – Entity Framework Core, explains in detail how your application can interact with various storage engines with the help of **Object-Relational Mappings** (**ORMs**) and, in particular, Entity Framework Core 8.0.

Chapter 14, Implementing Microservices with .NET, describes how to implement a microservice with .NET in practice and how to design communication among microservices. Here, you will learn also how to use the gRPC communication protocol and the RabbitMQ message broker in your .NET projects.

Chapter 15, Applying Service-Oriented Architectures with .NET, describes service-oriented architecture, which enables you to expose the functionalities of your applications as endpoints on the web or on a private network so that users can interact with them through various types of clients. Here, you will learn how to implement service-oriented architecture endpoints with ASP.NET Core and gRPC and how to self-document them with existing OpenAPI packages.

Chapter 16, Working with Serverless – Azure Functions, describes the serverless model of computation and how to use it in the Azure cloud. Here, you will learn how to allocate cloud resources just when they are needed to run some computation, thus paying only for the actual computation time.

Chapter 17, Presenting ASP.NET Core, describes the ASP.NET Core framework in detail. Here, you will learn also how to implement web applications based on the **Model-View-Controller** (**MVC**) pattern.

Chapter 18, Implementing Frontend Microservices with ASP.NET Core, is dedicated to frontend microservices, that is, to the microservices that fill the role of interacting with the world outside of the application. Here, you will learn in detail how to implement a frontend microservice based on ASP.NET Core.

Chapter 19, Client Frameworks: Blazor, describes the various client technologies for implementing presentation layers. The chapter focuses on and describes in detail both the browser-based Blazor WebAssembly and the .NET MAUI-based native Blazor. Here, you will learn how to implement single-page applications and native applications in C#.

Chapter 20, Kubernetes, describes Kubernetes, which is a de facto standard for microservices orchestration. Here, you will package and deploy microservices applications on Kubernetes. You will learn how to interact with Azure Kubernetes Service and how to simulate a Kubernetes cluster on your development machine with Minikube.

Chapter 21, Case Study, is dedicated to the book travel agency case study, which shows how technologies and architectural patterns learned in the book can be used in practice in the implementation of a microservice-based enterprise application.

Chapter 22, Case Study Extension: Developing .NET Microservices for Kubernetes, bridges the insights from *Chapter 21, Case Study*, which explores the practical implementation of .NET microservices, with the foundational knowledge of Kubernetes presented in *Chapter 20, Kubernetes*.

Answers contains answers to all the questions you can find at the end of all the chapters.

Appendix: Artificial Intelligence and Machine Learning, is an online-only chapter that contains an introduction to artificial intelligence and machine learning. The first part summarizes the basic principles and techniques, while the second part puts them into practice with a description of Azure Machine Learning Studio and a simple example based on ML .NET.

You can read the appendix at the following link: `https://static.packt-cdn.com/downloads/9781805127659_Appendix.pdf`

To get the most out of this book

- Do not forget to have Visual Studio Community 2022 or a later version installed.
- For a deeper understanding of any chapter's content, feel free to jump to the suggested section of *Chapter 21, Case Study*.
- Similarly, before diving into any section of *Chapter 21, Case Study*, please review the theory discussed in the corresponding suggested chapters.

Download the example code files

The code bundle for the book is hosted on GitHub at `https://github.com/PacktPublishing/Software-Architecture-with-C-Sharp-12-and-.NET-8-4E`. We also have other code bundles from our rich catalog of books and videos available at `https://github.com/PacktPublishing/`. Check them out!

Download the color images

We also provide a PDF file that has color images of the screenshots/diagrams used in this book. You can download it here: `https://packt.link/gbp/9781805127659`.

Conventions used

There are a number of text conventions used throughout this book.

`CodeInText`: Indicates code words in text, database table names, folder names, filenames, file extensions, pathnames, dummy URLs, user input, and Twitter handles. For example: "Mount the downloaded `WebStorm-10*.dmg` disk image file as another disk in your system."

A block of code is set as follows:

```
private static string ParseIntWithTryParse()
{
    string result = string.Empty;
    if (int.TryParse(result, out var value))
        result = value.ToString();
    else
        result = "There is no int value";
    return $"Final result: {result}";
}
```

When we wish to draw your attention to a particular part of a code block, the relevant lines or items are set in bold:

```
private static string ParseIntWithException()
{
    string result = string.Empty;
    try
    {
        result = Convert.ToInt32(result).ToString();
    }
    catch (Exception)
    {
        result = "There is no int value";
    }
    return $"Final result: {result}";
```

Any command-line input or output is written as follows:

```
sudo cp sample.service /lib/systemd/system
sudo systemctl daemon-reload
sudo systemctl enable sample
```

Bold: Indicates a new term, an important word, or words that you see on the screen. For instance, words in menus or dialog boxes appear in the text like this. For example: "Select **System info** from the **Administration** panel."

Warnings or important notes appear like this.

Tips and tricks appear like this.

Get in touch

Feedback from our readers is always welcome.

General feedback: Email `feedback@packtpub.com` and mention the book's title in the subject of your message. If you have questions about any aspect of this book, please email us at `questions@packtpub.com`.

Errata: Although we have taken every care to ensure the accuracy of our content, mistakes do happen. If you have found a mistake in this book, we would be grateful if you reported this to us. Please visit `http://www.packtpub.com/submit-errata`, search for this book, click **Submit Errata**, and fill in the form.

Piracy: If you come across any illegal copies of our works in any form on the internet, we would be grateful if you would provide us with the location address or website name. Please contact us at `copyright@packtpub.com` with a link to the material.

If you are interested in becoming an author: If there is a topic that you have expertise in and you are interested in either writing or contributing to a book, please visit `http://authors.packtpub.com`.

Share your thoughts

Once you've read *Software Architecture with C# 12 and .NET 8, Fourth Edition*, we'd love to hear your thoughts! Scan the QR code below to go straight to the Amazon review page for this book and share your feedback.

`https://packt.link/r/1805127659`

Your review is important to us and the tech community and will help us make sure we're delivering excellent quality content.

Download a free PDF copy of this book

Thanks for purchasing this book!

Do you like to read on the go but are unable to carry your print books everywhere?

Is your eBook purchase not compatible with the device of your choice?

Don't worry, now with every Packt book you get a DRM-free PDF version of that book at no cost.

Read anywhere, any place, on any device. Search, copy, and paste code from your favorite technical books directly into your application.

The perks don't stop there, you can get exclusive access to discounts, newsletters, and great free content in your inbox daily.

Follow these simple steps to get the benefits:

1. Scan the QR code or visit the link below.

`https://packt.link/free-ebook/9781805127659`

2. Submit your proof of purchase.
3. That's it! We'll send your free PDF and other benefits to your email directly.

1

Understanding the Importance of Software Architecture

We started writing this book in 2018. It has been five years since the publication of the first edition, and the importance of **software architecture** for creating **enterprise applications** (**EAs**) that attend to our customers' needs has only grown. Besides, technology itself is evolving at a speed that is hard to follow, and for this reason, new architectural opportunities keep emerging. So, we keep saying that the more we build complex and fantastic solutions, the more we need great software architectures to build and maintain them.

We are sure that is the reason why you decided to read this new edition of the book, and this is the reason why we decided to write it. It is not only a matter of how .NET 8 is different from .NET 6, because there are other incredible books that take this approach. It is truly the purpose of delivering to the community a book that can support developers and software architects in the difficult decision of what component to use while designing a solution. For this reason, in this new edition, we have reformulated the way we present all the content.

You will find while reading the chapters of this new edition that you will be given support for understanding the fundamentals and technology topics that are unavoidable when designing enterprise applications using .NET 8, C#, and cloud computing. Most of the examples will use Microsoft Azure, but we will always present this content in a way that you are not locked into a specific cloud platform.

It is important to remind you that it is not a simple task to write about this important subject, which offers so many alternative techniques and solutions. The main objective of this book is not to build an exhaustive and never-ending list of available techniques and solutions but to show how various families of techniques are related, and how they impact, in practice, the construction of a maintainable and sustainable solution. We hope you all enjoy this new journey!

Specifically, in *Chapter 1, Understanding the Importance of Software Architecture*, we will discuss how the need to keep our focus on creating effective enterprise solutions continuously increases; users always need more new features in their applications. Moreover, the need to deliver frequent application versions (due to a quickly changing market) increases our obligation to have sophisticated software architecture and development techniques.

The following topics will be covered in this chapter:

- What software architecture is
- Some software development process models that may help you as a software architect
- The process for gathering the right information to design high-quality software
- Design techniques for helping in the process of development
- Cases where the requirements impact the system results

For this new edition, we have also reformulated the way we will present the case study of the book. You will find it in a single chapter, at the end of the book, where it will be easy for you to understand the whole purpose of its implementation.

The case study of this book will take you through the process of creating the software architecture for a travel agency called **World Wild Travel Club** (**WWTravelClub**). The purpose of this case study is to help you understand the theory explained in each chapter and to provide an example of how to develop an enterprise application with Azure, Azure DevOps, GitHub, C# 12, .NET 8, ASP.NET Core, and other technologies that will be introduced in this book.

By the end of this chapter, you will understand exactly what the mission of software architecture is. You will also have learned what Azure is and how to create an account on the platform. You will also have received an overview of software processes, models, and other techniques that will enable you to lead your team.

What is software architecture?

That you are reading this book today is thanks to the computer scientists who decided to consider software development as an engineering area. This happened in the last century, more specifically, at the end of the sixties, when they proposed that the way we develop software is quite like the way we construct buildings. That is why we have the name **software architecture**. Just as an architect designs a building and oversees its construction based on that design, the main goal of a software architect is to ensure that the software application is implemented well; and good implementation requires the design of a great architectural solution.

In a professional development project, you must do the following things:

- Define the customer requirements for the solution.
- Design a great solution to meet those requirements.
- Implement the designed solution.
- Test the solution implementation.
- Validate the solution with your customer.
- Deliver the solution in the working environment.
- Maintain the solution afterward.

Software engineering defines these activities as the software development lifecycle fundamentals. All the theoretical software development process models (waterfall, spiral, incremental, agile, and so on) are somehow related to this cycle. No matter the model you use, if you do not perform the essential tasks in the initial stages of your project, you will not deliver acceptable software as a solution.

The main point about designing great solutions is foundational to the purpose of this book. You must understand that great real-world solutions bring with them a few fundamental constraints:

- The solution needs to meet user requirements.
- The solution needs to be delivered on time.
- The solution needs to adhere to the project budget.
- The solution needs to deliver good quality.
- The solution needs to guarantee safe and effective future evolution.

Great solutions need to be sustainable, and you must understand that there is no sustainable software without great software architecture. Nowadays, great software architecture depends on both modern tools and modern environments to perfectly fit users' requirements.

For this reason, this book will use some great tools provided by Microsoft. We decided to write the book always following the **long-term support** (**LTS**) versions, which is why we are now applying all the examples using .NET 8. This is the second LTS version as a unified platform for software development, which gives us a great opportunity to create fantastic solutions.

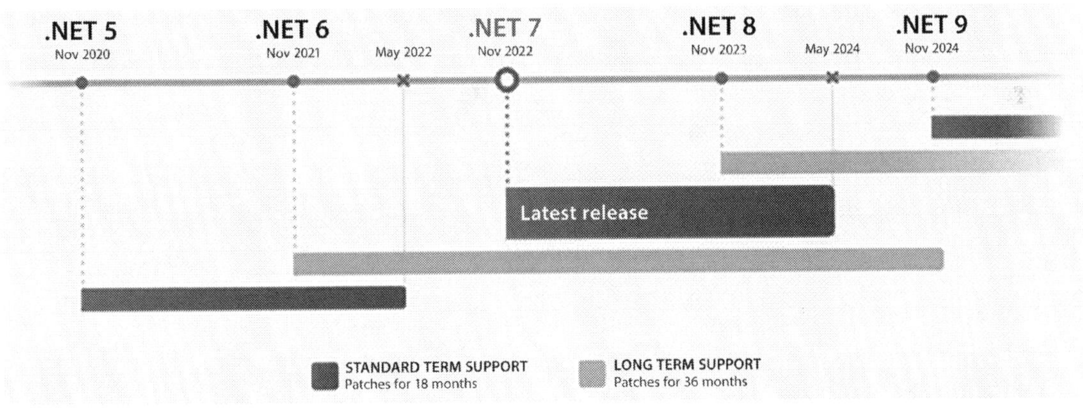

Figure 1.1: .NET support

.NET 8 is delivered together with C# 12. Considering the .NET approach of targeting so many platforms and devices, C# is now one of the most used programming languages in the world and runs on everything from small devices up to huge servers in different **operating systems** (**OSs**) and environments.

The book will also use **Microsoft Azure**, which is Microsoft's cloud platform, where you will find all the components the company provides to build advanced software architecture solutions.

It is worth mentioning that the use of .NET 8 with Azure was just an option chosen by the authors. .NET can work just as well using other cloud providers, and Azure can handle other coding frameworks very well.

To be a software architect, you need to be familiar with these technologies, and many others too. This book will guide you on a journey where, as a software architect working in a team, you will learn how to provide optimal solutions using these tools. Let us start this journey by creating your Azure account.

Creating an Azure account

Microsoft Azure is one of the best cloud solutions currently available on the market. It is important to know that, inside Azure, we will find a selection of components that can help us define the architecture of twenty-first-century solutions.

If you want to check Azure's current state, structure, and updates in a compact, digestible way, just go to `https://azurecharts.com/`, developed by Alexey Polkovnikov. The content is continuously updated so you can revisit it to learn, evaluate, or even just have fun with the dozens of Azure components described in this Azure encyclopedia.

This subsection will guide you in creating an Azure account. If you already have one, you can skip this part.

1. First, go to `https://azure.microsoft.com`. There, you will find the information you need to start your subscription. Translation to your native language is usually set automatically.
2. Once you have accessed this portal, it is possible to sign up. If you have never done this before, there is a **Start free** option, so you will be able to use some Azure features without spending any money. Please check the options for free plans at `https://azure.microsoft.com/free/`.
3. The process for creating a free account is quite simple, and you will be guided by a form that requires you to have a **Microsoft account** or **GitHub account**.
4. During the process, you will also be asked for a credit card number to verify your identity and to keep out spam and bots. However, you will not be charged unless you upgrade the account.
5. To finish the assignment, you will need to accept the subscription agreement, offer details, and privacy statement.
6. Once you have finished filling out the form, you will be able to access the Azure portal. As you can see in the following screenshot, the panel shows a dashboard that you can customize, and a menu on the left, where you can set up the Azure components you are going to use in your solution. Throughout this book, we will come back to this screen to set up the components needed to help us create modern software architecture. To find the next page, just select the hamburger menu icon and click on **All services**:

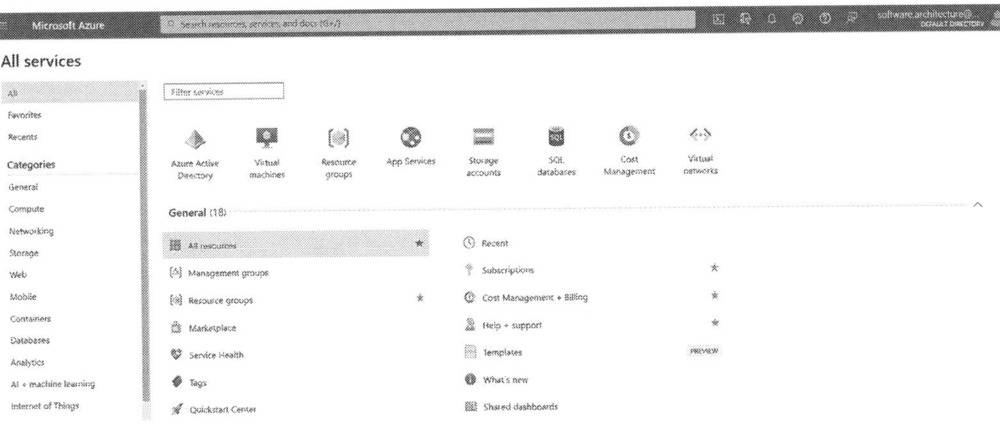

Figure 1.2: The Azure portal

Once you have created your Azure account, you are ready to find out how a software architect can lead a team to develop software, taking advantage of all the opportunities offered by Azure. However, it is important to keep in mind that a software architect needs to go beyond just technologies because they are expected to define how the software will be delivered.

Today, a software architect not only designs the basis of a piece of software but also determines how the whole software development and deployment process is conducted. The next section will cover some of the most widely used software development paradigms in the world. We will start by describing what the community refers to as traditional software engineering. After that, we will cover the agile models that have changed the way we build software nowadays.

Software development process models

As a software architect, it is important for you to understand some of the common development processes that are currently used in most enterprises. A software development process defines how people in a team produce and deliver software. In general, this process relates to a software engineering theory called the **software development process model**. Ever since software development was first defined as an engineering process, many process models for developing software have been proposed. Let us review the traditional software models, and then look at the agile ones that are currently common.

Reviewing traditional software development process models

Some of the models introduced in software engineering theory are already considered traditional and obsolete. This book does not aim to cover all of them, but here, we will give a brief explanation of the ones that are still used in some companies – the **waterfall** and **incremental** models.

Understanding the waterfall model principles

This topic may appear strange in a software architecture book from 2023, but yes, you may still find companies where the most traditional software process model remains the guideline for software development. This process executes all fundamental tasks in sequence. Any software development project consists of the following steps:

- **Requirements:** where a product requirements document is created, and it is the basis for the software development process
- **Design:** where the software architecture is developed according to the requirements
- **Implementation:** where the software is programmed
- **Verification:** where tests are performed in the application
- **Maintenance:** where the cycle starts again after delivery

Let us look at a diagrammatic representation of this:

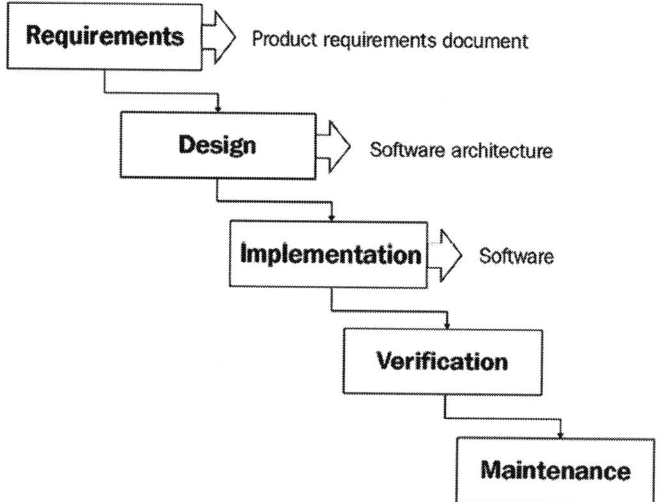

Figure 1.3: The waterfall development cycle (`https://en.wikipedia.org/wiki/Waterfall_model`*)*

Often, the use of waterfall models causes problems such as delays in the delivery of a functional version of the software and user dissatisfaction due to the distance between expectations and the final product delivered. Besides, in my experience, having application tests start only after the completion of development always feels terribly stressful.

Analyzing the incremental model

Incremental development is an approach that tries to overcome the biggest problem of the waterfall model: the user can test the solution only at the end of the project. The idea of a model following this approach is to give the users opportunities to interact with the solution as early as possible so that they can give useful feedback, which will help during the development of the software.

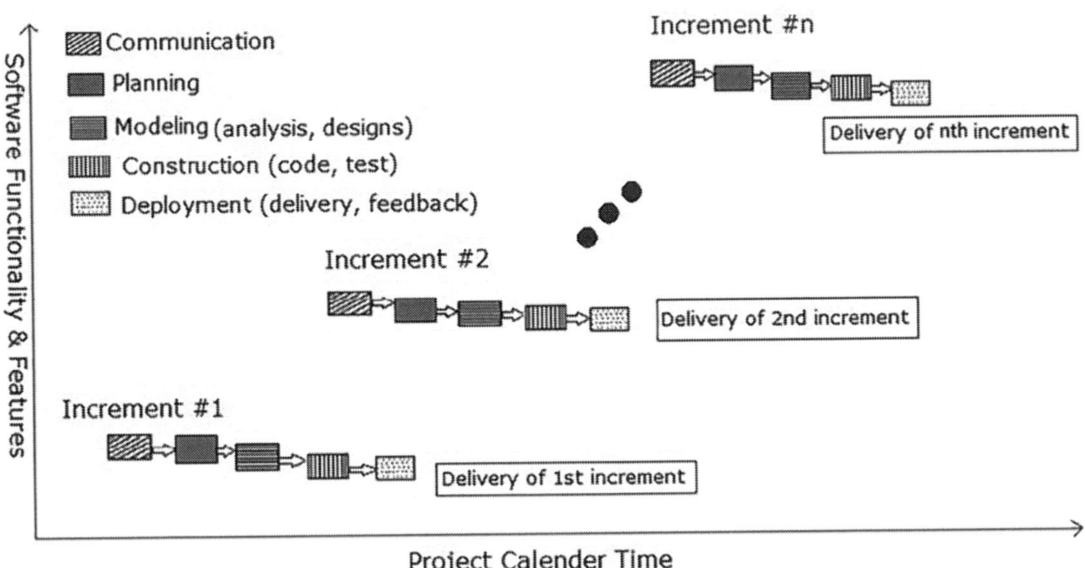

Figure 1.4: The incremental development cycle (`https://en.wikipedia.org/wiki/Incremental_build_model`*)*

The incremental model presented in the preceding picture was introduced as an alternative to the waterfall approach. The idea of the model is to run for each increment a set of practices related to software development (**communication**, **planning**, **modeling**, **construction**, and **deployment**). Although it mitigated problems related to the lack of communication with the customer, fewer increments were still a problem for big projects because the increments were still too long.

When the incremental approach was used on a large scale – mainly at the end of the last century – many problems related to project bureaucracy were reported, due to the large amount of documentation required. This clunky scenario caused the rise of a very important movement in the software development industry – **agile**.

Understanding agile software development process models

At the beginning of this century, developing software was considered one of the most chaotic activities in engineering. The percentage of software projects that failed was incredibly high, and this fact proved the need for a different approach to deal with the flexibility required by software development projects.

In 2001, the **Agile Manifesto** was introduced to the world, and from that time forward various agile process models were proposed. Some of them have survived up until now and are still very common.

The Agile Manifesto has been translated into more than 60 languages. You can check it out at `https://agilemanifesto.org/`.

One of the biggest differences between agile models and traditional models is the way developers interact with the customer. The message behind all agile models is that the faster you deliver software to the user, the better. This idea is sometimes confusing for software developers who understand this as – *Let's try coding, and that's all, folks!*

However, there is an important observation of the Agile Manifesto that many people do not read when they start working with agile:

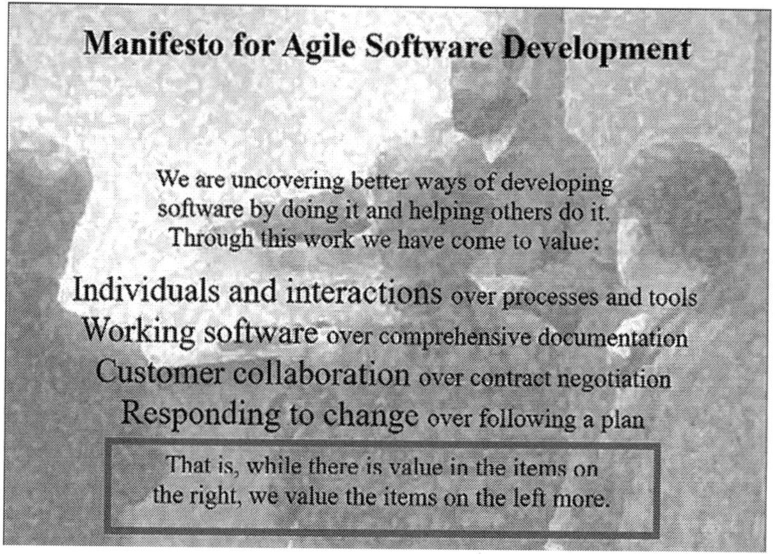

Figure 1.5: Manifesto for agile software development

A software architect always needs to remember this. Agile processes do not mean a lack of discipline. Moreover, when you use the agile process, you will quickly understand that there is no way to develop good software without discipline. On the other hand, as a software architect, you need to understand that *soft* means flexibility. A software project that refuses to be flexible tends to ruin itself over time.

The 12 principles behind agile are foundational to this flexible approach:

1. Continuously delivering valuable software to satisfy the customer must be the highest priority of any developer.
2. Changing requirements needs to be understood as an opportunity to make the customer more competitive.
3. Use a weekly timescale to deliver software.
4. A software team must be composed of businesspeople and developers.
5. A software team needs to be trusted and should have the correct environment to get the project done.
6. The best way to communicate with a software team is face to face.
7. You can see the greatest software team achievement when the software is really working in production.

8. Agile works properly when it delivers sustainable development.
9. The more you invest in techniques and good design, the more agile you are.
10. Simplicity is essential.
11. The more self-organized the teams are, the better-quality delivery you will have.
12. Software teams tend to improve their behavior from time to time, analyzing and adjusting their process.

Even 20 years after the launch of the Agile Manifesto, its importance and connection to the current needs of software teams remain intact. Certainly, there are many companies where this approach is not fully accepted, but as a software architect, you should understand this as an opportunity to transform practices and evolve the team you are working with.

There are many techniques and models that were presented to the software community with the agile approach. The next subsections will discuss **lean software development**, **extreme programming**, and **Scrum**, so that you can decide as a software architect which ones you might use to improve your software delivery.

Lean software development

After the Agile Manifesto, the approach of lean software development was introduced to the community as an adaptation of a well-known movement in automobile engineering, Toyota's model for building cars. The lean manufacturing method delivers a high level of quality even with few resources.

Mary and Tom Poppendieck mapped seven lean principles for software development, really connected to agile and the approach of many companies of this century, which are listed here:

- **Eliminate waste:** You may consider waste to be anything that will interfere with the delivery of the real need of the customer.
- **Build quality in:** An organization that wants to guarantee quality needs to promote it in processes from the very beginning, instead of only considering it when code is being tested.
- **Create knowledge:** All companies that have achieved excellence have a common pattern of generating new knowledge by disciplined experimentation, documenting that knowledge, and guaranteeing that it is spread all over the organization.
- **Defer commitment:** Plan decisions at the latest possible moment without causing damage to the project.
- **Deliver fast:** The faster you deliver software, the more elimination of waste you have. Companies that compete using time frequency have significant advantages over their competitors.
- **Respect people:** Giving reasonable objectives to the team, together with plans that will guide them to self-organize their routine, is a matter of respecting the people that you work with.
- **Optimize the whole:** A lean company improves the cycle of value; from the moment it receives a new requirement to the point at which it delivers the software.

Following the lean principles helps a team or company to improve the quality of the features that are delivered to the customer. It also creates a reduction in time spent on features that will not be used by the customer. In lean, deciding the features that are important to the customer guides the team in delivering software that matters, and this is exactly what the Agile Manifesto intends to promote in software teams.

Extreme programming

Just before the release of the Agile Manifesto, some of the participants who designed the document, especially Kent Beck, presented to the world the **extreme programming (XP) methodology** for developing software.

XP is based on the values of simplicity, communication, feedback, respect, and courage. It was considered later as a social change in programming, according to Beck in his second book about the topic. It certainly promotes a huge change in the flow of development.

XP states that every team should simply do only what it was asked to do, communicating face to face daily, demonstrating the software early to get feedback, respecting the expertise of each member of the team, and having the courage to tell the truth about progress and estimates, considering the team's work as a whole.

XP also delivers a set of rules. These rules may be changed by the team if they detect something is not working properly, but it is important to always maintain the values of the methodology.

These rules are divided into planning, managing, designing, coding, and testing. Don Wells has mapped XP at `http://www.extremeprogramming.org/`. Although some of the ideas of the methodology were criticized strongly by many companies and specialists, there are many good practices that are still used nowadays:

- **Writing software requirements using user stories:** User stories are considered an agile approach to describing user needs, together with acceptance tests, which are used to guarantee the correct implementation.
- **Divide software into iterations and deliver small releases:** The practice of iterating in software development is implemented by all methodologies aside from waterfall. The fact of delivering faster versions decreases the risk of not meeting the customer's expectations.
- **Avoid working overtime and guarantee a sustainable velocity:** Although this must be one of the hardest tasks a software architect may deal with, overtime indicates that something is not working properly in the process.
- **Keep things simple:** While developing solutions, it is quite common to try to anticipate features that the customer would like to have. This approach increases the complexity of the development and the time to market the solution. A different approach will cause high costs, and probably a low level of features that are used in the system you are developing.
- **Refactoring:** The approach of refactoring the code continuously is good because it enables the evolution of your software and guarantees the design improvement that will truly be necessary due to the normal technical changes of the platforms you use to develop.

- **Keep the customer always available:** If you follow XP, you should have an expert customer inside your team. This is certainly something that is hard to do, but the main idea of this approach is to guarantee that the customer is involved in all parts of development. As another bonus, having the customer close to your team means they understand the difficulties and expertise the team has, enabling an increase in trust between the parties.
- **Continuous integration:** This practice is one of the bases of the current DevOps approach. The less difference you have between your personal code repository and the main code repository, the better.
- **Code the unit test first:** A unit test is an approach where you program specific code for testing a single unit (class/method) of your project. This is discussed in a current development methodology called **Test-Driven Development** (**TDD**). The main goal here is to guarantee that every business rule has its own unit test case.
- **Code must be written to agreed standards:** The need to determine standards for coding is connected to the idea that no matter which developer you have working on a specific part of the project, the code must be written so that any of them will understand it.
- **Pair programming:** Pair programming is another difficult approach to achieve in every single minute of a software project, but the technique itself – one programmer coding and the other actively observing and offering comments, criticism, and advice – is useful in critical scenarios.
- **Acceptance tests:** The adoption of acceptance tests to meet user stories is a good way to guarantee that newly released versions of the software do not cause damage to its current needs. An even better option is to have these acceptance tests automated.

It is worth mentioning that many of these rules are today considered vital practices in different software development methodologies, including DevOps and Scrum. We will discuss DevOps later in this book, in *Chapter 8, Understanding DevOps Principles and CI/CD*. Let us get into the Scrum model right now.

Getting into the Scrum model

Scrum is an agile model for the management of software development projects. The model comes from lean principles and is one of the more widely used approaches for developing software nowadays.

Please check out this link for more information about the Scrum framework: `https://www.scrum.org/`.

As you can see in the following figure, the basis of Scrum is that you have a flexible backlog of user requirements (**Product Backlog**) that needs to be discussed in each agile cycle, called a **Sprint**. The Sprint goal (**Sprint Backlog**) is determined by the **Scrum Team**, composed of the **Product Owner**, the **Scrum Master**, and the **Development Team**. The Product Owner is responsible for prioritizing what will be delivered in that Sprint. During the Sprint, this person will help the team to develop the required features. The person who leads the team in the Scrum process is called the Scrum Master. All the meetings and processes are conducted by this person.

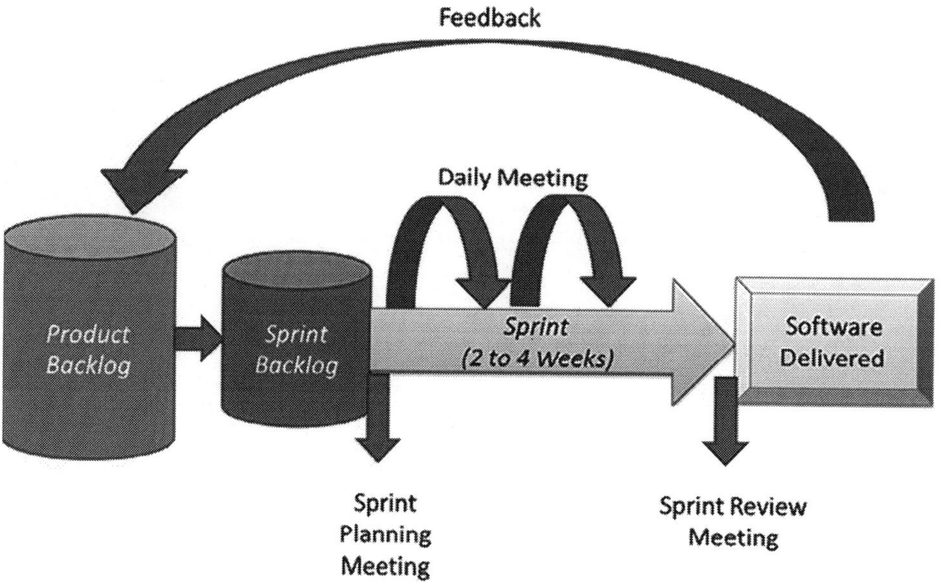

Figure 1.6: The Scrum process

It is common to apply Scrum together with another agile technique, called **Kanban**, also developed by Toyota for manufacturing cars and commonly used for software maintenance. The main purpose of Kanban is to enable a visual system to make sure everybody understands what is going on in the product that is being developed. The famous Kanban board is an incredible way to do so, where you define what the team must do, what they are doing, and the things that are already done.

It is important to note that the Scrum process does not discuss how the software needs to be implemented, nor which activities will be done. Again, you must remember the basis of software development, discussed at the beginning of this chapter; Scrum needs to be implemented together with a process model. DevOps is one of the approaches that may help you use a software development process model together with Scrum. Check out *Chapter 8, Understanding DevOps Principles and CI/CD*, to understand it better.

Scaling agile throughout a company

Today it is quite common to find companies where agility is being practiced and evolving in a good way, considering the results of the techniques presented in the previous sections. The mixture of Scrum, Kanban, and XP, together with the evolution of the maturity of the software development process, has brought good results for companies and we have a world where software development is one of the key strategies for the success of a business.

Some companies naturally need to scale up the number of teams, but the important question in this process is how to evolve without missing agility. And you can be sure that this question may be addressed to you, as a software architect. You may find in *SAFe® – Scaled Agile Framework* a good answer to this question:

> *SAFe® for LeanEnterprises is a knowledge base of proven, integrated principles, practices, and competencies for achieving business agility using Lean, Agile, and DevOps."*
>
> *– Dean Leffingwell, creator.*
>
> *© Scaled Agile, Inc.*

Based on the core values of alignment, built-in quality, transparency, and program execution, the framework provides a detailed path for delivering products with the agility needed in companies where you have one or more value streams. Its principles enable agility and incremental delivery, system thinking, fast and economic decisions, and mainly, organization around value.

As a software architect, you may find opportunities for growth, considering you can work as a software architect in a system team, a system architect in an agile release train, or even an enterprise architect in the company. For sure, this will require a lot of studying and dedication, but this structure is what you will find in big companies.

As with every framework, technique, or model that you will find in this book, the purpose of presenting SAFe to you is not to cover every single detail of the content. You will find excellent material and training on their website. But as a software architect, understanding how to scale up a company may be good knowledge to have in your toolbelt! Now that you know it, let us go back to the stages of designing software with high quality, discussing how to gather the right information to design it.

Gathering the right information to design high-quality software

Fantastic! You've just started a software development project. Now, it is time to use all your knowledge to deliver the best software you can. Your first question is probably – *How do I start?* Well, as a software architect, you are going to be the one to answer that question. And you can be sure that your answer is going to evolve with each software project you lead.

Defining a software development process is the first task. This is generally done during the project planning process, or it might happen before it starts.

Another very important task is to gather the software requirements. No matter which software development process you decide to use, collecting real user needs is part of a difficult and continuous job. Of course, there are techniques to help you with this, and you can be sure that gathering requirements will help you to define important aspects of your software architecture.

These two tasks are considered by most experts in software development as the keys to success at the end of the development project journey. As a software architect, you need to enable them so that you can avoid as many problems as possible while guiding your team.

Understanding the requirements gathering process

There are many ways to represent the requirements. The most traditional approach consists of you having to write a perfect specification before the beginning of the analysis. Agile methods suggest instead that you need to write user stories as soon as you are ready to start a development cycle.

Remember that you do not write requirements just for the user; you write them for you and your team too.

The truth is that no matter the approach you decide to adopt in your projects, you will have to follow some steps to gather requirements. This is what we call the **requirements engineering process.**

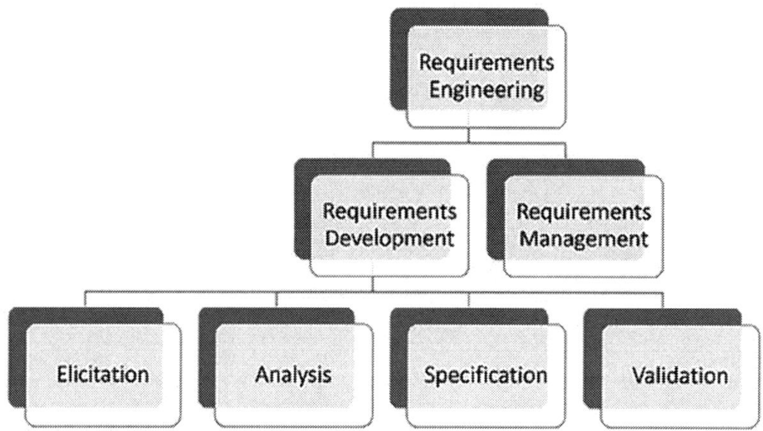

Figure 1.7: Requirements engineering process

During this process, you need to be sure that the solution is feasible. In some cases, the feasibility analysis is part of the project planning process too, and by the time you start the requirements elicitation, you will have the feasibility report already done. So, let us check the other parts of this process, which will give you a lot of important information about the software architecture.

Detecting exact user needs

There are a lot of ways to detect what exactly the user needs for a specific scenario. This process is known as *elicitation*. In general, this can be done using techniques that will help you to understand what we call user requirements. Here, you have a list of common techniques:

- **The power of imagination:** If you are an expert in the area where you are providing solutions, you may use your own imagination to find new user requirements. Brainstorming can be conducted collaboratively so that a group of experts can define the user's needs.
- **Questionnaires:** This tool is useful for detecting common and important requirements such as the number and kind of users, peak system usage, and the most commonly used **OS** and web browser.
- **Interviews:** Interviewing the users helps you as an architect to detect user requirements that perhaps questionnaires and your imagination will not cover.
- **Observation:** There is no better way to understand the daily routine of a user than observing them for a day.

As soon as you apply one or more of these techniques, you will have great and valuable information about the user's needs.

Remember that you can use these techniques in any situation where the real need is to gather requirements, no matter whether it is for the whole system or for a single story.

At that moment, you will be able to start analyzing these user needs and detecting the user and system requirements. Let us see how to do so in the next section.

Analyzing requirements

When you have detected the user needs, it is time to begin analyzing the requirements. To do so, you can use techniques such as the following:

- **Prototyping:** Prototypes are fantastic to clarify and materialize the system requirements. Today, we have many tools that can help you to mock interfaces. A nice open-source tool is the **Pencil Project**. You will find further information about it at `https://pencil.evolus.vn/`. **Figma** (`https://www.figma.com/`) is also a good tool for prototyping and they provide a starter pack that is free forever.
- **Use cases:** The **Unified Modeling Language** (**UML**) use case model is an option if you need detailed documentation. The model is composed of a detailed specification and a diagram. **Lucidchart** (`https://www.lucidchart.com/`) is another good tool that can help you out with this. You can see the model created in *Figure 1.8*:

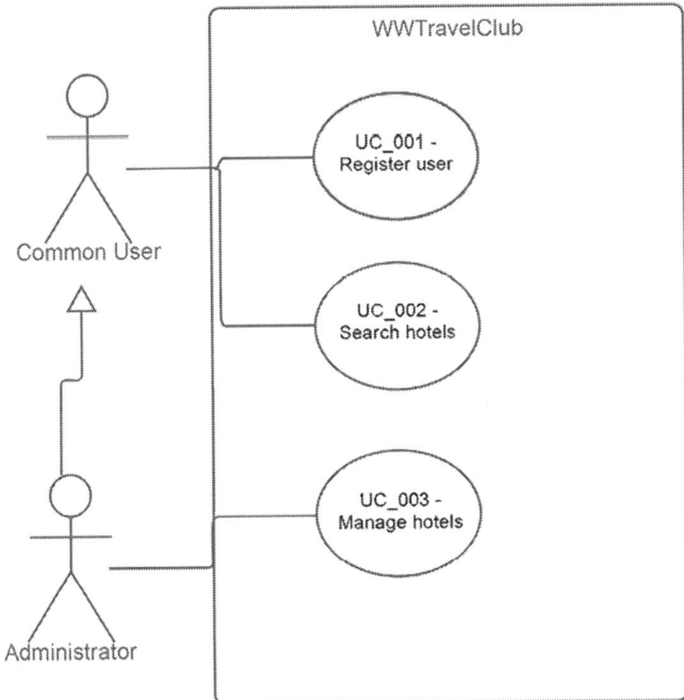

Figure 1.8: Use case diagram example

While you are analyzing the requirements of the system, you will be able to clarify exactly what the user's needs are. This is helpful when you are not sure about the real problem you need to solve, and it is much better than just starting to program the system and hoping for the best. Time invested in requirements analysis is time invested in better code later.

Writing the specifications

After you finish the analysis, it is important to register it as a specification. The specification document can be written using traditional requirements, or user stories, which are commonly used in agile projects.

A requirements specification represents the technical contract between the user and the team. There are some basic rules that this document needs to follow:

- All stakeholders need to understand exactly what is written in the technical contract, even if they are not technicians.
- The document needs to be clear.
- You need to classify each requirement.
- Use simple future tense to represent each requirement:
    - **Bad example:** A common user registers themselves.
    - **Good example:** A common user shall register themselves.
- Ambiguity and controversy need to be avoided.
- Some additional information can help the team to understand the context of the project they are going to work on. Here are some tips about how to add useful information:
    - Write an introductory chapter to give a full idea of the solution.
    - Create a glossary to make understanding easier.
    - Describe the kind of user the solution will cover.
- Write functional and non-functional requirements:

  Functional requirements are quite simple to understand because they describe exactly what the software will do. On the other hand, non-functional requirements determine the restrictions related to the software, which means scalability, robustness, security, and performance. We will cover these aspects in the next section.
- Attach documents that can help the user to understand the rules.

If you decide to write user stories, a good tip to follow is to write short sentences representing each moment in the system with each user, as follows:

As <user>, I want <feature>, so that <reason>

This approach will explain exactly the reason why that feature will be implemented. It is also a good tool to help you analyze the stories that are most important and prioritize the success of the project. They can also be great for informing the automated acceptance tests that should be built.

Understanding the principles of scalability, robustness, security, and performance

Detecting requirements is a task that will let you understand the software you are going to develop. However, as a software architect, you must pay attention to more than just the functional requirements for that system. Understanding the non-functional requirements is important, and one of the earliest activities for a software architect.

We are going to look at this in more detail in *Chapter 2, Non-Functional Requirements*, but at this point, it is important to know that the principles of scalability, robustness, security, and performance need to be applied to the requirements gathering process. Let us look at each concept:

- **Scalability:** The Internet gives you the opportunity to have a solution with a great number of users all over the world. This is fantastic, but you, as a software architect, need to design a solution that provides that possibility. Scalability is the possibility for an application to increase its processing power as soon as it is necessary, due to the number of resources that are being consumed.
- **Robustness:** No matter how scalable your application is, if it is not able to guarantee a stable and always-on solution, you are not going to get any peace. Robustness is important for critical solutions, where you do not have the opportunity to carry out maintenance at any time due to the kind of problem that the application solves. In many industries, the software cannot stop, and lots of routines run when nobody is available (overnight, during holidays, and so on). Designing a reliable solution will free you up to live your life while your software is running smoothly.
- **Security:** This is another really important area that needs to be discussed after the requirements stage. Everybody worries about security, and different laws dealing with it are in place in different parts of the world. You, as a software architect, must understand that security needs to be provided by design. This is the only way to cope with all the needs that the security community is discussing right now.
- **Performance:** The process of understanding the system you are going to develop will probably give you a good idea of what you will need to do to get the desired performance from the system. This topic needs to be discussed with the user, to identify most of the bottlenecks you will face during the development stage.

It is worth mentioning that all these concepts are requirements for the new generation of solutions that the world needs. What differentiates good software from incredible software is the amount of work done to meet the project requirements.

Reviewing the specification

Once you have the specification written, it is time to confirm with the stakeholders whether they agree with it. This can be done in a review meeting, or it can be done online using collaboration tools.

This is when you present all the prototypes, documents, and information you have gathered. As soon as everybody agrees with the specification, you are ready to start studying the best way to implement this part of your project.

It is worth mentioning that you might use the process described here for either the complete software or for just a small part of it.

Using design techniques as a helpful tool

Defining a solution is not easy. Determining which technology to use is also difficult. It is true that, during your career as a software architect, you will find many projects where your customer will bring you a solution *ready for development*. This can get quite complicated if you consider that solution as the correct solution; most of the time, there will be architectural and functional mistakes that will cause problems in the solution in the future.

There are some cases where the problem is worse – when the customer does not know the best solution for the problem. Some design techniques can help us with this, and we will introduce two of them here: **Design Thinking** and **Design Sprint**.

What you must understand is that these techniques can be a fantastic option to discover real requirements. As a software architect, you are committed to helping your team to use the correct tools at the correct time, and these tools may be the right options to ensure the project's success.

Design Thinking

Design Thinking is a process that allows you to collect data directly from the users, focusing on achieving the best results to solve a problem. During this process, the team will have the opportunity to discover all the *personas* that will interact with the system. This will have a wonderful impact on the solution since you can develop the software by focusing on the user experience, which can have a fantastic impact on the results.

The process is based on the following steps:

1. **Empathize**: In this step, you must execute field research to discover users' concerns. This is where you find out about the users of the system. The process is good for making you understand why and for whom you are developing this software.
2. **Define**: Once you have the users' concerns, it is time to define their needs to solve them.
3. **Ideate**: The needs will provide an opportunity to brainstorm some possible solutions.
4. **Prototype**: These solutions can be developed as mock-ups to confirm whether they are good ones.
5. **Test**: Testing the prototypes will help you to understand the prototype that is most connected to the real needs of the users.

The focus of a technique like this one is to accelerate the process of discerning the right product and considering the **Minimum Viable Product** (**MVP**). For sure, the prototype process will help stakeholders to understand the final product and, at the same time, engage the team to deliver the best solution.

Design Sprint

Design Sprint is a process focused on solving critical business questions through design in a five-day sprint. This technique was presented by Google, and it is something that allows you to quickly test and learn from an idea when you are looking to build and launch a solution to market.

The process involves experts spending a week to solve the problem at hand, in a war room prepared for that purpose. The week looks like this:

- **Monday:** The focus of this day is to identify the target of the sprint and map the challenge to achieve it.
- **Tuesday:** After understanding the goal of the sprint, participants start sketching solutions that may solve it. It is time to find customers to test the new solution that will be provided.
- **Wednesday:** This is when the team needs to decide on the solutions that have the greatest chance of solving the problem. The team must draw these solutions into a storyboard, preparing a plan for the prototype.
- **Thursday:** It is time to prototype the idea planned on the storyboard.
- **Friday:** Having completed the prototype, the team presents it to customers, learning by getting information from their reactions to the solution designed.

As you can see, in both techniques, the acceleration of collecting reactions from customers comes from prototypes that will materialize your team's ideas into something more tangible for the end user.

Common cases where the requirements gathering process impacts system results

All the information discussed up to this point in the chapter is useful if you want to design software following the principles of good engineering. Rather than advocating for traditional or agile development methods, the emphasis is on building software in a professional manner.

It is also a good idea to know about some cases in which failing to perform the activities you read about can cause some trouble for a software project. The following cases intend to describe what can go wrong, and how the preceding techniques can help a development team to solve the associated problems.

In most cases, very simple actions can guarantee better communication between the team and the customer, and this easy communication flow can transform a big problem into a real solution. Let us examine three common cases where requirements gathering can impact software performance, functionality, and usability.

Case 1 – my website is too slow to open that page!

Performance is one of the biggest problems that you as a software architect will deal with during your career. The reason why this aspect of any software is so problematic is that we do not have infinite computational resources to solve problems. The cost of computation is still high, especially if you are talking about software with a high number of simultaneous users.

You cannot solve performance problems by writing requirements. However, you will not end up in trouble if you write them correctly. The idea here is that requirements must present the desired performance of a system. A simple sentence describing this can help the entire team that works on the project:

Non-functional requirement: Performance – any web page of this software shall respond in at least 2 seconds, even when 1,000 users are accessing it concurrently.

The preceding sentence just lets everybody (users, testers, developers, architects, managers, and so on) know that any web page has a target to achieve. This is a good start, but it is not enough. A great environment for developing and deploying your application is also important. This is where .NET 8 can help you a lot; especially if you are talking about web apps, ASP.NET Core is considered one of the fastest options to deliver solutions today.

When it comes to performance, you, as a software architect, should consider the use of the techniques listed in the following sections together with specific tests to guarantee this non-functional requirement. It is also important to mention that ASP.NET Core will help you to use them easily, together with some **Platform as a Service** (**PaaS**) solutions delivered by Microsoft Azure.

Understanding backend caching

Caching is a great technique to avoid time-consuming and redundant queries. For instance, if you are fetching car models from a database, the number of cars in the database can increase, but the models themselves will not change. Once you have an application that constantly accesses car models, a good practice is to cache that information.

It is important to understand that a cache is stored in the backend and that cache is shared by the whole application (*in-memory caching*). A point to focus on is that when you are working on a scalable solution, you can configure a *distributed cache* using the Azure platform. In fact, ASP.NET provides both in-memory caching and distributed caching, so you can decide on the one that best fits your needs. *Chapter 2, Non-Functional Requirements*, covers scalability aspects in the Azure platform.

It is also important to mention that caching can happen in the frontend, in proxies along the way to the server, CDNs, and so on.

Applying asynchronous programming

When you develop ASP.NET applications, you need to keep in mind that your app needs to be designed for simultaneous access by many users. Asynchronous programming lets you do this simply, by giving you the keywords `async` and `await`.

The basic concept behind these keywords is that `async` enables any method to run asynchronously. On the other hand, `await` lets you synchronize the call of an asynchronous method without blocking the thread that is calling it. This easy-to-develop pattern will make your application run without performance bottlenecks and bring better responsiveness. This book will cover more about this subject in *Chapter 2, Non-Functional Requirements*.

Dealing with object allocation

One very good tip to avoid poor performance is to understand how the **Garbage Collector** (**GC**) works. The GC is the engine that will free memory automatically when you finish using it. There are some very important aspects of this topic, due to the complexity that the GC has.

Some types of objects are not collected by the GC if you do not dispose of them. The list includes any object that interacts with I/O, such as files and streaming. If you do not correctly use the C# syntax to create and destroy this kind of object, you will have memory leaks, which will deteriorate your application's performance.

The incorrect way of working with I/O objects is:

```
System.IO.StreamWriter file = new System.IO.StreamWriter(@"C:\sample.txt");
file.WriteLine("Just writing a simple line");
```

The correct way of working with I/O objects is:

```
using System.IO.StreamWriter file = new System.IO.StreamWriter(@"C:\sample.
txt");
file.WriteLine("Just writing a simple line");
```

It might be worth noting that this correct approach also ensures the file gets written (it calls `FileStream.Flush()` to dispose of its resources gracefully). In the incorrect example, the contents might not even be written to the file. Even though the preceding practice is mandatory for I/O objects, it is totally recommended that you keep doing this in all disposable objects. Indeed, using code analyzers in your solutions with warnings as errors will prevent you from accidentally making these mistakes! This will help the GC and will keep your application running with the right amount of memory. Depending on the type of object, mistakes here can snowball, and you could end up with other bad things on a bigger scale, for instance, port/connection exhaustion.

Another important aspect that you need to know about is that the time spent by the GC collecting objects will interfere with the performance of your app. Because of this, avoid allocating large objects and be careful with event handling and week references; otherwise, it can lead to you always waiting for the GC to finish its task.

Getting better database access

One of the most common performance Achilles' heels is database access. The reason why this is still a big problem is a lack of attention paid while writing queries or lambda expressions to get information from a database. This book will cover Entity Framework Core in *Chapter 13, Interacting with Data in C# – Entity Framework Core*, but it is important to know what to choose and the correct data information to read from a database. Filtering columns and rows is imperative for an application that wants to deliver on performance.

The good thing is that best practices related to caching, asynchronous programming, and object allocation fit completely into the environment of databases. It is only a matter of choosing the correct pattern to get better-performing software.

Case 2 – the user's needs are not properly implemented

The more technology is used in a wide variety of areas, the more difficult it is to deliver exactly what the user needs. Maybe this sentence sounds weird to you, but you must understand that developers, in general, study how to develop software, but they rarely study delivering the needs of a specific area. Of course, it is not easy to learn how to develop software, but it is even more difficult to understand a specific need in a specific area. Software development nowadays delivers software to all types of industries. The question here is *how can a developer, whether a software architect or not, evolve enough to deliver software in the area they are responsible for?*

Gathering software requirements will help you in this tough task; writing them will make you understand and organize the architecture of the system. There are several ways to minimize the risks of implementing something different from what the user really needs:

- Prototyping the interface to achieve an understanding of the user interface faster
- Designing the data flow to detect gaps between the system and the user operations
- Frequent meetings to stay up to date on the user's current needs and be aligned with incremental deliveries

Again, as a software architect, you will have to define how the software will be implemented. Most of the time, you are not going to be the one who programs it, but you will always be the one responsible for this. For this reason, some techniques can be useful to avoid the wrong implementation:

- Requirements are reviewed by the developers to guarantee that they understand what they need to develop.
- Code inspection to validate a predefined code standard. We will cover this in *Chapter 4, Best Practices in Coding C# 12*.
- Meetings to eliminate impediments.

Remember, making sure the implementation matches the user's needs is your responsibility. Use every tool you can to do so.

Case 3 – the usability of the system does not meet the user's needs

Usability is a key point for the success of a software project. The way the software is presented and how it solves a problem will determine whether the user wants to use it or not. As a software architect, you must keep in mind that delivering software with good usability is mandatory nowadays.

There are basic concepts of usability that this book does not intend to cover, but a good way to meet the user's needs when it comes to usability is by understanding who is going to use the software. Design Thinking can help you a lot with that, as was discussed earlier in this chapter.

Understanding the user will help you to decide whether the software is going to run on a web page, a cell phone, or even in the background. This understanding is very important to a software architect because the elements of a system will be better presented if you correctly map who will use them.

On the other hand, if you do not care about that, you will just deliver software that works. This can be good for a short time, but it will not exactly meet the real needs that made a person ask you to architect the software. You must keep in mind the options and understand that good software is software designed to run on many platforms and devices.

You will be happy to know that .NET 8 is an incredible cross-platform option for that. So, you can develop solutions to run your apps in Linux, Windows, Android, and iOS. You can run your applications on big screens, tablets, cell phones, and even drones! You can embed apps on boards for automation or in HoloLens for mixed reality. Software architects must be open-minded to design exactly what their users need.

Summary

In this chapter, you learned about the purpose of a software architect in a software development team. Also, this chapter covered the basics of software development process models and the requirements gathering process. You also had the opportunity to learn about how to create your Azure account, which will be used during the case study of this book. Moreover, you even learned about functional and non-functional requirements and how to create them using user stories. These techniques will help you deliver a better software project.

In the next chapter, you will have the opportunity to understand how important functional and non-functional requirements are to software architecture.

Questions

1. What is the expertise that a software architect needs to have?
2. How can Azure help a software architect?
3. How does a software architect decide on the best software development process model to use in a project?
4. How does a software architect contribute to gathering requirements?
5. What kind of requirements does a software architect need to check in a requirements specification?
6. How do Design Thinking and Design Sprint help a software architect in the process of gathering requirements?
7. How do user stories help a software architect in the process of writing requirements?
8. What are some good techniques to develop very good performance software?
9. How does a software architect check whether a user requirement is correctly implemented?

Further reading

Here, we have listed some books and links you may consider using to gather more information about the topics covered in this chapter.

- For information on Azure, check these out:
  - https://www.packtpub.com/virtualization-and-cloud/hands-azure-developers
  - https://azure.microsoft.com/overview/what-is-azure/
  - https://azure.microsoft.com/services/devops/
  - https://azurecharts.com/
- More information on .NET 8 can be found here:
  - https://docs.microsoft.com/dotnet/
  - https://docs.microsoft.com/aspnet/
  - https://docs.microsoft.com/aspnet/core/performance/performance-best-practices
- Software development process model links are listed here:
  - https://agilemanifesto.org/
  - https://www.amazon.com/Software-Engineering-10th-Ian-Sommerville/dp/0133943038
  - https://www.amazon.com/Software-Engineering-Practitioners-Roger-Pressman/dp/0078022126/
  - https://scrumguides.org/
  - https://www.packtpub.com/application-development/professional-scrummasters-handbook
  - https://en.wikipedia.org/wiki/Incremental_build_model
  - https://en.wikipedia.org/wiki/Waterfall_model
  - http://www.extremeprogramming.org/
  - https://www.gv.com/sprint/
- Here you can find SAFe® information:
  - https://www.scaledagileframework.com/
  - https://scaledagile.com/train-certify/
  - https://docs.microsoft.com/azure/devops/boards/plans/safe-concepts

Learn more on Discord

To join the Discord community for this book – where you can share feedback, ask questions to the authors, and learn about new releases – follow the QR code below:

https://packt.link/SoftwareArchitectureCSharp12Dotnet8

2

Non-Functional Requirements

Once you have gathered the system requirements, it is time to think about the impact they have on the architectural design. Scalability, availability, resiliency, performance, multithreading, interoperability, security, and other aspects need to be analyzed so that we can meet user needs. We refer to these aspects as non-functional requirements.

We will cover the following topics in this chapter:

- Enabling scalability, availability, and resiliency with Azure and .NET 8
- Performance issues that need to be considered when programming in C#
- Software usability: how to design effective user interfaces
- Interoperability with .NET 8
- Achieving security by design

The main purpose of discussing non-functional requirements here is that they are highly relevant to software architects: even though they are not so important to getting the software working in terms of functionality, they can make all the difference when comparing good software and bad software.

Technical requirements

The samples provided in this chapter require Visual Studio 2022 Community Edition with the .NET 8 SDK installed.

You can find the sample code for this chapter at `https://github.com/PacktPublishing/Software-Architecture-with-C-Sharp-12-and-.NET-8-4E`.

Enabling scalability, availability, and resiliency with Azure and .NET 8

A quick search online for a definition of "scalability" returns something along the lines of "the ability of a system to keep working well when there is an increase in demand." When developers go by this definition, many of them incorrectly conclude that scalability only means adding more hardware to keep things working without stopping their apps.

Scalability relies on hardware solutions to some extent. However, as a software architect, you need to be aware that good software will keep scalability in a sustainable model, which means that well-architected software can save a lot of money. Hence, scalability is not just a matter of hardware but also a matter of overall software design. The point here is that the running costs of a system should also be a factor in architectural decisions.

In *Chapter 1, Understanding the Importance of Software Architecture*, while discussing software performance, we presented some good tips to overcome performance issues. The same tips will help you with scalability, too. The fewer resources we spend on each process, the more users an application can handle.

Although scalability is important, cloud computing applications must be designed to work with system failures. Every time you guarantee that your application can recover from a failure without exposing the failure to the end user, you are creating a resilient application.

You may find cloud architecture resiliency patterns at `https://docs.microsoft.com/en-us/azure/architecture/framework/resiliency/reliability-patterns#resiliency`.

The reason why resiliency is especially important in cloud scenarios is that the infrastructure provided to you may need a small amount of time to manage updates, resets, and even hardware upgrades. You are also more likely to have to work with multiple systems, and transient errors are likely to occur in communicating with them. That is why the non-functional requirement of resiliency has gained a higher profile in recent years.

The possibility of having scalable and resilient solutions gets more exciting when you can enable high availability in the system. All the approaches presented in this book will help you to design solutions with good availability, but in some cases, you will need to design specific alternatives to achieve your specific goal.

It is worth knowing that Azure and .NET 8 web apps can be configured to achieve these non-functional requirements. Let us check this out in the following subsections.

Creating a scalable web app in Azure

It is simple to create a web app in Azure that is ready for scaling. The reason why you must do so is to be able to maintain different numbers of users during different seasons. The more users you have, the more hardware you will need. Let us show you how to create a scalable web application in Azure.

As soon as you log in to your Azure account, you will be able to create a new resource (web app, database, virtual machine, and so on), as you can see in the following screenshot:

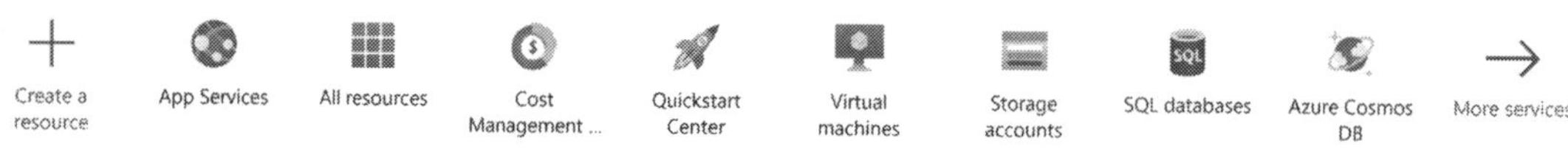

Figure 2.1: Microsoft Azure – Create a resource

After that, you can select **App Services in Popular Options** or even type it into the **Search the Marketplace** textbox. Then, you can choose to create a **web app.** This action will take you to the following screen:

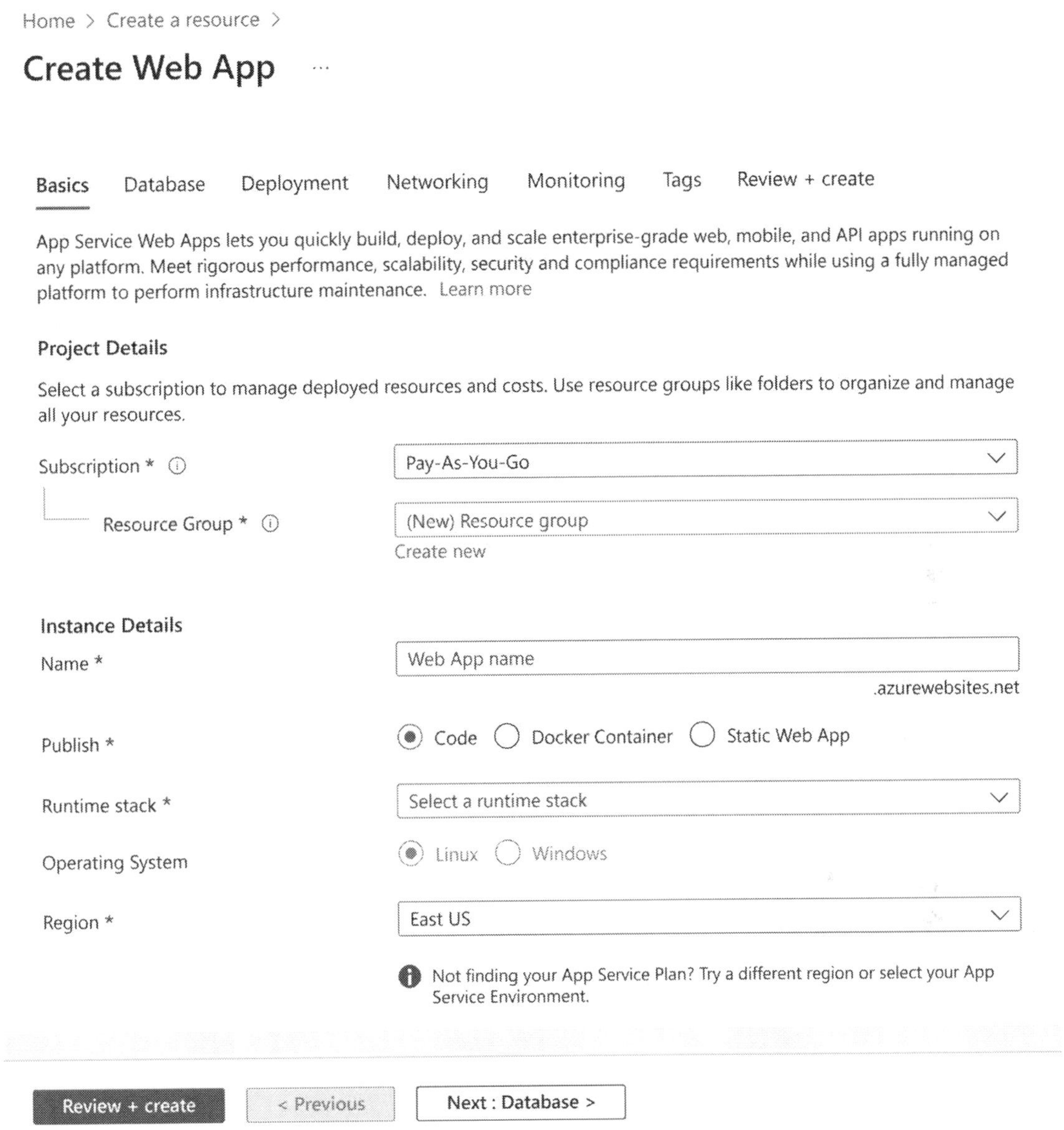

Home > Create a resource >

Create Web App ...

Basics Database Deployment Networking Monitoring Tags Review + create

App Service Web Apps lets you quickly build, deploy, and scale enterprise-grade web, mobile, and API apps running on any platform. Meet rigorous performance, scalability, security and compliance requirements while using a fully managed platform to perform infrastructure maintenance. Learn more

Project Details

Select a subscription to manage deployed resources and costs. Use resource groups like folders to organize and manage all your resources.

Subscription * Pay-As-You-Go

Resource Group * (New) Resource group

Create new

Instance Details

Name * Web App name

.azurewebsites.net

Publish * Code Docker Container Static Web App

Runtime stack * Select a runtime stack

Operating System Linux Windows

Region * East US

Not finding your App Service Plan? Try a different region or select your App Service Environment.

Review + create < Previous Next : Database >

Figure 2.2: Microsoft Azure – Creating a web app

The required **Project Details** are as follows:

- **Subscription:** This is the account that will be charged for all application costs.
- **Resource Group:** This is the collection of resources you can define to organize policies and permissions. You may specify a new resource group name or add the web app to a group specified during the definition of other resources.

Besides these, the **Instance Details** are as follows:

- **Name**: As you can see, the web app name is the URL that your solution will assume after its creation. The name must be globally unique and is checked to ensure it is available.
- **Publish**: This parameter indicates whether the web app will be delivered directly, a static web app, or whether it is going to use Docker technology to publish content. Docker will be discussed in more detail in *Chapter 11, Applying a Microservice Architecture to Your Enterprise Application*. If you opt for the Docker container publication, you will be able to configure the **Image Source**, **Access Type**, and **Image** and tag information to have it deployed to the web app.
- **Runtime stack**: This option is obviously only available when you decide to deliver code directly. You could define stacks for .NET, Go, Java, Node.js, PHP, Python, and Ruby.
- **Operating System**: This is the option for defining the OS that will host the web app. Both Windows and Linux may be used for .NET projects in the newest versions.
- **Region**: You may consider where you want to deploy your application; Azure has many different data centers all over the world.
- **Pricing Plans**: This is where you define the hardware plan that is used to handle the web app and the region of the servers. This choice defines application scalability, performance, and costs.
- **Zone redundancy:** Starting with premium pricing plans, you will be able to activate zone redundancy, which will increase the availability of the solution.
- **Deployment:** It is possible to define the GitHub repository that is responsible for continuously deploying the application.
- **Networking:** You may select the network behavior of the application according to its requirements and proposal.
- **Monitoring**: This is a useful Azure toolset for monitoring and troubleshooting web apps. In this section, you can enable **Application Insights**. It is always recommended that you keep the same regions for the different components of your solution since this will save costs in terms of traffic exchange from one data center to another.

Once you have created your web app, this application may be scaled in two conceptually different ways: vertically (**scale up**) and horizontally (**scale out**). Both are available in the web app settings, as you can see in the following screenshot:

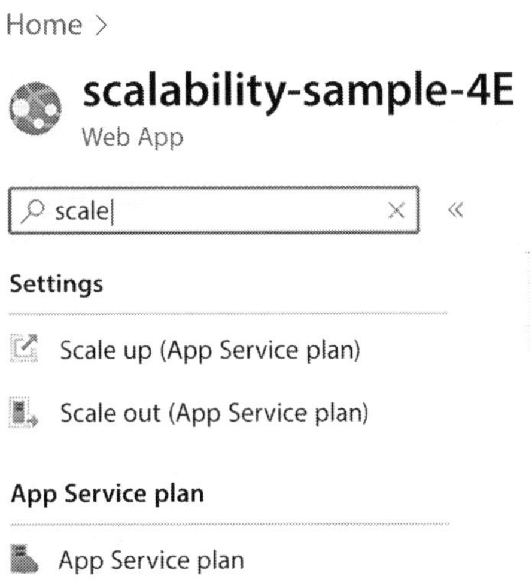

Home >

scalability-sample-4E

Web App

scale

Settings

Scale up (App Service plan)

Scale out (App Service plan)

App Service plan

App Service plan

Figure 2.3: Scaling options for web apps

Let us check out the two types of scaling.

Vertical scaling (scaling up)

Scaling up means changing the specification of the hardware that will host your application. In Azure, you have the opportunity to start with free, shared hardware and move to an isolated machine in a few clicks. The following screenshot shows the user interface for scaling up a web app:

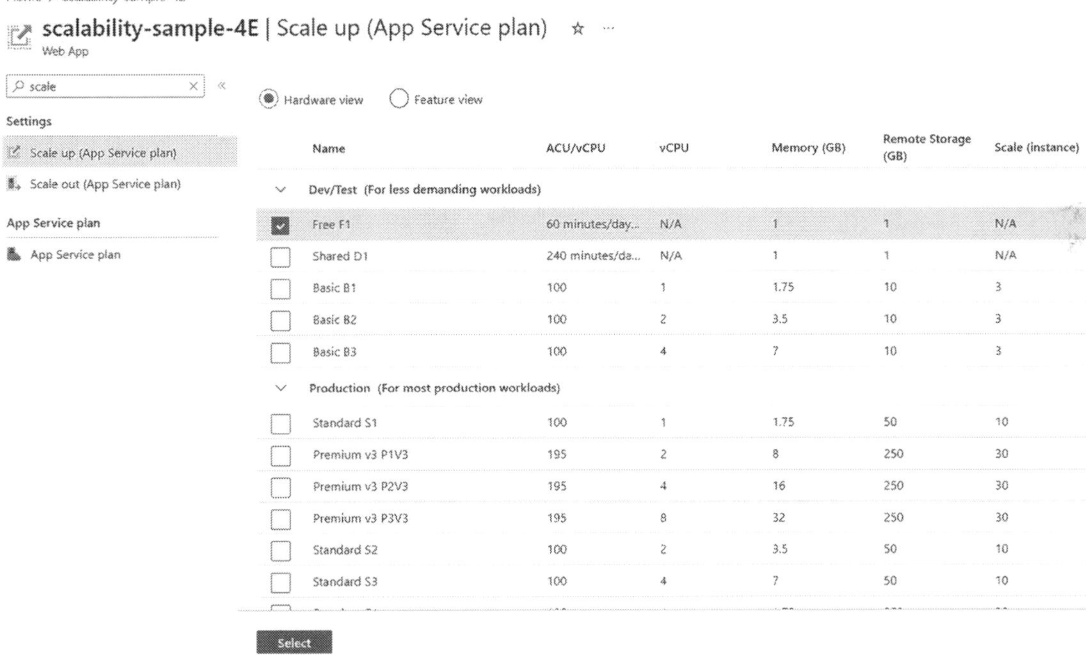

Figure 2.4: Vertical scaling options

By choosing one of the options provided, you can select more powerful hardware (machines with more CPUs, storage, and RAM). Monitoring your application and its App Service plan will guide you on how to decide the best infrastructure for running your solution. It will also offer key insights, such as possible CPU, memory, and I/O bottlenecks.

Horizontal scaling (scaling out)

Scaling out means splitting requests between more servers and using the same capacity instead of using more powerful machines. The load on all the servers is automatically balanced by the Azure infrastructure. This solution is advised when the overall load may change considerably in the future since horizontal scaling can automatically adapt to a given load. The following screenshot shows an automatic **Scale out** strategy defined by two simple rules, triggered by CPU usage:

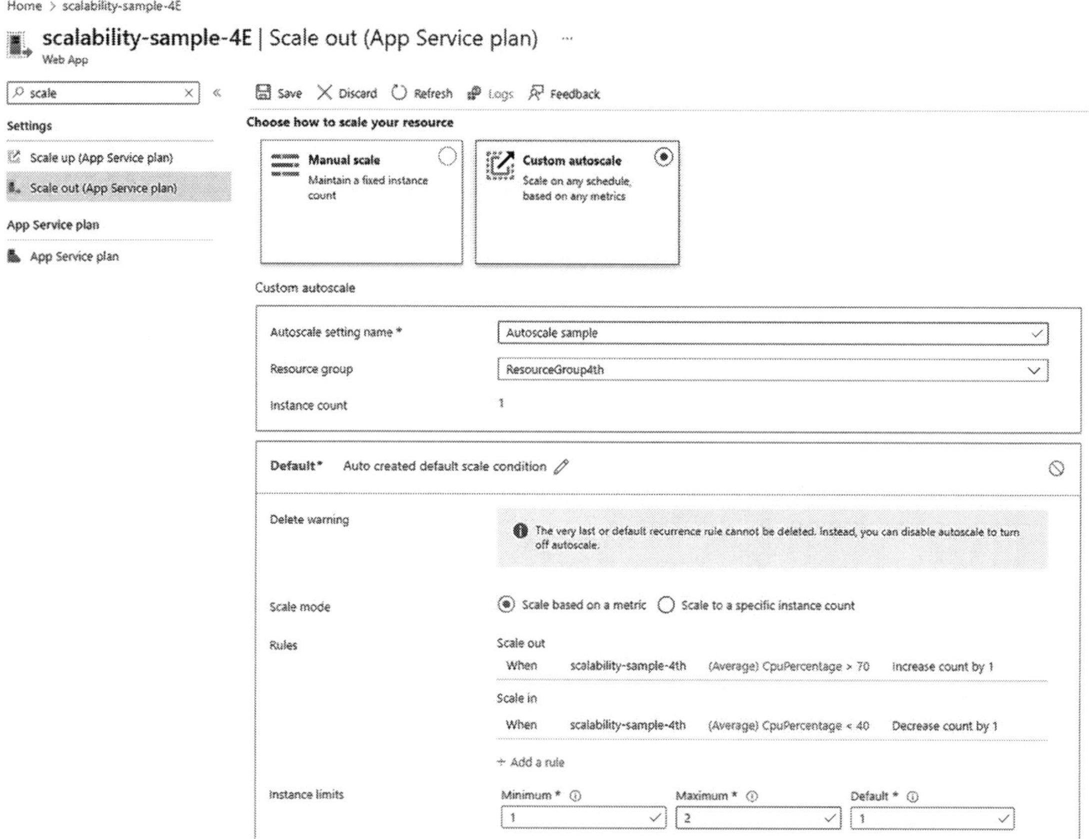

Figure 2.5: Horizontal scaling sample

It is worth highlighting that you can choose to have a hardcoded instance count or implement rules for automatic scale in/out.

A complete description of all the available autoscale rules is beyond the scope of this book. However, they are quite self-explanatory, and the *Further reading* section contains links to the full documentation.

The **Scale out** feature is only available in paid service plans.

In general, horizontal scaling is a way to guarantee availability in an application even with several simultaneous accesses. For sure, its use is not the only way to keep a system available, but it does help.

Creating a scalable web app with .NET 8

Among all the available frameworks for implementing web apps, running web apps with ASP.NET Core in .NET 8 ensures good performance, together with low production and maintenance costs. The union of C#, a strongly typed and advanced general-purpose language, and continuous performance improvements achieved in ASP.NET Core distinguish this option as one of the best for enterprise development.

The steps in this section will guide you through the creation of an ASP.NET Core Runtime 8-based web app. All the steps are quite simple, but some details require particular attention.

It is worth mentioning that .NET 8 gives you the opportunity to develop for any platform – desktops (WPF, Windows Forms, and UWP), web (ASP.NET), cloud (Azure), mobile (Xamarin), gaming (Unity), IoT (ARM32 and ARM64), or AI (ML.NET and .NET for Apache Spark). So, the recommendation from now on is to only use .NET 8. In this scenario, you can run your web app on either Windows servers or cheaper Linux servers.

Nowadays, Microsoft recommends classic .NET, just in case the features you need are not available in .NET Core/5+ or you are deploying your web app in an environment that does not support .NET Core. In any other case, you should prefer .NET Core/5+ because it allows you to do the following:

- Run your web app in Windows, Linux, macOS, or Docker containers
- Design your solution with microservices
- Have high-performance and scalable systems

Containers and microservices will be covered in *Chapter 11, Applying a Microservice Architecture to Your Enterprise Application*. There, you will get a better understanding of the advantages of these technologies. For now, it is enough to say that .NET 8 and microservices were designed for performance and scalability, which is why you should prefer .NET 8 in all your new projects. Besides, .NET 8 is guaranteed by Microsoft as a Long Term Support version, which means three years of patches and free support.

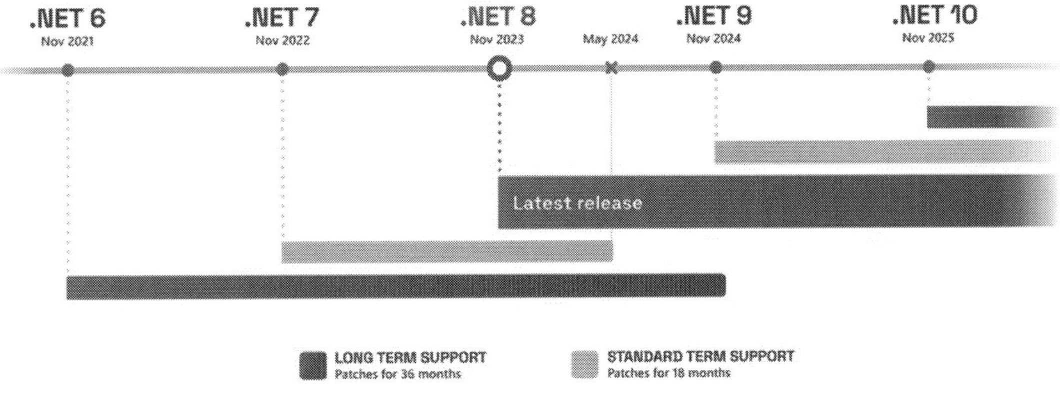

Figure 2.6: .NET 8 support policy

The following procedure will show you how to create an ASP.NET Core web app in Visual Studio 2022 with .NET 8:

1. As soon as you start VS 2022, you will be able to click on **Create a new project**.
2. Once you select **ASP.NET Core Web App**, you will be directed to a screen where you will be asked to set up **Project name, Location,** and **Solution name**:

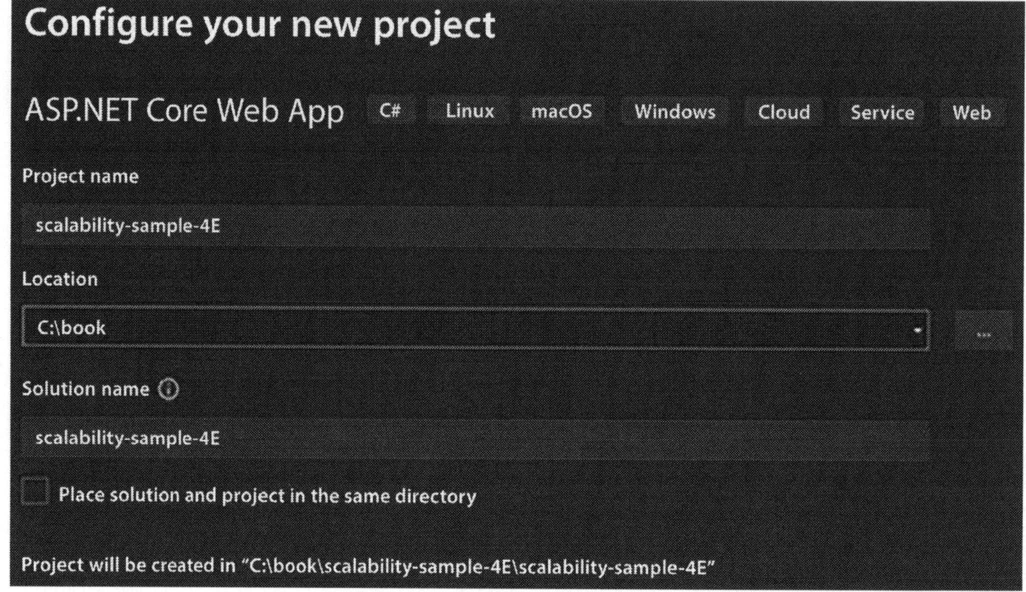

Figure 2.7: Creating an ASP.NET Core web application

3. After that, you will be able to select the .NET version to use. Select **.NET 8.0** to get the most advanced and up-to-date platform.
4. Click **Create** to create your ASP.NET Core 8 web app.
5. Now that you are done with adding the basic details, you can connect your web app project to your Azure account and publish it.

6. If you right-click the project you created in Solution Explorer, you have the option to **Publish**.
7. You will find different targets in terms of where to publish your web app. Select **Azure** as the target:

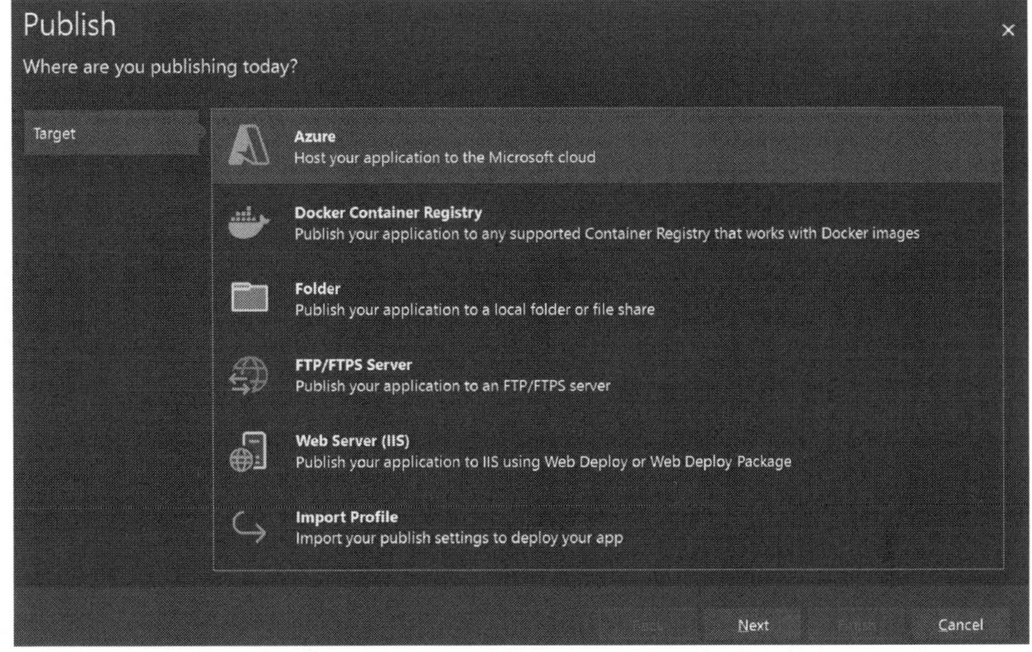

Figure 2.8: Targeting Azure to publish the app

8. Then, you will be able to decide the specific target to publish. Select **Azure App Service (Windows)** for this demo.

9. You may be required to define your Microsoft Account credentials at this time. This is because there is full integration between Visual Studio and Azure. This gives you the opportunity to view all the resources you created in the Azure portal in your development environment.

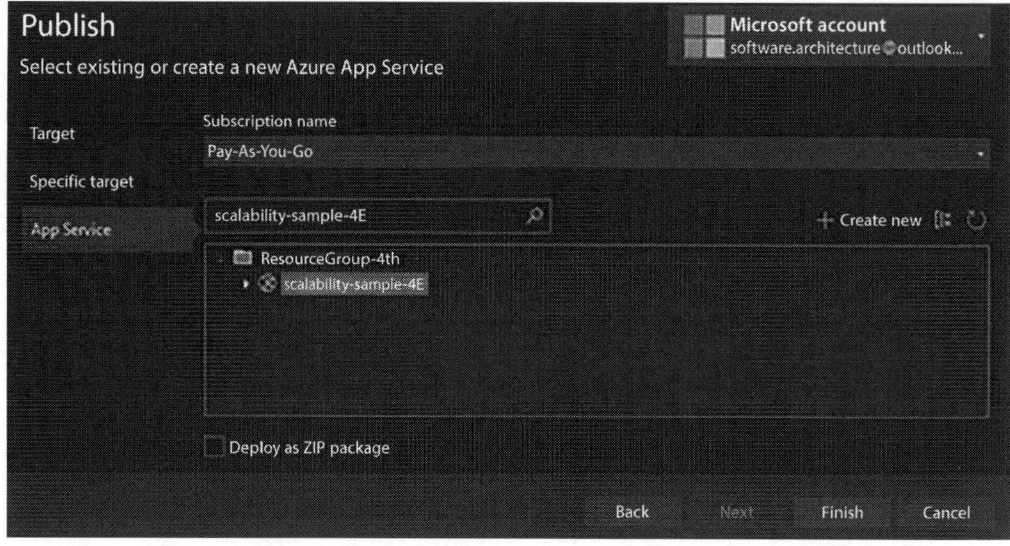

Figure 2.9: Integration between Visual Studio and Azure

10. If you want to create a new web app using Visual Studio, make sure to select the **Free Size** tier of pricing during the App Service creation process so that this does not incur any costs:

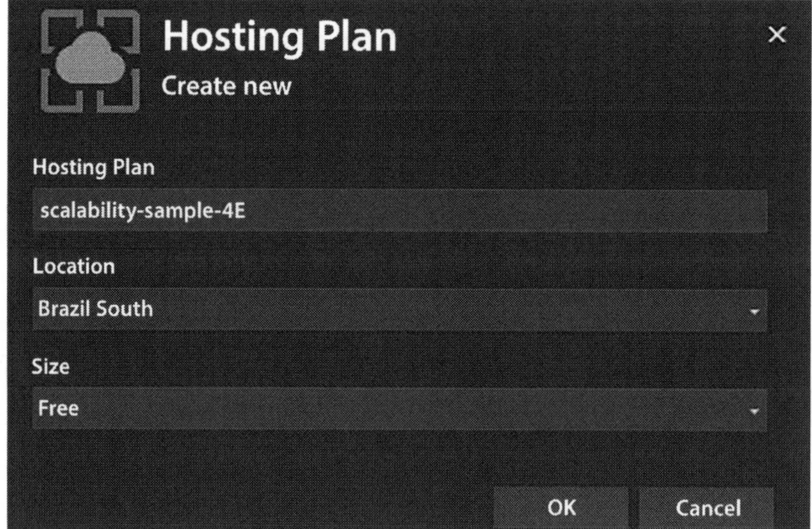

Figure 2.10: Creating a New Hosting Plan

11. The usual way to deploy using Visual Studio is by selecting **Publish Profile**, which generates a `.pubxml` file, which is a Visual Studio publish profile. In this case, you currently have two modes for deployment.

The first, **Framework-dependent**, will require a web app configured with the target framework. The second, **Self-contained**, will not need this feature since the binaries of the framework will be published together with the application. Once the file is created and the options are selected, you just click on the **Publish** button, and the process will start:

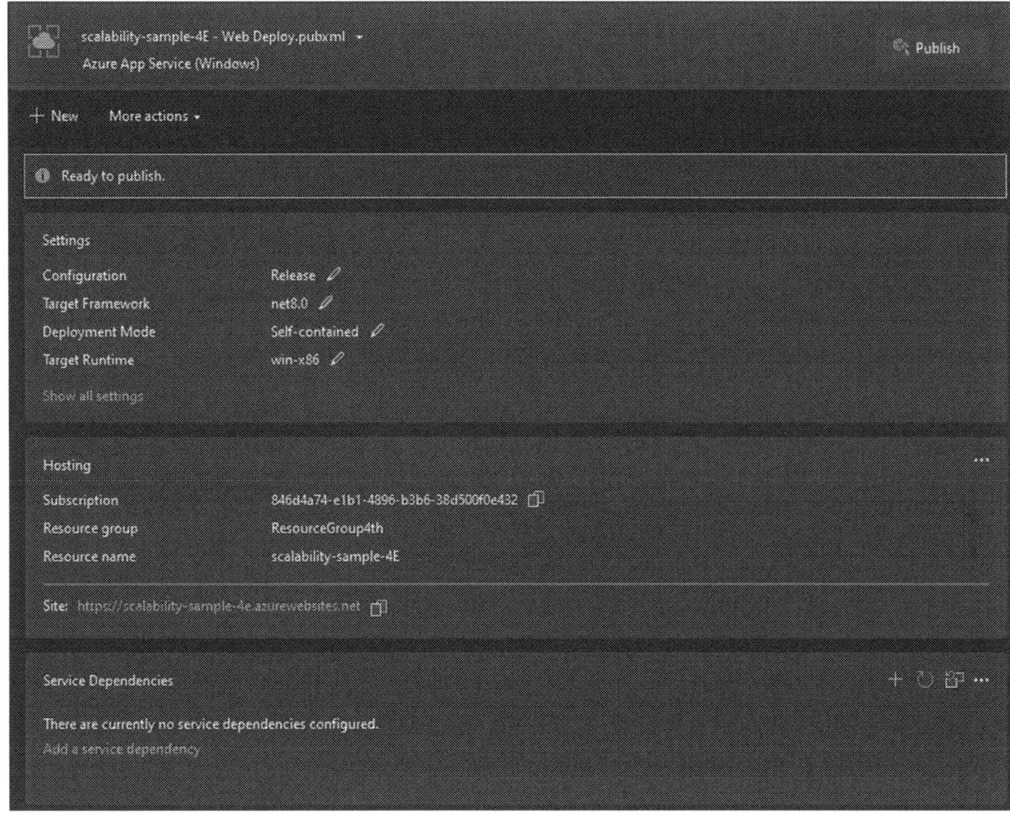

Figure 2.11: Publish profile web deploy

12. It is worth mentioning that to publish ASP.NET Preview versions in **Framework-dependent** mode, you must add an extension in the web app setup panel in the Azure portal, as shown in the following screenshot. However, consider using **Self-contained** mode, especially when you are under preview versions and using Windows apps:

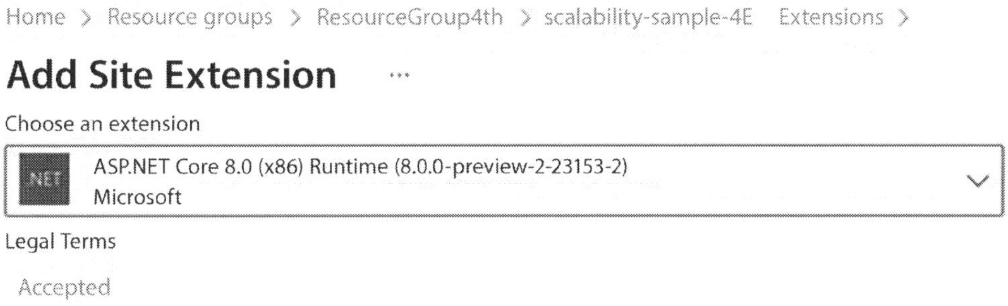

Home > Resource groups > ResourceGroup4th > scalability-sample-4E Extensions >

Add Site Extension ...

Choose an extension

.NET ASP.NET Core 8.0 (x86) Runtime (8.0.0-preview-2-23153-2)
Microsoft

Legal Terms

Accepted

Figure 2.12: Adding extensions in Azure App Service

For more information on deploying ASP.NET Core 8.0 to Azure App Service, please refer to the following link: `https://learn.microsoft.com/en-us/aspnet/core/host-and-deploy/azure-apps/?view=aspnetcore-8.0&tabs=visual-studio`.

Although publishing using Visual Studio 2022 may be considered a good option for demonstration, in the real world, it is almost impossible to keep your publishing strategy using it. For this reason, you might consider using a CI/CD flow based on GitHub Actions, which automatically enables deployment on the code being pushed to a GitHub repo. It is worth mentioning that you must be connected to a GitHub repo to access this new function. Let us use this new feature for this demonstration. We will discuss it in more depth in *Chapter 8, Understanding DevOps Principles and CI/CD*.

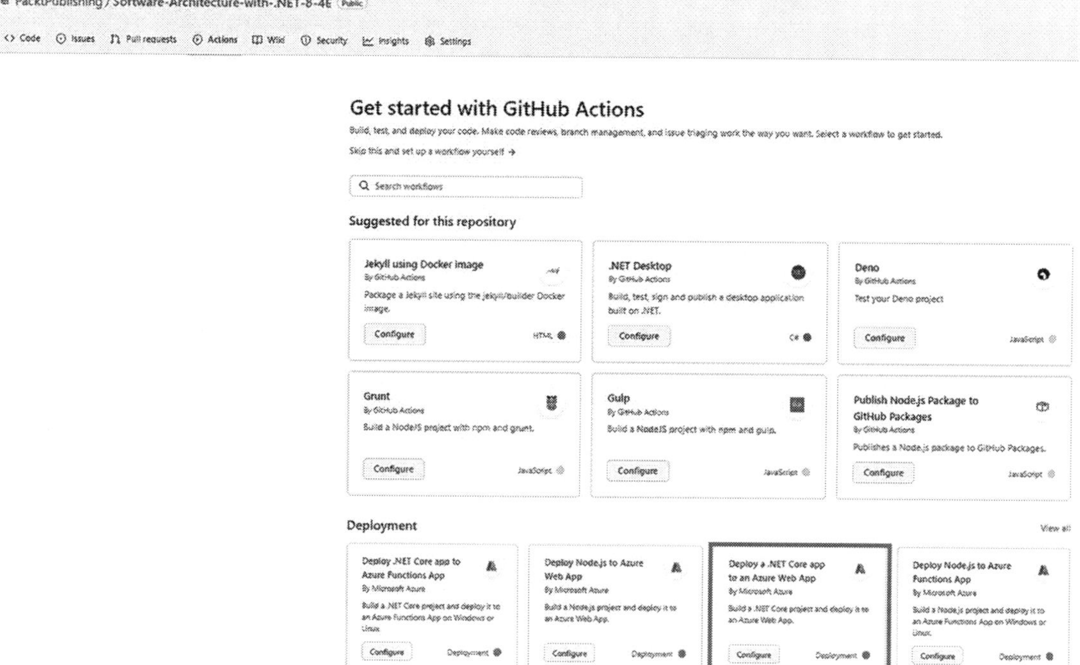

Figure 2.13: Deploying a web app using GitHub actions

1. Once you have pushed your code, you can go to the GitHub Actions pane and select the way you want to deploy the web app.
2. For this second demo, you can select **Deploy a .NET Core app to an Azure Web App**. With this option, you will have a YAML file created with all the instructions needed to connect your code to the web app.

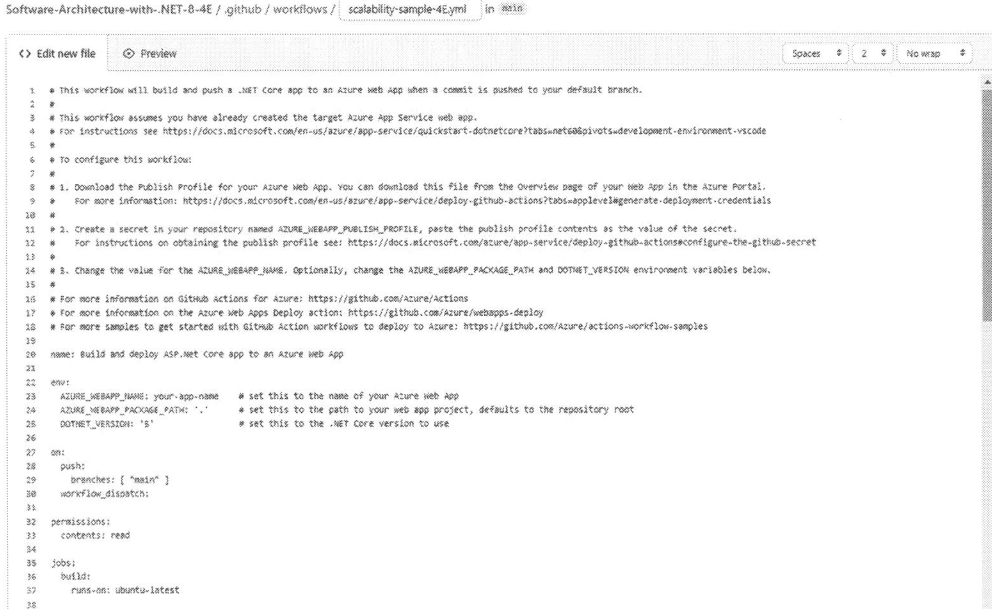

Figure 2.14: YAML file used to deploy the application

Depending on the web app you want to deploy, you will need a different script. These scripts are documented at `https://github.com/Azure/webapps-deploy`.

3. Once you have set the correct script, you will be able to check the execution of the GitHub Action:

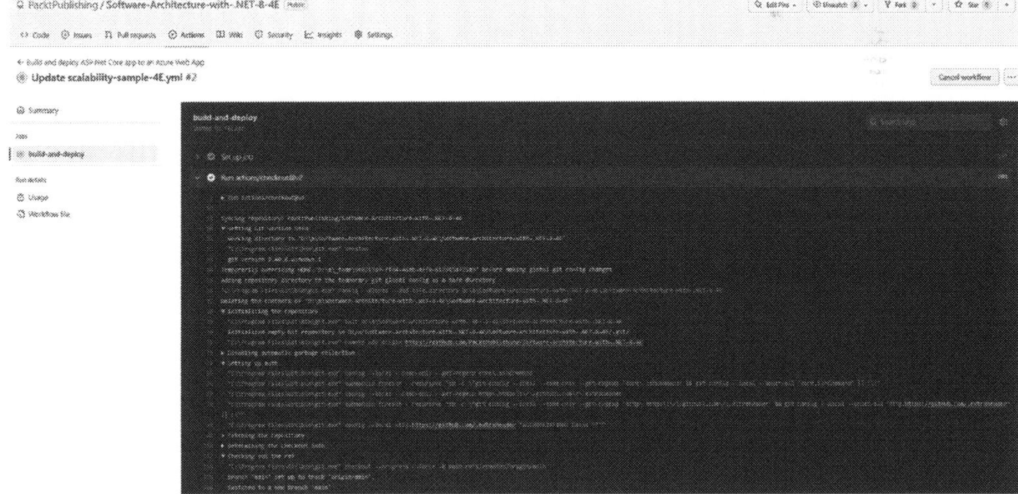

Figure 2.15: GitHub Actions tab

Here, we described two ways to deploy a web app. In *Chapter 8, Understanding DevOps Principles and CI/CD*, we will go further into **Continuous Integration/Continuous Delivery** (**CI/CD**) strategies to guarantee all the steps required to get an application to production, that is, building, testing, deployment to staging, and deployment to production.

Now that you have learned a great way to make your web apps run on Azure, using Visual Studio as a helpful tool, it is essential to understand some performance issues that may cause struggles while creating a solution.

Performance issues that need to be considered when programming in C#

Nowadays, C# is one of the most used programming languages in the world, so awareness of C# programming best practices is fundamental for the design of good architectures that satisfy the most common non-functional requirements.

The following sections mention a few simple but effective tips – the associated code samples are available in this book's GitHub repository. It is worth mentioning that .NET Foundation has developed a library dedicated to benchmarking called BenchmarkDotNet. You may find it useful for your scenarios. Check it out at `https://benchmarkdotnet.org/`.

String concatenation

This is a classic one! A naive concatenation of strings with the `+` string operator may cause serious performance issues since every time two strings are concatenated; their contents are copied into a new string.

So, if we concatenate, for instance, 10 strings that have an average length of 100, the first operation has a cost of 200, the second one has a cost of `200+100=300`, the third one has a cost of `300+100=400`, and so on. It is not difficult to convince yourself that the overall cost grows as $m*n^2$, where `n` is the number of strings and `m` is their average length. n^2 is not too big for small `n` (say, `n < 10`), but it becomes quite big when `n` reaches the magnitude of 100-1,000 and is unacceptable for magnitudes of 10,000-100,000.

Let us look at this with some test code that compares naive concatenation with the same operation but performed with the help of the `StringBuilder` class (the code is available in this book's GitHub repository):

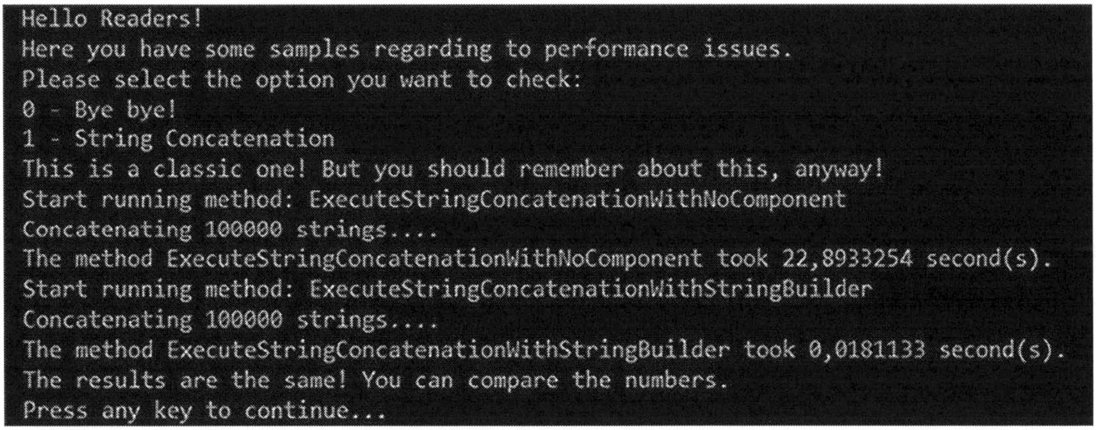

```
Hello Readers!
Here you have some samples regarding to performance issues.
Please select the option you want to check:
0 - Bye bye!
1 - String Concatenation
This is a classic one! But you should remember about this, anyway!
Start running method: ExecuteStringConcatenationWithNoComponent
Concatenating 100000 strings....
The method ExecuteStringConcatenationWithNoComponent took 22,8933254 second(s).
Start running method: ExecuteStringConcatenationWithStringBuilder
Concatenating 100000 strings....
The method ExecuteStringConcatenationWithStringBuilder took 0,0181133 second(s).
The results are the same! You can compare the numbers.
Press any key to continue...
```

Figure 2.16: Concatenation test code result

If you create a `StringBuilder` class with something like `var sb = new System.Text.StringBuilder()`, and then you add each string to it with `sb.Append(currString)`, the strings are not copied; instead, their pointers are queued in a list. They are copied in the final string just once when you call `sb.ToString()` to get the final result. Accordingly, the cost of `StringBuilder`-based concatenation grows simply as `m*n`.

Of course, you will probably never find a piece of software with a function like the preceding one that concatenates 100,000 strings. However, you need to recognize pieces of code like these where the concatenation of some 20-100 strings, say, in a web server that handles several requests simultaneously might cause bottlenecks that damage your non-functional requirements for performance.

Exceptions

Always remember that exceptions are much slower than normal code flow! So, the usage of `try-catch` needs to be concise and essential; otherwise, you will have big performance issues.

The following two samples compare the usage of `try-catch` and `Int32.TryParse` to check whether a string can be converted into an integer, as follows:

```
private static string ParseIntWithTryParse()
{
    string result = string.Empty;
    if (int.TryParse(result, out var value))
        result = value.ToString();
    else
        result = "There is no int value";
    return $"Final result: {result}";
}
private static string ParseIntWithException()
{
```

```
        string result = string.Empty;
        try
        {
            result = Convert.ToInt32(result).ToString();
        }
        catch (Exception)
        {
            result = "There is no int value";
        }
        return $"Final result: {result}";
    }
```

The second function does not look dangerous, but it is thousands of times slower than the first one:

```
Hello Readers!
Here you have some samples regarding to performance issues.
Please select the option you want to check:
0 - Bye bye!
1 - String Concatenation
2 - Exceptions
Always remember! Exceptions take too much time to handle!
Start running method: ParseIntWithException
The method ParseIntWithException took 0,0450462 second(s) (45,0462 ms)
Start running method: ParseIntWithTryParse
The method ParseIntWithTryParse took 5,6E-06 second(s) (0,0056 ms)
The results are the same! You can compare the numbers.
Press any key to continue...
```

Figure 2.17: Exception test code result

To sum this up, exceptions must be used to deal with exceptional cases that break the normal flow of control, for instance, situations when operations must be aborted for some unexpected reasons, and control must be returned several levels up in the call stack.

Multithreading environments for better results – dos and don'ts

If you want to take advantage of all the hardware that the system you are building provides, you must use multithreading. This way, when a thread is waiting for an operation to complete, the application can leave the CPU to other threads instead of wasting CPU time.

On the other hand, no matter how hard Microsoft works to help with this, parallel code is not as simple as eating a piece of cake: it is error-prone and difficult to test and debug. The most important thing to remember as a software architect when you start considering using threads is *does your system require them?* Non-functional and some functional requirements will answer this question for you.

As soon as you are sure that you need a multithreading system, you should decide on which technology is more adequate. There are a few options here, as follows:

- **Creating an instance of** `System.Threading.Thread`: This is a classic way of creating threads in C#. The entire thread life cycle will be in your hands. This is good when you are sure about what you are going to do, but you need to worry about every single detail of the implementation. The resulting code is hard to conceive and debug/test/maintain. So, to keep development costs acceptable, this approach should be confined to a few fundamental, performance-critical modules.
- **Managing threads using** `System.Threading.ThreadPool`: You can reduce the complexity of this implementation by using the `ThreadPool` class. Especially if you intend to develop a solution in which you will have many threads being executed, this could be a good option. It is worth mentioning that the .NET thread pool has been re-implemented in .NET 6 as a C# class, which will bring new possibilities for experimentation or customization.
- **Programming using** `System.Threading.Tasks.Parallel` classes: Since .NET Framework 4.0, you can use parallel classes to enable threads in a simpler way. This is good because you do not need to worry about the life cycle of the threads you create, but it will give you less control over what is happening in each thread.
- **Developing using asynchronous programming:** This is, for sure, the easiest way to develop multithreaded applications since the compiler takes on most of the work. Depending on the way you call an asynchronous method, you may have the `Task` created running in parallel with the `Thread` that was used to call it or even keep that `Thread` waiting without suspending for the `Task` that was created to conclude. This way, asynchronous code mimics the behavior of classical synchronous code while keeping most of the performance advantages of general parallel programming:
    - The overall behavior is deterministic and does not depend on the time taken by each task to complete, so non-reproducible bugs are less likely to happen, and the resulting code is easy to test/debug/maintain. Defining a method as an asynchronous task or not is the only choice left to the programmer; everything else is automatically handled by the runtime. The only thing you should be concerned about is which methods should have asynchronous behavior. It is worth mentioning that defining a method as `async` does not mean it will execute on a separate thread. You may find useful information in a great sample at `https://docs.microsoft.com/en-us/dotnet/csharp/programming-guide/concepts/async/`.
    - Later in this book, we will provide some simple examples of asynchronous programming. For more information about asynchronous programming and its related patterns, please check out *Task-Based Asynchronous Patterns* in the Microsoft documentation (`https://docs.microsoft.com/en-us/dotnet/standard/asynchronous-programming-patterns/task-based-asynchronous-pattern-tap`).

TAP is the evolution of **EAP (Event-Based Asynchronous Pattern)**, which, in turn, is the successor to **APM (Asynchronous Programming Model Pattern)**.

No matter the option you choose, there are some dos and don'ts that, as a software architect, you must pay attention to. These are as follows:

- **Do use concurrent collections** (`System.Collections.Concurrent`): As soon as you start a multithreading application, you have to use these collections. The reason for this is that your program will probably manage the same list, dictionary, and so on from different threads. The use of concurrent collections is the most convenient option for developing thread-safe programs.
- **Do worry about static variables:** It is not possible to say that static variables are prohibited in multithreading development, but you should pay attention to them. Again, multiple threads taking care of the same variable can cause a lot of trouble. If you decorate a static variable with the `[ThreadStatic]` attribute, each thread will see a different copy of that variable, hence solving the problem of several threads competing on the same value. However, `ThreadStatic` variables cannot be used for extra-thread communications since values written by a thread cannot be read by other threads. In asynchronous programming, `AsyncLocal<T>` is the option for doing something like that.
- **Do test system performance after multithreading implementations:** Threads give you the ability to take full advantage of your hardware, but in some cases, badly written threads can waste CPU time just doing nothing! Similar situations may result in almost 100% CPU usage and unacceptable system slowdowns. In some cases, the problem can be mitigated or solved by adding a simple `Thread.Sleep(1)` call in the main loop of some threads to prevent them from wasting too much CPU time, but you need to test this. A use case for this implementation is a Windows service with many threads running in the background.
- **Do not consider multithreading easy:** Multithreading is not as simple as it seems in some syntax implementations. While writing a multithreading application, you should consider things such as the synchronization of the user interface, threading termination, and coordination. In many cases, programs just stop working well due to bad implementation of multithreading.
- **Do not forget to plan the number of threads your system should have:** This is especially important for 32-bit programs. There is a limitation regarding how many threads you can have in any environment. You should consider this when you are designing your system.
- **Do not forget to end your threads:** If you do not have the correct termination procedure for each thread, you will probably have trouble with memory and handling leaks.

Scalability, performance tips, and multithreading are the main tools we can use to tune machine performance. However, the effectiveness of the system you design depends on the overall performance of the entire processing pipeline, which includes both humans and machines. For this reason, in the next section, we will discuss how to design effective user interfaces.

Software usability: how to design effective user interfaces

As a software architect, you cannot improve the performance of humans, but you can improve the performance of human-machine interaction by designing an effective **user interface** (UI), that is, a UI that ensures fast interaction with humans, which, in turn, means the following:

- The UI must be easy to learn to reduce the time that is needed for the target users to learn how to operate it. This constraint is fundamental if UI changes are frequent and for public websites that need to attract the greatest possible number of users.
- The UI must not cause any kind of slowdown in data insertion; data entry speed must be limited only by the user's ability to type, not by system delays or additional gestures that could be avoided.
- Today, we must also consider the accessibility aspects of our solutions since doing so allows us to include more users.

It is worth mentioning that we have UX experts in the market. As a software architect, you must decide when they are essential to the success of the project. The following are a few simple tips when it comes to designing *easy-to-learn* user interfaces:

- Each input screen must state its purpose clearly.
- Use the language of the user, not the language of developers.
- Avoid complications. Design the UI with the average case in mind; more complicated cases can be handled with extra inputs that appear only when needed. Split complex screens into more input steps.
- Use past inputs to understand user intentions and to put users on the right path with messages and automatic UI changes, for instance, cascading drop-down menus.
- Error messages are not bad notes that the system gives to the users who do something that's wrong, but they must explain how to insert the correct input.

Fast UIs result from efficacious solutions to the following three requirements:

- Input fields must be placed in the order they are usually filled, and it should be possible to move to the next input with the *Tab* or *Enter* key. Moreover, fields that often remain empty should be placed at the bottom of the form. Simply put, the usage of the mouse while filling in a form should be minimized. This way, the number of user gestures is kept to a minimum. In a web application, once the optimal placement of input fields has been decided, it is enough to use the `tabindex` attribute to define the right way for users to move from one input field to the next with the *Tab* key.
- System reactions to user input must be as fast as possible. Error messages (or information ones) must appear as soon as the user leaves the input field. The simplest way to achieve this is to move most of the help and input validation logic to the client side so that system reactions do not need to pass through both communication lines and servers.
- Efficacious selection logic: Selecting an existing item should be as easy as possible; for example, selecting one out of some thousands of products in an offer must be possible with a few gestures and with no need to remember the exact product name or its barcode. The next subsection analyzes techniques we can use to decrease complexity to achieve fast selection.

In *Chapter 19, Client Frameworks: Blazor*, we will discuss how this Microsoft technology can help us with the challenges of building web-based applications with C# code in the frontend.

Designing fast selection logic

When all possible choices are in the order of magnitude of 1-50, the usual drop-down menu is enough. For instance, take this currency selection drop-down menu:

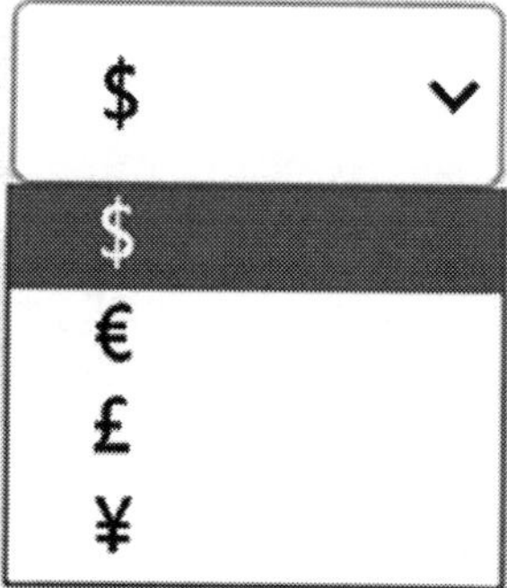

Figure 2.18: Simple drop-down menu

When the order of magnitude is higher but less than a few thousand, an autocomplete that shows the names of all the items that start with the characters typed by the user is usually a good choice:

Figure 2.19: Complex drop-down menu

A similar solution can be implemented with a low computational cost since all the main databases can efficiently select strings that start with a given substring.

When names are quite complex, when searching for the characters that were typed in by the user, they should be extended inside each item string. This operation cannot be performed efficiently with the usual databases and requires ad hoc data structures, nor can we forget the debouncing aspect that can happen while typing as a performance issue.

Finally, when we are searching inside descriptions composed of several words, more complex search patterns are needed. This is the case, for instance, with product descriptions. If the chosen database supports full-text search, the system can efficiently search for the occurrence of several words that have been typed by the user inside all the descriptions.

However, when descriptions are made up of names instead of common words, it might be difficult for the user to remember a few exact names contained in the target description. This happens, for instance, with multi-country company names. In these cases, we need algorithms that find the best match for the character that was typed by the user. Substrings of the string that was typed by the user must be searched in different places of each description. In general, similar algorithms cannot be implemented efficiently with databases based on indexes but require all the descriptions to be loaded in memory and ranked somehow against the string that was typed by the user.

The most famous algorithm in this class is probably the **Levenshtein** algorithm, which is used by most spellcheckers to find a word that best fits the one that was mistyped by the user. This algorithm minimizes the Levenshtein distance between the description and the string typed by the user, that is, the minimum number of character removals and additions needed to transform one string into another.

The Levenshtein algorithm works great but has a very high computational cost. Here, we use a faster algorithm that works well for searching character occurrences in descriptions. Characters typed by the user do not need to occur consecutively in the description but must occur in the same order. Some characters may be missing. Each description is given a penalty that depends on the missing characters and on how far the occurrences of the characters typed by the user are from the others.

More specifically, the algorithm ranks each description with two numbers:

- The number of characters typed by the user that occurs in the description: the more characters contained in the description, the higher its rank.
- Each description is given a penalty equal to the total distance among the occurrences of the characters typed by the user in the description.

The following screenshot shows how the word **Ireland** is ranked against the string **ilad**, which was typed by the user:

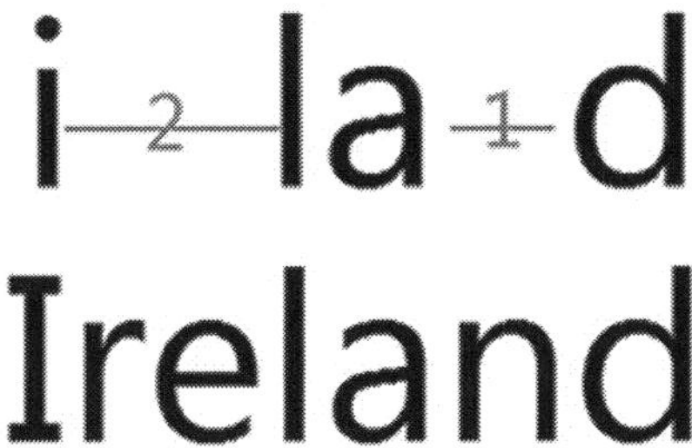

Figure 2.20: Sample of Levenshtein usage

The number of occurrences is four, while the total distance between character occurrences is three.

Once all the descriptions have been rated, they are sorted according to the number of occurrences. Descriptions with the same number of occurrences are sorted according to the lowest penalties. The following is an autocomplete that implements the preceding algorithm:

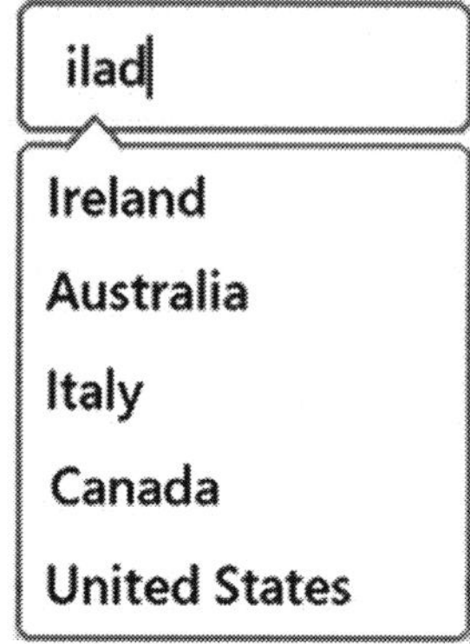

Figure 2.21: Levenshtein algorithm UI experience

The full class code, along with a test console project, is available in this book's GitHub repository.

Selecting from a huge number of items

Here, *huge* does not refer to the amount of space needed to store the data but to the difficulty the user has in remembering the features of each item. When an item must be selected from among more than 10,000-100,000 items, there is no hope of finding it by searching for character occurrences inside a description. Here, the user must be driven toward the right item through a hierarchy of categories.

In this case, several user gestures are needed to perform a single selection. In other words, each selection requires interaction with several input fields. Once it is decided that the selection can't be done with a single input field, the simplest option is cascading drop-down menus, that is, a chain of drop-down menus whose selection list depends on the values that were selected in the previous drop-down menus.

For example, if the user needs to select a town located anywhere in the world, we may use the first drop-down menu to select the country, and once the country has been chosen, we may use this choice to populate a second one with all the towns in the selected country. A simple example is as follows:

Figure 2.22: Cascading drop-down menu example

Clearly, each drop-down menu can be replaced by an autocomplete when required due to having a high number of options.

If making the right selection can be done by intersecting several different hierarchies, cascading drop-down menus become inefficient too, and we need a filter form, as follows:

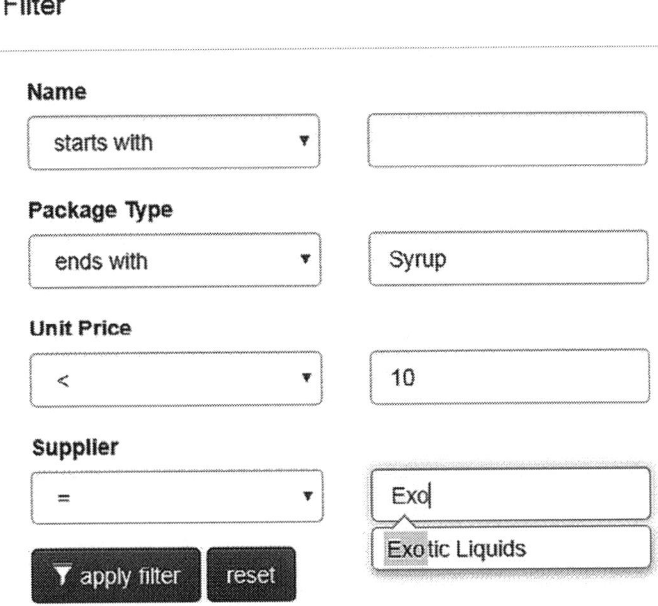

Figure 2.23: Filter form sample

Now, let us understand interoperability with .NET 6.

Interoperability with .NET 8

Since .NET Core, Microsoft has brought to C# developers the ability to deliver their software to various platforms. And you, as a software architect, need to pay attention to this, considering developing for Linux and macOS as a great opportunity to deliver new features to your customers. Therefore, we need to ensure performance and multi-platform support, two common non-functional requirements for many systems.

Both console applications and web apps designed with .NET 8 in Windows are almost completely compatible with Linux and macOS, too. This means you do not have to build the app again to run it on these platforms.

Microsoft offers scripts to help you install .NET on Linux and macOS. You can find them at `https://docs.microsoft.com/dotnet/core/tools/dotnet-install-script`. Once you have the SDK installed, you just need to call `dotnet` the same way you do in Windows.

However, you must be aware of some features that are not fully compatible with Linux and macOS systems. For instance, no equivalent to the Windows Registry exists in these OSes, and you must develop an alternative yourself. If needed, an encrypted JSON config file can be a good option.

Another important point is that Linux is case-sensitive, while Windows is not. Please remember this when you work with files. Another important thing is that the Linux path separator is different from the Windows separator. You can use the `Path.PathSeparator` field and all the other `Path` class members to ensure your code is multi-platform. `Environment.NewLine` can also be useful in some situations.

Besides, you can also adapt your code to the underlying OS by using the runtime checks provided by .NET 8, as follows:

```
using System.Runtime.InteropServices;
if (RuntimeInformation.IsOSPlatform(OSPlatform.Windows))
     Console.WriteLine("Here you have Windows World!");
else if(RuntimeInformation.IsOSPlatform(OSPlatform.Linux))
     Console.WriteLine("Here you have Linux World!");
else if (RuntimeInformation.IsOSPlatform(OSPlatform.OSX))
     Console.WriteLine("Here you have macOS World!");
```

Tip – creating a service in Linux

There are some good ways to create a service when you are developing on Windows, but how can we get the same result if we are developing for the Linux platform? The following script can be used to encapsulate a command-line .NET 8 app in Linux. The idea is that this service works like a Windows service. This can be useful, considering that most Linux installations are command-line-only and run without a user logged in:

1. The first step is to create a file that will run the command-line app. The name of the app is `app.dll`, and it is installed in `appfolder`. The application will be checked every 5,000 milliseconds. This service was created on a CentOS 7 system. Using a Linux terminal, you can type this:

   ```
   cat >sample.service<<EOF
   [Unit]
   Description=Your Linux Service
   After=network.target
   [Service]
   ExecStart=/usr/bin/dotnet $(pwd)/appfolder/app.dll 5000
   Restart=on-failure
   [Install]
   WantedBy=multi-user.target
   EOF
   ```

2. Once the file has been created, you must copy the service file to a system location. After that, you must reload the system and enable the service so that it will restart on reboots:

```
sudo cp sample.service /lib/systemd/system
sudo systemctl daemon-reload
sudo systemctl enable sample
```

3. Done! Now, you can start, stop, and check the service using the following commands. The whole input that you need to provide in your command-line app is as follows:

```
# Start the service
sudo systemctl start sample
# View service status
sudo systemctl status sample
# Stop the service
sudo systemctl stop sample
```

Now that we have learned about a few concepts, let us learn how to implement them in our use case.

Achieving security by design

As we have seen up to this point in the book, the opportunities and techniques we have for developing software are incredible. If you add all the information you will read about in relation to cloud computing in the next chapters, you will see that the opportunities just increase, as does the complexity involved in maintaining this computing environment.

As a software architect, you must understand that these opportunities come with many responsibilities. The world has changed a lot in recent years. The second decade of the 21st century has required lots of technology. Apps, social media, Industry 4.0, big data, and artificial intelligence are no longer future objectives but current projects that you will lead and deal with within your daily routine. However, the third decade of our century will require much more attention when it comes to cybersecurity.

The world now regulates companies that manage personal data. For instance, the GDPR – the General Data Protection Regulation – is mandatory not only for European territory but also for the whole world; it has changed the way software is developed. There are many initiatives comparable to the GDPR that must be added to your glossary of techniques and regulations, considering that the software you design will be impacted by them.

Security by design must be one of your areas of focus for designing new applications. This subject is huge, and it is not going to be completely covered in this book, but as a software architect, you must understand the necessity of having a specialist in the information security area in your team to guarantee the policies and practices needed to avoid cyber-attacks and maintain the confidentiality, privacy, integrity, authenticity, and availability of the services you architect.

When it comes to protecting your ASP.NET Core application, it is worth mentioning that the framework has many features to help you out with that. For instance, it includes authentication and authorization patterns. In the OWASP Cheat Sheet Series, you can read about many other .NET practices.

The **Open Web Application Security Project®** (**OWASP**) is a nonprofit foundation that works to improve the security of software. Check it out at `https://owasp.org/`.

ASP.NET Core also provides features to help us out with the GDPR. Basically, there are APIs and templates to guide you in the implementation of policy declaration and cookie usage consent.

List of practices for achieving a safe architecture

The following list of practices related to security certainly does not cover the entirety of the subject. However, these practices will help you, as a software architect, to explore some solutions related to this topic.

Authentication

Define an authentication method for your web app. There are many authentication options available nowadays, from ASP.NET Core Identity to external provider authentication methods, such as Facebook or Google. As a software architect, you must consider who the target audience of the application is. It would also be worth considering using Azure **Active Directory** (**AD**) as a starting point if you choose to go down this route.

You may find it useful to design authentication associated with Azure AD, a component for managing the Active Directory of the company you are working for. This alternative is pretty good in some scenarios, especially for internal usage. Azure currently offers Active Directory for usage as **B2B** (**Business to Business**) or B2C (**Business to Consumer**).

Depending on the scenario of the solution you are building, you might need to implement **MFA – Multi-Factor Authentication.** The idea of this pattern is to ask for at least two forms of proof of identity before allowing the solution to be used. It is worth mentioning that Azure AD facilitates this for you.

You may also find it useful to implement authentication to your platform using as basis **Microsoft Identity Platform**. In this case, the usage of the **Microsoft Authentication Library** (**MSAL**) will facilitate your work hugely. Check how to implement it by reading its documentation at `https://learn.microsoft.com/en-us/azure/active-directory/develop/msal-overview`.

Do not forget that you must determine an authentication method for the APIs you provide. JSON Web Token is a pretty good pattern, and its usage is totally cross-platform.

You must determine the authorization model you will use in your web app. There are four model options:

- **Simple**, where you just use the `[Authorize]` attribute in the class or method.
- **Role-based**, in which you may declare `Roles` for accessing the `Controller` you are developing.
- **Claims-based**, where you can define values that must be received during the authentication to indicate that the user is authorized.
- **Policy-based**, in which there is a policy established to define the access in that `Controller`.

You may also define a controller or method in a class as being fully accessible to any user by defining the `[AllowAnonymous]` attribute. Be sure this kind of implementation will not cause any vulnerabilities in the system you are designing.

The model you decide to use will define exactly what each user will be able to do in the application.

Sensitive data

While designing, you, as a software architect, will have to decide which part of the data you store is sensitive, and it will need to be protected. By connecting to Azure, your web app will be able to store protected data in components such as Azure Storage and Azure Key Vault. Storage in Azure will be discussed in *Chapter 12, Choosing Your Data Storage in the Cloud*.

It is highly recommended to check the **Data Protection Framework** that your solution will need to deal with, considering where it will be placed.

It is worth mentioning that Azure Key Vault is used to protect secrets your app may have. Consider using this solution when you have this kind of requirement.

Web security

It is totally unacceptable to have a production solution deployed without the HTTPS protocol enabled. Azure Web Apps and ASP.NET Core solutions have various options to not only use but enforce the usage of this security protocol.

There are many known attacks and malicious patterns, such as cross-site request forgery, open redirect, and cross-site scripting. ASP.NET Core provides APIs to solve them. You need to find the ones that are useful for your solution.

Good programming practices, such as avoiding SQL injection by using parameters in your queries, is another important goal to achieve.

You may find cloud architecture security patterns at `https://docs.microsoft.com/en-us/azure/architecture/patterns/category/security`.

To finish, it is worth mentioning that security needs to be treated using the onion approach, which means that there are many layers of security to be implemented. You must have determined a policy to guarantee a process to access the data, including physical access for people who use the system you are developing. In addition, you also must develop a disaster recovery solution in case the system is attacked. The disaster recovery solution will depend on your cloud solution. We will discuss this later, in *Chapter 10, Deciding on the Best Cloud-Based Solution*.

Summary

Functional requirements that describe system behavior must be complemented with non-functional requirements that constrain system performance, scalability, availability, resilience, interoperability, usability, and security.

Performance requirements come from response time and system load requirements. As a software architect, you should ensure you have the required performance at the minimum cost, building efficient algorithms and taking full advantage of the available hardware resources with multithreading.

Scalability is the ability of a system to be adapted to an increasing load. Systems can be scaled vertically by providing more powerful hardware or horizontally by replicating and load balancing the same hardware, which increases the availability. The cloud, in general, and Azure can help us implement strategies dynamically, with no need to stop your application.

Tools such as .NET 8 that run on several platforms can ensure interoperability, that is, the capability of your software to run on different target machines and with different operating systems (Windows, Linux, macOS, Android, and so on).

Usability is ensured by taking care of input field order, the effectiveness of the item selection logic, and how easy your system is to learn.

Besides, the more complex your solution is, the better resilience it should have. The idea of resilience is not to guarantee that the solution does not fail. Instead, the idea is to guarantee that the solution has an action defined when each part of the software fails.

As a software architect, you must consider security from the very beginning of the design. Following the guidelines to determine the correct patterns and having a security specialist on your team is the best way to comply with all the current regulations we have.

In the next chapter, you will learn how Azure DevOps and GitHub can help us when it comes to collecting, defining, and documenting our requirements.

Questions

1. What are the two conceptual ways to scale a system?
2. Can you deploy your web app automatically from Visual Studio to Azure?
3. What is multithreading useful for?
4. What are the main advantages of the asynchronous pattern over other multithreading techniques?
5. Why is the order of input fields so important?
6. Why is the `Path` class so important for interoperability?
7. What is the advantage of a .NET standard class library?
8. List the *most-used* types of .NET Visual Studio projects.

Further reading

The following are some books and links you may consider reading to gather more information in relation to this chapter:

- Cloud computing models
    - https://docs.microsoft.com/en-us/azure/architecture/best-practices/auto-scaling
    - https://docs.microsoft.com/en-us/aspnet/core/host-and-deploy/azure-apps/
- Parallel programming
    - https://docs.microsoft.com/en-us/dotnet/standard/parallel-processing-and-concurrency
    - https://docs.microsoft.com/en-us/dotnet/standard/parallel-programming/
- Performance improvements in .NET
    - https://devblogs.microsoft.com/dotnet/performance-improvements-in-net-8/
    - https://benchmarkdotnet.org/
- Security aspects
    - https://docs.microsoft.com/en-us/aspnet/core/security/
    - https://cheatsheetseries.owasp.org/cheatsheets/DotNet_Security_Cheat_Sheet.html
    - https://docs.microsoft.com/en-us/aspnet/core/security/gdpr
    - https://learn.microsoft.com/en-us/azure/active-directory/develop/msal-overview
- Service consistency aspects
    - https://docs.microsoft.com/en-us/azure/architecture/patterns/category/resiliency
    - https://docs.microsoft.com/en-us/azure/architecture/patterns/category/availability
- Dotnet support
    - https://dotnet.microsoft.com/platform/support/policy

Learn more on Discord

To join the Discord community for this book – where you can share feedback, ask questions to the authors, and learn about new releases – follow the QR code below:

`https://packt.link/SoftwareArchitectureCSharp12Dotnet8`

3

Managing Requirements

Based on what we covered in *Chapters 1* and *2*, the first steps of software development will direct you to create a software project. When it comes to software projects, the biggest challenge is how to organize them in a way where every single participant will understand what is needed. The best way to do so is to organize its requirements. But more than that, connecting these requirements to a code repository will deliver to everybody a fast and more collaborative view of the project that is being worked on. For years, Microsoft has invested in tools to help us to do this. Team Foundation Server and Visual Studio Teams Services are examples. Today, there are two good approaches we can use that we will discuss in this chapter: Azure DevOps and GitHub. Azure DevOps is an evolution of Visual Studio Team Services, and it offers a variety of new features that can help developers document and organize their software. GitHub is well known as an online code repository, but since Microsoft acquired it, a bunch of great tools for application lifecycle management have been integrated into it. For this reason, we can now find many different ways of using GitHub.

The following topics will be covered in this chapter:

- Creating a DevOps project using your Azure account
- Understanding the functionalities offered by Azure DevOps and GitHub to organize your project
- Organizing and managing requirements using Azure DevOps and GitHub

The first two sections of this chapter summarize all the functionalities offered by these tools, while the remaining sections focus specifically on the tools for documenting requirements and supporting the overall development process. Most of the functionality introduced in the first two sections will be analyzed in more detail in other chapters.

Technical requirements

This chapter requires you to create a new free Azure account or use an existing one. The *Creating an Azure account* section in *Chapter 1*, *Understanding the Importance of Software Architecture*, explains how to create one.

Introducing Azure DevOps

Azure DevOps is a Microsoft **Software-as-a-Service** (**SaaS**) platform that enables you to deliver continuous value to your customers. By creating an account there, you will be able to easily plan your project, store your code safely, test it, publish the solution to a staging environment, and then publish the solution to the actual production infrastructure.

The automation of all the steps involved in software production ensures the continuous enhancement and improvement of an existing solution to adapt it to market needs.

You can start the process by accessing `https://dev.azure.com`. There, you will be able to sign up using a new account or even sign in using your GitHub account. Once you have access to it, you will be asked to create an organization, as you can see in the following figure.

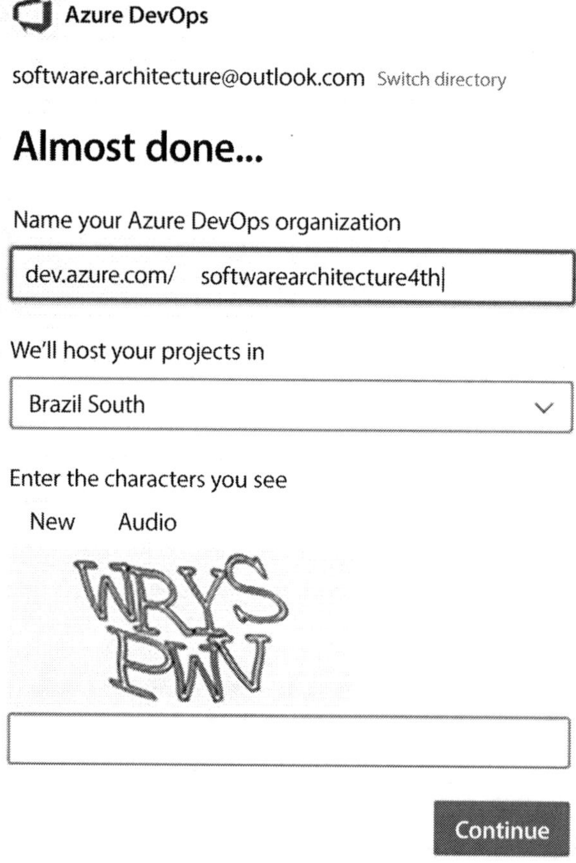

Figure 3.1: Creating an Azure DevOps organization

After the organization is created, you will be able to create a new project, as we can see in the following screenshot.

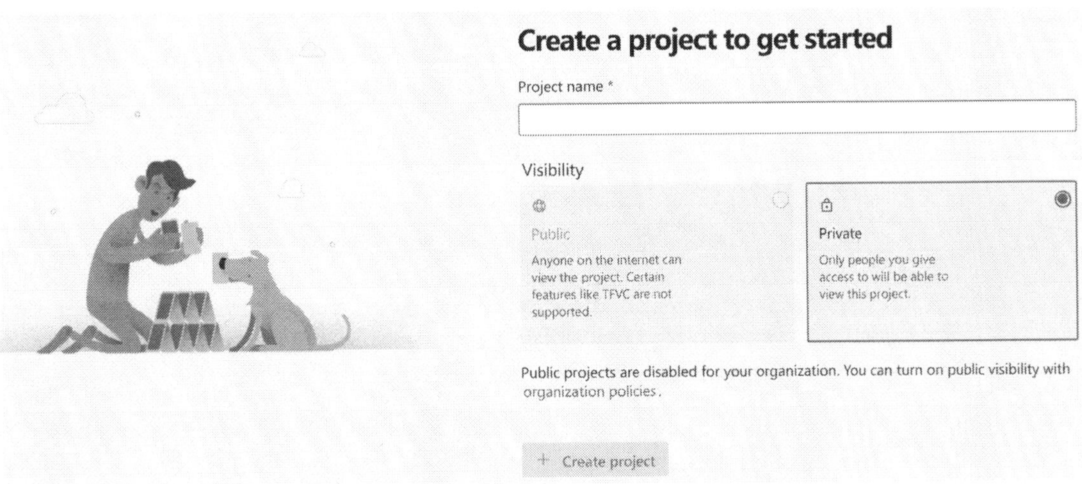

Figure 3.2: Creating a project using Azure DevOps

It is important to mention that public projects can be used so long as you comply with the Azure DevOps code of conduct. Once you define the name of the project and its visibility, you will have the project created in seconds.

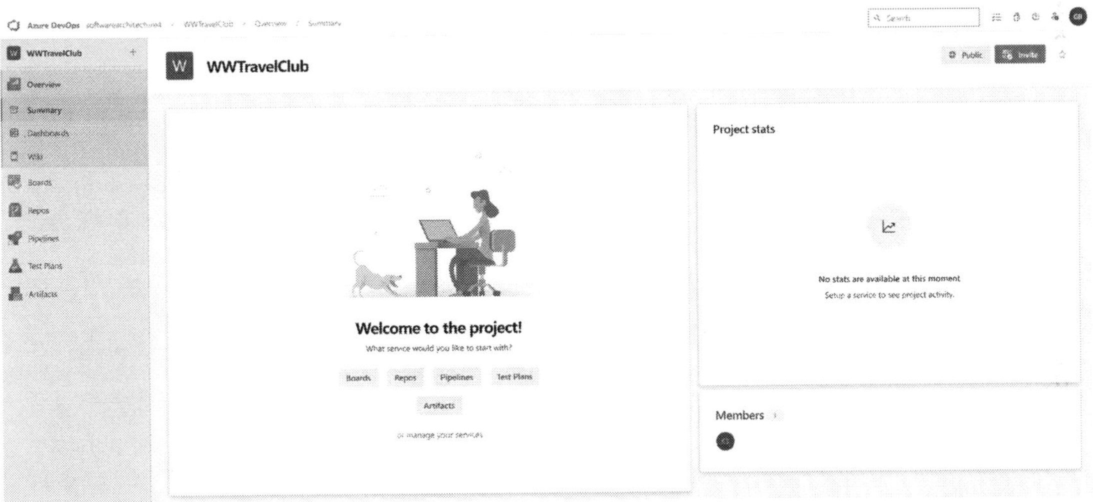

Figure 3.3: Azure DevOps project created

DevOps itself will be discussed in detail in *Chapter 8*, *Understanding DevOps Principles and CI/CD*, but you need to understand it as a philosophy that is focused on delivering value to customers. It is the union of people, processes, and products, where the **Continuous Integration and Continuous Deployment** (**CI/CD**) methodology is used to apply continuous improvements to a software application delivered to the production environment. Azure DevOps is a powerful tool whose range of applications encompasses all the steps involved in both the initial development of an application and its subsequent CI/CD process.

Azure DevOps contains tools for collecting requirements and organizing the whole development process. They can be accessed by clicking the **Boards** menu option on the Azure DevOps page.

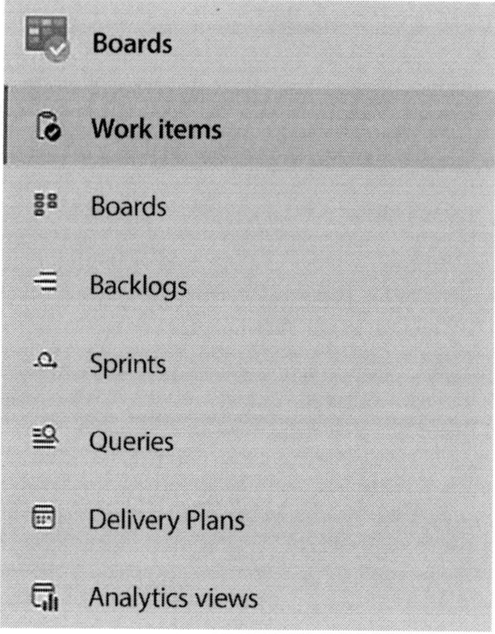

Figure 3.4: Azure DevOps Boards menu

All other functionalities available in Azure DevOps are briefly reviewed in the following subsections. They will be discussed in detail in other chapters. More specifically, DevOps principles and CI/CD are discussed in *Chapter 8*, *Understanding DevOps Principles and CI/CD*, and build/test pipelines can be reviewed in *Chapter 9*, *Testing Your Enterprise Application*.

Managing system requirements in Azure DevOps

Azure DevOps enables you to document system requirements using work items. Work items are stored in your project as chunks of information that can be assigned to a person. They are classified into various types and may contain a measure of the development effort required, a status, and the development stage (iteration) they belong to. Mainly, they are tasks or actions that need to be completed to deliver a product or service.

DevOps is usually combined with agile methodologies, so Azure DevOps uses iterations, and the whole development process is organized as a set of sprints. The work items available depend on the *work item process* you select while creating the Azure DevOps project.

You can check project types in Azure DevOps at `https://learn.microsoft.com/en-us/azure/devops/boards/work-items/guidance/choose-process`.

The following subsections contain a description of the most common work item types that appear when an **Agile** or **Scrum** work item process is selected (the default is **Agile**).

Epic work items

Imagine you are developing a system comprising various subsystems. You are probably not going to conclude the whole system in a single iteration. Therefore, we need an umbrella spanning several iterations to encapsulate all features of each subsystem. Each Epic work item represents one of these umbrellas that can contain several features to be implemented in various development iterations.

In the Epic work item, you can define the state and acceptance criteria as well as the start date and target date. Besides this, you can also provide a priority and an effort estimate. All this detailed information helps the stakeholders to follow the development process. This is useful as a macro view of the project.

Feature work items

All the information that you provide in an Epic work item can also be placed in a Feature work item. So, the difference between these two types of work items is not related to the kind of information they contain but rather to their respective roles and the goals your team aims to accomplish by completing. A feature is a shippable software component. Epics may span several iterations and are hierarchically above Features; that is, each Epic work item is linked to several children features, while each Feature work item is usually implemented in a few sprints and is part of a single Epic work item.

It is worth mentioning that all work items have sections for team discussions. There, you will be able to find a team member in the discussion area by typing the @ character (as in many forums/social media applications). Inside each work item, you can link and attach various information. You may also check the history of the current work item in a specific section.

Feature work items are the places to start recording user requirements. For instance, you can write a Feature work item called **Access Control** to define the complete functionality needed to implement the system access control.

Product Backlog items/User Story work items

Which of these work items is available depends on the working item process selected. There are minor differences between them, but their purpose is essentially the same. They contain detailed requirements for the features, described by the Feature work items they are connected to. More specifically, each Product Backlog/User Story work item specifies the requirements of a single functionality that is part of the behavior described in its parent Feature work item.

For instance, in a Feature work item for system access control, the maintenance of the users and the login interface should be two different User Story/Product Backlog items. These requirements will guide the creation of other child work items:

- **Tasks:** These are important work items that describe the job that needs to be done to meet the requirements stated in the father Product Backlog items/User Story work item. Task work items can contain time estimates, which help with team capacity management and overall scheduling.
- **Test cases:** These items describe how to test the functionality described by the requirements.

Considering that you will have many work items in a project, visualizing them is not an easy task. For this reason, you may consider **Work Item Visualization** to simplify your view. Check it out at `https://marketplace.visualstudio.com/items?itemName=ms-devlabs.WorkItemVisualization`.

The number of tasks and test cases you will create for each Product Backlog/User Story work item will vary according to the development and testing scenario you use.

Azure DevOps repository

There is no software without code, and the code that will be implemented according to a software requirement needs to be placed in a software repository. The **Repos** menu item gives you access to a default Git repository where you can place your project's code:

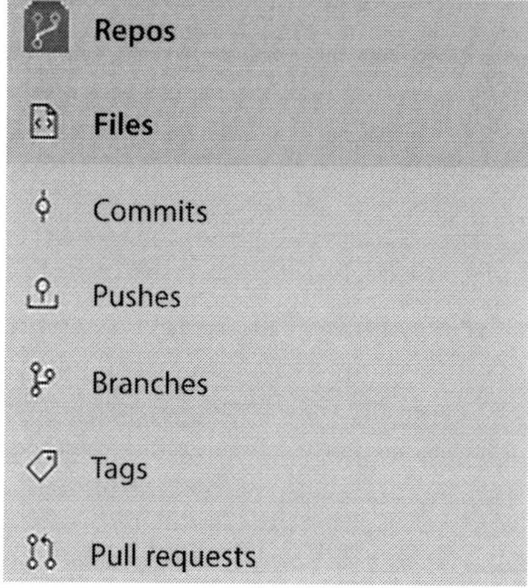

Figure 3.5: Azure DevOps Repos menu

By clicking the **Files** item, you enter the default repository initial page. It is empty and contains instructions on how to connect to this default repository.

You can add further repositories through the drop-down menu at the top of the page:

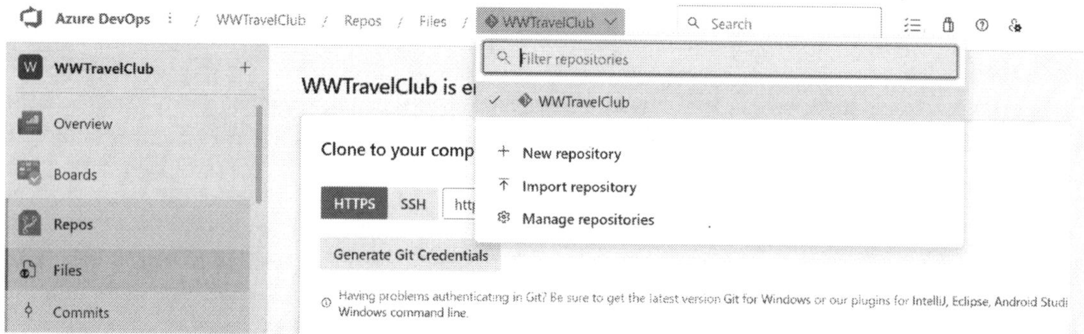

Figure 3.6: Adding a new repository

All repositories created are accessible through the same drop-down menu.

As shown in the preceding screenshot, each repository's initial page contains the repository address and a button to generate repository-specific credentials, so you can connect to your DevOps repositories with your favorite Git tools. However, you can also connect from inside Visual Studio in a very simple way:

1. Start Visual Studio and ensure you are logged in to it with the same Microsoft account used to define your DevOps project (or that was used to add you as a team member).
2. If the **Git Changes** window is not open, make it appear by going to the top menu in Visual Studio and selecting **View -> Git Changes**.

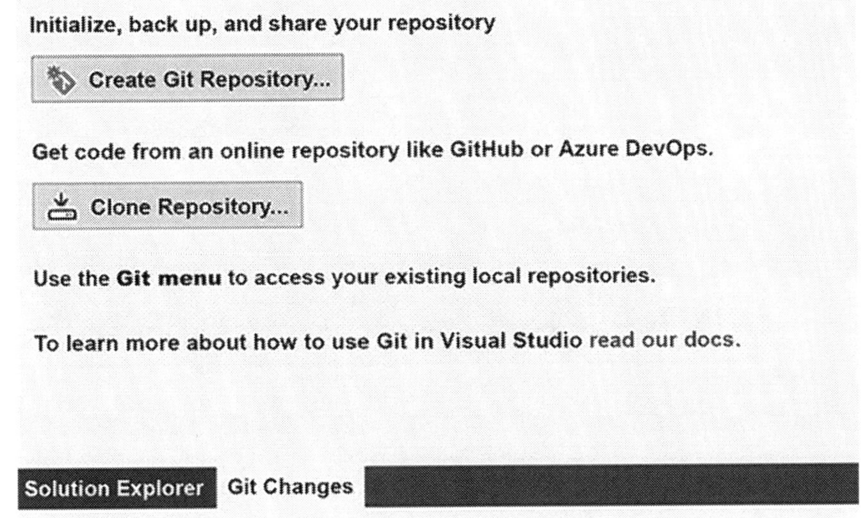

Figure 3.7: Git Changes window

3. Click the **Create Git Repository...** button in the Git Changes window.

4. In the window that opens, select **Existing remote** and insert the URL of the DevOps repository you created. Then, click **Create and Push**:

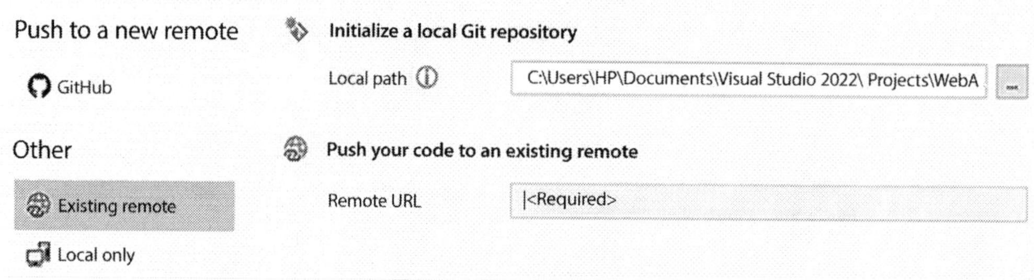

Figure 3.8: Connecting to the remote DevOps repository

Once connected to your DevOps remote repository, the Git Changes window will show several Git commands:

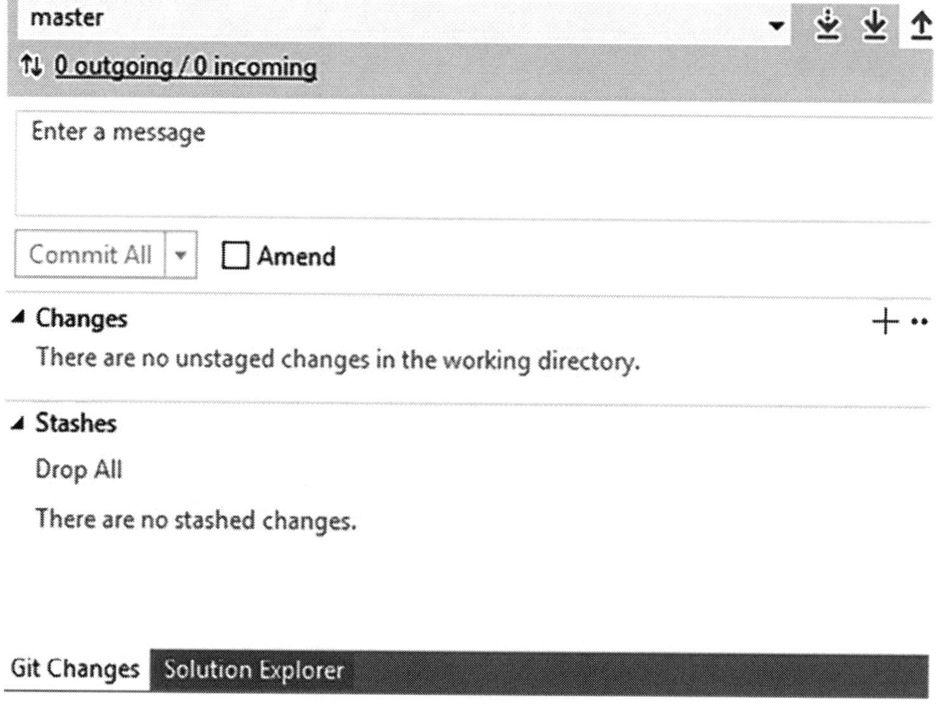

Figure 3.9: Git Changes window

When you have changes to commit, you can insert a message in the textbox at the top of the window and commit them locally by clicking the **Commit All** button, or you can click the dropdown next to this button to access more options:

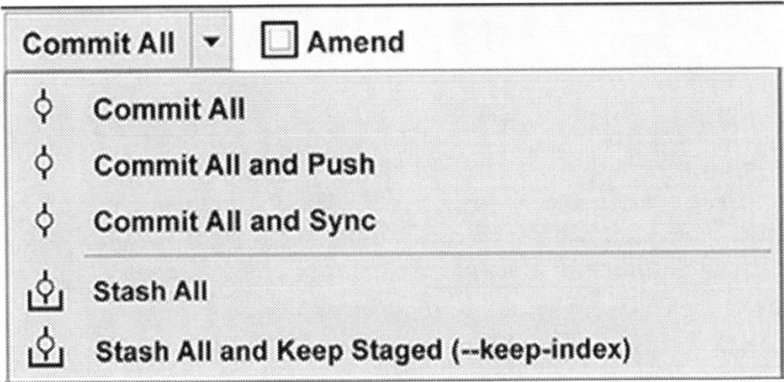

Figure 3.10: Commit options

You can commit and push or commit and sync, but you can also stage your changes. The three arrows in the top right of the Git Changes window trigger a fetch, pull, and push, respectively. Meanwhile, the dropdown at the top of the window takes care of operations on branches:

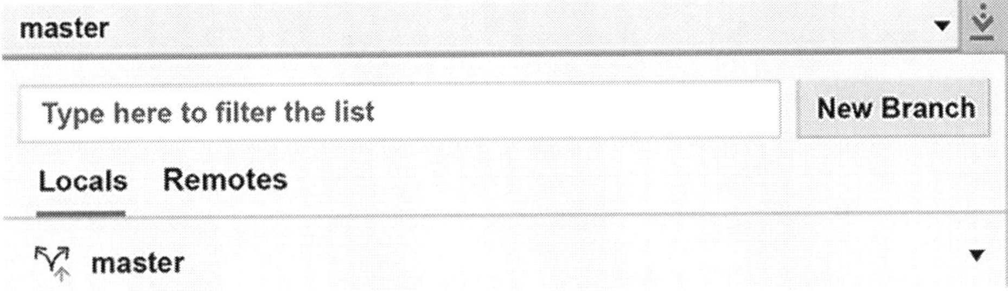

Figure 3.11: Branch operations

Package feeds

A great way to accelerate software development is by reusing code components that meet the user requirements. These components, in general, are placed into packages. We will discuss this further in *Chapter 5, Implementing Code Reusability in C# 12*. The **Artifacts** menu handles the software packages used or created by the project. There, you can define feeds for basically all types of packages, including NuGet, Node.js, and Python. Private feeds are required since commercial projects also use private packages, so you need a place to put them. Moreover, packages produced during builds are placed in these feeds, so other modules that have them as dependencies can immediately use them.

Once in the **Artifacts** area, you can create several feeds by clicking the **+ Create Feed** button, where each feed can handle several kinds of packages, as shown in *Figure 3.12*.

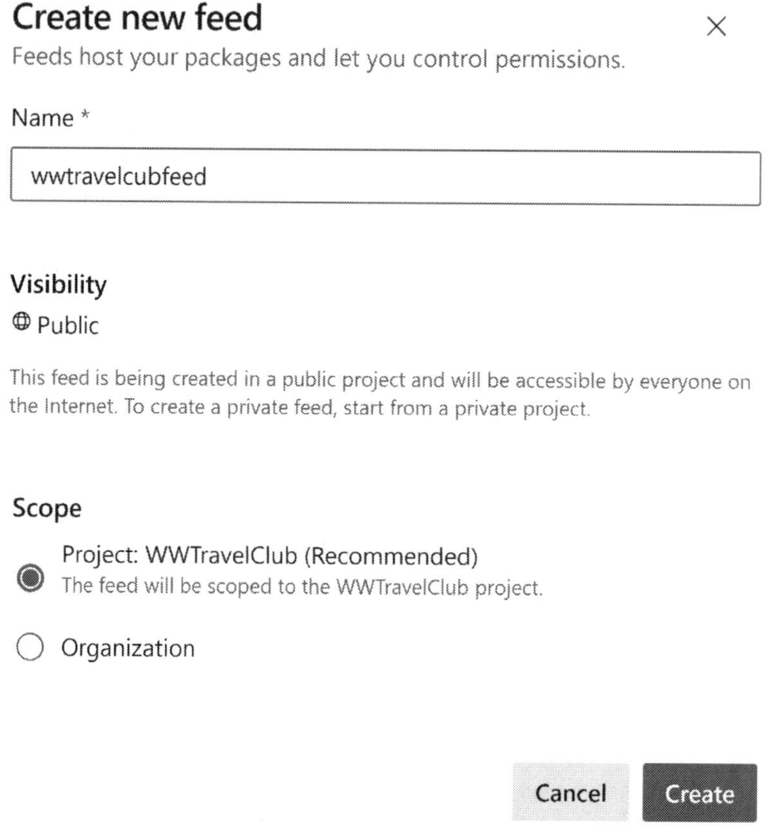

Figure 3.12: Feed creation

If you select the option to connect to packages from public sources, by default, the feed connects to `npmjs`, `nuget.org`, `pypi.org`, and `Maven`. However, you can go to the **Search Upstream sources** tab on the **Feed** settings page and remove/add package sources. The settings page can be reached by clicking the settings icon in the upper-right corner of the feed page.

A screenshot of the page of the newly created feed follows:

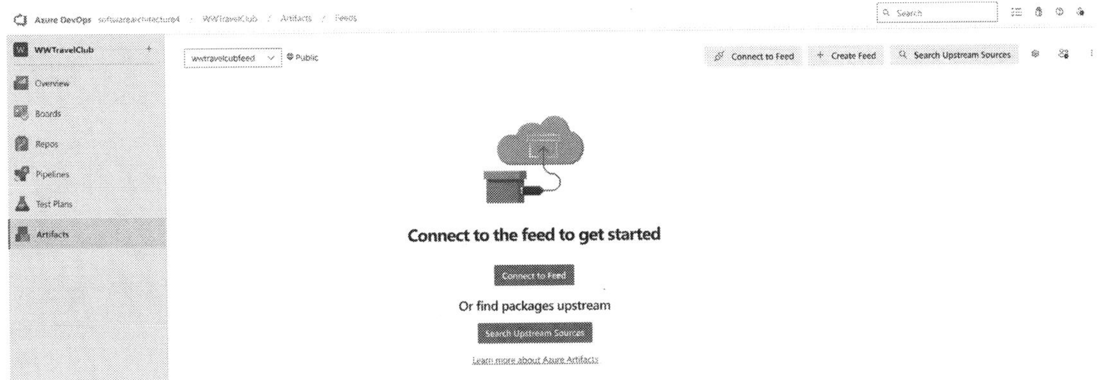

Figure 3.13: Feed page

The **Connect to Feed** button for each feed shows a window that explains how to connect to the feed for each package type.

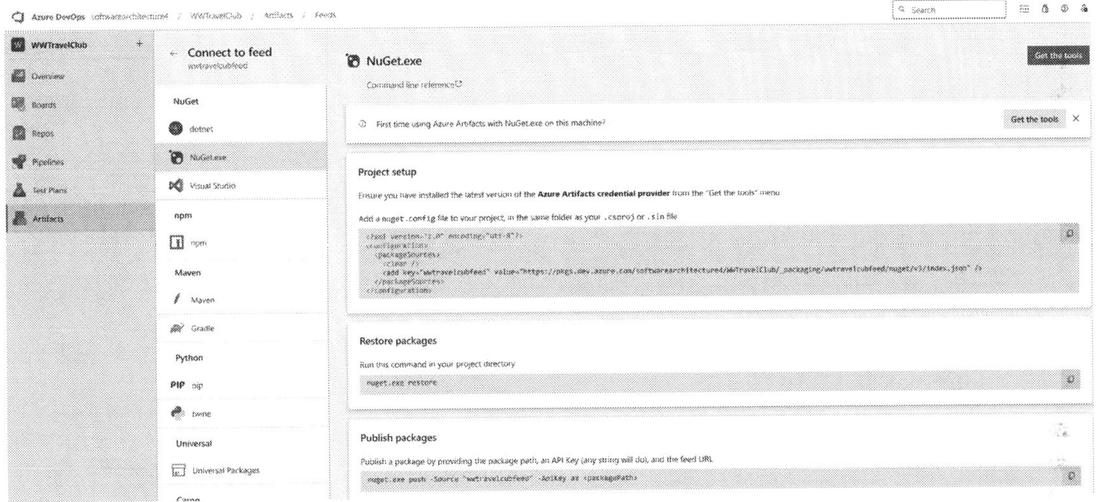

Figure 3.14: Feed connection information

For NuGet packages, you should add all project feeds to your Visual Studio projects'/solutions' `nuget.config` file so that local machines can also use them; otherwise, your local build will fail.

Test Plans

The **Test Plans** section allows you to define the test plans you want to use and their settings. Tests are discussed in detail in *Chapter 9, Testing Your Enterprise Application*, but here, we would like to summarize the opportunities offered by Azure DevOps. Test-related operations and settings can be accessed through the **Test Plans** menu item.

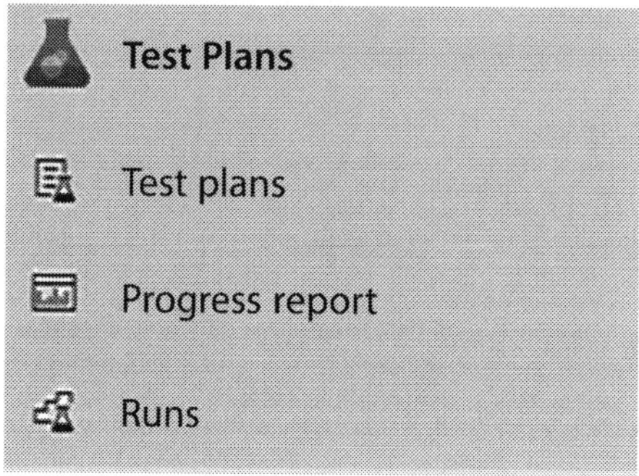

Figure 3.15: Test Plans menu

Here, you may define, execute, and track test plans made up of the following:

- Manual acceptance tests
- Automatic unit tests
- Load tests

Automatic unit tests must be defined in test projects contained in the Visual Studio solution and based on a framework such as NUnit, xUnit, and MSTest (the .NET SDK has project templates for all of them, so you may find them in Visual Studio). Test Plans gives you the opportunity to execute these tests on Azure and to define the following:

- Several configuration settings
- When to execute them
- How to track them and where to report their results in the overall project documentation

For manual tests, you may define complete instructions for the operator in the project documentation, covering the environment in which to execute them (for example, an operating system) and where to report their results. You can also define how to execute load tests and how to measure the results.

Pipelines

Pipelines are automatic action plans that specify all steps from the code build until the software deployment is in production. They can be defined in the **Pipelines** area, which is accessible through the **Pipelines** menu item:

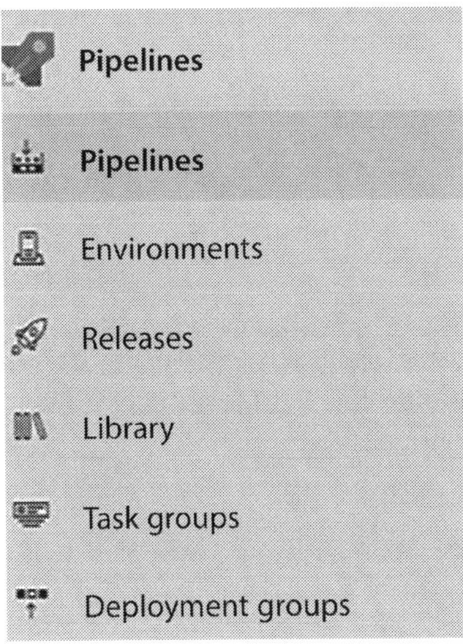

Figure 3.16: Pipelines menu

There, you can define a complete pipeline of tasks to be executed alongside their triggering events, which encompass steps such as code building, launching test plans, and what to do after the tests have passed.

Typically, after the tests have passed, the application is automatically deployed in a staging area where it can be beta-tested. You can also define the criteria for automatic deployment to production. Such criteria include, but are not limited to, the following:

- The number of days during which the application was beta-tested
- The number of bugs found during beta-testing and/or removed by the last code change
- Manual approval by one or more managers/team members

The criteria decision will depend on the way the company wants to manage the product that is being developed. You, as a software architect, must understand that when it comes to moving code to production, the safer, the better.

Usage

As you can see from the preceding screenshots, the process for creating an Azure DevOps account is extremely simple. It is worth mentioning that you can start using this fantastic tool at no cost if you have no more than five developers on your team, plus any number of stakeholders. However, it is worth mentioning that there is no limit on the number of users with a stakeholder role.

Introducing GitHub projects

Considering all the benefits of Azure DevOps presented, you may now be asking why we need to explore another tool. The reason is simple: GitHub has become, over the years, the main tool for the open-source world. So, we will find many initiatives and projects there that have changed the way we deliver software.

The main objective of GitHub is to manage code and guarantee that its users can create solutions in a collaborative way. For this, the platform presents features like version control, pull requests, code reviews, issue tracking, and CI/CD.

However, it would be impossible to design great projects without a platform to support them. That is why we have GitHub projects as an initiative that delivers an adaptable, flexible tool for planning and tracking work on GitHub.

You can find more information about GitHub projects at `https://docs.github.com/en/issues/planning-and-tracking-with-projects/learning-about-projects/about-projects`.

It is quite simple to set up a project on GitHub. Once you log in to the platform, you may find projects from your user menu.

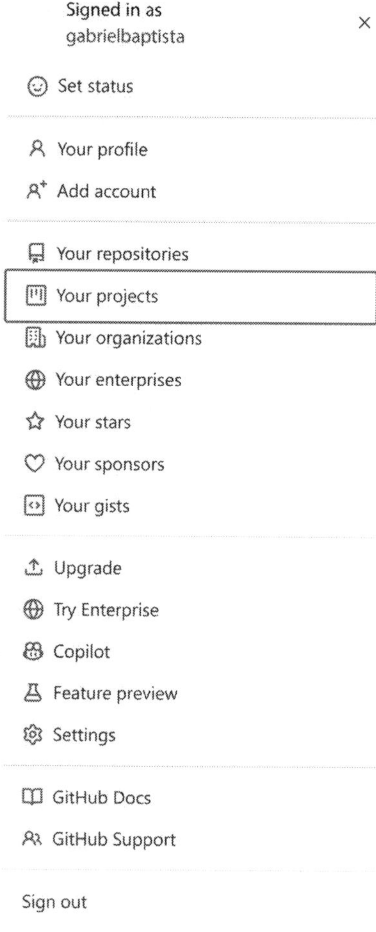

Figure 3.17: Accessing GitHub projects

There, you will find the option to create a **New project**. When you decide to create it, you will find different templates already provided by GitHub.

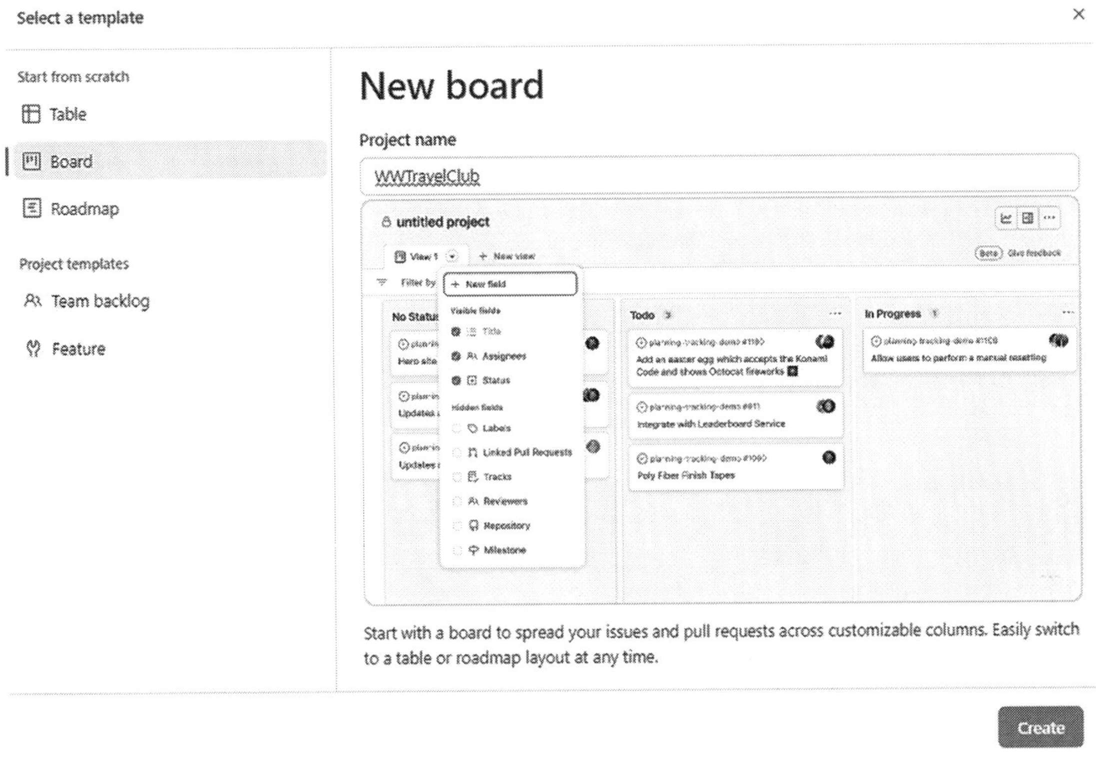

Figure 3.18: Creating a project on GitHub

The project needs to be linked to a repository. You can do this by accessing the **Projects** tab in your repo. There, you can also create a new project.

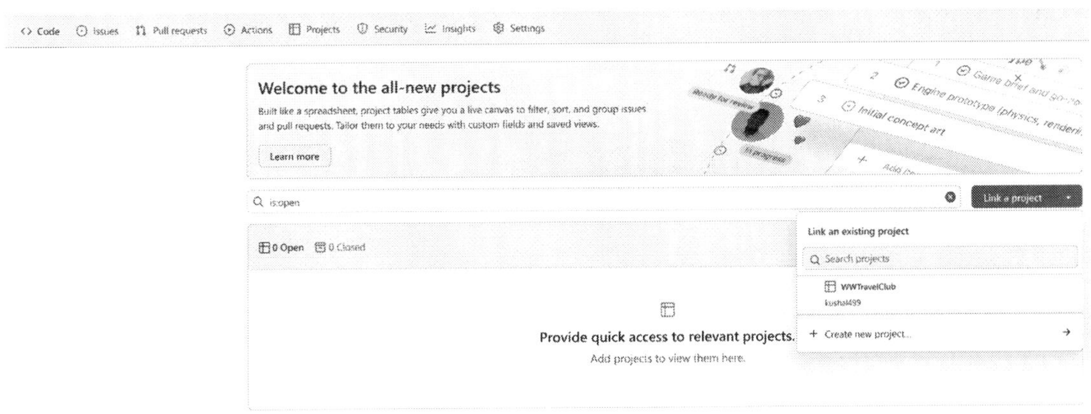

Figure 3.19: Connecting a GitHub repository to a project

It is worth mentioning that GitHub is more flexible than Azure DevOps, so you will find tools like the ones presented on Azure DevOps, but with different names/definitions. For instance, any task that you will need to define will be called an **issue**. Each issue can be placed in a **milestone**, which is a good way to define a feature or user story since it will describe an achievement with a date to be finished.

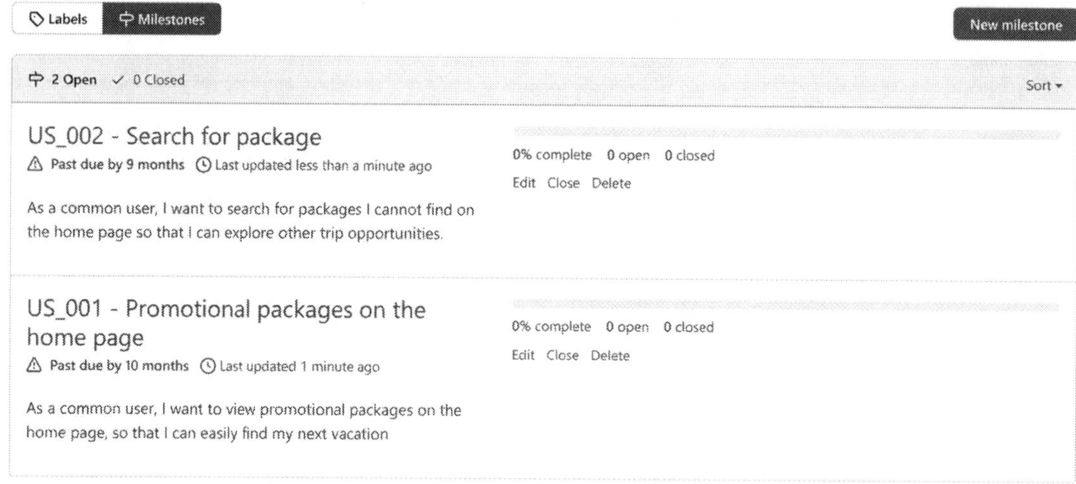

Figure 3.20: Setting milestones in a GitHub repository

Check out more about using issues at `https://docs.github.com/en/issues/tracking-your-work-with-issues/about-issues` and milestones at `https://docs.github.com/en/issues/using-labels-and-milestones-to-track-work/about-milestones`.

The idea of projects on GitHub is to define useful information for each item that will be used, which is documented in an issue. By default, only *Title*, *Assignees*, and *Status* are required. But you can add labels, linked pull requests, reviewers, repositories, and milestones to them. You can also define custom fields, like **Iteration**. For this, you will need to access **Project settings**.

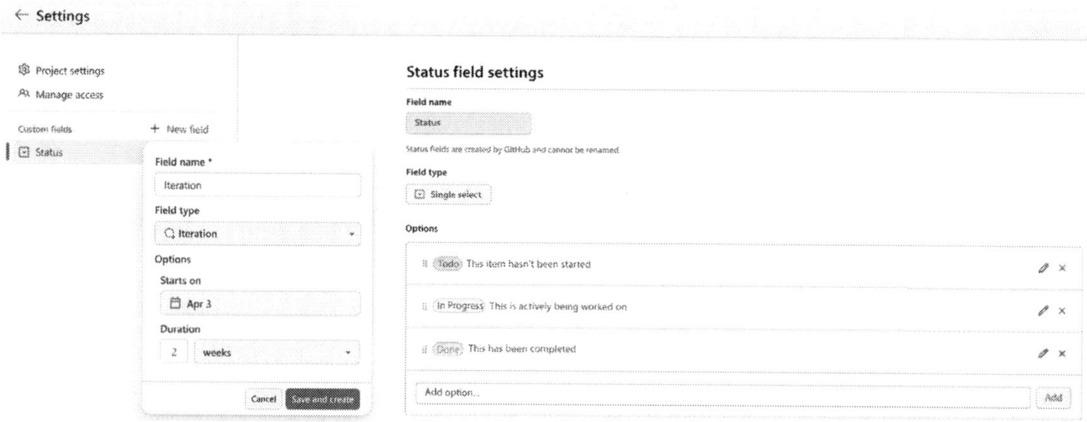

Figure 3.21: Creating custom fields for a GitHub project

In a GitHub project, you can also set different **Views**, such as **Table**, **Board**, or **Roadmap**. The Table view, in particular, offers a quick and efficient method for entering this project-related information, including the custom fields you've created, into the project. Once you've completed the design phase, you're ready to create issues for each item planned in your project.

Figure 3.22: GitHub project Table view

The **Board** view, together with a filter related to iteration, is a perfect way to conduct daily meetings because you will see exactly what is happening to the project.

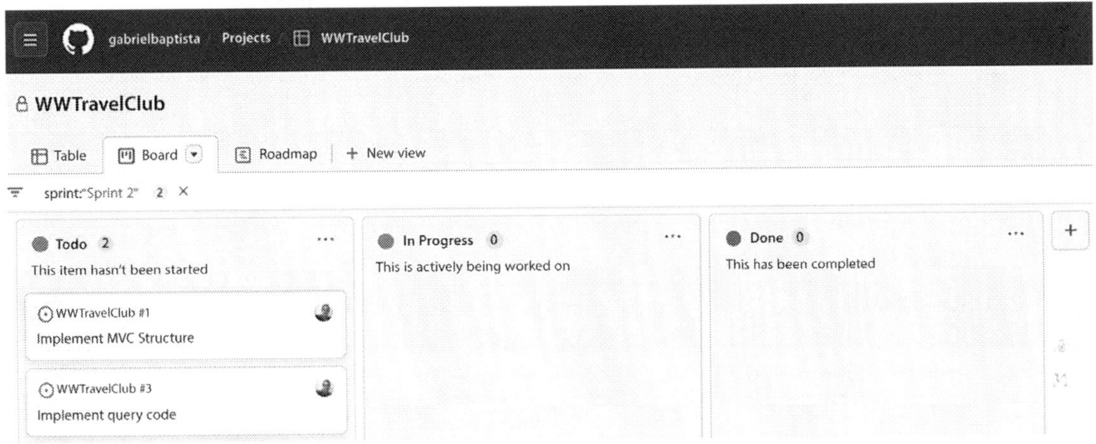

Figure 3.23: GitHub Board view

To finish, the **Roadmap** view will give you a perspective of the entire project over time.

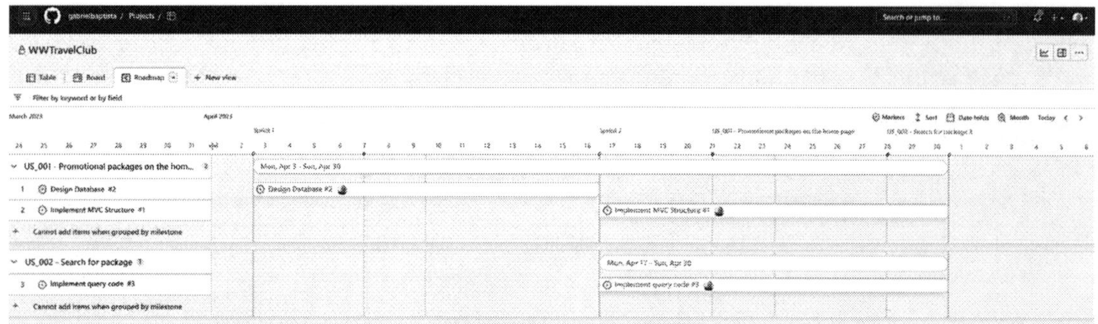

Figure 3.24: GitHub Roadmap view

As you can see, with GitHub projects, you will get almost the same results that we got when using Azure DevOps.

Summary

This chapter covered how you can create an Azure DevOps or GitHub account for a software development project and how to start managing your projects with Azure DevOps or GitHub projects.

It also gave a short review of all of Azure DevOps' functionalities, explaining how to access them through the Azure DevOps main menu.

To finish, it presented the GitHub project view options to plan and manage a project.

The chapter also described in more detail how to manage system requirements and how to organize the work necessary with various kinds of work items or issues, along with how to plan and organize sprints that will deliver epic solutions with many features.

The decision of whether to use Azure DevOps or GitHub in a project will vary according to the expertise of the team and the objective of the project itself. If you are designing an open-source solution, GitHub will definitely be a better option. On the other hand, if you are designing an enterprise solution and need everything to be connected, Azure DevOps is a fantastic tool to do so.

The next chapter discusses important approaches while writing code.

Questions

1. Is Azure DevOps only available for .NET projects?
2. What kinds of test plans are available in Azure DevOps?
3. Can DevOps projects use private NuGet packages?
4. Why do we use work items?
5. What is the difference between Epic and Feature work items?

6. What kind of relationship exists between Task and Product Backlog items/User Story work items?
7. How can GitHub projects be useful?
8. Which is the better option: Azure DevOps or GitHub?

Learn more on Discord

To join the Discord community for this book – where you can share feedback, ask questions to the authors, and learn about new releases – follow the QR code below:

`https://packt.link/SoftwareArchitectureCSharp12Dotnet8`

4

Best Practices in Coding C# 12

When you are the software architect on a project, it is your responsibility to define and/or maintain a coding standard that will direct the team to program according to the expectations of the company. This chapter covers some of the **best practices** in coding that will help developers like you program safe, simple, and maintainable software. It also includes tips and tricks for coding in **C#**. Although coding can be considered an art, writing understandable code is closer to a philosophy. In this chapter, we also discuss practices that you, as a software architect, need to propagate to your developers, with techniques and tools for code analysis, so that you have well-written code for your projects.

The following topics will be covered in this chapter:

- How the complexity of your code can affect performance
- The importance of using a version control system
- Writing safe code in C#
- .NET 8 tips and tricks for coding
- Identifying well-written code

C# 12 was launched together with **.NET 8**. However, the practices presented here can be used in many versions of .NET, since they refer to the basics of programming C#. By the end of the chapter, you will be able to define which tools you are going to incorporate into your software development life cycle to facilitate code analysis.

Technical requirements

This chapter requires, at least, the Visual Studio 2022 free *Community Edition*.

The simpler your code, the better a programmer you are

For many people, a good programmer is one who writes complex code. However, the evolution of maturity in software development means there is a different way of thinking about it. Complexity does not mean a good job; it means poor code quality. Some incredible scientists and researchers have confirmed this theory and emphasized that professional code needs to be focused on time, high quality, and budget.

Even when you have a complex scenario on your hands, if you reduce ambiguities and clarify the process of what you are coding, especially by using good names for methods and variables, which contribute to making your code "self-documented" and respect SOLID principles (**S**ingle Responsibility, **O**pen/Close, **L**iskov Substitution, **I**nterface Segregation, and **D**ependency Inversion), you will turn complexity into simple code.

So, if you want to write good code, you need to keep the focus on how to do it, considering you are not the only one who will read it later. This is a good tip that changes the way you write code. This is how we will discuss each point of this chapter.

If your understanding of the importance of writing good code is aligned with the idea of simplicity and clarity while writing it, you should look at the Visual Studio tool known as **Code Metrics**:

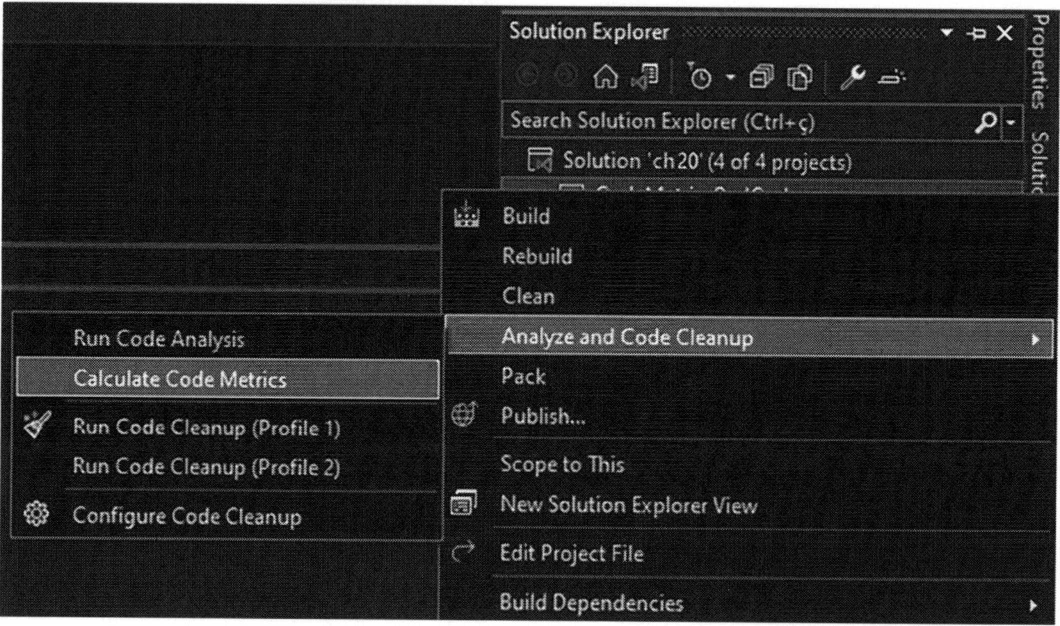

Figure 4.1: Calculating code metrics in Visual Studio

The **Code Metrics** tool will deliver metrics that will give you insights regarding the quality of the software you are delivering. The metrics that the tool provides can be found at this link: `https://docs.microsoft.com/en-us/visualstudio/code-quality/code-metrics-values`.

Once you have run the code metrics analysis, you will need to interpret each metric presented. The following subsections focus on describing how a **maintainability index**, **cyclomatic complexity**, **depth of inheritance**, **class coupling**, and the **number of lines of code** are useful in some real-life scenarios.

Maintainability index

The maintainability index represents a number from 0 to 100, which indicates how easy it is to maintain code – the easier the code, the higher the index. Easy maintenance is one of the key points to keeping software in good health. It is obvious that any software will require changes in the future since change is inevitable.

For this reason, consider refactoring your code to elevate the maintainability index if it currently has a low score. Writing classes and methods dedicated to a single responsibility, avoiding duplicate code, and limiting the number of lines of code of each method are examples of how you can improve the maintainability index.

Cyclomatic complexity

The creator of the cyclomatic complexity metric is Thomas J. McCabe. He defines the complexity of a software function according to the number of **code paths** available (**graph nodes**). The more paths you have, the more complex your function is. McCabe considers that each function must have a complexity score of less than 10. That means that if the code has more complex methods, you must refactor it, transforming parts of the code into separate methods. There are some real scenarios where this behavior is easily detected:

- Loops inside loops
- Lots of consecutive `if-else` statements
- `switch` with code processing for each case inside the same method

For instance, look at the first version of this method for processing different responses to a credit card transaction. As you can see, the cyclomatic complexity is bigger than the number considered by McCabe as a basis. The reason why this happens is because of the number of `if-else` statements inside each case of the main switch:

```
/// <summary>
/// This code is being used just for explaining the concept of
/// cyclomatic complexity.
/// It makes no sense at all. Please Calculate Code Metrics for
/// understanding
/// </summary>
private static void CyclomaticComplexitySample()
{
  var billingMode = GetBillingMode();
  var messageResponse = ProcessCreditCardMethod();
  switch (messageResponse)
    {
      case "A":
        if (billingMode == "M1")
          Console.WriteLine($"Billing Mode {billingMode} for " +
            $"Message Response {messageResponse}");
        else
          Console.WriteLine($"Billing Mode {billingMode} for " +
            $"Message Response {messageResponse}");
        break;
      case "B":
```

```
    if (billingMode == "M2")
      Console.WriteLine($"Billing Mode {billingMode} for " +
        $"Message Response {messageResponse}");
    else
      Console.WriteLine($"Billing Mode {billingMode} for " +
        $"Message Response {messageResponse}");
    break;
  case "C":
    if (billingMode == "M3")
      Console.WriteLine($"Billing Mode {billingMode} for " +
        $"Message Response {messageResponse}");
    else
      Console.WriteLine($"Billing Mode {billingMode} for " +
        $"Message Response {messageResponse}");
    break;
  case "D":
    if (billingMode == "M4")
      Console.WriteLine($"Billing Mode {billingMode} for " +
        $"Message Response {messageResponse}");
    else
      Console.WriteLine($"Billing Mode {billingMode} for " +
        $"Message Response {messageResponse}");
    break;
  case "E":
    if (billingMode == "M5")
      Console.WriteLine($"Billing Mode {billingMode} for " +
        $"Message Response {messageResponse}");
    else
      Console.WriteLine($"Billing Mode {billingMode} for " +
        $"Message Response {messageResponse}");
    break;
  case "F":
    if (billingMode == "M6")
      Console.WriteLine($"Billing Mode {billingMode} for " +
        $"Message Response {messageResponse}");
    else
      Console.WriteLine($"Billing Mode {billingMode} for " +
        $"Message Response {messageResponse}");
    break;
  case "G":
    if (billingMode == "M7")
      Console.WriteLine($"Billing Mode {billingMode} for " +
        $"Message Response {messageResponse}");
```

```
            else
              Console.WriteLine($"Billing Mode {billingMode} for " +
                $"Message Response {messageResponse}");
            break;
          case "H":
            if (billingMode == "M8")
              Console.WriteLine($"Billing Mode {billingMode} for " +
                $"Message Response {messageResponse}");
            else
              Console.WriteLine($"Billing Mode {billingMode} for " +
                $"Message Response {messageResponse}");
            break;
          default:
            Console.WriteLine("The result of processing is unknown");
            break;
      }
  }
```

If you calculate the code metrics of this code, you will find a bad result when it comes to cyclomatic complexity, as you can see in the following screenshot. A cyclomatic complexity number above 10 indicates that the code is difficult to read, and a developer will probably have trouble maintaining it in a future code change.

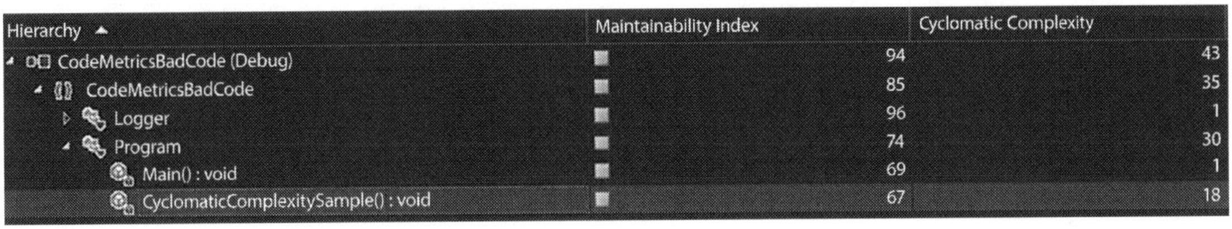

Hierarchy	Maintainability Index	Cyclomatic Complexity
CodeMetricsBadCode (Debug)	94	43
CodeMetricsBadCode	85	35
Logger	96	1
Program	74	30
Main() : void	69	1
CyclomaticComplexitySample() : void	67	18

Figure 4.2: High level of cyclomatic complexity

It is important to reinforce that the purpose of the code from this example is not the focus here. The point here is to show you the number of improvements that can be made to write better code:

- The options from switch-case could be written using Enum.
- Each case processing can be done:
    - In a specific method.
    - In a specific class, inheriting the action from the superclass, using the polymorphism concept.
    - In a specific class, implementing an interface to define a contract.
- switch-case can be substituted with Dictionary<Enum, Method> or by using the switch expression.

By refactoring this code with the preceding techniques, the result is a piece of code that is much easier to understand, as you can see in the following code snippet of its main method:

```
static void Main()
{
    var billingMode = GetBillingMode();
    var messageResponse = ProcessCreditCardMethod();
    Dictionary<CreditCardProcessingResult, CheckResultMethod>
        methodsForCheckingResult = GetMethodsForCheckingResult();
    if (methodsForCheckingResult.ContainsKey(messageResponse))
        methodsForCheckingResult[messageResponse](billingMode,
        messageResponse);
    else
        Console.WriteLine("The result of processing is unknown");
}
```

Using the `switch` expression available since C# 8.0, the code can be even simpler!

```
static void Main()
{
    var billingMode = GetBillingMode();
    var messageResponse = ProcessCreditCardMethod();
    CheckResult(messageResponse, billingMode);
}

private static CreditCardProcessingResult CheckResult(CreditCardProcessingResult
messageResponse, BillingMode billingMode) => messageResponse switch
{
    CreditCardProcessingResult.ResultA => CheckResultA(billingMode,
messageResponse),
    CreditCardProcessingResult.ResultB => CheckResultB(billingMode,
messageResponse),
```

```
    CreditCardProcessingResult.ResultC => CheckResultC(billingMode,
messageResponse),
    CreditCardProcessingResult.ResultD => CheckResultD(billingMode,
messageResponse),
    CreditCardProcessingResult.ResultE => CheckResultE(billingMode,
messageResponse),
    CreditCardProcessingResult.ResultF => CheckResultF(billingMode,
messageResponse),
    CreditCardProcessingResult.ResultG => CheckResultG(billingMode,
messageResponse),
    CreditCardProcessingResult.Succeed => CheckResultSucceed(billingMode,
messageResponse),
    _ => throw new ArgumentOutOfRangeException(nameof(messageResponse), $"Not
expected value: {messageResponse}"),
};
```

The full code can be found in the GitHub repository of this chapter at `https://github.com/PacktPublishing/Software-Architecture-with-C-Sharp-12-and-.NET-8-4E/tree/main/ch04` and demonstrates how lower-complexity code can be achieved. The following screenshot shows these results according to Code Metrics:

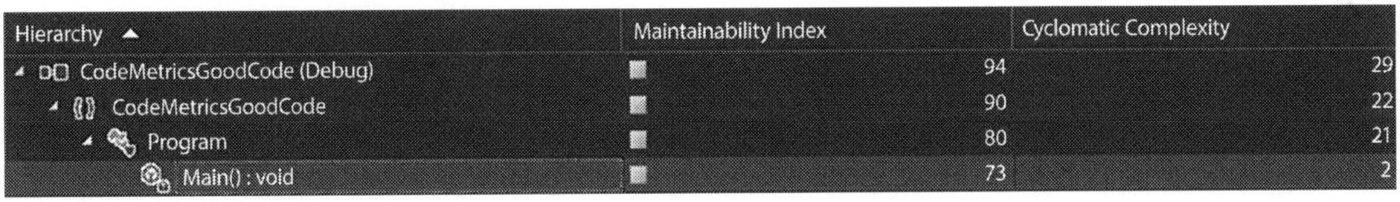

Hierarchy	Maintainability Index	Cyclomatic Complexity
CodeMetricsGoodCode (Debug)	94	29
CodeMetricsGoodCode	90	22
Program	80	21
Main() : void	73	2

Figure 4.3: Cyclomatic complexity reduction after refactoring

As you can see in the preceding screenshot, there is a considerable reduction in complexity after refactoring. In *Chapter 5, Implementing Code Reusability in C# 12*, we will discuss the importance of refactoring for code reuse. The reason we are doing this here is the same – we want to eliminate duplication. It is important to remember that when you are refactoring code, you are writing it in a better way while respecting the input and output data that this code will process.

The key point here is that with the applied techniques, our understanding of the code increased and the complexity index decreased, thus proving the importance of cyclomatic complexity.

Depth of inheritance

This metric represents the number of classes inherited by the one that is being analyzed. The more classes you have inherited, the worse the metric will be. This is like class coupling and indicates how difficult it is to change the code of this class without impacting other ones, which neglects the Open/Close principle stated by SOLID. For instance, the following screenshot shows four inherited classes:

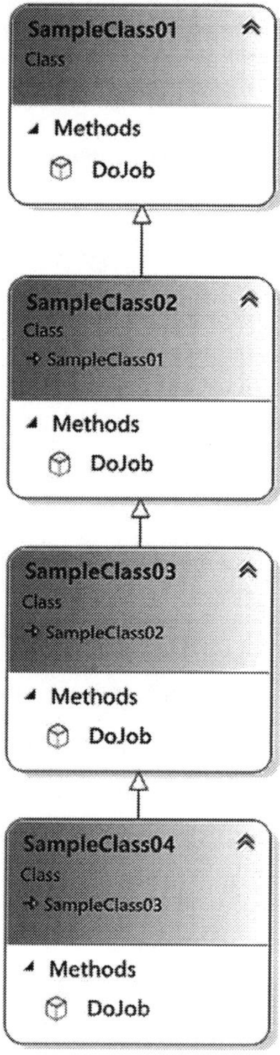

Figure 4.4: Depth of inheritance sample

You can see in the following screenshot that the deepest class has the worst metric, considering there are three other classes that can change its behavior:

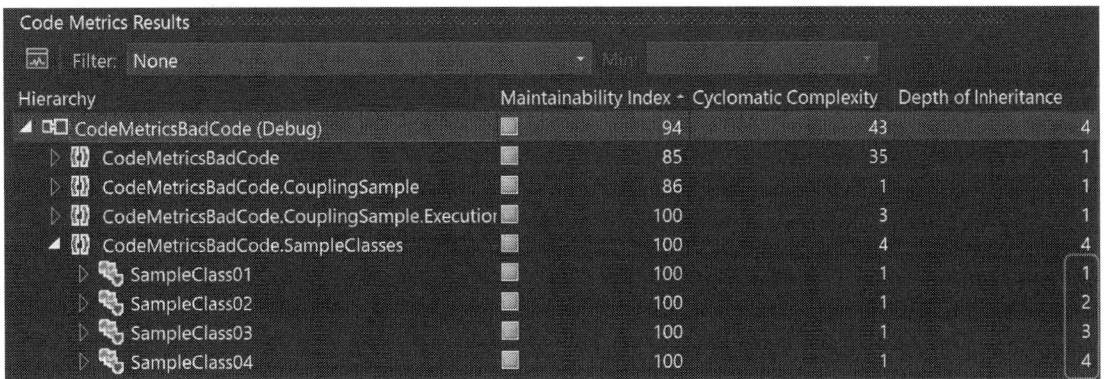

Figure 4.5: Depth of inheritance metric

Inheritance is one of the basic object-oriented analysis principles. However, it can sometimes be bad for your code in that it can cause dependencies. So, if it makes sense to do so, consider using composition or aggregation instead of inheritance, as we will explain in the following section.

Class coupling

When you connect too many classes in a single class, obviously you will get tight coupling, and changing a participant causes unintended consequences in others. For sure, this can cause bad maintenance of your code, resulting in bugs that will make you spend more time trying to deliver a great solution. For instance, refer to *Figure 4.6*. It shows a design where aggregation has been performed a lot. There is no sense to the code itself:

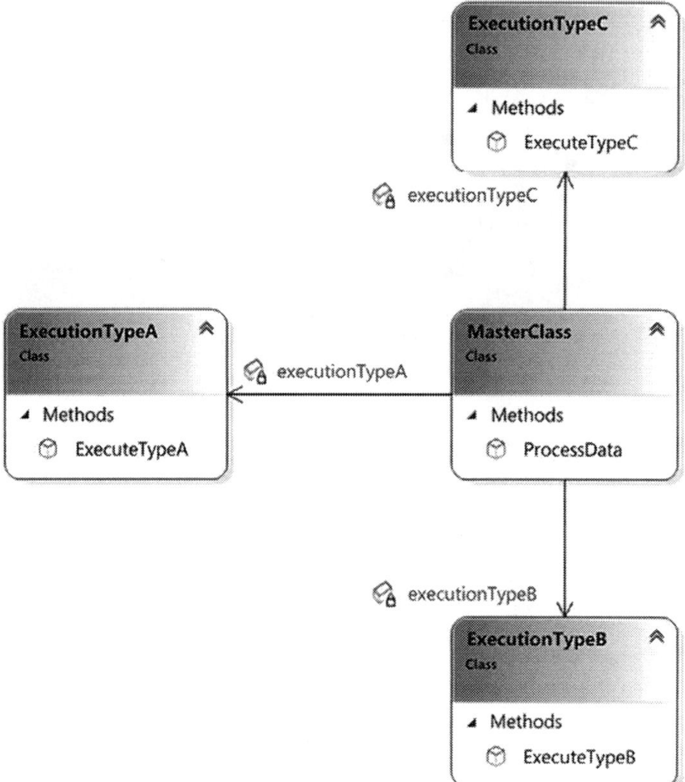

Figure 4.6: Class coupling example

Once you have calculated the code metrics for the preceding design, you will see that the number of class coupling instances for the `ProcessData()` method, which calls `ExecuteTypeA()`, `ExecuteTypeB()`, and `ExecuteTypeC()`, equals three:

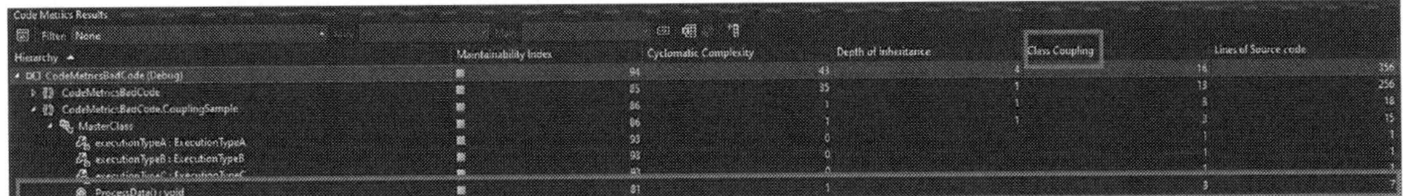

Figure 4.7: Class coupling metric

Microsoft suggests that the maximum number of class coupling instances should be nine, as presented at `https://learn.microsoft.com/en-us/visualstudio/code-quality/code-metrics-class-coupling?view=vs-2022`.

With composition/aggregation being a better practice than inheritance, and since you will decouple code written from your class, the use of interfaces will solve class coupling problems. For instance, the same code with the following design will give you a better result. Although the interface is not strictly required for this example, its usage enables us to evolve the solution for other **execution types** without impacting the classes already written, since you are not using inheritance to solve the problem.

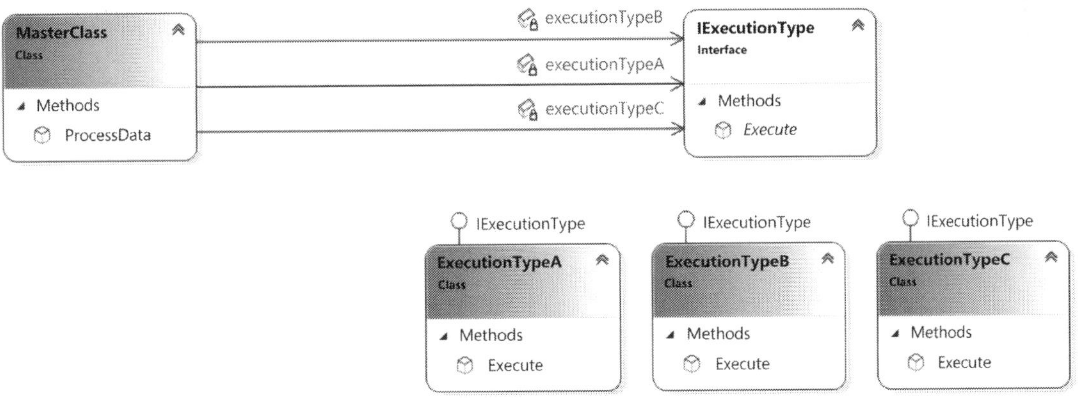

Figure 4.8: Reducing class coupling

Note that using the interface in the design will allow you to increase the number of execution types without increasing the class coupling of the solution:

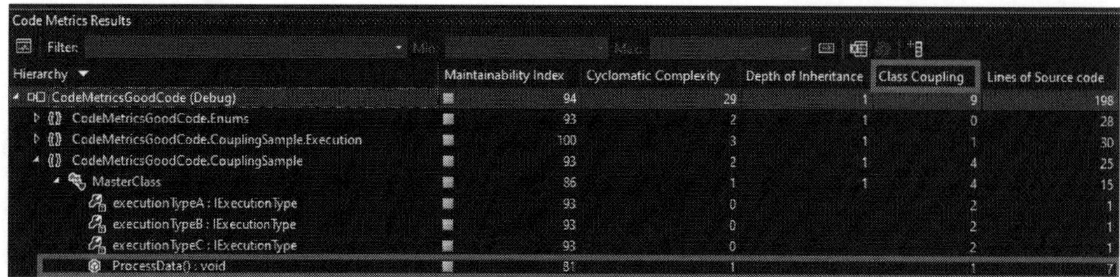

Hierarchy	Maintainability Index	Cyclomatic Complexity	Depth of Inheritance	Class Coupling	Lines of Source code
CodeMetricsGoodCode (Debug)	94	29	1	9	198
CodeMetricsGoodCode.Enums	93	2	1	0	28
CodeMetricsGoodCode.CouplingSample.Execution	100	3	1	1	30
CodeMetricsGoodCode.CouplingSample	93	2	1	4	25
MasterClass	86	1	1	4	15
executionTypeA : IExecutionType	93	0		2	1
executionTypeB : IExecutionType	93	0		2	1
executionTypeC : IExecutionType	93	0		2	1
ProcessData() : void	81	1		1	7

Figure 4.9: Class coupling results after applying aggregations

As a software architect, you must design your solution to have more cohesion than coupling. The literature indicates that good software has low coupling and high cohesion. In software development, high cohesion indicates that each class has its methods and data, with good relationships between them. Conversely, low coupling indicates that classes are not closely and directly connected. This is a basic principle that can guide you to a better architectural model.

Number of lines of code

This metric is useful in terms of making you understand the size of the code you are dealing with. There is no way to connect the number of lines of code and complexity, since the number of lines is not indicative of that. Conversely, the number of lines of code does show the software size and software design. For instance, if you have too many lines of code in a single class (more than 1,000 lines of code – 1 KLOC), this indicates that it is a bad design. Besides, if a class has too many methods, it obviously violates the Single Responsibility principle from SOLID.

In Visual Studio 2022, this metric was divided into **lines of source code** and **lines of executable code**. The first indicates the exact number of source lines, including blank lines. Conversely, the second one estimates the number of executable code lines.

As a software architect, you have the objective of delivering to your programmers a list of best practices that will enable each of them to improve their techniques for developing good software. Make sure they know the exact impacts of not achieving good metric results in their code. The metrics presented above are certainly a great way to start to achieve this objective. But let us see how using a version control system can be the difference between amateur and professional software development.

Using a version control system

You may find this topic a bit obvious, but many people and companies still do not regard a version control system as an essential tool for software development. A common reason why version control systems are not considered a priority, particularly in some situations, is the belief that they are unnecessary for solo coding projects or for study purposes. You may think that a version control system is only needed by teams inside companies. The purpose of addressing this is to force you to understand our point. There is no architectural model or best practice that can save software development if you do not use a **version control system**.

In the last few years, we have been enjoying the advantages of online version control systems, such as Azure DevOps, GitHub, and Bitbucket. The fact is, you must have a version control system in your software development life cycle, and there is no reason not to have one anymore, since most providers offer free versions for small groups. Even if you develop by yourself, these tools are useful for tracking your changes, managing your software versions, and guaranteeing the consistency and integrity of your code.

Dealing with version control systems in teams

The reason for using a version control system tool when you are alone is obvious. You want to keep your code safe. However, this kind of system was developed to solve team problems while writing code. For this reason, some features, such as branching and merging, were introduced to keep code integrity even in scenarios where the number of developers is quite large.

As a software architect, you will have to decide which branch strategy you will conduct in your team. Microsoft and GitHub suggest different ways to deliver that, and both are useful in some scenarios.

Information about how the Microsoft teams deal with DevOps can be found here: `https://learn.microsoft.com/en-us/devops/develop/how-microsoft-develops-devops`. The branching strategy presented in this article describes an approach where a branch is created for each release. They call it **the release flow**. The big difference here is that the master branch is not continuously deployed to production.

Conversely, GitHub describes its process at `https://guides.github.com/introduction/flow/`. This process is called **GitHub flow** and can be defined as a lightweight, branch-based workflow, where each development is created in a specific branch that will be reviewed by collaborators as soon as a pull request is created for feedback. As soon as the pull request is approved, the new code is merged to a master branch, so you can delete the development branch created before.

It is your choice; decide on the one that best fits your needs, but we do want you to understand that you need to have a strategy for controlling your code. In *Chapter 8, Understanding DevOps Principles and CI/CD*, we will discuss this in more detail. But now, let us see how to write safe code using C# so that you can develop a list of best practices to be shared with your developers.

Writing safe code in C#

C# can be considered a safe programming language by design. Unless you force it, there is no need for pointers, and memory release is, in most cases, managed by the garbage collector. Even so, some care should be taken so that you can get better and safer results from your code. Let us have a look at some common practices to ensure safe code in C#.

try-catch

Exceptions in coding are so frequent that you should have a way to manage them whenever they happen. `try-catch` statements are built to manage exceptions, and they are important for keeping your code safe. Be careful when they happen, since they can cause performance issues, as we discussed in *Chapter 2, Non-Functional Requirements*.

There are a lot of cases where an application crashes, and the reason for that is the lack of using `try-catch`. The following code shows an example of the lack of usage of the `try-catch` statement. It is worth mentioning that this is just an example of understanding the concept of an exception thrown without correct treatment. Consider using `int.TryParse(textToConvert, out int result)` to handle cases where a parse is unsuccessful:

```
private static int CodeWithNoTryCatch(string textToConvert)
{
    return Convert.ToInt32(textToConvert);
}
```

Conversely, bad `try-catch` usage can cause damage to your code too, especially because you will not see the correct behavior of that code and may misunderstand the results provided.

The following code shows an example of an empty `try-catch` statement:

```
private static int CodeWithEmptyTryCatch(string textToConvert)
{
    try
    {
        return Convert.ToInt32(textToConvert);
    }
    catch
    {
        return default;
    }
}
```

`try-catch` statements must be connected to logging solutions so that you can have a response from the system that will indicate the correct behavior and, at the same time, not cause application crashes. The following code shows an ideal `try-catch` statement with logging management. It is worth mentioning that specific exceptions should be caught whenever possible, since catching a general exception will hide unexpected exceptions:

```
private static int CodeWithCorrectTryCatch(string textToConvert)
{
    try
    {
        return Convert.ToInt32(textToConvert);
    }
    catch (FormatException err)
    {
        Logger.GenerateLog(err);
        return 0;
    }
}
```

It is very important to note that exceptions are, computationally speaking, expensive. No matter whether you are throwing them to indicate an error or catching them to manage errors, it takes a lot of computational processing. So, it is common, and preferable, to rely on a higher-level exception handler instead of trying to handle everything everywhere, as the code might become hard to reason about, particularly if there is not a good action to take when an exception happens. That means you may not handle the exceptions in every method, especially if you do not know what to do with them at that part of the code and you will throw it again to a higher-level handle. You should prioritize handling exceptions where meaningful actions can be taken.

However, it is also worth mentioning that exception errors delivered to the end user can cause the feeling that bad software was delivered. As a software architect, you should conduct code inspections to define the best behavior for code. Instability in a system, like unexpected crashes and high-memory usage, is often connected to the lack of `try-catch` statements in code.

try-finally and using

Memory leaks can be considered one of the worst software behaviors. They cause instability, bad usage of computer resources, and undesired application crashes. C# tries to solve this with **Garbage Collector**, which automatically releases objects from memory as soon as it realizes an object can be freed. The trigger for Garbage Collector is well explained at `https://learn.microsoft.com/en-us/dotnet/standard/garbage-collection/fundamentals`.

Objects that interact with I/O are the ones that generally are not managed by Garbage Collector: the filesystem, sockets, and so on. The following code is an example of the incorrect usage of a `FileStream` object because it thinks Garbage Collector will release the memory used, but it will not:

```
private static void CodeWithIncorrectFileStreamManagement()
{
    FileStream file = new ("C:\\file.txt", FileMode.CreateNew);
    byte[] data = GetFileData();
    file.Write(data, 0, data.Length);
}
```

Besides, it takes a while for Garbage Collector to interact with objects that need to be released, and sometimes, you may want to do it yourself. For both cases, the use of `try-finally` or `using` statements is the best practice:

```
private static void CorrectFileStreamManagementFirstOption()
{
    FileStream file = new ("C:\\file.txt",FileMode.CreateNew);
    try
    {
        byte[] data = GetFileData();
        file.Write(data, 0, data.Length);
    }
    finally
    {
        file.Dispose();
    }
}
private static void CorrectFileStreamManagementSecondOption()
{
    using (FileStream file = new ("C:\\file.txt", FileMode.CreateNew))
    {
        byte[] data = GetFileData();
        file.Write(data, 0, data.Length);
    }
}
private static void CorrectFileStreamManagementThirdOption()
{
    using FileStream file = new ("C:\\file.txt", FileMode.CreateNew);
    byte[] data = GetFileData();
    file.Write(data, 0, data.Length);
}
```

The preceding code shows exactly how to deal with objects that are not managed by Garbage Collector. Both `try-finally` and `using` are implemented. As a software architect, you do need to pay attention to this kind of code. The lack of `try-finally` or `using` statements can cause huge damage to software behavior when it is running. It is worth mentioning that using code analysis tools, such as **Sonar Lint** and **Code Analysis**, will automatically alert you to these sorts of problems.

The IDisposable interface

In the same way that you will have trouble if you do not manage objects created inside a method with `try-finally/using` statements, objects created in a class that does not properly implement the `IDisposable` interface may cause memory leaks in your application. For this reason, when you have a class that deals with and creates objects, you should implement the `Disposable` pattern to guarantee the release of all resources created by the class:

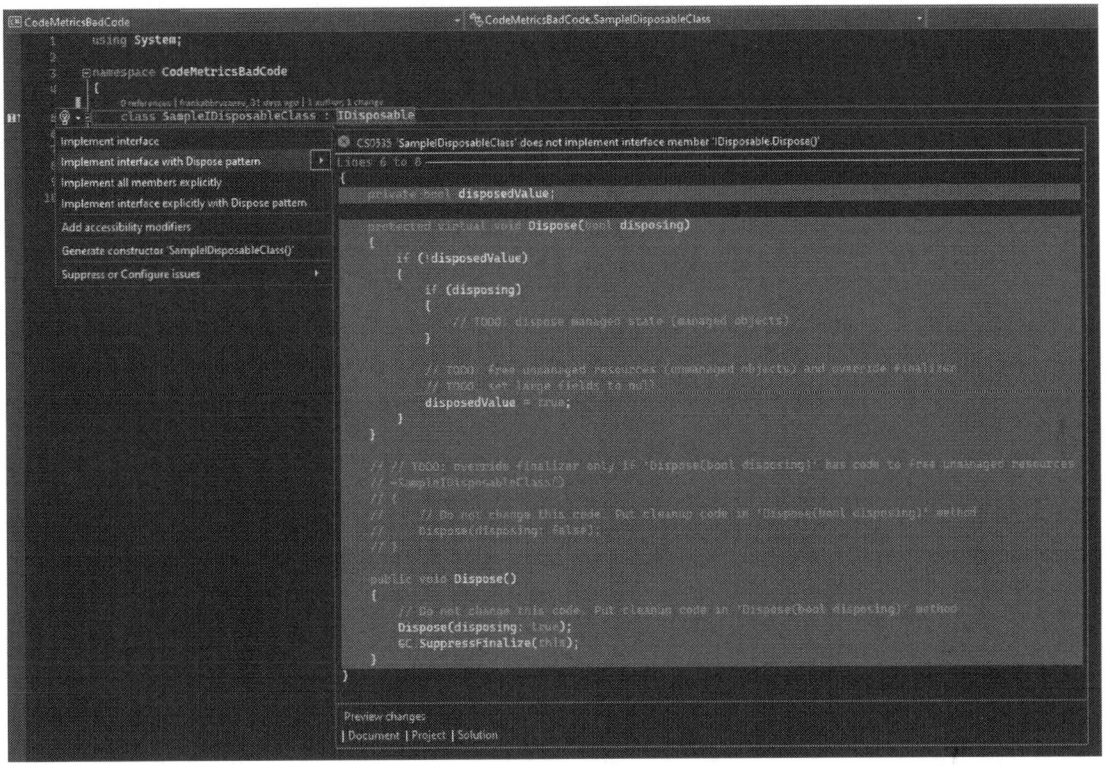

Figure 4.10: IDisposable interface implementation

The good news is that Visual Studio gives you a code snippet to implement this interface by simply indicating it in your code, and then you right-click on the **Quick Actions** and **Refactoring** options, as you can see in the preceding screenshot.

Once you have inserted the code, you need to follow the to-do instructions so that you have the correct pattern implemented.

As a software architect, you will be responsible not only for the architecture defined in a system but also for how this system performs in operation. Memory leaks and bad performance, in general, are caused by errors related to the `try-catch` strategy, a lack of `try-finally/using`, and wrong or no implementation of `IDisposable`. So be sure that your team knows how to deal with these techniques.

Since we have covered some important information about how to write safe code in C#, it would be nice to get some tips and tricks for coding in this programming language. Let us do so in the next topic of this chapter.

.NET 8 tips and tricks for coding

.NET 8 implements some good features that help us to write better code. One of the most useful things for having cleaner code is **dependency injection** (**DI**), which will be discussed in *Chapter 6, Design Patterns and .NET 8 Implementation*. There are some good reasons for considering this. The first one is that you will only need to worry about disposing of the injected objects if you are the creator of them.

Besides, DI enables you to inject `ILogger`, a useful tool for debugging exceptions that will need to be managed by `try-catch` statements in your code. Furthermore, programming in C# with .NET 8 must follow the common good practices of any programming language. The following list shows some of these:

- **Classes, methods, and variables should have understandable names:** The name should explain everything that the reader needs to know. There should be no need for an explanatory comment unless these declarations are public.
- **Methods should not have high complexity levels:** Cyclomatic complexity should be checked so that methods do not have too many lines of code.
- **Members must have the correct visibility:** As an object-oriented programming language, C# enables encapsulation with different visibility keywords. C# 9 has presented *init-only setters*, so you can create `init` property/index accessors instead of `set`, defining these members as read-only following the construction of the object.
- **Duplicate code should be avoided:** There is no reason for having duplicate code in a high-level programming language such as C#.
- **Objects should be checked before usage:** Since null objects can exist, code must have null type checking. It is worth mentioning that since C# 8, we have nullable reference types to avoid errors related to nullable objects. You can refer to `https://docs.microsoft.com/en-us/dotnet/csharp/nullable-references` for more information about nullable reference types.
- **Constants and enumerators should be used:** A good way of avoiding magic numbers and text inside code is to transform this information into constants and enumerators, which generally are more understandable.
- **Unsafe code should be avoided:** Unsafe code enables you to deal with pointers in C#. Unless there is no other way to implement the solution, unsafe code should be avoided.
- **try-catch statements cannot be empty:** There is rarely a reason to use a `try-catch` statement without treatment in the `catch` area. Moreover, the caught exceptions should be as specific as possible, and not just an "exception," to avoid swallowing unexpected exceptions.
- **Dispose of the objects that you have created, if they are disposable:** Even for objects where Garbage Collector will take care of the disposed-of object, consider disposing of objects that you were responsible for creating yourself.

- **At least public methods should be commented:** Considering that public methods are the ones used outside your library, they must be explained for their correct external usage.
- **switch-case statements must have a default treatment:** Since `switch-case` statements may receive an entrance variable unknown in some cases, the default treatment will guarantee that code will not break in such a situation.

As a software architect, you may consider a good practice of providing a code pattern for your developers that will be used to keep the style of code consistent as a team. You can also use this code pattern as a checklist for coding inspections, which will enrich software code quality.

Identifying well-written code

It is not easy to identify whether code is well written. The best practices described so far can certainly guide you as a software architect to define a standard for your team. However, even with a standard, mistakes will happen, and you will probably find them only after code is in production. The decision to refactor code in production just because it does not follow all the standards you define is not an easy one to take, especially if the code in question works properly. Some people conclude that well-written code is simply code that works well in production. However, this can surely cause damage to the software's life since developers might be influenced by that non-standard code.

For this reason, as a software architect, you need to find ways to enforce adherence to the coding standard you've defined. Luckily, nowadays, we have many options for tools that can help us with this task. They are called static code analysis tools, and using them provides a great opportunity to improve both the software developed and the team's programming knowledge.

The reason your developers will evolve with code analysis is that you start to disseminate knowledge between them during code inspections. The tools that we have now have the same purpose. Even better, with Roslyn, they do this task while you write the code. Roslyn is the compiler platform for .NET, and it enables you to develop some tools for analyzing code. These analyzers can check style, quality, design, and other issues.

For instance, look at the following code. It does not make any sense, but you can still see that there are some mistakes:

```
using System;
static void Main(string[] args)
{
    try
    {
        int variableUnused = 10;
        int variable = 10;
        if (variable == 10)
        {
            Console.WriteLine("variable equals 10");
        }
        else
        {
            switch (variable)
            {
                case 0:
                    Console.WriteLine("variable equals 0");
                    break;
            }
        }
    }
    catch
    {
    }
}
```

The idea of this code is to show you the power of some tools to improve the code you deliver. Let us study each of them in the next section, including how to set them up.

Understanding and applying tools that can evaluate C# code

The evolution of code analysis in Visual Studio is continuous. This means that Visual Studio 2022 certainly has more tools for this purpose than Visual Studio 2019, and so on.

One of the issues that you (as a software architect) need to deal with is the *coding style of the team*. This certainly results in a better understanding of the code. For instance, if you go to the **Visual Studio Menu**, then **Tools -> Options**, and then, in the left-hand menu, **Text Editor -> C#**, you will find ways to deal with different code style patterns, and a bad coding style is even indicated as an error in the **Code Style** options, as follows:

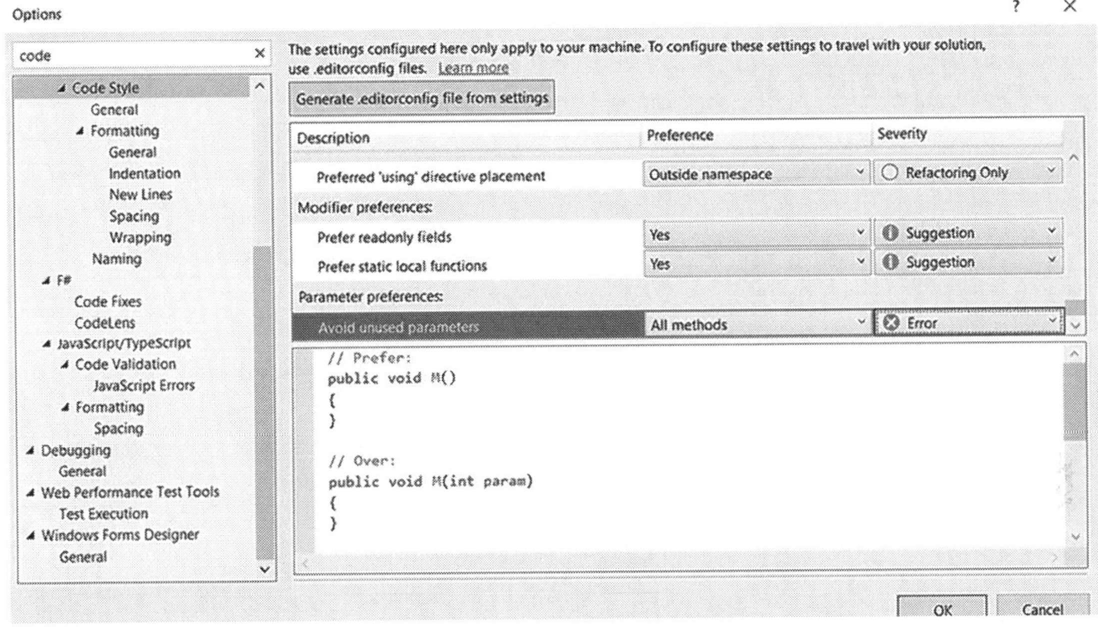

Figure 4.11: Code Style options

The preceding screenshot chnage that **Avoid unused parameters** was considered an error.

After this change, the result of the compilation of the code presented at the beginning of the chapter is different, as you can see in the following screenshot:

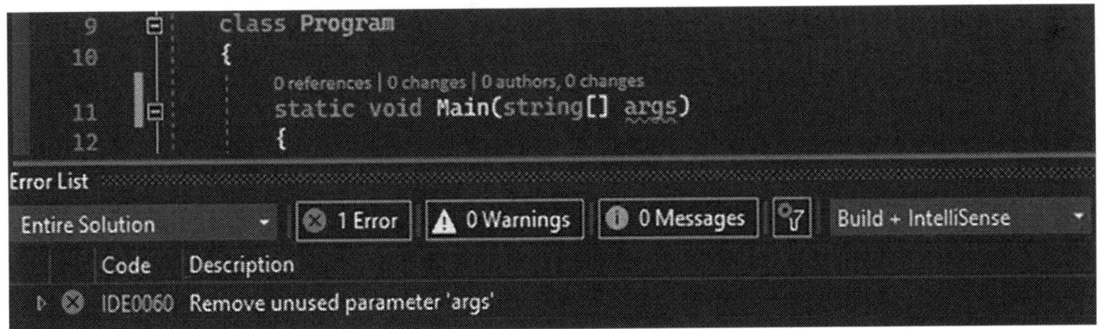

Figure 4.12: Code Style result

You can export your coding style configuration and attach it to your project so that it will follow the rules you have defined.

Another good tool that Visual Studio 2022 provides is **Analyze and Code Cleanup**. With this tool, you can set up some code standards that can clean up your code. For instance, in the following screenshot, it was set to remove unnecessary code:

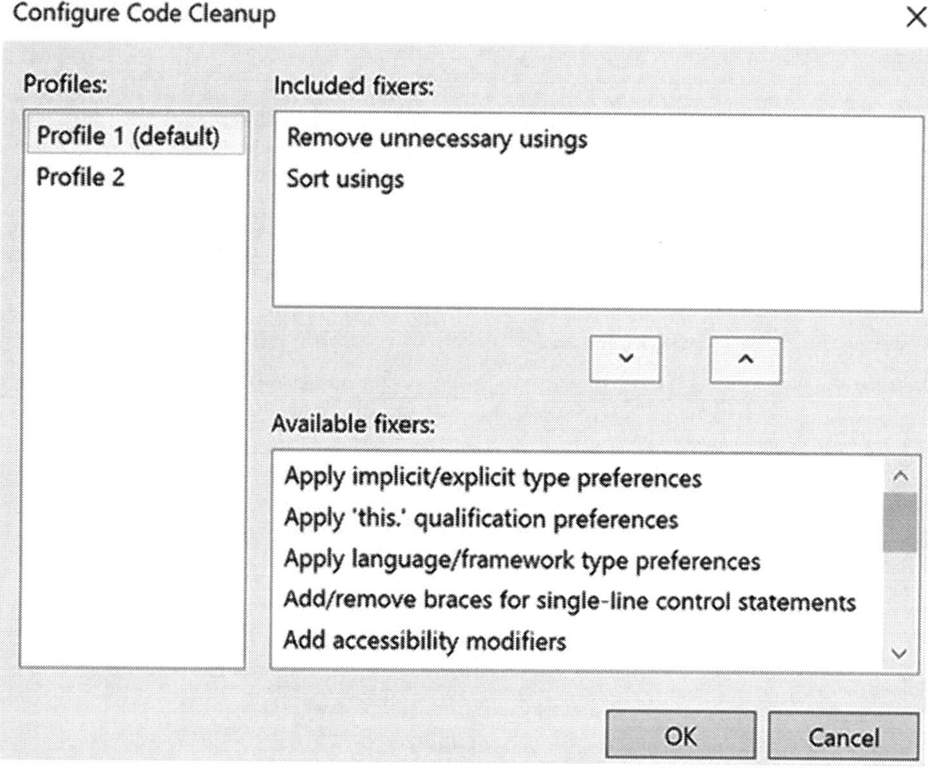

Figure 4.13: Configure Code Cleanup

The way to run Code Cleanup is by selecting it with the help of a right-click in the **Solution Explorer** area, over the project where you want to run it. After that, this process will run in all the code files you have:

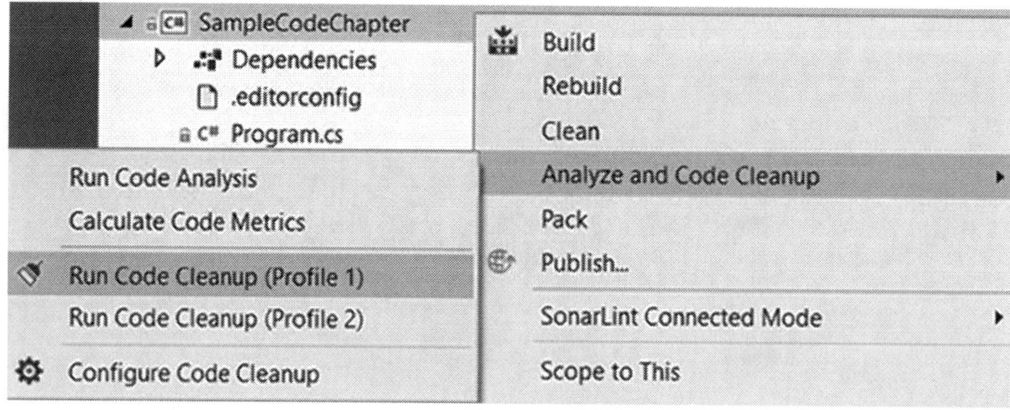

Figure 4.14: Run Code Cleanup

After solving the errors indicated by the **Code Style** and **Code Cleanup** tools, the sample code we are working on has some minimal simplifications, as follows:

```
using System;
try
{
    int variable = 10;
    if (variable == 10)
    {
        Console.WriteLine("variable equals 10");
    }
    else
    {
        switch (variable)
        {
            case 0:
                Console.WriteLine("variable equals 0");
                break;
        }
    }
}
catch
{
}
```

It is worth mentioning that the preceding code has many improvements that still need to be addressed. Visual Studio enables you to add additional tools for the IDE by installing extensions to it. These tools can help you to improve your code quality, since some of them were built to perform code analysis. This section will list some free options so that you can decide on the one that best fits your needs. There are certainly other options and even paid ones. The idea here is not to indicate a specific tool but to give you an idea of their abilities.

To install these extensions, you will need to find the **Extensions** menu in Visual Studio 2022. Here is a screenshot of the **Manage Extensions** option:

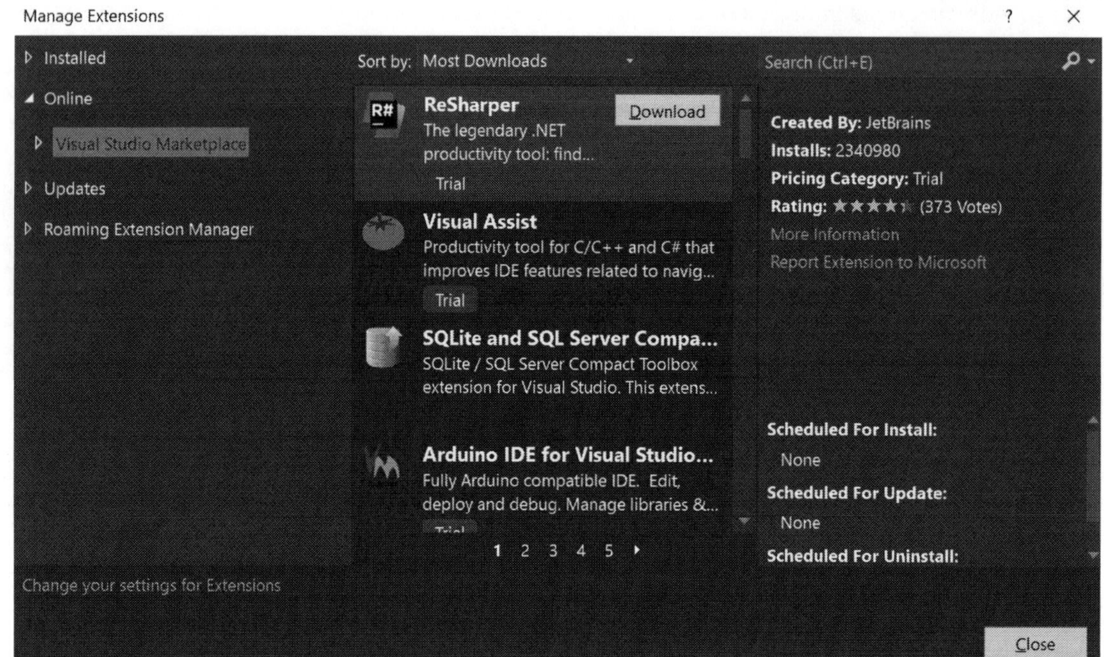

Figure 4.15: Extensions in Visual Studio 2022

There are many other great extensions that can improve the productivity and quality of your code and solutions. Search for them in this manager.

After you have selected the extension that will be installed, you will need to restart Visual Studio. Most of the extensions are easy to identify after installation, since they modify the behavior of the IDE. However, they need to be set in each developer environment. To resolve it, Visual Studio has introduced the option to include analyzers as NuGet packages, so all developers who work with the project will have their code analyzed.

Applying extension tools to analyze code

Although the sample code delivered after the Code Style and Code Cleanup tools is better than the code we presented at the beginning of the chapter, it is clearly far removed from the best practices discussed so far.

For this reason, Microsoft has divided analyzers into three groups:

- Code style, as mentioned before
- Code quality analyzers that are already included in .NET 5+ projects
- Third-party analyzers that can be installed as a NuGet package or Visual Studio extension

You can find an overview of source code analysis at `https://docs.microsoft.com/en-us/visualstudio/code-quality/roslyn-analyzers-overview`.

Let us study how these third-party analyzers can be useful, using as a reference the **SonarAnalyzer** package.

Applying SonarAnalyzer

SonarAnalyzer is an open-source initiative from the Sonar Source community to detect bugs and quality issues while you code. There is support for C#, VB.NET, C, C++, and JavaScript. They also offer an extension called **SonarLint**. The great thing about this extension is that it comes with explanations for resolving detected issues, and that is why we think developers learn how to code well while using these tools.

This extension can point out mistakes and, even better, there is an explanation for each warning. This is useful not only for detecting problems but also for training developers in good coding practices.

In Visual Studio 2022, the SonarLint extension is available. Besides that, you can also use the NuGet package, as we can see in the following screenshot:

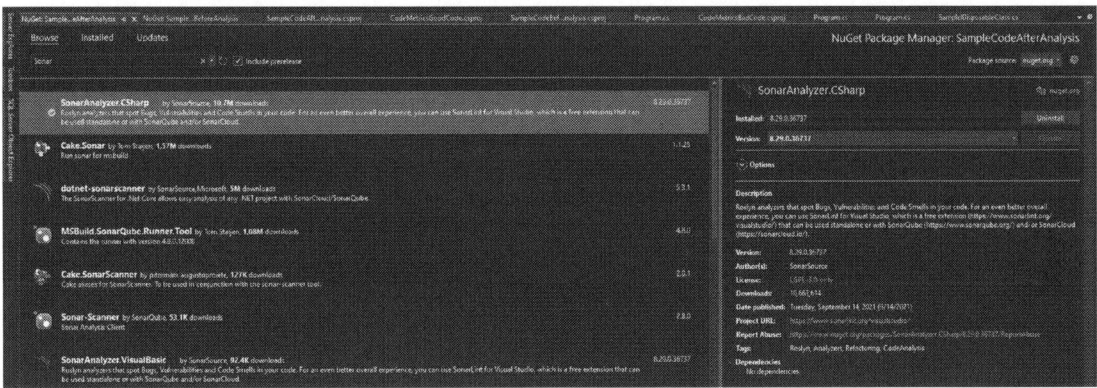

Figure 4.16: SonarAnalyzer.CSharp NuGet package

The result produced is the same as the one we got using the SonarLint extension, but the good thing about this option is that any developer who needs to code for this project will get their code analyzed.

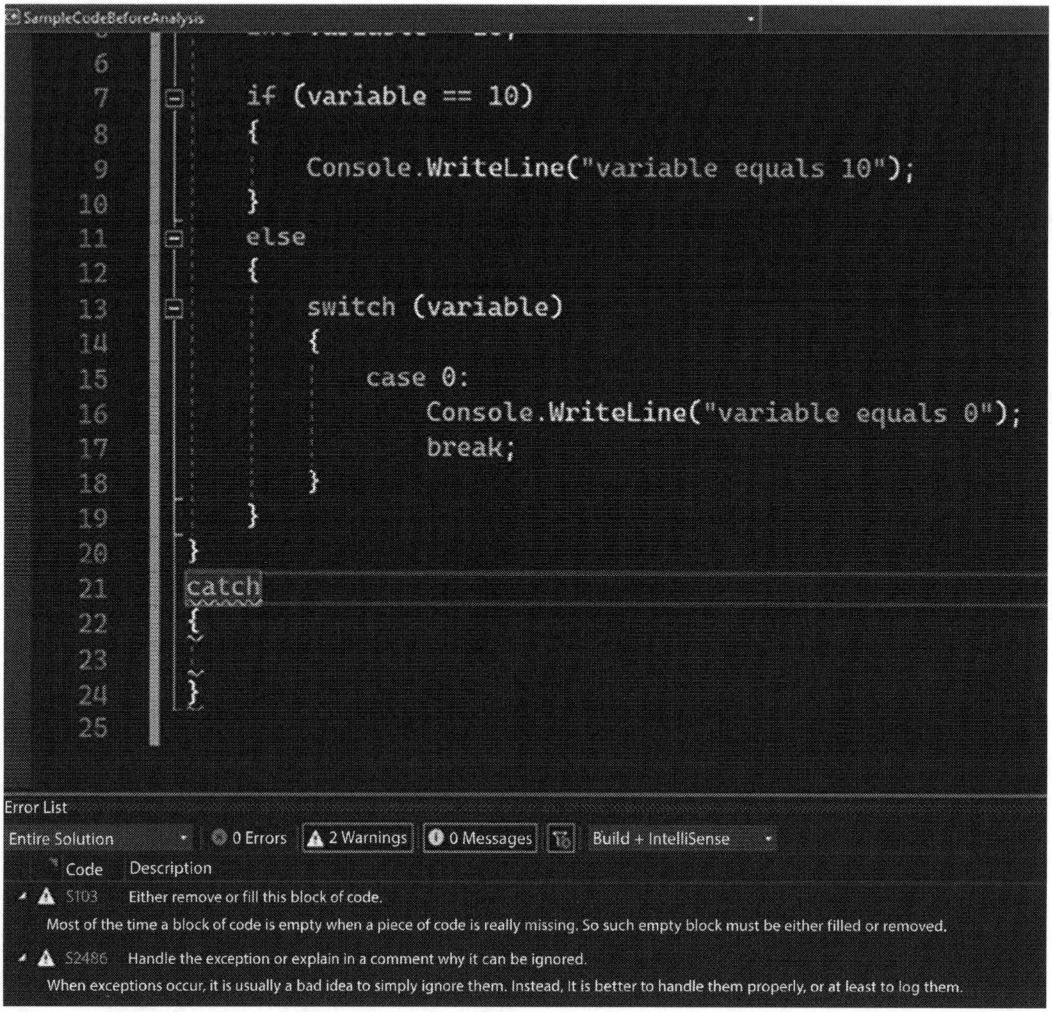

Figure 4.17: SonarAnalyzer.CSharp analysis result

As a software architect, you will always have to pay attention and take action to get projects unified with the same code standard, so the NuGet option may be useful for achieving this goal.

Checking the final code after analysis

Following the analysis of the two options presented, we have finally solved all the issues with the original code. Here is the final code:

```
using System;
try
{
    int variable = 10;
    if (variable == 10)
    {
        Console.WriteLine("variable equals 10");
    }
    else
    {
        switch (variable)
        {
            case 0:
                Console.WriteLine("variable equals 0");
                break;
            default:
                Console.WriteLine("Unknown behavior");
                break;
        }
    }
}
catch (Exception err)
{
    Console.WriteLine(err);
}
```

As you can see, the preceding code is not only easier to understand but is also safer and able to consider different paths of programming, since the default for `switch-case` was programmed. This pattern was discussed earlier in this chapter, which brings us to the happy conclusion that best practices can easily be followed by using one (or all) of the options discussed in this chapter.

Summary

In this chapter, we discussed some important tips for writing safe code. This chapter introduced a tool for analyzing code metrics so that you can manage the complexity and maintainability of the software you develop. To finish, we presented some good tips to guarantee that your software will not crash due to memory leaks and exceptions. In real life, a software architect will always be asked to solve this kind of problem.

The chapter also recommended tools that can be used to apply the best practices of the coding we discussed. We looked at the Roslyn compiler, which enables code analysis while a developer codes.

You will find in *Chapter 21, Case Study*, a way to evaluate C# code prior to publishing an application, which implements code analysis during the Azure DevOps building process, using SonarCloud.

When you apply all the content you have learned in this chapter to your projects, you will find that code analysis will give you the opportunity to improve the quality of the code you deliver to your customers. This is a very important part of your role as a software architect.

In the next chapter, you will learn about code reuse, which is an incredible technique to guarantee quality and velocity for your projects!

Questions

1. Why do we need to care about maintainability?
2. What is cyclomatic complexity?
3. List the advantages of using a version control system.
4. What is the garbage collector?
5. What is the importance of implementing the `IDisposable` interface?
6. What advantages do we gain from .NET 8 when it comes to coding?
7. What makes it possible for a piece of software to be described as having well-written code?
8. What is Roslyn?
9. What is code analysis?
10. What is the importance of code analysis?
11. How does Roslyn help with code analysis?
12. What are Visual Studio extensions?
13. What extension tools are available for code analysis?

Further reading

These are some books and websites where you will find more information about the topics of this chapter:

- *Clean Code: A Handbook of Agile Software Craftmanship*, by Martin, Robert C. Pearson Education, 2012.
- *The Art of Designing Embedded Systems*, by Jack G. Ganssle. Elsevier, 1999.
- *Refactoring*, by Martin Fowler. Addison-Wesley, 2018.
- *A Complexity Measure*, by Thomas J. McCabe. IEEE Trans. Software Eng. 2(4): 308–320, 1976 (`https://dblp.uni-trier.de/db/journals/tse/tse2.html`).
- Code metrics information:
    - `https://blogs.msdn.microsoft.com/zainnab/2011/05/25/code-metrics-class-coupling/`

    - https://docs.microsoft.com/en-us/visualstudio/code-quality/code-metrics-values?view=vs-2019

- Version control systems:
    - https://github.com/
    - https://bitbucket.org/
    - https://azure.microsoft.com/en-us/services/devops/
- Code branching techniques:
    - https://guides.github.com/introduction/flow/
- Logging fundamentals:
    - https://docs.microsoft.com/aspnet/core/fundamentals/logging/
- What is new in CSharp?:
    - https://docs.microsoft.com/en-us/dotnet/csharp/whats-new/csharp-9
    - https://docs.microsoft.com/en-us/dotnet/csharp/whats-new/csharp-10
    - https://learn.microsoft.com/en-us/dotnet/csharp/whats-new/csharp-11
    - https://learn.microsoft.com/en-us/dotnet/csharp/whats-new/csharp-12
- Source code analyzers:
    - https://marketplace.visualstudio.com/items?itemName=SonarSource.SonarLintforVisualStudio2019
    - https://marketplace.visualstudio.com/items?itemName=SonarSource.SonarLintforVisualStudio2022
    - https://github.com/dotnet/roslyn-analyzers
    - https://docs.microsoft.com/en-us/visualstudio/ide/code-styles-and-code-cleanup
    - https://docs.sonarcloud.io/
    - https://www.guidgenerator.com/

Learn more on Discord

To join the Discord community for this book – where you can share feedback, ask questions to the authors, and learn about new releases – follow the QR code below:

`https://packt.link/SoftwareArchitectureCSharp12Dotnet8`

5

Implementing Code Reusability in C# 12

Code reusability is one of the most important topics in software architecture. This chapter aims to discuss ways to enable code reuse, as well as help you understand how .NET 8 solves the problem of managing and maintaining a reusable library.

The following topics will be covered in this chapter:

- Understanding the principles of code reuse
- The advantages of working with .NET 8
- Creating reusable libraries using .NET 8

Although code reuse is an exceptional practice, as a software architect, you must be aware of when this is important for the scenario you are dealing with. Many good software architects agree that there is a lot of overengineering due to trying to make things reusable even though they are often single-use or not understood well enough, leading to unnecessary complexity and slowing down the development process.

Technical requirements

For this chapter, you will need the free Visual Studio 2022 Community Edition or above, with all the database tools installed.

Understanding the principles of code reusability

There is a single reason that you can always use to justify code reuse – you cannot spend your valuable time reinventing the wheel if it is already running well in other scenarios. That is why most engineering domains are based on reusability principles like modularity, standardization, abstraction, and documentation. Think about the light switches you have in your house. You can only change them without modifying other components of your house because it was built based on a standard, abstracting the idea of what a switch is according to a specification, providing modularity as a result.

Can you imagine the number of applications that can be made with the same interface components? The fundamentals of code reuse are the same. Again, it is a matter of planning a good solution so part of it can be reused later.

In software engineering, code reuse is one of the techniques that can bring a bunch of advantages to a software project, such as the following:

- There is confidence in the software, considering that the reused piece of code was already tested in another application.
- There is more efficient usage of software architects and the senior team since they can be dedicated to solving this kind of problem.
- There is the possibility of bringing to the project a pattern that is already accepted by the market.
- Development speed goes up due to the already-implemented components.
- Maintenance is easier.

These aspects suggest that code reuse should be done whenever possible. However, creating reusable components does carry higher costs initially. That is why you need to focus on creating it in situations where you recognize that this piece of code will really be reused in the future or where you are trying to reuse code that has not been created as a component. It is your responsibility, as a software architect, to ensure the preceding advantages are utilized and, more than that, that you incentivize your team to enable reuse in the software they are creating.

In the next section, we will discuss what can be considered code reuse and what cannot. The main purpose of discussing it is to help you define a code reuse strategy that will transform the efficiency of your team.

What code reuse is not

The first thing you must understand is that code reuse does not mean copying and pasting code from one class to another. Even if this code was written by another team or project, this does not indicate that you are properly working with reusability principles. Let us imagine a scenario that we will find in this book's use case, the **WWTravelClub** evaluation.

In this project scenario, you may want to evaluate different kinds of subjects, such as the **Package**, **DestinationExpert**, **City**, **Comments**, and so on. The process for getting the evaluation average is the same, no matter which subject you are referring to. Due to this, you may want to *enable* reuse by copying and pasting the code for each evaluation. The (bad) result will be something like this:

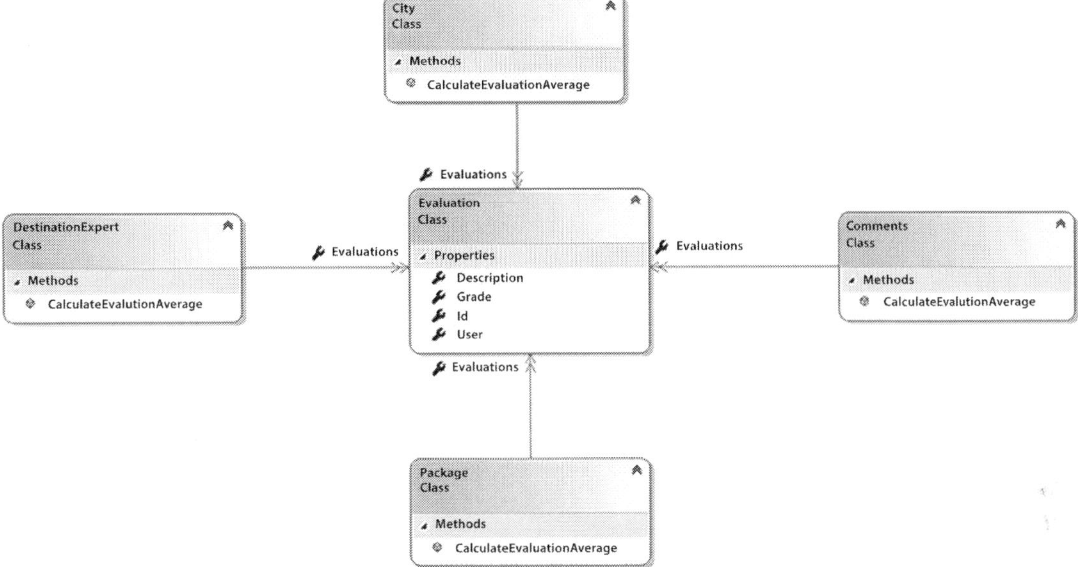

Figure 5.1: Bad implementation – there is no code reuse here

In the preceding diagram, the process of calculating the evaluation average is decentralized, which means that the same code will be duplicated in different classes. This will cause a lot of trouble, especially if the same approach is used in other applications. For instance, if there is a new specification covering how you must calculate the average, or even if you just get a bug in the calculation formula, you will have to fix it in all instances of the code. If you do not remember to update it everywhere, you will possibly end up with an inconsistent implementation.

In the next section, we will reorganize this code to respect some principles that you, as a software architect, should follow to avoid the issues we have mentioned here.

What code reuse is

The solution to the problem mentioned in the previous section is quite simple: you must analyze your code and select the parts of it that would be good to decouple from your application.

The most compelling reason you should decouple them is related to how you are sure that this code can be reused in other parts of the application or even in another application. This is exactly what Andrew Hunt and David Thomas present as the DRY principle (don't repeat yourself):

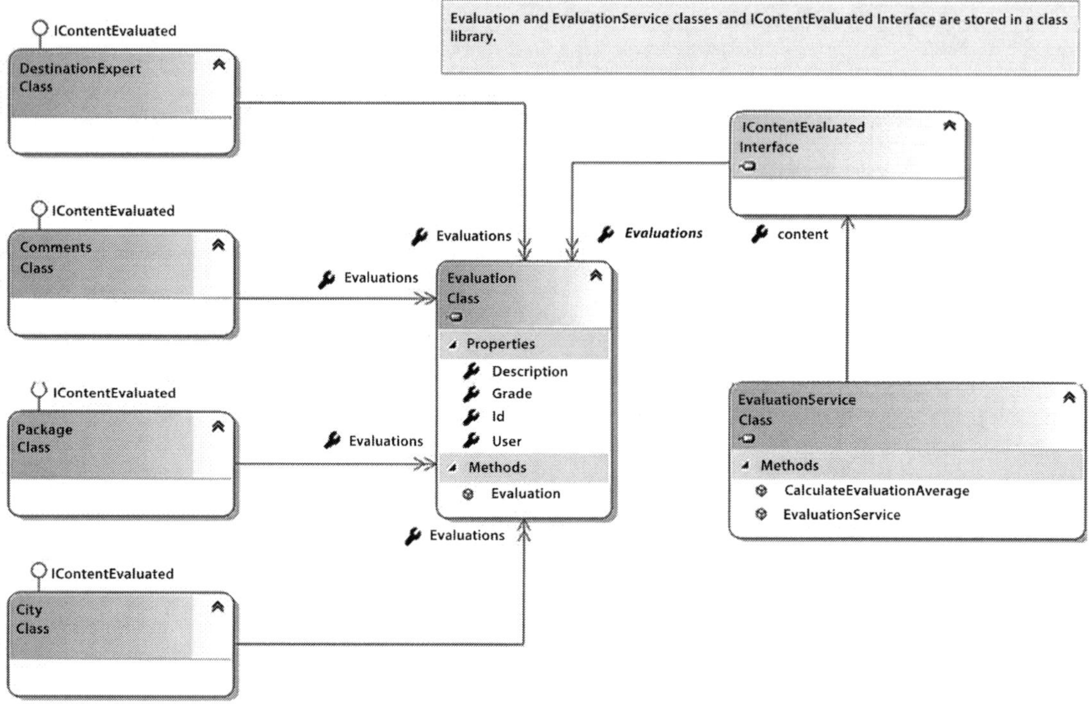

Figure 5.2: An implementation focused on code reuse

The centralization of the code brings with it a different responsibility for software architects such as yourself. You must keep in mind that if there is a mistake or problem in this code, it can cause issues in many parts of the application or even other applications that use it. On the other hand, once you have this code tested and running, you will be able to reuse this code again in new projects with no worries. Besides, let's remember the use case we are implementing here: you may want to evaluate different kinds of subjects, such as the **Package**, **DestinationExpert**, **City**, **Comments**, and so on. The process for getting the evaluation average is the same, no matter which subject you are referring to. What if you need to evolve the average calculation process? In the design now provided, you will have to change the code in a single class. Considering what we have already learned, we could also:

- Make a base class implementing the logic of the method.
- Inherit all other classes from the newly created base class and eventually augment/modify the method's behavior.
- Turn the inheritance into an association (as discussed in the previous chapter).

It is worth mentioning that the more you use the same code, the cheaper this development will become. Although it might seem like developing reusable code costs more initially, the more you use it, the more cost-effective and efficient the development process becomes over time. Cost needs to be mentioned because, in general, the concept of reusable software costs more in the beginning.

Reusability in the development life cycle

If you understand that code reusability will take you to another level of coding, improving the way you write and use code, then it's time to think about how to make this technique available in your development life cycle.

As a matter of fact, creating and maintaining a component library is not very easy due to the responsibility you will take on and the lack of good tools to support the search for existing components.

On the other hand, there are some practices that you may consider implementing in your software development process every time you initiate a new development:

- **Use** the already-implemented components from your user library, selecting features that need them in the software requirements specification.
- **Identify** features in the software requirements specification that are candidates to be designed as library components.
- **Modify** the specification, considering that these features will be developed using reusable components.
- **Design** the reusable components and be sure that they have the appropriate interfaces to be used in many projects.
- **Build** the project architecture with the new component library version.
- **Document** the component library version so that every developer and team knows about it.

The *use-identify-modify-design-build* process is a technique that you may consider implementing every time you need to enable software reuse. As soon as you have the components you need to write for this library, you will need to decide on the technology that will provide these components.

During the history of software development, there have been many approaches to enable code reuse, from **dynamic link libraries** (**DLLs**) to microservices, as we will discuss in *Chapter 11, Applying a Microservice Architecture to Your Enterprise Application*, in the *Microservices and the evolution of the concept of modules* section. The methodology explained in the section can be used by you, as a software architect, to implement this strategy to accelerate software development. Now, let us check how .NET 8 can help us with it.

Using .NET 8 for code reuse

.NET has evolved a lot since its first version. This evolution is related not only to the number of commands and performance issues but also to the supported platforms. As we discussed in *Chapter 1, Understanding the Importance of Software Architecture*, you can run C# .NET on billions of devices, even if they are running Linux, Android, macOS, or iOS. For this reason, .NET Standard was first announced together with .NET Core 1.0, but .NET Standard became particularly important with .NET Standard 2.0 when .NET Framework 4.7.2, .NET Core, and Xamarin became compatible with it.

The key point is that .NET Standard was not only a Visual Studio project. More than that, it was a formal specification available to all .NET implementations. As you can see in the following table, .NET Standard 2.0, which is recommended by Microsoft, covers everything in .NET. You can find a full .NET Standard overview at `https://docs.microsoft.com/en-us/dotnet/standard/net-standard`.

.NET implementation	Version support
.NET and .NET Core	2.0, 2.1, 2.2, 3.0, 3.1, 5.0, 6.0, 7.0, 8.0
.NET Framework 1	4.6.1 2, 4.6.2, 4.7, 4.7.1, 4.7.2, 4.8, 4.8.1
Mono	5.4, 6.4
Xamarin.iOS	10.14, 12.16
Xamarin.Mac	3.8, 5.16
Xamarin.Android	8.0, 10.0
Universal Windows Platform	10.0.16299, TBD
Unity	2018.1

Table 5.1: .NET Standard 2.0 support

This indicates that if you build a class library that is compatible with this standard, you will be able to reuse it on any of the platforms presented. Think about how fast your development process could become if you plan to do this in all your projects.

Obviously, some components are not included in .NET Standard, but its evolution is continuous. It is worth mentioning that Microsoft's official documentation indicates that *the higher the version, the more APIs are available to you.*

The initiative of having a single framework for all platforms brought us to .NET 5. Microsoft indicated that from .NET 5.0, the framework would run everywhere. The next question you, as a software architect, might have is *what is going to happen to .NET Standard?*

The answer to this question is well explained by Immo Landwerth at the dotnet blog: `https://devblogs.microsoft.com/dotnet/the-future-of-net-standard/`. The basic answer is that .NET 5.0 (and future versions) needs to be thought of as the foundation for sharing code moving forward. Considering .NET 8 is an **LTS** (**Long-Term Support**) version, we can now understand the framework as the best option to share code for new applications.

Bearing this scenario in mind, it is time to check how to create reusable class libraries. So, let us move to the next topic.

Creating a reusable class library

If you want to make useful functionalities to be used by multiple applications, you will need to create a **class library** project. So, creating class libraries is the best way to reuse code using .NET. It is quite simple to create a **class library**. Basically, you need to choose the following project when creating the library:

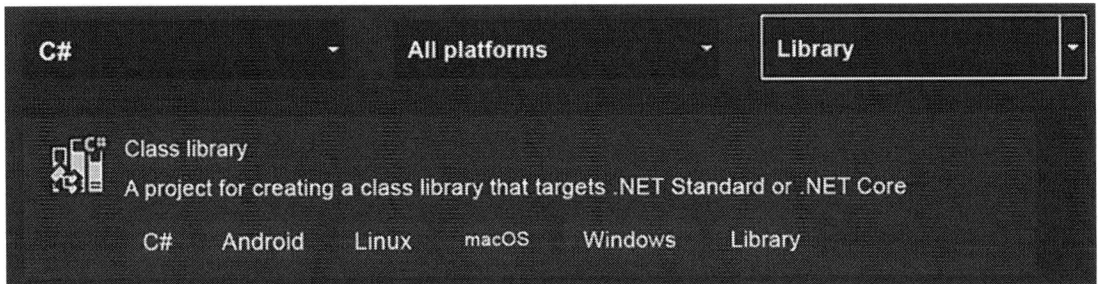

Figure 5.3: Creating a class library

Once you have concluded this part, you will notice that the project file keeps the information about the **target framework moniker** (**TFM**). The idea of the TFM is to define the set of APIs that will be available to the library. You can find a list of the available TFMs at `https://docs.microsoft.com/en-us/dotnet/standard/frameworks`:

```
<Project Sdk="Microsoft.NET.Sdk">
  <PropertyGroup>
    <TargetFramework>net8.0</TargetFramework>
    <Nullable>enable</Nullable>
  </PropertyGroup>
</Project>
```

As soon as your project is loaded, you can start coding the classes that you intend to reuse. The advantage of building reusable classes using this approach is that you will be able to reuse the written code in all the project types we checked previously. On the other hand, you will find out that some APIs that are available in .NET Framework do not exist in this type of project.

Considering that you already have the correct project type selected for creating reusable code, let us check how C# deals with code reuse in the next section.

How does C# deal with code reuse?

Considering you are writing class libraries using C#.NET, there are many approaches where **C#** helps us deal with code reuse. The ability to build libraries, as we did in the previous section, is one of them. One of the most important ones is the fact that the language is **object-oriented**. Besides this, it is also worth mentioning the facilities that generics brought to the C# language. This section will discuss object-oriented analysis and generics principles.

Object-oriented analysis

The object-oriented analysis approach gives us the ability to reuse code in different ways, from the facility of inheritance to the changeability of polymorphism. Complete adoption of object-oriented programming will let you implement abstraction and encapsulation, too.

It is important to mention that in *Chapter 4, Best Practices in Coding C# 12*, we discuss how inheritance can cause complexity in your code. Although the following example presents a valid way to reuse code, consider using composition over inheritance in real-life applications.

The following diagram shows how using the object-oriented approach makes reuse easier. As you can see, there are different ways to calculate the grades of an evaluation, considering that you can be a basic or a prime user of this example system:

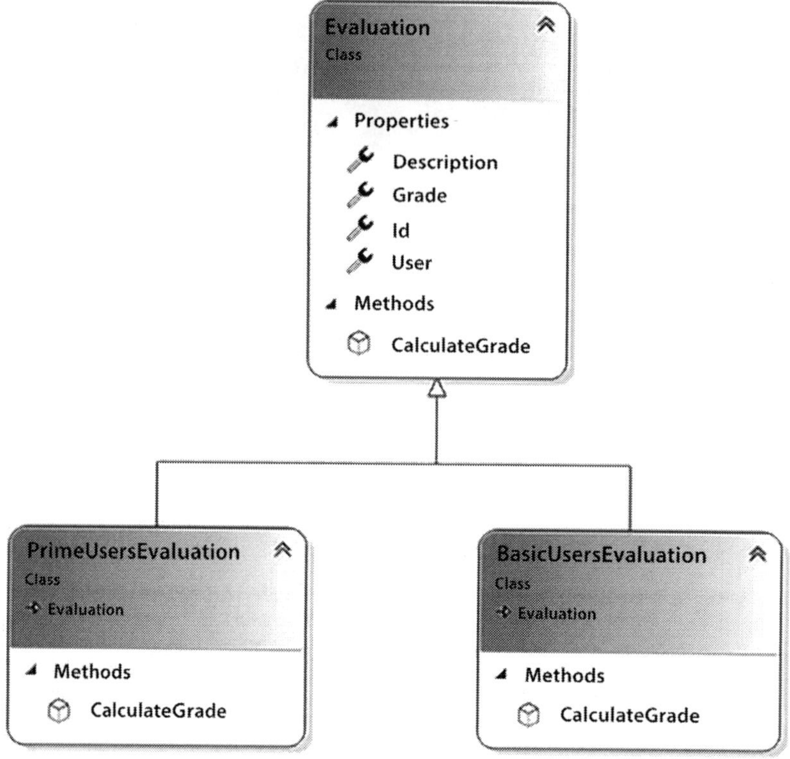

Figure 5.4: Object-oriented case analysis

There are two aspects to be analyzed as code reuse in this design. The first is that there is no need to declare the properties in each child class since inheritance does it for you.

The second is the opportunity to use polymorphism, enabling different behaviors for the same method:

```
public class PrimeUsersEvaluation : Evaluation
{
    /// <summary>
    /// The business rule implemented here indicates that grades
    /// that came from prime users have 20% of increase
    /// </summary>
    /// <returns>the final grade from a prime user</returns>
    public override double CalculateGrade()
    {
        return Grade * 1.2;
    }
}
```

In the preceding code, you can see the usage of the polymorphism principle, where the calculation of evaluation for prime users will increase by 20%. Now, look at how easy it is to call different objects inherited by the same class. Since the collection content implements the same interface, `IContentEvaluated`, it can have basic and prime users, too:

```
public class EvaluationService
{
    public IContentEvaluated Content { get; set; }
    /// <summary>
    /// No matter the Evaluation, the calculation will always get
    /// values from the method CalculateGrade
    /// </summary>
    /// <returns>The average of the grade from
    /// Evaluations
    /// </returns>
    public double CalculateEvaluationAverage()
    {
            return Content.Evaluations
                .Select(x => x.CalculateGrade())
                .Average();
    }
}
```

Object-oriented adoption can be considered mandatory when using C#. However, more specific usage requires study and practice. You, as a software architect, should always incentivize your team to study object-oriented analysis. The more abstract abilities they have, the easier code reuse will become.

Generics

Generics were introduced in C# in version 2.0 and are considered an approach that increases code reuse. It also maximizes type safety and performance.

The basic principle of generics is that you can define in an interface, class, method, property, event, or even delegate a placeholder that will be replaced with a specific type later when one of the preceding entities is used. The opportunity you have with this feature is incredible since you can use the same code to run different generic versions of the type.

The following code is a modification of `EvaluationService`, which was presented in the previous section. The idea here is to enable the generalization of the service, giving us the opportunity to define the goal of evaluation since its creation:

```
public class EvaluationService<T> where T: IContentEvaluated, new()
```

This declaration indicates that any class that implements the `IContentEvaluated` interface can be used for this service. The new constraint indicates this class must have a public parameter-less default constructor.

The service will be responsible for creating the evaluated content:

```
public EvaluationService()
{
    var name = GetTypeOfEvaluation();
    content = new T();
}
```

It is worth mentioning that this code works because all the classes are in the same assembly. The result of this modification can be checked in the instance creation of the service:

```
var service = new EvaluationService<CityEvaluation>();
```

The good news is that now, you have a generic service that will automatically instantiate the `list` object with the evaluations of the content you need. It's worth mentioning that generics will obviously need more time dedicated to the first project's construction. However, once the design is done, you will have good, fast, and easy-to-maintain code. This is what we call reuse!

What if the code is not reusable?

In fact, any code can be reusable. The key point here is that the code you intend to reuse must be well-written and follow good patterns for reuse. There are several reasons why code should be considered not ready for reuse:

- **The code has not been tested before**: Before reusing code, it is a good approach to guarantee that it works.
- **The code is duplicated**: If you have duplicate code, you will need to find each place where it is used so you only have a single version of the code being reused. If you find different versions of the code duplicated, you will need to define the best version of it to be considered the reusable one, and, at the same time, you will need to retest every replacement of the duplicated code to guarantee that the functionality of the software remains the same.
- **The code is too complex to understand:** Code that is reused in many places needs to be written with simplicity to enable easy understanding.
- **The code has tight coupling**: This is a discussion related to composition versus inheritance when building separate class libraries. Classes (with interfaces) are usually much easier to reuse than base classes that can be inherited.

In any of these cases, considering a refactoring strategy can be a great approach. When you refactor code, you write it in a better way, guaranteeing the code standards, reducing complexity, and respecting the input and output data that this code will process. This enables more comprehensive and lower-cost changes to be made to the code when the time comes. Martin Fowler, in his book *Refactoring* of 2018, indicates some reasons why you should consider refactoring:

- **It improves software design**: The more expert your team becomes, the better the design will be. A better software design will not only deliver faster coding but also bring us the opportunity to process more tasks in less time.

- **It makes the software easier to understand:** Regardless of whether we are talking about juniors or seniors, good software needs to be understood by every developer in your team.
- **It helps us find bugs:** While you are refactoring, you are reviewing code. During this process, you will find business rules that may not have been well programmed, so you will probably find bugs. However, do not forget that the basis of refactoring is keeping the behavior, so be sure that it is the correct moment for fixing issues.
- **It makes our program quicker:** The result of refactoring will be code that will enable faster development in the future.

When refactoring, we can guarantee good results and minimize the errors that occur during the journey by following these steps:

- **Be sure you have a set of tests to guarantee the correct processing:** This set of tests will eliminate the fear of breaking the code.
- **Eliminate duplication:** Refactoring is a good opportunity to eliminate code duplication.
- **Minimize complexity:** Given that one goal is to make the code more understandable, following the best practices of programming, as mentioned in *Chapter 4, Best Practices in Coding C# 12*, will help you reduce the complexity of the code.
- **Clean up the design:** Refactoring is a good time to reorganize the design of your libraries, too. Do not forget to update them as well. This can be a great way to eliminate bugs and security issues.

As a software architect, you will receive many refactoring demands from your team. The incentive for refactoring must be continuous, but you must remind your team that refactoring without following the preceding steps might be risky once it may cause bugs during the process. So, it is your responsibility to ensure that refactoring happens in a way that both enables fast programming and reduces the impact of unnecessary bugs caused by the refactoring process, thus delivering real business value.

I have my libraries. How do I promote them?

Once you have made all the necessary effort to guarantee you have good libraries that can be reused in many of your projects, you will find another difficult situation arises when enabling reusability: it is not so easy to let programmers know you have libraries ready to reuse.

There are some simple approaches to documenting a library. As we mentioned when we talked about the development life cycle, documenting is a good way to help developers take notice of the libraries they have. There are two examples of documenting reusable code that we would like to mention in the following subsections.

Documenting .NET libraries using DocFX

DocFX is a good option for documenting a library using comments made in its code. By simply adding the `docfx.console` NuGet package, the tool allows you to create a task that will run once your library has been built:

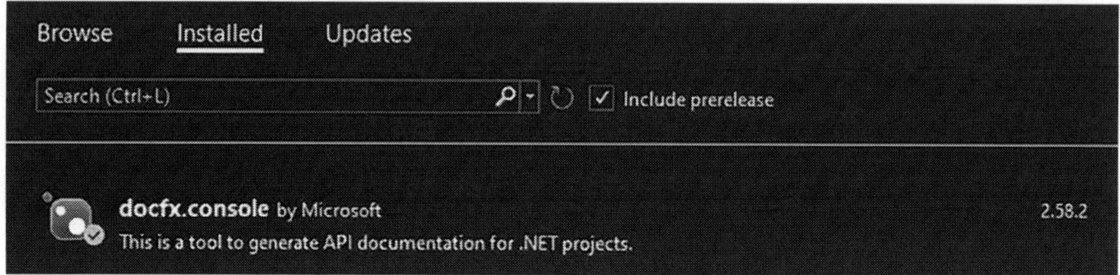

Figure 5.5: docfx.console NuGet library

The output of this compilation is a stylish static website that contains the documentation of your code:

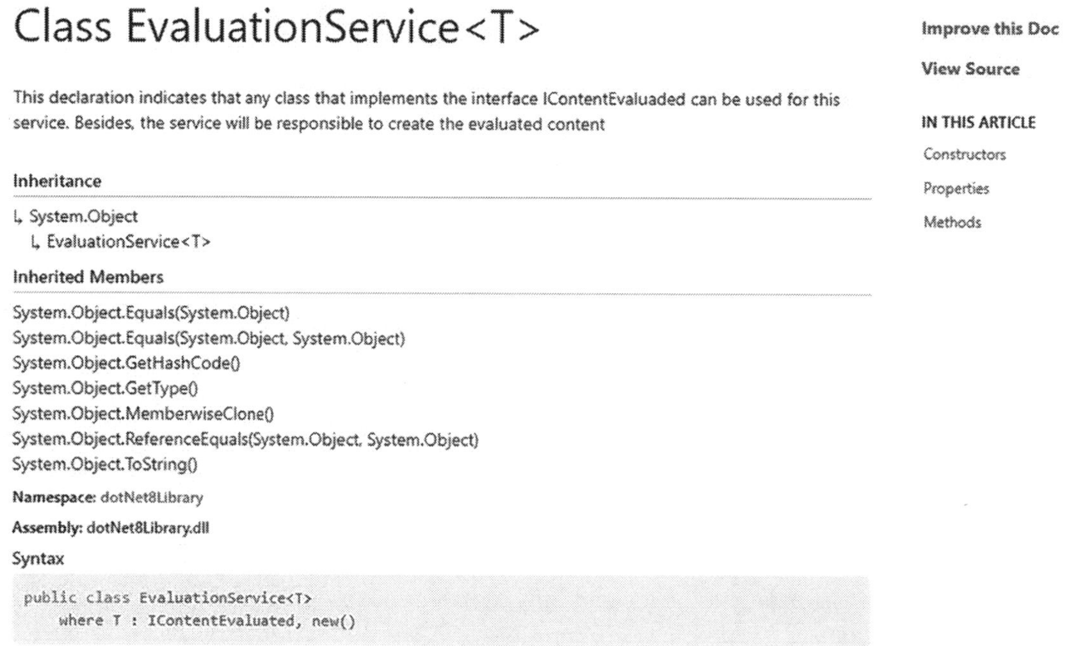

Figure 5.6: DocFx result

This website is useful because you can distribute the documentation to your team so that they can search for the libraries you have. You can check the customizations of the output and find more information about it at `https://dotnet.github.io/docfx/`.

Documenting a web API using Swagger

There is no doubt that a web API is one of the technologies that facilitates and promotes code reuse. For this reason, ensuring good documentation and, more than that, respecting a standard is good practice and indicates that you are up to date with the approach to delivering reusable APIs. To do this, we have **Swagger**, which respects the **OpenAPI Specification**.

The OpenAPI Specification is known as the standard for describing modern APIs. One of the most widely used tools for documenting APIs in an **ASP.NET Core Web API** is `Swashbuckle.AspNetCore`.

The good thing about using the `Swashbuckle.AspNetCore` library is where you can set the **Swagger UI** viewer for your web API, which is a good, graphical way to distribute the APIs.

We will learn how to use this library in ASP.NET Core web APIs in *Chapter 15, Applying Service-Oriented Architectures with .NET*. Until then, it is important to understand that this documentation will help not only your team but any developer who might use the APIs you are developing.

Summary

This chapter aimed to help you understand the advantages of code reuse. It also gave you an idea about what code is not appropriate for reuse. This chapter also presented approaches for reusing and refactoring code.

Considering that technology without processes does not take you anywhere, a process was presented that helps enable code reuse. This process is related to using already completed components from your library, identifying features in the software requirements specification that are candidates to be designed as library components, modifying the specification considering these features, designing the reusable components, and building the project architecture with the new component library version.

Concluding this chapter, we presented .NET Standard libraries as an approach to reusing code for different C# platforms, indicating that .NET 8 and new versions allow the reuse of code across different platforms. This chapter also reinforced the principles of object-oriented programming when reusing code and presented generics as a sophisticated implementation to simplify the treatment of objects with the same characteristics.

Questions

1. Can copy-and-paste be considered code reuse? What are the impacts of this approach?
2. How can you reuse code without copying and pasting it?
3. Is there a process that can help with code reuse?
4. What is the difference between .NET Standard and .NET Core?
5. What are the advantages of creating a .NET Standard library?
6. How does object-oriented analysis help with code reuse?
7. How do generics help with code reuse?
8. Will .NET Standard be replaced by .NET 6?
9. What are the challenges related to refactoring?

Further reading

The following are some books and websites where you will find more information about the topics covered in this chapter:

- *Clean Code: A Handbook of Agile Software Craftmanship* by Martin, Robert C. Pearson Education, 2012.
- *Clean Architecture: A Craftsman's Guide to Software Structure and Design* by Martin, Robert C. Pearson Education, 2018.
- *Design Patterns: Elements of Reusable Object-Oriented Software* by Eric Gamma [et al.] Addison-Wesley, 1994.
- *Design Principles and Design Patterns* by Robert C. Martin, 2000.
- *Refactoring* by Martin Fowler, 2018.
- If you need more information about .NET Standard:
    - `https://devblogs.microsoft.com/dotnet/introducing-net-standard/`
    - `https://www.packtpub.com/application-development/net-standard-20-cookbook`
    - `https://devblogs.microsoft.com/dotnet/the-future-of-net-standard/`
    - `https://devblogs.microsoft.com/dotnet/the-future-of-net-standard/`
- A great guide for programming using the generics concept: `https://docs.microsoft.com/pt-br/dotnet/csharp/programming-guide/generics/`
- Some links that may help you with the documentation of libraries and APIs:
    - `https://dotnet.github.io/docfx/`
    - `https://github.com/domaindrivendev/Swashbuckle.AspNetCore`
    - `https://docs.microsoft.com/en-us/aspnet/core/tutorials/web-api-help-pages-using-swagger`

Learn more on Discord

To join the Discord community for this book – where you can share feedback, ask questions to the authors, and learn about new releases – follow the QR code below:

`https://packt.link/SoftwareArchitectureCSharp12Dotnet8`

6

Design Patterns and .NET 8 Implementation

Design patterns can be defined as ready-to-use architectural solutions for common problems you encounter during software development. They are essential for understanding the .NET architecture and useful for solving ordinary problems that we face when designing any piece of software. In this chapter, we will look at the implementation of some design patterns. It is worth mentioning that this book does not explain all the known patterns we can use. The focus here is to explain the importance of studying and applying them.

In this chapter, we will cover the following topics:

- Understanding design patterns and their purpose
- Understanding the design patterns available in .NET

By the end of this chapter, you will have learned about some of the use cases that you can implement with design patterns.

Technical requirements

To complete this chapter, you will need the free Visual Studio 2022 Community Edition or better.

You can find the sample code for this chapter at `https://github.com/PacktPublishing/Software-Architecture-with-C-Sharp-12-and-.NET-8-4E/tree/main/ch06`.

Understanding design patterns and their purpose

Deciding on the design of a system is challenging, and the responsibility associated with this task is enormous. As software architects, we must always keep in mind that features such as great reusability, good performance, and good maintainability are important for delivering a good solution. This is where design patterns help and accelerate the design process.

As we mentioned previously, design patterns are solutions that have already been discussed and defined so that they can solve common software architectural problems. This approach grew in popularity after the release of the book *Design Patterns – Elements of Reusable Object-Oriented Software*, where the **Gang of Four** (**GoF**) divided these patterns into three types: creational, structural, and behavioral.

A little bit later, Uncle Bob introduced the SOLID principles to the developer community, giving us the opportunity to efficaciously organize the functions and data structures of each system. The SOLID design principles indicate how the components of software should be designed and connected. It is worth mentioning that, compared to the design patterns presented by GoF, the SOLID principles do not deliver code recipes. Instead, they give you the basic principles to follow when you design your solutions, keeping the software's structure strong and reliable. They can be defined as follows:

- **Single Responsibility**: A module or function should be responsible for a single purpose.
- **Open-Closed**: A software artifact should be open for extension but closed for modification.
- **Liskov Substitution**: The behavior of a program needs to remain unchanged when you substitute one of its components for another component that has been defined by a supertype of the primer object.
- **Interface Segregation**: Depending on the way you create interfaces, you will promote dependencies that do not necessarily occur when you build their concrete objects, causing harm to the system architecture.
- **Dependency Inversion**: The most flexible systems are the ones where object dependencies only refer to abstractions.

As technologies and software problems change, more patterns are conceived. The advance of cloud computing has brought a bunch of them, and some can be found at `https://docs.microsoft.com/en-us/azure/architecture/patterns`. The content is organized into three different challenge areas: Data Management, Design and Implementation, and Messaging. Many of them are described in the chapters of this book, as we can see in the list below:

- **Asynchronous Request-Reply**: This pattern is presented while discussing Azure Durable Functions in *Chapter 16, Working with Serverless - Azure Functions*; the orchestrator function for **async HTTP APIs** solves this pattern.
- **Bulkhead Isolation**: This pattern is presented while discussing microservices design principles in *Chapter 11, Applying a Microservice Architecture to Your Enterprise Application*.
- **Cache-Aside**: Caching was presented in *Chapter 1, Understanding the Importance of Software Architecture*. Its usage with Azure Redis is also presented in *Chapter 12, Choosing Your Data Storage in the Cloud*.

- **Circuit-Breaker:** The strategy necessary to implement this is presented in *Chapter 11, Applying a Microservice Architecture to Your Enterprise Application.*
- **Command Query Responsibility Segregation (CQRS):** CQRS is described in *Chapter 7, Understanding the Different Domains in Software Solutions.*
- **Publisher/Subscriber:** This pattern will be explained in the subsections below and discussed in *Chapter 7, Understanding the Different Domains in Software Solutions.*
- **Retry:** The *resilient task execution* subsection of *Chapter 11, Applying a Microservice Architecture to Your Enterprise Application*, shows how to use Polly, a general framework for applying retries.
- **Queue-Based Load Leveling:** The scenario presented in *Chapter 16, Working with Serverless – Azure Functions*, uses a queue that acts as a buffer between a task and a service.

The reason why new patterns emerge is related to the challenges we face when new solutions are developed. Today, availability, data management, messaging, monitoring, performance, scalability, resiliency, and security are aspects we must deal with when delivering cloud solutions.

The reason why you should always consider using design patterns in development is quite simple—as a software architect, you cannot spend time reinventing the wheel. However, there is another great reason for using and understanding them—you will find many of these patterns already implemented in .NET.

In the next few subsections, we will cover some of the most well-known patterns. The idea of this chapter is just to let you know that they exist and need to be studied so that you can accelerate and simplify your projects. Moreover, each pattern will be presented with a C# code snippet so that you can implement it in your projects while always remembering that we are talking about samples, not code ready for production.

Builder pattern

There are cases where you will have a complex object with different behaviors due to its configuration. Instead of setting this object up while using it, you may want to decouple its configuration from its usage, using a customized configuration that is already built. This way, you have different representations of the instances you are building. This is where you should use the Builder pattern.

The following class diagram shows the pattern that has been implemented for a scenario from this book's use case, presented in *Chapter 21, Case Study*. The idea behind this design choice is to simplify the way rooms from WWTravelClub are described.

The Fluent API implemented in the `Room` class enables us to have the construction of each kind of room defined in each builder (`SimpleRoomBuilder` and `FamilyRoomBuilder`) more simply.

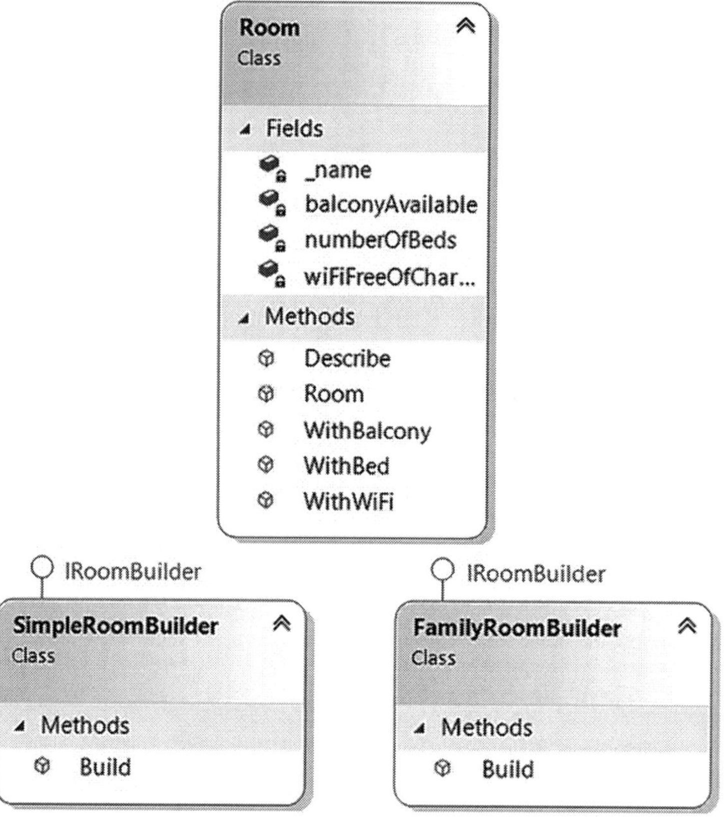

Figure 6.1: Builder pattern

As shown in the following snippet, the code for this is implemented in a way where the configurations of the instances are not set in the main program. Instead, you just build the objects using the `Build()` method. This example simulates the creation of different room styles (a single room and a family room) in WWTravelClub:

```
using DesignPatternsSample.BuilderSample;
using System;
namespace DesignPatternsSample
{
    class Program
    {
        static void Main()
        {
          #region Builder Sample
          Console.WriteLine("Builder Sample");
```

```
            var simpleRoom = new SimpleRoomBuilder().Build();
            simpleRoom.Describe();

            var familyRoom = new FamilyRoomBuilder().Build();
            familyRoom.Describe();
            #endregion
            Console.ReadKey();
        }
    }
}
```

The result of this implementation is quite simple but clarifies the reason why you need to implement a pattern:

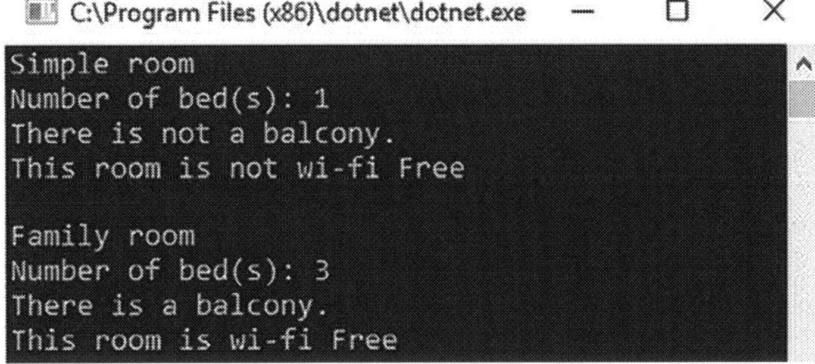

Figure 6.2: Builder pattern sample result

As soon as you have the implementation, evolving this code becomes simpler. For example, if you need to build a different style of room, you can just create a new builder for that type of room, and you will be able to use it.

The reason why this implementation becomes quite simple is related to the usage of chaining methods, as we can see in the `Room` class:

```
    public class Room
    {
        private readonly string _name;
        private bool wiFiFreeOfCharge;
        private int numberOfBeds;
        private bool balconyAvailable;
        public Room(string name)
        {
            _name = name;
        }
        public Room WithBalcony()
        {
```

```
            balconyAvailable = true;
            return this;
        }
        public Room WithBed(int numberOfBeds)
        {
            this.numberOfBeds = numberOfBeds;
            return this;
        }
        public Room WithWiFi()
        {
            wiFiFreeOfCharge = true;
            return this;
        }
    ...
    }
```

Fortunately, if you need to add the configuration settings for the product, all the concrete classes you used previously will be defined in the Builder interface and stored there so that you can update them with ease.

We will see a great implementation of the Builder pattern in .NET in the *Understanding the design patterns available in .NET* section. There, you will be able to understand how Generic Host was implemented using `HostBuilder`.

Factory pattern

The Factory pattern is useful in situations where you have multiple objects from the same abstraction, and you only know which one needs to be created at runtime. This means you will have to create the instance according to a certain configuration or according to where the software lives now.

For instance, let us check out the WWTravelClub sample. Here, there is a user story that describes that this application will have customers from all over the world paying for their trips. However, in the real world, there are different payment services available for each country. The process of paying is similar for each country, but this system will have more than one payment service available. A good way to simplify this payment implementation is by using the Factory pattern.

The following diagram shows the basic idea of its architectural implementation:

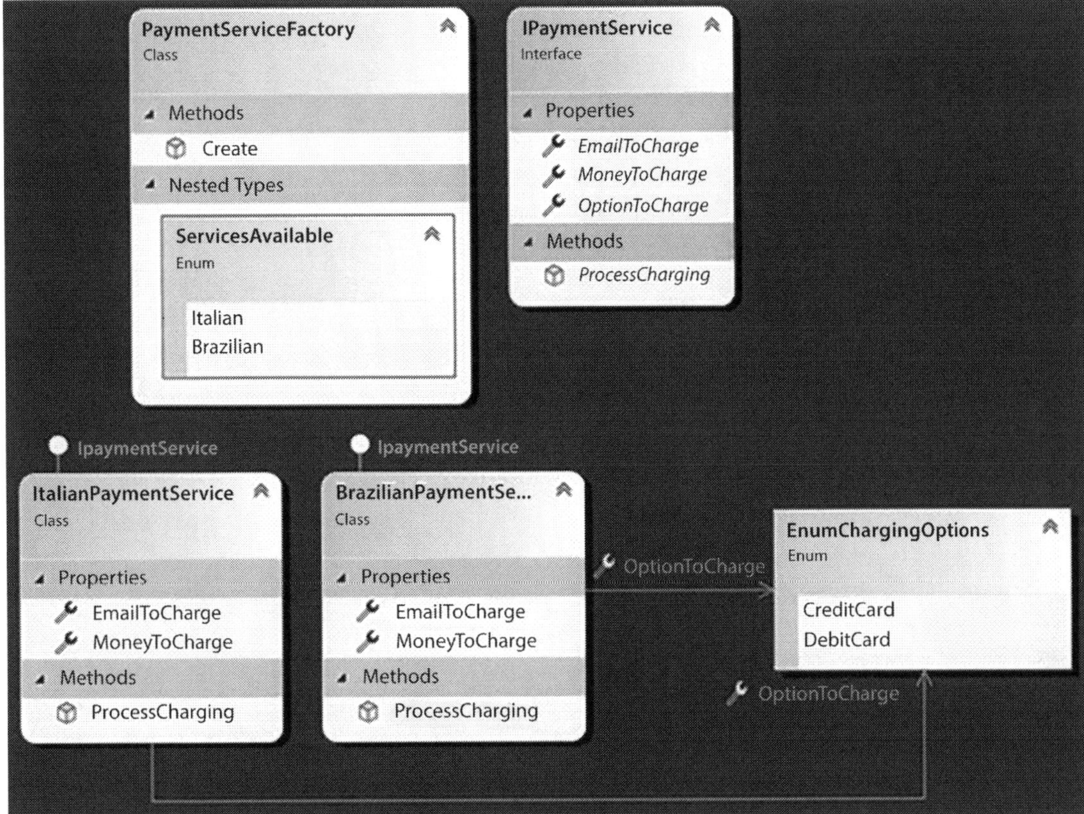

Figure 6.3: Factory pattern

Notice that since you have an interface that describes what the payment service for the application is, you can use the Factory pattern to change the concrete class according to the services that are available:

```
static void Main()
{
    #region Factory Sample
      // In this sample, we will use the Factory Method Pattern
      // to create a Payment Service to charge a Brazilian
      // customer
    ProcessCharging(
    PaymentServiceFactory.ServicesAvailable.Brazilian,
```

```
        "gabriel@sample.com",
         178.90m,
         EnumChargingOptions.CreditCard);
        // In this sample, we will use the Factory Method Pattern
        // to create a Payment Service to charge an Italian
        // customer
         ProcessCharging(
         PaymentServiceFactory.ServicesAvailable.Italian,
        "francesco@sample.com",
         188.70m,
         EnumChargingOptions.DebitCard);
        #endregion

        Console.ReadKey();
    }

    private static void ProcessCharging
        (PaymentServiceFactory.ServicesAvailable serviceToCharge,
        string emailToCharge, decimal moneyToCharge,
        EnumChargingOptions optionToCharge)
    {
        PaymentServiceFactory factory = new PaymentServiceFactory();
        IPaymentService service = factory.Create(serviceToCharge);
        service.EmailToCharge = emailToCharge;
        service.MoneyToCharge = moneyToCharge;
        service.OptionToCharge = optionToCharge;
        service.ProcessCharging();
    }
```

Once again, the service's usage has been simplified due to the implemented pattern. If you had to use this code in a real-world application, you would change the instance's behavior by defining the service you needed in the Factory pattern.

Singleton pattern

When you implement Singleton in your application, you will have a single instance of the object implemented in the entire solution. This is one of the most used patterns in every application. The reason is simple—there are many use cases where you need some classes to have just one instance. Singletons solve this by providing a better solution than a global variable does.

In the Singleton pattern, the class is responsible for creating and delivering a single object that will be used by the application. In other words, the Singleton class creates a single instance:

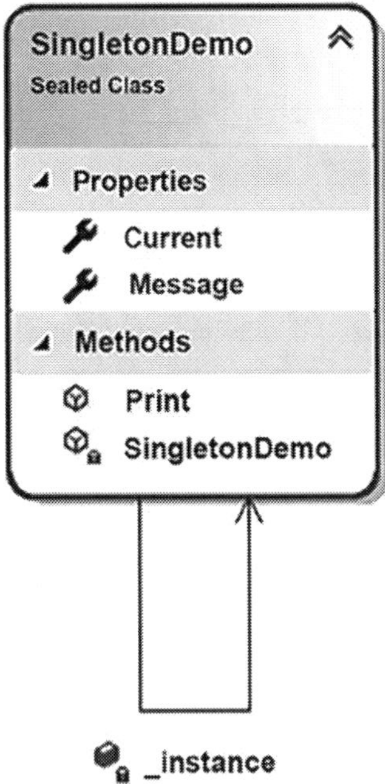

Figure 6.4: Singleton pattern

To do so, the object that is created is `static` and delivered in a static property or method. The `??=` operator assigns the value of its right operand to its left one if its value is null.

The following code implements the Singleton pattern, which has a `Message` property and a `Print()` method:

```
public sealed class SingletonDemo
{
    #region This is the Singleton definition
    private static SingletonDemo _instance;
    public static SingletonDemo Current => _instance ??= new
        SingletonDemo();
    #endregion
    public string Message { get; set; }
    public void Print()
    {
        Console.WriteLine(Message);
    }
}
```

Its usage is simple–you just need to call the static property every time you need to use the Singleton object:

```
SingletonDemo.Current.Message = "This text will be printed by " +
  "the singleton. Be careful with concurrency.";
SingletonDemo.Current.Print();
```

Be careful because the sample can have concurrency issues according to the usage defined! Please refer to *Chapter 2, Non-Functional Requirements,* to read a bit more about concurrency and multithreading.

One of the situations where you can use this pattern is when you need to deliver the app configuration in a way that can be easily accessed from anywhere in the solution. For instance, let us say you have some configuration parameters that are stored in a table, which your app needs to query at several decision points. Although we have standard solutions like `appsettings.json` or `web.config`, where caching is out of the box, you may want to use this custom solution. In this case, instead of querying the configuration table directly, you can create a Singleton class to help you:

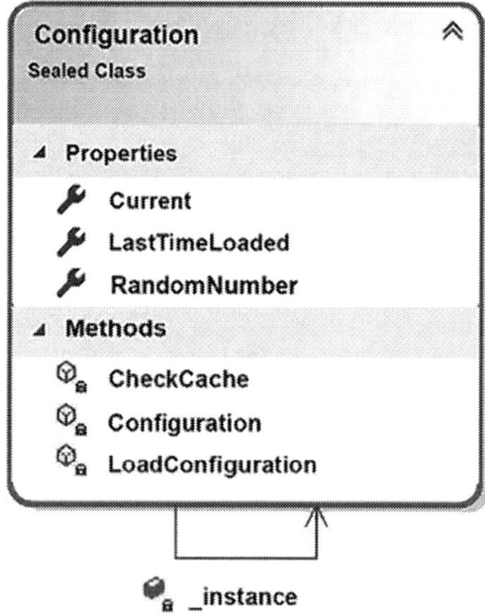

Figure 6.5: Singleton pattern usage

Moreover, you will need to implement a cache in this Singleton, thus improving the performance of the system since you will be able to decide whether the system will check each configuration in the database every time it needs it or if the cache will be used. The following screenshot shows the implementation of the cache, where the configuration is loaded every 5 seconds. The parameter that is read in this case is just a random number:

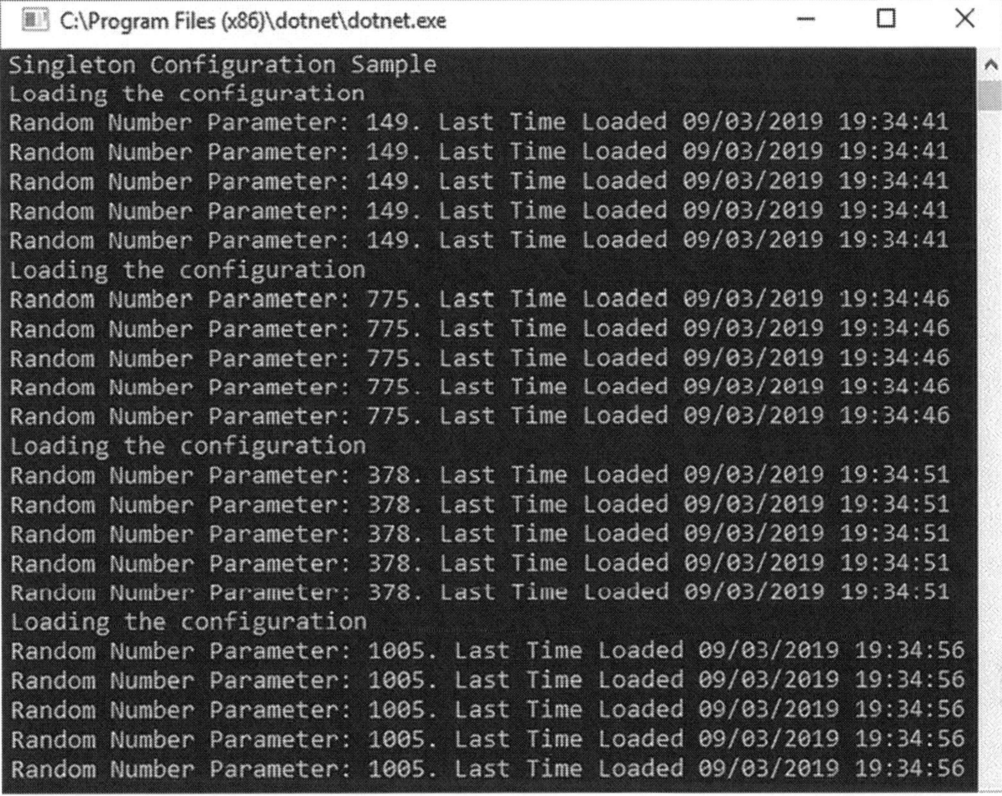

Figure 6.6: Cache implementation inside the Singleton pattern

This is great for the application's performance. Besides, using parameters in several places in your code is simpler since you do not have to create configuration instances everywhere in the code.

It is worth mentioning that due to the dependency injection implementation in .NET, Singleton pattern usage has become less common since you can set dependency injection to handle your Singleton objects. We will cover dependency injection in .NET in later sections of this chapter.

Proxy pattern

The Proxy pattern is used when you need to provide an object that controls access to another object. One of the biggest reasons why you should do this is related to the cost of creating the object that is being controlled. For instance, if the controlled object takes too long to be created or consumes too much memory, a proxy can be used to guarantee that the largest part of the object will only be created when it is required.

The following class diagram is of a **Proxy** pattern implementation for loading pictures from **Room** (see *Figure 6.1*), but only when requested:

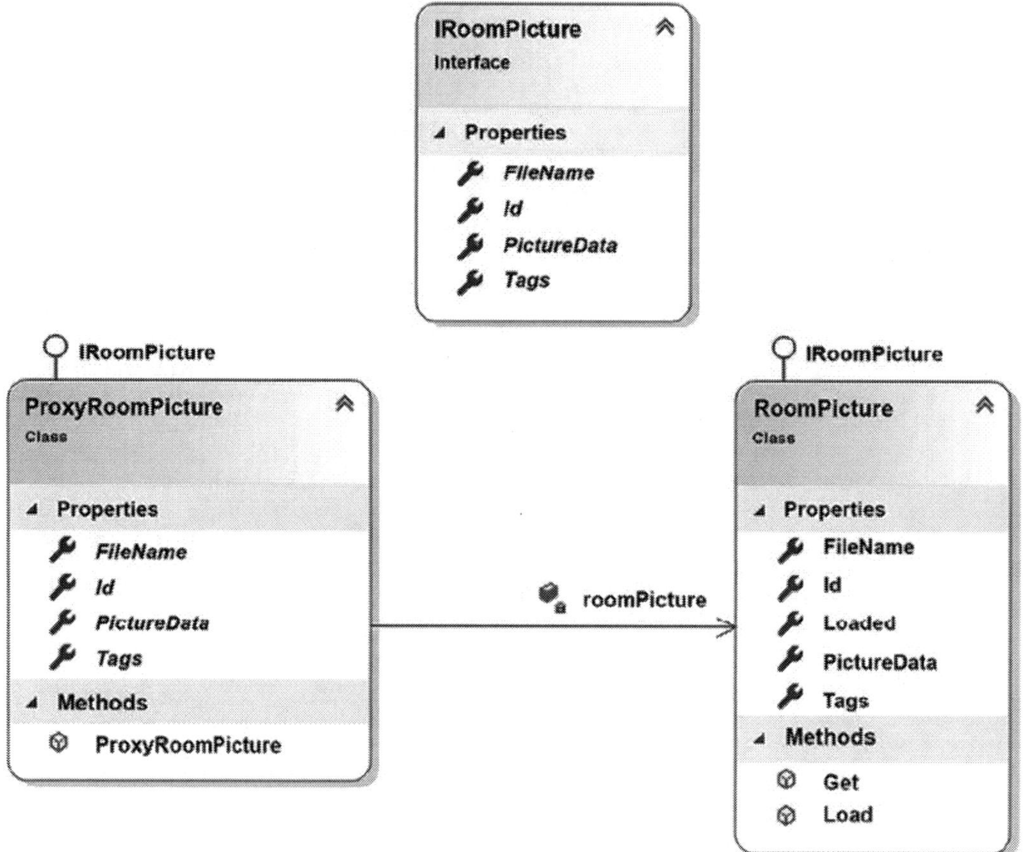

Figure 6.7: Proxy pattern implementation

The client of this proxy will request its creation. Here, the proxy will only gather basic information (`Id`, `FileName`, and `Tags`) from the real object and will not query `PictureData`.

Only when `PictureData` is requested in the first call will the proxy load it, as we can confirm with the message Now the picture is loaded!. After that, in the second picture data request, the proxy will not load the `PictureData` again, which causes a better performance, as we can see in *Figure 6.8*:

```
static void Main()
{
    Console.WriteLine("Proxy Sample");
    ExecuteProxySample(new ProxyRoomPicture());
}
private static void ExecuteProxySample(IRoomPicture roomPicture)
{
    Console.WriteLine($"Picture Id: {roomPicture.Id}");
```

```
        Console.WriteLine($"Picture FileName: {roomPicture.FileName}");
        Console.WriteLine($"Tags: {string.Join(";", roomPicture.Tags)}");
        Console.WriteLine($"1st call: Picture Data");
        Console.WriteLine($"Image: {roomPicture.PictureData}");
        Console.WriteLine($"2nd call: Picture Data");
        Console.WriteLine($"Image: {roomPicture.PictureData}");
    }
```

If `PictureData` is requested again, since the image data is already in place, the proxy will guarantee that image reloading will not be repeated. The following screenshot shows the result of running the preceding code:

```
C:\Program Files (x86)\dotnet\dotnet.exe
Proxy Sample
Picture Id: a60ebbef-f734-43c3-a962-a24e34ebd9e1
Picture FileName: picture.jpg
Tags: incredible picture;must seeing!
1st call: Picture Data
Now the picture is loaded!
Image: [DATA FROM PICTURE]
2nd call: Picture Data
Image: [DATA FROM PICTURE]
```

Figure 6.8: Proxy pattern result

This technique can be referred to by another name: **lazy loading**. In fact, the Proxy pattern is a way of implementing lazy loading. Another approach for implementing lazy loading is the usage of the `Lazy<T>` type. For instance, in Entity Framework Core, as discussed in *Chapter 13, Interacting with Data in C# – Entity Framework Core*, you can turn on lazy loading using proxies. You can find out more about this at `https://docs.microsoft.com/en-us/ef/core/querying/related-data#lazy-loading`.

Command pattern

There are many cases where you need to execute a **command** that will affect the behavior of an object. The Command pattern can help you with this by encapsulating this kind of request in an object. The pattern also describes how to handle undo/redo support for a request.

There is another design pattern called Memento that also has the purpose of implementing undo actions. However, the Command pattern focuses on encapsulating requests as objects, whereas Memento focuses on capturing and externalizing an object's internal state for the purpose of restoring it later.

For instance, let us imagine that, on the WWTravelClub website, users can evaluate packages by specifying whether they liked, disliked, or even loved their experience.

The following class diagram is an example of what can be implemented to create this rating system with the Command pattern:

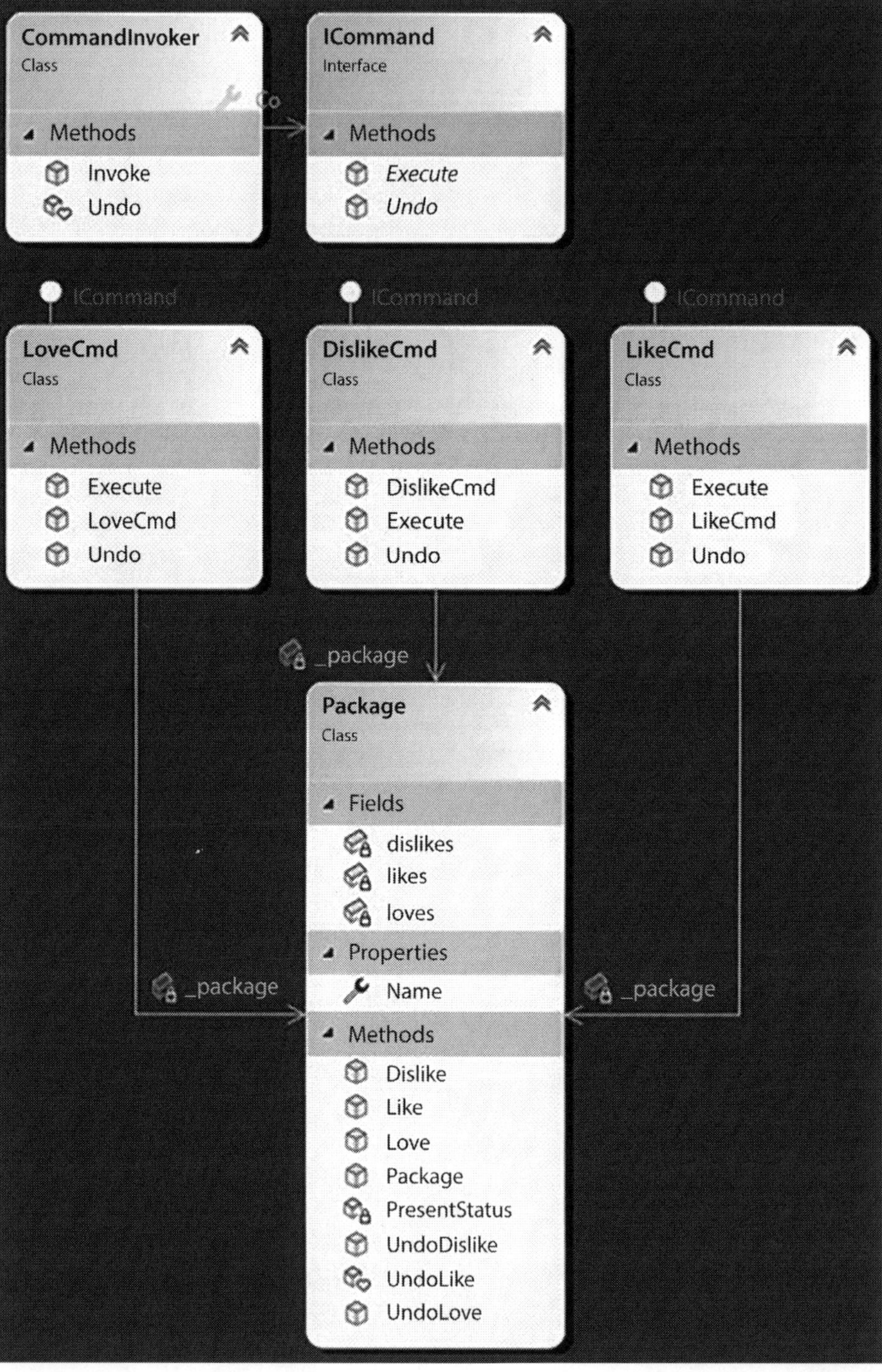

Figure 6.9: Command pattern

Notice the way this pattern works – if you need a different command, such as `Hate`, you will only implement a new class based on the `ICommand` interface. You do not need to change the code from other action classes. The change in the `Package` class will not impact the commands already implemented. Besides that, if you want to implement the `Redo` method, it can be added in a similar way to the `Undo` method. The full code sample for this is available in this book's GitHub repository.

It might also help to mention that ASP.NET Core MVC uses the Command pattern for its `IActionResult` hierarchy. The business operation described in *Chapter 7, Understanding the Different Domains in Software Solutions*, will make use of this pattern to execute business rules.

Publisher/Subscriber pattern

Providing information from an object to a group of other objects is common in all applications. The Publisher/Subscriber pattern is almost mandatory when there is a large volume of components (subscribers) that will receive a message containing the information that was sent by the object (publisher).

The concept here is quite simple to understand and is shown in the following diagram:

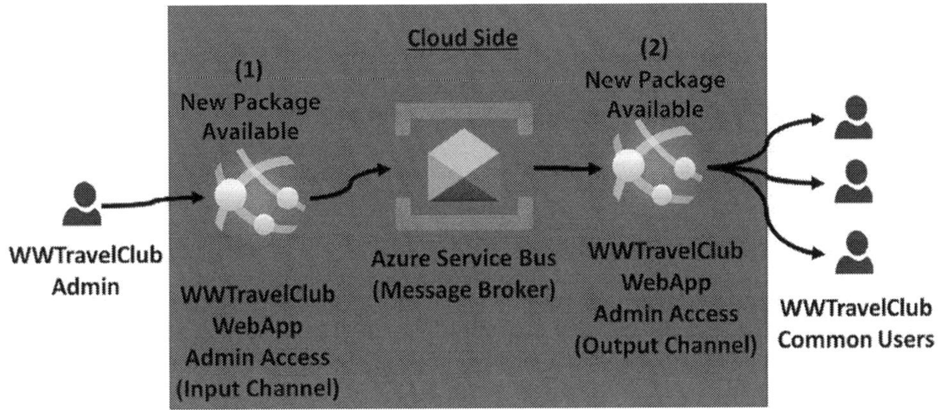

Figure 6.10: Publisher/Subscriber sample case

When you have an indefinite number of different possible subscribers, it is essential to decouple the component that broadcasts information from the components that consume it. The Publisher/Subscriber pattern does this for us.

Implementing this pattern is complex since distributing environments is not a trivial task. Therefore, it is recommended that you consider pre-existing technologies for implementing the message broker that connects the input channel to the output channels instead of building it from scratch. Azure Service Bus is a reliable infrastructure component where you can find this pattern provided, so all you need to do is connect to it.

RabbitMQ, which we mention in *Chapter 11, Applying a Microservice Architecture to Your Enterprise Application*, and in *Chapter 14, Implementing Microservices with .NET*, is another service that can be used to implement a message broker, but it is a lower-level infrastructure and requires several manual implementations, such as retries in errors.

Dependency Injection pattern

The Dependency Injection pattern is considered a good way to implement the Dependency Inversion principle, guiding you to implement this SOLID principle.

The concept is quite simple. Instead of creating instances of the objects that the component depends on, you just need to define their dependencies, declare their interfaces, and enable the reception of the objects by **injection**.

There are three ways to perform dependency injection:

- Use the constructor of the class to receive the objects
- Tag some class properties to receive the objects
- Define an interface with a method to inject all the necessary components

The following diagram shows the implementation of the Dependency Injection pattern using the constructor of the class to receive the objects. In this case, it receives `UserAddress` and `DestinationAddress` classes, which can be completely different, but both of them implement the `IAddress` interface, which enables the **DistanceCalculator** to work:

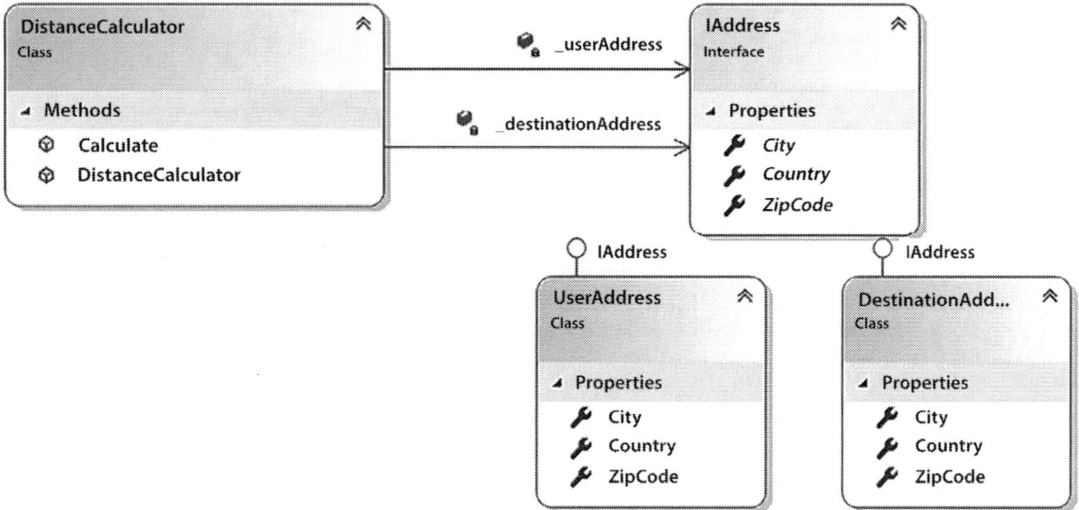

Figure 6.11: Dependency Injection pattern

Apart from these three ways mentioned above, Dependency Injection can be used with an **Inversion of Control** (**IoC**) container. This container enables the automatic injection of dependencies whenever they are asked for. There are several IoC container frameworks available on the market, but with .NET 8, for most cases, there is no need to use third-party software since it contains a set of libraries to solve this in the `Microsoft.Extensions.DependencyInjection` namespace.

This IoC container is responsible for creating and disposing of the objects that are requested. The implementation of Dependency Injection is based on constructor types. There are three options for the injected component's lifetime:

- **Transient:** The objects are created each time they are requested.
- **Scoped:** The objects are created for each scope defined in the application. In a web app, a **scope** is identified with a web request unless you create a custom scope. A good example where custom scope can be used is in multi-tenant applications. In this case, you may want to manage dependencies per tenant.
- **Singleton:** Each object has the same application lifetime, so a single object is reused to serve all the requests for a given type. If your object contains state, you should not use this one unless it is thread-safe. Remember to refer to *Chapter 2, Non-Functional Requirements*, to learn more about multithreading.

The way you use these options depends on the business rules of the project you are developing. It is also a matter of how you register the services of the application. You need to be careful in deciding on the correct one since the behavior of the application will change according to the type of object you are injecting.

Understanding the design patterns available in .NET

As we discovered in the previous sections, C# allows us to implement any of the patterns. .NET provides many implementations in its SDK that follow all the patterns we have discussed, such as Entity Framework Core proxy lazy loading. Another good example that has been available since .NET Core 2.1 is .NET Generic Host, which does not directly implement a specific pattern but combines many of them, providing a flexible and extensible host environment for .NET applications.

In *Chapter 17, Presenting ASP.NET Core MVC*, we will detail the hosting that's available for web apps in .NET 8. This web host helps us since the startup of the app and lifetime management are set up alongside it. The idea of .NET Generic Host is to enable this way of working for applications that do not need HTTP implementation. With this Generic Host, any .NET program can have a startup class where we can configure the dependency injection engine. This can be useful for creating multi-service apps, using Composite patterns as a basis for that.

You can find out more about .NET Generic Host at `https://docs.microsoft.com/en-us/aspnet/core/fundamentals/host/generic-host`, which contains some sample code and is the current recommendation from Microsoft.

The code provided in the GitHub repository is simple, but it focuses on the creation of a console app that can run a service for monitoring. The great thing about this is the way the console app is set up to run, where the builder configures the services that will be provided by the application and the way logging will be managed.

This is shown in the following code:

```
public static void Main()
{
    CreateHostBuilder().Build().Run();
    Console.WriteLine("Host has terminated. Press any key to finish the App.");
    Console.ReadKey();
}
public static IHostBuilder CreateHostBuilder() =>
    Host.CreateDefaultBuilder()
    .ConfigureServices((hostContext, services) =>
    {
          services.AddHostedService<HostedService>();
          services.AddHostedService<MonitoringService>();
    })
    .ConfigureLogging((hostContext, configLogging) =>
    {
          configLogging.AddConsole();
    });
```

The preceding code gives us an idea of how .NET uses design patterns. Using the Builder pattern, .NET Generic Host allows you to set the classes that will be injected as services. In addition to this, the Builder pattern helps you configure some other features, such as the way logs will be shown/stored. This configuration allows the services to inject `ILogger<outTCategoryName>` objects into any instance.

Other examples of Generic Host usage are worker services, described in *Chapter 14, Implementing Microservices with .NET*, and Blazor's Generic Host, described in *Chapter 19, Client Frameworks: Blazor*.

Summary

In this chapter, we understood why design patterns help with the maintainability and reusability of the parts of the system you are building. We also looked at some typical use cases and code examples that you can consider in your projects, always remembering that they need to evolve to achieve professional delivery. Finally, we presented .NET Generic Host, which is a good example of how .NET uses design patterns to enable code reusability and enforce best practices.

All this content will help you while architecting new software or even maintaining something existing since design patterns are already-known solutions for some real-life problems in software development.

In *Chapter 7, Understanding the Different Domains in Software Solutions*, we will cover the domain-driven design approach. We will also learn how to use the SOLID design principles so that we can map different domains to our software solutions.

Questions

1. What are design patterns?
2. What is the difference between design patterns and design principles?
3. When is it a good idea to implement the Builder pattern?
4. When is it a good idea to implement the Factory pattern?
5. When is it a good idea to implement the Singleton pattern?
6. When is it a good idea to implement the Proxy pattern?
7. When is it a good idea to implement the Command pattern?
8. When is it a good idea to implement the Publisher/Subscriber pattern?
9. When is it a good idea to implement the Dependency Injection pattern?

Further reading

The following are some books and websites where you can find out more about what was covered in this chapter:

- *Clean Architecture: A Craftsman's Guide to Software Structure and Design*, Martin, Robert C., Pearson Education, 2018.
- *Design Patterns: Elements of Reusable Object-Oriented Software*, Erich Gamma, et al., Addison-Wesley, 1994.
- *Design Principles and Design Patterns*, Martin, Robert C., 2000.
- If you need to get more info about design patterns and architectural principles, please check out these links:
  - `https://www.packtpub.com/application-development/design-patterns-using-c-and-net-core-video`
  - `https://docs.microsoft.com/en-us/dotnet/standard/modern-web-apps-azure-architecture/architectural-principles`
- If you want to check specific cloud design patterns, you can find them at:
  - `https://docs.microsoft.com/en-us/azure/architecture/patterns/`
- If you want to better understand the idea of a Generic Host, follow this link:
  - `https://docs.microsoft.com/en-us/aspnet/core/fundamentals/host/generic-host`
- There is a very good explanation about Service Bus messaging at this link:
  - `https://docs.microsoft.com/en-us/azure/service-bus-messaging/service-bus-dotnet-how-to-use-topics-subscriptions`

- You can learn more about dependency injection by checking out these links:
  - https://docs.microsoft.com/en-us/aspnet/core/fundamentals/dependency-injection
  - https://www.martinfowler.com/articles/injection.html

Learn more on Discord

To join the Discord community for this book – where you can share feedback, ask questions to the authors, and learn about new releases – follow the QR code below:

https://packt.link/SoftwareArchitectureCSharp12Dotnet8

7

Understanding the Different Domains in Software Solutions

This chapter is dedicated to a modern software development technique called **domain-driven design** (**DDD**), which was first proposed by Eric Evans (see *Domain-Driven Design*: `https://www.amazon.com/exec/obidos/ASIN/0321125215/domainlanguag-20`). While DDD has existed for more than 15 years, it has achieved great success in the last few years because of its ability to cope with two important problems.

The main problem is modeling complex systems that involve several domains of knowledge. No single expert has in-depth knowledge of the whole domain; this knowledge is instead split among several people. The second problem is that each expert speaks a language that is specific to his domain of expertise, so for effective communication between the experts and the development team, objects, interfaces, and methods must mimic the language of the domain experts. This means that the different modules that compose an application must use a different vocabulary for each domain of expertise. Consequently, the application must be split into modules that reflect the different domains of knowledge, and the interface between modules that deal with the different domains of knowledge must be carefully designed to carry out the necessary translations.

DDD copes with this problem by splitting the whole CI/CD cycle into independent parts, assigned to different teams. This way, each team can focus on a specific domain of knowledge by interacting only with the experts in that domain.

That's why the evolution of DDD is interleaved with the evolution of microservices and DevOps. Thanks to DDD, big projects can be split among several development teams, with each team having a different domain of knowledge. There are many reasons why a project is split among several teams, with the most common being the team's size and all of its members having different skills and/or being in different locations. In fact, experience has proven that teams of more than 6–8 people are not effective, and, clearly, different skills and locations prevent tight interaction from occurring.

In turn, the importance of the two aforementioned problems has grown in the last few years. Software systems have always taken up a lot of space inside every organization, and they have become more and more complex and geographically distributed.

At the same time, the need for frequent updates has increased so that these complex software systems can be adapted to the needs of a quickly changing market.

As a result of the increasing complexity and need for frequent updates in software systems, we now face a scenario where it's common to implement complex software systems with associated fast CI/CD cycles that always require more people to evolve and maintain them. In turn, this created a need for technologies that were adequate for high-complexity domains and for the cooperation of several loosely coupled development teams.

In this chapter, we will analyze the basic principles, advantages, and common patterns related to DDD, as well as how to use them in our solutions.

More specifically, we will cover the following topics:

- What are software domains?
- Understanding DDD
- Common DDD patterns and architectures

Let's get started.

As you progress through the second part of the book, you might find it enriching to revisit this particular chapter. Reflecting on these concepts with a deeper understanding can offer new insights and enhance your overall experience. Feel free to come back to this chapter as a resource whenever you encounter related ideas later on.

Technical requirements

This chapter requires the free Visual Studio 2022 Community Edition or better, with all the database tools installed.

All the code snippets in this chapter can be found in the GitHub repository associated with this book: `https://github.com/PacktPublishing/Software-Architecture-with-C-Sharp-12-and-.NET-8-4E`.

What are software domains?

As we discussed in *Chapter 2, Non-Functional Requirements*, and *Chapter 3, Managing Requirements*, the transfer of knowledge from domain experts to the development team plays a fundamental role in software design. Developers try to communicate with experts and describe their solutions in a language that domain experts and stakeholders can also understand. However, often, the same word has a different meaning in various parts of an organization, and what appears to be the same conceptual entities have completely different shapes in different contexts.

For instance, in our WWTravelClub use case, the order-payment and package-handling subsystems use completely different models for customers. The order-payment subsystem characterizes a customer by their payment methods, currency, bank accounts, and credit cards, while package-handling is more concerned with the locations that have been visited and/or the packages that have been purchased, the user's preferences, and their geographical location. Moreover, while order-payment refers to various concepts with a language that we may roughly define as a **bank language**, package-handling uses a language that is typical of travel agencies/operators.

The classic way to cope with these discrepancies is to use a unique abstract entity called **customer**, which projects into two different views—the order-payment view and the package-handling view. Each projection operation takes some operations and some properties from the **customer** abstract entity and changes their names. Since domain experts only give us the projected views, our main task as system designers is to create a conceptual model that can explain all the views. The following diagram shows how different views are handled:

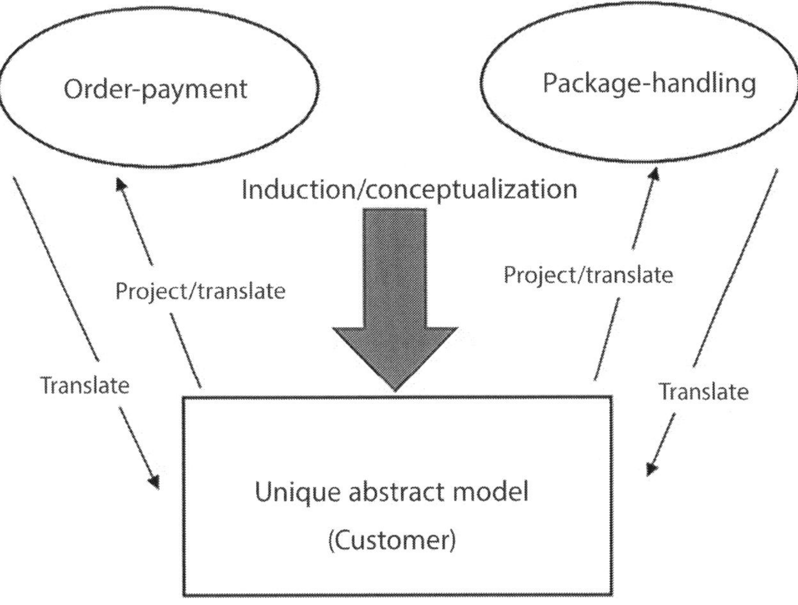

Figure 7.1: Creating a unique model

The main advantage of the classic approach is that we have a unique and coherent representation of the data of the domain. If this conceptual model is built successfully, all the operations will have a formal definition and purpose and the whole abstraction will be a rationalization of the way the whole organization should work, possibly highlighting and correcting errors and simplifying some procedures.

However, what are the downsides of this approach?

The sharp adoption of a new monolithic data model may cause an acceptable impact in a small organization when the software is destined for a small part of the overall organization, or when the software automates a small enough percentage of the data flow. However, if the software becomes the backbone of a complex, geographically distributed organization, sharp changes become unacceptable and unfeasible. On the one hand, big structured companies need to react quickly to market changes, but on the other hand, due to the complexity of their organizations, only gradual changes are feasible. Therefore, the changes in their organizations and information systems that are needed to adapt to the market must be gradual. In turn, a gradual transition is possible only if old data models can coexist with new data models, and if each of the various components of the organization is allowed to change at its own speed—that is, if each component of the organization can evolve independently of the others.

Moreover, as the complexity of a software system grows, several other issues make the unique data model of classical architectures hard to maintain:

- **Coherency issues**: Arriving at a uniquely coherent view of data becomes more difficult since we can't retain the complexity when we break these tasks into smaller, loosely coupled tasks.
- **Difficulties updating**: As complexity grows, there is a need for frequent system changes, but it is quite difficult to update and maintain a unique global model. Moreover, bugs/errors that are introduced by changes in small subparts of the system may propagate to the whole organization through the uniquely shared model.
- **Team organization issues**: System modeling must be split among several teams, and only loosely coupled tasks can be given to separate teams; if two tasks are strongly coupled, they need to be given to the same team.
- **Parallelism issues**: As we will discuss in more detail in *Chapter 11, Applying a Microservice Architecture to Your Enterprise Application*, the need to move to a microservice-based architecture often makes the bottleneck of a unique database unacceptable.
- **Language issues**: As the system grows, we need to communicate with more domain experts, each speaking a different language and each with a different view of that data model. Thus, we need to translate our unique model's properties and operations to/from more languages to be able to communicate with them.

As the system grows, it becomes more inefficient to deal with records with hundreds/thousands of fields that project in smaller views. Such inefficiencies originate in database engines that inefficiently handle big records with several fields (memory fragmentation, problems with too many related indices, and so on). However, the main inefficiencies take place in **object-relational mappings** (**ORMs**) and business layers that are forced to handle these big records in their update operations. In fact, while query operations usually require just a few fields that have been retrieved from the storage engine, updates and business processing involve the whole entity. ORMs are described in detail in *Chapter 13, Interacting with Data in C# – Entity Framework Core.*

As the traffic in the data storage subsystem grows, we need read and update/write parallelism in all the data operations. As we will discover in *Chapter 12, Choosing Your Data Storage in the Cloud,* while read parallelism is easily achieved with data replication, write parallelism requires sharding; that is, splitting database records among several distributed databases, and it is difficult to shard a uniquely monolithic and tightly connected data model.

These issues are the reason for DDD's success in the last few years because they were characterized by more complex software systems that became the backbones of entire organizations. DDD's basic principles will be discussed in detail in the next section.

Understanding DDD

According to DDD, we should not construct a unique domain model that projects into different views in each application subsystem. Instead, the whole application domain is split into smaller domains, each with its own data model. These separate domains are called **Bounded Contexts**. Each Bounded Context is characterized by the language used by the experts and used to name all the domain concepts and operations.

Thus, each Bounded Context defines a common language used by both the experts and the development team called a **Ubiquitous Language**. Translations are not needed anymore, and if the development team uses C# interfaces as bases for its code, the domain expert is able to understand and validate them since all the operations and properties are expressed in the same language that's used by the expert.

Here, we're getting rid of a cumbersome unique abstract model, but now we have several separate models that we need to relate somehow. DDD proposes that we handle all these separate models (that is, all the Bounded Contexts) as follows:

- **We need to add Bounded Context boundaries whenever the meanings of the language terms change.** For instance, in the WWTravelClub use case, order-payment and package-handling belong to different Bounded Contexts because they give a different meaning to the word **customer**.
- **We need to explicitly represent relations among Bounded Contexts.** Different development teams may work on different Bounded Contexts, but each team must have a clear picture of the relationship between the Bounded Context it is working on and all the other models. For this reason, such relationships are represented in a unique document that's shared with every team.
- **We need to keep all the Bounded Contexts aligned with CI.** Meetings are organized and simplified system prototypes are built in order to verify that all the Bounded Contexts are evolving coherently—that is, that all the Bounded Contexts can be integrated into the desired application behavior.

The following diagram shows how the WWTravelClub example that we discussed in the previous section changes with the adoption of DDD:

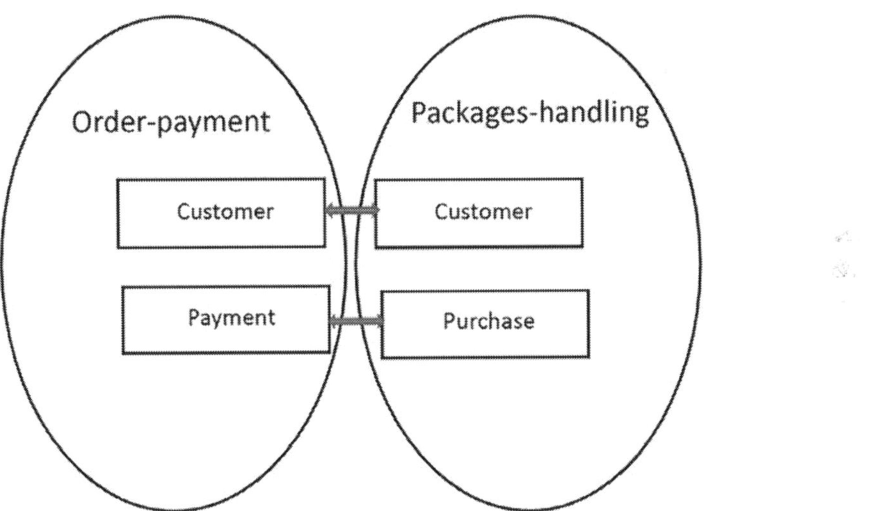

Figure 7.2: Relationships between DDD-Bounded Contexts

There is a relationship between the Customer entities of each Bounded Context, while the Purchase entity of the package-handling Bounded Context is related to the Payments. Identifying entities that map to each other in the various Bounded Contexts is the first step of formally defining the interfaces that represent all the possible communications among the contexts.

For instance, in the previous diagram, since payments are made after purchases, we can deduce that the order-payment Bounded Context must have an operation to create a payment for a specific customer. In this domain, new customers are created if they don't already exist.

The payment creation operation is triggered immediately after purchase. Since several more operations are triggered after an item is purchased, we can implement all the communication related to a purchase event with the Publisher/Subscriber pattern we explained in *Chapter 6, Design Patterns and .NET 8 Implementation*. In DDD, these are known as **domain events**. Using events to implement communications between Bounded Contexts is very common since it helps keep Bounded Contexts loosely coupled.

Once an instance of either an event or an operation that's been defined in the Bounded Context's interface crosses the context boundary, it is immediately translated into the Ubiquitous Language of the receiving context. It is important that this translation be performed before the input data starts interacting with the other domain entities to prevent the Ubiquitous Language of the receiving domain from becoming contaminated by extra-contextual terms. An inadequate translation is usually evidenced by the domain experts complaining about "strange words."

Each Bounded Context implementation must contain a domain model completely expressed in terms of the Bounded Context Ubiquitous Language (class and interface names and property and method names), with no contamination from other Bounded Contexts' Ubiquitous Languages, and without contamination from technical programming stuff. This is necessary to ensure good communication with domain experts and to ensure that domain rules are translated correctly into code so that they can be easily validated by domain experts.

When there is a strong mismatch between the communication language and the target Ubiquitous Language, an anti-corruption layer is added to the receiving Bounded Context boundary. The only purpose of this anti-corruption layer is to perform a language translation.

Relationships among Bounded Contexts

The document that contains a representation of all the Bounded Contexts, along with the Bounded Contexts' mutual relationships and interface definitions, is called a **context map**. The relationships between contexts contain organizational constraints that specify the kind of cooperation required among the teams that are working on the different Bounded Contexts. Such relationships don't constrain the Bounded Context interfaces but do affect the way they may evolve during the software CI/CD cycle. They represent patterns of team cooperation.

The most common patterns are as follows:

- **Partner**: This is the original pattern suggested by Eric Evans. The idea is that the two teams have a mutual dependency on each other for delivery. In other words, they decide together the Bounded Context's mutual communication specifications during the software development lifecycle.
- **Customer/supplier development teams**: In this case, one team acts as a customer and another one acts as a supplier. In the preliminary stage, both teams define the interface of the customer side of the Bounded Context and some automated acceptance tests to validate it. After that, the supplier can work independently.

This pattern works when the customer's Bounded Context is the only active part that invokes the interface methods exposed by the other Bounded Context. This is adequate for the interaction between the order-payment and the package-handling contexts, where order-payment acts as a supplier since its functions are subordinate to the needs of package-handling. When this pattern can be applied, it decouples both the implementation and the maintenance of the two Bounded Contexts completely.

- **Conformist**: This is similar to the customer/supplier pattern, but in this case, the customer side accepts an interface that's been imposed by the supplier side with no preliminary negotiation stage. This pattern offers no advantages to the other patterns, but sometimes we are forced into the situation depicted by the pattern since either the supplier's Bounded Context is implemented in a preexisting product that can't be configured/modified too much, or because it is a legacy subsystem that we don't want to modify.

It is worth pointing out that the separation in Bounded Contexts is only effective if the resulting Bounded Contexts are loosely coupled; otherwise, the reduction of complexity that's obtained by breaking a whole system into parts would be overwhelmed by the complexity of the coordination and communication processes.

However, if Bounded Contexts are defined with the language criterion—that is, Bounded Context boundaries are added whenever the Ubiquitous Language changes—this should actually be the case. In fact, different languages may arise as a result of a loose interaction between an organization's subparts since the more each subpart has tight interactions inside of it and loose interactions with other subparts, the more each subpart ends up defining and using its own internal language, which differs from the language used by the other subparts.

Moreover, as all human organizations grow just by evolving into loosely coupled subparts, similarly, complex software systems may be implemented just as the cooperation of loosely coupled submodules: this is the only way humans are able to cope with complexity. From this, we can conclude that complex organizations/artificial systems can always be decomposed into loosely coupled subparts. We just need to understand *how*.

Beyond the basic principles we've mentioned so far, DDD provides a few basic primitives to describe each Bounded Context, as well as some implementation patterns. While Bounded Context primitives are an integral part of DDD, the patterns are simply useful heuristics we can use in our implementation, so their usage in some or all Bounded Contexts is not obligatory once we opt for DDD adoption.

In the next section, we will describe Bounded Context primitives, while the various patterns will be described in the remaining sections of the chapter.

Entities

DDD entities represent domain objects that have a well-defined identity, as well as all the operations that are defined on them. They don't differ too much from the entities of other, more classical approaches.

The main difference is that DDD stresses the entities' object-oriented nature, while other approaches use them mainly as **records** whose properties can be written/updated without too many constraints.

DDD, on the other hand, forces strong SOLID principles on them to ensure that only certain information is encapsulated inside of them and that only certain information is accessible from outside of them, to stipulate which operations are allowed on them, and to set which business-level validation criteria apply to them.

In other words, DDD entities are richer than the entities of record-based approaches.

In the record-based approach, operations that manipulate entities are defined outside of them in classes that represent business and/or domain operations. In DDD, these operations are moved into the entity definitions as their class methods. The reason for this is that this approach offers better modularity and keeps related chunks of software in the same place so that they can be maintained and tested easily.

More details on the difference between the record-based approach and the DDD approach will be given later on, in the *Repository pattern* subsection of this chapter.

For the same reason, business validation rules that are specific for each entity are moved inside of DDD entities. DDD entity validation rules are business-level rules, so they must not be confused with database integrity rules or user-input validation rules. They contribute to the way entities represent domain objects by encoding the constraints the represented objects must obey.

For instance, it might be obligatory to provide an entity property such as "Shipping Address" on a web page (user input validation rule), even though property is not obligatory in general (no corresponding business validation rule). In fact, the "Shipping Address" property becomes obligatory only if we need to ship something, so if the context of the web page is about shipping something, then "Shipping Address" must be obligatory as a user input in that specific web page but not as a general business rule.

User input validation will be discussed in more detail in *Chapter 17, Presenting ASP.NET Core,* which will show, in practice, how user input validation and business validation have different and complementary purposes. While business-level validation rules encode domain rules, input validation rules enforce the format of every single input (string length, correct email and URL formats, and so on), ensure that all the necessary input has been provided, enforce the execution of the chosen user machine interaction protocols, and provide fast and immediate feedback that drives the user to interact with the system.

It is worth pointing out that not all business validation rules can be encoded inside DDD entities. Business rules that are not specific to single DDD entities but involve the interaction of several entities must be encoded in the software module that handles and coordinates the interaction among entities. We will speak more about the software module that coordinates entity interactions later on in this chapter.

The subsection that follows gives more details on entity-level validation rules.

Entity-level validation in .NET

In .NET, business validation can be carried out with one of the following techniques:

- Calling the validation methods in all the class methods that modify the entity.
- Hooking the validation methods to all the property setters.

- Decorating the class and/or its properties with custom validation attributes and then invoking the `TryValidateObject` static method of the `System.ComponentModel.DataAnnotations.Validator` class on the entity each time it is modified. The .NET `System.ComponentModel.DataAnnotations` namespace contains predefined validation attributes (see `https://learn.microsoft.com/en-us/aspnet/core/mvc/models/validation?view=aspnetcore-8.0#built-in-attributes`), but the developer can define also custom validation attributes by inheriting from the `System.ComponentModel.DataAnnotations.ValidationAttribute` abstract class (see `https://makolyte.com/aspnetcore-create-a-custom-model-validation-attribute/`).

More details on validation attributes will be given in *Chapter 17, Presenting ASP.NET Core*.

Once detected, validation errors must be handled somehow; that is, the current operation must be aborted and the error must be reported to an appropriate error handler. The simplest way to handle validation errors is by throwing an exception. This way, both purposes are easily achieved and we can choose where to intercept and handle them. Unfortunately, as we discussed in the *Performance issues that need to be considered while programming in C#* section of *Chapter 2, Non-Functional Requirements*, exceptions imply big performance penalties and must be used to deal just with "exceptional circumstances" so, often, different options are considered. Handling errors in the normal flow of control would break modularity by spreading the code that's needed to handle the error all over the stack of methods that caused the error, with a never-ending set of conditions all over that code. Therefore, more sophisticated options are needed.

A good alternative to exceptions is to notify errors to an error handler that is unique for each processing request. For instance, it can be implemented as a scoped service in the dependency injection engine. Being scoped, the same service instance is returned while each request is being processed so that the handler that controls the execution of the whole call stack can inspect possible errors when the flow of control returns to it, and can handle them appropriately. Unfortunately, this sophisticated technique can't automatically abort the operation's execution and return immediately to the most adequate controlling handler that is in the call stack.

This is why exceptions are often used for this scenario, notwithstanding their performance issues. The other option is the usage of a **result object** that informs the caller of the success of the operation in all method calls. However, result objects have their cons: they imply more coupling between the methods involved in the call stack, so during software maintenance, each change might require modifications in several methods.

DDD entities in .NET

Since DDD entities must have a well-defined identity, they must have properties that act as primary keys. It is common to override the `Object.Equals` method of all the DDD entities in such a way that two objects are considered equal whenever they have the same primary keys. This is easily achieved by letting all the entities inherit from an abstract `Entity` class, as shown in the following code:

```
public abstract class Entity<K>: IEntity<K>
{

    public virtual K Id { get; protected set; }
    public bool IsTransient()
    {
        return Object.Equals(Id, default(K));
    }
    public override bool Equals(object obj)
    {
        return obj is Entity<K> entity &&
          Equals(entity);
    }
    public bool Equals(IEntity<K>? other)
    {
        if (other == null ||
            other.IsTransient() || this.IsTransient())
            return false;
        return Object.Equals(Id, other.Id);
    }
    int? _requestedHashCode;
    public override int GetHashCode()
    {
        if (!IsTransient())
        {
            if (!_requestedHashCode.HasValue)
                _requestedHashCode = HashCode.Combine(Id);
            return _requestedHashCode.Value;
        }
        else
            return base.GetHashCode();
    }
    public static bool operator ==(Entity<K> left, Entity<K> right)
    {
```

```
        if (Object.Equals(left, null))
            return Object.Equals(right, null);
        return left.Equals(right);
    }
    public static bool operator !=(Entity<K> left, Entity<K> right)
    {
        return !(left == right);
    }
}
```

Note the following things in the code:

- It is worth implementing an `IEntity<K>` interface that defines all the properties/methods of `Entity<K>`. This interface is useful whenever we need to hide data classes behind interfaces.
- The `IsTransient` predicate returns `true` whenever the entity has been recently created and hasn't been recorded in the permanent storage, so its primary key is still undefined.
- In .NET, it is good practice that, whenever you override the `Object.Equals` method of a class, you also override its `Object.GetHashCode` method so that class instances can be efficiently stored in data structures such as dictionaries and sets. That's why the `Entity` class overrides it.
- It is worth pointing out that once we've redefined the `Object.Equals` method in the `Entity` class, we can also override the == and != operators.

Entities are not the only data ingredient of DDD. Domain modeling also requires data with no unique identities. That's why value objects were conceived.

Value objects

Value objects, in contrast to entities, represent complex types that can't be encoded with numbers or strings. Therefore, they have no identity and no principal keys. They have no operations defined on them and are immutable; that is, once they've been created, all their fields can be read but cannot be modified. For this reason, they are usually encoded with classes whose properties have protected/private setters.

Two value objects are considered equal when all their independent properties are equal. Some properties are not independent since they just show data that's been encoded by other properties in a different way, as is the case for the ticks of `DateTime` and its representation of the date and time fields.

Value objects are easily implemented with C# 12 `record` types since all `record` types automatically override the `Equals` method so that it performs a property-by-property comparison. Record types can also be made immutable by adequately defining their properties; once immutable objects are initialized, the only way to change their values is to create a new instance. Here is an example of how to modify a `record`:

```
var modifiedAddress = myAddress with {Street = "new street"}
```

Here is an example of how to define a record:

```
public record Address
{
    public string Country {get; init;}
    public string Town {get; init;}
    public string Street {get; init;}
}
```

The init keyword is what makes record type properties immutable since it means they can only be initialized.

If we pass all the properties in the constructor instead of using initializers, the preceding definition can be simplified as follows:

```
public record Address(string Country, string Town, string Street) ;
```

Typical value objects include costs represented as a number and a currency symbol, locations represented as longitude and latitude, addresses, and contact information.

The way both entities and value objects typically interact with data storage in .NET applications is explained in *Chapter 13, Interacting with Data in C# – Entity Framework Core.*

Aggregates

So far, we have talked about entities as the **units** that are processed by a DDD-based business layer. However, several entities can be manipulated and made into single entities. An example of this is a purchase order and all of its items. In fact, it makes absolutely no sense to process a single order item independently of the order it belongs to. This happens because order items are actually subparts of an order, not independent entities.

There is no transaction that may affect a single order item without it affecting the order that the item is in. Imagine that two different people in the same company are trying to increase the total quantity of cement, but one increases the quantity of type-1 cement (item 1) while the other increases the quantity of type-2 cement (item 2). If each item is processed as an independent entity, both quantities will be increased, which could cause an incoherent purchase order since the total quantity of cement would be increased twice.

On the other hand, if the whole order, along with all its order items, is loaded and saved with every single transaction by both people, one of the two will overwrite the changes of the other one, so whoever makes the final change will have their requirements set.

A purchase order, along with all its subparts (its order items), is called an **aggregate**, while the order entity is called the **root** of the aggregate. Aggregates always have roots since they are hierarchies of entities connected by **subpart** relationships.

Since each aggregate represents a single complex entity, all the operations on it must be exposed by a unique interface. Therefore, the aggregate root usually represents the whole aggregate, and all the operations on the aggregate are defined as methods of the root entity.

When the aggregate pattern is used, the units of information that are transferred between the business layer and the data layer are called aggregates, queries, and query results. Thus, aggregates replace single entities.

In a few words, aggregates are in-memory representations of storage information that need to be dealt with as a single object. Being an in-memory representation based on an object-oriented paradigm, they take full advantage of all the benefits of object-oriented programming.

Domain events

Domain events are the main communication ingredient of DDD. While DDD doesn't impose constraints on the way communication among bounded contexts is achieved, a communication based on the publisher/subscriber pattern described in *Chapter 6, Design Patterns and .NET 8 Implementation*, maximizes independence among bounded contexts. Each bounded context publishes all information that might interest other bounded contexts, and interested bounded contexts subscribe. This way, the publisher doesn't need to know about each subscriber and how it works, but just publish the result of its job in a general format. More implementation details will be given in the *Command handlers and domain events* subsection of this chapter.

Common DDD patterns and architectures

In this and the sections that follow, we will describe some of the patterns and architectures that are commonly used with DDD. Some of them can be adopted in all projects, while others can only be used for certain Bounded Contexts.

Before we begin, we should note that, from a conceptual point of view, the functionality of each application can be classified into three groups:

- Handling the interaction with the user
- Performing business-related processing
- Interacting with the storage engine

Each of the above groups uses a different language and different technologies. The first group uses the language of the target users and user interface technologies, the second group uses the language of the domain expert and is focused on application domain modeling, and the third group uses both language and technologies related to databases.

Each of the architectures we will look at organize these functionalities in different ways. We will start with the classic layers architecture since it is simpler to understand, and then we will describe the more sophisticated onion architecture.

Classic layers architecture

The classic layers architecture organizes the three groups of functionalities as three loosely coupled sets of classes/interfaces called **layers**, put one after the other:

- The first layer in the sequence is the one that takes care of user interaction and is called the **presentation layer**.
- The second layer in the sequence is the one that performs business-related processing and is called the **business layer**.
- The third layer is the one dedicated to database interaction and is called the **data layer**.

Each layer can communicate directly just with the layer that precedes it and the layer that follows it, as shown in the figure below:

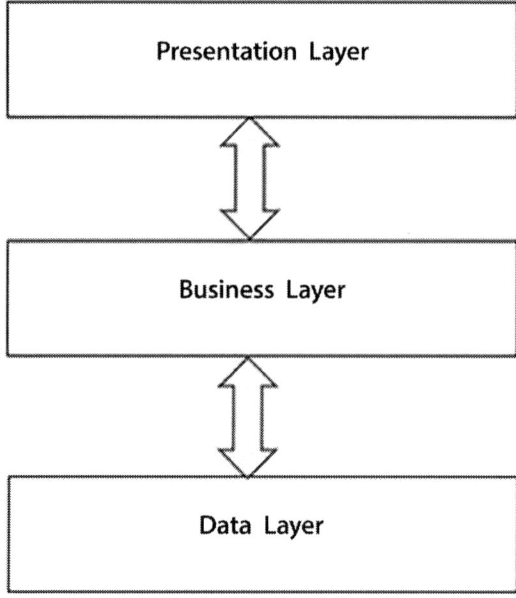

Figure 7.3: Classic layers architecture

Each layer call can pass data to methods of public objects in the layer that follows it and receive the resulting data back.

The presentation layer handles not only graphics but also the whole user-machine interaction protocol. During its interaction protocol, the presentation layer uses business layer methods either to present data to the user or to update the application state.

In turn, the business layer uses data layer methods to retrieve all data it needs to prepare the user answer from the data storage and to update the application state.

Each layer offers a well-defined interface to the layer that precedes it while hiding all implementation details.

The layer architecture promotes modularity since each layer doesn't depend on how the layers that precede it are implemented, and avoids the possibility of the language used by each layer contaminating the language used by the others.

However, data exchanged in the classic layer architecture are record-type objects with no methods that encode any processing logic, since the whole processing logic is contained in the objects and methods that compose the three layers.

Since record-like objects used by the classic layers architecture are very different from DDD domain objects, which are rich objects that encode most of the business logic in their methods, the classic layers architecture has a poor match with DDD. That's why an improvement on the classic layers architecture, called the onion architecture, has been proposed.

Onion architecture

In the onion architecture, layers obey different rules and are defined in a slightly different way. There is:

- An outermost layer that takes care of all interactions with the application environment—that is, user interface, test software, and interaction with operating system and data storage
- An application layer
- A domain layer

Here, the domain layer is an abstraction of the classical data layer based on the Ubiquitous Language. It is where DDD entities and value objects are defined, together with abstractions of the operations that retrieve and save them. For better modularity, all or some domain layer classes may be made internal and hidden behind public interfaces.

The application layer, instead, defines operations that use the domain layer public interface (public interfaces and public classes) to get DDD entities and value objects and manipulate them to implement the application business logic. The DDD application layer is called **application services** since it exposes its functionalities through an API that is completely independent of the outermost layers. This way, for instance, any user interface layer and a test suite both call exactly the same methods to interact with the application logic.

The outermost layer contains the user interface, the functional test suites (if any), and the application interface with the infrastructure that hosts the application.

The infrastructure represents the environment in which the application runs and includes the operating system, any devices, filesystem services, cloud services, and databases. The infrastructure interface is placed on the outermost level to ensure that no other onion layer depends on it. This maximizes both usability and modifiability.

The infrastructure layer contains all the drivers needed to adapt the application to its environment. Infrastructure resources communicate with the application through these drivers, and, in turn, drivers expose the infrastructure resources to all application layers through interfaces that are associated with the drivers implementing them in the dependency injection engine. This way, adapting the application to a different environment just requires changing the drivers.

Here's a sketch of the onion architecture:

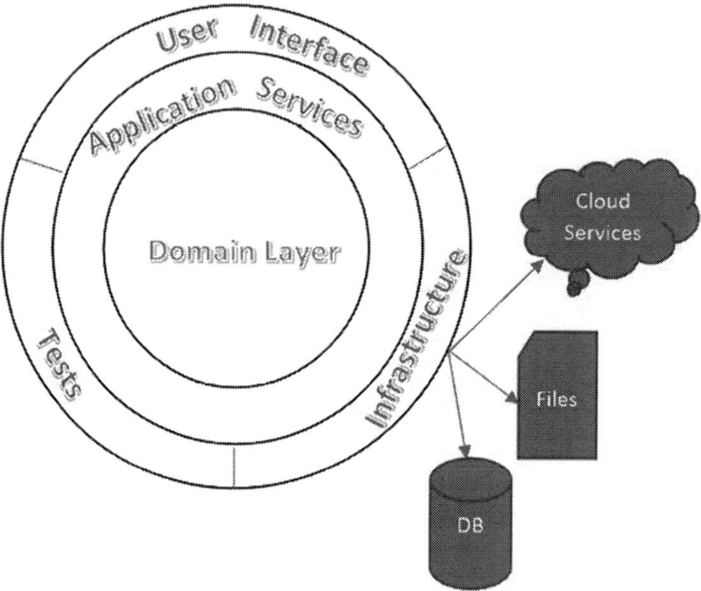

Figure 7.4: Onion architecture

Each ring is a layer. Inward from the outermost layer are the **application services**, and inward from the application services we have the **domain layer**, which contains the representation of the entities involved in the Bounded Context knowledge.

Both the application services and the domain layer can be split into sublayers, and all layers/sublayers must conform to the following rule: *Each layer may depend only on the inner layers.*

For instance, the domain layer may be split into **Domain Model** and **Domain Services**, where Domain Model is below Domain Services. The *Domain Model* layer contains the classes and interfaces that represent all domain objects, while the *Domain Services* layer contains the so-called repositories that are explained later on in this chapter in the *Repository pattern* and *Unit of work pattern* sections.

As we will see later on in this chapter, it is common to interact with the domain layer through interfaces that are defined in a separate library and implemented in the domain layer. Thus, the domain layer must have a reference to the library containing all domain layer interfaces since it must implement those interfaces, while the application layer is where each domain layer interface is connected with its implementation through a record of the application layer dependency injection engine. More specifically, the only data layer objects referenced by the application layer are these interface implementations that are only referenced in the dependency injection engine.

Outer layers that implement interfaces defined in the next inner layer are a common pattern used in the onion architecture.

Each application layer operation requires the interfaces it needs from the dependency engine, uses them to get DDD entities and value objects, manipulates them, and possibly saves them through the same interfaces.

Here is a diagram that shows the relationships among the three layers discussed in this section:

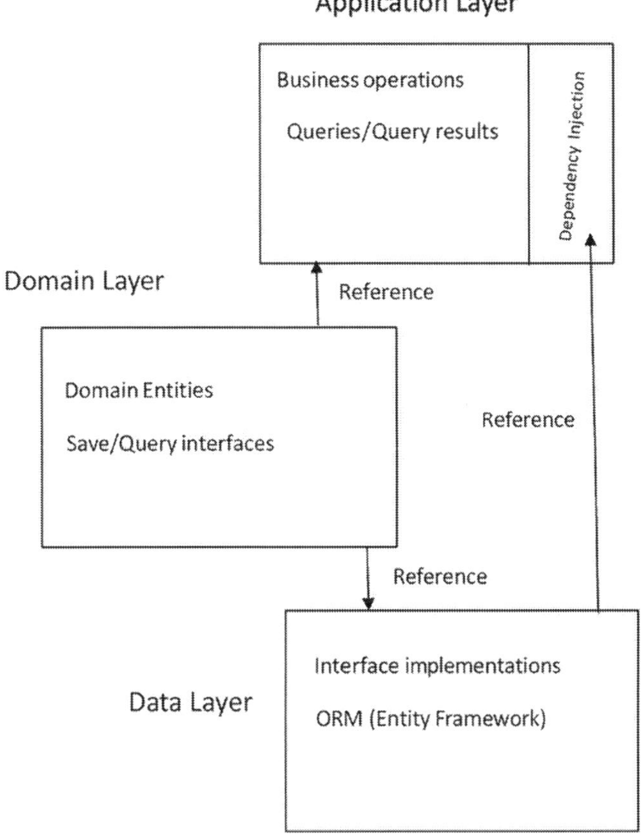

Figure 7.5: Relationships among the layers

Thus, the domain layer contains the representation of the domain objects, the methods to use on them, validation constraints, and the domain layer's relationship with various entities. To increase modularity and decoupling, communication among entities is usually encoded with events—that is, with the **Publisher/Subscriber pattern**. This means entity updates can trigger events that have been hooked to business operations, and these events act on other entities.

This layered architecture allows us to change the whole data layer without affecting the domain layer, which only depends on the domain specifications and language and doesn't depend on the technical details of how the data is handled.

The application layer contains the definitions of all the operations that may potentially affect several entities and the definitions of all the queries that are needed by the applications. Both business operations and queries use the interfaces defined in the domain layer to interact with the data layer.

However, while business operations manipulate and exchange entities with these interfaces, queries send query specifications and receive generic **Data Transfer Objects** (**DTOs**) from them. In fact, the purpose of queries is just to show data to the user, not to act on them; accordingly, query operations don't need whole entities with all their methods, properties, and validation rules, but just property tuples.

Business operations are invoked either by other layers (typically the presentation layer) or by communication operations.

Summing up, the application layer operates on the interfaces defined in the domain layer instead of interacting directly with their data layer implementations, which means that the application layer is decoupled from the data layer. More specifically, data layer objects are only mentioned in the dependency injection engine definitions. All the other application layer components refer to the interfaces that are defined in the domain layers, and the dependency injection engine injects the appropriate implementations.

The application layer communicates with other application components through one or more of the following patterns:

- ***It exposes business operations and queries on a communication endpoint***, such as an HTTP Web API (see *Chapter 15, Applying Service-Oriented Architectures with .NET*). In this case, the presentation layer may connect to this endpoint or to other endpoints that, in turn, take information from this and other endpoints. Application components that collect information from several endpoints and expose them in a unique endpoint are called **gateways**. They may be either custom or general-purpose, such as Ocelot.
- ***It is referenced as a library by an application that directly implements the presentation layer***, such as an ASP.NET Core MVC Web application.
- ***It doesn't expose all the information through endpoints and communicates some of the data it processes/creates to other application components that, in turn, expose endpoints***. Such communication is often implemented with the Publisher/Subscriber pattern to increase modularity.

Repository pattern

The repository pattern is an entity-centric approach to the definition of the domain layer interfaces: each entity—or better, each aggregate—has its own repository interface that defines how to retrieve and create it, and defines all queries that involve entities in the aggregate. The implementation of each repository interface is called a repository. Repositories are associated with aggregates instead of entities, since, as discussed in the *Aggregates* subsection, aggregates represent the minimum granularity that makes sense to consider in each data operation.

With the repository pattern, each operation has an easy-to-find place where it must be defined: the interface of the aggregate the operation works on, or, in the case of a query, the aggregate that contains the root entity of the query.

The repository pattern was initially conceived for the classical layer architecture and its record-like objects. Then, it was adapted to work with rich DDD entities/aggregates.

Classical repositories contain all methods needed to handle record-like objects—that is, modification, creation and delete methods since record-like objects have no modification methods. DDD-adapted repositories, instead, only contain create and delete methods since all methods that modify each aggregate are defined as aggregate methods. Moreover, applications based on classic repositories and record-like objects do not have a unique record-like object that represents each domain aggregate, but there are several record-like objects, each containing a different view of the overall domain aggregate. Therefore, classic repositories have modification methods for several different record-like objects.

Both classic and DDD-adapted repositories have methods to retrieve data to be returned to the user. In both cases, this data is represented by record-like objects, since aggregates are built only when domain entities must be modified or created.

The diagram below summarizes the differences between classical and DDD-adapted repository patterns.

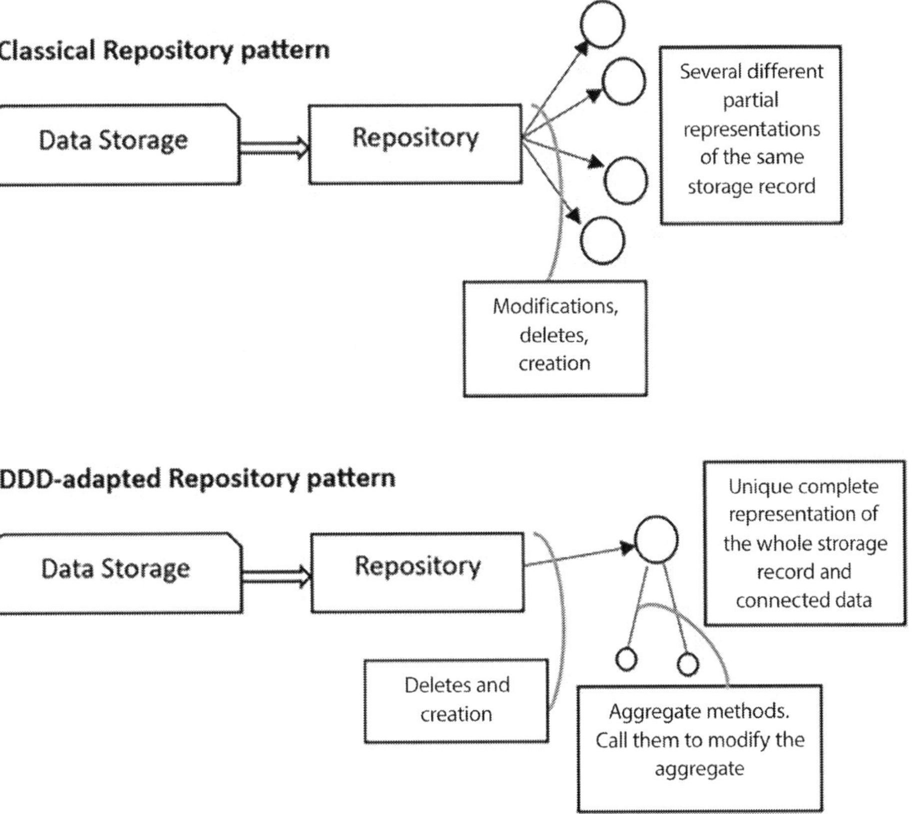

Figure 7.6: Classical and DDD-adapted repository pattern

Unit of work pattern

While it is preferable for transactions to be confined within the boundary of a single aggregate design, sometimes application layer transactions might span several aggregates and, accordingly, might use several different repository interfaces.

For instance, buying a travel involves the simultaneous modifications of the following entities:

- Hotel/travel available places
- Customer shopping basket

Both operations must be accomplished in a single transaction since either they are both successful or they must both fail. Therefore, we need a way to execute operations on several entities/aggregates in a single transaction, while keeping the methods/code of the involved entities decoupled, according to object-oriented programming best practices.

The **Unit of Work** pattern is a solution that maintains the independence of the domain layer from the underlying domain layer implementation. It states that each repository interface must also contain a reference to a Unit of Work interface that represents the identity of the current transaction. This means that several repositories with the same Unit of Work reference belong to the same transaction.

The Unit of Work pattern can be used with both aggregates and record-like entities.

Both the repository and the Unit of Work patterns can be implemented by defining some seed interfaces:

```
public interface IUnitOfWork
{
    Task<bool> SaveEntitiesAsync();
    Task StartAsync();
    Task CommitAsync();
    Task RollbackAsync();
}
public interface IRepository<T>: IRepository
{
   IUnitOfWork UnitOfWork { get; }
}
```

All repository interfaces inherit from `IRepository<T>` and bind `T` to the aggregate root or entity they are associated with, while Unit of Work simply implements `IUnitOfWork`. When `SaveEntitiesAsync()` is called, all pending modifications, deletions, and creations done on aggregates or record-like objects are saved in a single transaction in the storage engine. If a wider transaction that starts when some data is retrieved from the storage engine is needed, it must be started and committed/aborted by the application layer handler, which takes care of the whole operation with the help of the `IUnitOfWork` `StartAsync`, `CommitAsync`, and `RollbackAsync` methods. `IRepository<T>` inherits from an empty `IRepository` interface to help automatic repository discovery.

The GitHub repository associated with this book contains a `RepositoryExtensions` class whose `AddAllRepositories` `IServiceCollection` extension method automatically discovers all the repository implementations contained in an assembly and adds them to the dependency injection engine.

Classic repository pattern versus DDD aggregates

The DDD patterns discussed so far, such as aggregates and DDD-adapted repositories, ensure modularity and modifiability, and, since whole domain aggregates are loaded in memory, they also prevent various kinds of bugs due to wrong partial updates. However, each addition of new functionality is cumbersome since it usually involves a complex modeling activity, the reengineering or creation of whole aggregates, and the definition of several classes.

On the one hand, record-like objects are easier to define and we may define different classes for different usages. So, adding a new functionality simply requires the definition of an independent repository method, and possibly the definition of a new record-like class.

Suppose we need just to maintain travel descriptions and features. It is a very simple domain, and we need just to perform CRUD operations—that is, creating and deleting travels and modifying their features. In this case, there is no advantage in loading the whole aggregates in memory and performing all operations as methods of a unique entity class.

On the other hand, with the classical repository pattern, we can load just the features of the travel we would like to modify, say a marketing-optimized description in some web pages, price in other pages where the user is an administrator with the power of deciding on prices, and so on. This way each operation uses a different object that is specific and optimized for that operation.

Suppose now we are designing a complex resource allocation software for an industrial application. All properties of each entity are constrained by complex business rules, and also several entities are constrained by several complex business rules. Therefore, a partial update of a few properties has consequences that propagate to the whole entity and to other connected entities.

In this case, each classical repository method would be forced to take into account all possible consequences of each property change, resulting in complex spaghetti code and in the recoding of the same operations several times in different repository methods.

In this case, a DDD approach performs much better. We load in memory the full aggregates involved and let their methods handle the business rule complexity with the help of object-oriented best practices. It is enough that each aggregate encodes the behavior of the real word object it represents, with no need to care about consequences on other entities.

Summing up, when a Bounded Context is quite simple, meaning a few entities with a few interactions among them and a few different update operations, there is no doubt that the classic repository pattern is more convenient. On the other hand, when there are many entities, or complex entities, and many different update operations are added, repositories turn into spaghetti code with several partially overlapping methods, code duplication, and no easy-to-understand interaction rules.

A full example showing the DDD-adapted repository pattern is given in the *A frontend microservice* section of *Chapter 21, Case Study*, while a full example showing the classical repository pattern is given in the *Using client technologies* section of the same chapter.

Moreover, as already pointed out, partial updates performed by several record-like projections of domain aggregates may cause bugs due to simultaneous modifications performed by different users.

Therefore, when the probability of similar bugs becomes high because of complex update patterns, it is very dangerous to use the classic repository pattern.

Thus, again, complexity is the main factor that drives us to the usage of DDD patterns. Moreover, the need to centralize the triggering of domain events used to synchronize Bounded Context data stores (review the previous *Understanding domain-driven design* section) forces the loading of whole aggregates in memory, and the usage of DDD patterns. Therefore, when a Bounded Context needs to trigger several domain events in complex circumstances, we can't use the simpler classic repository pattern.

Now that we've discussed the basic patterns of DDD, we can discuss some more advanced DDD patterns. In the next section, we will introduce the CQRS pattern.

Command Query Responsibility Segregation (CQRS) pattern

In its general form, the usage of this pattern is quite easy: *use different structures to store/update and query data*. Here, the requirements regarding how to store and update data differ from the requirements of queries. This means that both the domain layer and application services of queries and store/update operations must be designed in completely different ways.

In the case of DDD, the unit of storage is the aggregate, so additions, deletions, and updates involve aggregates. On the other hand, differently from storages/updates, queries don't perform business operations but involve transformations of properties that have been taken from several aggregates (projections, sums, averages, and so on).

Therefore, while updates require entities enriched with business logic and constraints (methods, validation rules, encapsulated information, and so on), query results just need sets of property/value pairs, so DTOs with only public properties and no methods work well.

In its common form, the pattern can be depicted as follows:

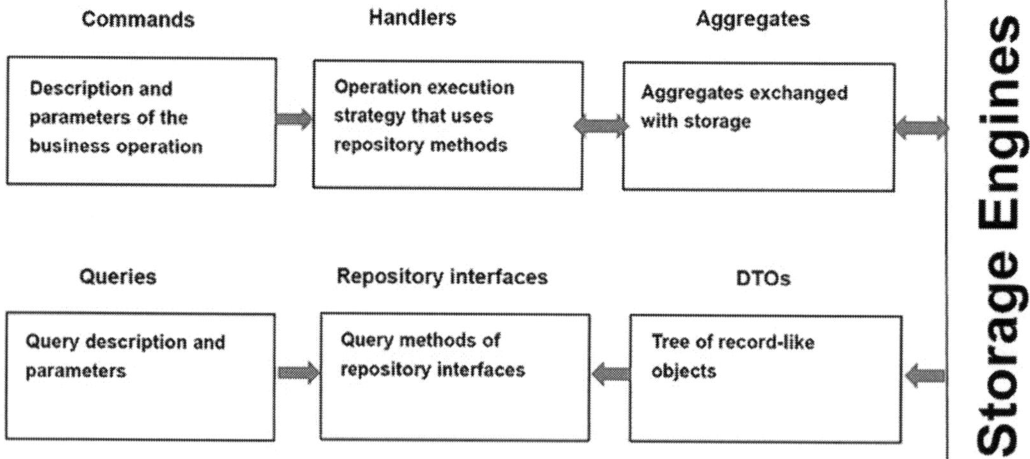

Figure 7.7: Command and query processing

Where:

- The middle boxes (Handlers and Repository interfaces) represent operations.
- The leftmost and rightmost boxes represent data.
- Arrows simply represent the direction of data.

The main takeaway from this is that the extraction of query results doesn't need to pass through the construction of entities and aggregates, but the fields shown in the query must be extracted from the storage engine and projected into ad hoc DTOs.

However, in more complex situations, CQRS may be implemented in a stronger form. Namely, we can use different Bounded Contexts to store preprocessed query results.

In fact, the other option would be an aggregator microservice that queries all the necessary microservices in order to assemble each query result. However, recursive calls to other microservices to build an answer may result in unacceptable response times. Moreover, factoring out some preprocessing ensures better usage of the available resources.

This pattern is implemented as follows:

- Query handling is delegated to separated and specialized components.
- Each query-handling component uses a database table for each query it must handle. There, it stores all fields to be returned by the query. This means that queries are not computed at each request, but precomputed and stored in specific database tables. Clearly, queries with child collections need additional tables, one for each child collection.
- All components that process updates forward all changes to the interested query-handling components. Records are versioned so the query-handling components that receive the changes can apply them in the right order to their query-handling tables. In fact, since communication is asynchronous to improve performance, changes are not guaranteed to be received in the same order they were sent.
- Changes received by each query-handling microservice are cached while they wait for the changes to be applied. Whenever a change has a version number that immediately follows the last change applied, it is applied to the right query-handling table.

It is worth noticing that the software "components" we mentioned above run as separate processes on possibly different machines, and are called microservices. They will be discussed in detail in *Chapter 11, Applying a Microservice Architecture to Your Enterprise Application*.

The usage of this stronger form of the CQRS pattern transforms typical local database transactions into complex time-consuming distributed transactions since a failure in a single query preprocessor microservice should invalidate the whole transaction. As we will discuss in *Chapter 11, Applying a Microservice Architecture to Your Enterprise Application*, implementing distributed transactions is usually unacceptable for performance reasons and sometimes is not supported at all, so the common solution is to renounce the idea of a database that is immediately consistent overall and to accept that the overall database will eventually be consistent after each update.

Transient failures can be solved with retry policies, which we will discuss in *Chapter 11, Applying a Microservice Architecture to Your Enterprise Application*, while permanent failures are handled by performing corrective actions on the already committed local transactions instead of pretending to implement an overall globally distributed transaction.

At this point, you may be asking the following question:

"Why do we need to keep the original data once we have all the preprocessed query results? We will never use it to answer queries!"

Some of the answers to this question are as follows:

- They are the source of truth that we may need to recover from failures.
- We need them to compute new preprocessed results when we add new queries.
- We need them to process new updates. In fact, processing updates usually requires that some of the data is retrieved from the database, possibly shown to the user, and then modified.

For instance, to modify an item in an existing purchase order, we need the whole order so that we can show it to the user and compute the changes so that we can forward it to other microservices. Moreover, whenever we modify or add data to the storage engine, we must verify the coherence of the overall database (unique key constraints, foreign key constraints, and so on).

The next subsection is dedicated to an extreme implementation of the CQRS pattern.

Event sourcing

Event sourcing is a more advanced implementation of the stronger form of CQRS. It is useful when the original Bounded Context is a **source of truth**—that is, for recovering from failures and for software maintenance. In this case, instead of updating data, we simply add events that describe the operation that was performed, such as *deleted record Id 15, changed the name to John in Id 21*, and so on. These events are immediately sent to all the dependent Bounded Contexts, and in the case of failures and/or the addition of new queries, all we have to do is reprocess some of them. For performance reasons, together with the events representing all changes, the current state is also maintained; otherwise, each time it is needed, it will need to be recomputed, replaying all events. Moreover, usually, the full state is cached after, say, every *N* changes. This way, if there is a crash or any kind of failure, only a few events must be replayed.

Replaying events can't cause problems if events are **idempotent**—that is, if processing the same event several times has the same effect as processing it once.

As we will discuss in *Chapter 11, Applying a Microservice Architecture to Your Enterprise Application*, idempotency is a standard requirement for microservices that communicate through events.

In the next section, we will describe a common pattern that's used for handling operations that span several aggregates and several Bounded Contexts.

Command handlers and aggregate events

According to the Command pattern, each application domain operation is handled by a so-called command handler. Since each command handler encodes a single application domain operation, all of its actions must take place in the same transaction because the operation must succeed or fail as a whole. Command handlers perform their job by calling aggregates and repository methods. However, some actions might be triggered by state changes inside aggregates, so they can't be called by command handlers but must rely on some form of direct aggregate-to-aggregate communication.

To keep aggregates separated, usually, communication among aggregates and also with other Bounded Contexts is done through events. We already discussed domain events used to communicate with other bounded contexts in the *Domain events* subsection. However, direct communication among aggregates can also take advantage of the publisher/subscriber pattern to keep the code more modular and easy to modify. It is good practice to store all the events when they are triggered during the processing of each aggregate, instead of executing them immediately, in order to prevent event execution from interfering with the ongoing aggregate processing. This is easily achieved by adding the following code to the abstract `Entity` class defined in the *Entities* subsection of this chapter, as follows:

```
public List<IEventNotification> DomainEvents { get; private set; }
public void AddDomainEvent(IEventNotification evt)
{
    DomainEvents ??= new List<IEventNotification>();
    DomainEvents.Add(evt);
}
public void RemoveDomainEvent(IEventNotification evt)
{
    DomainEvents?.Remove(evt);
}
```

Here, `IEventNotification` is an empty interface that's used to mark classes as events.

Event processing is usually performed immediately before changes are stored in the storage engine. Accordingly, a good place to perform event processing is immediately before the command handler calls the `SaveEntitiesAsync()` method of each `IUnitOfWork` implementation (see the *Repository pattern* subsection). Similarly, if event handlers can create other events, they must process them after they finish processing all their aggregates.

Subscriptions to an event, `T`, can be provided as an implementation of the `IEventHandler<T>` interface:

```
public interface IEventHandler<T>: IEventHandler
    where T: IEventNotification
{
    Task HandleAsync(T ev);
}
```

Analogously, the command pattern is implemented with a `command` object, which contains all the input data of the application domain operation, while the code that implements the actual operation can be provided through a command handler that is an implementation of an `ICommandHandler<T>` interface:

```
public interface ICommandHandler<T>: ICommandHandler
    where T: ICommand
{
    Task HandleAsync(T command);
}
```

Here, `ICommand` is an empty interface that's used to mark classes as commands. `ICommandHandler<T>` and `IEventHandler<T>` are examples of the **Command pattern** we described in *Chapter 6, Design Patterns and .NET 8 Implementation.*

Each `ICommandHandler<T>` can be registered in the dependency injection engine so that classes that need to execute a command, `T`, can use `ICommandHandler<T>` in their constructor. This way, we decouple the abstract definition of a command (the class that implements `ICommand`) from the way it is executed.

The same construction can't be applied to events, `T`, and their `IEventHandler<T>`, because when an event is triggered, we need to retrieve several instances of `IEventHandler<T>` and not just one. We need to do this since each event may have several subscriptions. However, a few lines of code can easily solve this difficulty. First, we need to define a class that hosts all the handlers for a given event type:

```
public class EventTrigger<T>
    where T: IEventNotification
{
    private IEnumerable<IEventHandler<T>> handlers;
    public EventTrigger(IEnumerable<IEventHandler<T>> handlers)
    {
        this.handlers = handlers;
    }
    public async Task Trigger(T ev)
    {
        foreach (var handler in handlers)
            await handler.HandleAsync(ev);
    }
}
```

Declaring a `handlers` `IEnumerable<IEventHandler<T>>` parameter in the `EventTrigger<T>` constructor lets a .NET dependency injection engine pass all `IEventHandler<T>` implementations available in the dependency injection container to this `handlers` parameter.

The idea is that each class that needs to trigger event `T` requires `EventTrigger<T>` and then passes the event to be triggered to its `Trigger` method, which, in turn, invokes all the handlers.

Then, we need to register EventTrigger<T> in the dependency injection engine. A good idea is to define the dependency injection extensions that we can invoke to declare each event, as follows:

```
service.AddEventHandler<MyEventType, MyHandlerType>()
```

This AddEventHandler extension must automatically produce a dependency injection definition for EventTrigger<T> and must process all the handlers that are declared with AddEventHandler for each type, T.

The following extension class does this for us:

```
public static class EventDIExtensions
{
    public static IServiceCollection AddEventHandler<T, H>
        (this IServiceCollection services)
        where T : IEventNotification
        where H: class, IEventHandler<T>
    {
        services.AddScoped<H>();
        services.TryAddScoped(typeof(EventTrigger<>));
        return services;
    }
    ...
    ...
}
```

The H type passed to AddEventHandler is recorded in the dependency injection engine, and the first time AddEventHandler is called, EventTrigger<T> is also added to the dependency injection engine. Then, when an EventTrigger<T> instance is required by the dependency injection engine, all IEventHandler<T> types added to the dependency injection engine are created, collected, and passed to the EventTrigger(IEnumerable<IEventHandler<T>> handlers) constructor.

When the program starts up, all the ICommandHandler<T> and IEventHandler<T> implementations can be retrieved with reflection and registered automatically. To help with automatic discovery, they inherit from ICommandHandler and IEventHandler, which are both empty interfaces.

The EventDIExtensions class, which is available in this book's GitHub repository, contains methods for the automatic discovery and registration of command handlers and event handlers. The GitHub repository also contains an IEventMediator interface and its EventMediator implementation, whose TriggerEvents(IEnumerable<IEventNotification> events) method retrieves all the handlers associated with the events it receives in its argument from the dependency injection engine and executes them. It is sufficient to have IEventMediator injected into a class so that it can trigger events. EventDIExtensions also contains an extension method that discovers all the queries that implement the empty IQuery interface and adds them to the dependency injection engine.

A more sophisticated implementation is given by the `MediatR` NuGet package.

Summary

In this chapter, we analyzed the main reasons for the adoption of DDD and why and how it meets the needs of the market. We described how to identify domains and how to coordinate the teams that work on different domains of the same application with domain maps. Then, we analyzed the way DDD represents data with entities, value objects, and aggregates, providing advice and code snippets so that we can implement them in practice.

We also described the onion architecture frequently used in conjunction with DDD-based projects, and compared it with the classical layer architecture.

We also covered some typical patterns that are used with DDD—that is, the repository and Unit of Work patterns, domain event patterns, CQRS, and event sourcing. Then, we learned how to implement them in practice. We also showed you how to implement domain events and the command pattern with decoupled handling so that we can add code snippets to real-world projects.

Questions

1. What provides the main hints so that we can discover domain boundaries?
2. What is the main tool that's used for coordinating the development of a separate Bounded Context?
3. Is it true that each entry that composes an aggregate communicates with the remainder of the system with its own methods?
4. Why is there a single aggregate root?
5. How many repositories can manage an aggregate?
6. How does a repository interact with the application layer?
7. Why is the Unit of Work pattern needed?
8. What are the reasons for the light form of CQRS? What about the reasons for its strongest form?
9. What is the main tool that allows us to couple commands/domain events with their handlers?
10. Is it true that event sourcing can be used to implement any Bounded Context?

Further reading

- Eric Evans, Domain-Driven Design: `https://www.amazon.com/exec/obidos/ASIN/0321125215/domainlanguag-20`
- More resources on DDD can be found here: `https://domainlanguage.com/ddd/`
- A detailed discussion of CQRS design principles can be found here: `http://udidahan.com/2009/12/09/clarified-cqrs/`
- More information on MediatR can be found on MediatR's GitHub repository: `https://github.com/jbogard/MediatR`
- A good description of event sourcing, along with an example of it, can be seen in the following blog post by Martin Fowler: `https://martinfowler.com/eaaDev/EventSourcing.html`

Learn more on Discord

To join the Discord community for this book – where you can share feedback, ask questions to the authors, and learn about new releases – follow the QR code below:

`https://packt.link/SoftwareArchitectureCSharp12Dotnet8`

8

Understanding DevOps Principles and CI/CD

Although many people define DevOps as a process, the more you work with it, the better you understand it as a philosophy. This chapter will cover the main concepts, principles, and tools you need to develop and deliver your software with DevOps.

By considering the DevOps philosophy, this chapter will focus on **service design thinking**, that is, keeping in mind that the software you design is a service offered to an organization or part of an organization. The main takeaway of this approach is that the highest priority is the value your software gives to the target organization. Moreover, you are not just offering working code and an agreement to fix bugs but also a solution for all the needs that your software was conceived for. In other words, your job includes everything it needs to satisfy those needs, such as monitoring users' satisfaction and quickly adapting the software when the user needs change, due to issues or new requirements.

Service design thinking is strictly tied to the **Software as a Service** (**SaaS**) model, which is discussed in *Chapter 10, Deciding on the Best Cloud-Based Solution*. In fact, the simplest way to offer solutions based on web services is to offer the usage of web services as a service, instead of selling the software that implements them.

Continuous Integration (**CI**) and **Continuous Delivery** (**CD**) are sometimes stated as prerequisites for DevOps. So, the purpose of this chapter is also to discuss how to enable CI/CD in a real scenario, considering the challenges that you, as a software architect, will need to deal with.

The following topics will be covered in this chapter:

- Understanding DevOps principles: CI, CD, and continuous feedback
- Understanding how to implement DevOps using Azure DevOps and GitHub
- Understanding the risks and challenges when using CI/CD

The `WWTravelClub` project case, presented in *Chapter 21, Case Study*, will be discussed during these topics, giving you the opportunity to understand how the DevOps philosophy can be implemented. All the screenshots exemplifying the DevOps principles come from the main use case of the book, so you will be able to understand the DevOps principles easily.

By the end of this chapter, you will be able to design software according to service design thinking principles and use Azure Pipelines to deploy your application. You will be able to decide whether to use CI/CD in your project environment. Additionally, you will be able to define the tools needed for the successful use of this approach.

Technical requirements

This chapter requires Visual Studio 2022 Community Edition or better, with all the Azure tools installed. You may also need an Azure DevOps account, as described in *Chapter 3, Managing Requirements*. It requires a free Azure account too. If you have not already created one, the *Creating an Azure account* subsection of *Chapter 1, Understanding the Importance of Software Architecture*, explains how to do so. This chapter uses the same code as *Chapter 9, Testing Your Enterprise Application*.

Describing DevOps

DevOps is a term that is derived from the combination of the words *Development* and *Operations*, and the DevOps process simply unifies actions in these two areas. However, when you start to study a little bit more about it, you will realize that just connecting these two areas is not enough to achieve the true goals of this philosophy.

We can also say that DevOps is the process that answers the current needs of people, regarding software delivery.

Donovan Brown has a spectacular definition of what DevOps is: *DevOps is the union of people, process, and products to enable continuous delivery of value to our end users* (`http://donovanbrown.com/post/what-is-devops`).

A way to deliver value continuously to our end users, using processes, people, and products: this is the best description of the DevOps philosophy. We need to develop and deliver customer-oriented software. As soon as all areas of a company understand that the key point is the end user, your task as a software architect is to present the technology that will facilitate the process of delivery.

All the content in this book is connected to this approach. It is never a matter of knowing a bunch of tools and technologies. As a software architect, you must understand that there is always a way to bring faster solutions to your end user easily, linked to their real needs. For this reason, you need to learn the DevOps principles, which will be discussed in this chapter.

Understanding DevOps principles

Considering DevOps as a philosophy, there are some principles that enable the process to work well in your team. These principles are **CI**, **CD**, and **continuous feedback**.

Microsoft has a specific web page for defining the DevOps overview, culture, practices, tools, and its relation to the cloud. Please check this out at `https://azure.microsoft.com/en-us/overview/what-is-devops/`.

DevOps is represented by the symbol of infinity in many books and technical articles. This represents the necessity for a continuous approach in the software development life cycle. During the cycle, you will need to plan, build, continuously integrate, deploy, operate, and get feedback, and then start all over again. The process must be a collaborative one since everybody has the same focus—to deliver value to the end user. Together with these principles, you "as a software architect" will need to decide on the best software development process that fits this approach. We discussed these processes in *Chapter 1, Understanding the Importance of Software Architecture*.

CI

When you start building enterprise solutions, collaboration is the key to getting things done faster and meeting the users' needs. Version control systems, as we discussed in *Chapter 4, Best Practices in Coding C# 12*, are essential for this process, but these tools do not do the job by themselves, especially if they are not well configured.

As a software architect, you must know that **CI** will help you to adopt a concrete approach to software development collaboration. When you implement it, as soon as a developer commits their code, the main code is automatically compiled and tested, according to unit and functional tests available in the project.

The good thing when you apply CI is that you can motivate developers to merge their changes as fast as they can to minimize merge conflicts. They can also share unit tests, which will improve the quality of software. This will make your master branch stable and safe after every commit from your team.

The key point of CI is the ability to identify problems faster. You will have this opportunity when you allow code to be tested and analyzed by others. The only thing the DevOps approach helps with is making sure this happens as quickly as possible.

CD

Once every single commit of your application is built and this code is tested with both unit tests and functional tests, you may also want to enable **CD**. Doing this is not just a matter of configuring the tool. As a software architect, you need to be sure that the team and the process are ready to go to this step.

The CD approach needs to guarantee that the production environment will be kept safe in each new deployment. To do so, a multi-stage pipeline is a great practice to be adopted.

The following screenshot shows an approach with common stages, using this book's use case, **WWTravelClub**, as a demonstration:

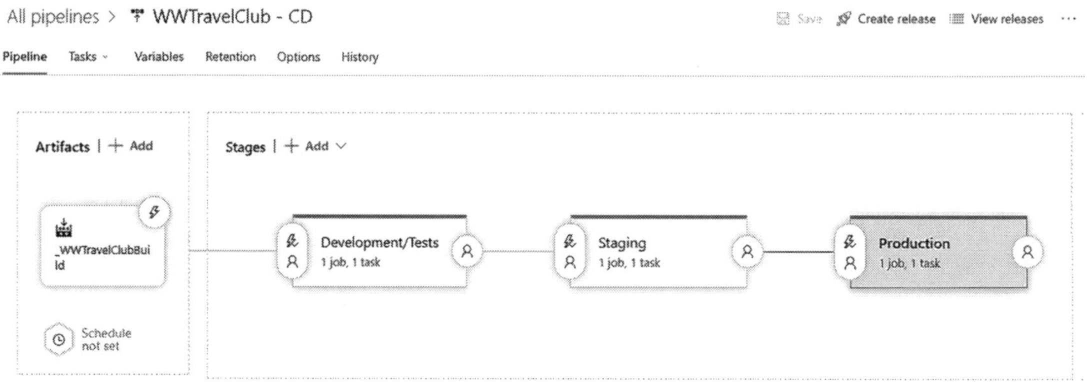

Figure 8.1: Release stages using Azure DevOps

As you can see, these stages were configured using the Azure DevOps release pipeline, which will be explained soon. Each stage has its own purpose, which will affect the quality of the product ultimately delivered. Let's look at the stages:

- **Development/tests:** This stage is used by developers and testers to build new functionality. This environment will certainly be the one that is most exposed to bugs and incomplete functions.
- **Staging:** This environment gives a brief version of new functionalities to areas of the team not related to development and tests. Program managers, marketing, vendors, and others can use it as an area of study, validation, and even preproduction. Additionally, quality assurance teams can guarantee that the new releases are correctly deployed, considering both functionality and infrastructure.
- **Production:** This is the stage where customers have their solution running. The goal for a good production environment, according to CD, is to have it updated as quickly as possible. The frequency will vary according to team size, but there are some approaches where this process happens more than once a day.

The adoption of these three stages of deploying your application will positively impact the quality of the solution. It will also enable the team to have a safer deployment process, with fewer risks and better product stability. This approach may look a bit expensive at first sight, but without it, the results of bad deployment will generally be more expensive than this investment.

Risks and challenges when using CI/CD

Now that we have an idea of how useful CI/CD is, it would be nice to think about the risks and challenges you may encounter while implementing it. The goal of this section is to help you, as a software architect, mitigate the risks and find a better way to overcome the challenges, using good processes and techniques.

The list of risks and challenges that will be discussed in this section are as follows:

- Continuous production deployment
- Incomplete features in production
- Unstable solutions for testing

Once you have the techniques and the processes defined to deal with them, there is no reason not to use CI/CD.

Remember that DevOps does not depend on CI/CD. You can use a process where code integration and software deployment are human-based. However, CI/CD does make DevOps work more smoothly.

Now, let us have a look at them.

Disabling continuous production deployment

Continuous production deployment is a process where, after a commit of a new piece of code and some pipeline steps, you will have this code in the **production** environment. This is not impossible, but it is hard and expensive to do. Besides, you need to have well-established, sophisticated processes, as well as a team with substantial experience and expertise to enable it. The problem is that most of the demos and samples you will find on the internet presenting CI/CD will show you a fast track to deploying code. The demonstrations of CI/CD make it look so simple! This *simplicity* might suggest that you should implement it as soon as possible. However, if you think a little more, this scenario can be dangerous if you deploy directly into production! In a solution that needs to be available 24 hours a day, 7 days a week, this is impractical. So you will need to worry about that and think of different solutions.

The first one is the use of a multi-stage scenario, as we described before. The multi-stage scenario can bring more security to the ecosystem of the deployment you are building. Besides, you will get more options to avoid incorrect deployments into production, such as pre-deployment approvals,

You can build a deployment pipeline where all your code and software structure will be updated by this tool. However, if you have something outside of this scenario, such as database scripts and environment configurations, an incorrect publication into production may cause damage to end users. Besides, the decision of when the production environment will be updated needs to be planned, and in many scenarios, all the platform users need to be notified of the upcoming change. It is worth mentioning that, in these hard-to-decide cases, it is a good idea to use a **change management** procedure, based on the **Information Technology Infrastructure Library** (**ITIL**) or ISO 20000.

So the challenge of delivering code to production will make you think about a schedule to do so. It does not matter whether your cycle is monthly, daily, or even at each commit. The key point here is that you need to create a process and a pipeline that guarantees that only good and approved software is at the production stage. It is worth noting, however, that the longer you leave deployments, the scarier they are, as the deviation between the previously deployed version and the new one will be greater, and more changes will be pushed out in one go. The more frequently you can deploy, the better.

Incomplete features

While a developer of your team is creating a new feature or fixing a bug, you will probably consider generating a branch, which means they can avoid the use of the branch designed for CD. A branch can be considered a feature available in code repositories to enable the creation of an independent line of development, since it isolates code.

As you can see in the following screenshot, creating a branch for **wwtravelclub** using Visual Studio is quite simple:

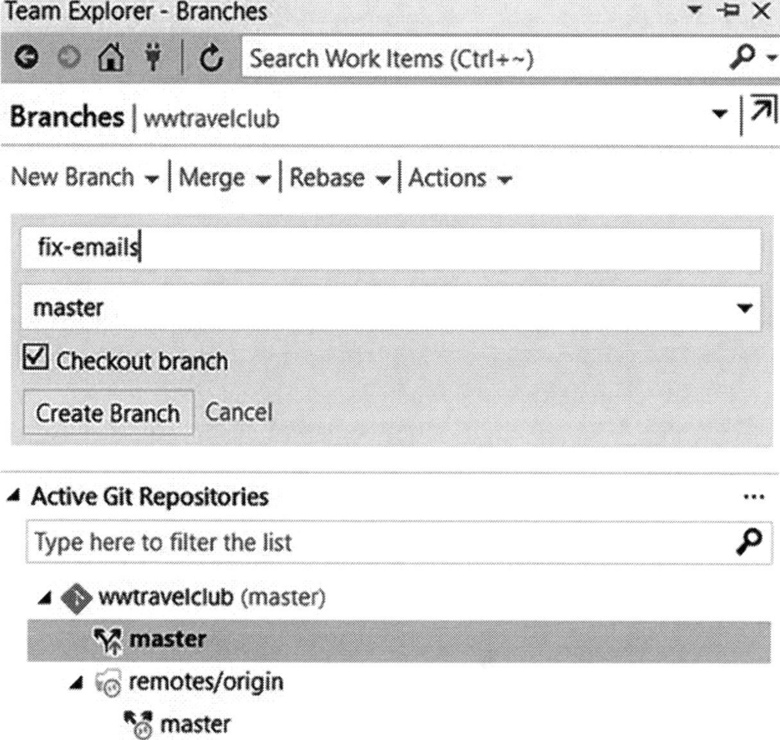

Figure 8.2: Creating a branch in Visual Studio

This seems to be a good approach, but let us suppose that the developer has considered the implementation ready for deployment and has just merged the code into the master branch, although this is also considered a bad practice. What if this feature is not ready yet, just because a requirement was omitted? What if the bug has caused incorrect behavior? The result could be a release with an incomplete feature or an incorrect fix.

One of the good practices to avoid broken features and even incorrect fixes in the master branch is the use of **Pull Requests** (**PRs**). PRs will let other team developers know that the code you developed is ready to be merged. The following screenshot shows how you can use the Azure DevOps WWTravelClub repository to create a **New pull request** for a change you have made.

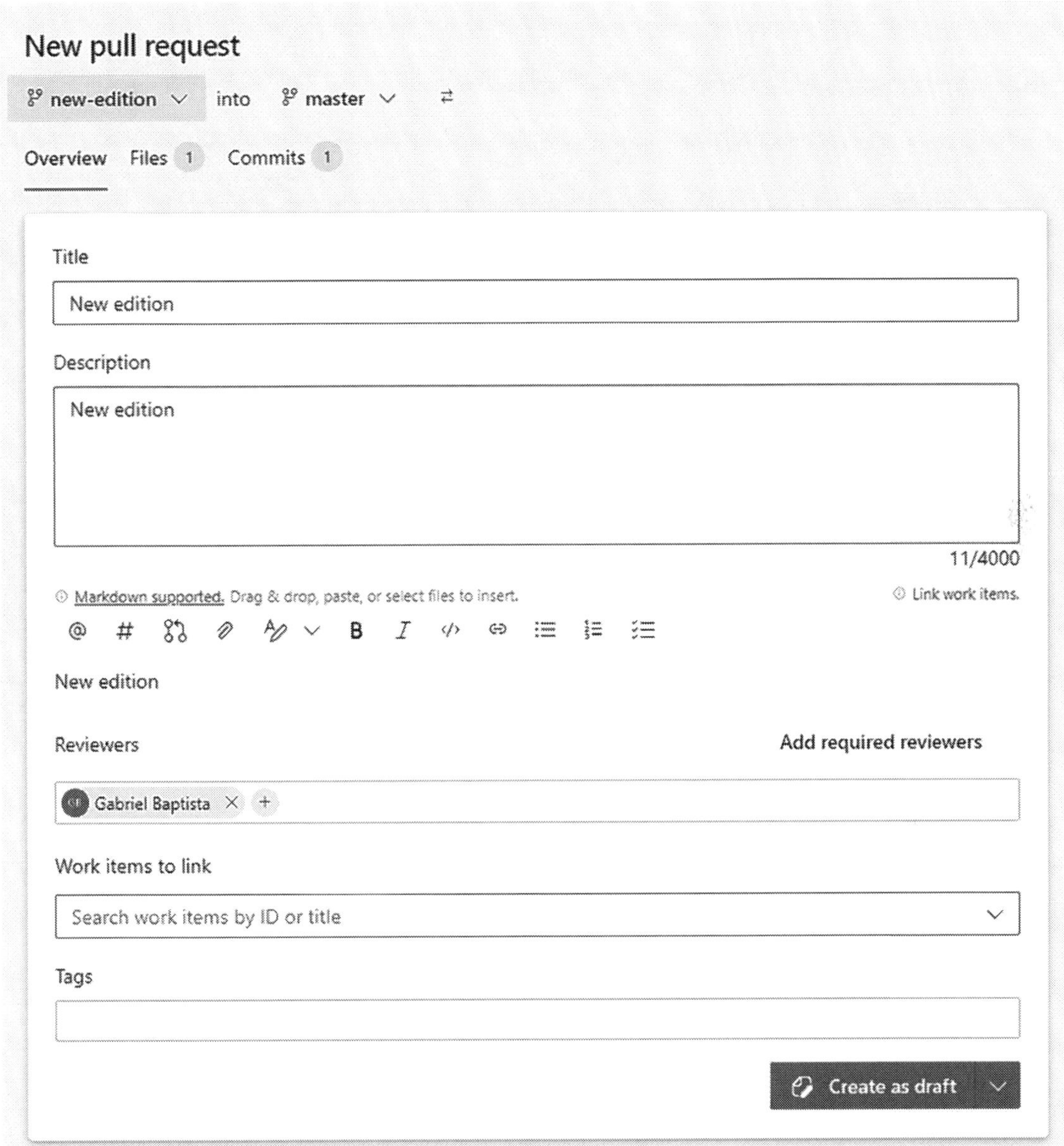

Figure 8.3: Creating a PR

Once the PR is created and the reviewers are defined, each reviewer will be able to analyze the code and decide whether it is healthy enough to be in the master branch.

The following screenshot shows a way to check the code, by using the compare tool to analyze the change in the **WWTravelClub** code:

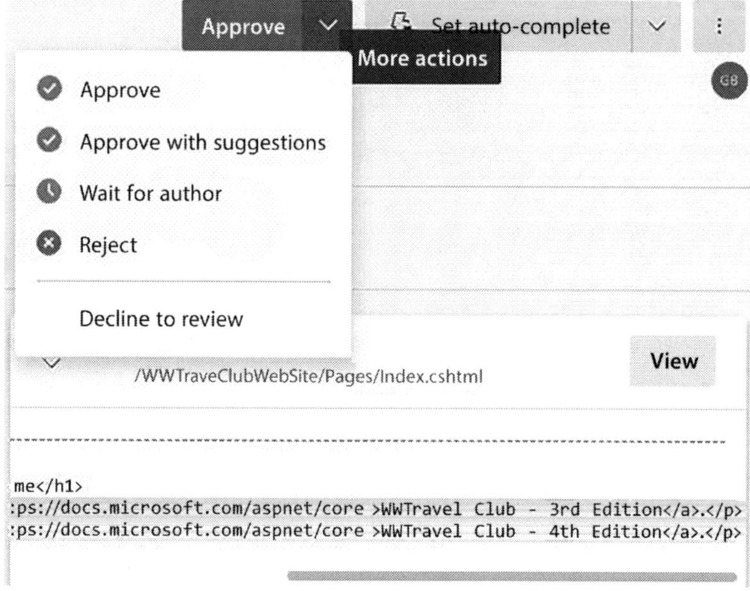

Figure 8.4: Analyzing the PR

Once all approvals are done, you will be able to safely merge the code to the master branch, as you can see in the following screenshot. To merge the code, you will need to click on **Complete merge**. It is important to mention that you can also do this in Visual Studio, which has a better user interface. If the CI trigger is enabled in the WWTravelClub project, as we will show in this chapter, Azure DevOps will start a build pipeline:

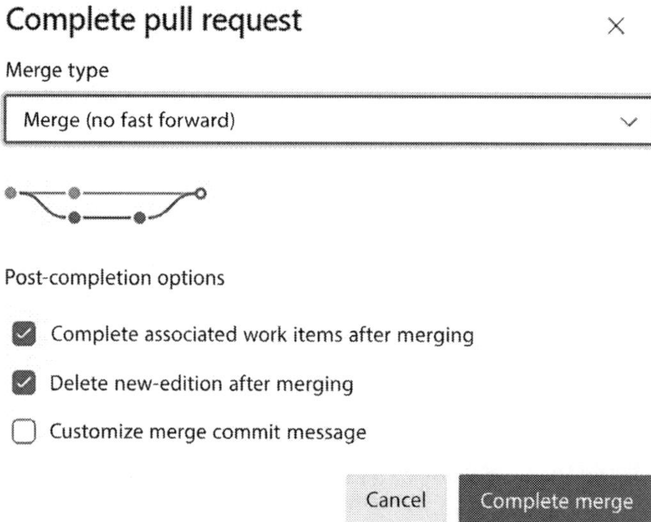

Figure 8.5: Merging the PR

Without a process like this, there is a great chance of having a master branch with a lot of bad code, and this code being deployed there may cause damage together with CD. A code review is an excellent practice in CI/CD scenarios, and it is considered a wonderful practice to create good quality software in general.

The challenge that you need to focus on here is guaranteeing that only entire features will appear to your end users. You can use the **feature flag** principle to solve this, which is a technique that makes sure only features that are ready are presented to end users.

In the **Feature Flag** or **Feature Toggle** technique, you must create a solution that has, in each feature, the possibility to test it in a setup to see whether it is enabled or not. According to this, all the functionalities will be presented to the user.

It is worth mentioning that to control feature availability in an environment, feature flags are much safer than using branching/PRs. Both have their place, but PRs are about controlling the quality of code at the CI stage, and feature flags are for controlling feature availability at the CD stage.

Again, we are not talking about CI/CD as a *tool* but as a *process*, to be defined and used every single time you need to deliver code for production.

An unstable solution for testing

If you have already mitigated the two other risks presented in this section, you may find it uncommon to have bad code after CI/CD. It is true that the worries presented earlier will certainly reduce if you work with a multi-stage scenario and PRs before pushing to the final stage. But the risk of having unstable code, especially when it comes to business logic rules, remains even if you apply all the recommendations we will discuss later.

But is there a way to accelerate the evaluation of a release while being sure that this new release is ready for your stakeholders' tests? Yes, there is! Technically, the way you can do so is by automating unit and functional testing. This technique is explained in more detail in *Chapter 9*, *Testing Your Enterprise Application*.

However, it is worth saying that it is impracticable to automate every single part of a piece of software, considering the efforts needed to do so. Besides, the maintenance of automation can be more expensive in scenarios where the user interface or the business rules change a lot. Although this is a tough decision, as a software architect, you must always incentivize the usage of automated testing.

To exemplify it, let us have a look at the following screenshot, which shows the unit and functional test samples for WWTravelClub, created by an Azure DevOps project template:

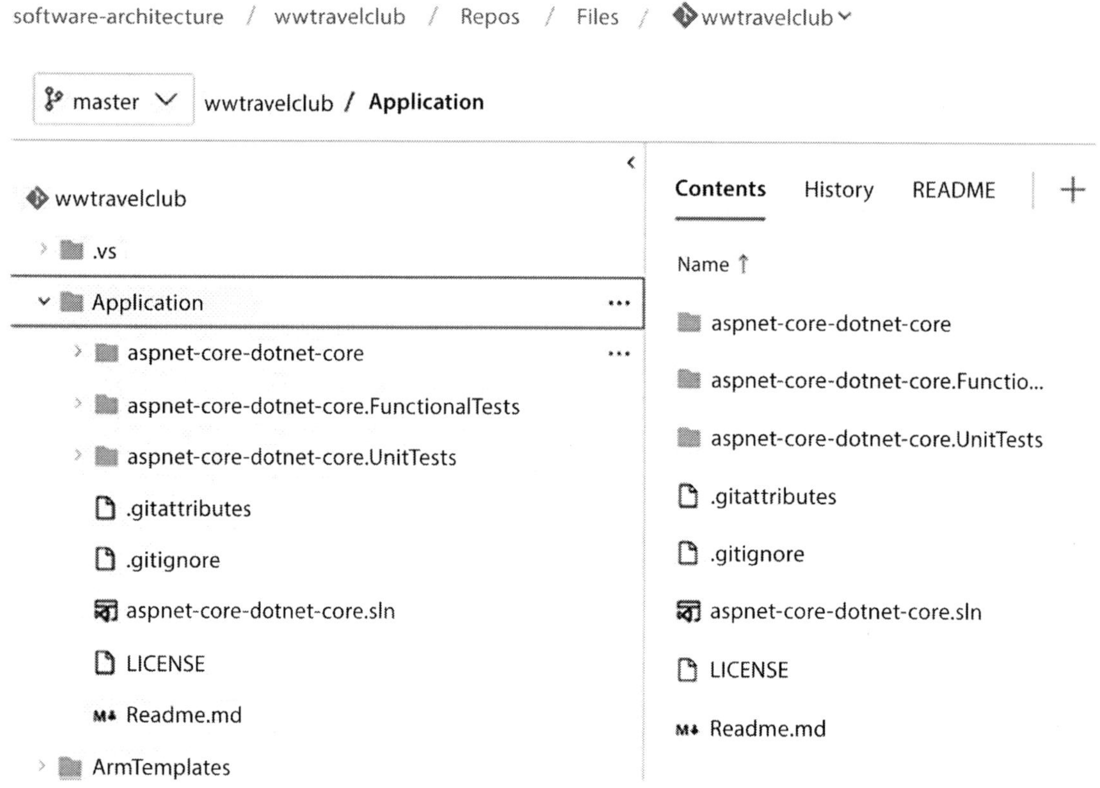

Figure 8.6: Unit and functional tests projects

There are some architectural patterns, such as SOLID, presented in *Chapter 6*, and quality assurance approaches, such as peer review, that will give you better results than software testing. However, these approaches do not invalidate automation practice. The truth is that all of them will be useful for getting a stable solution, especially when you run a CI scenario. In this environment, the best thing you can do is to detect errors and incorrect behaviors as fast as you can. Both unit and functional tests, as shown earlier, will help you with this.

Unit tests will help you a lot in discovering business logic errors before deployment, during the build pipeline. For instance, in the following screenshot from the WWTravelClub build process, you will find a simulated error that canceled the build, since the unit test did not pass:

Certain free services on Azure may be deactivated due to the possibility of misuse. However, you have the option to request the reactivation of these services by submitting a request.

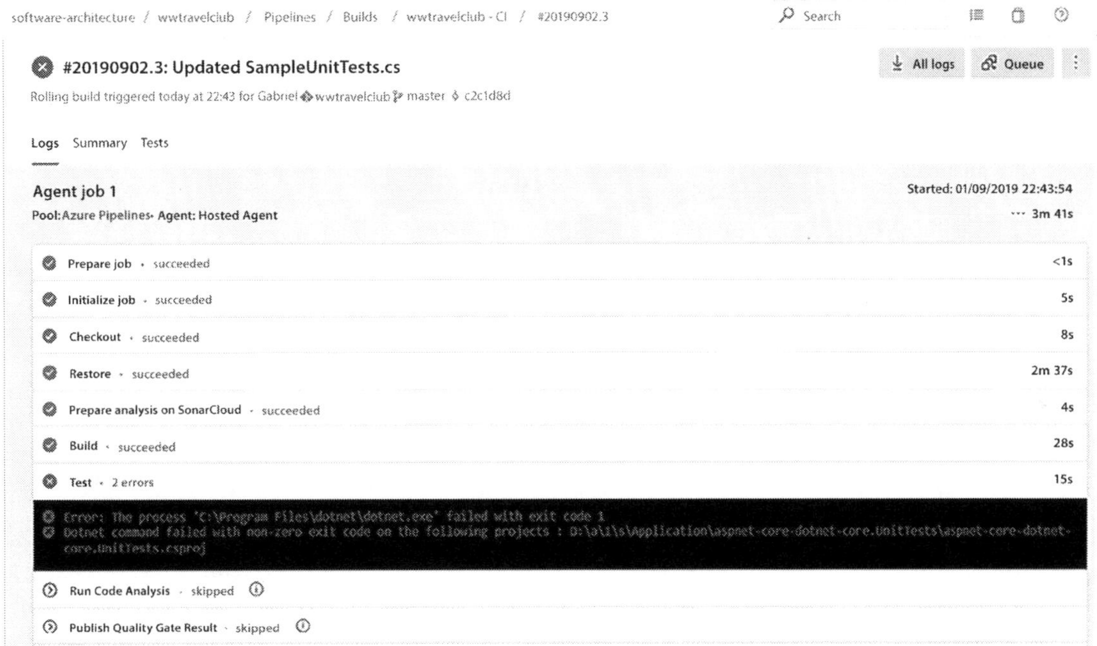

Figure 8.7: Unit test result

The way to get this error is quite simple. You need to code something that does not respond according to what the unit tests are checking. Once you commit it, assuming you have the trigger for CD on, you will build the code in the pipeline. So after the build of the code, the unit tests will run. If the code does not match the tests anymore, you will get an error.

The following screenshot shows an error during the functional tests in the **Development/Tests** stage of the WWTravelClub project. In this instance, the **Development/Tests** environment has a bug that was rapidly detected by functional tests:

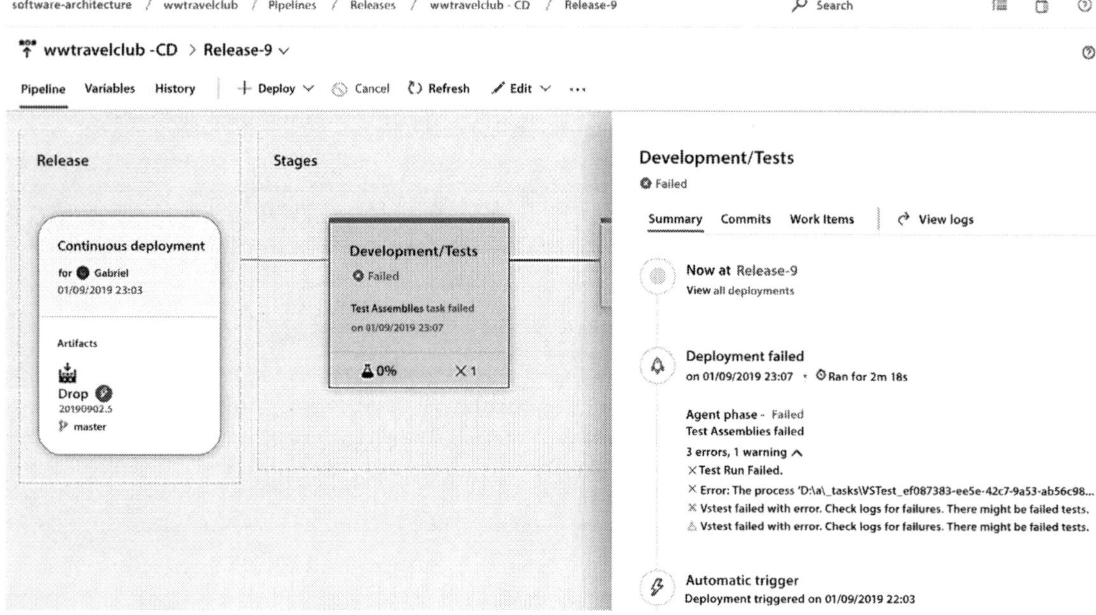

Figure 8.8: Functional test result

But this is not the only good thing about applying functional tests during CI/CD. Let us look at the following screenshot from the **Releases** pipeline interface in Azure DevOps. If you look at **Release-9**, you will realize that, since this error happened after the publication in the **Development/Tests** environment, the multi-stage environment will protect the other stages of the wrong deployment, especially the WWTravelClub production stage:

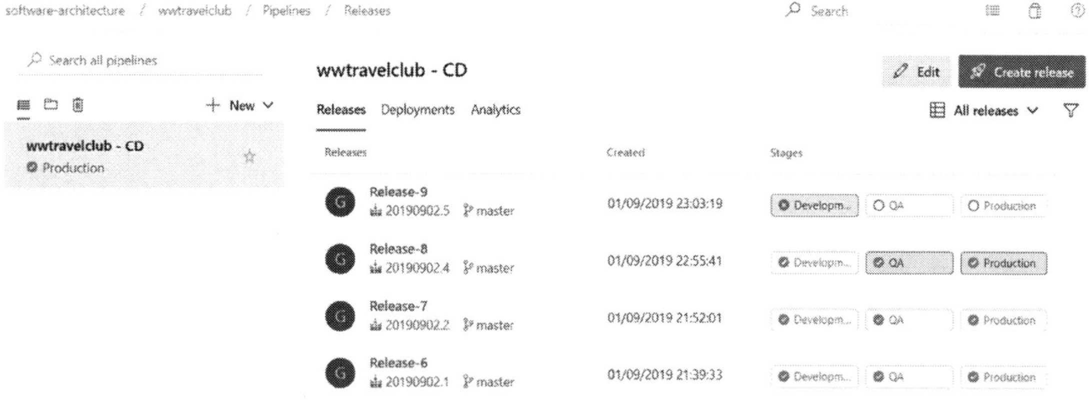

Figure 8.9: Multi-stage environment protection

The key point for success in the CI process is to think about it as a useful tool to accelerate the delivery of software and to not forget that a team always needs to deliver value to its end users. With this approach, the techniques presented earlier will provide incredible ways to achieve the results that your team aims for.

Continuous feedback

Once you have a solution that runs perfectly in the deployment scenario described in the previous section, feedback will be essential for your team to understand the results of the release and how the version works for customers. To get this feedback, there are some tools that can help both developers and customers, bringing them together to fast-track the process of feedback.

The main purpose of continuous feedback is to enable developers to get information about the application running in production, enabling the team to improve the infrastructure of the environment deployed and, at the same time, detect improvements that can be made in the source code and user interface.

Tools to facilitate DevOps implementation

Considering that DevOps is a philosophy, there are many tools that can be used to help you with its implementation. The following topics will present some of the most-used ones in a Microsoft environment.

Azure DevOps

As soon as you start working with a platform such as Azure DevOps, enabling CI/CD will be easy when it comes to clicking on the options to do so. So technology is not the Achilles' heel for implementing this process.

The following screenshot shows an example of how easy it is to turn on CI/CD using the Azure DevOps WWTravelClub pipeline. By clicking in the **Pipelines** and editing it, you will be able to set a trigger that enables CI/CD after some clicks:

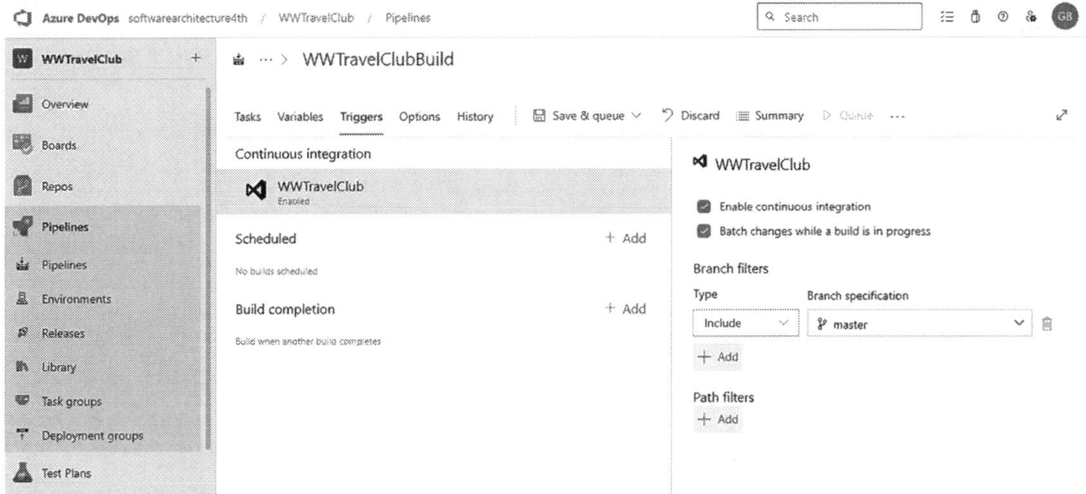

Figure 8.10: Enabling the CI trigger

CI/CD will help you solve some problems. For instance, it will force you to test your code, since you will need to commit the changes faster so that other developers can make use of the code you are programming.

Conversely, you will not do CI/CD just by enabling a CI build in Azure DevOps. For sure, you will turn on the possibility of starting a build as soon as you get a commit done and the code is complete, but this is far from saying you have CI/CD available in your solution.

The reason you, as a software architect, need to worry a bit more about it is related to a real understanding of what DevOps is. The need to deliver value to the end user will always be a good way to decide how the development life cycle will work. So even if turning on CI/CD is easy, what is the real business impact of this feature being enabled for your end users? Once you have all the answers to this question and you know how to reduce the risks of its implementation, then you will be able to say that you have a CI/CD process implemented.

CI/CD is a principle that will make DevOps work better and faster. However, DevOps can live without it, if you are not sure if your process is mature enough to enable code to be continuously delivered.

Moreover, if you turn on CI/CD in a team that is not mature enough to deal with its complexity, you will probably cause a bad understanding of DevOps, since you will start incurring some risks while deploying your solution. The point is that CI/CD is not a prerequisite for DevOps.

When you have CI/CD enabled, you can make things faster in DevOps. However, you can practice DevOps without it.

Deployments and other release artifacts are added to different pipelines, called release pipelines, to decouple them from build-related artifacts. With Release Pipelines, you cannot edit a `.yaml` file, but you will work with a graphic interface, as follows:

1. Click the **Releases** left menu tab to create a new **Release Pipeline**. As soon as you click **Add a new pipeline**, you will be prompted to add the first task of the first pipeline stage. In fact, the whole release pipeline is composed of different stages, each grouping sequences of tasks. While each stage is just a sequence of tasks, the stages diagram can branch, and we can add several branches after each stage. This way, we can deploy to different platforms that each require different tasks. In our simple example, we will use a single stage.
2. Select the **Azure App Service Deployment** task. As soon as you add this task, you will be prompted to fill in the missing information.
3. Select your subscription, and then, if an **Authorization** button appears, click it to authorize Azure Pipelines to access your subscription. Then, select **Windows** as the deployment platform, and finally, select the app service you created from the **App service name** drop-down list. Task settings are automatically saved while you write them, so you just need to click the **Save** button for the whole pipeline.
4. Now, we need to connect this pipeline to a source artifact. Click the **Add Artifact** button and then select **Build** as the source type, because we need to connect the new release pipeline with the ZIP file created by our build pipeline. A settings window appears:

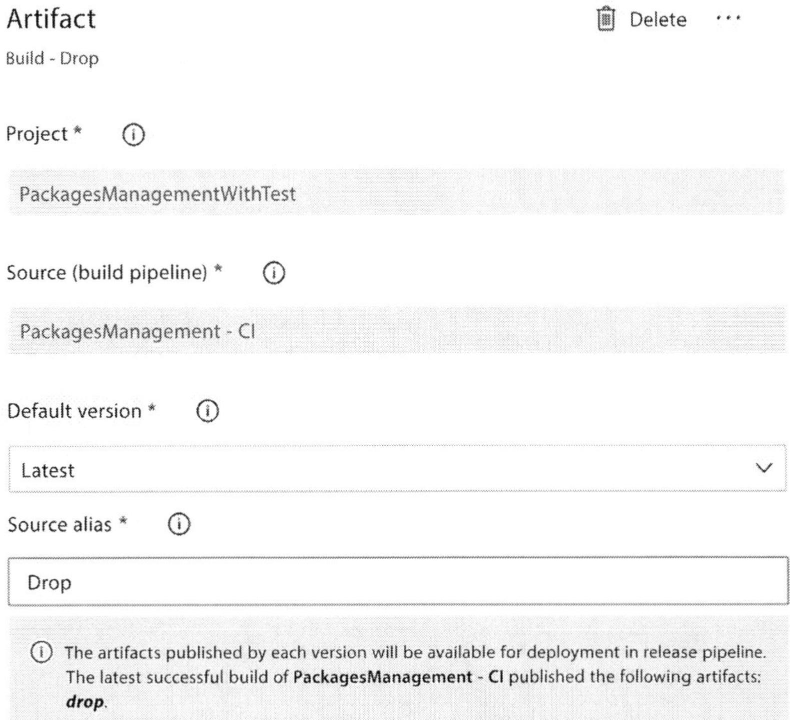

Figure 8.11: Defining the artifact to publish

5. Select our previous build pipeline from the drop-down list, and keep **Latest** as the version. Accept the suggested name under **Source alias.**
6. Our release pipeline is ready and can be used as-is. The image of the source artifact you just added contains a trigger icon in its top-right corner, as follows:

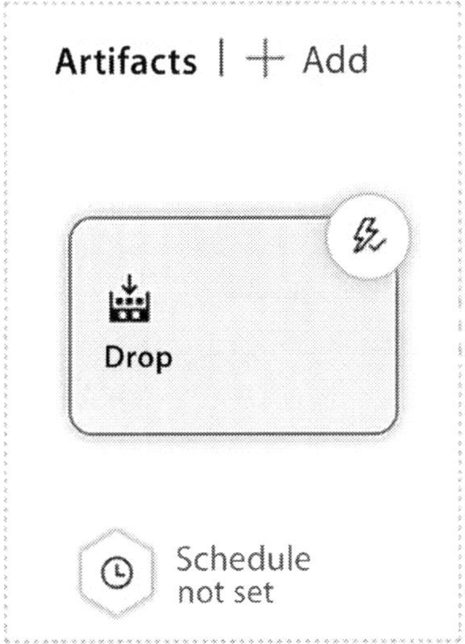

Figure 8.12: Artifact ready to publish

7. If you click on the trigger icon, you are given the option to automatically trigger the release pipeline as soon as a new build is available:

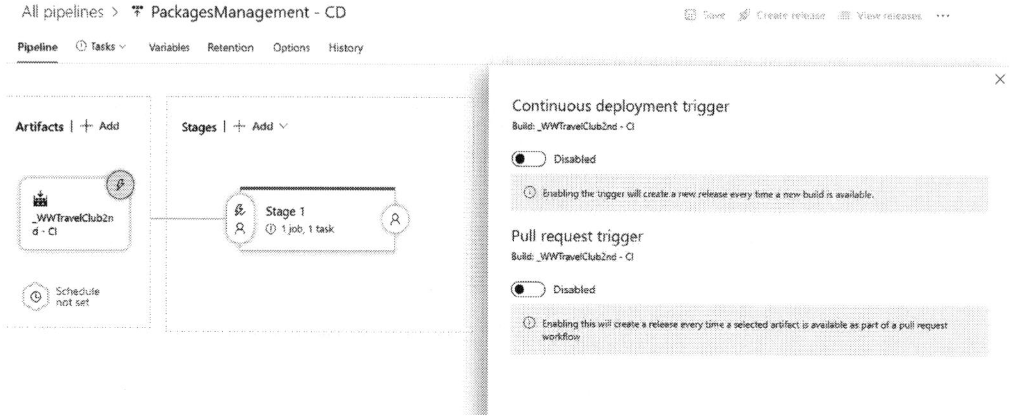

Figure 8.13: Enabling the continuous deployment trigger

8. Keep it disabled; we can enable it after we have completed and manually tested the release pipeline.

As we mentioned earlier, in preparation for an automatic trigger, we need to add a human approval task before the application is deployed. Let's add it with the following steps:

1. Click the three dots on the right of the **Stage 1** header:

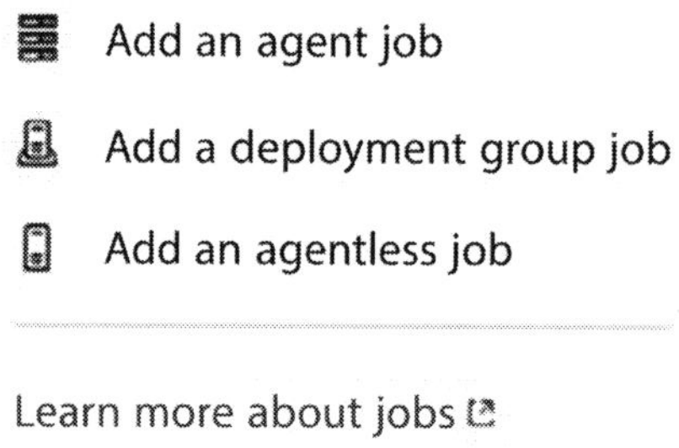

Add an agent job

Add a deployment group job

Add an agentless job

Learn more about jobs

Figure 8.14: Adding human approval to a stage

2. Then, select **Add an agentless job**. Once the agentless job has been added, click the **Add** button and add a **Manual intervention** task. The following screenshot shows the **Manual intervention** settings:

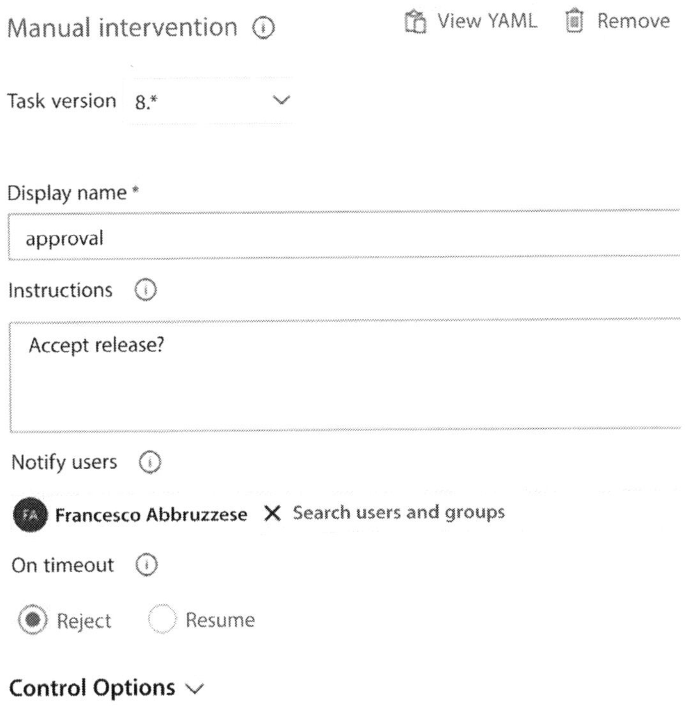

Manual intervention
View YAML
Remove
Task version
8.*
Display name *
approval
Instructions
Accept release?
Notify users
Francesco Abbruzzese
Search users and groups
On timeout
Reject
Resume
Control Options

Figure 8.15: Configuring human approval for a stage

Add instructions for the operator, and select your account in the **Notify users** field.

3. Now, drag the whole **Agentless job** with the mouse, and place it before the application deployment task. It should look like this:

Pipeline
Tasks
Variables
Retention
Options
History
Stage 1
Deployment process
Agentless job
Run on server
approval
Manual intervention
Run on agent
Run on agent
Deploy Azure App Service
Azure App Service deploy

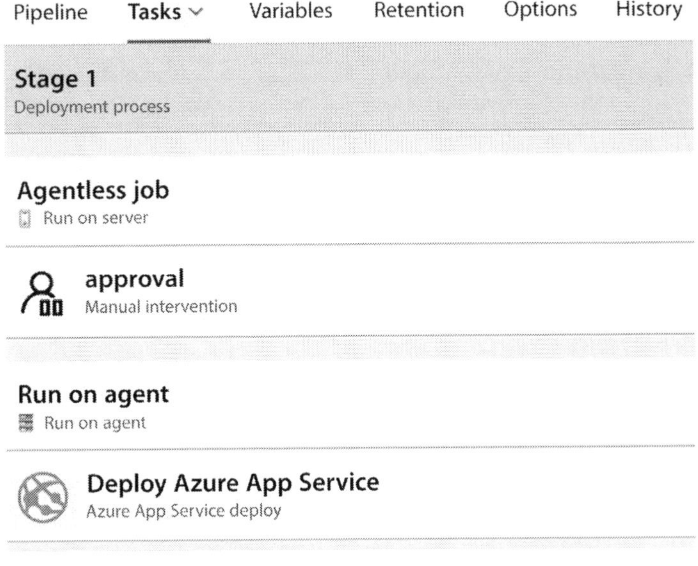

Figure 8.16: Setting the human approval deployment tasks list

4. Finished! Click the **Save** button in the top-left corner to save the pipeline.

Now, everything is ready to create our first automatic release. And to do so, a new release can be prepared and deployed as follows:

1. Click the **Create release** button to start the creation of a new release, as shown in the following screenshot:

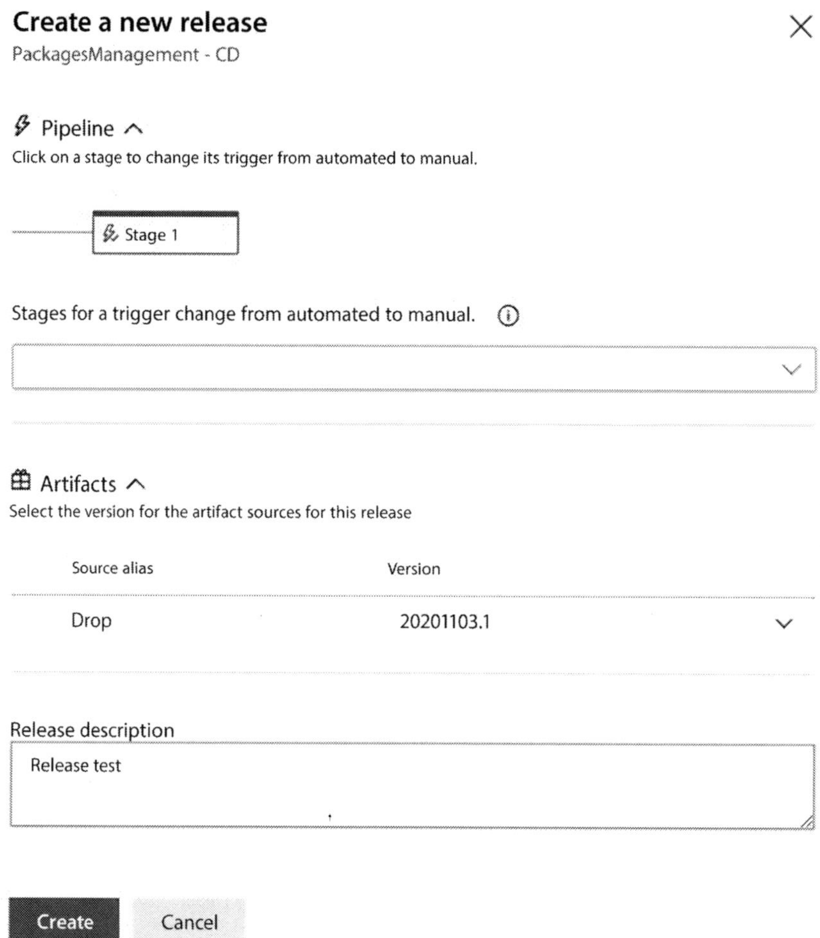

Figure 8.17: Creating a new release

2. Verify that the **Source alias** is the last available one, add a **Release description**, and then click **Create**. In a short time, you should receive an email for release approval. Click the link it contains and go to the approval page:

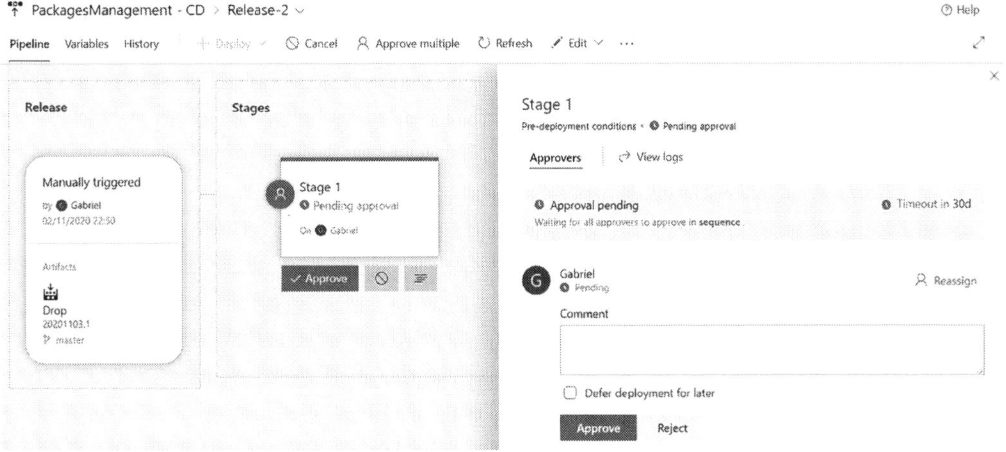

Figure 8.18: Approving a release

3. Click the **Approve** button to approve the release. Wait for the deployment to complete. You should have all the tasks successfully completed, as shown in the following screenshot:

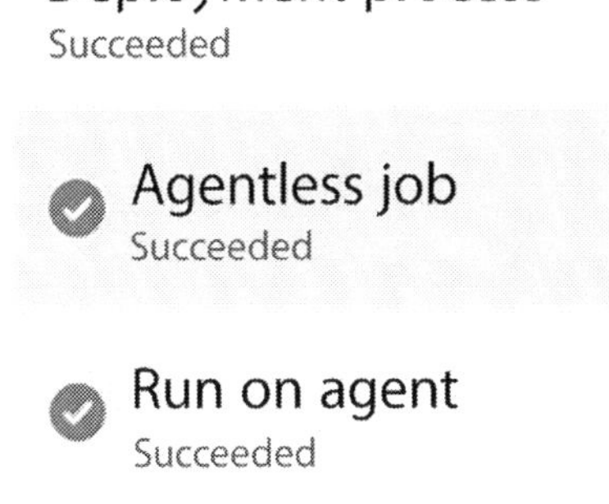

Figure 8.19: Release deployed

4. You have run your first successful release pipeline!

In a real-life project, the release pipeline would contain more tasks. In fact, applications (before being deployed in the actual production environment) are deployed in a **staging environment** where they are beta-tested. Hence, after this first deployment, there would probably be some manual tests, manual authorization for the deployment in production, and the final deployment in production.

Considering the multistage scenario, you can set up the pipeline in a way where only with defined authorizations will you be able to move from one stage to another:

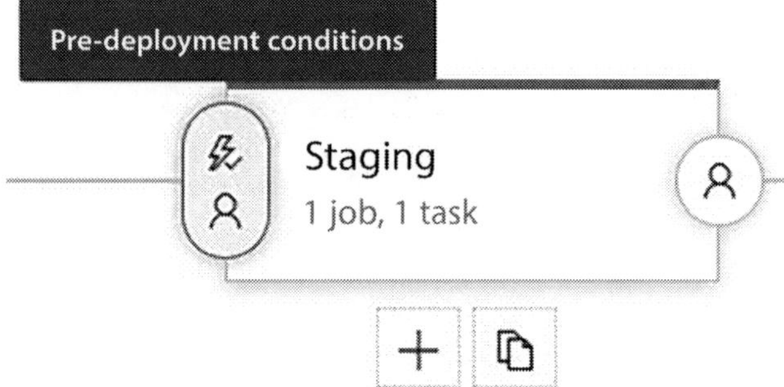

Figure 8.20: Defining pre-deployment conditions

As you can see in the preceding screenshot, it is quite simple to set up pre-deployment conditions, and there is more than a single option to customize the authorization method. This allows you to refine the CD approach, exactly meeting the needs of the project you are dealing with.

The following screenshot shows the options provided by Azure DevOps for pre-deployment approval. You can define the people who can approve the stage and set policies for them, that is, revalidate the approver identity before completing the process. You, as a software architect, will need to identify the configuration that fits the project you are creating with this approach:

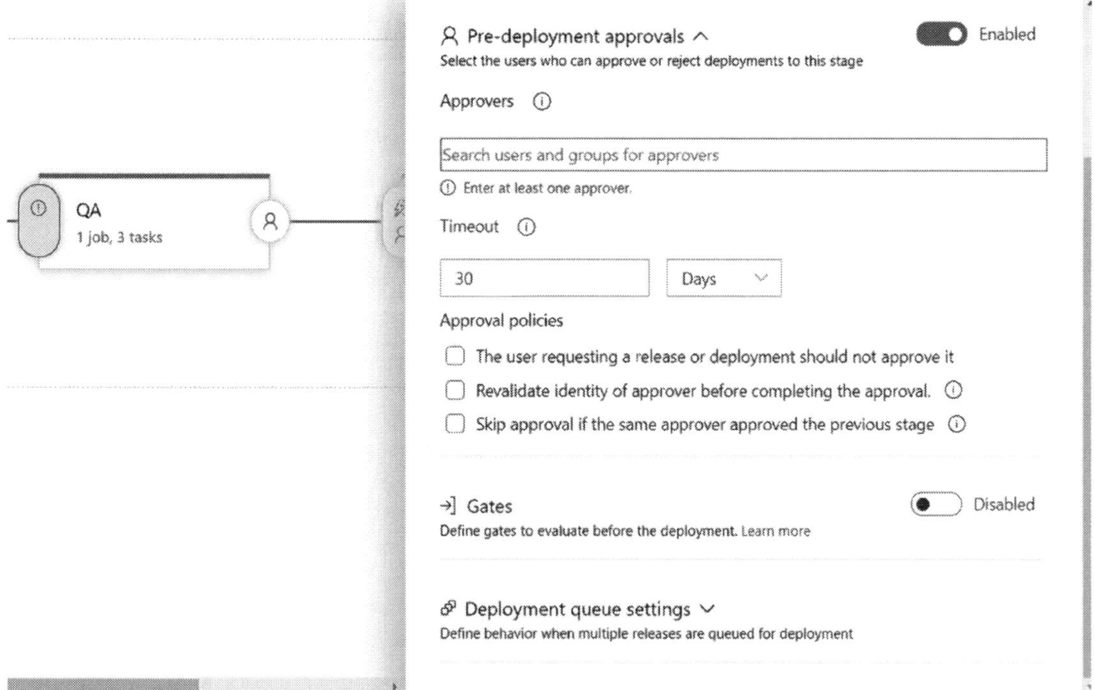

Figure 8.21: Pre-deployment approval options

It is worth mentioning that although this approach is far better than a single-stage deployment, a DevOps pipeline will direct you, as a software architect, to another stage of monitoring. App Insights, which will be presented later, is an incredible tool for this.

GitHub

Since GitHub's acquisition by Microsoft, many features have evolved and new options have been delivered, enhancing the power of this powerful tool. These integrations can be explored using the Azure portal and, particularly, GitHub Actions.

GitHub Actions is a set of tools that helps with the automation of software development. It enables a fast CI/CD service on any platform, using YAML files to define its workflows. You can consider GitHub Actions a new approach presented by Microsoft as a substitute for Azure DevOps Pipelines. You can automate any GitHub event using GitHub Actions, with thousands of actions available on GitHub Marketplace:

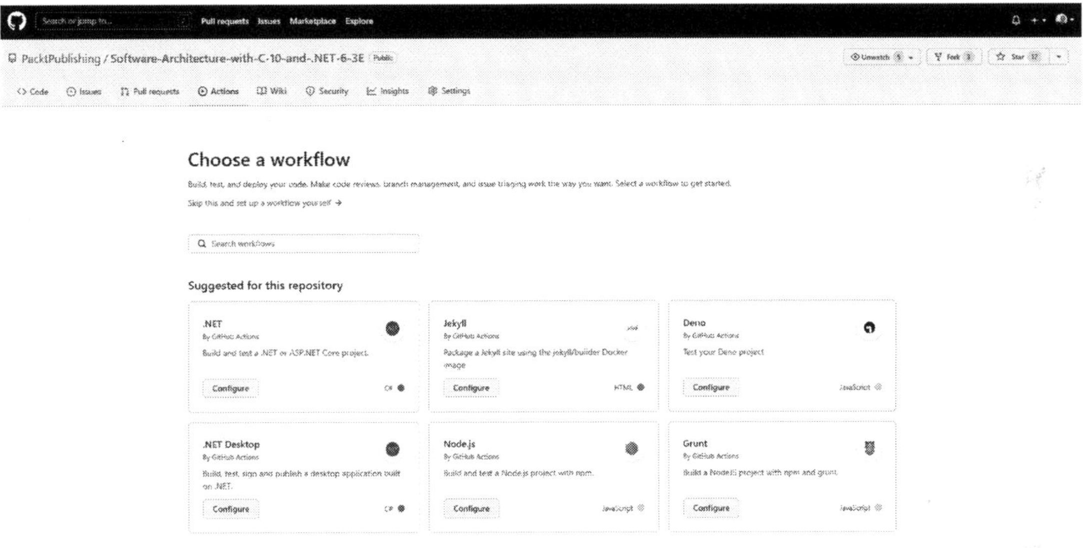

Figure 8.22: GitHub Actions

Creating a workflow to build a .NET web app is quite simple via the GitHub Actions interface. As you can see in the preceding screenshot, there are some workflows that have already been created to help us out.

The YAML we have below was generated by clicking the **Set up this workflow** option in the **Configure** options under **.NET**:

```
name: .NET
on:
  push:
    branches: [ main ]
  pull_request:
```

```
    branches: [ main ]
jobs:
  build:
    runs-on: ubuntu-latest
    steps:
    - uses: actions/checkout@v2
    - name: Setup .NET
      uses: actions/setup-dotnet@v1
      with:
        dotnet-version: 8.0.x
    - name: Restore dependencies
      run: dotnet restore
    - name: Build
      run: dotnet build --no-restore
    - name: Test
      run: dotnet test --no-build --verbosity normal
```

With the adaptations made below, it can build the application specifically created for this chapter:

```
name: .NET 8 Chapter 08
on:
  push:
    branches:
    - main
env:
  DOTNET_CORE_VERSION: 8.0.x
jobs:
  build:
    runs-on: ubuntu-latest
    steps:
      - uses: actions/checkout@v2
      - name: Setup .NET 8
        uses: actions/setup-dotnet@v1
        with:
          include-prerelease: True
          dotnet-version: ${{ env.DOTNET_CORE_VERSION }}
      - name: Install dependencies
        run: dotnet restore ./ch08
      - name: Build
        run: dotnet build ./ch08 --configuration Release --no-restore
      - name: Test
        run: dotnet test ./ch08 --no-restore --verbosity normal
```

As you can see below, once the script is updated, it is possible to check the result of the workflow. It is also possible to enable CD if you want to. It is just a matter of defining the correct script:

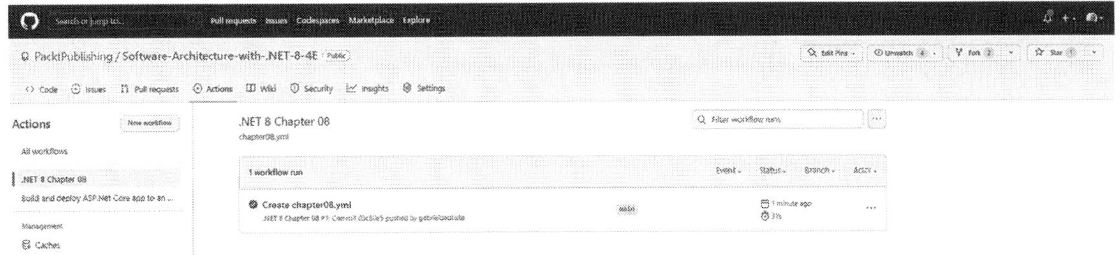

Figure 8.23: Simple application compilation using GitHub Actions

Microsoft provides documentation specifically covering Azure and GitHub integration. Check this out at `https://docs.microsoft.com/en-us/azure/developer/github`.

As a software architect, you need to understand which tool best fits your development team. Azure DevOps has a wonderful environment for enabling CI/CD, and so does GitHub. The key point here is that no matter the option you decide on, there are risks and challenges that you will face once CI/CD is enabled. Let's check them out in the next topic.

Application Insights

Application Insights is a feature that any software architect must have for continuous feedback on their solution. Application Insights is part of **Azure Monitor**, a wider suite of monitoring features that also includes alerting, dashboards, and workbooks. As soon as you connect your app to it, you start receiving feedback on each request made to the software. This enables you to monitor not only the requests made but also your database performance, the errors that the application may be suffering from, and the calls that take the most time to process.

Obviously, you will have costs relating to having this tool plugged into your environment, but the facilities that the tool provides will be worth it. It might be worth noting that, for simple applications, it could even be free because you pay for data ingested, for which there is a free quota. Aside from financial cost, you need to understand that there is a very small performance cost, since all the requests to store data in **Application Insights** run in a separate thread.

Several services, such as App Services, Functions, and so on, will give you the option to add Application Insights as part of the initial creation process, so you may have already created it while following along with this book.

The following screenshot shows how easily you can create a tool in your environment:

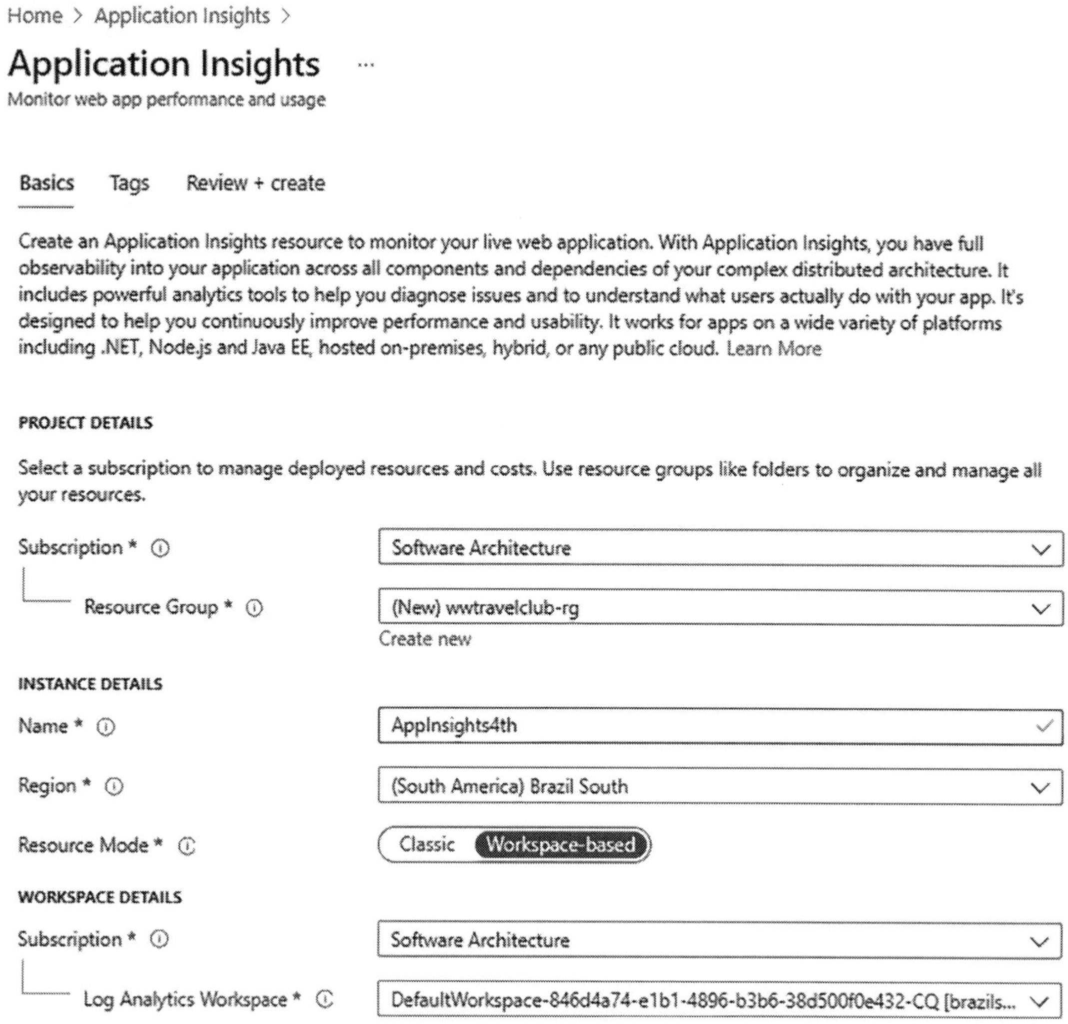

Home > Application Insights >

Application Insights ...

Monitor web app performance and usage

Basics Tags Review + create

Create an Application Insights resource to monitor your live web application. With Application Insights, you have full observability into your application across all components and dependencies of your complex distributed architecture. It includes powerful analytics tools to help you diagnose issues and to understand what users actually do with your app. It's designed to help you continuously improve performance and usability. It works for apps on a wide variety of platforms including .NET, Node.js and Java EE, hosted on-premises, hybrid, or any public cloud. Learn More

PROJECT DETAILS

Select a subscription to manage deployed resources and costs. Use resource groups like folders to organize and manage all your resources.

Subscription * ⓘ — Software Architecture

Resource Group * ⓘ — (New) wwtravelclub-rg

Create new

INSTANCE DETAILS

Name * ⓘ — AppInsights4th

Region * ⓘ — (South America) Brazil South

Resource Mode * ⓘ — Classic | Workspace-based

WORKSPACE DETAILS

Subscription * ⓘ — Software Architecture

Log Analytics Workspace * ⓘ — DefaultWorkspace-846d4a74-e1b1-4896-b3b6-38d500f0e432-CQ [brazils...

Figure 8.24: Creating Application Insights resources in Azure

For instance, let's suppose you need to analyze the requests that are taking more time in your application. The process of attaching Application Insights to your web app is quite simple: it can be done as soon as you set it up. If you are not sure whether Application Insights is configured for your web app, you can find out using the Azure portal. Navigate to **App Services** and look at the **Application Insights** settings, as shown in the following screenshot:

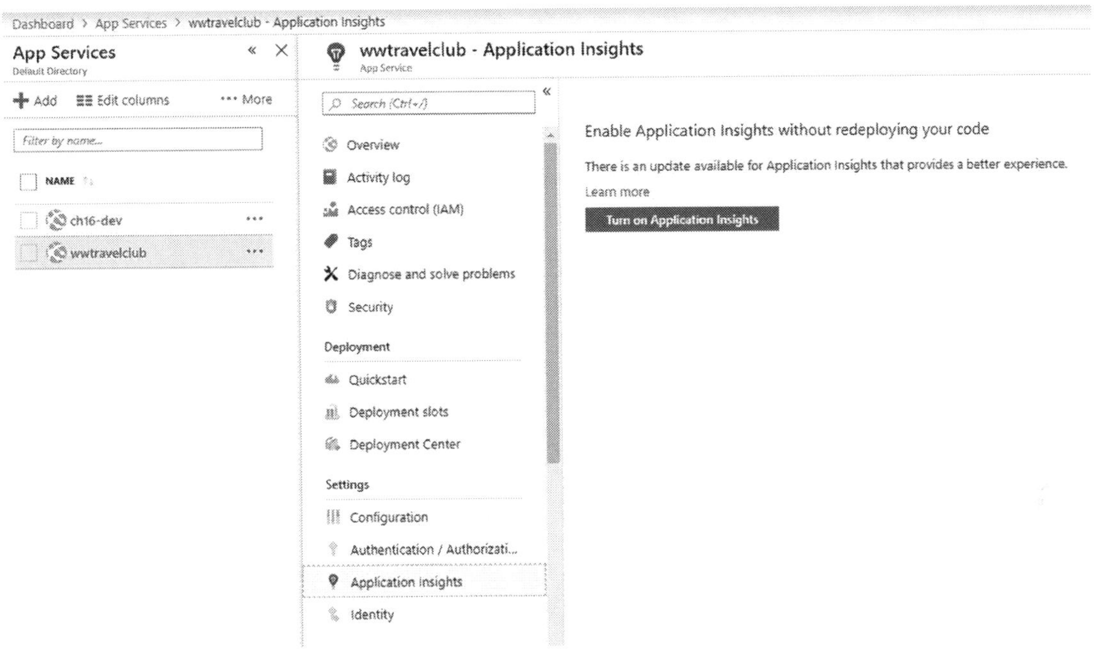

Figure 8.25: Enabling Application Insights in App Services

The interface will give you the opportunity to create or attach an already-created monitoring service to your web app. You can connect more than one web app to the same **Application Insights** component.

The following screenshot shows how to add a web app to an already-created **Application Insights** resource:

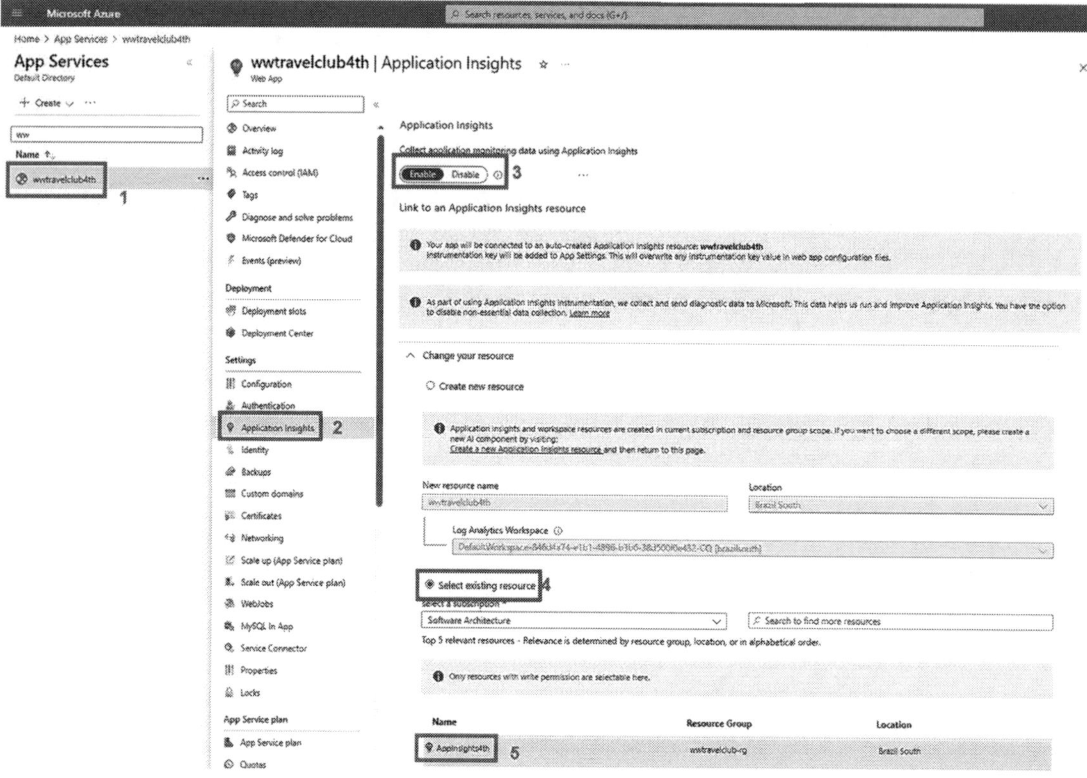

Figure 8.26: Enabling App Insights in App Services

Once you have Application Insights configured for your web app, you will see the following screen in App Services:

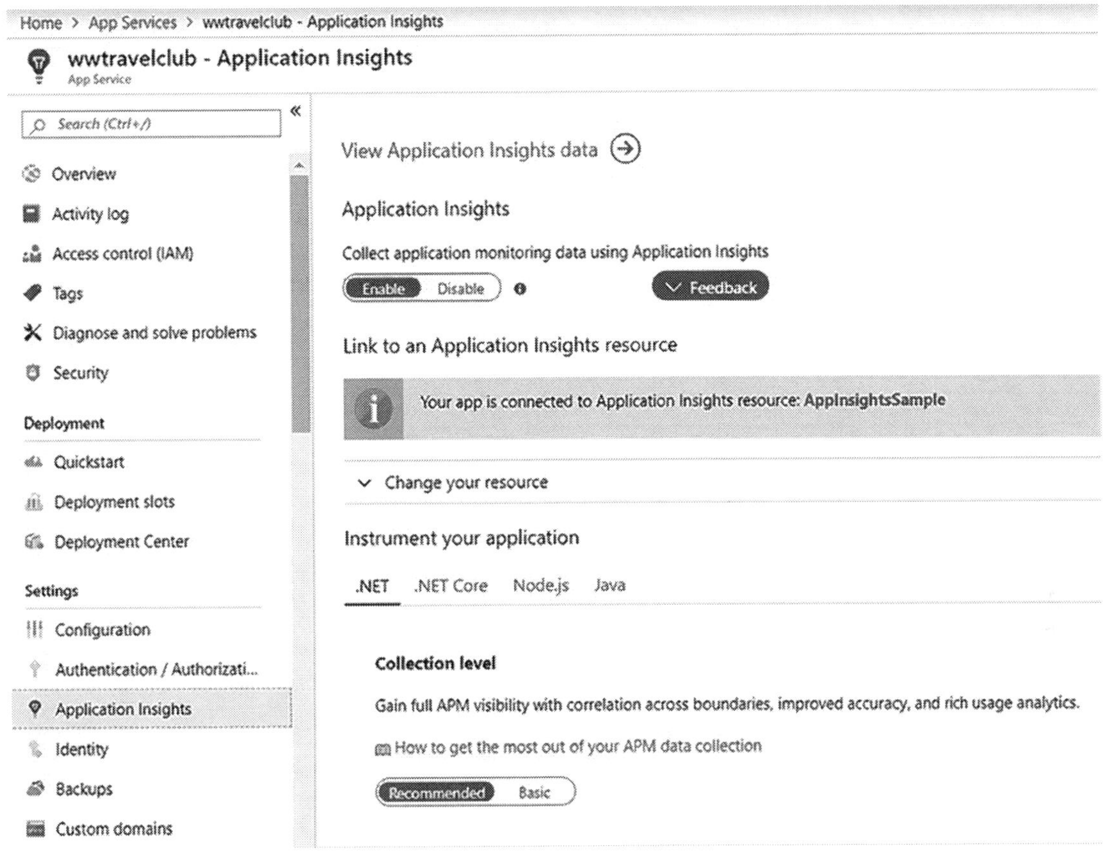

Figure 8.27: Application Insights in App Services

Once it is connected to your solution, the data collection will happen continuously, and you will see the results in the dashboard provided by the component. You can find this screen in two places:

- In the same place where you configured Application Insights, inside the web app portal
- In the Azure portal, after navigating through the Application Insights resource

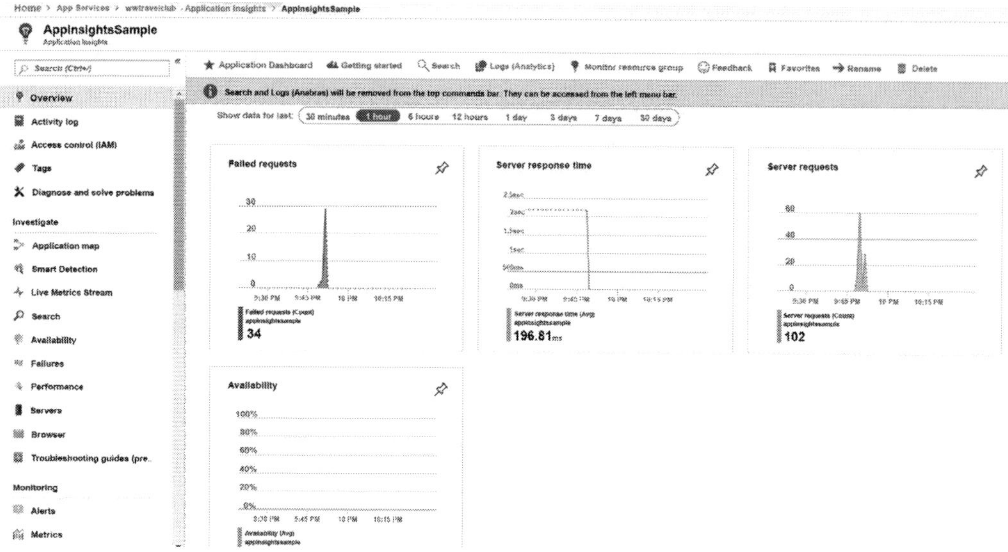

Figure 8.28: Application Insights in action

This dashboard gives you an idea of failed requests, server response time, and server requests. You can also turn on the availability check, which will make requests to your selected URL from any of the Azure data centers.

The beauty of Application Insights is in how deeply it analyzes your system. In the following screenshot, for instance, it gives you feedback on the number of requests made on the website. You can analyze this feedback by ranking the requests by the ones that took more time to process or the ones that were called more often.

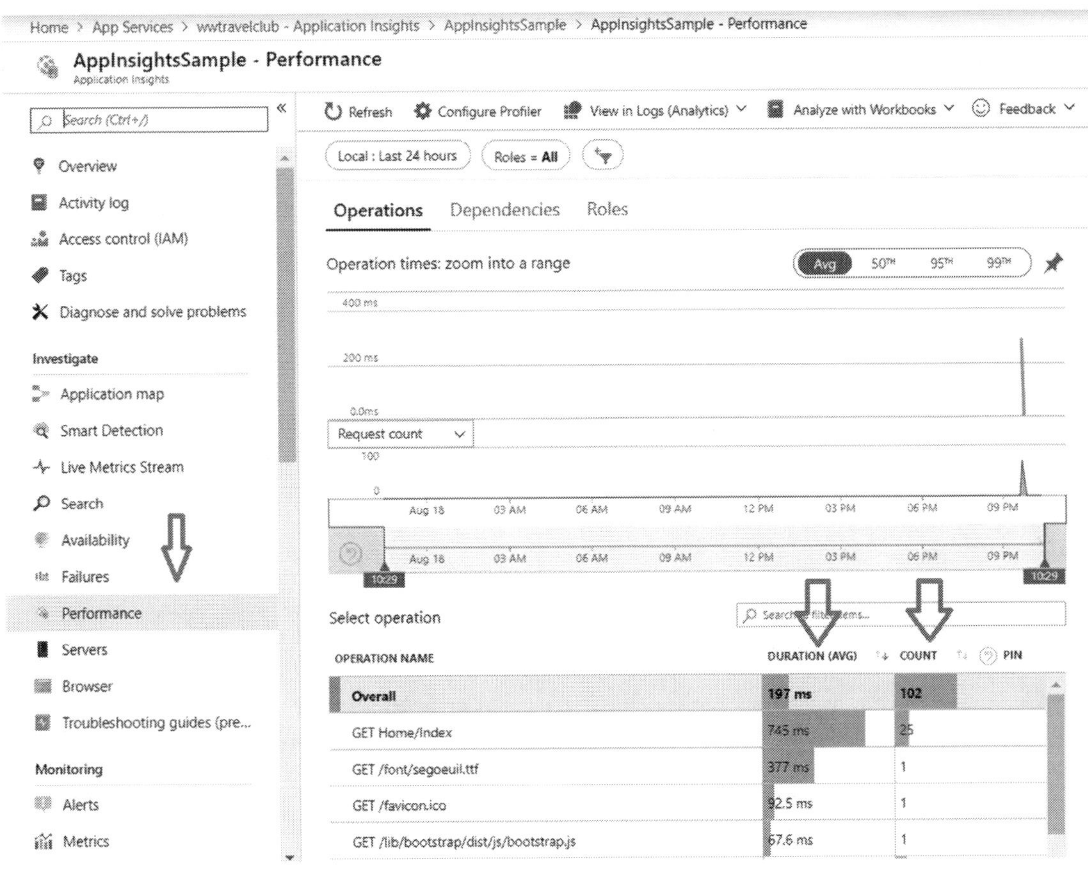

Figure 8.29: Analyzing app performance using Application Insights

Considering this view can be filtered in different ways and you receive the information just after it happens in your web app, this is certainly a tool that defines continuous feedback. This is one of the best ways you can use DevOps principles to achieve exactly what your customer needs.

Test and Feedback

Another useful tool in the process of continuous feedback is the **Test and Feedback** tool, designed by Microsoft to help product owners and quality assurance users with the process of analyzing new features.

Using Azure DevOps, you can ask for feedback from your team by selecting an option inside each work item, as you can see in the following screenshot:

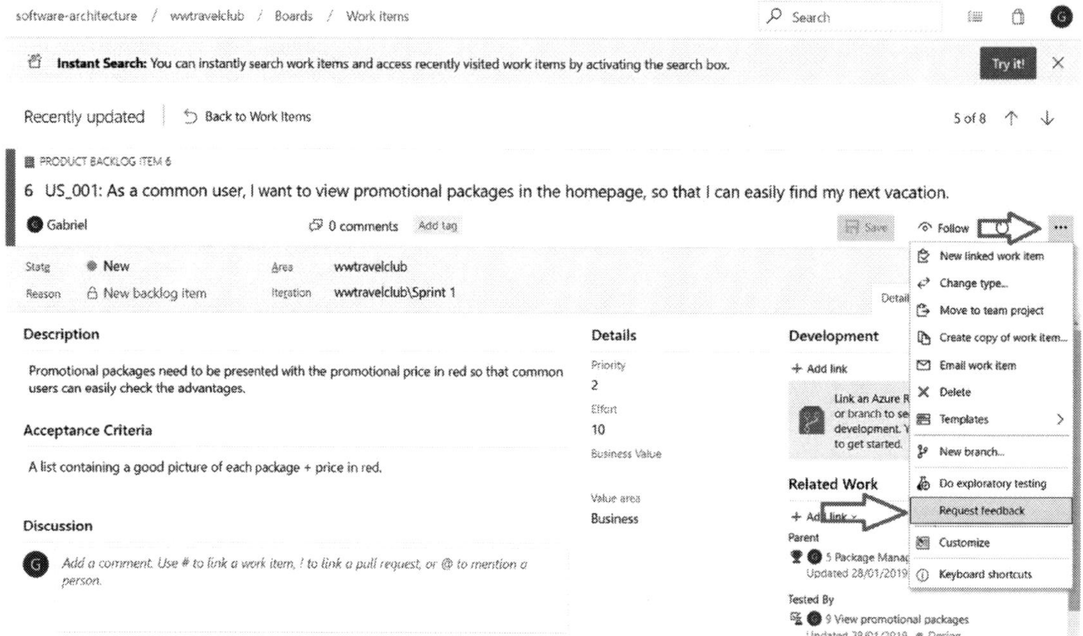

Figure 8.30: Requesting feedback using Azure DevOps

Once someone receives a feedback request, they can use the **Test and Feedback** tool to analyze and give the correct feedback to the team. They will be able to connect the tool to your Azure DevOps project, giving you more features while analyzing the feedback request.

You can download this tool from `https://marketplace.visualstudio.com/items?itemName=ms.vss-exploratorytesting-web`.

This tool is a web browser extension that you will need to install before use. The following screenshot shows how to set up an Azure DevOps project URL for the **Test and Feedback** tool:

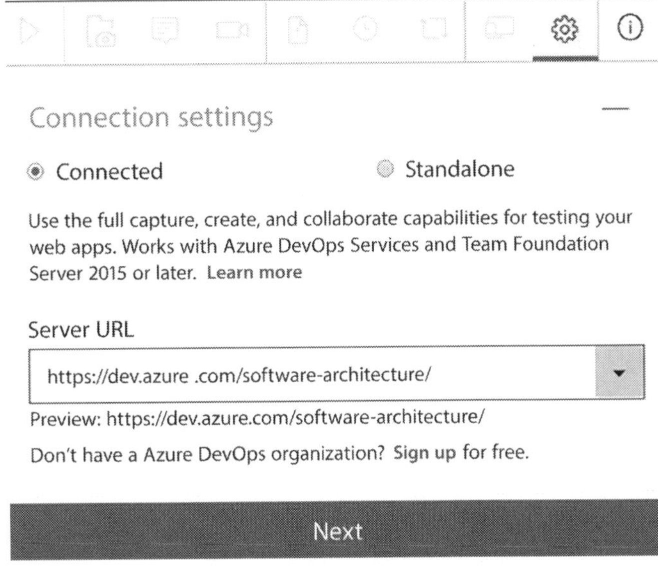

Figure 8.31: Connecting Test and Feedback to an Azure DevOps organization

The tool is quite simple. You can take screenshots, record a process, or even make a note. The following screenshot shows how easily you can write a message inside a screenshot:

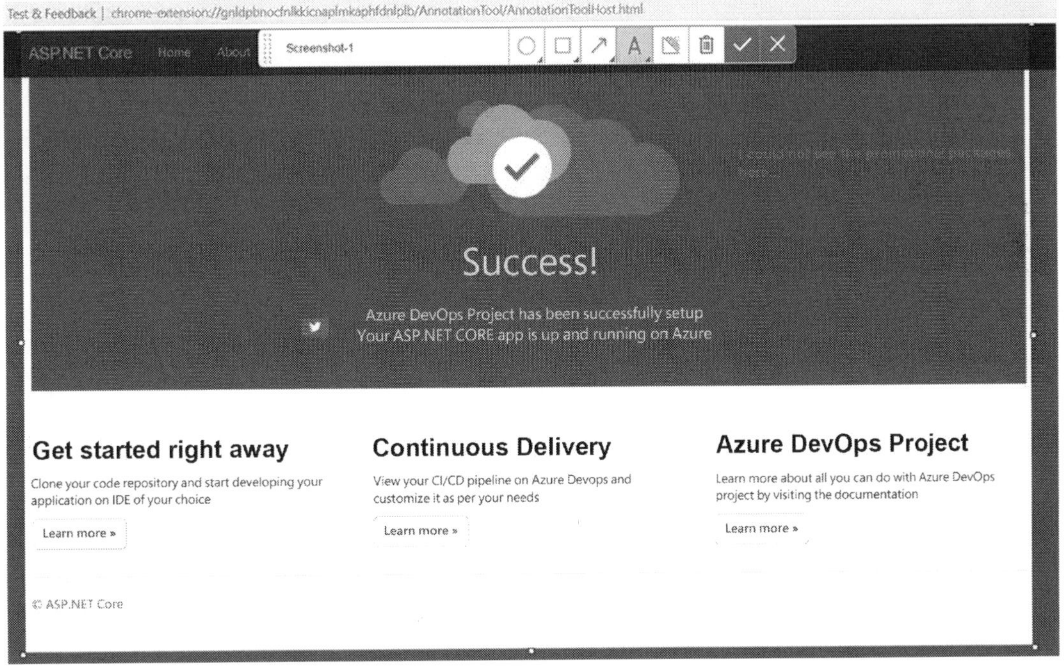

Figure 8.32: Giving feedback with the Test and Feedback tool

The good thing is that you record all this analysis in a session timeline. As you can see in the next screenshot, you can have multiple pieces of feedback in the same session, which is good for the analysis process:

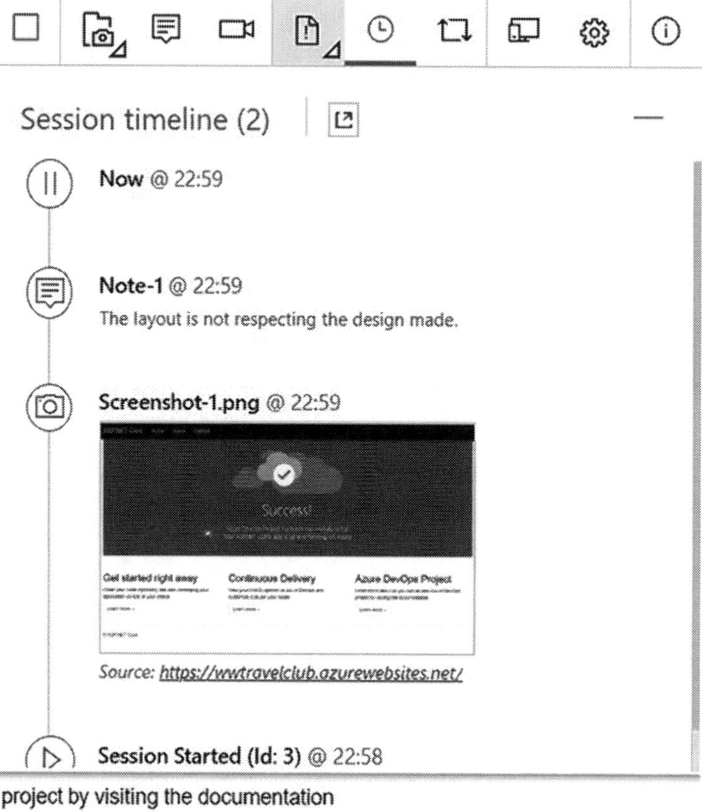

Figure 8.33: Giving feedback with the Test and Feedback tool

Once you have done the analysis and you are connected to Azure DevOps, you will be able to report a bug (as shown in the following screenshot), create a task, or even start a new test case:

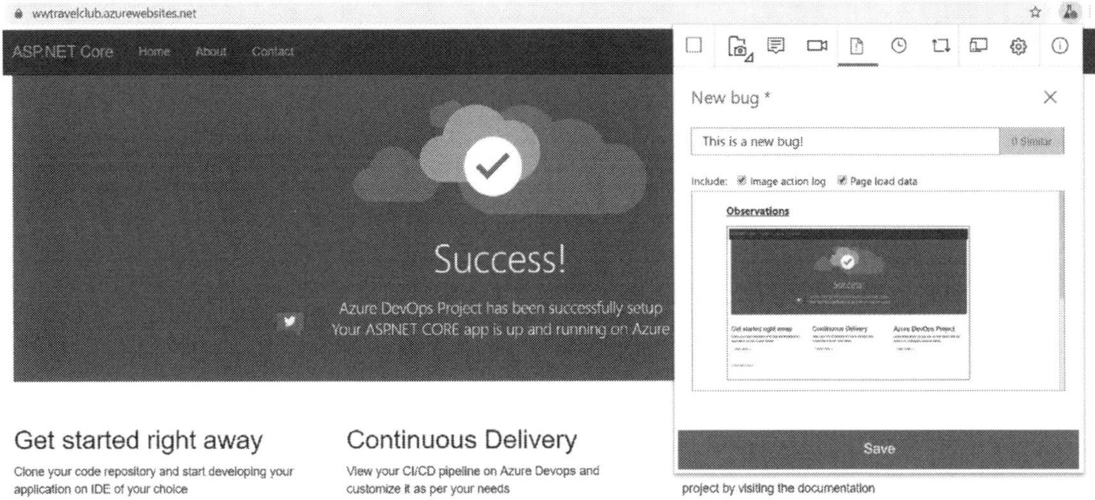

Figure 8.34: Opening a bug in Azure DevOps

The result of the bug created can be checked on the **Work items** board in Azure DevOps. It is worth mentioning that you do not need an Azure DevOps developer license to have access to this area of the environment. This enables you, as a software architect, to share this basic and useful tool with as many key users of the solution as you have.

The following screenshot shows the bug created by the tool once you have connected it to your Azure DevOps project:

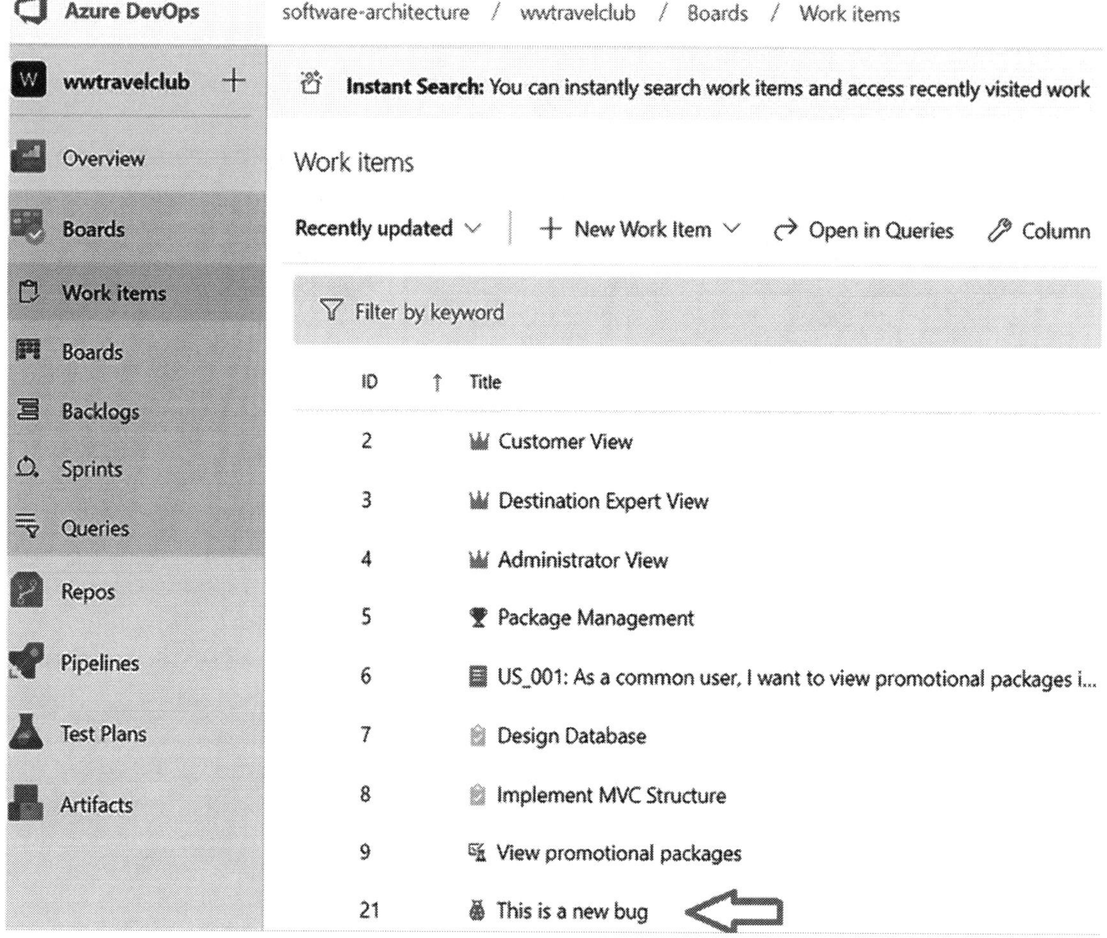

Figure 8.35: New reported bug in Azure DevOps

It is important to have a tool like this to get good feedback on your project. But, as a software architect, you may have to find the best solutions to hasten the feedback process.

Summary

In this chapter, we have learned that DevOps is not only a bunch of techniques and tools used together to deliver software continuously but also a philosophy to enable continuous delivery of value to the end user of the project you are developing.

Considering this approach, we saw how CI/CD and continuous feedback are essential to the purpose of DevOps. We also saw how Azure, Azure DevOps, GitHub, and Microsoft tools help you to achieve your goals.

The chapter also covered the importance of understanding when you can enable CI/CD in the software development life cycle, considering the risks and challenges you will take as a software architect once you decide to use it for your solution.

Additionally, the chapter introduced some solutions and concepts that can make this process easier, such as multi-stage environments, PR reviews, feature flags, peer reviews, and automated tests. Understanding these techniques and processes will enable you to guide your project toward safer behavior when it comes to CI/CD in a DevOps scenario.

We also described *service design thinking* principles. Now, you should be able to analyze all the implications of these approaches for an organization, and you should be able to adapt pre-existing software development processes and hardware/software architectures to take advantage of the opportunities they offer.

We also explained the need for, and the techniques involved in, the automation of the software cycle, cloud hardware infrastructure configuration, and application deployment.

Once you have implemented the examples shown, you should be able to use Azure Pipelines to automate infrastructure configuration and application deployment. This chapter elucidated this approach using WWTravelClub as an example, enabling CI/CD inside Azure DevOps, and using Application Insights and the Test and Feedback tool for both technical and functional feedback. In real life, these tools will enable you to understand the current behavior of the system you are developing more quickly, as you will have continuous feedback on it.

In the next chapter, we will see how automation for software testing works.

Questions

1. What is DevOps?
2. What is continuous integration (CI)?
3. What is continuous delivery (CD)?
4. Can you have DevOps without CI/CD?
5. What are the risks of enabling CI/CD in a non-mature team?
6. How can a multi-stage environment help CI/CD?
7. How can automated tests help CI/CD?
8. How can PRs help CI/CD?
9. Do PRs only work with CI/CD?
10. What is continuous feedback?
11. What is the difference between the build and release pipelines?
12. What is the main purpose of Application Insights in the DevOps approach?
13. How can the Test and Feedback tool help in the process of DevOps?
14. What is the main goal of service design thinking?
15. What is the preferred Azure tool for the automation of the whole application life cycle?

Learn more on Discord

To join the Discord community for this book – where you can share feedback, ask questions to the authors, and learn about new releases – follow the QR code below:

`https://packt.link/SoftwareArchitectureCSharp12Dotnet8`

Testing Your Enterprise Application

When developing software, it is essential to ensure that an application is as bug-free as possible and that it satisfies all requirements. This can be done by testing all the modules while they are being developed or when the overall application has been either completely or partially implemented. This need has become more and more compelling in today's agile and DevOps-driven software development landscape, where integrating testing at every stage of the development process is essential for the continuous delivery of reliable software.

While most of the key concepts covered by this chapter apply to a wide range of applications and environments, this chapter focuses on essential testing strategies for enterprise-level applications in C# and .NET environments.

Performing all the tests manually is not a feasible option since most of the tests must be executed each time the application is modified, and, as explained throughout this book, modern software is continuously being modified to adapt applications to the needs of a fast-changing market. Therefore, automated tests are indispensable in today's fast-paced environment of continuous development.

This chapter discusses the most common types of tests needed to deliver reliable software and how to organize and automate them. More specifically, this chapter covers the following topics:

- Understanding unit and integration tests and their usage, which are the main tools to ensure software reliability and stability
- Understanding the basics of **test-driven development** (**TDD**) and how and why it can dramatically reduce the probability of undiscovered bugs
- Functional tests, which are the main tool for enforcing software specifications
- Defining C# test-specific projects in Visual Studio to take full advantage of the testing tools available in the .NET ecosystem
- Automating functional tests in C#

This chapter will not only teach you the different types of tests and how to implement them but also how to effectively apply these techniques in your role as a .NET software architect to build robust, scalable enterprise applications.

Technical requirements

This chapter requires the Visual Studio 2022 free Community Edition or better, with all database tools installed. The code for this chapter is available at `https://github.com/PacktPublishing/Software-Architecture-with-C-Sharp-12-and-.NET-8-4E`.

Understanding unit and integration tests

Testing is an essential part of software development since it verifies both that the software is bug-free and that it conforms to the agreed specification. Delaying application testing until immediately after most of the application's functionalities have been implemented in their entirety must be avoided for the following reasons:

- If a class or module has been incorrectly designed or implemented, it might have already influenced the way other modules were implemented. Therefore, at this point, fixing the problem might have a very high cost.
- The possible combination of input that is needed to test all possible paths that execution can take grows exponentially with the number of modules or classes that are tested together. Thus, for instance, if the execution of a class method `A` can take three different paths, while the execution of another method `B` can take four paths, then testing `A` and `B` together would require 3 x 4 different inputs. In general, if we test several modules together, the total number of paths to test is the product of the number of paths to test in each module. If modules are tested separately, instead, the number of inputs required is just the sum of the paths needed to test each module. That's why so-called unit tests verify each class method separately in an exhaustive way as soon as each class is designed. After that, the overall behavior correctness can be verified with an acceptably small number of so-called *integration tests, because integration tests* just need to verify the various classes' interaction patterns without analyzing all methods' execution paths.
- If a test of an aggregate made of *N* modules fails, then locating the origin of the bug among the *N* modules is usually a very time-consuming activity.
- When *N* modules are tested together, we have to redefine all tests involving the *N* modules, even if just one of the *N* modules changes during the application's life cycle.

These considerations show that we need both to test each class method separately as soon as possible and to test for correct module integration.

That is why tests are organized into three stages, as follows:

- **Unit tests:** These verify that all or almost all execution paths of each method behave properly. They should be free from external dependencies, such as storage and databases, and should be quite complete; that is, they should cover most of the possible paths. This is usually feasible at an acceptable time cost because there are not too many possible execution paths for each method as compared to the possible execution paths of the whole application.

- **Integration tests:** These are executed once the software passes all its unit tests. Integration tests verify that all modules interact properly to get the expected results. Integration tests do not need to be complete since unit tests will have already verified that all the execution paths of each module work properly. They need to verify as many patterns of interaction as possible, that is, as many ways in which the various modules may cooperate.
- **Acceptance tests:** These are executed at the end of each sprint and/or before releasing the application. They verify that the output of a sprint or the final application satisfies both functional and non-functional requirements. Tests that verify functional requirements are called **functional tests**, while tests that verify performance requirements are called **performance tests**.

Usually, each interaction pattern has more than one test associated with it: a typical activation of a pattern and some extreme cases of activation. For instance, if a whole pattern of interaction receives an array as input, we will write a test for the typical size of the array, a test with a `null` array, a test with an empty array, and a test with a very big array. This way, we verify that the way the single module was designed is compatible with the needs of the whole interaction pattern. It is worth pointing out that, in our array example, `null`, `0`, `1`, and *many* are equivalence classes that represent the whole universe of array values in an efficacious way.

With the preceding strategy in place, if we modify a single module without changing its public interface, we need to change the unit tests for that module.

If, instead, the change involves the way some modules interact, then we also have to add new integration tests or modify existing ones. However, usually, this is not a big problem since most of the tests are unit tests, so rewriting a large percentage of all integration tests does not require too much effort. Moreover, if the application was designed according to the **Single Responsibility**, **Open/Closed**, **Liskov Substitution**, **Interface Segregation**, or **Dependency Inversion** (**SOLID**) principles, the number of integration tests that must be changed after a single code modification should be small since the modification should affect just a few classes that interact directly with the modified method or class.

Automating unit and integration tests

At this point, it should be clear that both unit tests and integration tests will be reused during the entire lifetime of the software. That is why it is worth automating them. The automation of unit and integration tests avoids the possible errors of manual test execution and saves time. A whole battery of several thousand automated tests can verify software integrity following each small modification in a few minutes, thereby enabling the frequent changes needed in the CI/CD cycles of modern software.

As new bugs are found, new tests are added to discover them so that they cannot reappear in future versions of the software. This way, automated tests always become more reliable and protect the software more from bugs added as a result of new changes. Thus, the probability of adding new bugs (that are not immediately discovered) is greatly reduced.

The next subsection will give us the basics for organizing and designing automated unit and integration tests, as well as practical details on how to write a test in C# in the *Defining C# test projects in Visual Studio* section.

Writing automated (unit and integration) tests

Tests are not written from scratch; all software development platforms have tools that help us to both write tests and launch them (or some of them). Once the selected tests have been executed, these tools usually show a report and offer the possibility to debug the code of all failed tests.

More specifically, by and large, all unit and integration test frameworks are composed of three important parts:

1. **Facilities for defining all tests:** They verify whether the actual results correspond to the expected results. Usually, a test is organized into test classes, where each test call tests either a single application class or a single class method. Each test is split into three stages:
    1. **Test preparation** (*Arrange*): The general environment needed by the test is prepared. This stage only prepares the global environment for tests, such as objects to inject into class constructors or simulations of database tables; it doesn't prepare the individual inputs for each of the methods we're going to test. Usually, the same preparation procedure is used in several tests, so test preparations are factored out into dedicated modules.
    2. **Test execution** (*Act/Assert*): The methods to test are invoked with adequate input (*Act*), and all results of their executions are compared with expected results (*Assert*) with constructs such as `Assert.Equal(x,y)` and `Assert.NotNull(x)`.
    3. **Tear-down:** The whole environment is cleaned up to avoid the execution of a test influencing other tests. This step is the converse of *step 1*.
2. **Mock facilities:** While integration tests use all (or almost all) classes involved in a pattern of object cooperation, in unit tests, the use of other application classes should be avoided because their purpose is to test each isolated method. Thus, if a class under test, say, `A`, uses a method of another application class, `B`, that is injected into its constructor in one of its methods, `M`, and then, in order to test `M`, we must inject a fake implementation of `B`. It is worth pointing out that only classes that do some processing cannot be used by other classes being unit tested, while pure data classes can. Mock frameworks contain facilities to define implementations of interfaces and interface methods that return data that can be defined by the test designer. Typically, mock implementations are also able to report information on all mock method calls. Such mock implementations do not require the definition of actual class files but are done online in the test code by calling methods such as `new Mock<IMyInterface>()`.
3. **Execution and reporting tool:** This is a visual configuration-based tool that the developer may use to decide which tests to launch and when to launch them. Moreover, it also shows the final outcome of the tests as a report containing all successful tests, all failed tests, each test's execution time, and other information that depends on the specific tool and how it was configured. Usually, execution and reporting tools that are executed in development IDEs, such as Visual Studio, also give you the possibility of launching a debug session on each failed test.

Since only interfaces allow a complete mock definition of all their methods, we should inject interfaces or pure data classes (that don't need to be mocked) in class constructors and methods if we want to mock all dependencies in our unit tests. Therefore, for each cooperating class that we want to inject into another class and that we want to mock, we must define a corresponding interface.

Moreover, classes should use instances that are injected in their constructors or methods and not class instances available in the public static fields of other classes; otherwise, the results of the unit tests might appear not to be deterministic since these static values might not be set properly during the tests.

The subsection that follows focuses on functional and performance tests.

Acceptance tests: writing functional and performance tests

Acceptance tests define the contract between the project stakeholders and the development team. They are used to verify that the software developed actually behaves as it was agreed it would. Acceptance tests verify not only functional specifications but also constraints on the software usability and **user interface** (UI). Since they also have the purpose of showing how the software appears and behaves on actual computer monitors and displays, they are never completely automatic but consist mainly of lists of recipes and verifications that must be followed by an operator.

Sometimes, automatic **functional tests** are developed to verify just functional requirements, but some of these tests may also bypass the UI and inject the test input directly into the logic that is immediately behind the user interface. For instance, in the case of an ASP.NET Core MVC application (see *Chapter 17, Presenting ASP.NET Core*), the whole website can be run in a complete environment that includes all the necessary storage filled with test data. Input is not provided to HTML pages but is injected directly into the ASP.NET Core controllers. Tests that bypass the user interface are called subcutaneous tests. ASP.NET Core supplies various tools to perform subcutaneous tests.

If possible, most automated acceptance tests should be defined as subcutaneous tests for the following reasons:

1. Automating the actual interaction with the user interface is a very time-consuming task.
2. User interfaces are changed frequently to improve their usability and to add new features, and small changes in a single application screen may force a complete rewrite of all tests that operate on that screen.

In a few words, user interface tests are very expansive and have low reusability, so usually, complete adherence to specifications is tested with subcutaneous tests, and full tests involving the whole user interface are performed just to test the more common and/or more error-prone scenarios.

A common approach for testing the user interface is the usage of playback tools like **Selenium IDE** (`https://www.selenium.dev/selenium-ide/`) during manual tests so that each manual test can be repeated automatically. It's likely that the code generated automatically by such tools is not robust enough to resist non-trivial changes in the HTML. The Selenium IDE playback code tries to resist HTML changes by attempting several selectors to identify each HTML element, but this only helps with small changes. Therefore, in general, playback code can be reused only for the parts of the application UI that are not affected by changes.

The Selenium software may also be used programmatically, that is, by describing user interface tests directly in the code. Selenium will be discussed in more detail in the *Automating functional tests in C#* section, while functional tests, in general, are discussed in the *Functional tests* section.

Performance tests apply a fake load to an application to see whether it can handle the typical production load, discover its load limits, and locate bottlenecks. The application is deployed in a staging environment that is a copy of the actual production environment in terms of hardware resources.

Then, fake requests are created and applied to the system, and response times and other metrics are collected. Fake request batches should have the same composition as the actual production batches. They can be generated from the actual production request logs if they are available.

If response times are not satisfactory, other metrics are collected to discover possible bottlenecks (low memory, slow storage, or slow software modules). Once located, a software component that is responsible for the problem can be analyzed in the debugger to measure the execution time of the various method calls involved in a typical request.

Failures in the performance tests may lead either to a redefinition of the hardware needed by the application or to the optimization of some software modules, classes, or methods.

Both Azure and Visual Studio offer tools to create fake loads and to report execution metrics. However, they have been declared obsolete and will be discontinued, so we will not describe them. As an alternative, there are both open-source and third-party tools that can be used. Some of them are listed in the *Further reading* section.

The next section describes a software development methodology that plays a central role in tests.

Understanding the basics of test-driven development

Test-driven development (TDD) is a software development methodology that gives a central role to unit tests. According to this methodology, unit tests are a formalization of the specifications of each class, so they must be written before the code of the class. Actually, a full test that covers all code paths univocally defines the code behavior, so it can be considered a specification for the code. It is not a formal specification that defines the code behavior through some formal language but a specification based on examples of behavior.

The ideal way to test software would be to write formal specifications of the whole software behavior and to verify with some wholly automatic tools whether the software that was actually produced conforms to them. In the past, some research effort was spent defining formal languages for describing code specifications, but expressing the behavior the developer has in mind with similar languages was a very difficult and error-prone task. Therefore, these attempts were quickly abandoned in favor of approaches based on examples. At that time, the main purpose was the automatic generation of code.

Nowadays, automatic code generation has been largely abandoned and survives in small application areas, such as the creation of device drivers. In these areas, the effort of formalizing the behavior in a formal language is worth the time saved in trying to test difficult-to-reproduce behaviors of parallel threads.

Unit tests were initially conceived as a way to encode example-based specifications in a completely independent way as part of a specific agile development methodology called **extreme programming**. However, since TDD proved to be very efficacious in preventing bugs, nowadays, TDD is used independently of extreme programming and is included as an obligatory prescription in other agile methodologies.

The practice of TDD proved that well-designed initial unit tests are enough to ensure an acceptable level of software stability, despite the fact that, usually, initial tests are not a "perfect" specification of the code. However, it is undoubtedly true that unit tests refined after finding hundreds of bugs act as reliable and substantially perfect code specifications.

Well-designed unit tests can't be based on random inputs since you might need an infinite or at least an immense number of examples to define a code's behavior this way univocally. However, the behavior can be defined with an acceptable number of inputs if you have all possible execution paths in mind. In fact, at this point, it is enough to select a typical example for each execution path.

That's why writing a unit test for a method after that method has been completely coded is easy: it simply requires the selection of a typical instance for each execution path of the already-existing code. However, writing unit tests this way does not protect from errors in the design of the execution paths themselves.

Therefore, a unit test must be written before a method has been completely coded, but while writing unit tests, the developer must somehow forecast all execution paths by looking for extreme cases and by possibly adding more examples than are strictly needed.

For instance, while writing the code that sorts an array, we might start considering all possible extreme cases we are able to forecast before any line of useful method code has been written, that is:

- An empty array
- A null array
- A single-element array
- An array with a few elements
- An array with several elements
- An already-ordered array
- A partially ordered array
- An extremely unordered array

After the first version of the algorithm has been written and passes all of the above tests, other inputs that might cause different execution paths might be discovered by analyzing all execution paths. If this is the case, we add a new unit test for each different execution path discovered.

For instance, in the case of the array sorting method, suppose that we use a divide-and-conquer algorithm, like merge-sort, that recursively splits the array into two halves to recursively reduce the problem to a simpler one. For sure, the way that arrays with even or odd lengths are processed will be different, so we must add at least two new tests, one with an even-length array and the other with an odd-length array.

However, as developers can make mistakes while writing application code, they can also make mistakes in forecasting all possible execution paths while designing unit tests!

It seems we have identified a possible drawback of TDD: unit tests themselves may be wrong. That is, not only application code but also its associated TDD unit tests may be inconsistent with the behavior the developer has in mind. Therefore, in the beginning, unit tests can't be considered software specifications but rather a possibly incorrect and incomplete description of the software behavior.

Therefore, we have two descriptions of the behavior we have in mind: the application code itself and its TDD unit tests that were written before the application code. However, this is not an issue because the theory of probability helps us!

What makes TDD work well in practice is the fact that the probability of making exactly the same error while writing the tests and while writing the code is very low. Therefore, whenever a test fails, there is an error either in the tests or in the application code, and conversely, if there is an error either in the application code or in the test, there is a very high probability that a test will fail. That is, the use of TDD ensures that most bugs are found immediately!

Now that we have understood why TDD is efficacious in preventing bugs and have learned how to select the inputs for our unit tests, we can move to the description of the TDD-based code-writing process.

Writing a class method or a chunk of code, say for finding the maximum of an array of integers with TDD, is a loop composed of three stages:

1. **Red stage:** At this stage, the developer writes an empty method, say `MaximumGrade`, that throws `NotImplementedException`, and also writes new unit tests for this method. These tests must necessarily fail because, at this time, no code implements the behavior they describe:

```
public int MaximumGrade(int[] grades)
{
    throw new NotImplementedException();
}
```

2. **Green stage:** In this stage, the developer writes the minimum code or makes the minimum modifications to existing code necessary to make all unit tests pass. Say we test `MaximumGrade` with a null array, an array with `0` elements, an array with just one element, and an array with several elements; the code that passes all tests might be:

```
int MaximumGrade(int[] grades)
{
    if(grades == null) return 0;
    int result= 0;
    for(int i = 0; i < grades.Length; i++)
    {
        if (grades[i]> result) result= grades[i];
    }
    return result;
}
```

3. **Refactoring stage:** Once the test is passed, the code is refactored to ensure good code quality and the application of best practices and patterns. In particular, in this stage, some code can be factored out in other methods or other classes. During this stage, we may also discover the need for other unit tests because new execution paths or new extreme cases are discovered or created. In the case of `MaximumGrade`, at this stage, we might notice the following:
    - Instead of returning 0 when the array is `null`, it would be better to define a new exception and throw it.
    - `foreach` is more efficient and more readable than `for`.
    - What if all numbers are negative? We must create a new test with an array of negative numbers:

```
int MaximumGrade(int[] grades)
{
    if(grades == null) throw new ArgumentException();
    int result= 0;
    foreach(int grade in grades)
    {
        if (grade > result) result= grade;
    }
    return result;
}
```

The loop stops as soon as all tests pass without writing new code or modifying the existing code.

When we repeat the red stage, the newly added test for the negative array will fail because of our inadequate initialization:

```
int result=0;
```

So, we need to replace it with:

```
int result= int.MinValue;
```

At this point, all tests pass again, and we move to the green stage again. There is no need for further refactoring, so the refactoring stage doesn't modify our code, meaning we can exit the test loop: we are done!

Sometimes, it is very difficult to design the initial unit tests because it is quite difficult to imagine how the code might work and the execution paths it might take. In this case, you can get a better understanding of the specific algorithm to use by writing an initial sketch of the method code. In this initial stage, we need to focus just on the main execution path, completely ignoring extreme cases and input verifications. Once we get a clear picture of the main ideas behind an algorithm that should work, we can enter the standard three-stage TDD loop.

The next section discusses functional tests in detail.

Functional tests

These tests use the same techniques and tools as unit and integration tests but differ from them in that they are run only at the end of each sprint. They have the fundamental role of verifying that the current version of the entire software complies with its specifications.

Since functional tests also involve the UI, they need further tools to simulate, somehow, how the user acts in the UI. The need for extra tools is not the only challenge the UI brings with it because UIs also see frequent and major changes. Thus, we mustn't design tests that depend on the UI's graphical details, or we might be forced to rewrite all the tests completely at each UI change. We will discuss both the tools and the best practices for optimizing UI tests in the *Automating functional tests in C#* section.

Anyway, it is worth pointing out that sometimes it is better to renounce automated testing for some UI-related features and fall back to manual tests because the time investment is not justified by the short life of the UI code.

Whether automatic or manual, functional testing must be a formal process that is performed for the following purposes:

1. Functional tests represent the most important part of the contract between stakeholders and the development team, the other part being the verification of non-functional specifications. The way this contract is formalized depends on the nature of the relationship between the development team and stakeholders.
2. In the case of a supplier-customer relationship, the functional tests become part of the supplier-customer business contract for each sprint, and a team that works for the customer writes them. If the tests fail, then the sprint is rejected, and the supplier must run a supplementary sprint to fix all problems.
3. If there is no supplier-customer business relationship because the development team and the stakeholder belong to the same company, there is no business contract. In this case, the stakeholder, together with the team, writes an internal document that formalizes the requirements of the sprint. If the tests fail, usually, the sprint is not rejected, but the results of the tests are used to drive the specifications for the next sprints. Of course, if the failure percentage is high, the sprint may be rejected and should be repeated.
4. Formalized functional tests that run at the end of each sprint prevent any results achieved in previous sprints from being destroyed by new code.
5. When using an agile development methodology, maintaining an updated battery of functional tests is the best way to get a formal representation of the final system specifications since, during agile development, the specifications of the final system are not decided before development starts but are the result of the system's evolution. Agile development and sprints are discussed in detail in *Chapter 1, Understanding the Importance of Software Architecture*.

Since the output of the first sprints may differ a lot from the final system in these early stages, it is not worth spending too much time writing detailed manual tests and/or automatized tests. Therefore, you may limit the user stories to just a few examples that will be used both as inputs for software development and as manual tests.

As system functionalities become more stable, it is worth investing time in writing detailed and formal functional tests for them. For each functional specification, we must write tests that verify their operation in extreme cases. For instance, in a cash withdrawal use case, we must write tests that verify all possibilities:

1. Not enough funds
2. Card expired
3. Wrong credentials
4. Repeated wrong credentials

The following diagram sketches the whole process with all possible outcomes:

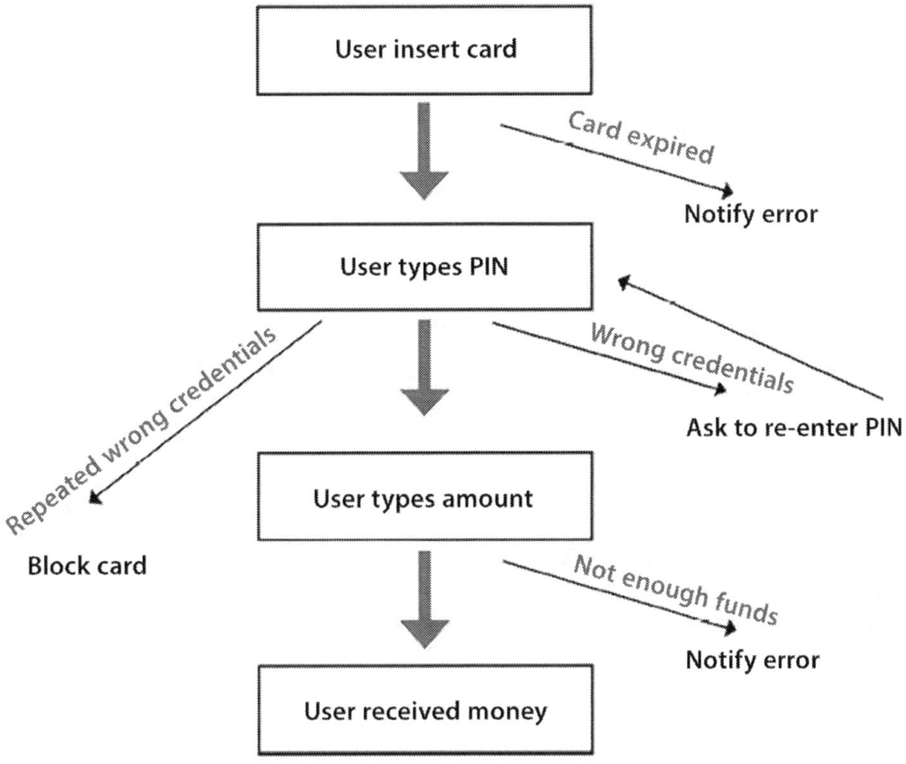

Figure 9.1: Withdrawal example

The user inserts their card, and the card may be accepted or rejected because it has expired. Then, the user tries their PIN with possible errors, so they might repeat the PIN entry till either they succeed or they reach a maximum number of attempts. Finally, the user enters the amount to withdraw and may get their money or a "Not enough funds" error.

In the case of manual tests, for each of the preceding scenarios, we must give all the details of all the steps involved in each operation and, for each step, the expected result.

An important decision is whether you want to automate all or a part of the functional tests since it is very expensive to write automated tests that simulate a human operator that interacts with a system's UI. The final decision depends on the cost of the test implementation divided by the expected number of times it will be used.

In the case of CI/CD, the same functional test can be executed several times, but unluckily, functional tests are strictly tied to the way the UI is implemented, and, in modern systems, the UI is changed frequently. Therefore, in this case, a test is executed with exactly the same UI no more than a couple of times.

In order to overcome most of the problems related to the UI, some functional tests can be implemented as **subcutaneous tests**. Subcutaneous tests are a specific type of functional test designed to bypass the UI layer of an application. Instead of interacting with the application through its UI, like a user would, these tests directly interact with the application's underlying logic. For example, in an ASP.NET Core application, a subcutaneous test might directly invoke the methods of a controller – the part of the application that handles incoming requests – rather than going through the process of sending these requests via a browser. This approach helps us focus on testing the core functionality of the application without the complexities of the UI.

In the user case in *Chapter 21*, *Case Study*, we will see in practice how to design subcutaneous tests for an ASP.NET Core application.

Unfortunately, subcutaneous tests can't verify all possible implementation errors since they can't detect errors in the UI itself. Moreover, in the case of a web application, subcutaneous tests usually suffer from other limitations because they bypass the whole HTTP protocol.

In particular, in the case of ASP.NET Core applications, which will be described in *Chapter 17*, *Presenting ASP.NET Core*, if we call controller action methods directly, we bypass the whole ASP.NET Core pipeline that processes each request before passing it to the right action method. Therefore, authentication, authorization, CORS, and the behavior of other middleware in the ASP.NET Core pipeline will not be analyzed by the tests.

A complete automated functional test of a web application should do the following things:

1. Start an actual browser on the URL to be tested.
2. Wait so that any JavaScript on the page completes its execution.
3. Then, send commands to the browser that simulate the behavior of a human operator.
4. Finally, after each interaction with the browser, automatic tests should wait so that any JavaScript that was triggered by the interaction completes.

Such tests can be executed using browser automatization tools like **Selenium**, which will be discussed in the *Automating functional tests in C#* section of this chapter.

It is worth pointing out that not all user interface tests can be automated since no automatic test can verify how the user interface appears and how usable it is.

As we've explored the intricacies of functional and subcutaneous testing, it's become clear that a comprehensive testing strategy must encompass not only how the tests are performed but also how they are conceptualized and communicated. This brings us to **Behavior-Driven Development** (**BDD**), a methodology that builds upon the principles of functional testing by emphasizing business value and client-side behavior. BDD offers a structured approach to creating tests that are more closely aligned with user requirements and business objectives.

Behavior-Driven Development (BDD)

BDD conforms to the rules of TDD we already described but focuses mainly on business value and client-side behavior.

We discussed that the strength of unit tests is as follows: "It is very unlikely that when describing a behavior in two completely different ways, that is, with code and with examples, we might make exactly the same errors, so errors are discovered with a probability that is close to 100%."

BDD uses the same approach, but the examples used in TDD must not depend on the specific way the functionality might be implemented. That is, examples must be as close as possible to pure specifications. This way, we are sure tests can't influence the way functionality is implemented and vice versa; we are not influenced by pure technical facilities or constraints when writing specifications but focus mainly on the user needs.

Moreover, tests should use a vocabulary that can be understood by stakeholders. For these reasons, tests are described by a Given-When-Then syntax. The following is an example:

```
Given the first number is 50
And the second number is 70
When the two numbers are added
Then the result should be 120
```

`Given`, `And`, `When`, and `Then` are keywords, while the remaining text is just natural language containing the example data.

The Given-When-Then formal language is called Gherkin. It can be translated into code either manually or with tools that are part of toolsets like Cucumber (`https://cucumber.io/`) or SpecFlow in the case of .NET projects. SpecFlow is a Visual Studio extension that can be installed from the Visual Studio **Extensions** menu. Once installed, it adds a new kind of test project, a SpecFlow project.

In SpecFlow, Given-When-Then tests are defined in `.feature` files, while natural language clauses contained in the description are transformed into code in the so-called step files. Step files are automatically created, but the code inside of them must be written by the developer. Below is the method that is in charge of translating into code the `"Given the first number is 50"` clause:

```
[Given("the first number is (.*)")]
public void GivenTheFirstNumberIs(int number)
{
    _calculator.FirstNumber = number;
}
```

The attribute on top of the method is automatically created by SpecFlow, but the (.*) regular expression that extracts the datum from the natural language clause must be written by the developer.

`_calculator` is a variable that must be created by the developer and that contains a class to test:

```
private readonly Calculator _calculator = new Calculator();
```

Once completely defined, SpecFlow tests are run by exploiting an underlying test framework supported by .NET. The underlying test framework to use is specified when the SpecFlow project is created.

While BDD and the Gherkin syntax can be used in unit, integration, and functional tests, the effort of writing tests in natural language and turning them into code is worth it only for functional tests because functional tests must be easily understood by stakeholders.

When writing unit tests, the BDD rule of the independence of tests from the implementation improves the tests' quality and lifetime (fewer tests depend on implementation. Thus, they need to be updated less frequently). However, keep in mind that the classes that we are unit testing are themselves the result of implementation choices, so an excessive obsession with test independence might result in a waste of time.

After having described the theory behind testing, we are ready to move to practical implementations in C#. In the next section, we will list all test projects available in Visual Studio and describe xUnit in detail.

Defining C# test projects in Visual Studio

The .NET SDK contains project templates for three types of unit testing frameworks: MSTest, xUnit, and NUnit. When starting the new project wizard in Visual Studio, if you want to see the compatible versions of these testing frameworks for .NET C# applications, set the **Project type** to **Test**, the **Language** to **C#**, and the **Platform** as **Linux**. This configuration will allow you to identify and select the appropriate versions of MSTest, xUnit, and NUnit for your project.

The following screenshot shows the selection that should appear:

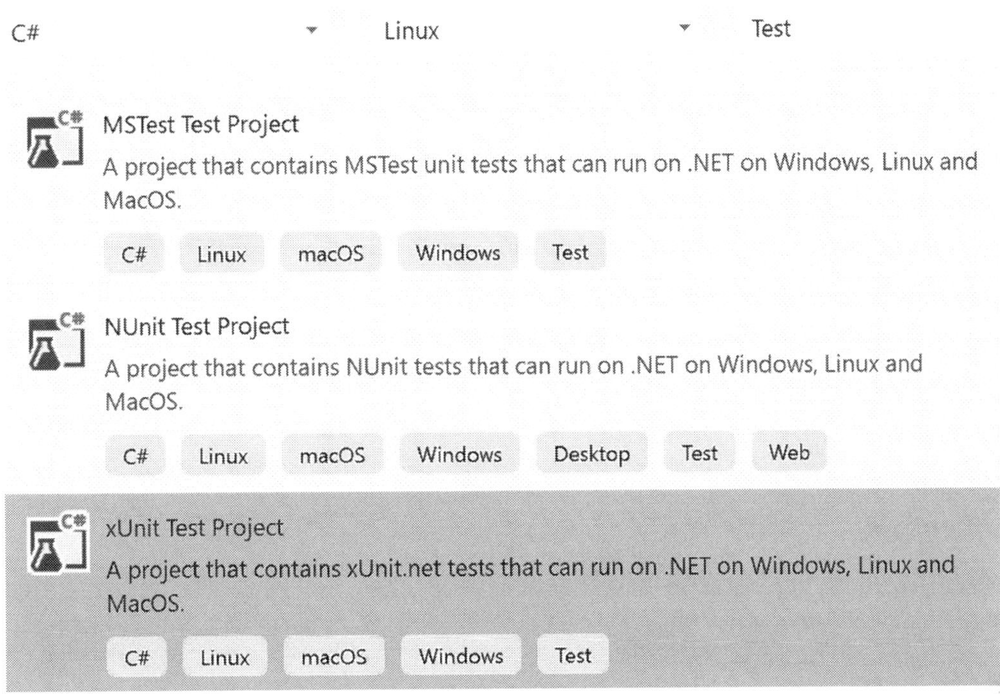

Figure 9.2: Adding a test project

All the preceding projects automatically include the NuGet package for running all the tests in the Visual Studio test user interface (Visual Studio test runner). However, they do not include any facility for mocking interfaces, so you need to add the `Moq` NuGet package, which contains a popular mocking framework.

All these test projects must contain a reference to the project to be tested.

In the next subsection, we will describe **xUnit**, but all three frameworks are quite similar and differ mainly in the names of the assert methods and the names of the attributes used to decorate various testing classes and methods.

Using the xUnit test framework

In xUnit, tests are methods decorated with either the `[Fact]` or `[Theory]` attributes. Tests are automatically discovered by the test runner, which lists all of them in the user interface so the user can run either all of them or just a selection of them.

A new instance of the test class is created before running each test, so the *test preparation* code contained in the class constructor is executed before each test of the class. If you also require *tear-down code*, the test class must implement the `IDisposable` interface so that the tear-down code can be included in the `IDisposable.Dispose` method.

The test code invokes the methods to be tested and then tests the results with methods from the `Assert` static class, such as `Assert.NotNull(x)`, `Assert.Equal(x, y)`, and `Assert.NotEmpty(IEnumerable x)`. Some methods verify whether a call throws an exception of a specific type, for instance:

```
Assert.Throws<MyException>(() => {/* test code */ ...}).
```

When an assertion fails, an exception is thrown. A test fails if a not-intercepted exception is thrown either by the test code or by an assertion.

The following is an example of a method that defines a single test:

```
[Fact]
public void Test1()
{
    var myInstanceToTest = new ClassToTest();
    Assert.Equal(5, myInstanceToTest.MethodToTest(1));
}
```

The `[Fact]` attribute is used when a method defines just one test, while the `[Theory]` attribute is used when the same method defines several tests, each on a different tuple of data. Tuples of data can be specified in several ways and are injected into the test as method parameters.

The previous code can be modified to test `MethodToTest` on several inputs as follows:

```
[Theory]
[InlineData(1, 5)]
[InlineData(3, 10)]
[InlineData(5, 20)]
public void Test1(int testInput, int testOutput)
{
    var myInstanceToTest = new ClassToTest();
      Assert.Equal(testOutput,
         myInstanceToTest.MethodToTest(testInput));
}
```

Each `InlineData` attribute specifies a tuple to be injected into the method parameters. Since just simple constant data can be included as attribute arguments, xUnit also gives you the possibility to take all data tuples from a class that implements `IEnumerable`, as shown in the following example:

```
public class Test1Data: IEnumerable<object[]>
{
    public IEnumerator<object[]> GetEnumerator()
    {
        yield return new object[] { 1, 5};
        yield return new object[] { 3, 10 };
        yield return new object[] { 5, 20 };
```

```
    }
    IEnumerator IEnumerable.GetEnumerator()=>GetEnumerator();
}
...
[Theory]
[ClassData(typeof(Test1Data))]
public void Test1(int testInput, int testOutput)
{
    var myInstanceToTest = new ClassToTest();
    Assert.Equal(testOutput,
    myInstanceToTest.MethodToTest(testInput));
}
```

The type of class that provides the test data is specified with the `ClassData` attribute.

It is also possible to take data from a static method of a class that returns `IEnumerable` with the `MemberData` attribute, as shown in the following example:

```
[Theory]
[MemberData(nameof(MyStaticClass.Data),
    MemberType= typeof(MyStaticClass))]
public void Test1(int testInput, int testOutput)
{
    ...
```

The `MemberData` attribute is passed the method name as the first parameter, and the class type in the `MemberType` named parameter. If the static method is part of the same test class, the `MemberType` parameter can be omitted.

The next subsection shows how to deal with some advanced preparation and tear-down scenarios.

Advanced test preparation and tear-down scenarios

Sometimes, the preparation code contains very time-consuming operations, such as opening a connection with a database that doesn't need to be repeated before each test but that can be executed once before all the tests contained in the same class. In xUnit, this kind of test preparation code can't be included in the test class constructor; since a different instance of the test class is created before every single test, it must be factored out in a separate class called a fixture class.

If we also need corresponding tear-down code, the fixture class must implement `IDisposable`. In other test frameworks, such as NUnit, the test class instances are created just once instead, so they don't need the fixture code to be factored out in other classes. However, test frameworks such as **NUnit**, which do not create a new instance before each test, may suffer from bugs because of unwanted interactions between test methods.

The following is an example of an xUnit fixture class that opens and closes a database connection:

```
public class DatabaseFixture : IDisposable
{
    public DatabaseFixture()
    {
        Db = new SqlConnection("MyConnectionString");
    }
    public void Dispose()
    {
        Db.Close()
    }
    public SqlConnection Db { get; private set; }
}
```

Since a fixture class instance is created just once before all tests associated with the fixture are executed and the same instance is disposed of immediately after the tests, then the database connection is created just once when the fixture class is created and is disposed of immediately after the tests when the fixture object is disposed of.

The fixture class is associated with each test class by letting the test class implement the empty `IClassFixture<T>` interface as follows:

```
public class MyTestsClass : IClassFixture<DatabaseFixture>
{
    private readonly DatabaseFixture fixture;
    public MyDatabaseTests(DatabaseFixture fixture)
    {
        this.fixture = fixture;
    }
    ...
}
```

A fixture class instance is automatically injected into the test class constructor in order to make all data computed in the fixture test preparation available for the tests. This way, for instance, in our previous example, we can get the database connection instance so that all test methods of the class can use it.

If we want to execute some test preparation code on all tests contained in a collection of test classes instead of a single test class, we must associate the fixture class with an empty class that represents the collection of test classes, as follows:

```
[CollectionDefinition("My Database collection")]
public class DatabaseCollection : ICollectionFixture<DatabaseFixture>
{
    // this class is empty, since it is just a placeholder
}
```

The `CollectionDefinition` attribute declares the name of the collection, and the `IClassFixture<T>` interface has been replaced with `ICollectionFixture<T>`.

Then, we declare that a test class belongs to the previously defined collection by applying it to the `Collection` attribute with the name of the collection, as follows:

```
[Collection("My Database collection")]
public class MyTestsClass
{
    DatabaseFixture fixture;
    public MyDatabaseTests(DatabaseFixture fixture)
    {
        this.fixture = fixture;
    }
    ...
}
```

The `Collection` attribute declares which collection to use, while the `DataBaseFixture` argument in the test class constructor provides an actual fixture class instance, so it can be used in all class tests.

Now that we have seen how to leverage fixture classes to share setup and cleanup code across multiple tests, enhancing our test organization and efficiency, we turn our attention to another powerful technique in our testing arsenal. The following section introduces the use of the `Moq` framework, a tool that allows us to simulate the behavior of complex dependencies in our tests through mocking. This approach is crucial for isolating the component we are testing and verifying its behavior under controlled conditions without the need for the actual implementations of its dependencies.

Mocking interfaces with Moq

Mocking is a technique used in both unit testing to isolate classes from dependencies they have on other classes, so we can impute each test failure to the class under test. Classes are isolated from their dependencies by creating a mock or a fake version of each dependency.

Mocking capabilities are not included in any of the test frameworks we listed in this section, as they are not included in xUnit, so we must add another library that offers mocking capability. The `Moq` framework, a popular tool in .NET, makes the mocking process super-easy.

Let's explore how to use `Moq` to create mocks and set up our tests effectively. Here, we will discuss just how to use `Moq` to create mock classes. A practical and complete example that shows how to use `Moq` in your tests in practice is in the *Testing the WWTravelClub application* section of *Chapter 21, Case Study*.

As a first step, we need to install the `Moq` NuGet package. Then, we need to add a `using Moq` statement to our test files. A mock implementation is easily defined as follows:

```
var myMockDependency = new Mock<IMyInterface>();
```

The behavior of the mock dependency on specific inputs of the specific method can be defined with the `Setup/Return` method pair as follows:

```
myMockDependency.Setup(x=>x.MyMethod(5)).Returns(10);
```

We can add several `Setup/Return` instructions for the same method. This way, we can specify an indefinite number of input/output behaviors.

Instead of specific input values, we may also use wildcards that match a specific type as follows:

```
myMockDependency.Setup(x => x.MyMethod(It.IsAny<int>()))
                  .Returns(10);
```

Where we replaced `5` with its type, `int`.

Once we have configured the mock dependency, we may extract the mocked instance from its `Object` property and use it as if it were an actual implementation, as follows:

```
var myMockedInstance=myMockDependency.Object;
...
myMockedInstance.MyMethod(10);
```

However, mocked methods are usually called by the code under test, so we just need to extract the mocked instance and use it as an input in our tests.

We may also mock properties and **async** methods as follows:

```
myMockDependency.Setup(x => x.MyProperty)
                  .Returns(42);
...
myMockDependency.Setup(x => x.MyMethodAsync(1))
                   .ReturnsAsync("aasas");
var res=await myMockDependency.Object
    .MyMethodAsync(1);
```

With `async` methods, `Returns` must be replaced by `ReturnsAsync`.

Each mocked instance records all calls to its methods and properties, so we may use this information in our tests. The following code shows an example:

```
myMockDependency.Verify(x => x.MyMethod(1), Times.AtLeast(2));
```

The preceding statement asserts that `MyMethod` has been invoked with the given arguments at least twice. There are also `Times.Never`, and `Times.Once` (which asserts that the method was called just once), and more.

The `Moq` documentation summarized up to now should cover 99% of the needs that may arise in your tests, but `Moq` also offers more complex options. The *Further reading* section contains the link to the complete documentation.

The *Testing the WWTravelClub application* section of *Chapter 21, Case Study*, shows the practical usage of Moq in a complex example.

After exploring the capabilities of Moq and how it enhances our unit testing with effective mock implementations, we now turn our attention to a different facet of C# application testing - automating functional tests in ASP.NET Core applications. In this next section, we'll dive into how various testing tools and techniques, including some we've just discussed, are applied to ensure our ASP.NET Core applications function as intended, both in isolation and when integrated with other systems and interfaces.

Automating functional tests in C#

Automated functional tests use the same test tools as unit and integration tests. That is, these tests can be embedded in the same xUnit, NUnit, or MSTest projects that we described in the previous section. However, in this case, we must add further tools that can interact with and inspect the UI.

In the remainder of this chapter, we will focus on web applications since they are the main focus of this book. Accordingly, if we are testing web APIs, we just need `HttpClient` instances since they can easily interact with web API endpoints in both XML and JSON.

In the case of applications that return HTML pages, the interaction is more complex since we also need tools for parsing and interacting with the HTML page DOM tree.

The *Selenium* toolset is a great solution since it has drivers for simulating user interaction in all mainstream browsers and for programmatically accessing the browser DOM.

There are two basic options for testing a web application with the `HttpClient` class:

1. **Staging application**: An `HttpClient` instance connects with the actual *staging* web application through the internet/intranet, together with all other humans who are beta-testing the software. The advantage of this approach is that you are testing the *real stuff*, but tests are more difficult to conceive since you can't control the initial state of the application before each test.
2. **Controlled application**: An `HttpClient` instance connects with a local application that is configured, initialized, and launched before every single test. This scenario is completely analogous to the unit test scenario. Test results are reproducible, the initial state before each test is fixed, tests are easier to design, and the actual database can be replaced by a faster and easier-to-initialize in-memory database. However, in this case, you are far from the actual system's operation.

A good strategy is to use a **controlled application**, where you have full control of the initial state, for testing the extreme cases, and then use a **staging application** for testing random average cases on the *real stuff*.

The two subsections that follow describe both approaches. The two approaches differ only in the way that you define the fixtures of your tests.

Testing the staging application

In the case of staging applications, your tests just need a class that can issue HTTP requests, which in the case of .NET is the `HttpClient` class. It is enough to define an efficient fixture that supplies the needed `HttpClient` instances, avoiding the risk of running out of operating system connections. Efficient management of the underlying operating system connections can be achieved through the `IHttpClientFactory` interface.

It is enough to add an `HttpClient` management factory to a dependency injection container that will be used by the tests with:

```
services.AddHttpClient(),
```

where the `AddHttpClient` extension belongs to the `Microsoft.Extensions.DependencyInjection` namespace and is defined in the `Microsoft.Extensions.Http` NuGet package. Therefore, our test fixture must create a dependency injection container, call the `AddHttpClient` extension method, and finally build the container. The following fixture class does this job:

```
public class HttpClientFixture
{
    public HttpClientFixture()
    {
        var serviceCollection = new ServiceCollection();
        serviceCollection
            .AddHttpClient();
         ServiceProvider = serviceCollection.BuildServiceProvider();
    }
    public ServiceProvider ServiceProvider { get; private set; }
}
```

After the preceding definition, your tests should look as follows:

```
public class MyUnitTestClass:IClassFixture<HttpClientFixture>
{
    private readonly ServiceProvider _serviceProvider;
    public UnitTest1(HttpClientFixture fixture)
    {
        _serviceProvider = fixture.ServiceProvider;
    }
    [Fact]
    public void MyTest()
    {
        var factory =
            _serviceProvider.GetService<IHttpClientFactory>())
```

```
            HttpClient client = factory.CreateClient();
        }
    }
```

In `Test1`, once you get an HTTP client, you can test the application by issuing an HTTP request and then by analyzing the response returned by the application.

The approach described above is adequate when the HTTP endpoints return data, for instance, in JSON format that can be turned into .NET data by a data serializer/deserializer and then compared with the expected data.

The next subsection describes how to test endpoints that return HTML.

Testing the staging application with Selenium

Most endpoints that return HTML are tested either manually or with playback tools, like Selenium IDE, on various browsers. Playback tools record all user actions performed on an actual browser and generate code that repeats the same action sequences with the help of browser drivers.

However, the code generated by playback tools is too sensitive to the DOM structure of each page, so most of the tests must be replaced after each relevant change in the user interface.

Therefore, the code of important and stable UI tests is better created manually in a way that is more robust to DOM changes.

For this purpose, the Selenium toolset contains the `Selenium.WebDriver` NuGet package and a driver for each browser that you would like to adopt, such as, for instance, the `Selenium.WebDriver.ChromeDriver` NuGet package for the Chrome browser.

Manual tests based on Selenium WebDriver look like this:

```
using OpenQA.Selenium;
using OpenQA.Selenium.ChromeDriver;
public class MyUnitTestClass:IClassFixture<HttpClientFixture>
{
    [Fact]
    public void MyTest()
    {
        Using (IWebDriver driver = new ChromeDriver())
        {
            driver.Navigate().GoToUrl("https://localhost:5001/mypage");
            //use driver to interact with the loaded page here
            ...
            var title = driver.Title;
           Assert().Equal("My Application - My Page", title);
           ...
        var submitButton =
            driver.FindElement(By.ClassName("confirm-changes"));
```

```
        submitButton.Clikck();
        ...
        }

    }
}
```

Once the page to test has been loaded, `driver` is used to explore the page content and to interact with page elements, like buttons, links, and input fields. As shown in the preceding code, the syntax for interacting with the browser is quite simple and intuitive. `driver.FindElement` can find elements by CSS class name, by ID, and also through generic CSS selectors.

Adding CSS classes that characterize their role with HTML elements is a good technique for building robust UI tests.

The next subsection explains how to test an application that runs in a controlled environment.

Testing a controlled application

In this case, we create an ASP.NET Core server within the test application and test it with an `HttpClient` instance. The `Microsoft.AspNetCore.Mvc.Testing` NuGet package contains all that we need to create both an HTTP client and the server running the application.

`Microsoft.AspNetCore.Mvc.Testing` contains a fixture class that does the job of launching a local web server and furnishing a client to interact with it. The predefined fixture class is `WebApplicationFactory<T>`. The generic `T` argument must be instantiated with the `Program` class of your web project, that is, with an entry point for the web application.

Tests look like the following class:

```
public class MynitTest
    : IClassFixture<WebApplicationFactory<MyProject.Program>>
{
    private readonly
        WebApplicationFactory<MyProject.Program> _factory;
    public UnitTest1 (WebApplicationFactory<MyProject.Program> factory)
    {
        _factory = factory;
    }
    [Theory]
    [InlineData("/")]
    [InlineData("/Index")]
    [InlineData("/About")]
    ....
    public async Task MustReturnOK(string url)
    {
```

```
        var client = _factory.CreateClient();
        // here both client and server are ready
        var response = await client.GetAsync(url);
        //get the response
        response.EnsureSuccessStatusCode();
        // verify we got a success return code.
    }
    ...
    ---
}
```

The `Program` class must exist and must be defined as public. Otherwise, `WebApplicationFactory` has no entry point for starting the application. Therefore, if the code in `Program.cs` is not enclosed in a public class, as in the default project scaffolded by Visual Studio, you must turn the internal `Program` class automatically generated by the C# compile into a public class. This is easily achieved by adding the following code at the end of the `Program.cs` file:

```
public partial class Program { }
```

If you want to analyze the HTML of the returned pages, you must also reference **Selenium** NuGet packages, as shown in the previous subsection. We will see how to use them in the example in the next section.

The simplest way to cope with databases in this type of test is to replace them with in-memory databases that are faster and automatically cleared whenever the local server is shut down and restarted.

Unfortunately, in-memory databases are not 100% compatible with the actual database used, so some tests might fail. Therefore, at least some of the tests might require the actual database.

When performing tests with actual databases, we must also add all the required instructions to clear or recreate from scratch a standard database in the constructor of a custom fixture that inherits from `WebApplicationFactory<T>`. Note that deleting all database data is not as easy as it might appear, owing to integrity constraints. You have various options, but none is the best for all cases:

1. Delete the whole database and recreate it using SQL scripts or Entity Framework Core migrations, which will be analyzed in *Chapter 13, Interacting with Data in C# – Entity Framework Core*. This always works, but it is slow and requires a database user with high privileges.
2. Enclose a test database in a Docker image and recreate a new container at each new test (Docker will be discussed in *Chapter 11, Applying a Microservice Architecture to Your Enterprise Application*). This is faster than recreating a new database from scratch but still slow.
3. Disable the database constraints and then clear all tables in any order. This technique sometimes doesn't work and requires a database user with high privileges.

4. Delete all data in the right order, thus without violating all database constraints. This is not difficult if you keep an ordered delete list of all tables while the database grows and you add tables to the database. This delete list is a useful resource that you may also use to fix issues in database update operations and to remove old entries during production database maintenance. Unfortunately, this method also fails in the rare case of circular dependencies, such as a table that has a foreign key referring to itself.

I prefer method 4 and revert to method 3 only in the rare case of difficulties due to circular dependencies.

Recording tests with Selenium IDE

The Selenium toolset contains browser extensions for recording and replaying browser tests. These are called Selenium IDE. You can download the extensions for Chrome and Firefox from `https://www.selenium.dev/selenium-ide/`, while the extension for Microsoft Edge is available from `https://microsoftedge.microsoft.com/addons/detail/selenium-ide/ajdpfmkffanmkhejnopjppegokpogffp`.

In Chrome, once installed, Selenium IDE can be run by clicking the extensions icon and then selecting the Selenium extension from the menu that appears, as shown in the screenshot below:

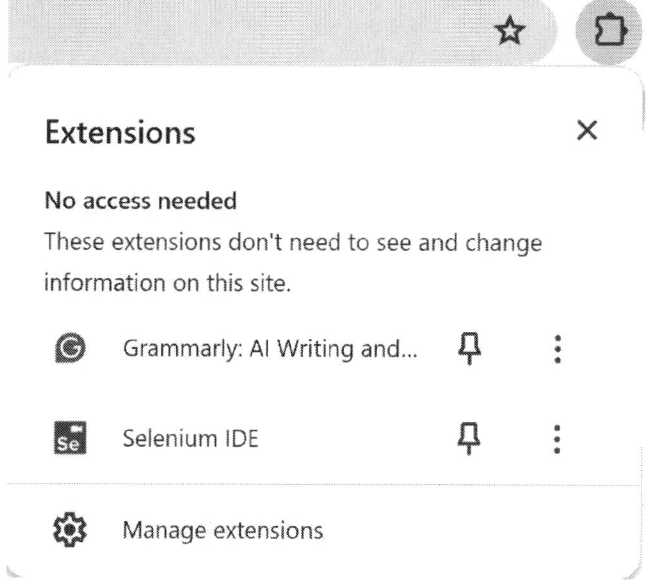

Figure 9.3: Running Selenium IDE

You are prompted for the action you would like to perform, whether to create a new project, access an existing project, etc.

When you create a new project, you are prompted for the project name. At this point, Selenium IDE opens, and you can insert the application URL.

New tests can be created by clicking the plus button next to the tests list.

In order to record a test, select the test name and then click the record icon. A new browser window will open with the application URL. From this point, every action you perform on the application and its results will be recorded.

You can make assertions on the page content by right-clicking on a page element and selecting the appropriate action from the **Selenium IDE > Assert** submenu. For instance, if you select the **Selenium IDE > Assert > Text** command on a text element, the text value will be stored. When the test is executed, the content of the same text element will be compared with the previously stored value, and the test will fail if the two values are different.

Once all desired actions and assertions have been performed, return to the Selenium IDE window, click the stop recording button, and save the project.

Selenium IDE offers the option to run either a selected test or all tests.

Summary

In this chapter, we explained why it is worth automating software tests, and then we focused on the importance of unit tests. We also listed the various types of tests and their main features, focusing mainly on unit tests and functional tests. We analyzed the advantages of **TDD** and how to use it in practice. With this knowledge, you should be able to produce software that is both reliable and easy to modify.

Then, this chapter analyzed when it is worth automating some or all functional tests and described how to automate them in `ASP.NET` Core applications.

Finally, we analyzed the main test tools available for .NET projects, focusing on xUnit, `Moq`, `Microsoft.AspNetCore.Mvc.Testing`, and *Selenium*, and showed how to use them in practice with the help of the book's use case.

Chapter 21, *Case Study*, applies all the test concepts described in this chapter to the book's case study.

Questions

1. Why is it worth automating unit tests?
2. What is the main reason why TDD is able to discover most bugs immediately?
3. What is the difference between the `[Theory]` and `[Fact]` attributes of xUnit?
4. Which xUnit static class is used in test assertions?
5. Which methods allow the definition of the `Moq` mocked dependencies?
6. Is it possible to mock `async` methods with `Moq`? If so, how?
7. Is it always worth automating UI functional tests in the case of quick CI/CD cycles?
8. What is the disadvantage of subcutaneous tests for ASP.NET Core applications?
9. What is the suggested technique for writing code-driven ASP.NET Core functional tests?
10. What is the suggested way of inspecting the HTML returned by a server?

Further reading

- While the documentation on xUnit included in this chapter is quite complete, it doesn't include a few configuration options offered by xUnit. The full xUnit documentation is available at `https://xunit.net/`. Documentation for MSTest and NUnit can be found at `https://github.com/microsoft/testfx` and `https://docs.nunit.org/`, respectively.
- For more information on BDD and SpecFlow, refer to the Cucumber official website at `https://cucumber.io/` and to the SpecFlow documentation at `https://docs.specflow.org/`.
- The full Moq documentation is available at `https://github.com/moq/moq4/wiki/Quickstart`.
- Here are some links to performance test frameworks for web applications:
    - `https://jmeter.apache.org/ (free and open source)`
    - `https://www.neotys.com/neoload/overview`
    - `https://www.microfocus.com/en-us/products/loadrunner-load-testing/overview`
- `https://www.microfocus.com/en-us/products/silk-performer/overview`
- More details on the `Microsoft.AspNetCore.Mvc.Testing NuGet` package can be found in the official documentation at `https://docs.microsoft.com/en-US/aspnet/core/test/integration-tests`.
- More information on Selenium IDE can be found on the official website: `https://www.selenium.dev/selenium-ide/`.
- More information on Selenium WebDriver can be found on the official website: `https://www.selenium.dev/documentation/webdriver/`.

Learn more on Discord

To join the Discord community for this book – where you can share feedback, ask questions to the authors, and learn about new releases – follow the QR code below:

`https://packt.link/SoftwareArchitectureCSharp12Dotnet8`

10

Deciding on the Best Cloud-Based Solution

When designing your application to make it cloud-based, you must understand different architectural designs – from the simplest to the most sophisticated. In fact, cloud technology not only enables cost optimization but also significantly reduces the time it takes to launch your solution to the market. Also, it effectively enhances your application's ability to tolerate faults and scale. However, optimizing for cost, speed, resilience, and scalability often involves trade-offs in terms of constraints and flexibility, so you must choose the right compromise for your needs.

This chapter discusses different software architecture models and teaches you how to take advantage of the opportunities offered by the cloud in your solutions. This chapter will also discuss the different types of cloud service that we can consider while developing our infrastructure, what the ideal scenarios are, and where we can use each of them.

The following topics will be covered in this chapter:

- Infrastructure as a Service solutions
- Platform as a Service solutions
- Software as a Service solutions
- Serverless solutions
- How to use hybrid solutions and why they are so useful

It is worth mentioning that the choice to be made between these options depends on different aspects of the project scenario, such as the need for flexibility and/or highly customized solutions versus simplicity, low maintenance costs, and low time-to-market. These trade-offs will be discussed throughout the whole chapter.

Technical requirements

For the practical content in this chapter, you must create or use an Azure account. We can find the detailed procedure for creating an Azure account in *Chapter 1, Understanding the Importance of Software Architecture*, in the *Creating an Azure account* section.

Different software deployment models

Let's begin our exploration with **Infrastructure as a Service** (**IaaS**), the foundational layer of cloud computing. IaaS offers a flexible and scalable infrastructure, which is crucial for businesses with specific hardware requirements or those transitioning from on-premises solutions to the cloud.

In companies where you have infrastructure engineers, you will probably find more people working with **IaaS**. On the other hand, in companies where IT is not the core business, you will find a bunch of **Software as a Service** (**SaaS**) systems. It is common for developers to decide to use the **Platform as a Service** (**PaaS**) option or to go serverless, as they have no need to deliver infrastructures in this scenario.

As a software architect, you must cope with this environment and be sure that you are optimizing the cost and work factors, not only during the initial development of the solution but also during its maintenance. Also, as an architect, you must understand the needs of your system and work hard to connect those needs to best-in-class peripheral solutions, speeding up delivery and keeping the solution as close as possible to the customer's specifications.

IaaS and Azure opportunities

IaaS was the first generation of cloud services provided by many different cloud players. Its definition is easily found in many places, but we can summarize it as "your computing infrastructure delivered on the internet, hosted somewhere that you do not manage." In the same way that we have virtualization of services in a local data center, IaaS will also give you virtualized components, such as servers, storage, and firewalls, in the cloud.

In a few words, all the hardware you need is hosted in the cloud and maintained by the cloud provider instead of being hosted in your private data center. This includes servers delivered as virtual machines, possibly connected to private networks, disk storage, and also firewalls. You don't buy the hardware but pay for its usage, and you can scale to a more powerful configuration at zero cost.

You can access your cloud hardware as if it were hosted in your private data center, but hardware maintenance is taken care of by the cloud provider. Moreover, you can scale your hardware gradually as your application traffic increases without installation and purchase costs and without migrating data to new hardware. Scaling is performed with simple configuration instructions.

Among the various cloud providers, Azure is the one with the most complete and varied offer, so you can easily find a perfect match with any hardware need. Most Azure **IaaS** solutions are paid for, and you should pay attention to this when it comes to testing. It is worth mentioning that this book does not set out to describe all IaaS services that Azure provides in detail. However, as a software architect, you do need to understand that you will find services such as the following:

- **Virtual machines**: Windows Server, Linux, Oracle, data science, and machine learning
- **Network**: Virtual networks, load balancers, and DNS zones
- **Storage**: Files, tables, databases, and Redis

Obviously, these are not the only ones available as IaaS models, so the first step is to look at the service options available in Azure. To create any service in Azure, you must find the service that best fits your needs and then create a resource. The following screenshot shows a Windows Server virtual machine being configured.

Basics Disks Networking Management Monitoring Advanced Tags Review + create

Create a virtual machine that runs Linux or Windows. Select an image from Azure marketplace or use your own customized image. Complete the Basics tab then Review + create to provision a virtual machine with default parameters or review each tab for full customization. Learn more

Project details

Select the subscription to manage deployed resources and costs. Use resource groups like folders to organize and manage all your resources.

Subscription * : Sottoscrizione di Azure 1

Resource group * : (New) WWTravelC_group

Create new

Instance details

Virtual machine name * : WWTravelC

Region * : (Europe) West Europe

Availability options : No infrastructure redundancy required

Security type : Standard

Image * : Windows Server 2022 Datacenter: Azure Edition - x64 Gen2

See all images | Configure VM generation

This image is compatible with additional security features. Click here to swap to the Trusted launch security type.

VM architecture : Arm64 / x64

Arm64 is not supported with the selected image.

Run with Azure Spot discount

Size * : Standard_D2s_v3 - 2 vcpus, 8 GiB memory (154,76 USD/month)

See all sizes

Review + create < Previous Next : Disks >

Figure 10.1: Creating a virtual machine in Azure

Following the wizard provided by Azure to set up your virtual machine, you will be able to connect to it by using **Remote Desktop Protocol (RDP)**. The next screenshot presents some of the hardware options you have for deploying a virtual machine. It is interesting to consider the vast array of hardware options at our disposal for deploying a virtual machine, especially when considering that these can be accessed just by clicking on the **Select** button.

Showing 334 VM sizes. | Subscription: Pay-As-You-Go | Region: Brazil South | Current size: Standard_DS1_v2 | Image: Windows Server 2019 Datacenter | Learn more about VM sizes

VM Size ↑↓	Family ↑↓	vCPUs ↑↓	RAM (GiB) ↑↓	Data disks ↑↓	Max IOPS ↑↓	Temp storage (GiB) ↑↓
Most used by Azure users		The most used sizes by users in Azure				
DS1_v2	General purpose	1	3.5	4	3200	7
D2s_v3	General purpose	2	8	4	3200	16
D2as_v4	General purpose	2	8	4	3200	16
B2s	General purpose	2	4	4	1280	8
B1s	General purpose	1	1	2	320	4
B2ms	General purpose	2	8	4	1920	16
DS2_v2	General purpose	2	7	8	6400	14
B4ms	General purpose	4	16	8	2880	32
D4s_v3	General purpose	4	16	8	6400	32
DS3_v2	General purpose	4	14	16	12800	28
D8s_v3	General purpose	8	32	16	12800	64

Figure 10.2: Virtual machine sizes available in Azure

If you compare the on-premises velocity to deliver hardware with the cloud velocity, you will realize that there is nothing better than the cloud when it comes to time-to-market. For instance, there are machines with 64 CPUs, 256 GB of RAM, and temporary storage of 512 GB. This is something you probably will not find in an on-premises data center, for instance, if you have a temporary workload, or it will take you a lot to deliver if you have a brand-new business idea that needs this computing power. Besides, in the temporary workload scenario, this machine will be underutilized, so it would be impossible to justify its purchase in an on-premises scenario.

IaaS can be adopted when you want full control over your infrastructure while still benefiting from cloud computing advantages like redundancy and scalability. However, the time-to-market for IaaS solutions is similar to that for on-premises solutions. Therefore, it is convenient to start with options that allow for a quicker launch in the short run and consider transitioning to IaaS for long-term objectives.

Security responsibility in IaaS

Security is an essential aspect of all hardware solutions because hacker attacks might cause both service interruptions and leaks or loss of important business data.

Security responsibility is another important thing to know about an IaaS platform. Many people think that once you decide to go on the cloud, all the security is done by the provider. However, this is not true, as you can see in the following screenshot:

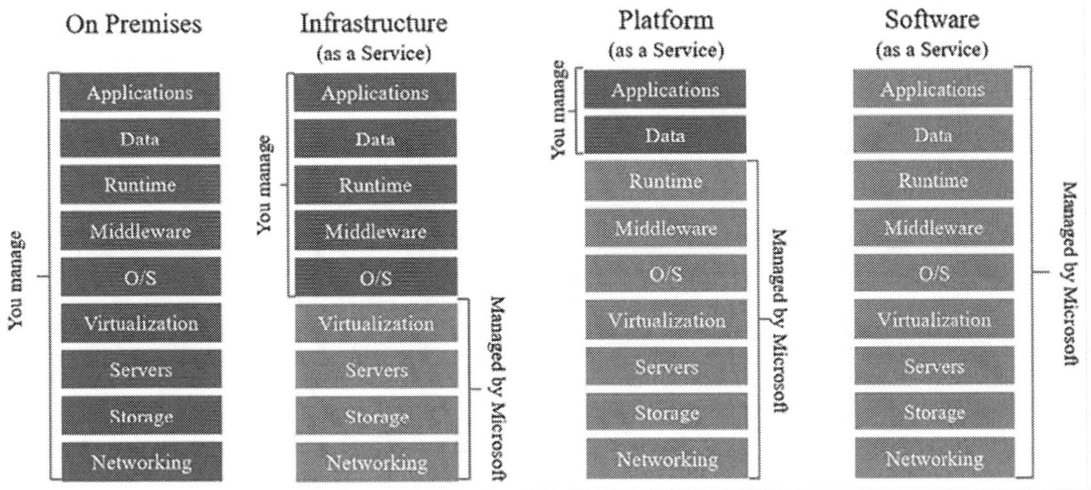

Figure 10.3: Managing security in cloud computing

IaaS will force you to take care of security from the operating system to the application. In some cases, this is inevitable, but you must understand that this will increase your system cost.

IaaS can be a good option if you just want to move an already existing on-premises structure to the cloud. This enables scalability due to the tools that Azure gives you, along with all the other services. However, if you are planning to develop an application from scratch, you should also consider other options available on Azure.

Shifting our focus to **PaaS**, we enter a realm where speed and efficiency in software development take center stage. PaaS provides an environment where businesses can develop, run, and manage applications without the complexity of building and maintaining the infrastructure.

PaaS – a world of opportunities for developers

If you are studying or have studied software architectures, you will probably perfectly understand the meaning of the next sentence. The world demands high speed when it comes to software development! This demand for speed is precisely where **PaaS** becomes invaluable, offering rapid development and deployment capabilities.

As you can see in the preceding screenshot, PaaS allows you to worry about security only in terms of aspects that are closer to your business: your data and applications. For developers, this represents freedom from having to implement a bunch of configurations that make your solution work safely.

Security handling is not the only advantage of PaaS. As a software architect, you can introduce these services as an opportunity to deliver richer solutions faster. Time-to-market can surely justify the cost of many applications that run on a PaaS basis.

PaaS solutions free you from managing all details involved in your solution deployment without creating an excessive dependency on the PaaS supplier. In fact, your software need not depend too much on the chosen PaaS and small dependencies can be isolated in adequately designed drivers. In other words, it is always easy to move to a different PaaS solution or an IaaS solution if the software is designed with driver-based architecture, like the Onions architecture we described in the *Layers and the Onion architecture* section of *Chapter 7, Understanding the Different Domains in Software Solutions*. Therefore, PaaS may be a good choice to reduce time-to-market also when one plans to move to IaaS in the long run.

Delving deeper into PaaS, let's examine how Azure implements this model through its diverse range of services. Azure's PaaS offerings are designed to cater to various development needs, from web applications to complex data processing.

There are lots of services delivered as PaaS nowadays in Azure, and the array of available services is continuously expanding, reflecting the evolving needs of developers and businesses.

Again, it is not the purpose of this book to list all of them. However, some do need to be mentioned. The list keeps growing, and the recommendation here is to use and test these services as much as you can! Make sure that you will deliver better-designed solutions with this thought in mind.

On the other hand, it is worth mentioning that, with PaaS solutions, you will not have full control of the operating system. In fact, in many situations, you do not even have to have a way to connect to it. This is fine most of the time, but in some debugging situations, you may miss this feature. The good thing is that PaaS components are evolving every single day, and one of Microsoft's biggest concerns is making them widely visible.

The following subsections introduce the most common PaaS components delivered by Microsoft for .NET web apps, that is, Azure Web Apps and Azure SQL Server. We also describe Azure Cognitive Services, a very powerful PaaS platform that demonstrates how wonderful development is in the PaaS world. We will explore some of them in greater depth in the remainder of this book.

Of the many PaaS services, web apps stand out for their versatility and ease of use. Azure's web app service simplifies the deployment of various types of applications, demonstrating the practicality and accessibility of PaaS solutions.

Web apps

A web app is a PaaS option you can use to deploy your web app. You can deploy different types of applications, such as .NET, .NET Core, Java, PHP, Node.js, and Python. An example of this was presented in *Chapter 1, Understanding the Importance of Software Architecture*.

The good thing is that creating a web app does not require any structure and/or IIS web server setup. In some cases, where you are using Linux to host your .NET application, you do not have IIS at all. Web apps' flexibility in hosting options, such as not requiring IIS for Linux-based deployments, underscores their adaptability to various development and deployment environments.

Moreover, web apps have a plan option where you do not need to pay for usage. Of course, there are limitations, such as only running 32-bit apps and failing to enable scalability. This free tier is ideal for learning and initial application prototyping, offering essential features without the financial commitment.

SQL databases

Imagine how quickly you can deploy a solution if you have the complete power of an SQL server without needing to pay for a big server to deploy this database. This applies to SQL databases. With them, you can use Microsoft SQL Server for what you need the most – storage and data processing. In this scenario, Azure assumes responsibility for backing up the database.

Here, we will discuss briefly the advantages of having your databases in the cloud. Databases are discussed in detail in both *Chapter 12, Choosing Your Data Storage in the Cloud*, and *Chapter 13, Interacting with Data in C# – Entity Framework Core*.

Say you are starting a new business application, and say, initially, your data storage and traffic requirements are quite low, but you need advanced features such as data replication to safeguard your data and offer high performance to geographically distributed users. Without Azure SQL databases, you would be forced to buy several SQL licenses since the SQL Server free edition doesn't cover similar scenarios.

With Azure SQL databases, instead, you can have the top features of the SQL Server Enterprise edition without paying for an expensive license, paying instead just for your initially small storage and traffic needs.

The SQL database even gives you the option to manage performance by itself. This is called automatic tuning – that is, your traffic requirements are automatically scaled to keep response time acceptable as requests increase. This means that your costs might automatically increase, but you can also define maximum expense limits.

Again, with PaaS components, you will be able to focus on what is important to your business: a very fast time-to-market.

The steps to create a SQL database for testing are quite simple, like what we have seen with other components. However, there are two things you need to pay attention to: the creation of the server and how you will be charged. In fact, understanding the various configurations and their costs is essential to finding the best trade-off between your application and maximum cost requirements.

When you create a resource, you can search for `SQL Database`, and you will find this wizard to help you:

Microsoft Azure
Search resources, services, and docs (G+/)
Home > Create a resource > SQL Database >
Create SQL Database ...
Microsoft
Basics Networking Security Additional settings Tags Review + create
Create a SQL database with your preferred configurations. Complete the Basics tab then go to Review + Create to provision with smart defaults, or visit each tab to customize. Learn more
Project details
Select the subscription to manage deployed resources and costs. Use resource groups like folders to organize and manage all your resources.
Subscription * Pay-As-You-Go
Resource group * Select a resource group
Create new
Database details
Enter required settings for this database, including picking a logical server and configuring the compute and storage resources
Database name * Enter database name
Server * Select a server
Create new
The value must not be empty.
Want to use SQL elastic pool? * Yes No
Compute + storage * Please select a server first.
Configure database
Backup storage redundancy
Choose how your PITR and LTR backups are replicated. Geo restore or ability to recover from regional outage is only available when geo-redundant storage is selected
Review + create Next : Networking >

Figure 10.4: Creating a SQL database in Azure

The SQL database depends on an SQL server to host it. For this reason, as you can see, you must create (at least for the first database) a `database.windows.net` server, where your databases will be hosted. This server will provide all the parameters you need to access the SQL server database using current tools, such as Visual Studio, SQL Server Management Studio, and Azure Data Studio. It is worth mentioning that you have a bunch of security features, such as Transparent Data Encryption and IP firewalls.

As soon as you decide on the name of your database server, you will be able to choose the pricing tier on which your system will be charged. Especially in SQL databases, there are several different pricing options, as you can see in the following screenshot. You should study each of them carefully because, depending on your scenario, you can save money by optimizing a pricing tier:

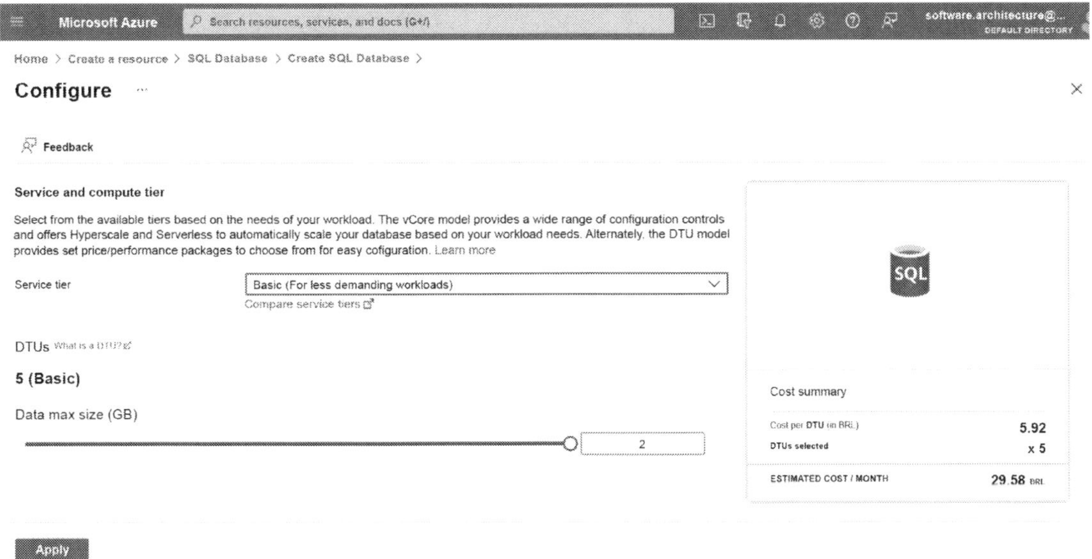

Figure 10.5: Configuring the Azure SQL Database Pricing Tier

For more information about SQL configuration, you can use this link: `https://azure.microsoft.com/en-us/services/sql-database/`.

More details on database solutions are discussed in *Chapter 12, Choosing Your Data Storage in the Cloud*, and *Chapter 13, Interacting with Data in C# - Entity Framework Core*.

Once you have completed the configuration, you will be able to connect to this server database in the same way you did when your SQL server was installed on-premises. The only detail that you must pay attention to is the configuration of the Azure SQL Server firewall, but this is quite simple to set up and a good demonstration of how safe the PaaS service is.

Azure Cognitive Services

Artificial Intelligence (**AI**) is one of the most frequently discussed topics in software architecture. We are a step away from a really great world where AI will be everywhere.

For instance, AI is gaining ever more importance in the field of automatic help centers, data analysis to drive business decisions, and user interfaces based on natural language. The economic value added to these areas by AI is enormous, both in the decrease of service costs and in the increase in profit due to optimized decision-making.

To realize this, as a software architect, you cannot think about AI as software you need to invent from scratch all the time.

Azure Cognitive Services can help you with this. These APIs empower developers to create advanced features, like voice recognition in apps or language translation in customer service tools, with relative ease.

The great thing about PaaS is evident from this scenario. The cost of developing an in-house AI solution would require both enormous investments and hard-to-find competencies. With Azure Cognitive Services' PaaS, instead, you just don't need to worry about AI techniques. Instead, you may remain focused on what really matters to you as a software architect: the solution to your business problem.

Setting up Azure Cognitive Services in your Azure account is also quite simple. First, you will need to add Cognitive Services like any other Azure component. You can choose a specific cognitive service or a multi-service account that will enable you to access all cognitive services. In the screenshot below, we have chosen a multi-service account:

Project Details

Subscription * | Sottoscrizione di Azure 1

Resource group * | Create new

Cognitive Services resource creation requires subscription registration, we detected that your selected subscription did not register Cognitive Services resource type before, we will help you to register Cognitive Services resource type when you select a subscription in subscription dropdown. Click to learn more how to check registration state for your selected subscription.

Instance Details

Region | East US

Name * | WWTravelClubCS

Location specifies the region only for included regional services. This does not specify a region for included non-regional services. Click here for more details.

Pricing tier * | Standard S0

View full pricing details

By checking this box I acknowledge that I have read and understood all the terms below *

Responsible AI Notice

Review + create | < Previous | Next : Network >

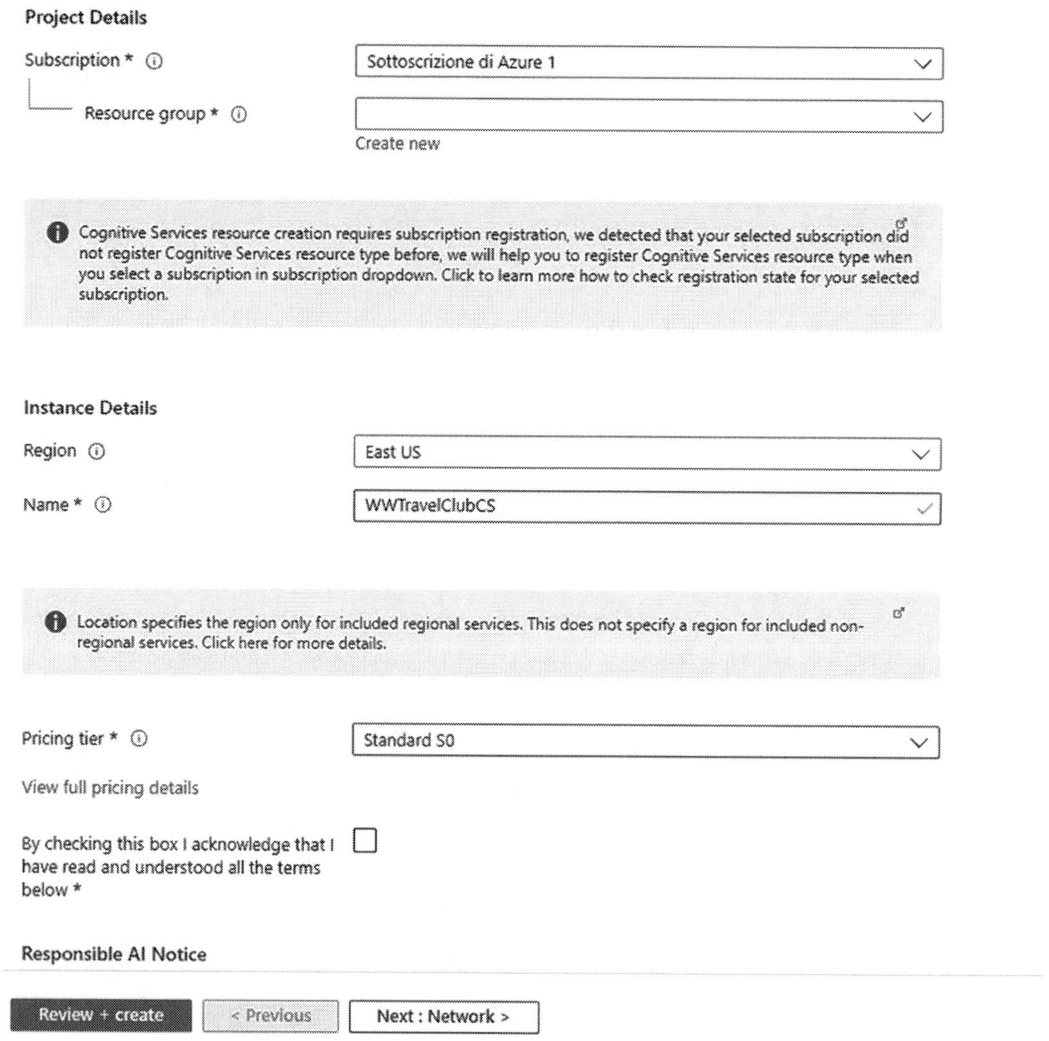

Figure 10.6: Creating a Cognitive Services API account in Azure

As soon as you have done this, you will be able to use the APIs provided by the server. You will find two important features in the service that you have created: endpoints and access keys. They are going to be used in your code to access APIs.

The following code sample shows how you can use the Cognitive Services API to translate sentences. The main concept underlying this translation service is that you can post the sentence you want to translate according to the key and region where the service was set. The following code enables you to post a request to the service API:

```
private static async Task<string> CSTranslate(string api, string key, string
region, string textToTranslate)
{
    using var client = new HttpClient();
    client.DefaultRequestHeaders.Add("Ocp-Apim-Subscription-Key", key);
    client.DefaultRequestHeaders.Add("Ocp-Apim-Subscription-Region", region);
    client.Timeout = TimeSpan.FromSeconds(5);
    var body = new[] { new { Text = textToTranslate } };
    var requestBody = JsonConvert.SerializeObject(body);
    var content = new StringContent(requestBody, Encoding.UTF8, "application/
json");
    var response = await client.PostAsync(api, content);
    response.EnsureSuccessStatusCode();
    return await response.Content.ReadAsStringAsync();
}
```

It is worth mentioning that the preceding code will allow you to post requests to translate any text into any language, provided you define it in the parameters. The following is the main program that calls the previous method:

```
static async Task Main()
{
    var host = "https://api.cognitive.microsofttranslator.com";
    var route = "/translate?api-version=3.0&to=es";
    var subscriptionKey = "[YOUR KEY HERE]";
    var region = "[YOUR REGION HERE]";
    if (subscriptionKey == "[YOUR KEY HERE]")
    {
        Console.WriteLine("Please, enter your key: ");
        subscriptionKey = Console.ReadLine();
    }
    if (region  == "[YOUR REGION HERE]")
    {
        Console.WriteLine("Please, enter your region: ");
        region = Console.ReadLine();
```

```
        }
        var translatedSentence = await PostAPI(host + route, subscriptionKey,
    region, "Hello World!");
        Console.WriteLine(translatedSentence);
        Console.WriteLine("Press any key to continue...");
        Console.ReadKey();
    }
```

For further information, visit `https://docs.microsoft.com/en-us/azure/cognitive-services/translator/reference/v3-0-languages`.

This is a perfect example of how easily and quickly you can use services such as this to architect your projects. This ease of use not only accelerates project development but also opens up new possibilities for innovation and enhanced user experiences.

SaaS — just sign in and get started!

SaaS is probably the easiest way to use cloud-based services. The application you need is already available on the cloud, and you need just to configure and use it! Cloud players provide many good options that solve common problems for their end users in a company. From email services to comprehensive business management tools, SaaS offers a wide array of applications that you can tailor to your various business needs.

A good example of this type of service is Office 365. The key point with these platforms is that you do not need to worry about application maintenance. This is particularly convenient in scenarios where your team is totally focused on developing the core business of the application. For example, if your solution needs to deliver good reports, maybe you can design them using Power BI (which is included in Office 365). Thus, integrating Office 365 into your solution allows for seamless data analysis and reporting, immediately enhancing the overall efficiency and productivity of your business operations.

A SaaS solution can be customized in various ways. The most powerful technique is the addition of custom plugins. For instance, you can customize your Office 365 tenant by adding various kinds of plugins that are available in public repositories and/or by developing your own custom plugins.

It is also worth pointing out that if you decide to invest in custom plugins, you already have, say, 90% of the application running and stable, so both the initial investment and the time to market are incredibly reduced.

In summary, on the one hand, SaaS offers immediately sophisticated and proven solutions, but on the other hand, SaaS offers very limited customization options. So, how do you decide whether to use a SaaS solution?

1. **Evaluate existing solutions**: First of all, you need to verify if a SaaS that matches your needs already exists.
2. **Consider customization and integration:** Then, you need to verify if the selected options can be adapted to your needs and the investment required to adapt them.

3. **Analyze cost implications:** At this point, you must analyze the impact of the inevitable compromises you will be forced to accept, as well as the overall cost implied by each candidate SaaS adoption, which includes the overall cost of the impact it has on your organization.
4. **Review security and compliance:** You also need to verify that the users/security model used by the SaaS is compatible with your needs and that, in general, the application fulfills all constraints required by your organization.
5. **Assess vendor reliability and support:** The impact of having a strong dependency on the SaaS supplier is a key factor in your final decision. Keep in mind that once you incorporate a SaaS solution into your business, it might be very difficult to move to a different solution – that is, the contractual power of your supplier might rise over time to unacceptable levels. For the same reason, an unreliable supplier (for instance, a young start-up) or a supplier that can't offer adequate product support might cause unacceptable damage.
6. **Plan for scalability and future growth:** You must also consider the future of your organization. Thus, you must also verify if the candidate options are scalable and can be adapted to your growing needs and traffic.
7. **Test the solution:** Finally, you need to test the chosen solution in practice in a staging environment, verifying that your overall analysis and predictions are correct.

Another pretty good example of a SaaS platform is Azure DevOps. As a software architect, before Azure DevOps, you needed to install and configure **Team Foundation Server** (**TFS**) (or even older tools like Microsoft Visual SourceSafe) for your team to work with a common repository and an application life cycle management tool.

We used to spend a lot of time just working either on preparing the server for TFS installation or upgrading and continuously maintaining the TFS already installed. This is no longer needed due to the simplicity of SaaS Azure DevOps.

Understanding what serverless means

A serverless solution is a solution where the focus is not on where the code runs. Even in a "serverless" solution, there is always a server. The thing is that you just do not know or care which server your code executes on. The main advantage of serverless is that you have zero fixed monthly costs, and you are billed just for your traffic.

However, there are also other advantages. For instance, in a serverless solution, you have a very fast, simple, and agile application life cycle since almost all serverless code is stateless and loosely coupled with the remainder of the system. Some authors refer to this as **Function as a Service** (**FaaS**).

Of course, the server runs somewhere. The key point here is that you do not need to worry about this or even scalability. This will enable you to focus completely on your app's business logic. Again, the world needs fast development and good customer experiences at the same time. The more you focus on customer needs, the better!

FaaS offers the shortest time-to-market and the lowest cost threshold, together with large scalability possibilities. So, they are convenient in situations where it is extremely difficult to forecast the application workload or when the application workload has a high and difficult-to-forecast variance.

Suppose, for instance, you are looking for a solution for mass email sending to connect to your application. If your applications also handle marketing campaigns, there would be traffic peaks that might also be 100 times your average traffic. A FaaS solution might be able to easily cover these huge peaks without impacting the average costs you have outside of them.

Conversely, in a similar situation, PaaS or IaaS would force you to move to a higher price tier if you don't need it during your average periods, just during your marketing campaign peaks.

If the workload becomes more stable, and it is easier to draw reliable lower and higher bounds, FaaS becomes less convenient due to its higher cost on higher workloads. As an example, Amazon Prime recently publicized its savings by switching from FaaS to IaaS.

Unluckily, moving from FaaS to PaaS or IaaS is not easy since FaaS code is strictly tied to the chosen FaaS solution.

This issue can be partially mitigated by avoiding overly fragmented FaaS code made of small functions and, instead, using a few functions that trigger the execution of bigger conventional software modules enclosed inside the FaaS solution. This way, moving to a different FaaS, or to IaaS/PaaS, would require just rewriting a few FaaS mains while keeping the bigger software modules they call unchanged. Unfortunately, the performance penalty of waking up an inactive function is incompatible with the usage of complex frameworks inside each function, so fragmentation is unavoidable.

In my experience, FaaS proves to be useful either in the early stages of a presumably high-traffic but low-complexity application or for low-complexity applications like our previous email-sending application, which are specifically designed to handle high and difficult-to-forecast peaks. In fact, in these applications, near-complete code rewrites are acceptable since the investment for the code development is low compared with the savings implied by an almost immediate time-to-market and by efficacious handling of big and hard-to-forecast traffic peeks.

In *Chapter 16, Working with Serverless – Azure Functions*, you will explore one of the best serverless implementations that Microsoft provides in Azure – Azure Functions. There, we will focus on how you can develop serverless solutions and learn about their advantages and disadvantages.

The following subsections compare IaaS, PaaS, SaaS, and FaaS along several axes.

Comparing IaaS, PaaS, SaaS, and FaaS

In the previous sections, we described various types of solutions offered by all main cloud providers, with their advantages and disadvantages. The table below summarizes the main advantages offered by each of them, assigning a note between 1 (less good) and 4 (very good) to five axes.

	Time-to-Market	Customization possibility	Maintenance effort	Scalability	Cost
IaaS	1	4	1	1	4
PaaS	2	3	2	2	3
SaaS	4	1	4	Depends on application	1
FaaS	3	2	3	4	2

Why are hybrid applications so useful in many cases?

In its general meaning, the word *hybrid* means something whose parts do not share a uniform architectural choice; each part makes a different architectural choice. However, in the case of cloud solutions, the word *hybrid* refers mainly to solutions that mix cloud subsystems with on-premises subsystems. However, it can also refer to mixing web subsystems with device-specific subsystems, such as mobiles or any other device that runs code.

Due to the number of services Azure can provide and the number of design architectures that can be implemented, hybrid applications are probably the best answer to the main question addressed in this chapter: how to use the opportunities offered by the cloud in your projects.

Nowadays, many current projects are moving from an on-premises solution to a cloud architecture, and depending on where you are going to deliver these projects, you will still find many bad preconceptions regarding moving to the cloud. Most of them are related to cost, security, and service availability.

You need to understand that there is some truth in these preconceptions, but not in the way people think. For sure, you, as a software architect, cannot ignore them. Especially when you develop a critical system, you must decide whether everything can go on the cloud or whether it is better to deliver part of the system on the edge. Therefore, understanding these factors is key to navigating the hybrid landscape, which ensures that you balance cost, security, and availability according to your specific needs.

It is worth mentioning a real-life example that might clarify the need for hybrid solutions. Recently, several customers of a SaaS solution we offer objected to the fact that they couldn't move reserved and business-critical documents to the cloud. Our solution was equipping our SaaS with file-handling drivers capable of retrieving files from an in-house document server located in the customer's private intranet.

A completely different kind of hybrid solution is the edge computing paradigm. According to this paradigm, parts of the system must be deployed on machines or devices close to the location where they are needed. This helps to reduce response times and bandwidth.

Mobile solutions can be considered another classic example of hybrid applications since they mix a web-based architecture with a device-based architecture to offer a better user experience. There are lots of scenarios where you can replace a mobile application with a responsive website. However, when it comes to interface quality and performance, maybe a responsive website will not give the end user what they really need.

Summary

In this chapter, you learned how to take advantage of the services offered by the cloud in your solutions, as well as the various options you can choose from.

This chapter covered different ways to deliver the same application in a cloud-based structure. We also noted how rapidly Microsoft is delivering all these options to its customers, as you can experience all of these options in actual applications and choose the one that best fits your needs, since there is no *silver bullet* that works in all situations. As a software architect, you need to analyze your environment and your team, and then decide on the best cloud architecture to implement in your solution.

The next chapter is dedicated to building a flexible architecture comprising small, scalable software modules called microservices.

Questions

1. Why should you use IaaS in your solution?
2. Why should you use PaaS in your solution?
3. Why should you use SaaS in your solution?
4. Why should you use serverless in your solution?
5. What is the advantage of using an Azure SQL Server database?
6. How can you accelerate AI in your application with Azure?
7. How can hybrid architectures help you to design a better solution?

Further reading

You can check out these web links to study the topics covered in this chapter in greater depth:

- `https://visualstudio.microsoft.com/xamarin/`
- `https://www.packtpub.com/application-development/xamarin-cross-platform-application-development`
- `https://www.packtpub.com/virtualization-and-cloud/learning-azure-functions`
- `https://azure.microsoft.com/overview/what-is-iaas/`
- `https://docs.microsoft.com/en-us/azure/security/azure-security-iaas`
- `https://azure.microsoft.com/services/app-service/web/`
- `https://azure.microsoft.com/services/sql-database/`
- `https://azure.microsoft.com/en-us/services/virtual-machines/data-science-virtual-machines/`
- `https://docs.microsoft.com/azure/sql-database/sql-database-automatic-tuning`
- `https://azure.microsoft.com/en-us/services/cognitive-services/`
- `https://docs.microsoft.com/en-us/azure/architecture/`
- `https://powerbi.microsoft.com/`
- `https://office.com`
- `https://azure.microsoft.com/en-us/overview/what-is-serverless-computing/`
- `https://azure.microsoft.com/en-us/pricing/details/sql-database/`
- `https://www.packtpub.com/virtualization-and-cloud/professional-azure-sql-database-administration`

Learn more on Discord

To join the Discord community for this book – where you can share feedback, ask questions to the authors, and learn about new releases – follow the QR code below:

`https://packt.link/SoftwareArchitectureCSharp12Dotnet8`

11

Applying a Microservice Architecture to Your Enterprise Application

This chapter is dedicated to describing highly scalable architectures based on small modules called microservices. The microservice architecture allows for fine-grained scaling operations where every single module can be scaled as required without affecting the remainder of the system. Moreover, they allow for better **Continuous Integration/Continuous Deployment** (CI/CD) by permitting every system subpart to evolve and be deployed independently of the others.

In this chapter, we will cover the following topics:

- What are microservices?
- When do microservices help?
- How does .NET deal with microservices?
- Which tools are needed to manage microservices?

By the end of this chapter, you will have learned how to implement a single microservice in .NET. *Chapter 20, Kubernetes,* also explains how to deploy, debug, and manage a whole microservices-based application. *Chapter 14, Implementing Microservices with .NET,* and *Chapter 18, Implementing Frontend Microservices with ASP.NET Core,* are step-by-step guides to the practical implementation of microservices with .NET.

Technical requirements

The code for this chapter is available at `https://github.com/PacktPublishing/Software-Architecture-with-C-Sharp-12-and-.NET-8-4E`.

In this chapter, you will require the following:

- Visual Studio 2022 free Community Edition or better with all the database tools installed.
- A free Azure account. The *Creating an Azure account* section in *Chapter 1, Understanding the Importance of Software Architecture*, explains how to create one.
- **Docker Desktop for Windows** if you want to debug Docker containerized microservices in Visual Studio (`https://www.docker.com/products/docker-desktop`).

In turn, **Docker Desktop for Windows** requires at least Windows 10 with either **Windows Subsystem for Linux** (**WSL**) or **Windows Containers** installed.

WSL enables Docker containers to run on a Linux virtual machine and can be installed as follows (see also `https://learn.microsoft.com/en-us/windows/wsl/install`):

1. Type `powershell` in the Windows 10/11 search bar.
2. When **Windows PowerShell** is proposed as a search result, click on **Run as an administrator**.
3. In the Windows PowerShell administrative console that appears, run the command `wsl --install`.

Windows Containers enable Docker containers to run directly on Windows, but they require at least the Windows Professional edition. They can be installed as follows:

1. Type `Windows features` in the Windows 10/11 search bar.
2. The search results will propose running the panel to enable/disable Windows features.
3. Click on it, and in the window that opens, select **Containers**.

What are microservices?

Microservices are essentially small, independent units that make up a larger software application, each with its specific role and functionality. Splitting a software application into independent microservices allows each module that makes up a solution to be scaled independently from the others to achieve the maximum throughput with minimal cost. In fact, scaling whole systems instead of their current bottlenecks inevitably results in a remarkable waste of resources, so fine-grained control of subsystem scaling has a considerable impact on the system's overall cost.

However, microservices are more than scalable components – they are software building blocks that can be developed, maintained, and deployed independently of each other. Splitting development and maintenance among modules that can be independently developed, maintained, and deployed improves the overall system's CI/CD cycle (CI/CD was described in detail in *Chapter 8, Understanding DevOps Principles and CI/CD*).

The CI/CD improvement is due to microservice *independence* because it enables the following:

- Scaling and distributing microservices on different types of hardware.
- Since each microservice is deployed independently from the others, there can't be binary compatibility or database structure compatibility constraints. Therefore, there is no need to align the versions of the different microservices that compose the system. This means that each of them can evolve as needed without being constrained by the others.

However, attention must be paid to the choice of communication protocols and messages and to their versions, which must be supported by all involved microservices. Protocols that are widely supported and that facilitate backward compatibility with previous versions of messages should be preferred.

- Assigning their development to completely separate smaller teams, thus simplifying job organization and reducing all the inevitable coordination inefficiencies that arise when handling large teams.
- Implementing each microservice with more adequate technologies and in a more adequate environment since each microservice is an independent deployment unit. This means choosing tools that best fit your requirements and an environment that minimizes development efforts and/or maximizes performance.
- Since each microservice can be implemented with different technologies, programming languages, tools, and operating systems, enterprises can use all available human resources by matching environments with developers' competencies. For instance, all available Java and .NET developers can cooperate in the same application, thus exploiting all available resources.
- Legacy subsystems can be embedded in independent microservices, thus enabling them to cooperate with newer subsystems. This way, companies may reduce the time to market new system versions. Moreover, in this way, legacy systems can evolve slowly toward more modern systems with an acceptable impact on costs and the organization.

The next subsection explains how the concept of microservices was conceived. Then, we will continue this introductory section by exploring basic microservice design principles and analyzing why microservices are often designed as Docker containers.

Microservices and the evolution of the concept of modules

For a better understanding of the advantages of microservices, as well as their design techniques, we must keep the two-fold nature of software modularity and software modules in mind:

- **Code modularity** refers to code organization that makes it easy for us to modify a chunk of code without affecting the remainder of the application. It is usually enforced with object-oriented design, where modules can be identified with classes.
- **Deployment modularity** depends on what your deployment units are and which properties they have. The simplest deployment units are executable files and libraries. Thus, for instance, **dynamic link libraries (DLLs)** are, for sure, more modular than static libraries since they must not be linked with the main executable before being deployed.

While the fundamental concepts of code modularity have reached stasis, the concept of deployment modularity is still evolving, and microservices are currently state-of-the-art along this evolution path.

As a short review of the main milestones on the path that led to microservices, we can say that, first, monolithic executables were broken into static libraries. Later on, DLLs replaced static libraries.

A great change took place when .NET (and other analogous frameworks, such as Java) improved the modularity of executables and libraries. In fact, with .NET, they can be deployed on different hardware and different operating systems since they are deployed in an intermediary language that is compiled when the library is executed for the first time. Moreover, they overcome some versioning issues of previous DLLs since any executable can bring with it a DLL with a version that differs from the version of the same DLL that is installed on the operating system.

However, .NET can't accept two referenced DLLs – let's say, *A* and *B* – using two different versions of a common dependency – let's say, *C*. For instance, suppose there is a newer version of *A* with many new features we would like to use that, in turn, relies on a newer version of *C* that is not supported by *B*. In this situation, we should renounce the newer version of *A* because of the incompatibility of *C* with *B*. This difficulty has led to two important changes:

- Packages: The development world moved from using single DLLs and/or single files as deployment units to using *packages* composed of both DLLs and metadata as deployment units. Packages are handled by *package management systems* such as NuGet and npm, which use package metadata to automatically check version compatibility with the help of semantic versioning.
- **Service-Oriented Architecture (SOA)**: Deployment units started being implemented as SOAP-based web services and later transition to REST web services. This solves the version compatibility problem since each web service runs in a different process and can use the most adequate version of each library with no risk of causing incompatibilities with other web services. Moreover, the interface that is exposed by each web service is platform-agnostic; that is, web services can connect with applications using any framework and run on any operating system since web service protocols are based on universally accepted standards. SOAs and protocols will be discussed in more detail in *Chapter 15, Applying Service-Oriented Architectures with .NET.*

Microservices are an evolution of SOA and add more features and more constraints that improve the scalability and the modularity of services to improve the overall CI/CD cycle. It's sometimes said that microservices are SOA done well. Moreover, as we will see in the next section, microservices are strictly tied with the DDD methodology described in *Chapter 7, Understanding the Different Domains in Software Solutions.*

To sum things up, the microservice architecture is an SOA that maximizes independence and fine-grained scaling. Now that we've clarified all the advantages of microservice independence and fine-grained scaling, as well as the very nature of independence, we are in a position to look at microservice design principles.

Microservice design principles

In this section, you will learn about the microservices' basic design principles. These principles are the basis for designing each microservice's code and architecture, and for designing the whole application architecture.

Let's start with principles that arise from the independence constraint. We will discuss them each in a separate subsection.

The independence of design choices

A fundamental design principle is the *independence of design choices*, which can be stated as follows:

The design of each microservice must not depend on the design choices that were made in the implementation of other microservices.

This principle enables the full independence of each microservice CI/CD cycle and leaves us with more technological choices on how to implement each microservice. This way, we can choose the best available technology to implement each microservice.

Another consequence of this principle is that different microservices can't connect to the same shared storage (database or filesystem) since sharing the same storage also means sharing all the design choices that determine the structure of the storage subsystem (database table design, database engine, and so on). Thus, either a microservice has its own data storage, or it has no storage at all and communicates with other microservices that take care of handling storage.

Dedicated data storage can be implemented either by physically including the database service within the boundary of the microservice or with an external database that the microservice has exclusive access to. Both are acceptable design choices. However, external databases are usually adopted because, for performance reasons, database engines are better run on dedicated hardware and with OS and hardware features that are optimized for their storage functionalities.

Usually, the *independence of design choices* is interpreted in a lighter form by distinguishing between logical and physical microservices. More specifically, logical microservices are the result of splitting the application into logical independent modules. If the application is designed with a **domain-driven design** (**DDD**) methodology, logical microservices correspond to DDD-bounded contexts, which we discussed in detail in *Chapter 7, Understanding the Different Domains in Software Solutions*.

In turn, each logical microservice may be split into various physical microservices that use the same data storage but that are load-balanced independently to achieve a better load balance.

For instance, in the book case study, travel payments are handled by the Payments Bounded Context described in the *Understanding the domains of the WWTravelClub application* section of *Chapter 21, Case Study*, which gives rise to a unique logical microservice. However, its practical implementation requires two main submodules:

- A customer credit card verification and authorization module, which takes care of all credit card verifications
- A user credits management module, which handles credits that the user already purchased, card information already loaded in the platform, and new credit card info loading

Since the process of credit card verification and authorization might be very time-consuming, it is convenient to implement the two submodules above as independent physical microservices, so they can be load-balanced separately.

Independence from the deployment environment

During load-balancing, microservices can be moved from very busy hardware nodes to more idle nodes. However, dependencies of each microservice on other software/files of the destination hardware nodes constrain the possible destination nodes.

Therefore, the more we reduce microservice dependencies, the more we have the freedom to move them from busy nodes to idle nodes, achieve a better load balance, and exploit the available hardware nodes.

This is the reason microservices are often containerized and use Docker. Containers will be discussed in more detail in the *Containers and Docker* subsection of this chapter, but basically, containerization is a technique that allows each microservice to bring its dependencies with it so that it can run anywhere. However, this is not a must because, in some applications, one might verify that all dependencies requirements of all microservices can be easily satisfied by all available nodes.

As we explore how microservices operate within their containerized environments, another key architectural principle comes into play – the concept of loose coupling.

Loose coupling

Each microservice must be loosely coupled with all the other microservices. This principle has a two-fold nature. On the one hand, this means that, according to object-oriented programming principles, the interface that's exposed by each microservice must not be too specific but as general as possible. However, it also means that communications among microservices must be minimized in order to reduce communication costs since microservices don't share the same address space and run on different hardware nodes.

For instance, suppose we are implementing a distributed web video game with a microservice architecture. Each microservice might take care of different functionalities, like collisions, visibility, user input handling, and so on. Some modules, like the collision and visibility modules, must know the whole game state, such as places where the user avatars are, the state of each avatar, and also the state of each reactive object that is in the game (such as obstacles, bullets shot by avatars, and so on). Therefore, either all the modules with a hard dependency on the whole game state are collapsed into a unique microservice or we must find an efficient way to share the overall game state between them with just a few message exchanges.

Both options have advantages and disadvantages and are actually adopted by real-world video games. Fewer messages might cause temporary incongruences, but melting too many modules into a unique microservice might impact the overall game performance so that the game might appear too "slow" to the users.

This concept of minimal inter-service communication naturally leads us to another consideration: the avoidance of chained requests/responses in a microservice architecture

No chained requests/responses

When a request reaches a microservice, it must not cause a recursive chain of nested requests/responses to other microservices since a similar chain would result in an unacceptable response time.

For instance, suppose that microservice A issues a request to microservice B and then waits for B to answer, and B does the same with C, and C does the same with D, and so on. As a result, A remains blocked waiting for its answer for the whole time the request propagates first to B, then to C, and then to D, and then the answer propagates back from D to C, then from C to B, and finally reaches A. That is, four request propagation times sum to the other four answer propagation times to get the overall A wait time. This way, the time a user waits to get an answer from the application might easily become unacceptable.

Chained requests/responses can be avoided if the private data models of all the microservices synchronize with push events each time they change. In other words, as soon as the data that is handled by a microservice changes, those changes are sent to all the microservices that may need them to serve their requests. This way, each microservice has all the data it needs to serve all its incoming requests in its private data storage, with no need to ask other microservices for the data that it lacks.

Figure 11.1 shows how updates are sent to all interested microservices as soon as they are produced and how each microservice combines all received updates in a local database. This way, each query microservice has all the data it needs to answer queries in its local database.

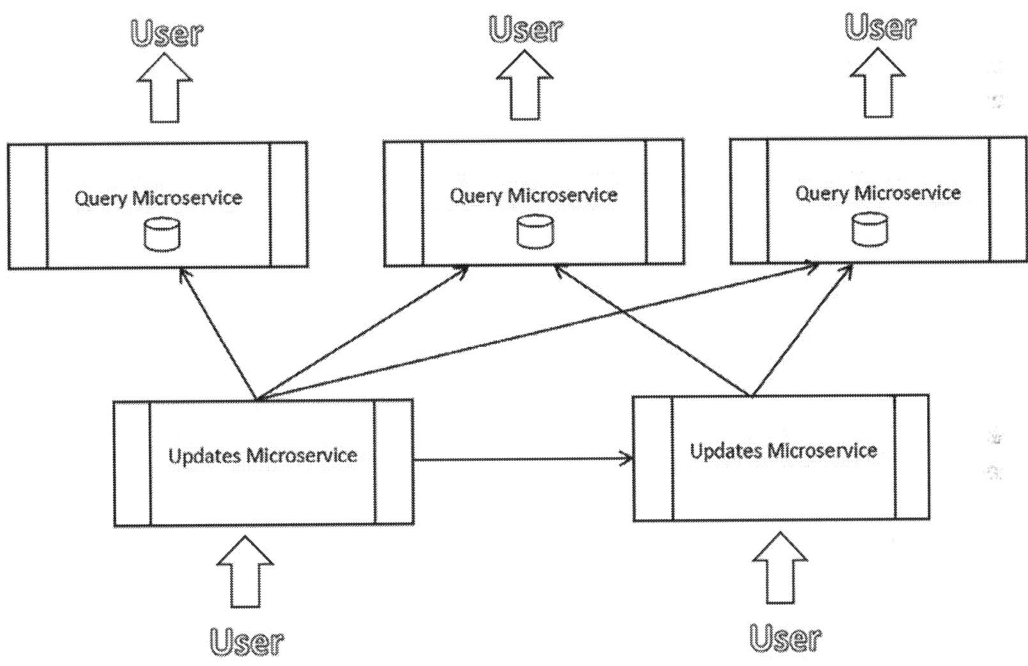

Figure 11.1: Push events

In conclusion, every microservice must contain all the data it needs to serve incoming requests and ensure fast responses. To keep their data models up to date and ready for incoming requests, microservices must communicate their data changes as soon as they take place. These data changes should be communicated through asynchronous messages since synchronous nested messages cause unacceptable performance because they block all the threads involved in the call tree until a result is returned.

It is worth pointing out that the *independence of design choices* principle is substantially the bounded context principle of DDD, which we discussed in detail in *Chapter 7, Understanding the Different Domains in Software Solutions*. In this chapter, we have seen that, often, a full DDD approach is useful for the *update* subsystem of each microservice.

It's not trivial that, in general, all systems that have been developed according to the bounded context principle are better implemented with a microservice architecture. In fact, once a system has been decomposed into several completely independent and loosely coupled parts, it is very likely that these different parts will need to be scaled independently because of different traffic and different resource requirements.

At the preceding constraints, we must also add some best practices for building a reusable SOA. More details on these best practices will be given in *Chapter 15, Applying Service-Oriented Architectures with .NET*, but nowadays, most SOA best practices are automatically enforced by tools and frameworks that are used to implement web services.

Fine-grained scaling is a key aspect of microservices architecture, involving several critical software and infrastructure requirements:

- First of all, microservices must be small enough to isolate well-defined functionalities.
- We also need a complex infrastructure that takes care of automatically instantiating microservices and allocating instances on various hardware computational resources, commonly called **nodes**.
- The same infrastructure must take care of scaling microservices and load-balancing them on the available nodes.

These kinds of structures will be introduced in the *Which tools are needed to manage microservices?* section of this chapter, and discussed in detail in *Chapter 20, Kubernetes*.

Moreover, fine-grained scaling of distributed microservices that communicate through asynchronous communication requires each microservice to be resilient. In fact, communication that's directed to a specific microservice instance may fail due to a hardware fault or for the simple reason that the target instance was killed or moved to another node during a load-balancing operation.

Temporary failures can be overcome with exponential retries. This is where we retry the same operation after each failure with a delay that increases exponentially until a maximum number of attempts is reached. For instance, first, we would retry after 10 milliseconds, and if this retry operation results in a failure, a new attempt is made after 20 milliseconds, then after 40 milliseconds, and so on.

On the other hand, long-term failures often cause an explosion of retry operations that may saturate all system resources in a way that is similar to a denial-of-service attack. Therefore, usually, exponential retries are used together with a *circuit break strategy*: after a given number of failures, a long-term failure is assumed, and access to the resource is prevented for a given time by returning an immediate failure without attempting the communication operation.

It is also fundamental that the congestion of some subsystems, due to either failure or a request peak, does not propagate to other system parts in order to prevent overall system congestion. *Bulkhead isolation* prevents congestion propagation in the following ways:

- Only a maximum number of similar simultaneous outbound requests are allowed; let's say, 10. This is similar to putting an upper bound on thread creation.
- Requests exceeding the previous bound are queued.
- If the maximum queue length is reached, any further requests result in exceptions being thrown to abort them.

The practical .NET implementation of exponential retries, circuit break, and bulkhead isolation is described in the *Resilient task execution subsection* of this chapter.

Retry policies may make it so that the same message is received and processed several times because the sender has received no confirmation that the message has been received, or simply because it has timed out the operation while the receiver actually received the message. The only possible solution to this problem is designing all messages so that they're idempotent – that is, designing messages in such a way that processing the same message several times has the same effect as processing it once.

Updating a database table field to a value, for instance, is an idempotent operation since repeating it once or twice has exactly the same effect. However, incrementing a decimal field is not an idempotent operation. Microservice designers should make an effort to design the overall application with as many idempotent messages as possible.

An idempotent message is also a message that, if processed twice, doesn't cause malfunctions. For instance, a message that modifies the price of travel is idempotent because if we process it another time, we just set again the price to the same price as before. However, a message whose purpose is to add a new travel booking is not idempotent since if we process it twice, we add two travel bookings instead of one.

The remaining non-idempotent messages must be transformed into idempotent in the following way or with other similar techniques:

1. Attach both a time and some identifier that uniquely identifies each message.
2. Store all the messages that have been received in a dictionary that's been indexed by the unique identifier attached to the message mentioned in the previous point.
3. Reject old messages.
4. When a message that may be a duplicate is received, verify whether it's contained in the dictionary. If it is, then it has already been processed, so reject it.
5. Since old messages are rejected, they can be periodically removed from the dictionary to prevent it from growing exponentially.

In *Chapter 14, Implementing Microservices with .NET*, we will use this technique in practice and discuss communication and coordination problems in more detail.

It is worth pointing out that some message brokers, such as Azure Service Bus, offer facilities for implementing the technique described previously. However, the receiver must always be able to recognize duplicate messages since, due to time-outs in the reception of acknowledgments, messages might be resent. Azure Service Bus is discussed in the *.NET communication facilities* subsection.

In the next subsection, we will talk about microservice containerization based on Docker.

Containers and Docker

We've already discussed the advantages of having microservices that don't depend on the environment where they run; microservices can be moved from busy nodes to idle nodes without constraints, thus achieving a better load balance and, consequently, better usage of the available hardware.

However, if we need to mix legacy software with newer modules, the ability to mix several development stacks in order to use the best stack for each module implementation, and so on, we are faced with the problem that the various microservices have different hardware/software prerequisites. In these cases, the independence of each microservice from the hosting environment can be restored by deploying each microservice with all its dependencies on a private virtual machine.

However, starting a virtual machine with its private copy of the operating system takes a lot of time, and microservices must be started and stopped quickly to reduce load-balancing and fault recovery costs. In fact, new microservices may be started either to replace faulty ones or because they were moved from one hardware node to another to perform load-balancing. Moreover, adding a whole copy of the operating system to each microservice instance would be an excessive overhead.

Luckily, microservices can rely on a lighter form of technology: containers. Containers provide a lightweight, efficient form of virtualization. Unlike traditional virtual machines that virtualize an entire machine, including the operating system, containers virtualize at the OS filesystem level, sitting on top of the host OS kernel. They use the operating system of the hosting machine (kernel, DLLs, and drivers) and use the OS's native features to isolate processes and resources, creating an isolated environment for the images they run.

As a consequence, containers are tied to a specific OS, but they don't suffer the overhead of copying and starting a whole OS in each container instance.

On each host machine, containers are handled by a runtime that takes care of creating them from *images* and creating an isolated environment for each of them. The most popular container image format is Docker, which is a *de facto* standard for container images.

Images contain files needed to create each container and specify which container resources, such as communication ports, to expose outside of the container. However, they need not explicitly contain all involved files since they can be layered. This way, each image is built by adding new files and configuration information on top of another existing image that is referenced from inside the newly defined image.

For instance, if you want to deploy a .NET application as a Docker image, it is enough to just add your software and files to your Docker image and then reference an already existing .NET Docker image.

To allow for easy image referencing, images are grouped into registries that may be either public or private. They are similar to NuGet or npm registries. Docker offers a public registry (`https://hub.docker.com/_/registry`) where you can find most of the public images you may need to reference in your own images. However, each company can define private registries. For instance, Microsoft offers Azure Container Registry, where you can define your private container registry service: `https://azure.microsoft.com/en-us/services/container-registry/`. There, you can also find most of the .NET-related images you might need to reference in your code.

Before instantiating each container, the Docker runtime must solve all the recursive references. This cumbersome job is not performed each time a new container is created since the Docker runtime has a cache where it stores the fully assembled images that correspond to each input image and that it has already processed.

Since each application is usually composed of several modules to be run in different containers, a tool called **Docker Compose** also allows `.yml` files, known as **composition files**, that specify the following information:

- Which images to deploy.
- How the internal resources that are exposed by each image must be mapped to the physical resources of the host machine. For instance, how communication ports that are exposed by Docker images must be mapped to the ports of the physical machine.

We will analyze Docker images and `.yml` files in the *How does .NET deal with microservices?* section of this chapter.

The Docker runtime handles images and containers on a single machine, but usually, containerized microservices are deployed and load-balanced on clusters that are composed of several machines. Clusters are handled by pieces of software called **orchestrators**. Orchestrators will be introduced in the *Which tools are needed to manage microservices?* section of this chapter, and described in detail in *Chapter 20, Kubernetes*.

Now that we understand what microservices are, what problems they can solve, and their basic design principles, we are ready to analyze when and how to use them in our system architecture. The next section analyzes when we should use them.

When do microservices help?

The answer to this question requires us to understand the roles microservices play in modern software architectures. We will look at this in the following two subsections:

- Layered architectures and microservices
- When is it worth considering microservice architectures?

Let's start with a detailed look at layered architectures and microservices.

Layered architectures and microservices

As discussed in *Chapter 7, Understanding the Different Domains in Software Solutions*, enterprise systems are usually organized in logical independent layers. The outermost layer is the one that interacts with the user and is called the presentation layer (in the onion architecture, the outermost layer also contains drivers and test suites), while the last layer (the innermost layer in the onion architecture) takes care of application permanent data handling and is called the data layer (the domain layer in the onion architecture). Requests originate in the presentation layer and pass through all the layers until they reach the data layer (and then come back, traversing all the layers in reverse until they reach the outermost layer again).

In the case of classical layered architecture (the onion architecture is quite different, as discussed in *Chapter 7, Understanding the Different Domains in Software Solutions*), each layer takes data from the previous layer, processes it, and passes it to the next layer. Then, it receives the results from its next layer and sends them back to its previous layer. Also, thrown exceptions can't jump layers – each layer must take care of intercepting all the exceptions and either *solve them* somehow or transform them into other exceptions that are expressed in the language of its previous layer. The layered architecture ensures the complete independence of the functionalities of each layer from the functionalities of all the other layers.

For instance, we can change the **Object-Relational Mapping** (**ORM**) software that interfaces the database without affecting all the layers that are above the data layer (ORM software is discussed in *Chapter 13, Interacting with Data in C# – Entity Framework Core*). In the same way, we can completely change the user interface (that is, the presentation layer) without affecting the remainder of the system.

Moreover, each layer implements a different kind of system specification. The data layer takes care of what the system *must remember*, the presentation layer takes care of the system-user interaction protocol, and all the layers that are in the middle implement the domain rules, which specify how data must be processed (for instance, how an employee paycheck must be computed). Typically, the data and presentation layers are separated by just one domain rule layer, called the business or application layer.

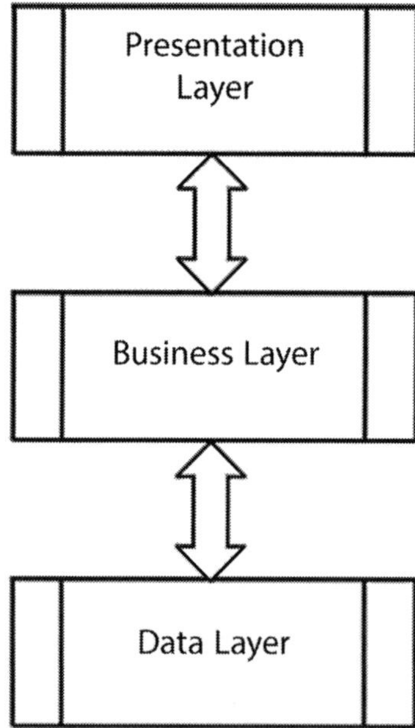

Figure 11.2: Layers of classic architectures

Each layer *speaks* a different language: the data layer speaks the language of relation among entities, the business layer speaks the language of domain experts, and the presentation layer speaks the language of users. So, when data and exceptions pass from one layer to another, they must be translated into the language of the destination layer.

That being said, how do microservices fit into a layered architecture? Are they adequate for the functionalities of all the layers or just some layers? Can a single microservice span several layers?

The last question is the easiest to answer: yes! In fact, we've already stated that microservices should store the data they need within their logical boundaries. Therefore, there are microservices that span the business and data layers, for sure.

However, since we said that each logical microservice can be implemented with several physical microservices for pure load-balancing reasons, one microservice might take care of encapsulating data used by another microservice that might remain confined in the data layer.

Moreover, we said also that while each microservice must have its exclusive storage, it can use also external storage engines. This is shown in the diagram below:

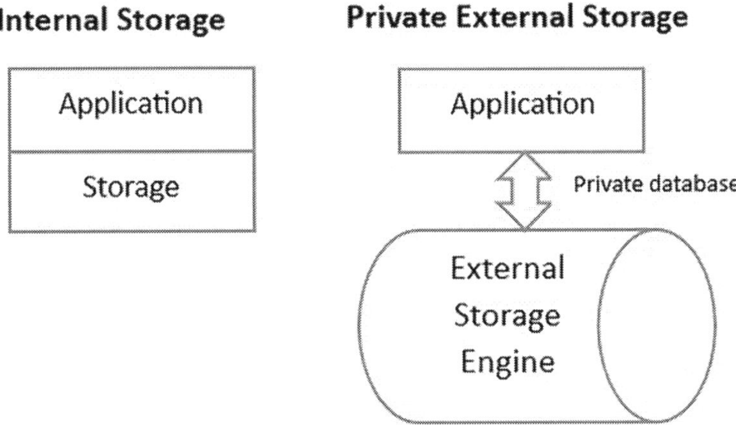

Figure 11.3: External or internal storage

It is worth pointing out that the storage engine itself can be implemented as a set of physical microservices that are associated with no logical microservice since they may be considered part of the infrastructure.

This is the case, for instance, for storage engines based on the distributed Redis in-memory cache, where we use microservice facilities offered by the infrastructure to implement scalable one-master/many-read-only replicas, or sophisticated many-master/many-read-only replicas distributed in memory storage. Redis and Redis Cloud services are described in the *Redis* section *of Chapter 12, Choosing Your Data Storage in the Cloud,* while many-master/many-read-only replicas architectures are described in *Chapter 20, Kubernetes*. The diagram below shows how microservice-based many-master/many-read-only replicas storage engines work.

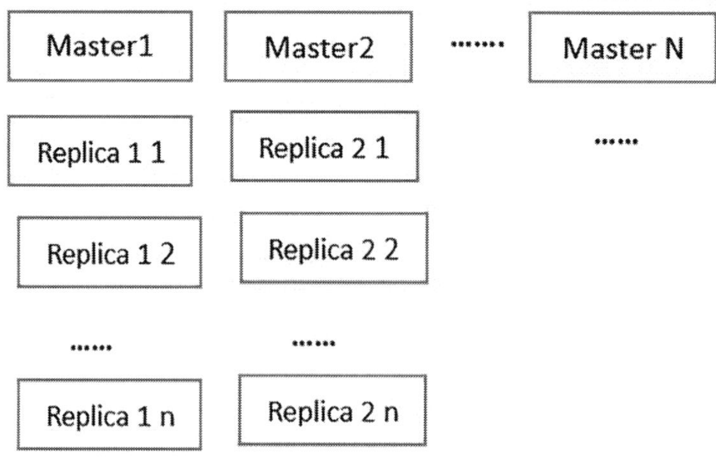

Figure 11.4: Many-master/many-read-only replicas storage engine

Each master has its associated read-only replicas. Storage updates can be passed just to masters that replicate their data to all their associated read-only replicas.

Each master takes care of a portion of the storage space, for instance, all products whose name starts with "A," and so on. In this way, the load is balanced between all masters.

Thus, we may have business layer microservices, data layer microservices, and microservices that span both layers. So, what about the presentation layer?

The presentation layer

This layer can also fit into a microservice architecture if it is implemented on the server side – that is, if the whole graphic that interacts with the user is built on the server side and not in the user client machine (mobile device, desktop, etc.).

When there are microservices that interact directly with the user, we speak of server-side implementation of the presentation layer since the HTML and/or all elements of the user interface are created by the frontend, which sends the response to the user.

These kinds of microservices are called frontend microservices, while microservices that do back-office work without interacting with the user are called worker microservices. The diagram below summarizes the frontend/worker organization.

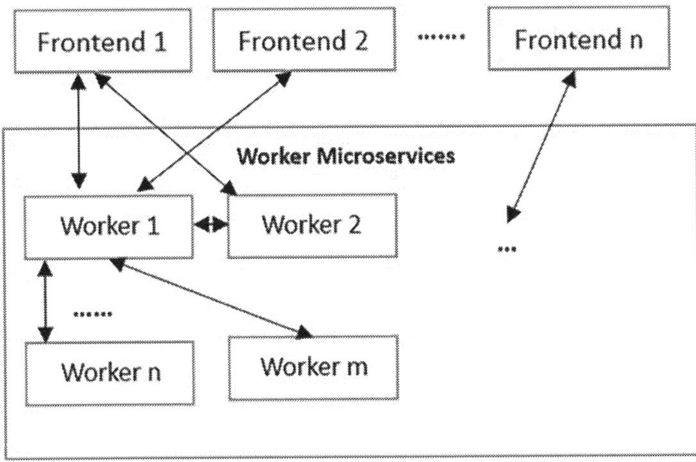

Figure 11.5: Frontend and worker microservices

When, instead, the HTML and/or all elements of the user interface are generated on the user machine, we speak of client-side implementation of the presentation layer. The so-called single-page applications and mobile applications run the presentation layer on the client machine and interact with the application through communication interfaces exposed by dedicated microservices. These dedicated microservices are completely analogous to the frontend microservices depicted in *Figure 11.5* and are called *API gateways,* to underline their role of exposing a public API for connecting client devices with the whole microservices infrastructure. Also, API gateways interact with worker microservices in a way that is completely analogous to frontend microservices.

Single-page applications and mobile/desktop client applications are discussed in *Chapter 19, Client Frameworks: Blazor*.

In a microservice architecture, when the presentation layer is a website, it can be implemented with a set of several microservices. However, if it requires heavy web servers and/or heavy frameworks, containerizing them may not be convenient. This decision must also consider the loss of performance that happens when containerizing the web server and the possible need for hardware firewalls between the web server and the remainder of the system.

ASP.NET Core is a lightweight framework that runs on the Kestrel web server, so it can be containerized efficiently and used as is in the worker microservices. The usage of ASP:NET Core in the implementation of worker microservices is described in great detail in *Chapter 14, Implementing Microservices with .NET*.

Instead, frontend and/or high-traffic websites have more compelling security and load-balancing requirements that can be satisfied just with fully-featured web servers. Accordingly, architectures based on microservices usually offer specialized components that take care of interfacing with the outside world. For instance, in *Chapter 20, Kubernetes*, we will see that in microservices-dedicated infrastructures like **Kubernetes** clusters, this role is played by so-called **ingresses**. These are fully-featured web servers interfaced with the microservices infrastructure. Thanks to the integration with the microservices infrastructure, the whole web server traffic is automatically routed to the interested microservices. More details on this will be given in *Chapter 20, Kubernetes*. The diagram below shows the role of Ingresses.

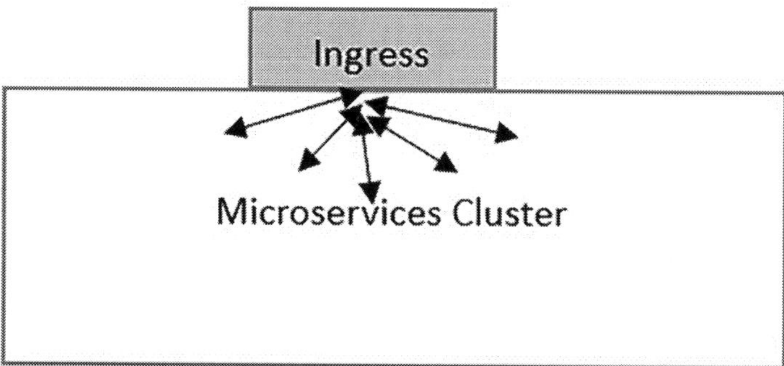

Figure 11.6: Ingresses based on load-balanced web servers

Monolithic websites can be easily broken into load-balanced smaller subsites without microservice-specific technologies, but a microservice architecture can bring all the advantages of microservices into the construction of a single HTML page. More specifically, different microservices may take care of different areas of each HTML page. Microservices that cooperate in the construction of the HTML of application pages, and, in general, in the construction of any kind of user interface, are named micro-frontends.

When the HTML is created on the server side, the various micro-frontends create HTML chunks that are combined either on the server side or directly in the browser.

When, instead, the HTML is created directly on the client, each micro-frontend provides a different chunk of code to the client. These code chunks are run on the client machine, and each of them takes care of different pages/page areas. We will speak more of this kind of micro-frontend in *Chapter 18, Implementing Frontend Microservices with ASP.NET Core*.

Now that we've clarified which parts of a system can benefit from the adoption of microservices, we are ready to state the rules when it comes to deciding how they're adopted.

When is it worth considering microservice architectures?

Microservices can improve the implementation of both the business and data layers, but their adoption has some costs:

- Allocating instances to nodes and scaling them has a cost in terms of cloud fees or internal infrastructures and licenses.

- Splitting a unique process into smaller communication processes increases communication costs and hardware needs, especially if the microservices are containerized.
- Designing and testing software for a microservice requires more time and increases engineering costs, both in time and complexity. In particular, making microservices resilient and ensuring that they adequately handle all possible failures, as well as verifying these features with integration tests, can increase the development time by more than one order of magnitude (that is, about 10 times).

So, when are microservices worth the cost of using them? Are there functionalities that must be implemented as microservices?

A rough answer to the second question is yes when the application is big enough in terms of traffic and/or software complexity. In fact, as an application grows in complexity and its traffic increases, it's recommended that we pay the costs associated with scaling it since this allows for more scaling optimization and better handling when it comes to the development team. The costs we pay for these would soon exceed the cost of microservice adoption.

Thus, if fine-grained scaling makes sense for our application, and if we can estimate the savings that fine-grained scaling and development give us, we can easily compute an overall application throughput limit that makes the adoption of microservices convenient.

Microservice costs can also be justified by an increase in the market value of our products/services. Since the microservice architecture allows us to implement each microservice with a technology that has been optimized for its use, the quality that's added to our software may justify all or part of the microservice costs.

However, scaling and technology optimizations are not the only parameters to consider. Sometimes, we are forced to adopt a microservice architecture without being able to perform a detailed cost analysis.

If the size of the team that takes care of the CI/CD of the overall system grows too much, the organization and coordination of this big team cause difficulties and inefficiencies. In this type of situation, it is desirable to move to an architecture that breaks the whole CI/CD cycle into independent parts that can be taken care of by smaller teams.

Moreover, since these development costs are only justified by a high volume of requests, we probably have high traffic being processed by independent modules that have been developed by different teams. Therefore, scaling optimizations and the need to reduce interaction between development teams make the adoption of a microservice architecture very convenient.

From this, we may conclude that if the system and the development team grow too much, it is necessary to split the development team into smaller teams, each working on an efficient bounded context subsystem. It is very likely that, in a similar situation, a microservice architecture is the only possible option.

Another situation that forces the adoption of a microservice architecture is the integration of newer subparts with legacy subsystems based on different technologies, as containerized microservices are the only way to implement an efficient interaction between the legacy system and the new subparts in order to gradually replace the legacy subparts with newer ones. Similarly, if our team is composed of developers with experience in different development stacks, an architecture based on containerized microservices may become a *must*.

In the next section, we will analyze the building blocks and tools that are available for the implementation of .NET-based microservices.

How does .NET deal with microservices?

The new .NET, which evolved from .NET Core, was conceived as a multi-platform framework that was light and fast enough to implement efficient microservices. In particular, ASP.NET Core is the ideal tool for implementing text REST and binary gRPC APIs to communicate with a microservice since it can run efficiently with lightweight web servers such as Kestrel and is itself light and modular.

The whole .NET stack evolved with microservices as a strategic deployment platform in mind and has facilities and packages for building efficient and light HTTP and gRPC communication to ensure service resiliency and to handle long-running tasks. The following subsections describe some of the different tools or solutions that we can use to implement a .NET-based microservice architecture.

.NET communication facilities

Microservices need two kinds of communication channels.

The first communication channel receives external requests, either directly or through an API gateway. HTTP is the usual protocol for external communication due to available web service standards and tools. .NET's main HTTP/gRPC communication facility is ASP.NET Core since it's a lightweight HTTP/gRPC framework, which makes it ideal for implementing web APIs in small microservices. We will describe ASP.NET REST API apps in detail in *Chapter 15, Applying Service-Oriented Architectures with .NET*, and we will describe gRPC services in *Chapter 14, Implementing Microservices with .NET*. .NET also offers an efficient and modular HTTP client solution that is able to pool and reuse heavy connection objects. Also, the `HttpClient` class will be described in more detail in *Chapter 15*.

The second channel is a different type of communication channel to push updates to other microservices. In fact, we have already mentioned that intra-microservice communication cannot be triggered by an ongoing request since a complex tree of blocking calls to other microservices would increase request latency to an unacceptable level. As a consequence, updates must not be requested immediately before they're used and should be pushed whenever state changes take place. Ideally, this kind of communication should be asynchronous to achieve acceptable performance. In fact, synchronous calls would block the sender while they are waiting for the result, thus increasing the idle time of each microservice. However, synchronous communication that just puts the request in a processing queue and then returns confirmation of the successful communication instead of the final result is acceptable if communication is fast enough (low communication latency and high bandwidth). A publisher/subscriber communication would be preferable since, in this case, the sender and receiver don't need to know each other, thus increasing the microservices' independence. In fact, all the receivers that are interested in a certain type of communication merely need to register to receive a specific *event*, while senders just need to publish those events. All the wiring is performed by a service that takes care of queuing events and dispatching them to all the subscribers. The publisher/subscriber pattern was described in *Chapter 6, Design Patterns and .NET 8 Implementation*, along with other useful patterns.

While .NET doesn't directly offer tools that may help in asynchronous communication or client/server tools that implement publisher/subscriber communication, Azure offers a similar service with *Azure Service Bus* (`https://docs.microsoft.com/en-us/azure/service-bus-messaging/`). Azure Service Bus handles both queued asynchronous communication through Azure Service Bus *queues* and publisher/subscriber communication through Azure Service Bus *topics*.

Once you've configured the Azure Service Bus on the Azure portal, you can connect to it in order to send messages/events and receive messages/events through a client contained in `Microsoft.Azure.ServiceBus` NuGet package.

Azure Service Bus has two types of communication: queue-based and topic-based. In queue-based communication, each message that's placed in the queue by a sender is removed from the queue by the first receiver that pulls it from the queue. Topic-based communication, on the other hand, is an implementation of the publisher/subscriber pattern. Each topic has several subscriptions, and a different copy of each message sent to a topic can be pulled from each topic subscription.

The design flow is as follows:

1. Define an Azure Service Bus private namespace.
2. Get the root connection strings that were created by the Azure portal and/or define new connection strings with fewer privileges.
3. Define queues and/or topics where the sender will send their messages in binary format.
4. For each topic, define names for all the required subscriptions.
5. In the case of queue-based communication, the sender sends messages to a queue, and the receivers pull messages from the same queue. Each message is delivered to one receiver. That is, once a receiver gains access to the queue, it reads and removes one or more messages.
6. In the case of topic-based communication, each sender sends messages to a topic while each receiver pulls messages from its private subscription associated with that topic.

There are also other commercial and free open-source alternatives to Azure Service Bus, such as NServiceBus (`https://particular.net/nservicebus`), MassTransit (`https://masstransit-project.com/`), and Brighter (`https://www.goparamore.io/`). They enhance existing brokers (like Azure Service Bus itself) with higher-level functionalities.

There is also a completely independent option that can be used on on-premises platforms: RabbitMQ. It is free and open source and can be installed locally, on a virtual machine, or in a Docker container. Then, you can connect with it through the client contained in the `RabbitMQ.Client` NuGet package.

The functionalities of RabbitMQ are similar to the ones offered by Azure Service Bus, but you have to take care of more implementation details, like serialization, reliable messages, and error handling, while Azure Service Bus takes care of all the low-level operations and offers you a simpler interface. However, there are clients that build a more powerful abstraction on top of RabbitMQ, like, for instance, EasyNetQ. The publisher/subscriber-based communication pattern used by both Azure Service Bus and RabbitMQ was described in *Chapter 6, Design Patterns and .NET 8 Implementation*. RabbitMQ will be described in more detail in *Chapter 14, Implementing Microservices with .NET*.

Resilient task execution

Resilient communication and, in general, resilient task execution can be implemented easily with the help of a .NET library called Polly, whose project is a member of the .NET Foundation. Polly is available through the `Polly` NuGet package.

In Polly, you define policies and then execute tasks in the context of those policies, as follows:

```
var myPolicy = Policy
  .Handle<HttpRequestException>()
  .Or<OperationCanceledException>()
  .RetryAsync(3);
....
....
await myPolicy.ExecuteAsync(()=>{
    //your code here
});
```

The first part of each policy specifies the exceptions that must be handled. Then, you specify what to do when one of those exceptions is captured. In the preceding code, the `Execute` method is retried up to three times if a failure is reported either by an `HttpRequestException` exception or by an `OperationCanceledException` exception.

The following is the implementation of an exponential retry policy:

```
var retryPolicy= Policy
    ...
    //Exceptions to handle here
    .WaitAndRetryAsync(6,
        retryAttempt => TimeSpan.FromSeconds(Math.Pow(2,
            retryAttempt)));
```

The first argument of `WaitAndRetryAsync` specifies that a maximum of six retries is performed in the event of failure. The lambda function passed as the second argument specifies how much time to wait before the next attempt. In this specific example, this time grows exponentially with the number of attempts by a power of 2 (2 seconds for the first retry, 4 seconds for the second retry, and so on).

The following is a simple circuit breaker policy:

```
var breakerPolicy =Policy
    .Handle<SomeExceptionType>()
    .CircuitBreakerAsync (6, TimeSpan.FromMinutes(1));
```

After six failures, the task can't be executed for one minute since an exception is returned.

The following is the implementation of the Bulkhead Isolation policy (see the *Microservices design principles* section for more information):

```
Policy
  .BulkheadAsync(10, 15)
```

A maximum of 10 parallel executions is allowed in the `Execute` method. Further tasks are inserted in an execution queue. This has a limit of 15 tasks. If the queue limit is exceeded, an exception is thrown.

For the Bulkhead Isolation policy to work properly and, in general, for every strategy to work properly, task executions must be triggered through the same policy instance; otherwise, Polly is unable to count how many executions of a specific task are active.

Policies can be combined with the `Wrap` method:

```
var combinedPolicy = Policy
  .Wrap(retryPolicy, breakerPolicy);
```

Polly offers several more options, such as generic methods for tasks that return a specific type, timeout policies, task result caching, the ability to define custom policies, and so on. It is also possible to configure Polly as part of an `HttpClient` definition in the dependency injection section of any ASP.NET Core and .NET application. This way, it is quite immediate to define resilient clients.

Polly's official documentation can be found in its GitHub repository here: `https://github.com/App-vNext/Polly`.

The practical usage of Polly is explained in the *A worker microservice with ASP.NET Core* section of *Chapter 21, Case Study*.

The resilience and robustness provided by tools like Polly are crucial components of microservice architecture, particularly when managing complex tasks and processes.

This brings us to another fundamental aspect of microservices: the implementation of generic hosts.

Using generic hosts

Each microservice may need to run several independent threads, with each performing a different operation on requests received. Such threads need several resources, such as database connections, communication channels, specialized modules that perform complex operations, and so on. Moreover, all processing threads must be adequately initialized when the microservice is started and gracefully stopped when the microservice is stopped as a consequence of either load-balancing or errors.

All of these needs led the .NET team to conceive and implement *hosted services* and *hosts*. A host creates an adequate environment for running several tasks, known as **hosted services**, and provides them with resources, common settings, and a graceful start/stop.

The concept of a web host was initially conceived to implement the ASP.NET Core web framework, but, with effect from .NET Core 2.1, the host concept was extended to all .NET applications.

At the time of writing this book, a `Host` is automatically created for you in any ASP.NET Core, Blazor, and Worker Service project. The simplest way to test .NET Host features is to select a **Service -> Worker Service** project.

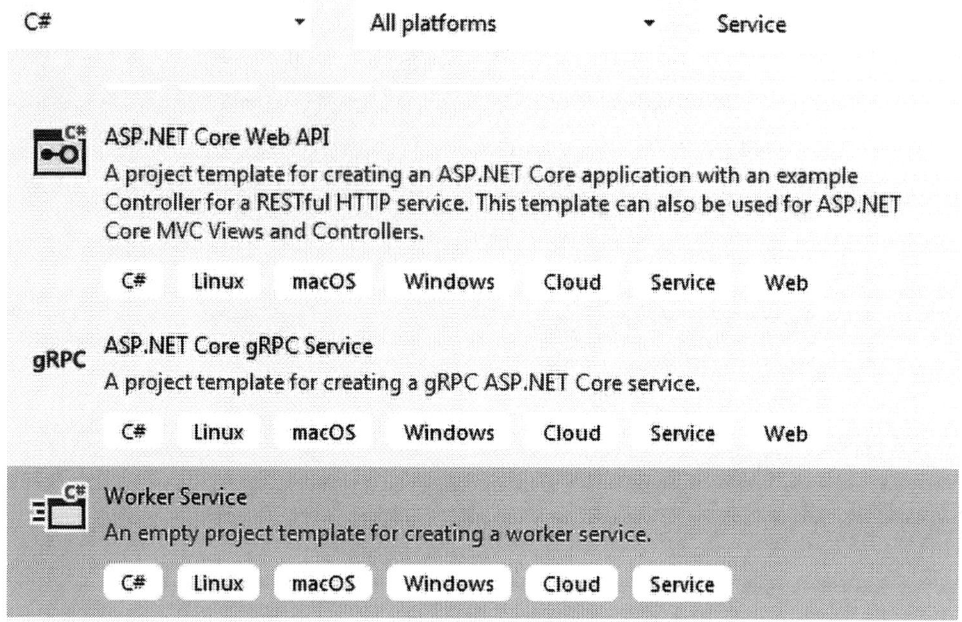

Figure 11.7: Creating a Worker Service project in Visual Studio

All features related to the concept of a `Host` are contained in the `Microsoft.Extensions.Hosting` NuGet package.

`Program.cs` contains some skeleton code for configuring the host with a fluent interface, starting with the `CreateDefaultBuilder` method of the `Host` class. The final step of this configuration is calling the `Build` method, which assembles the actual host with all the configuration information we provided:

```
...
var myHost=Host.CreateDefaultBuilder(args)
 .ConfigureServices(services =>
    {
        //some configuration
        ...
    })
    .Build();
...
```

Host configuration includes defining the common resources, defining the default folder for files, loading the configuration parameters from several sources (JSON files, environment variables, and any arguments that are passed to the application), and declaring all the hosted services.

It is worth pointing out that ASP.NET Core and Blazor projects use methods that perform pre-configuration of the `Host`, including several of the tasks listed previously.

Then, the host is started, which causes all the hosted services to be started:

```
await host.RunAsync();
```

The program remains blocked on the preceding instruction until the host is shut down. The host is automatically shut down when the operating system kills the process. However, the host can also be shut down manually either by one of the hosted services or externally by calling `await host.StopAsync(timeout)`. Here, `timeout` is a time span defining the maximum time to wait for the hosted services to stop gracefully. After this time, all the hosted services are aborted if they haven't been terminated. We will explain how a hosted service can shut down the host later on in this subsection.

When the thread contains a `host.RunAsync` is launched from within another thread instead of `Program.cs`. The fact that the host thread is being shut down can be signaled by a `cancellationToken` passed to `RunAsync`:

```
await host.RunAsync(cancellationToken)
```

This way of shutting down is triggered as soon as the `cancellationToken` enters a canceled state by another thread.

By default, the host has a 5-second timeout for shutting down; that is, it waits 5 seconds before exiting once a shutdown has been requested. This time can be changed within the `ConfigureServices` method, which is used to declare *hosted services* and other resources:

```
var myHost = Host.CreateDefaultBuilder(args)
    .ConfigureServices(services =>
    {
        services.Configure<HostOptions>(option =>
        {
            option.ShutdownTimeout = System.TimeSpan.FromSeconds(10);
        });
        ....
        ....
        //further configuration
    })
    .Build();
```

However, increasing the host timeout doesn't increase the orchestrator timeout, so if the host waits too long, the whole microservice is killed by the orchestrator.

If no cancellation token is explicitly passed to `Run` or `RunAsync`, a cancellation token is automatically generated and is automatically signaled when the operating system informs the application it is going to kill it. This cancellation token is passed to all hosted services to give them the opportunity to stop gracefully.

Hosted services are implementations of the `IHostedService` interface, whose only methods are `StartAsync(cancellationToken)` and `StopAsync(cancellationToken)`.

Both methods are passed a `cancellationToken`. The `cancellationToken` in the `StartAsync` method signals that a shutdown was requested. The `StartAsync` method periodically checks this `cancellationToken` while performing all operations needed to start the host, and if it is signaled, the host start process is aborted. On the other hand, the `cancellationToken` in the `StopAsync` method signals that the shutdown timeout expired.

Hosted services can be declared in the same `ConfigureServices` method that's used to define host options, as follows:

```
services.AddHostedService<MyHostedService>();
```

Most declarations inside `ConfigureServices` require the addition of the following namespace:

```
using Microsoft.Extensions.DependencyInjection;
```

Usually, the `IHostedService` interface isn't implemented directly but can be inherited from the `BackgroundService` abstract class, which exposes the easier-to-implement `ExecuteAsync(CancellationToken)` method, which is where we can place the whole logic of the service. A shutdown is signaled by passing `cancellationToken` as an argument, which is easier to handle. We will look in more detail at an implementation of `IHostedService` in *Chapter 14, Implementing Microservices with .NET*.

To allow a hosted service to shut down the whole host, we need to declare an `IApplicationLifetime` interface as its constructor parameter:

```
public class MyHostedService: BackgroundService
{
    private readonly IHostApplicationLifetime _applicationLifetime;
    public MyHostedService(IHostApplicationLifetime applicationLifetime)
    {
        _applicationLifetime=applicationLifetime;
    }
    protected Task ExecuteAsync(CancellationToken token)
    {
        ...
        _applicationLifetime.StopApplication();
```

```
        ...
    }
}
```

When the hosted service is created, it is automatically passed an implementation of `IHostApplicationLifetime`, whose `StopApplication` method will trigger the host shutdown. This implementation is handled automatically, but we can also declare custom resources whose instances will be automatically passed to all the host service constructors that declare them as parameters. Therefore, say we define a constructor like this one:

```
Public MyClass(MyResource x, IResourceInterface1 y)
{
    ...
}
```

There are several ways to define the resources needed by the preceding constructor:

```
services.AddTransient<MyResource>();
services.AddTransient<IResourceInterface1, MyResource1>();
services.AddSingleton<MyResource>();
services.AddSingleton<IResourceInterface1, MyResource1>();
```

When we use `AddTransient`, a different instance is created and passed to all the constructors that require an instance of that type. On the other hand, with `AddSingleton`, a unique instance is created and passed to all the constructors that require the declared type. The overload with two generic types allows you to pass an interface and a type that implements that interface. This way, a constructor requires the interface and is decoupled from the specific implementation of that interface.

If resource constructors contain parameters, they will be automatically instantiated with the types declared in `ConfigureServices` in a recursive fashion. This pattern of interaction, called **dependency injection** (**DI**), has already been discussed in detail in *Chapter 6, Design Patterns and .NET 8 Implementation*.

`IHostBuilder` also has a method we can use to define the default folder – that is, the folder used to resolve all relative paths mentioned in all .NET methods:

```
.UseContentRoot("c:\\<deault path>")
```

It also has methods that we can use to add logging targets:

```
.ConfigureLogging((hostContext, configLogging) =>
    {
        configLogging.AddConsole();
        configLogging.AddDebug();
    })
```

The previous example shows a console-based logging source, but we can also log in to Azure targets with adequate providers. The *Further reading* section contains links to some Azure logging providers that can work with microservices that have been deployed in Azure. Once you've configured logging, you can enable your hosted services and log custom messages by adding an `ILogger<T>` parameter in their constructors. `ILogger<T>` has methods for logging messages with several severity levels: Trace, Debug (lowest), Information, Warning, Error, Critical, and None (highest). In turn, the application configuration specifies the minimum severity level needed to actually output log messages. All messages that pass the severity filter are simultaneously sent to all configured targets.

The only purpose of the type `T` is to classify the message through its full name.

The developer can specify the minimum severity level in a configuration file. We may have different severity levels for each type of `T`.

For instance:

```
{
  "Logging": {
    "LogLevel": {
      "Default": "Information",
      "Microsoft.AspNetCore": "Warning"
    }
  }
}
```

In the above configuration file, the default severity level is "`Information`", but all types whose name starts with "`Microsoft.AspNetCore`" have a "`Warning`" severity level.

Finally, `IHostBuilder` has methods we can use to read configuration parameters from various sources:

```
.ConfigureAppConfiguration(configHost =>
    {
        configHost.AddJsonFile("settings.json", optional: true);
        configHost.AddEnvironmentVariables(prefix: "PREFIX_");
        configHost.AddCommandLine(args);
    })
```

The way parameters defined in configuration streams can be used from inside the application will be explained in more detail in *Chapter 17, Presenting ASP.NET Core*, which is dedicated to ASP.NET.

As we transition from the specificities of ASP.NET Core to the broader realm of application deployment and environment setup, an important tool comes into play – Visual Studio Docker support.

Visual Studio support for Docker

Visual Studio offers support for creating, debugging, and deploying Docker images. Docker deployment requires us to install *Docker Desktop for Windows* on our development machine so that we can run Docker images.

The download link can be found in the *Technical requirements* section at the beginning of this chapter. Before we start any development activity, we must ensure it is installed and running (you should see a Docker icon in the window notification bar when the Docker runtime is running).

Docker support will be described with a simple ASP.NET Core MVC project. Let's create one. To do so, follow these steps:

1. Name the project `MvcDockerTest`.
2. For simplicity, disable authentication if it is not already disabled.
3. You are given the option to add Docker support when you create the project, but please don't check the **Docker support** checkbox. You can test how Docker support can be added to any project after it has been created.
4. Once you have your ASP.NET MVC application scaffolded and running, right-click on its project icon in **Solution Explorer**, select **Add**, and then select **Container Orchestrator Support | Docker Compose**. If you installed both **WSL** and **Windows Containers**, a dialog for choosing between **Linux** and **Windows** will appear. Otherwise, **Linux** will be automatically chosen if you installed just **WSL**, and **Windows** if you installed just **Windows Containers**.
5. If you installed **WSL**, please select **Linux**, since it is the default used by the Docker server when WSL is available.

The advantage of enabling Docker Compose instead of just Docker is that you can manually configure how the image is run on the development machine, as well as how Docker image ports are mapped to external ports by editing the Docker Compose files that are added to the solution.

If your Docker runtime has been installed properly and is running, you should be able to run the Docker image from Visual Studio. Please try it!

Now that we have explored how to configure and run Docker images, let's delve deeper into the structure and composition of these images. Understanding the Docker file created by Visual Studio is key to grasping how it orchestrates the creation and management of these images.

Analyzing the Docker file

Let's analyze the Docker file that was created by Visual Studio. It is a sequence of image creation steps. Each step enriches an existing image with something else with the help of the `From` instruction, which is a reference to an already existing image. The following is the first step:

```
FROM mcr.microsoft.com/dotnet/aspnet:x.x AS base
WORKDIR /app
EXPOSE 80
EXPOSE 443
```

The first step uses the `mcr.microsoft.com/dotnet/aspnet:x.x` ASP.NET (Core) runtime that was published by Microsoft in the Docker public repository (where `x.x` is the ASP.NET (Core) version that was selected in your project).

The WORKDIR command creates the directory that follows the command within the image that is going to be created. The two EXPOSE commands declare which ports will be exposed outside the image and mapped to ports of the actual hosting machine. Mapped ports are decided in the deployment stage either as command-line arguments of a Docker command or within a Docker Compose file. In our case, there are two ports: one for HTTP (80) and another for HTTPS (443).

This intermediate image is cached by Docker, which doesn't need to recompute since it doesn't depend on the code we write but only on the selected version of the ASP.NET (Core) runtime.

The second step produces a different image that will not be used to deploy. Instead, it will be used to create application-specific files that will be deployed:

```
FROM mcr.microsoft.com/dotnet/core/sdk:x.x  AS build
WORKDIR /src
COPY ["MvcDockerTest/MvcDockerTest.csproj", "MvcDockerTest/"]
RUN dotnet restore MvcDockerTest/MvcDockerTest.csproj
COPY . .
WORKDIR /src/MvcDockerTest
RUN dotnet build MvcDockerTest.csproj -c Release -o /app/build
FROM build AS publish
RUN dotnet publish MvcDockerTest.csproj -c Release -o /app/publish
```

This step starts from the ASP.NET SDK image, which contains parts we don't need to add for deployment; these are needed to process the project code. The new src directory is created in the build image and made the current image directory. Then, the project file is copied into /src/MvcDockerTest.

The RUN command executes an operating system command on the image. In this case, it calls the dotnet runtime, asking it to restore the NuGet packages that were referenced by the previously copied project file.

Then, the COPY.. command copies the whole project file tree into the src image directory. Finally, the project directory is made the current directory, and the dotnet runtime is asked to build the project in release mode and copy all the output files into the new /app/build directory. Finally, the dotnet publish task is executed in a new image called publish, outputting the published binaries into /app/publish.

The final step starts from the image that we created in the first step, which contains the ASP.NET (Core) runtime and adds all the files that were published in the previous step:

```
FROM base AS final
WORKDIR /app
COPY --from=publish /app/publish .
ENTRYPOINT ["dotnet", "MvcDockerTest.dll"]
```

The ENTRYPOINT command specifies the operating system command that's needed to execute the image. It accepts an array of strings. In our case, it accepts the dotnet command and its first command-line argument – that is, the DLL we need to execute. With that out of the way, let's now publish our little project!

Publishing the project

If we right-click on our project and click **Publish**, we are presented with several options:

- Publish the image to an existing or new web app (automatically created by Visual Studio)
- Publish to one of several Docker registries, including a private registry in Azure Container Registry that, if it doesn't already exist, can be created from within Visual Studio

Docker Compose support allows you to run and publish a multi-container application and add further images, such as a containerized database that is available everywhere.

The following Docker Compose file instructs the Docker server to run two containerized ASP.NET applications:

```
version: '3.4'
services:
  mvcdockertest:
    image: ${DOCKER_REGISTRY-}mvcdockertest
    build:
      context: .
      dockerfile: MvcDockerTest/Dockerfile
  mvcdockertest1:
    image: ${DOCKER_REGISTRY-}mvcdockertest1
    build:
      context: .
      dockerfile: MvcDockerTest1/Dockerfile
```

You can add another ASP:NET Core MVC application to our previous docker-compose file by just adding another ASP:NET Core MVC application named MvcDockerTest 1 to the solution and by enabling docker-compose on it. However, you must pay attention to the fact that the newly created project folder is placed inside the same solution folder as MvcDockerTest.

The preceding code references existing Docker files. Any environment-dependent information is placed in the `docker-compose.override.yml` file, which is merged with the `docker-compose.yml` file when the application is launched from Visual Studio:

```
version: '3.4'
services:
  mvcdockertest:
    environment:
      - ASPNETCORE_ENVIRONMENT=Development
      - ASPNETCORE_URLS=https://+:443;http://+:80
    ports:
      - "80"
      - "443"
    volumes:
```

```
      -${APPDATA}/Microsoft/UserSecrets:/root/.microsoft/usersecrets:ro
      - ${APPDATA}/ASP.NET/Https:/root/.aspnet/https:ro
  mvcdockertest1:
    environment:
      - ASPNETCORE_ENVIRONMENT=Development
      - ASPNETCORE_URLS=https://+:443;http://+:80
    ports:
      - "80"
      - "443"
    volumes:
      - ${APPDATA}/Microsoft/UserSecrets:/root/.microsoft/usersecrets:ro
      - ${APPDATA}/ASP.NET/Https:/root/.aspnet/https:ro
```

For each image, the file specifies some environment variables (which will be defined in the image when the application is launched), the port mappings, and some host files.

The files in the host are directly mapped into the images. Each declaration contains the path in the host, how the path is mapped in the image, and the desired access rights. In our case, `volumes` are used to map the machine key used for all encryption needs of the application and the self-signed HTTPS certificate that's used by Visual Studio.

When you launch the application in Visual Studio, just the browser window opens and shows the **MvcDockerTest** application. However, both applications are launched, so you just need to discover which port **MvcDockerTest1** is running on and open another browser window. You can discover the port by clicking on **MvcDockerTest1** in the Containers tab in Visual Studio and looking at its HTTPS **Host Port** (60072), as shown in the figure below:

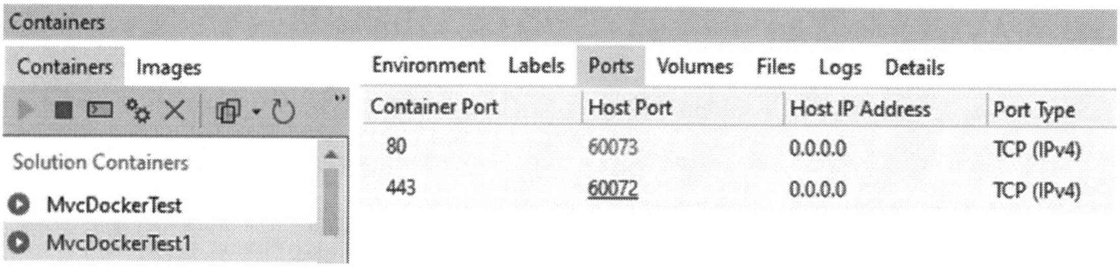

Container Port	Host Port	Host IP Address	Port Type
80	60073	0.0.0.0	TCP (IPv4)
443	60072	0.0.0.0	TCP (IPv4)

Figure 11.8: Discovering the MvcDockerTest1 host port

Now, suppose we want to add a containerized SQL Server instance. We would need something like the following instructions split between `docker-compose.yml` and `docker-compose.override.yml`:

```
sql.data:
  image: mcr.microsoft.com/mssql/server:2022-latest
  environment:
  - SA_PASSWORD=Pass@word
  - ACCEPT_EULA=Y
```

```
      - MSSQL_PID=Express
    ports:
      - "5433:1433"
```

Here, the preceding code specifies the properties of the SQL Server container, as well as the SQL Server configuration and installation parameters. More specifically, the preceding code contains the following information:

- `sql.data` is the name that's given to the container.
- `image` specifies where to take the image from. In our case, the image is contained in a public Docker registry.
- `environment` specifies the environment variables that are needed by SQL Server – that is, the administrator password, the acceptance of a SQL Server license, and the SQL Server edition.
- As usual, `ports` specify the port mappings.
- `docker-compose.override.yml` is used to run the images from within Visual Studio.

If you need to specify parameters for either the production environment or the testing environment, you can add further `docker-compose-xxx.override.yml` files, such as `docker-compose-staging.override.yml` and `docker-compose-production.override.yml`, and then launch them manually in the target environment with something like the following code:

```
docker-compose -f docker-compose.yml -f docker-compose-staging.override.yml up
```

Then, you can destroy all the containers with the following code:

```
docker-compose -f docker-compose.yml -f docker-compose.staging.yml down
```

While `docker-compose` has a limited capability when it comes to handling node clusters, it is mainly used in testing and development environments. For production environments, more sophisticated tools, called orchestrators, are needed. A de facto standard for the production environment is Kubernetes, which will be analyzed in detail in *Chapter 20, Kubernetes*.

Azure and Visual Studio support for microservice orchestration

Visual Studio has extensions for debugging a single microservice while it communicates with other microservices deployed in Kubernetes.

Also available are tools for testing and debugging several communicating microservices in the development machine and for deploying them automatically on Azure Kubernetes Service with just minimal configuration information.

All Visual Studio tools for Kubernetes and the whole process of developing for Kubernetes with Visual Studio will be described in the practical example in *Chapter 22, Developing .NET Microservices for Kubernetes*.

Moving on from Visual Studio's features for Kubernetes, let's dive into the key tools offered, in general, by all microservices orchestrators like Kubernetes.

Which tools are needed to manage microservices?

Effectively handling microservices in your CI/CD cycles requires both a private Docker image registry and a state-of-the-art microservice orchestrator that's capable of doing the following:

- Allocating and load-balancing microservices on available hardware nodes
- Monitoring the health state of services and replacing faulty services if hardware/software failures occur
- Logging and presenting analytics
- Allowing the designer to dynamically change requirements such as hardware nodes allocated to a cluster, the number of service instances, and so on

The following subsection describes the Azure facilities we can use to store Docker images. The microservices orchestrators available in Azure are described in a dedicated chapter – namely, *Chapter 20, Kubernetes*.

Having learned about the essential functionalities offered by microservices orchestration, let's now turn our attention to how Azure facilitates these processes, starting with the setup of a private Docker registry.

Defining your private Docker registry in Azure

Defining your private Docker registry in Azure is easy. Just type `Container registries` into the Azure search bar and select **Container registries**. On the page that appears, click on the **Create** button.

The following form will appear:

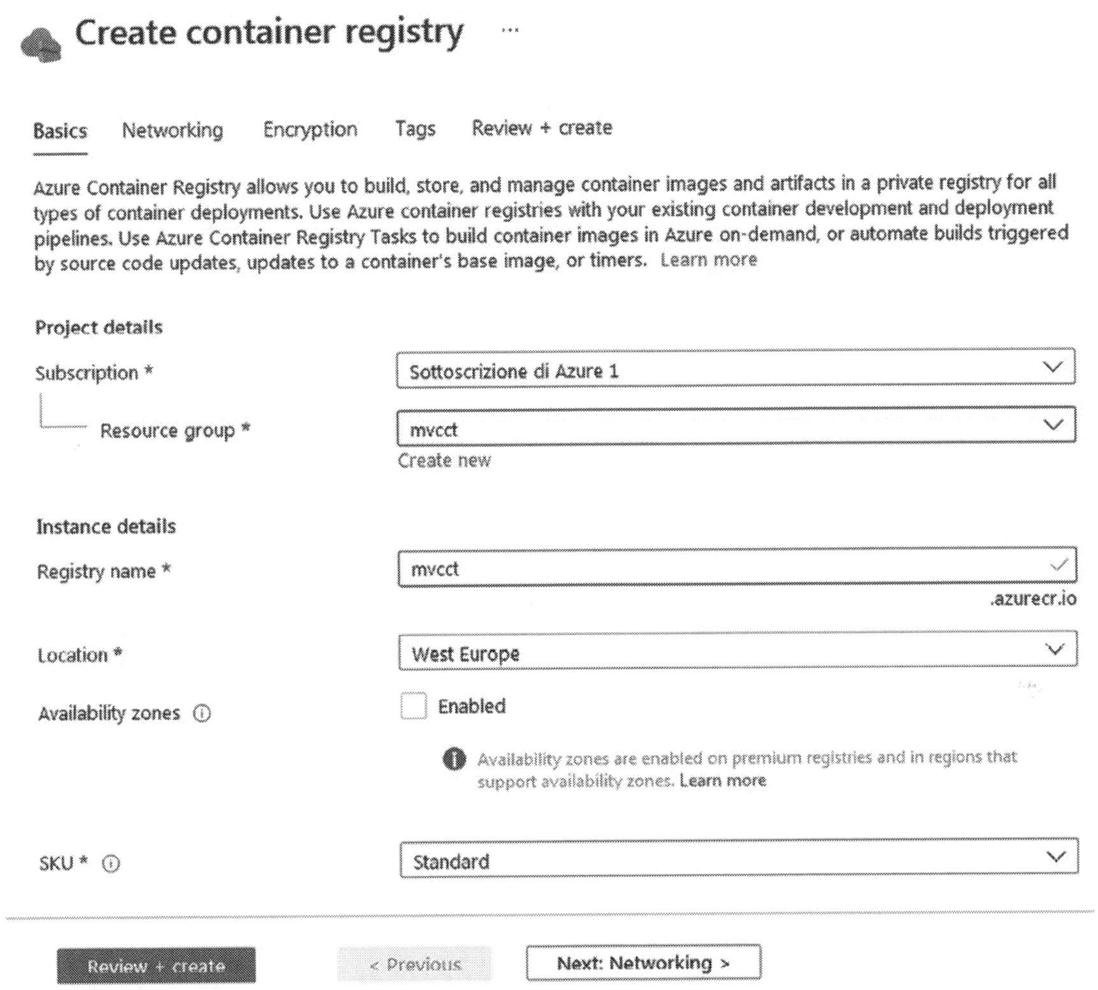

Figure 11.9: Creating an Azure private Docker registry

The name you select is used to compose the overall registry URI: `<name>.azurecr.io`. As usual, you can specify the subscription, resource group, and location. The **SKU** dropdown lets you choose from various levels of offerings that differ in terms of performance, available memory, and a few other auxiliary features.

Whenever you mention image names in Docker commands or in a Visual Studio publish form, you must prefix them with the registry URI: `<name>.azurecr.io/<my imagename>`.

If images are created with Visual Studio, then they can be published by following the instructions that appear once you publish the project. Otherwise, you must use Docker commands to push them into your registry.

The easiest way to use Docker commands that interact with the Azure registry is by installing the Azure CLI on your computer. Download the installer from `https://aka.ms/installazurecliwindows` and execute it. Once the Azure CLI has been installed, you can use the `az` command from Windows Command Prompt or PowerShell. In order to connect with your Azure account, you must execute the following `login` command:

```
az login
```

This command should start your default browser and should drive you through the manual login procedure.

Once logged in to your Azure account, you can log in to your private registry by typing the following command:

```
az acr login --name {registryname}
```

Now, let's say you have a Docker image in another registry. As a first step, let's pull the image on your local computer:

```
docker pull other.registry.io/samples/myimage
```

If there are several versions of the preceding image, the latest will be pulled since no version was specified. The version of the image can be specified as follows:

```
docker pull other.registry.io/samples/myimage:version1.0
```

Using the following command, you should see `myimage` within the list of local images:

```
docker images
```

Then, tag the image with the path you want to assign in the Azure registry:

```
docker tag myimage myregistry.azurecr.io/testpath/myimage
```

Both the name and destination tag may have versions (`:<version name>`).

Finally, push it to your registry with the following command:

```
docker push myregistry.azurecr.io/testpath/myimage
```

In this case, you can specify a version; otherwise, the latest version is pushed.

By doing this, you can remove the image from your local computer using the following command:

```
docker rmi myregistry.azurecr.io/testpath/myimage
```

Summary

In this chapter, we described what microservices are and how they have evolved from the concept of a module. Then, we talked about the advantages of microservices and when it is worth using them, as well as general criteria for their design. We also explained what Docker containers are and analyzed the strong connection between containers and microservice architectures.

Then, we took on a more practical implementation by describing all the tools that are available in .NET so that we can implement microservice-based architectures. We also described infrastructures that are needed by microservices and how Azure offers both container registries and container orchestrators.

This chapter was just a general introduction to microservices. Further chapters will discuss most of the subjects introduced here in more detail while showing practical implementation techniques and code examples.

This ends the first part of the book dedicated to fundamentals. The next chapter, *Choosing Your Data Storage in the Cloud*, starts the second part of the book, which is dedicated to specific technologies.

Questions

1. What is the two-fold nature of the module concept?
2. Is scaling optimization the only advantage of microservices? If not, list some further advantages.
3. What is Polly?
4. What Docker support is offered by Visual Studio?
5. What is an orchestrator, and what orchestrators are available on Azure?
6. Why is publisher/subscriber-based communication so important in microservices?
7. What is RabbitMQ?
8. Why are idempotent messages so important?

Further reading

The following are links to the official documentation for Azure Service Bus, RabbitMQ, and other event bus technologies:

- **Azure Service Bus:** `https://docs.microsoft.com/en-us/azure/service-bus-messaging/`
- **NServiceBus:** `https://particular.net/nservicebus`
- **MassTransit:** `https://masstransit-project.com/`
- **Brighter:** `https://www.goparamore.io/`
- **RabbitMQ:** `https://www.rabbitmq.com/getstarted.html`
- **EasyNetQ:** `https://easynetq.com/`
- The following are also links for Polly and Docker:
    - The documentation for Polly, a tool for reliable communication/tasks, can be found here: `https://github.com/App-vNext/Polly`
    - More information on Docker can be found on Docker's official website: `https://docs.docker.com/`

Learn more on Discord

To join the Discord community for this book – where you can share feedback, ask questions to the authors, and learn about new releases – follow the QR code below:

`https://packt.link/SoftwareArchitectureCSharp12Dotnet8`

12

Choosing Your Data Storage in the Cloud

Azure, like other clouds, offers a wide range of storage services. The first approach that we may consider is defining a scalable set of virtual machines hosted in the cloud where we can implement our custom solutions. For instance, we can create a SQL Server cluster on our cloud-hosted virtual machines to increase reliability and computational power. However, usually, custom architectures are not the optimal solution and do not take full advantage of the opportunities offered by cloud infrastructure. Scalability, fast setup, focus on the business, and security are some of the criteria that you might consider while deciding on your data storage on Azure. To help you with this, many of the **platform-as-a-service** (**PaaS**) options for storing data can be a great solution.

Therefore, this chapter will not discuss such custom architectures but will focus mainly on the various PaaS storage offerings that are available in the cloud and on Azure. These offerings include scalable solutions based on plain disk space, relational databases, NoSQL databases, and in-memory data stores such as Redis.

Choosing a more adequate storage type is based not only on the application's functional requirements but also on performance and scaling-out requirements. In fact, while scaling out when processing resources causes a linear increase in performance, scaling out storage resources does not necessarily imply an acceptable increase in performance. In short, no matter how much you duplicate your data storage devices, if several requests affect the same chunk of data, they will always queue for the same amount of time to access it!

Scaling out data causes linear increases in read operation throughput since each copy can serve a different request, but it doesn't imply the same increase in throughput for write operations since all copies of the same chunk of data must be updated! Accordingly, more sophisticated techniques are required to scale out storage devices, and not all storage engines scale equally well.

Relational databases do not scale well in all scenarios. Therefore, scaling needs and the need to distribute data geographically play a fundamental role in the choice of a storage engine, as well as in the choice of SaaS offering.

In this chapter, we will cover the following topics:

- Understanding the different repositories for different purposes
- Choosing between SQL and NoSQL document-oriented databases
- Azure Cosmos DB – an opportunity to manage a multi-continental database

Let us get started!

Technical requirements

This chapter requires that you have the following:

- Visual Studio 2022 free Community edition or better, with all the database tool components installed.
- A free Azure account. The *Creating an Azure account* subsection in *Chapter 1, Understanding the Importance of Software Architecture*, explains how to create one.
- For a better development experience, we advise that you also install the local emulator of Cosmos DB, which can be found at `https://aka.ms/cosmosdb-emulator`.
- You can find the sample code for the chapter at `https://github.com/PacktPublishing/Software-Architecture-with-C-Sharp-12-and-.NET-8-4E`.

Understanding the different repositories for different purposes

This section describes the functionalities that are offered by the most popular data storage techniques. We will mainly focus on the functional requirements they are able to satisfy. Performance and scaling-out features will be analyzed in the next section, which is dedicated to comparing relational and NoSQL databases.

In Azure, the various offerings can be found by typing product names into the search bar at the top of all Azure portal pages.

The following subsections describe the various kinds of databases that we can use in our C# projects.

Relational databases

These databases are the most common and studied type of storage. They guarantee a high level of service and store an immeasurable amount of data. Dozens of applications have been designed to store data in this kind of database, and we can find them in banks, stores, industries, and so on. When you store data in a relational database, the basic principle is to define the entities and properties you will save in each of them, defining the correct relationship between these entities.

For decades, relational databases were the only option imagined for designing great projects. Many big companies around the world have built their own database management system. Oracle, MySQL, and MS SQL Server would be listed by many as the ones you can trust to store your data.

Usually, clouds offer several database engines. Azure offers a variety of popular database engines, such as Oracle, MySQL, PostgreSQL, and SQL Server (Azure SQL).

Regarding the Oracle database engine, Azure offers configurable virtual machines with various Oracle editions installed on them, which you can easily verify by the suggestions you get after typing `Oracle` into the Azure portal search bar. Azure fees do not include Oracle licenses; they just include computation time, so you must bring your own license to Azure.

With MySQL on Azure, you pay to use a private server instance. The fees you incur depend on the number of cores you have, how much memory must be allocated, and backup retention time.

MySQL instances are redundant, and you can choose between local or geographically distributed redundancy:

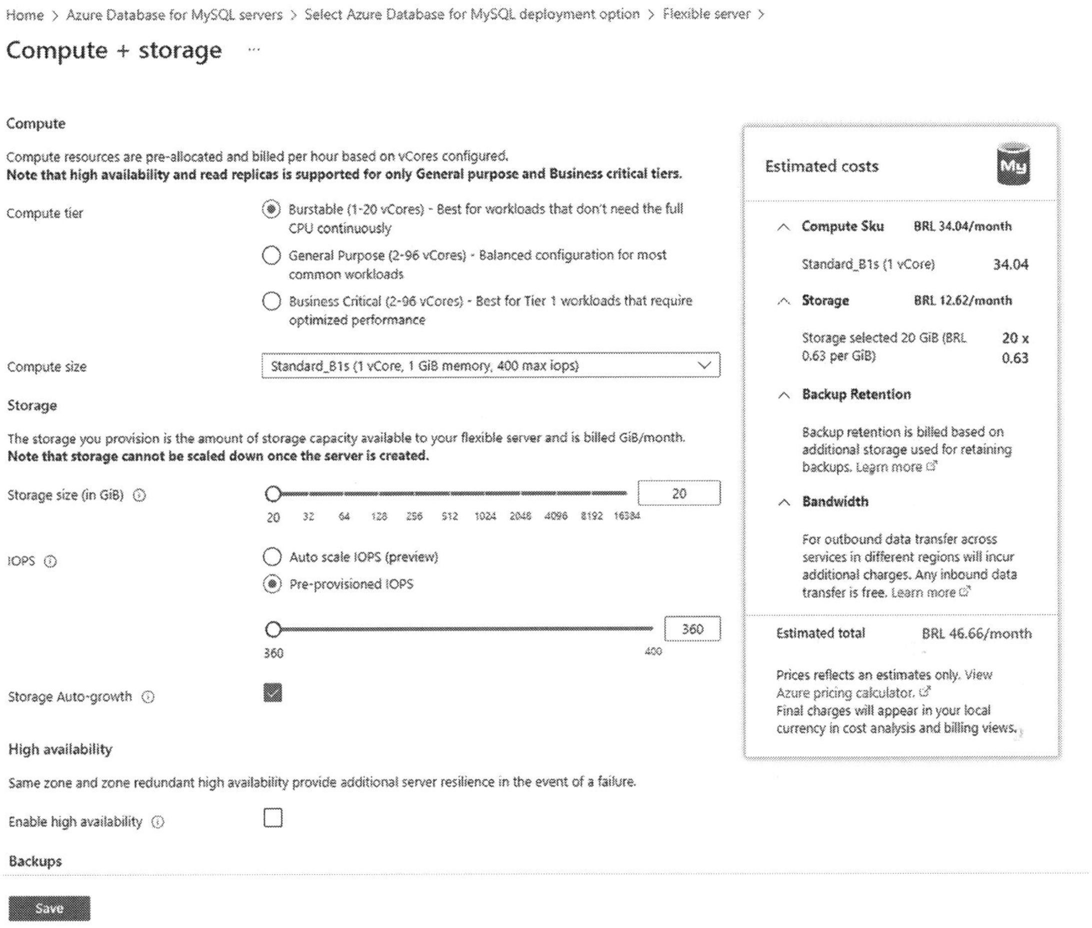

Figure 12.1: Creating a MySQL server on Azure

Azure SQL Database was one of the first PaaS options available on Azure, and for this reason, it has evolved a lot in recent years, which has made it one of the most flexible offers. Today, it also includes a serverless pricing model, where you are billed for the compute used per second. Here, you can configure resources that are used by every single database. When you create a database, you have the option to place it on an existing server instance or create a new instance.

There are several pricing options that you may choose while defining your solution, and Azure keeps incrementing them to make sure you will be able to handle your data in the cloud. Basically, they vary due to the computing capacity you need.

For instance, in the **Database Transaction Units** (**DTUs**) model, fees are based on the database storage capacity that has been reserved and a linear combination of I/O operations, CPU usage, and memory usage that is determined by a reference workload. Considering the difficulty of understanding exactly how DTUs are calculated, Azure also offers **vCore-based** models, where you have flexibility, control, and transparency of individual resource consumption.

Roughly, maximal database performance increases linearly when you increase the DTUs.

You can find detailed information about the options you have for purchasing Azure SQL Database at `https://learn.microsoft.com/en-us/azure/azure-sql/database/purchasing-models?view=azuresql`.

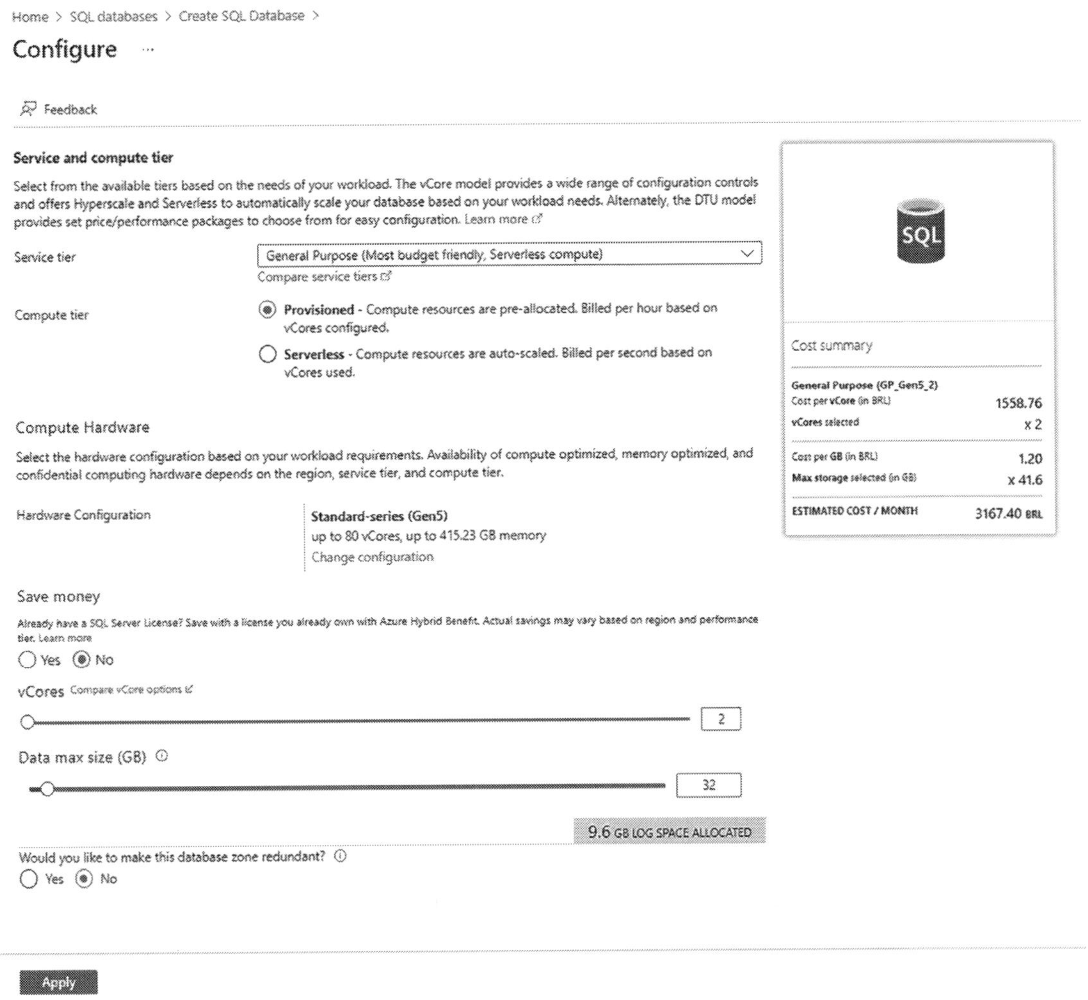

Home > SQL databases > Create SQL Database >

Configure ...

Feedback

Service and compute tier

Select from the available tiers based on the needs of your workload. The vCore model provides a wide range of configuration controls and offers Hyperscale and Serverless to automatically scale your database based on your workload needs. Alternately, the DTU model provides set price/performance packages to choose from for easy configuration. Learn more

Service tier: General Purpose (Most budget friendly, Serverless compute)

Compare service tiers

Compute tier:

- (selected) **Provisioned** - Compute resources are pre-allocated. Billed per hour based on vCores configured.
- **Serverless** - Compute resources are auto-scaled. Billed per second based on vCores used.

Compute Hardware

Select the hardware configuration based on your workload requirements. Availability of compute optimized, memory optimized, and confidential computing hardware depends on the region, service tier, and compute tier.

Hardware Configuration: **Standard-series (Gen5)** up to 80 vCores, up to 415.23 GB memory

Change configuration

Save money

Already have a SQL Server License? Save with a license you already own with Azure Hybrid Benefit. Actual savings may vary based on region and performance tier. Learn more

Yes / No (selected)

vCores Compare vCore options: 2

Data max size (GB): 32

9.6 GB LOG SPACE ALLOCATED

Would you like to make this database zone redundant?

Yes / No (selected)

Apply

Cost summary

General Purpose (GP_Gen5_2)	
Cost per vCore (in BRL)	1558.76
vCores selected	x 2
Cost per GB (in BRL)	1.20
Max storage selected (in GB)	x 41.6
ESTIMATED COST / MONTH	3167.40 BRL

Figure 12.2: Creating an Azure SQL Database

You can also configure data replication by enabling read scale-out. This way, you can improve the performance of read operations. Backup retention is fixed for each offering level (basic, standard, and premium).

If you select **Yes** for **Want to use SQL elastic pool?**, the database will be added to an elastic pool. Databases that are added to the same elastic pool will share their resources, so resources that are not used by a database can be used during the usage CPU peaks of other databases. It is worth mentioning that elastic pools can only contain databases hosted on the same server instance. Elastic pools are an efficient way to optimize resource usage to reduce costs.

NoSQL databases

One of the biggest challenges that relational databases have caused software architects is related to how we deal with database structural schema changes. The agility of changes needed at the beginning of this century brought the opportunity to use a new database style called NoSQL. The next subtopics will present several types of NoSQL databases.

Document-oriented database

The most common type of database, where you have the key and complex data, is called a document.

For instance, in NoSQL document-oriented databases, relational tables are replaced with more general collections that can contain heterogeneous JSON objects. That is, collections have no predefined structure and no predefined fields with length constraints (in the case of strings) but can contain any type of object. The only structural constraint associated with each collection is the name of the property that acts as a primary key.

More specifically, each collection entry can contain nested objects and object collections nested in object properties, that is, related entities that, in relational databases, are contained in different tables and connected through external keys. In NoSQL, databases can be nested in their parent entities. Since collection entries contain complex nested objects instead of simple property/value pairs, as is the case with relational databases, entries are not called tuples or rows but *documents*.

No relations and/or external key constraints can be defined between documents that belong to the same collection or to different collections. If a document contains the primary key of another document in one of its properties, it does so at its own risk. The developer is responsible for maintaining and keeping these coherent references. This is a tradeoff that you, as a software architect, must analyze. If you design a system that is generally dependent on relational databases, the gain of NoSQL will not be achieved, and you are at the same time sacrificing data integrity and redundancy. However, if you have a scenario where flexibility is needed, you must consider NoSQL as an option.

Finally, NoSQL storage is quite cheap. You can store a great amount of data as Base64 string properties. The developer can define rules to decide what properties to index in a collection. Since documents are nested objects, properties are tree paths. It is worth saying that you can specify which collection of paths and subpaths are indexed.

Almost all NoSQL databases are queried either with a subset of SQL or with a JSON-based language where queries are JSON objects whose paths represent the properties to query and whose values represent the query constraints that have been applied to them.

The possibility of nesting children objects inside documents can be simulated in relational databases with the help of one-to-many relationships. However, with relational databases, we are forced to redefine the exact structure of all the related tables, while NoSQL collections do not impose any predefined structure on the objects they contain. The only constraint is that each document must provide a unique value for the primary key property.

It is true that today, we have the possibility to define JSON columns in relational databases such as Azure SQL, so we can take a hybrid approach when defining our data model, having a schema for part of it but being flexible on other parts of it. However, NoSQL databases continue to be the best option when the structure of our objects is extremely variable, like social media and **Internet of Things** (**IoT**) solutions.

However, often, they are chosen for the way they scale out read and write operations and, more generally, for their performance advantages in distributed environments. Their performance features, which compare them to relational databases, will be discussed in the next section.

Graph database

Social media sites tend to use this kind of database since the data is stored as graphs.

The graph data model is an extreme case of a completely unstructured document. The whole database is a graph where queries can add, change, and delete graph documents.

In this case, we have two kinds of documents: nodes and relationships. While relationships have a well-defined structure (the primary key of the nodes connected by the relationship, plus the relationship's name), nodes have no structure at all since properties and their values are added together during node update operations.

It is important to you, as a software architect, to decide if this kind of structure presented in graph databases is the best one for the use case for which you are designing the system, always remembering that such a decision can make the system more complicated than needed.

Graph data models were conceived to represent the features of people and the objects they manipulate (media, posts, and so on), along with their relationships in *social applications*. The Gremlin language was conceived specifically to query graph data models. We will not discuss this in this chapter, but references are available in the *Further reading* section.

Key-value database

This is a useful database for implementing caches since you can store key-value pairs. Redis is a great example of it and it will be detailed soon in this chapter.

Wide-column store database

This is a type of database where the same column in each row can store different data.

NoSQL databases will be analyzed in detail in the remaining sections of this chapter, which are dedicated to describing Azure Cosmos DB and comparing it with relational databases.

Redis

Redis is a distributed in-memory storage based on key-value pairs and supports distributed queuing. It can be used as permanent in-memory storage and as a web application cache for database data. Alternatively, it can be used as a cache for pre-rendered content.

Redis can also be used to store a web application's user session data. This was done originally with Microsoft SQL Server, but due to the performance provided by memory databases, Redis is the best alternative today.

In fact, ASP.NET Core supports session data to overcome the fact that the HTTP protocol is stateless. More specifically, user data that is kept between page changes is maintained in server-side stores such as Redis and indexed by a session key stored in cookies.

Interaction with the Redis server in the cloud is typically based on a client implementation that offers an easy-to-use interface. The client for .NET is available through the `StackExchange.Redis` NuGet package. The basic operations of the `StackExchange.Redis` clients have been documented in `https://stackexchange.github.io/StackExchange.Redis/Basics`, while the full documentation can be found at `https://stackexchange.github.io/StackExchange.Redis`.

The user interface for defining a Redis server on Azure is quite simple:

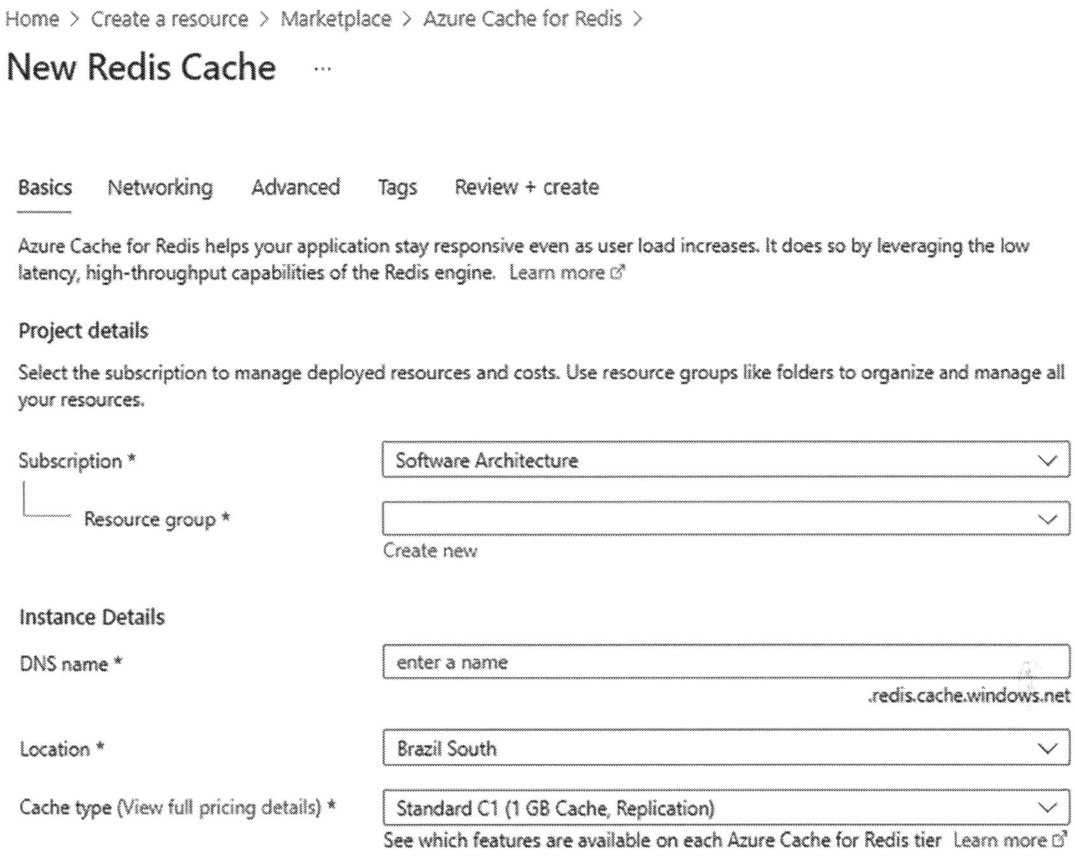

Home > Create a resource > Marketplace > Azure Cache for Redis >

New Redis Cache ...

Basics Networking Advanced Tags Review + create

Azure Cache for Redis helps your application stay responsive even as user load increases. It does so by leveraging the low latency, high-throughput capabilities of the Redis engine. Learn more

Project details

Select the subscription to manage deployed resources and costs. Use resource groups like folders to organize and manage all your resources.

Subscription * Software Architecture

Resource group *

Create new

Instance Details

DNS name * enter a name .redis.cache.windows.net

Location * Brazil South

Cache type (View full pricing details) * Standard C1 (1 GB Cache, Replication)

See which features are available on each Azure Cache for Redis tier Learn more

Figure 12.3: Creating a Redis cache

The **Pricing tier** dropdown allows us to select one of the available memory/replication options. A quick-start guide that explains how to use Azure Redis credentials and the URI with the `StackExchange.Redis` .NET client can be found at `https://docs.microsoft.com/en-us/azure/azure-cache-for-redis/cache-dotnet-core-quickstart`.

Azure storage accounts

All clouds offer scalable and redundant general-purpose disk memory that you can use as virtual disks in virtual machines and/or as external file storage. Azure *storage account* disk space can also be structured in **tables** and **queues**. Consider using this option if you need cheap blob storage. However, there are more sophisticated options, as we have mentioned before. Depending on the scenario you have, Azure NoSQL databases are a better option than tables, and Azure Redis is a better option than Azure storage queues.

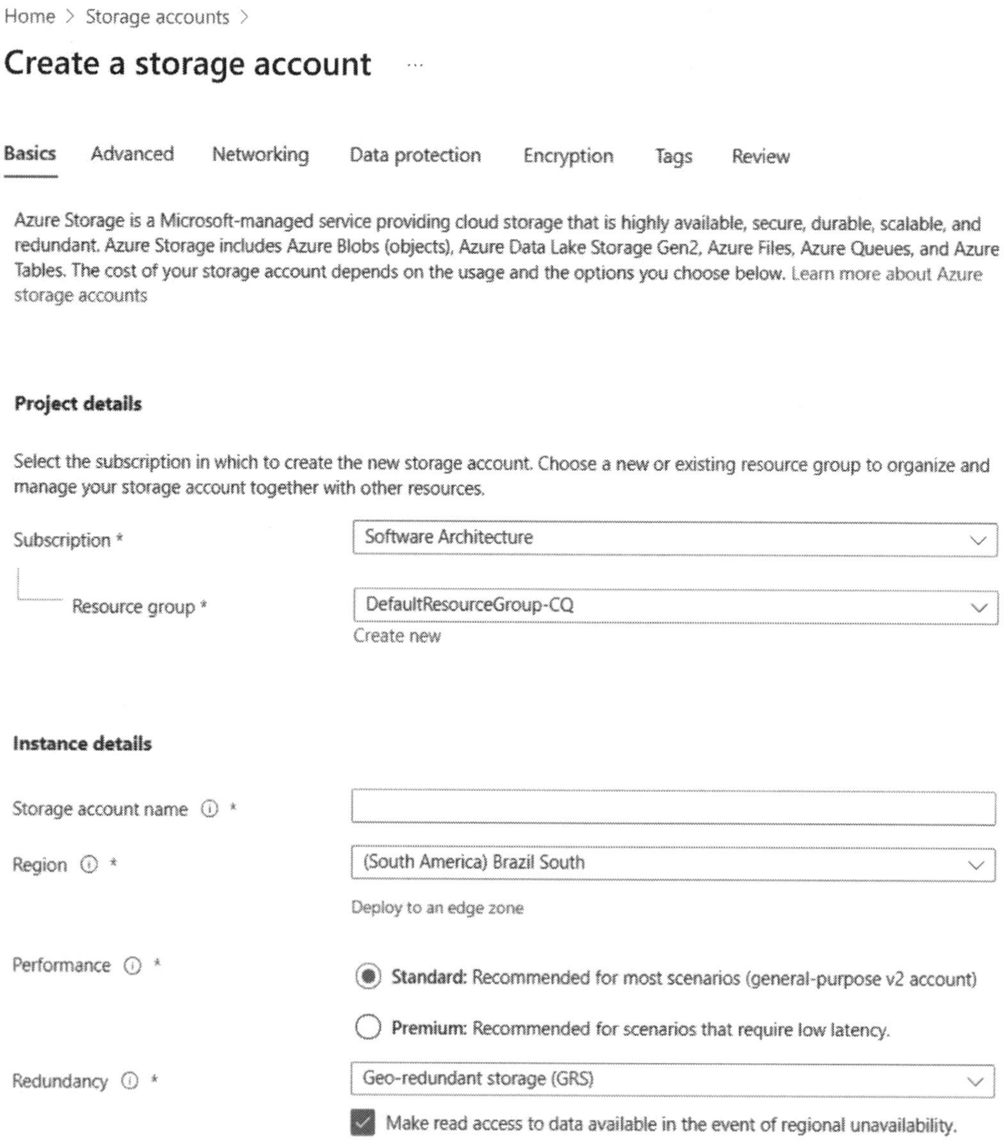

Home > Storage accounts >

Create a storage account ...

Basics Advanced Networking Data protection Encryption Tags Review

Azure Storage is a Microsoft-managed service providing cloud storage that is highly available, secure, durable, scalable, and redundant. Azure Storage includes Azure Blobs (objects), Azure Data Lake Storage Gen2, Azure Files, Azure Queues, and Azure Tables. The cost of your storage account depends on the usage and the options you choose below. Learn more about Azure storage accounts

Project details

Select the subscription in which to create the new storage account. Choose a new or existing resource group to organize and manage your storage account together with other resources.

Subscription * Software Architecture

Resource group * DefaultResourceGroup-CQ

Create new

Instance details

Storage account name *

Region * (South America) Brazil South

Deploy to an edge zone

Performance *

Standard: Recommended for most scenarios (general-purpose v2 account)

Premium: Recommended for scenarios that require low latency.

Redundancy * Geo-redundant storage (GRS)

Make read access to data available in the event of regional unavailability.

Figure 12.4: Creating a storage account

In the rest of this chapter, we will focus on NoSQL databases and how they differ from relational databases. Next, we will look at how to choose one over the other.

Choosing between SQL and NoSQL document-oriented databases

As a software architect, you may consider some aspects of SQL and NoSQL databases to decide the best storage option for you. In many cases, both will be needed. The key point here will surely be how organized your data is and how big the database will become.

In the previous section, we stated that NoSQL document-oriented databases should be preferred by you, as a software architect, when data has almost no predefined structure. They not only keep variable attributes close to their owners, but they also keep some related objects close since they allow related objects to be nested inside properties and collections.

Unstructured data can be represented in relational databases if variable properties of a tuple (`t`) can be placed in a connected table containing the property name, property value, and the external key of `t`. However, the problem in this scenario is performance. In fact, property values that belong to a single object would be spread all over the available memory space. In a small database, *all over the available memory space* means far away but on the same disk; in a bigger database, it means far away but in different disk units; in a distributed cloud environment, it means far away but in different – and possibly geographically distributed – servers.

On the other hand, in the NoSQL document-oriented database design, we always try to put all related objects that are likely to be processed together into a single entry. Related objects that are accessed less frequently are placed in different entries. Since external key constraints are not enforced automatically, and NoSQL transactions are very flexible, the developer can choose the best compromise between performance and coherence.

It is important to mention that today, we can store unstructured data as columns with JSON (or XML) types in relational databases. This approach allows the use of patterns typically implemented in document databases to also be achievable in relational databases, such as avoiding joins by inserting complete objects in a JSON column. However, the adoption of the NoSQL document-oriented database can be considered the best option since it was designed for this purpose.

Therefore, we can conclude that relational databases perform well when tables that are usually accessed together can be stored close together. NoSQL document-oriented databases, on the other hand, automatically ensure that related data is kept close together since each entry keeps most of the data it is related to inside it as nested objects. Therefore, NoSQL document-oriented databases perform better when they are distributed to a different memory and to different geographically distributed servers.

Unfortunately, the only way to scale out storage write operations is to split collection entries across several servers according to the values of *shard keys*. For instance, we can place all the records containing usernames that start with **A** on a server, the records containing usernames that start with **B** on another server, and so on. This way, write operations for usernames with different start letters may be executed in parallel, ensuring that the write throughput increases linearly with the number of servers.

However, if a *shard* collection is related to several other collections, there is no guarantee that related records will be placed on the same server. Also, putting different collections on different servers without using collection sharding increases write throughput linearly until we reach the limit of a single collection per server, but it doesn't solve the issue of being forced to perform several operations on different servers to retrieve or update data that are usually processed together.

This issue becomes catastrophic for performance in relational databases if access to related distributed objects must be transactional and/or must ensure structural constraints (such as external key constraints) are not violated. In this case, all related objects must be blocked during the transaction, preventing other requests from accessing them during the whole lifetime of a time-consuming distributed operation.

NoSQL document-oriented databases do not suffer from this problem and perform better with sharding and, consequently, with write-scaled output. This is because they do not distribute related data to different storage units and instead store them as nested objects of the same database entry. On the other hand, they suffer from different problems, like not supporting transactions by default.

It is worth mentioning that there are situations where relational databases perform well with sharding. A typical instance is a multi-tenant application. In a multi-tenant application, all entry collections can be partitioned into non-overlapping sets called **tenants**. Only entries belonging to the same tenant can refer to each other, so if all the collections are sharded in the same way according to their object tenants, all related records end up in the same shard, that is, in the same server, and can be navigated efficiently.

In this chapter, we did not talk about how to define sharding with Azure SQL. Here is the link to the official documentation if you want to find out more: `https://docs.microsoft.com/en-us/azure/sql-database/sql-database-elastic-scale-introduction`.

Multi-tenant applications are not rare in the cloud since all applications that offer the same services to several different users are often implemented as multi-tenant applications, where each tenant corresponds to a user subscription. Accordingly, relational databases, such as Azure SQL Server, are conceived to work in the cloud and usually offer sharding options for multi-tenant applications. Typically, sharding is not a cloud service and must be defined with database engine commands. Here, we will not describe how to define shards with Azure SQL Server, but the *Further reading* section contains a link to the official Microsoft documentation. The following table presents the pros and cons of each database approach:

Subject	SQL	NoSQL document-oriented DB
Schema	Easy to deal with in well-structured schemas. Today, it is possible to design hybrid solutions with JSON/XML columns to store unstructured data.	Preferred when data has almost no predefined structure.

Performance	In general, bad performance in distributed environments.	In general, good performance for reading and writing distributed data.
Language	Declarative to query and update data, standard.	Procedural to query and update operations.
Consistency	Strong use of foreign keys.	Weak and left to the developer's decision. All related objects that are likely to be processed together into a single entry.
Transactions	Supported.	By default, they are not supported.
Scale	Vertically upgrading hardware.	Horizontally with data sharding.

Table 12.1: Pros and cons for each database approach

In conclusion, relational databases offer a pure, logical view of data that is independent of the way they are stored and use declarative language to query and update them. This simplifies development and system maintenance, but it may cause performance issues in a distributed environment that requires write scale-out. It is also worth noting that tools like Entity Framework, presented in *Chapter 13, Interacting with Data in C# – Entity Framework Core*, help in bridging the gap between objects and relational data, making development more intuitive for relational databases.

In NoSQL document-oriented databases, you must handle more details about how to store data, as well as some procedural details for all the update and query operations, manually, but this allows you to optimize performance in distributed environments that require both read and write scale-out. On the flip side, working with NoSQL data, especially when it involves deserializing formats like JSON or XML, can be tricky. It often requires careful mapping to ensure data integrity, which can be both challenging and error-prone. In the next section, we will look at Azure Cosmos DB, the main Azure NoSQL offering, which, fortunately, can be integrated with Entity Framework for a more streamlined development experience.

Azure Cosmos DB – an opportunity to manage a multi-continental database

Azure Cosmos DB is Azure's main NoSQL offering. Azure Cosmos DB has its own interface that is a subset of SQL, but it can be configured with a MongoDB interface, a Table API, or a Cassandra API. It can also be configured as a graph data model that can be queried with Gremlin.

You can find further details about Cosmos DB in the official documentation: `https://docs.microsoft.com/en-us/azure/cosmos-db/`.

Cosmos DB allows replication for fault tolerance and read scale-out, and replicas can be distributed geographically to optimize communication performance. Moreover, you can specify which data center all the replicas are placed in. The user also has the option to write-enable all the replicas so that writes are immediately available in the geographical area where they are done. Write scale-up is achieved with sharding, which the user can configure by defining which properties to use as shard keys.

Creating an Azure Cosmos DB account

You can define a Cosmos DB account by typing `Cosmos DB` into the Azure portal search bar and clicking **+ Create**. The following page will appear:

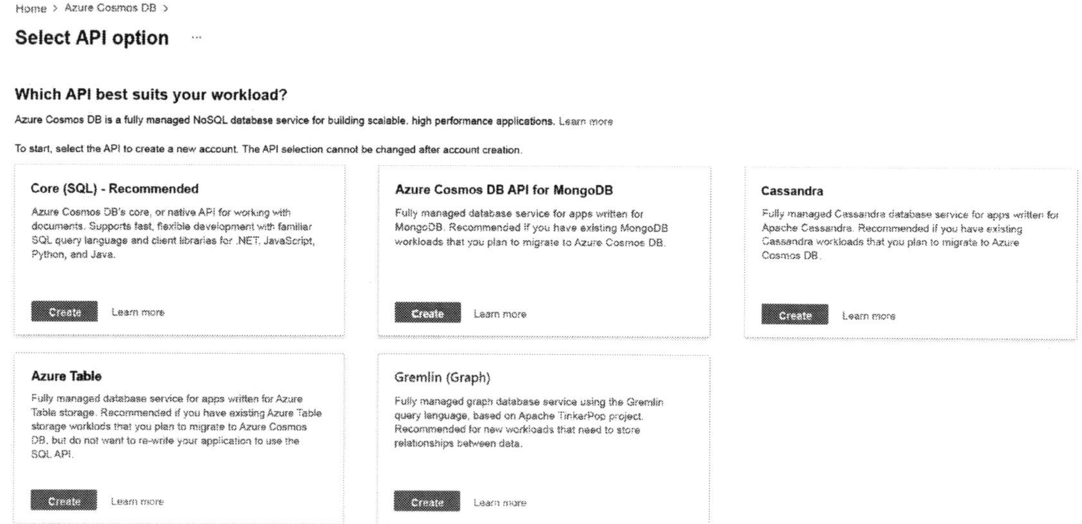

Figure 12.5: Creating an Azure Cosmos DB account

For instance, if you select the **Core (SQL)** option, the account name you choose is used in the resource URI as `{account_name}.documents.azure.com`. Then, you can decide which location the main database will be placed in and the capacity mode. You can check more information about the capacity modes available at `https://docs.microsoft.com/en-us/azure/cosmos-db/throughput-serverless`.

Microsoft keeps improving many of its Azure services. The best way to keep updated about new features of any Azure component is by checking its documentation from time to time.

On the **Global Distribution** tab, the **Multi-region Writes** toggle lets you enable writes on geographically distributed replicas. If you do not do this, all write operations will be routed to the main location. Finally, you may also define network connectivity, backup policies, and encryption during the creation process.

Creating an Azure Cosmos DB container

Once you have created your Azure Cosmos DB – Core SQL account, select **Data Explorer** to create your databases and containers inside of them. A container is the unit of scalability both for provisioned throughput and storage, available when you decide by provisioned throughput capacity mode.

Since databases just have a name and no configuration, you can **Add a container** directly and then place the database where you wish:

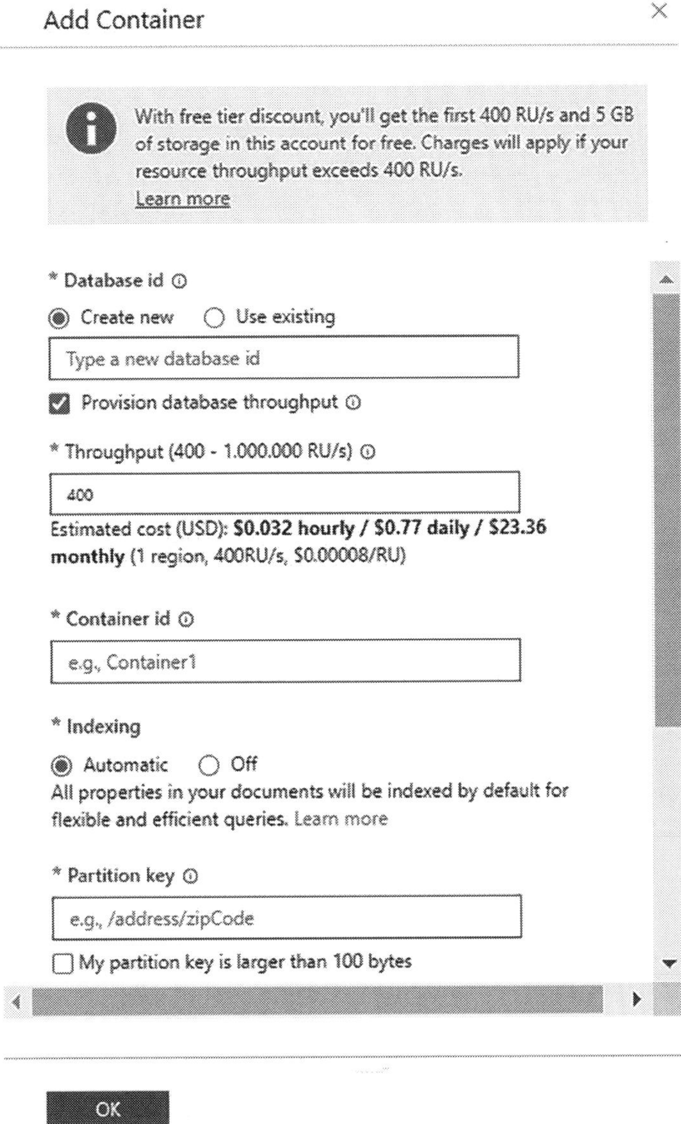

Figure 12.6: Adding a container in Azure Cosmos DB

Here, you can decide on database and container names and the property to use for sharding (the partition key). Since NoSQL entries are object trees, property names are specified as paths. You can also add properties whose values are required to be unique.

However, the uniqueness of IDs is checked inside each partition, so this option is only useful in certain situations, such as multi-tenant applications (where each tenant is included in a single shard). The fees depend on the collection throughput that you choose.

This is where you need to target all resource parameters to your needs. Throughput is expressed in request units per second, where request units per second are defined as the throughput we have when performing a read of 1 KB per second. Hence, if you check the **Provision database throughput** option, the chosen throughput is shared with the whole database instead of being reserved as a single collection.

Accessing Azure Cosmos DB

After creating the Azure Cosmos container, you will be able to access data. To get connection information, you can select the **Keys** menu. There, you will see all the information you need to connect with your Cosmos DB account from your application. The connection information page will provide you with the account URI and two connection keys, which can be used interchangeably to connect with the account.

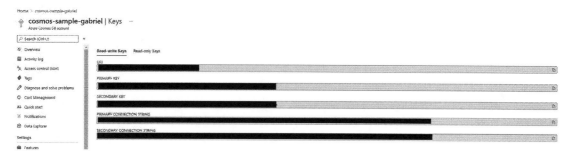

Figure 12.7: Connection information page

There are also keys with read-only privileges. Every key can be regenerated, and each account has two equivalent keys, like many other Azure components. This approach enables operations to be handled efficiently; that is, when a key is changed, the other one is kept. Therefore, existing applications can continue using the other key before upgrading to the new key.

Defining database consistency

Considering that you are in the context of a distributed database, Azure Cosmos DB enables you to define the default read consistency level you will have. By selecting **Default consistency** in the main menu of your Cosmos DB account, you can choose the default replication consistency that you wish to apply to all your containers.

This default can be overridden in each container, either from Data Explorer or programmatically. Consistency problems in read/write operations are a consequence of data replication. More specifically, the results of various read operations may be incoherent if the read operations are executed on different replicas that have received different partial updates.

The following are the available consistency levels. These have been ordered from the weakest to the strongest:

- **Eventual:** After enough time has passed, if no further write operations are done, all the reads converge and apply all the writes. The order of writes is also not guaranteed, so while writes are being processed, you could also end up reading an earlier version than the one you have previously read.

- **Consistent prefix:** All the writes are executed in the same order on all the replicas. So, if there are `n` write operations, each read is consistent with the result of applying the first `m` writes for some `m` less than or equal to `n`.
- **Session:** This is the same as the consistency prefix but also guarantees that each writer sees the result of its own writes in all subsequent read operations and that subsequent reads of each reader are coherent (either the same database or a more updated version of it).
- **Bounded staleness:** This is associated either with a delay time, `Delta`, or with several operations, `N`. Each read sees the results of all the write operations that were performed before a time `Delta` (or before the last `N` operations). That is, its reads converge with the result of all the writes with a maximum time delay of `Delta` (or a maximum operations delay of `N`).
- **Strong:** This is bounded staleness combined with `Delta = 0`. Here, each read reflects the result of all previous write operations.

The strongest consistency can be obtained to the detriment of performance. By default, the consistency is set to **Session**, which is a good compromise between coherence and performance. A lower level of consistency is difficult to handle in applications and is only usually acceptable if sessions are either read-only or write-only.

If you select the **Settings** option in the **Data Explorer** menu of the container of your database, you can configure which paths to index and which kind of indexing to apply to each data type of each path. The configuration consists of a JSON object. Let us analyze its various properties:

```
{
    "indexingMode": "consistent",
    "automatic": true,
    ...
```

If you set `indexingMode` to `none` instead of `consistent`, no index is generated, and the collection can be used as a key-value dictionary that is indexed by the collection's primary key. In this scenario, no secondary indexes are generated, so the primary key cannot efficiently be searched.

When `automatic` is set to `true`, all document properties are automatically indexed:

```
{
    ...
    "includedPaths": [
        {
            "path": "/*",
            "indexes": [
                {
                    "kind": "Range",
                    "dataType": "Number",
                    "precision": -1
                },
                {
```

```
                    "kind": "Range",
                    "dataType": "String",
                    "precision": -1
                },
                {
                    "kind": "Spatial",
                    "dataType": "Point"
                }
            ]
        }
    ]
},
...
```

Each entry in `includedPaths` specifies a path pattern such as `/subpath1/subpath2/?` (settings apply just to the `/subpath1/subpath2/property`) or `/subpath1/subpath2/*` (settings apply to all the paths starting with `/subpath1/subpath2/`).

Patterns contain the `[]` symbol when settings must be applied to child objects contained in collection properties; for example, `/subpath1/subpath2/[]/?`, `/subpath1/subpath2/[]/childpath1/?`, and so on. Settings specify the index type to apply to each data type (string, number, geographic point, and so on). Range indexes are needed for comparison operations, while hash indices are more efficient if we need equality comparisons.

It is possible to specify a precision, that is, the maximum number of characters or digits to use in all the index keys. `-1` means the maximum precision and is always recommended:

```
    ...
    "excludedPaths": [
   {
          "path": "/\"_etag\"/?"
      }
    ]
```

Paths contained in `excludedPaths` are not indexed at all. Index settings can also be specified programmatically.

Here, you have two options to connect to Cosmos DB: use a version of its official client for your preferred programming language or use Cosmos DB's Entity Framework Core provider. In the following subsections, we will have a look at both options. Then, we will describe how to use Cosmos DB's Entity Framework Core provider with a practical example.

The Cosmos DB client

The Cosmos DB client for .NET 8 is available through the `Microsoft.Azure.Cosmos` NuGet package. It offers full control of all Cosmos DB features, while the Cosmos DB Entity Framework provider is easier to use but hides some Cosmos DB peculiarities. Follow these steps to interact with Cosmos DB through the official Cosmos DB client for .NET 8.

The following code sample shows the creation of a database and a container using the client component. Any operation requires the creation of a client object. Do not forget that the client must be disposed of by calling its `Dispose` method (or by enclosing the code that references it in a `using` statement) when you do not need it anymore:

```
public static async Task CreateCosmosDB()
{
    using var cosmosClient = new CosmosClient(endpoint, key);
    Database database = await
        cosmosClient.CreateDatabaseIfNotExistsAsync(databaseId);
    ContainerProperties cp = new ContainerProperties(containerId,
        "/DestinationName");
    Container container = await database.CreateContainerIfNotExistsAsync(cp);
    await AddItemsToContainerAsync(container);
}
```

During collection creation, you can pass a `ContainerProperties` object, where you can specify the consistency level, how to index properties, and all the other collection features.

Then, you must define the .NET classes that correspond to the structure of the JSON document you need to manipulate in your collections. You can also use the `JsonProperty` attribute to map class property names to JSON names if they are not equal:

```
public class Destination
{
    [JsonPropertyName("id")]
    public string Id { get; set; }
    public string DestinationName { get; set; }
    public string Country { get; set; }
    public string Description { get; set; }
    public Package[] Packages { get; set; }
}
```

NoSQL means Not Only SQL, so it is also possible to map properties. The great thing about NoSQL is that you must map these properties without causing damage to other properties or information you have in the document you are connecting to.

Once you have all the necessary classes, you can use client methods to `ReadItemAsync`, `CreateItemAsync`, and `DeleteItemAsync`. You can also query data using a `QueryDefinition` object that accepts SQL commands. You can find a complete introduction to this library at `https://docs.microsoft.com/en-us/azure/cosmos-db/sql-api-get-started`.

The Cosmos DB Entity Framework Core provider

The Cosmos DB provider for Entity Framework Core is contained in the `Microsoft.EntityFrameworkCore.Cosmos` NuGet package. Once you've added this to your project, you can proceed in a similar way to when you used the SQL Server provider in *Chapter 13, Interacting with Data in C# – Entity Framework Core*, but with a few differences. Let us take a look:

- There are no migrations since Cosmos DB databases have no structure to update. Instead, they have a method that ensures that the database, along with all the necessary collections, is created:

  ```
  context.Database.EnsureCreated();
  ```

- By default, the `DbSet<T>` properties from `DBContext` are mapped to a unique container since this is the cheapest option. You can override this default by explicitly specifying which container you want to map some entities to by using the following configuration instruction:

  ```
  builder.Entity<MyEntity>()
       .ToContainer("collection-name");
  ```

- The only useful annotation on entity classes is the `Key` attribute, which becomes obligatory when the primary keys are not called `Id`.
- Primary keys must be strings and cannot be auto-incremented to avoid synchronization issues in a distributed environment. The uniqueness of primary keys can be ensured by generating GUIDs and transforming them into strings.
- When defining relationships between entities, you can specify that an entity or a collection of entities is owned by another entity, in which case it is stored together with the parent entity.

We will look at the usage of Cosmos DB's Entity Framework provider in the *How to choose your data storage in the cloud* section of *Chapter 21, Case Study*.

Summary

In this chapter, we looked at the main storage options available in Azure and learned when to use them. Then, we compared relational and NoSQL databases. We pointed out that relational databases offer automatic consistency checking and transaction isolation, but NoSQL databases are cheaper and offer better performance, especially when distributed writes form a high percentage of the average workload.

Then, we described Azure's main NoSQL option, Cosmos DB, and explained how to configure it and how to connect with a client.

Finally, we learned how to interact with Cosmos DB with Entity Framework Core. Here, we learned how to decide whether to use relational or NoSQL databases for all families of data involved in an application. So, you can choose the kind of data storage that ensures the best compromise between data coherence, speed, and parallel access to data in each of your applications.

In the next chapter, we will learn all about how to interact with data in C#–Entity Framework Core.

Questions

1. Is Redis a valid alternative to relational databases?
2. Are NoSQL databases a valid alternative to relational databases?
3. What operation is more difficult to scale out in relational databases?
4. What is the main weakness of NoSQL databases? What is their main advantage?
5. Can you list all Cosmos DB consistency levels?
6. Can we use auto-increment integer keys with Cosmos DB?
7. Which Entity Framework configuration method is used to store an entity inside its related father document?
8. Can nested collections be searched efficiently with Cosmos DB?

Further reading

- The following is a reference to the Gremlin language, which is supported by Cosmos DB: `http://tinkerpop.apache.org/docs/current/reference/#graph-traversal-steps`.
- The following is a general description of the Cosmos DB graph data model: `https://docs.microsoft.com/en-us/azure/cosmos-db/graph-introduction`.
- Details on how to use Cosmos DB's official .NET client can be found at `https://docs.microsoft.com/en-us/azure/cosmos-db/sql-api-dotnetcore-get-started`. A good introduction to the `MvcControlsToolkit.Business.DocumentDB` NuGet package that we mentioned in this chapter is the *Fast Azure Cosmos DB Development with the DocumentDB Package* article contained in Issue 34 of *DNCMagazine*. This can be downloaded from `https://www.dotnetcurry.com/microsoft-azure/aspnet-core-cosmos-db-documentdb`.

Learn more on Discord

To join the Discord community for this book – where you can share feedback, ask questions to the authors, and learn about new releases – follow the QR code below:

`https://packt.link/SoftwareArchitectureCSharp12Dotnet8`

13

Interacting with Data in C# – Entity Framework Core

As we mentioned in *Chapter 7, Understanding the Different Domains in Software Solutions*, software systems are organized into layers that communicate with each other through interfaces and classes that don't depend on how the peculiarities of each layer are implemented. When the software is a business/enterprise system, it usually contains at least three layers: the data layer, the business layer, and the presentation layer, if the software is based on a classical layer architecture (see the *Classic layers architecture* section of *Chapter 7*.

If, instead, the application is based on an onion architecture, an outermost layer contains presentation logic, drivers, and testing logic, then there is an application layer, and finally, a domain layer (see the *Onion architecture* section of *Chapter 7*). While, in the onion architecture, layers are defined in a slightly different way, the functionalities of the three layers of the onion architecture are basically the same as the ones of the three layers of the classical layer architecture.

However, notwithstanding the differences among all possible architectural choices, experience has proved that the main functionalities needed to handle data efficaciously are quite standard.

More specifically, in all architectures described in *Chapter 7,* data-processing layers have the main purpose of mapping data from a data storage subsystem into objects and vice versa.

In the case of the classical data layer, these objects are plain objects with no methods, while in the case of the domain layer, they are rich objects whose methods implement the application's domain logic. Data layers, instead, implement the application's domain logic within repository classes that are associated with their plain objects (see the *The Repository and Unit of Work patterns* section of *Chapter 7*).

This led to the conception of general-purpose frameworks for implementing data layers in a substantially declarative way. These tools are called **Object-Relational Mapping** (**ORM**) tools since they are data storage subsystems based on relational databases. However, they also work well with modern non-relational storage classified as NoSQL databases (such as MongoDB and Azure Cosmos DB) since their data model is closer to the target object model than a purely relational model.

ORMs improve and simplify the whole development process since they factor out and take away the burden of mapping data into objects and vice versa, so developers can focus just on the peculiarity of the business domain.

In this chapter, we will cover the following topics:

- Understanding ORM basics
- Configuring Entity Framework Core
- Entity Framework Core migrations
- Compiled models
- Querying and updating data with Entity Framework Core
- Deploying your data layer
- Understanding Entity Framework Core advanced features

This chapter describes ORMs and how to configure them, and then focuses on Entity Framework Core, the ORM included in .NET 8.

Before delving into ORM basics, let's look at the technical requirements needed to follow the practical examples in this chapter.

Technical requirements

This chapter requires the free Visual Studio 2022 Community Edition or better with all the database tools installed.

All the concepts in this chapter will be clarified with practical examples. You will find the code for this chapter at `https://github.com/PacktPublishing/Software-Architecture-with-C-Sharp-12-and-.NET-8-4E`.

Understanding ORM basics

ORMs map relational DB tables into in-memory collections of objects where object properties correspond to DB table columns. Types from C#, such as Booleans, numeric types, and strings, have corresponding DB types. If GUIDs are not available in the mapped DB, then types such as GUIDs are mapped to their equivalent string representations. All date and time types are mapped either to C# `DateTime` when the date/time contains no time zone information, to `DateTimeOffset` when the date/time also contains explicit time zone information, to `DateOnly` when the type contains just date information, or to `TimeOnly` when the type contains just time information. Any DB time duration is mapped to a `TimeSpan`. Finally, single characters should not be mapped at all to DB fields.

Since the string properties of most object-oriented languages have no length limits associated with them (while DB string fields usually have length limits), the DB limits are taken into account in the DB mapping configuration. In general, when the mapping between DB types and object-oriented language types needs options to be specified, these options are declared in the mapping configuration.

The way the whole configuration is defined depends on the specific ORM. Entity Framework Core offers three options:

- Data annotations (property attributes)
- Name conventions
- A fluent configuration interface based on configuration objects and methods

While the fluent interface can be used to specify any configuration option, the data annotations and name conventions can be used for a smaller subset of them.

Personally, I prefer using the fluent interface for most settings. I use name conventions only for specifying the principal key with an ID property name since I find that relying on name conventions for more complex settings is very dangerous. In fact, there are no compilation-time checks on name conventions, so a re-engineering operation might erroneously change or destroy some ORM settings.

I use data annotations mainly for specifying constraints on the possible values of properties, such as the maximum length of a value or the fact that a property is obligatory and can't be null. In fact, these constraints restrict the type specified in each property, so placing them next to the properties they are applied to increases the code's readability.

All other settings are better grouped and organized by using the fluent interface in order to increase code readability and maintainability.

Each ORM adapts to a specific DB type (Oracle, MySQL, SQL Server, and so on) with DB-specific adapters called **providers** or **connectors**. Entity Framework Core has providers for most of the available DB engines.

A complete list of providers can be found at `https://docs.microsoft.com/en-US/ef/core/providers/`.

Adapters are necessary for the differences in DB types, for the way transactions are handled, and for all other features that are not standardized by the SQL language.

Relationships among tables are represented with object pointers. For instance, in a one-to-many relationship, the class that's mapped to the *one* side of the relationship contains a collection that is populated with the related objects on the *many* side of the relationship. On the other hand, the class mapped to the *many* side of the relationship has a simple property that is populated with a uniquely related object on the *one* side of the relationship.

While, in the case of a one-to-one relationship, both classes have a property populated with the companion object, in the case of many-to-many relationships, both classes contain a collection that is populated with the related objects.

The whole database (or just a part of it) is represented by an in-memory cache class that contains a collection for each mapped DB table. First, the query and update operations are performed on an instance of an in-memory cache class, and then this instance is synchronized with the database.

The in-memory cache class that's used by Entity Framework Core is called `DbContext` and it also contains the mapping configuration.

Developers can customize the `DbContext` class furnished by Entity Framework Core by inheriting from it and by adding their database-mapping instructions inside overridden methods.

Summing up, `DbContext` subclass instances contain partial snapshots of the DB that are synchronized with the database to get/update the actual data.

DB queries are performed with a query language made of method calls on the collections of the in-memory cache class. The actual SQL is created and executed during the synchronization stage. For instance, Entity Framework Core performs **Language Integrated Query** (**LINQ**) queries on the collections mapped to the DB tables.

In general, LINQ queries produce `IEnumerable` instances, that is, collections whose elements are not computed when the is created at the end of the query, but when you actually attempt to retrieve the collection elements from the. This is called lazy evaluation or deferred execution. It works as follows:

- LINQ queries that start from a mapped collection of a `DbContext` create a specific subtype of `IEnumerable` called `IQueryable`.
- An `IQueryable` contains all the information that's needed to issue a query to the database, but the actual SQL is produced and executed when the first element of the `IQueryable` is retrieved.
- Typically, each Entity Framework query ends with a `ToListAsync` or `ToArrayAsync` operation that transforms the `IQueryable` into a list or array, thereby causing the actual execution of the query on the database.
- If the query is expected to return just a single element or no element at all, we typically execute a `SingleOrDefaultAsync` operation that returns a single element, if any, or `null`. This operation may be used also when several results are expected but we need just one. In this case, we might also use `LastOrDefaultAsync`.
- If we need just to count the total results, for instance, for adequately organizing paging information, we can use `CountAsync()`.

Also, updates, deletions, and the addition of new entities to a DB table are performed by mimicking these operations on a `DbContext` collection property that represents the database table. However, entities may only be updated or deleted this way after they have been loaded in that memory collection by means of a query. Typically, an update query requires the in-memory representation of the entity to be modified as needed, while a delete query requires the in-memory representation of the entity to be removed from its in-memory mapped collection. In Entity Framework Core, the removal operation is performed by calling the `Remove(entity)` method of the collection.

The addition of a new entity has no further requirements. It is enough to add the new entity to the in-memory collection. Updates, deletions, and additions that are performed on various in-memory collections are actually passed to the database with an explicit call to a DB synchronization method.

For instance, Entity Framework Core passes all the changes that are performed on a `DbContext` instance to the database when you call the `DbContext.SaveChangesAsync()` method.

Changes that are passed to the database during a synchronization operation are executed in a single transaction. Moreover, for ORMs, such as Entity Framework Core, that have an explicit representation of transactions, if a synchronization operation is executed in the scope of a transaction then it uses that transaction instead of creating a new transaction.

The remaining sections in this chapter explain how to use Entity Framework Core, along with some example code based on this book's WWTravelClub use case.

Configuring Entity Framework Core

Since, as detailed in *Chapter 7, Understanding the Different Domains in Software Solutions*, database handling is confined within a dedicated application layer, it is good practice to define your Entity Framework Core (`DbContext`) in a separate library. Accordingly, we need to define a .NET class library project.

We have two different kinds of library projects: **.NET Standard** and **.NET Core**. Please refer to *Chapter 5, Implementing Code Reusability in C# 12,* for a discussion on the various kinds of libraries.

While .NET libraries are tied to a specific .NET Core version, .NET Standard 2.0 libraries have a wide range of applications since they work with any .NET version greater than 2.0 and also with the old .NET Framework 4.7 and above.

Since our library is not a general-purpose library (it's just a component of a specific .NET 8 application), instead of choosing a .NET Standard library project, we can simply choose a .NET 8 library. Our .NET 8 library project can be created and prepared as follows:

1. Open Visual Studio, click **Create new project** and then select **Class Library**.
2. Name the new project `WWTravelClubDB` and accept the same name for the whole Visual Studio solution.
3. In the window that follows, choose .NET 8 as the target framework.
4. We must install all Entity Framework Core-related dependencies. The simplest way to have all the necessary dependencies installed is to add the NuGet package for the provider of the database engine we are going to use – in our case, SQL Server – as we mentioned in *Chapter 10, Deciding on the Best Cloud-Based Solution.*
5. In fact, any provider will install all the required packages since it has all of them as dependencies. So, let's add the latest stable version of `Microsoft.EntityFrameworkCore.SqlServer`. If you plan to use several database engines, you can also add other providers since they can work side by side. Later in this chapter, we will install other NuGet packages that contain tools that we need to process our Entity Framework Core configuration.
6. Let's rename the default `Class1` class to `MainDbContext`. The `Class1` class is automatically added to the class library. Now, let's replace its content with the following code:

```
using System;
using Microsoft.EntityFrameworkCore;
namespace WWTravelClubDB
{
```

```
    public class MainDbContext: DbContext
    {
        public MainDbContext(DbContextOptions options)
            : base(options)
        {
        }
        protected override void OnModelCreating(ModelBuilder
        builder)
        {
        }
    }
}
```

7. We inherit from `DbContext`, and we pass a `DbContextOptions` to the `DbContext` constructor. `DbContextOptions` contains creation options, such as the database connection string, which depends on the target DB engine.
8. All the collections that have been mapped to database tables will be added as properties of `MainDbContext`. The mapping configuration will be defined inside of the overridden `OnModelCreating` method with the help of the `ModelBuilder` object passed as a parameter.

The next step is the creation of all the classes that represent the tables. These are called entities. We need an entity class for each DB table we want to map. Let's create a `Models` folder in the project root for all of them. The next subsection explains how to define all the required entities.

Defining DB entities

DB design, like the whole application design, is organized in iterations (see *Chapter 1, Understanding the Importance of Software Architecture*). Let's suppose that, in the first iteration, we need a prototype with two database tables: one for all the travel packages and another one for all the locations referenced by the packages. Each package covers just one location, while a single location may be covered by several packages, so the two tables are connected by a one-to-many relationship.

So, let's start with the location database table. As we mentioned at the end of the previous section, we need an entity class to represent the rows of this table. Let's call the entity class `Destination`:

```
namespace WWTravelClubDB.Models
{
    public class Destination
    {
        public int Id { get; set; }
        public required string Name { get; set; }
        public required string Country { get; set; }
        public string? Description { get; set; }
    }
}
```

In the code above, all the DB fields must be represented by read/write C# properties. Since both the `Name` and `Country` properties are obligatory but we are not going to define a constructor, we added the `required` keyword to instruct the compiler to signal an error whenever an instance is created without initializing them.

Suppose that each destination is something like a town or a region that can be defined by just its name and the country it is in and that all the relevant information is contained in its `Description`. In future iterations, we will probably add several more fields. `Id` is an auto-generated key.

However, now, we need to add information about how all the fields are mapped to DB fields. In Entity Framework Core, all the primitive types are mapped automatically to DB types by the DB engine-specific provider that's used (in our case, the SQL Server provider).

Our only preoccupations are as follows:

- **Length limits on the string**: They can be taken into account by applying adequate `MaxLength` and `MinLength` attributes to each string property. All the attributes that are useful for the entity's configuration are contained in the `System.ComponentModel.DataAnnotations` and `System.ComponentModel.DataAnnotations.Schema` namespaces. Therefore, it's good practice to add both of them to all the entity definitions.
- **Specifying which fields are obligatory and which ones are optional**: If the project is not using the new **Nullable Reference Type** feature, by default, all the reference types (such as all the strings) are assumed to be optional, while all the value types (numbers and GUIDs, for instance) are assumed to be obligatory. If we want a reference type to be obligatory, then we must decorate it with the `Required` attribute. On the other hand, if we want a `T` type property to be optional, and `T` is a value type, or the Nullable Reference Type feature is on, then we must replace `T` with `T?`. As a default, .NET 8 projects have the new Nullable Reference Type feature set.
- **Specifying which property represents the primary key**: The key may be specified by decorating a property with the `Key` attribute. However, if no `Key` attribute is found, a property named `Id` (if there is one) is taken as the primary key. In our case, there is no need for the `Key` attribute.

Since each destination is on *one* side of a one-to-many relationship, it must contain a collection of the related package entities; otherwise, it will be difficult to refer to the related entities in the clauses of our LINQ queries. This collection will have a fundamental role in our LINQ queries and will be populated by Entity Framework Core. However, as we will see later in this chapter, it must be ignored in most of the database update operations. Therefore, the best option to avoid compiler warnings is to assign them the null-forgiving fake default value: `null!`.

Putting everything together, the final version of the `Destination` class is as follows:

```
using System.Collections.Generic;
using System.ComponentModel.DataAnnotations;
using System.ComponentModel.DataAnnotations.Schema;
namespace WWTravelClubDB.Models
{
    public class Destination
```

```
    {
        public int Id { get; set; }
        [MaxLength(128)]
        Public required string Name { get; set; }
        [MaxLength(128)]
        Public required string Country { get; set; }
        public string? Description { get; set; }
        public ICollection<Package> Packages { get; set; } = null!
    }
}
```

Since the `Description` property has no length limits, it will be implemented with a SQL Server `nvarchar(MAX)` field of indefinite length. We can write the code for the `Package` class in a similar way:

```
using System;
using System.ComponentModel.DataAnnotations;
using System.ComponentModel.DataAnnotations.Schema;
namespace WWTravelClubDB.Models
{
    public class Package
    {
        public int Id { get; set; }
        [MaxLength(128)]
        Public required string Name { get; set; }
        [MaxLength(128)]
        public string? Description { get; set; }
        public decimal Price { get; set; }
        public int DurationInDays { get; set; }
        public DateTime? StartValidityDate { get; set; }
        public DateTime? EndValidityDate { get; set; }
        public Destination MyDestination { get; set; } = null!

        public int DestinationId { get; set; }
    }
}
```

Each package has a duration in days, as well as optional start and stop dates in which the package offer is valid. `MyDestination` connects packages with their destinations in the many-to-one relationship that they have with the `Destination` entity, while `DestinationId` is the external key of the same relation.

While it is not obligatory to specify the external key, it is good practice to do so since this is the only way to specify some properties of the relationship. For instance, in our case, since `DestinationId` is an `int` (not nullable type), it is obligatory.

Therefore, the relationship here is one-to-many and not (0, 1)-to-many. Defining `DestinationId` as `int?` instead of `int` would turn the one-to-many relationship into a (0, 1)-to-many relationship. Moreover, as we will see later in this chapter, having an explicit representation of the foreign key simplifies the update operations a lot, and some queries.

In the next section, we will explain how to define the in-memory collection that represents the database tables.

Defining the mapped collections

Once we have defined all the entities that are object-oriented representations of the database rows, we need to define the in-memory collections that represent the database tables themselves. As we mentioned in the *Understanding ORM basics* section, all the database operations are mapped to the operations on these collections (the *Querying and updating data with Entity Framework Core* section of this chapter explains how). It is enough to add a `DbSet<T>` collection property to our `DbContext` for each entity, `T`. Usually, the name of each of these properties is obtained by pluralizing the entity name. Thus, we need to add the following two properties to our `MainDbContext`:

```
public DbSet<Package> Packages { get; set; }
public DbSet<Destination> Destinations { get; set; }
```

Up until now, we've translated database stuff into properties, classes, and data annotations. However, Entity Framework needs further information to interact with a database. The next subsection explains how to provide it.

Completing the mapping configuration

The mapping configuration information that we couldn't specify in the entity definitions must be added with configuration code based on a fluent interface. The simplest way to add this configuration information is to add it using the `OnModelCreating DbContext` method. Each piece of configuration information relative to an entity, `T`, starts with `builder.Entity<T>()` and continues with a call to a method that specifies that kind of constraint. Further nested calls specify further properties of the constraint. For instance, our one-to-many relationship may be configured as follows:

```
builder.Entity<Destination>()
    .HasMany(m => m.Packages)
    .WithOne(m => m.MyDestination)
    .HasForeignKey(m => m.DestinationId)
    .OnDelete(DeleteBehavior.Cascade);
```

The two sides of the relationship are specified through the navigation properties that we added to our entities. `HasForeignKey` specifies the external key. Finally, `OnDelete` specifies what to do with packages when a destination is deleted. In our case, it performs a cascade delete of all the packages related to that destination.

The same configuration can be defined by starting from the other side of the relationship, that is, starting with `builder.Entity<Package>()`. Clearly, the developer must choose just one of the options:

```
builder.Entity<Package>()
    .HasOne(m => m.MyDestination)
    .WithMany(m => m.Packages)
    .HasForeignKey(m => m.DestinationId)
    .OnDelete(DeleteBehavior.Cascade);
```

The only difference is that the previous statement's `HasMany-WithOne` methods are replaced by the `HasOne-WithMany` methods since we started from the other side of the relationship. Here, we can also choose the precision with which each decimal property is represented in its mapped database field. As a default, decimals are represented by 18 digits and 2 decimals. You can change this setting for each property with something like:

```
...
.Property(m => m.Price)
        .HasPrecision(10, 3);
```

The `ModelBuilder builder` object allows us to specify database indexes with something such as the following:

```
builder.Entity<T>()
   .HasIndex(m => m.PropertyName);
```

Multi-property indexes are defined as follows:

```
builder.Entity<T>()
    .HasIndex("propertyName1", "propertyName2", ...);
```

Starting from version 5, indexes can also be defined with attributes applied to the class. The following is the case of a single property index:

```
[Index(nameof(Property), IsUnique = true)]
public class MyClass
{
    public int Id { get; set; }
    [MaxLength(128)]
    public string Property { get; set; }
}
```

The following is the case of a multi-property index:

```
[Index(nameof(Property1), nameof(Property2), IsUnique = false)]
public class MyComplexIndexClass
{
```

```
    public int Id { get; set; }
    [MaxLength(64)]
    public string Property1 { get; set; }
    [MaxLength(64)]
    public string Property2 { get; set; }
}
```

Configuration options that are specific to an entity can also be grouped into separate configuration classes, one for each entity:

```
internal class DestinationConfiguration :
    IEntityTypeConfiguration<Destination>
{
    public void Configure(EntityTypeBuilder<Destination> builder)
    {
        builder
            .HasIndex(m => m.Country);
        builder
            .HasIndex(m => m.Name);
        ...
    }
}
```

Each of these classes must implement the `IEntityTypeConfiguration<>` interface, whose unique method is `Configure`. Then, the configuration class can be declared with a class-level attribute:

```
[EntityTypeConfiguration(typeof(DestinationConfiguration))]
public class Destination
{
  ...
```

The configuration class can also be recalled from within the `OnModelCreating` method of the context class:

```
new DestinationConfiguration()
        .Configure(builder.Entity<Destination>());
```

It is also possible to add all configuration information defined in the assembly with:

```
builder.ApplyConfigurationsFromAssembly(typeof(MainDbContext).Assembly);
```

If we add all the necessary configuration information, then our `OnModelCreating` method will look as follows:

```
protected override void OnModelCreating(ModelBuilder builder)
{
    builder.Entity<Destination>()
```

```
        .HasMany(m => m.Packages)
        .WithOne(m => m.MyDestination)
        .HasForeignKey(m => m.DestinationId)
        .OnDelete(DeleteBehavior.Cascade);
    new DestinationConfiguration()
                .Configure(builder.Entity<Destination>());
    new PackageConfiguration()
                .Configure(builder.Entity<Package>());
}
```

Together with the two configuration classes:

```
using Microsoft.EntityFrameworkCore;
using Microsoft.EntityFrameworkCore.Metadata.Builders;
namespace WWTravelClubDB.Models
{
    internal class DestinationConfiguration :
        IEntityTypeConfiguration<Destination>
    {
        public void Configure(EntityTypeBuilder<Destination> builder)
        {
            builder
                .HasIndex(m => m.Country);
            builder
                .HasIndex(m => m.Name);
        }
    }
}
using Microsoft.EntityFrameworkCore;
using Microsoft.EntityFrameworkCore.Metadata.Builders;
namespace WWTravelClubDB.Models
{
    internal class PackageConfiguration : IEntityTypeConfiguration<Package>
    {
        public void Configure(EntityTypeBuilder<Package> builder)
        {
            builder
                .HasIndex(m => m.Name);
            builder
                .HasIndex(nameof(Package.StartValidityDate),
                 nameof(Package.EndValidityDate));
        }
    }
}
```

I prefer to define just general configuration and relationships in the context class. It is also convenient to use data annotation just for restricting property values (maximum and minimum length, required fields, and so on). This way, entities don't depend on the specific ORM used and can be exported outside of the data layer, if needed.

The best place for other entity-specific configurations is the configuration class. I also avoid using the `EntityTypeConfiguration` attribute and call entity configuration classes from within the context class since this attribute ties the entity to a specific ORM.

The previous example shows a one-to-many relationship, but Entity Framework Core 8 also supports many-to-many relationship:

```
modelBuilder
   .Entity<Teacher>()
   .HasMany(e => e.Classrooms)
   .WithMany(e => e.Teachers)
```

In the preceding case, the join entity and the database join table are created automatically, but you can also specify an existing entity as the join entity. In the previous example, the join entity might be the course that the teacher teaches in each classroom:

```
modelBuilder
   .Entity<Teacher>()
   .HasMany(e => e.Classrooms)
   .WithMany(e => e.Teachers)
       .UsingEntity<Course>(
            b => b.HasOne(e => e.Teacher).WithMany()
            .HasForeignKey(e => e.TeacherId),
            b => b.HasOne(e => e.Classroom).WithMany()
            .HasForeignKey(e => e.ClassroomId));
```

Once you've configured Entity Framework Core, we can use all the configuration information we have to create the actual database and put all the tools we need in place in order to update the database's structure as the application evolves. The next section explains how.

Entity Framework Core migrations

Now that we've configured Entity Framework and defined our application-specific `DbContext` subclass, we can use the Entity Framework Core design tools to generate the physical database and create the database structure snapshot that's needed by Entity Framework Core to interact with the database.

Entity Framework Core design tools must be installed in each project that needs them as NuGet packages. There are two equivalent options:

- **Tools that work in any operating system console**: These are available through the `Microsoft.EntityFrameworkCore.Design` NuGet package. All Entity Framework Core commands are in `dotnet ef .....` format since they are contained in the `ef` command line's .NET Core application.

- **Tools that are specific to the Visual Studio Package Manager Console:** These are contained in the `Microsoft.EntityFrameworkCore.Tools` NuGet package. They don't need the `dotnet ef` prefix since they can only be launched from the **Package Manager Console** inside Visual Studio.

Entity Framework Core's design tools are used within the design/update procedure. This procedure is as follows:

1. We modify `DbContext` and the entities' definitions as needed.
2. We launch the design tools to ask Entity Framework Core to detect and process all the changes we made.
3. Once launched, the design tools update the database structure snapshot and generate a new *migration*, that is, a file containing all the instructions we need in order to modify the physical database to reflect all the changes we made.
4. We launch another tool to update the database with the newly created migration.
5. We test the newly configured DB layer, and if new changes are necessary, we go back to *step 1*.
6. When the data layer is ready, it is deployed in staging or production, where all the migrations are applied once more to the actual staging/production database.

This is repeated several times in the various software project iterations and during the lifetime of the application.

If we operate on an already existing database, we need to configure `DbContext` and its models to reflect the existing structure of all the tables we want to map. This can be done automatically with the `Scaffold-DbContext` command (see `https://learn.microsoft.com/en-us/ef/core/managing-schemas/scaffolding/?tabs=vs` for more details).

All classes generated by .NET are partial classes, so the user can enrich them with further methods without modifying the scaffolded classes by adding the new methods to partial classes with the same names.

Then, if we want to start using migration instead of continuing with direct database changes, we can call the design tools with the `IgnoreChanges` option so that they generate an empty migration. Also, this empty migration must be passed to the physical database so that it can synchronize a database structure version associated with the physical database with the version that's been recorded in the database snapshot. This version is important because it determines which migrations must be applied to a database and which ones have already been applied.

However, developers may also choose to continue manually modifying the database and repeating the scaffold operation after each change.

The whole design process needs a test/design database, and if we operate on an existing database, the structure of this test/design database must reflect the actual database – at least in terms of the tables we want to map. To enable design tools so that we can interact with the database, we must define the `DbContextOptions` options that they pass to the `DbContext` constructor. These options are important at design time since they contain the connection string of the test/design database. The design tools can be informed about our `DbContextOptions` options if we create a class that implements the `IDesignTimeDbContextFactory<T>` interface, where `T` is our `DbContext` subclass:

```
using Microsoft.EntityFrameworkCore;
using Microsoft.EntityFrameworkCore.Design;
namespace WWTravelClubDB
{
    public class LibraryDesignTimeDbContextFactory
        : IDesignTimeDbContextFactory<MainDbContext>
    {
        private const string connectionString =
            @"Server=(localdb)\mssqllocaldb;Database=wwtravelclub;
                Trusted_Connection=True;MultipleActiveResultSets=true";
        public MainDbContext CreateDbContext(params string[] args)
        {
            var builder = new DbContextOptionsBuilder<MainDbContext>();

            builder.UseSqlServer(connectionString);
            return new MainDbContext(builder.Options);
        }
    }
}
```

`connectionString` will be used by Entity Framework to create a new database in the local SQL Server instance that's been installed in the development machine and connects with Windows credentials. You are free to change it to reflect your needs.

Now, we are ready to create our first migration! Let's get started:

1. Let's go to the **Package Manager Console** and ensure that **WWTravelClubDB** is selected as our default project.
2. Now, type `Add-Migration initial` and press *Enter* to issue this command. Verify that you added the `Microsoft.EntityFrameworkCore.Tools` NuGet package before issuing this command; otherwise, you might get an "unrecognized command" error:

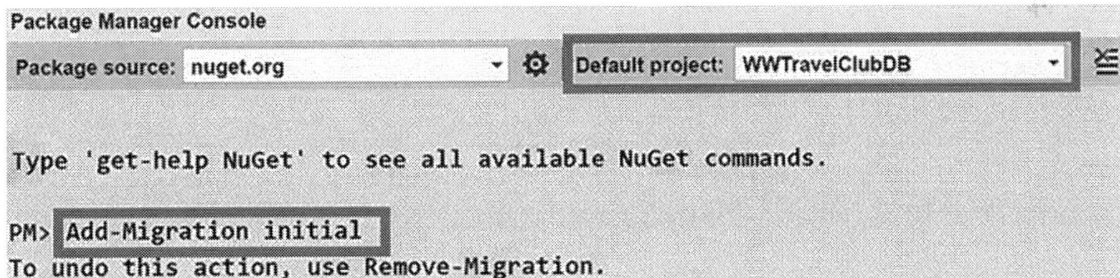

Figure 13.1: Adding the first migration

`initial` is the name we gave our first migration. So, in general, the command is `Add-Migration <migration name>`. When we operate on an existing database, we must add the `-IgnoreChanges` option to the first migration (and just to that) so that an empty migration is created. References to the whole set of commands can be found in the *Further reading* section.

3. If, after having created the migration but before having applied the migration to the database, we realize we made some errors, we can undo our action with the `Remove-Migration` command. If the migration has already been applied to the database, the simplest way to correct our error is to make all the necessary changes to the code and then apply another migration.
4. As soon as the `Add-Migration` command is executed, a new folder appears in our project:

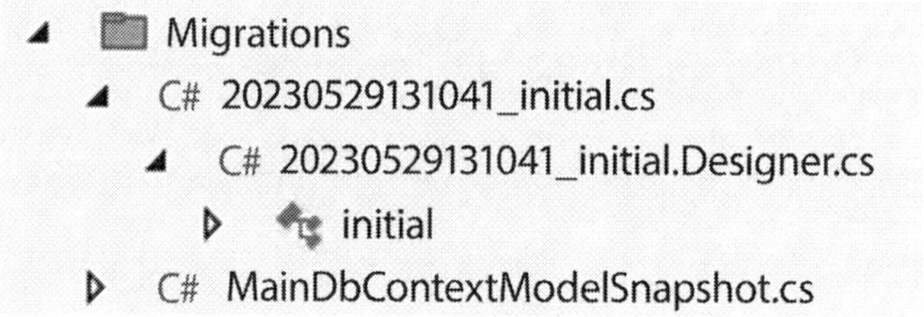

Migrations
C# 20230529131041_initial.cs
C# 20230529131041_initial.Designer.cs
initial
C# MainDbContextModelSnapshot.cs

Figure 13.2: Files created by the Add-Migration command

`20210924143018_initial.cs` is our migration expressed in an easy-to-understand language.

You may review the code to verify that everything is okay. You may also modify the migration content (only if you are enough of an expert to do it reliably) or simply undo the migration with the `in Remove-Migration` `Remove-Migration` command, which is the advised way to proceed when we discover errors.

Each migration contains an `Up` method and a `Down` method.

The `Up` method implies the migration, while the `Down` method undoes its changes. Accordingly, the `Down` method contains the reverse actions of all the actions included in the `Up` method in reverse order.

`20210924143018_initial.Designer.cs` is the Visual Studio designer code, which you must not modify, while `MainDbContextModelSnapshot.cs` is the overall database structure snapshot. If you add further migrations, new migration files and their designer counterparts will appear, and the unique `MainDbContextModelSnapshot.cs` database structure snapshot will be updated to reflect the database's overall structure.

The same command can be issued in an operating system console by typing `dotnet ef migrations add initial`. This command must be issued from within the project's root folder (not from within the solution's root folder).

However, if `Microsoft.EntityFrameworkCore.Design` is installed globally with `dotnet tool install --global dotnet-ef`, then we can use it in a project after adding it to that project by typing `dotnet add package --project <project path> Microsoft.EntityFrameworkCore.Design`. In this case, commands can be issued from any folder by specifying the `--project <project path>` option.

Migrations can be applied to the database by typing `Update-Database` in the Package Manager Console. The equivalent console command is `dotnet ef database update`. Let's try using this command to create the physical database!

The next subsection explains how to create database stuff that Entity Framework is unable to create automatically. After that, in the next section, we will use Entity Framework's configuration and the database we generated with `dotnet ef database update` to create, query, and update data.

Understanding stored procedures and direct SQL commands

Some database structures, like, for instance, stored procedures, can't be generated automatically by the Entity Framework Core commands and declarations we described previously. Stored procedures such as generic SQL strings can be included manually in the `Up` and `Down` methods through the `migrationBuilder.Sql("<sql command>")` method.

The safest way to do this is by adding a migration without performing any configuration changes so that the migration is empty when it's created. Then, we can add the necessary SQL commands to the empty `Up` method of this migration and their converse commands in the empty `Down` method. It is good practice to put all the SQL strings in the properties of resource files (`.resx` files).

Stored procedures should replace `Entity Framework` commands in the following circumstances:

- When we need to perform manual SQL optimizations to increase the performance of some operations.
- When `Entity Framework` doesn't support the SQL operation, we need to perform. A typical example is the increment or decrement of a numeric field that occurs in all booking operations (air travel, hotels, and so on). Actually, we might replace the increment/decrement operation with a database read, an in-memory increment/decrement, and finally, a database update, all enclosed in the same transaction scope. However, this might be overkill for performance.

Before starting to interact with our database, we can perform a further optional step: model optimizations.

Compiled models

Starting from version 6, Entity Framework Core introduced the possibility to create precompiled data structures that improve Entity Framework Core's performance by about 10 times in the case of models with hundreds of entities (see the reference in the *Further reading* section for more details). This step is accomplished by generating some code that, once compiled together with the data layer project, creates data structures that our context classes can use to improve performance.

The usage of pre-compilation is advised just after you verify the system experiences slow-downs and also on very simple queries. In other words, it is better to start without pre-compilation and then possibly add it in case of slow-downs caused by the EF infrastructure.

Code is generated with the `Optimize-DbContext` command provided by the `Microsoft.EntityFrameworkCore.Tool` NuGet package that we already installed. The command accepts the folder name to place the code and the namespace to place all classes. In our case, let's choose the `Optimization` folder and the `WWTravelClubDB.Optimization` namespace:

```
Optimize-DbContext -Context MainDBContext -OutputDir Optimization -Namespace
WWTravelClubDB.Optimization
```

Here, the `-Context` parameter must be passed the name of our context class. The `Optimization` folder is automatically created and filled with classes.

The optimization code depends on the ORM configuration, so the `Optimize-DbContext` command must be repeated each time a new migration is created.

Optimizations are enabled by passing the root of our optimization model as an option when an instance of the context class is created. Let's open the `LibraryDesignTimeDbContextFactory.cs` file and add the line below:

```
builder.UseSqlServer(connectionString);
//Line to add. Add it after that the optimization model has been created
builder.UseModel(Optimization.MainDbContextModel.Instance);
return new MainDbContext(builder.Options);
```

Now, you are ready to interact with the database through Entity Framework Core.

Querying and updating data with Entity Framework Core

To test our DB layer, we need to add a console project based on the same .NET Core version as our library to the solution. Let's get started:

1. Let's call the new console project `WWTravelClubDBTest`.
2. Now, we need to add our data layer as a dependency of the console project by right-clicking on the **Dependencies** node of the console project and selecting **Add Project Reference**.
3. Remove the content of the `Program.cs` file and start by writing the following:

   ```
   Console.WriteLine("program start: populate database, press a key to
   continue");
   Console.ReadKey();
   ```

4. Then, add the following namespaces at the top of the file:

   ```
   using WWTravelClubDB;
   using WWTravelClubDB.Models;
   using Microsoft.EntityFrameworkCore;
   using WWTravelClubDBTest;
   ```

Now that we have finished preparing our test project, we can experiment with queries and data updates. Let's start by creating some database objects, that is, some destinations and packages. Follow these steps to do so:

1. First, we must create an instance of our `DbContext` subclass with an appropriate connection string. We can use the same `LibraryDesignTimeDbContextFactory` class that's used by the design tools to get it:

   ```
   var context = new LibraryDesignTimeDbContextFactory()
   .CreateDbContext();
   ```

2. New rows can be created by simply adding class instances to the mapped collections of our `DbContext` subclass. If a `Destination` instance has packages associated with it, we can simply add them to its `Packages` property:

```
var firstDestination= new Destination
{
    Name = "Florence",
    Country = "Italy",
    Packages = new List<Package>()
    {
        new Package
        {
            Name = "Summer in Florence",
            StartValidityDate = new DateTime(2019, 6, 1),
            EndValidityDate = new DateTime(2019, 10, 1),
            DurationInDays=7,
            Price=1000
        },
        new Package
        {
            Name = "Winter in Florence",
            StartValidityDate = new DateTime(2019, 12, 1),
            EndValidityDate = new DateTime(2020, 2, 1),
            DurationInDays=7,
            Price=500
        }
    }
};
context.Destinations.Add(firstDestination);
await context.SaveChangesAsync();
Console.WriteLine(
 $"DB populated: first destination id is {firstDestination.Id}");
Console.ReadKey();
```

There is no need to specify primary keys since they are auto-generated and will be filled in by the database. In fact, after the `SaveChangesAsync()` operation synchronizes our context with the actual DB, the `firstDestination.Id` property has a non-zero value. The same is true for the primary keys of `Package`. Key auto-generation is the default behavior for all integer types.

When we declare that an entity (in our case, `Package`) is a child of another entity (in our case, `Destination`) by inserting it in a parent entity collection (in our case, the `Packages` collection), there is no need to explicitly set its external key (in our case, `DestinationId`) since it is inferred automatically by Entity Framework Core. Once created and synchronized with the `firstDestination` database, we can add further packages in two different ways:

- Create a `Package` class instance, set its `DestinationId` external key to `firstDestination.Id`, and add it to `context.Packages`
- Create a `Package` class instance, with no need to set its external key, and then add it to the `Packages` collection of its parent `Destination` instance

The latter approach should be preferred when the two entities do not belong to the same aggregate since, in this case, the whole aggregate must be loaded in memory before operating on it to be sure all business rules are correctly applied and to prevent incoherences caused by simultaneous operations on different parts of the same aggregates (see the *Aggregates* subsection of *Chapter 7, Understanding the Different Domains in Software Solutions*).

Moreover, the latter option is the only possibility when a child entity (`Package`) is added with its parent entity (`Destination`) and the parent entity has an auto-generated principal key since, in this case, the external key isn't available at the time we perform the additions.

In most of the other circumstances, the former option is simpler since the second option requires the parent `Destination` entity to be loaded in memory, along with its `Packages` collection, that is, together with all the packages associated with the `Destination` object (by default, connected entities aren't loaded by queries).

Now, let's say we want to modify the `Florence` destination and give a 10% increment to all `Florence` package prices. How do we proceed? Follow these steps to find out how:

1. First, comment out all previous instructions for populating the database while keeping the `DbContext` creation instruction:

```
Console.WriteLine("program start: populate database, press a key to
continue");
Console.ReadKey();
var context = new LibraryDesignTimeDbContextFactory()
    .CreateDbContext();
//var firstDestination = new Destination
//{
//    Name = "Florence",
//    Country = "Italy",
//    Packages = new List<Package>()
//    {
//        new Package
//        {
//            Name = "Summer in Florence",
//            StartValidityDate = new DateTime(2019, 6, 1),
//            EndValidityDate = new DateTime(2019, 10, 1),
//            DurationInDays=7,
//            Price=1000
//        },
```

```
//          new Package
//          {
//              Name = "Winter in Florence",
//              StartValidityDate = new DateTime(2019, 12, 1),
//              EndValidityDate = new DateTime(2020, 2, 1),
//              DurationInDays=7,
//              Price=500
//          }
//      }
//};
//context.Destinations.Add(firstDestination);
//await context.SaveChangesAsync();
//Console.WriteLine(
//    $"DB populated: first destination id is {firstDestination.Id}");
//Console.ReadKey();
```

2. Then, we need to load the entity into memory with a query, modify it, and call `await SaveChangesAsync()` to synchronize our changes with the database.
3. If we want to modify, say, just its description, a query such as the following is enough:

```
var toModify = await context.Destinations
    .Where(m => m.Name == "Florence").FirstOrDefaultAsync();
```

4. We need to load all the related destination packages that are not loaded by default. This can be done with the `Include` clause, as follows:

```
var toModify = await context.Destinations
    .Where(m => m.Name == "Florence")
    .Include(m => m.Packages)
    .FirstOrDefaultAsync();
```

5. After that, we can modify the description and package prices, as follows:

```
toModify.Description =
  "Florence is a famous historical Italian town";
foreach (var package in toModify.Packages)
   package.Price = package.Price * 1.1m;
await context.SaveChangesAsync();
var verifyChanges= await context.Destinations
    .Where(m => m.Name == "Florence")
    .FirstOrDefaultAsync();
Console.WriteLine(
    $"New Florence description: {verifyChanges.Description}");
Console.ReadKey();
```

If entities included with the Include method themselves contain a nested collection we would like to include, we can use ThenInclude, as shown here:

```
.Include(m => m.NestedCollection)
.ThenInclude(m => m.NestedNestedCollection)
```

Since Entity Framework always tries to translate each LINQ into a single SQL query, sometimes the resulting query might be too complex and slow. In such cases, starting from version 5, we can give Entity Framework the permission to split the LINQ query into several SQL queries, as shown here:

```
.AsSplitQuery().Include(m => m.NestedCollection)
.ThenInclude(m => m.NestedNestedCollection)
```

Performance issues can be addressed by inspecting the SQL generated by a LINQ query with the help of the ToQueryString method:

```
var mySQL = myLinQQuery.ToQueryString ();
```

Starting from version 5, the included nested collection can also be filtered with Where, as shown here:

```
.Include(m => m.Packages.Where(l-> l.Price < x))
```

So far, we've performed queries whose unique purpose is to update the retrieved entities. Next, we will explain how to retrieve information that will be shown to the user and/or used by complex business operations.

Returning data to the presentation layer

To keep the layers separated and to adapt queries to the data that's actually needed by each *use case*, DB entities aren't sent as they are to the presentation layer. Instead, the data is projected into smaller classes that contain the information that's needed by the *use case*. These are implemented by the presentation layer's caller method. Objects that move data from one layer to another are called **Data Transfer Objects** (**DTOs**).

As an example, let's create a DTO containing the summary information that is worth showing when returning a list of packages to the user (we suppose that, if needed, the user can get more details by clicking the package they are interested in):

1. Let's add a DTO to our WWTravelClubDBTest project that contains all the information that needs to be shown in a list of packages:

```
namespace WWTravelClubDBTest
{
    public record PackagesListDTO
    {
        public int Id { get; init; }
        public required string Name { get; init; }
        public decimal Price { get; init; }
        public int DurationInDays { get; init; }
```

```
        public DateTime? StartValidityDate { get; init; }
        public DateTime? EndValidityDate { get; init; }
        public required string DestinationName { get; init; }
        public int DestinationId { get; init; }
        public override string ToString()
        {
         return string.Format("{0}. {1} days in {2}, price: {3}",
                Name, DurationInDays, DestinationName, Price);
        }
    }
}
```

2. We don't need to load entities in memory and then copy their data into the DTO, but database data can be projected directly into the DTO, thanks to the LINQ `Select` clause. This minimizes how much data is exchanged with the database.
3. As an example, we can populate our DTOs with a query that checks all the packages that are available around August 10:

```
var period = new DateTime(2019, 8, 10);
var list = await context.Packages
    .Where(m => period >= m.StartValidityDate
    && period <= m.EndValidityDate)
    .Select(m => new PackagesListDTO
    {
        StartValidityDate=m.StartValidityDate,
        EndValidityDate=m.EndValidityDate,
        Name=m.Name,
        DurationInDays=m.DurationInDays,
        Id=m.Id,
        Price=m.Price,
        DestinationName=m.MyDestination.Name,
        DestinationId = m.DestinationId
    })
    .ToListAsync();
foreach (var result in list)
    Console.WriteLine(result.ToString());
Console.ReadKey();
```

4. In the `Select` clause, we can also navigate to any related entities to get the data we need. For instance, the preceding query navigates to the related `Destination` entity to get the `Package` destination name.

5. The programs stop at each `Console.ReadKey()` method, waiting for you to hit any key. This way, you have time to analyze the output that's produced by all the code snippets that we added to the `Main` method.
6. Now, right-click on the `WWTravelClubDBTest` project in Solution Explorer and set it as the start project. Then, run the solution.

Now, we will learn how to handle operations that can't be efficaciously mapped to the immediate operations in the in-memory collections that represent the database tables.

Issuing direct SQL commands

Not all database operations can be executed efficiently by querying the database with LINQ and updating in-memory entities. For instance, counter increments can be performed more efficiently with a single SQL instruction. Moreover, some operations can be executed with acceptable performance if we define adequate stored procedures/SQL commands. In these cases, we are forced to either issue direct SQL commands to the database or call database-stored procedures from our Entity Framework code. There are two possibilities: SQL statements that perform database operations but do not return entities, and SQL statements that do return entities.

SQL commands that don't return entities can be executed with the `DbContext` method as follows:

```
Task<int> DbContext.Database.ExecuteSqlRawAsync(string sql, params object[]
parameters)
```

Parameters can be referenced in the string as `{0}, {1}, ..., {n}`. Each `{m}` is filled with the object contained at the `m` index of the `parameters` array, which is converted from a .NET type into the corresponding SQL type. The method returns the number of affected rows.

SQL commands that return collections of entities must be issued through the `FromSqlRaw` method of the mapped collection associated with those entities:

```
context.<mapped collection>.FromSqlRaw(string sql, params object[] parameters)
```

Thus, for instance, a command that returns `Package` instances would look something like this:

```
var results = await context.Packages.FromSqlRaw("<some sql>", par1, par2,
...).ToListAsync();
```

SQL strings and parameters work like this in the `ExecuteSqlRaw` method. The following is a simple example:

```
var allPackages = await context.Packages.FromSqlRaw(
    "SELECT * FROM Products WHERE Name = {0}",
    myPackageName).ToListAsync();
```

We can also use string interpolation:

```
var allPackages = await context.Packages.FromSqlRaw(
  $"SELECT * FROM Products WHERE Name = {myPackageName}").ToListAsync();
```

In case the objects to be returned by the SQL query are not mapped objects represented by a collection added to the DB context, like `context.Packages`, we can use a new method added in .NET 7:

```
IQueryable<TResult> DbContext.Database.SqlQueryRaw<TResult> (string sql, params
object[] parameters)
```

`SqlQueryRaw` is a method of the `Database` property of the `DbContext` object, and it accepts the class of the objects to return as a generic parameter (`TResult`). However, in this case, Entity Framework Core is able to transform the SQL tuples returned by the database into objects only if the column names in the tuples are equal to the property names in `TResult`. Name mismatches in some properties can be overcome by decorating these properties with the names of the columns they must be mapped from with the `[Column("<column name")]` attribute. This is also possible using fluent API configuration: `.HasColumnName(<column name")`.

It is good practice to put all the SQL strings in resource files and encapsulate all the `ExecuteSqlRawAsync` and `FromSqlRaw` calls inside the public methods that you defined in your `DbContext` subclasses, in order to keep the dependence from a specific database inside of your Entity Framework Core-based data layer.

Handling transactions

All the changes that are made to a `DbContext` instance are passed in a single transaction at the first `SaveChangesAsync` call. However, sometimes, it is necessary to include queries and updates in the same transaction. In these cases, we must handle the transaction explicitly. Several Entity Framework Core commands can be included in a transaction if we put them inside a `using` block associated with a transaction object:

```
using (var dbContextTransaction = context.Database.BeginTransaction())
try{
    ...
    ...
    dbContextTransaction.Commit();
  }
  catch
  {
    dbContextTransaction.Rollback();
  }
```

In the preceding code, `context` is an instance of our `DbContext` subclass. Inside the `using` block, the transaction can be aborted and committed by calling its `Rollback` and `Commit` methods. Any `SaveChanges` calls that are included in the transaction block use the transaction they are already in, instead of creating new ones.

Deploying your data layer

When your database layer is deployed in production or in staging, usually, an empty database already exists, so you must apply all the migrations in order to create all the database objects. This can be done by calling `context.Database.Migrate()`. The `Migrate` method applies the migrations that haven't been applied to the databases yet, so it may be called safely several times during the application's lifetime.

`context` is an instance of our `DbContext` class that must be passed through a connection string with enough privileges to create tables and perform all the operations included in our migrations. Thus, typically, this connection string is different from the string we will use during normal application operations.

During the deployment of a web application on Azure, we are given the opportunity to check migrations with a connection string we provide. We can also check migrations manually by calling the `context.Database.Migrate()` method when the application starts. This will be discussed in detail in *Chapter 18, Implementing Frontend Microservices with ASP.NET Core*, which is dedicated to frontend applications based on ASP.NET Core MVC.

In some production environments, it is not possible to apply migrations during the application deployment because the person in charge of the deployment doesn't have enough privileges to create a new database and/or to create and modify tables. In this case, we must transform migrations into SQL commands and pass them to the database administrator who, after having verified they will not damage the existing database and data, applies them.

We can transform all migrations in a given interval into SQL with the `Script-Migration` command (see `https://learn.microsoft.com/en-us/ef/core/cli/powershell`):

```
Script-Migration -From <initial migration> -To <final migration> -Output <name
of output file>
```

For desktop applications, we can apply migrations during the installation of the application and its subsequent updates.

At the first application installation and/or in subsequent application updates, we may need to populate some tables with initial data. For web applications, this operation can be performed at application startup, while for desktop applications, this operation can be included in the installation.

Database tables can be populated with Entity Framework Core commands. First, though, we need to verify whether the table is empty in order to avoid adding the same table rows several times. This can be done with the `Any()` LINQ method, as shown in the following code:

```
if(!context.Destinations.Any())
{
    //populate here the Destinations table
}
```

Let's take a look at a few advanced features that Entity Framework Core has to share.

How data and domain layers communicate with other layers

As discussed in *Chapter 7, Understanding the Different Domains in Software Solutions*, classical layer architectures use plain objects and repositories to communicate with the other layers.

Therefore, the entities that define Entity Framework Core configuration themselves can be used as they are to communicate with other layers, since they are just record-like lists of public properties, as prescribed for plain objects.

The case of domain layers and onion architectures is slightly more complex, since, in this case, the domain layer communicates with the application layer through rich objects whose methods represent application domain rules. Accordingly, in general, the remainder of the application can't access all domain layer objects' properties but is forced to modify them through their own methods, in order to enforce domain rules.

In other words, Entity Framework entities are record-like lists of public properties with almost no methods, while DDD entities should have methods that encode domain logic, more sophisticated validation logic, and read-only properties. While further validation logic and methods can be added without breaking Entity Framework's operations, adding read-only properties that must not be mapped to database properties can create problems that must be handled adequately. Preventing properties from being mapped to the database is quite easy–all we need to do is decorate them with the `NotMapped` attribute or, using the fluent API, as `.Ignore(e => e.PropertyName)`.

The issues that read-only properties have are a little bit more complex and can be solved in three fundamental ways:

- **Map Entity Framework entities to different classes:** Define the DDD entities as different classes and copy data to/from them when entities are returned/passed to repository methods. This is the easiest solution, but it requires that you write some code so that you can convert the entities between the two formats. DDD entities are defined in the domain layer, while the Entity Framework entities continue to be defined in the data layer. This is the cleaner solution, but it causes a non-trivial overhead in both code writing and maintenance. I recommend it when you have complex aggregates with several complex methods.
- **Map table fields to private properties:** Let Entity Framework Core map fields to private class fields so that you can decide how to expose them to properties by writing custom getters and/or setters. It is sufficient to give either the `_<property name>` name or the `_<property name in camel case>` name to these private fields, and Entity Framework will use them instead of their associated properties. In this case, DDD entities defined in the domain layer are also used as data layer entities. The main disadvantage of this approach is that we can't use data annotations to configure each property because DDD entities can't depend on how the underlying data layer is implemented.

  Therefore, we must configure all database mapping in the `OnModelCreating` `DbContext` method, or in configuration classes associated with each entity (see *Chapter 13, Interacting with Data in C# – Entity Framework Core*). Both options look less readable than data annotations to me, so I don't like this technique, but other professionals use it.

- **Hide Entity Framework entities behind interfaces:** Hide each Entity Framework entity with all its public properties behind an interface that, when needed, only exposes property getters. Entities are defined as `internal` so outer layers can access them just through the interfaces they implement. This way, we can force the usage of methods that implement business logic rules to modify entity properties. Also, `DbContext` is defined as `internal`, so it can be accessed through the `IUnitOfWork` interface that it implements from the outer levels. Interfaces can be defined in a different library for better decoupling from the outer layers. In terms of the onion architecture, the library that defines all interfaces is the next layer in from the Entity Framework layer. As usual, interfaces are coupled with their implementations in the dependency injection engine. This is the solution I prefer when there are several simple entities.

Let's suppose that we would like to define a DDD interface called `IDestination` for the `Destination` entity, and suppose we would like to expose the `Id`, `Name`, and `Country` properties as read-only since, once a destination is created, it can't be modified anymore. Here, it is sufficient to let `Destination` implement `IDestination` and to define `Id`, `Name`, `Country`, and `Description` as read-only in `IDestination`:

```
public interface IDestination
{
    int Id { get; }
    string Name { get; }
    string Country { get; }
    string Description { get; set; }
    ...
}
```

Another difference between DDD with onion architectures and a classical data layer is that, in classical data layers, all operations and queries on data are exposed as repository methods, while in domain layers, repository methods just encode creations, deletions, and queries, while modification operations are performed by methods of the rich domain layer classes.

A complete example of domain layer implementation is described in *Chapter 18, Implementing Frontend Microservices with ASP.NET Core*.

Understanding Entity Framework Core advanced features

An interesting Entity Framework advanced feature that is worth mentioning is global filters, which were introduced at the end of 2017. They enable techniques such as soft delete and multi-tenant tables that are shared by several users, where each user just *sees* its records.

Global filters are defined with the `modelBuilder` object, which is available in the `DbContext` `OnModelCreating` method. The syntax for this method is as follows:

```
modelBuilder.Entity<MyEntity>().HasQueryFilter(m => <define filter condition
here>);
```

For instance, if we add an `IsDeleted` property to our `Package` class, we may soft delete a `Package` without removing it from the database by defining the following filter:

```
modelBuilder.Entity<Package>().HasQueryFilter(m => !m.IsDeleted);
```

However, filters contain `DbContext` properties. Thus, for instance, if we add a `CurrentUserID` property to our `DbContext` subclass (whose value is set as soon as a `DbContext` instance is created), then we can add a filter like the following one to all the entities that refer to a user ID:

```
modelBuilder.Entity<Document>().HasQueryFilter(m => m.UserId == CurrentUserId);
```

With the preceding filter in place, the currently logged-in user can only access the documents they own (the ones that have their `UserId`). Similar techniques are very useful in the implementation of multi-tenant applications.

Another interesting feature that is worth mentioning is mapping entities to un-updatable database queries, which was introduced in version 5.

When you define an entity, you can define explicitly either the name of the mapped database table or the name of a mapped updatable view:

```
modelBuilder.Entity<MyEntity1>().ToTable("MyTable");
modelBuilder.Entity<MyEntity2>().ToView("MyView");
```

When an entity is mapped to a view, no table is generated by database migration, so the database view must be defined manually by the developer.

If the view we would like to map our entity in is not updatable, LINQ cannot use it to pass updates to the database. In this case, we can map the same entity simultaneously to a view and a table:

```
modelBuilder.Entity<MyEntity>().ToTable("MyTable").ToView("MyView");
```

Entity Framework will use the view for the queries and the table for the updates. This is useful when we create a newer version of a database table but we want to also take data from the old version of the table in all queries. In this case, we may define a view that takes data from both the old and the new tables but passes all updates only on the new table.

The option to set property defaults is also interesting. This can be done by specifying an override for the `ConfigureConventions` `DbContext` method. For instance, we can set a default precision for all decimal properties:

```
protected override void ConfigureConventions(
    ModelConfigurationBuilder configurationBuilder)
{
    configurationBuilder.Properties<decimal>()
        .HavePrecision(10, 3);
        ...
}
```

Specifying a default maximum length for all string properties is also useful:

```
protected override void ConfigureConventions(
    ModelConfigurationBuilder configurationBuilder)
{
      configurationBuilder.Properties<decimal>()
          .HavePrecision(10, 3);
      configurationBuilder.Properties<string>()
          .HaveMaxLength(128);
       ...
}
```

Another interesting feature that was gradually introduced in the last versions of Entity Framework Core is the mapping of JSON database columns. In particular, JSON data contained in a single JSON column can be queried, and the JSON objects mapped to .NET types.

Suppose that an `Author` class that must be mapped to a database table has a `Contact` property containing a complex object, and suppose we would like to store this object in a database JSON column of the `Author` table. We can do it with the help of the `OwnsOne` configuration method, as follows:

```
modelBuilder.Entity<Author>().OwnsOne(
            author => author.Contact, ownedNavigationBuilder =>
            {
                ownedNavigationBuilder.ToJson();
            });
```

After this configuration, the `contact` object can be queried as a standard navigation property:

```
context.Authors
 .Where(m => m.Contact.Email == searchEmail).FirstOrDefaultAsync();
```

We can recursively also map sub-objects contained in the `contact` object, such as a collection of addresses, but in this case, we must use `OwnsMany`:

```
modelBuilder.Entity<Author>().OwnsOne(
            author => author.Contact, ownedNavigationBuilder =>
            {
                ownedNavigationBuilder.ToJson();
              ownedNavigationBuilder.OwnsMany(
                   contactDetails => contactDetails.Addresses);
            });
```

After that, the nested Addresses JSON collection can also be queried with the usual LINQ syntax:

```
context.Authors
  .Where(m => m.Contact.Addresses.Any()).FirstOrDefaultAsync();
```

The above query returns all authors with a nonempty addresses list.

Summary

In this chapter, we looked at the essentials of ORM basics and why they are so useful. Then, we described Entity Framework Core. In particular, we discussed how to configure database mappings with class annotations and other declarations and commands that are included in `DbContext` subclasses, and in configuration classes associated with each entity.

Then, we discussed how to create data structures for improving ORM performance and how to automatically create and update the physical database with the help of migrations, as well as how to query and pass updates to the database through Entity Framework Core. Finally, we learned how to pass direct SQL commands and transactions through Entity Framework Core, as well as how to deploy a data layer based on Entity Framework Core.

This chapter also reviewed some advanced features that were introduced in the latest Entity Framework Core releases.

In the next chapter, we move on to microservices orchestrators and will learn how to deploy and manage microservices on Kubernetes.

Questions

1. How does Entity Framework Core adapt to several different database engines?
2. How are primary keys declared in Entity Framework Core?
3. How is a string field's length declared in Entity Framework Core?
4. How are indexes declared in Entity Framework Core?
5. How are relations declared in Entity Framework Core?
6. What are the two important migration commands?
7. By default, are related entities loaded by LINQ queries?
8. Is it possible to return database data in a class instance that isn't a database entity? If yes, how?
9. How are migrations applied in production and staging?

Further reading

- More details about migration commands can be found at `https://docs.microsoft.com/en-US/ef/core/miscellaneous/cli/index` and the other links contained there
- More details about Entity Framework Core compiled models can be found in the official Microsoft documentation: `https://docs.microsoft.com/en-us/ef/core/what-is-new/ef-core-6.0/whatsnew#compiled-models`
- More details about Entity Framework Core can be found in the official Microsoft documentation: `https://docs.microsoft.com/en-us/ef/core/`
- An exhaustive set of examples of complex LINQ queries can be found here: `https://learn.microsoft.com/en-us/samples/dotnet/try-samples/101-linq-samples/`

Learn more on Discord

To join the Discord community for this book – where you can share feedback, ask questions to the authors, and learn about new releases – follow the QR code below:

`https://packt.link/SoftwareArchitectureCSharp12Dotnet8`

14

Implementing Microservices with .NET

In *Chapter 11, Applying a Microservice Architecture to Your Enterprise Application*, you learned the theory and basic concepts of microservices. In this chapter, you will learn how to put into practice those general concepts and tools to implement microservices in .NET. This way, you will have a practical understanding of how high-level architectural decisions translate into concrete .NET code.

The focus of this chapter is on worker microservices; that is, microservices that are not part of the public interface of your application. Other kinds of microservices will be focused on in other chapters. Worker microservices process jobs that are not connected to a specific user. They somehow prepare the data that will be used by frontend microservices to satisfy all user requests. They are the assembly line of each application, so their design priorities are efficiency in both communication and local processing, together with protocols that ensure data coherence and fault tolerance.

You will learn how to implement a frontend service in *Chapter 18, Implementing Frontend Microservices with ASP.NET Core*, after having learned about techniques for implementing a presentation layer in *Chapter 17, Presenting ASP.NET Core*. Other techniques for implementing presentation layers are described in *Chapter 19, Client Frameworks: Blazor*, while techniques for implementing public APIs will be discussed in *Chapter 15, Applying Service-Oriented Architectures with .NET*.

This chapter explains the structure of a .NET microservice and discusses the options for exchanging messages and serializing .NET data structures. In particular, we will put into practice a lot of concepts analyzed in *Chapter 11, Applying a Microservice Architecture to Your Enterprise Application*, such as the concept of Generic Host, the techniques for ensuring reliable communication (exponential retry, etc.), forward communication, and idempotency of messages.

More specifically, in this chapter, you will learn about the following subjects:

- Communication and data serialization
- Implementing worker microservices with ASP.NET Core
- Implementing microservices with .NET worker services and message brokers

Each point will be discussed in depth, and the reader can find further practical details in the section *A worker microservice with ASP .NET core* of *Chapter 21, Case Study*, which describes in detail three complete implementations of worker microservices.

The first section of the chapter discusses the main coordination and queuing problems that arise in microservices communication and how to solve them with either message brokers or custom permanent queues. These topics are fundamental in the design of efficient and fault-tolerant communication, which, in turn, are essential requirements for ensuring coherent behavior and low response times of the overall application.

The remaining sections include examples of how to implement the same microservice with two different techniques. The techniques in the second section are based on the ASP.NET Core implementation of gRPC and an SQL Server-based permanent queue. It is worth pointing out that this technique requires HTTP/2. The example in the third section shows how to use message brokers and two serialization techniques.

Message brokers are fundamental for three main reasons:

- They take care of most of the communication overhead.
- They support the publisher/subscriber pattern, which promotes the independence of communicating microservices.
- All main cloud providers offer message broker services. The example uses **RabbitMQ**, but RabbitMQ can be replaced by **Azure Service Bus**, the message broker offered by Azure. The chapter also explains the pros and cons of different serialization techniques.

Technical requirements

This chapter requires the free Visual Studio 2022 Community edition or better with all database tools installed. The code for this chapter is available at `https://github.com/PacktPublishing/Software-Architecture-with-C-Sharp-12-and-.NET-8-4E`.

Experimenting with message brokers also requires the installation of the RabbitMQ message broker (version 3.9 or higher), which in turn requires the previous installation of a 64-bit version of Erlang. An adequate Erlang version for RabbitMQ 3.9 can be downloaded from `https://github.com/erlang/otp/releases/download/OTP-24.0.6/otp_win64_24.0.6.exe`. The RabbitMQ Windows installer can be downloaded from `https://github.com/rabbitmq/rabbitmq-server/releases/download/v3.9.5/rabbitmq-server-3.9.5.exe`. We recommend you launch both installations from an administrative account.

Three complete examples of worker microservices are in the *A worker microservice with ASP.NET core* and *A worker microservice based on RabbitMQ* sections of *Chapter 21, Case Study*. Each of them exemplifies a technique described in this chapter and shows an alternative way of collecting travel statistics in the case study application.

Communication and data serialization

As explained in the *Microservice design principles* subsection of *Chapter 11, Applying a Microservice Architecture to Your Enterprise Application*, requests to a microservices-based application can't cause long chains of recursive microservices calls.

In fact, each call adds both a wait time and a communication time to the actual processing time, thus leading to unacceptable levels of overall response time, as shown in the following figure.

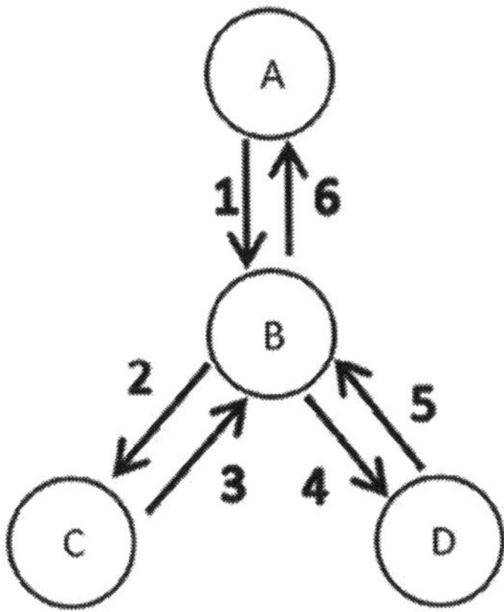

Figure 14.1: Tree of blocking RPC calls

Messages **1-6** are triggered by a request to the **A** microservice and are sent in sequence, so their processing times sum up to the response time. Moreover, once sent, message **1** from microservice **A** remains blocked until it receives the last message (**6**); that is, it remains blocked for the whole lifetime of the overall recursive communication process.

Microservice **B** remains blocked twice, waiting for an answer to a request it issued. The first time is during the 2-3 communication and then the second is during the **4-5** communication. To sum up, **Remote Procedure Calls** (**RPCs**) involve high response times and a waste of microservices computation time.

That's why microservices avoid blocking recursive RPCs and prefer a data-driven approach that starts from the leaves of the procedure calls tree. Put simply, tree nodes, instead of waiting for requests from their parent nodes, send pre-processed data to all their possible callers each time their private data changes, as shown in the following figure.

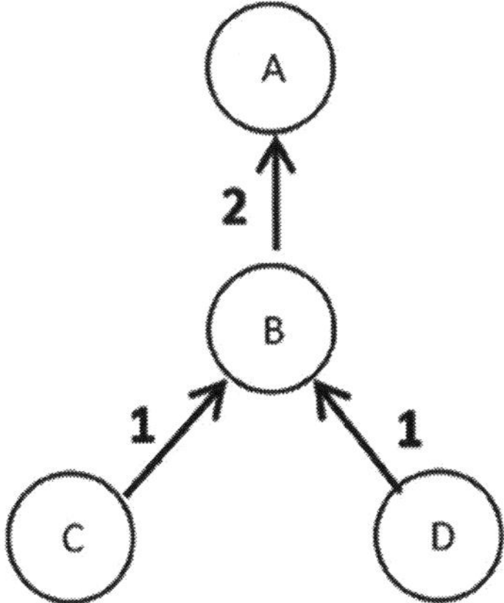

Figure 14.2: Data-driven asynchronous communication

Both communications labeled **1** are triggered when the data of the **C/D** microservices changes, and they may occur in parallel. Moreover, once a communication is sent, each microservice can return to its job without waiting for a response. Finally, when a request arrives at microservice **A**, **A** already has all the data it needs to build the response with no need to interact with other microservices.

In general, microservices based on the data-driven approach pre-process data and send it to whichever other service might be interested. This way, each microservice already contains pre-computed data it can use to respond immediately to user requests with no need for further request-specific communications.

More specifically, as new data becomes available, each microservice does its job and then sends the results to all interested microservices with asynchronous communications; that is, a microservice doesn't wait for any acknowledgment from its recipients. Asynchronous communication is a must since each communication act usually triggers other communication acts recursively for the recipient, so we can't block the whole tree of microservices until the final acknowledgment arrives from all the tree leaves, as in the case of RPC.

However, while being the only acceptable option for high-traffic microservices, the data-driven approach is more difficult to implement. In particular, the absence of acknowledgments creates complex coordination problems that increase the application development and testing time. We will discuss how to face coordination problems later on in the chapter.

Here it is just worth stating the following rule of thumb.

Use the data-driven approach for all high-traffic worker microservices, but for services with shorter request-response cycles and experiencing low to moderate amounts of requests, use utilizing RPC (Remote Procedure Call).

Therefore, actual applications mix efficient short-path RPC calls with the data-driven approach.

Another point that is worth mentioning is communication security. When security is needed, and communication relies on an underlying TCP/IP connection, we can simply use TLS/SSL (the same protocol used by HTTPS connections). However, in this case, since we are speaking of communications among servers, so there is no actual client, it is common that both communicating microservices authenticate each other with private key certificates, and then agree on a cryptographic protocol and key to secure their TLS/SS communication. .NET furnishes all tools for negotiating a TLS/SSL connection based on reciprocal authentication based on servers.

However, when all microservices are part of the same private network, it is common to secure just the communication in/out of this private network and not secure all the intranet communications, both to simplify the design of the overall communication strategy and to save the performance cost of encryption.

Another typical optimization of inter-application communications is the usage of binary serialization, which produces shorter messages and requires less bandwidth and less processing time. In fact, for instance, representing an integer within an object with a binary serialization costs about 4 bytes, that is, basically the same number of bytes needed to store it in the computer memory (there is a small overhead, for protocol-handling metadata), while representing the same integer as a text requires a byte for each digit, plus the bytes needed for the field name.

Binary serialization is discussed in detail in the next subsection. Then, also, RPC- and data-driven asynchronous communication will be analyzed in dedicated subsections.

Efficient and flexible binary serialization

Serialization is the process of transforming data in a way that they can be sent on a communication channel, or stored in a file. Therefore, the way data are serialized has a strong impact on the quantity of data that will be sent.

The .NET echo system contains several fast, platform-specific binary serializers, which are able to produce compact, short messages with very low computational costs. In the *Implementing microservices with .NET worker services and message brokers* section, we will test one of the fastest, the *Binaron* package.

Unfortunately, efficient binary serializers suffer from a couple of well-known problems:

- Since the most performant binary serializers are tied to a specific platform, they are not interoperable. Thus, for instance, the Java binary format is not compatible with the .NET binary format. This constraint creates problems when your application microservices are heterogeneous and use different technologies.
- If one uses the same platform-specific, in-memory binary format, adding/removing properties to/from an object breaks compatibility. Thus, a microservice that uses an old version of a class is not able to de-serialize data created with a newer version of the same class. This constraint creates dependencies between the microservices' CI/CD cycles because when a microservice changes to meet new requirements, it causes recursive changes in all other microservices that communicate with it.

In *Chapter 15, Applying Service-Oriented Architectures with .NET*, we will see that the JSON format was widely adopted because it avoids these two problems since it is not tied to any specific language/runtime, and added properties can simply be ignored, while removed properties are handled by assigning default values.

The **ProtoBuf** binary format was conceived to ensure the same JSON serialization/deserialization advantages for binary formats.

ProtoBuf achieves interoperability by defining abstract elementary types and their binary representations. Then, each framework takes care of converting its native types to/from them. Elementary types are combined into complex structures called **messages**, which represent classes.

Compatibility between different versions of the same message is ensured by assigning a unique integer number to each property. This way, when a message is de-serialized into an object, just the integers that mark the property of the given message version are searched in the serialized data and de-serialized. When a property number is not found in the serialized data, the default value is taken for the associate property. This way, ProtoBuf messages have the same serialization/deserialization advantages as JSON objects. In a few words compatibility among different versions is ensured if the developer doesn't change the number associated with each property. The developer can also remove properties, but without assigning their numbers to new properties, because these numbers have the purpose of naming (with very short names) all fields. The receiver uses these integer names to restore the messages.

There are also other serialization proposals similar to ProtoBuf. Some of them also ensure better performance, but at the moment, ProtoBuf, which was created by Google, is the de facto standard for interoperable binary communication.

ProtoBuf messages are defined in `.proto` files and are then compiled into code in the target language by language-specific tools. The section that follows describes the ProtoBuf data description language.

The ProtoBuf language

Each `.proto` file starts with a declaration of the version of ProtoBuf. At the moment, the highest available version is `proto3`:

```
syntax = "proto3";
```

Since .NET SDK will generate classes out of ProtoBuf definitions, then, if the target language is .NET, you can specify the namespace where you generate all the .NET classes corresponding to the ProtoBuf types defined in the file:

```
option csharp_namespace = "FakeSource";
```

Then, you can import definitions contained in other `.proto` files, with one or more `import` declarations:

```
import "google/protobuf/timestamp.proto";
```

The above definition imports the definition of the `TimeStamp` type, which encodes both the `DateTime` and `DateTimeOffset` .NET types. `TimeStamp` is not a ProtoBuf simple type but is defined in a standard ProtoBuf types library.

Finally, we can scope all message definitions to a `package` to avoid name collisions. ProtoBuf packages have the same role as a .NET namespace but are not automatically converted into .NET namespaces during .NET code generation, since .NET namespaces are specified with the `option C#` declaration:

```
package purchase;
```

Each `.proto` file can contain several message definitions. Here is an example message:

```
message PurchaseMessage {
  string id = 1;
  google.protobuf.Timestamp time = 2;
```

```
    string location = 3;
    int32 cost =4;
    google.protobuf.Timestamp purchaseTime = 5;
  }
```

Each property is specified by the property type followed by the property name, and then by the unique integer associated with that property. Property names must be in camel case, but they are converted to Pascal case during .NET code generation.

If a new version of `PurchaseMessage` is created, compatibility with the past version can be maintained by not reusing the integers assigned to the properties of the old version, and by removing just unused properties, as in the following example:

```
message PurchaseMessage {
  string id = 1;
  int32 cost =4;
  google.protobuf.Timestamp purchaseTime = 5;
  Reseller reseller = 7;
}
```

The new version of `PurchaseMessage` doesn't contain properties `2` and `3`, but it contains the new `reseller` property, marked with the new `7` integer. The `Reseller` type is defined by another message that can be contained either in the same `.proto` file or an imported file.

Clearly, compatibility is maintained just with clients that don't use the removed properties, while clients directly affected by the changes must be updated.

Collections are represented by prefixing the name of the collection element type with the `repeated` keyword:

```
message PurchaseMessage {
  ...
  repeated Product products = 3;
  ...
}
```

Repeated data are translated into the `Google.Protobuf.Collections.RepeatedField<T>` .NET type, which implements `IList<T>`.

Dictionaries are represented with the `map<T1, T2>` type:

```
message PurchaseMessage {
  ...
  map<string, int> attributes = 3;
  ...
}
```

Messages can be nested in other messages, in which case they generate classes defined in other .NET classes during code generation:

```
message PurchaseMessage {
  message Product {
    int32 id = 1;
    string name = 2;
    uint32 cost = 3;
    uint32 quantity = 4;
  }
  ...
  repeated Product products = 3;
  ...
}
```

We can also define `enum` types that translate directly to .NET `enum` types:

```
enum ColorType {
    RED = 0;
    GREEN = 1;
    ...
  }
```

It is also possible to define messages with conditional content. This is useful for sending either a response or error information:

```
message Payload {
    ...
}
message Error {
    ...
}
message ResponseMessage {
  one of result {
    Error error = 1;
    Person payload = 2;
  }
}
```

Once a microservice receives a .NET object of the `ResponseMessage` type, it can process it as follows:

```
ResponseMessage  response = ...;
switch (response.ResultCase)
{
```

```
        case ResponseMessage.ResultOneofCase.Payload:
            HandlePayload(response. Payload);
            break;
        case ResponseMessage.ResultOneofCase.Error:
            HandleError(response.Error);
            break;
        default:
            throw new ArgumentException();
    }
```

The table below summarizes all the ProtoBuf simple types and their equivalent .NET types:

.NET types	Protobuf types
`double`	`double`
`float`	`float`
`string`	`string`
`bool`	`bool`
`ByteString`	`bytes`
`int`	`int32, sint32, sfixed32`
`uint`	`uint32, fixed32`
`long`	`int64, sint64, sfixed64`
`ulong`	`uint64, fixed64`

Table 14.1: Mapping Protobuf Simple Types to .NET Equivalents

The `ByteString` .NET type is defined in the `Google.Protobuf` namespace contained in the `Google.Protobuf` NuGet package. It can be converted to `byte[]` with its `.ToByteArray()` method. A `byte[]` object can be converted into a `ByteString` with the `ByteString.CopyFrom(byte[] data)` static method.

`int32`, `sint32`, and `sfixed32` encode .NET `int`. Now, `sint32` is convenient when the integer is more likely to be negative, while the `sfixed32` type is convenient when the integer is likely to contain more than 28 bits. Similar considerations apply to `uint32` and `fixed32`.

The same criteria apply to 64-bit integers, but in this case, the threshold for the convenience of `sfixed64` and `fixed64` is 56 bits.

ProtoBuf simple types are not nullable. This means that they can't have a null value, and if no value is assigned to them, they take a default value. The default value of a `string` is an empty `string`, while the default value of a `ByteString` is an empty `ByteString`.

If you need nullable types, you must include a predefined `.proto` file:

```
import "google/protobuf/wrappers.proto"
```

Here is a table that details the correspondence between .NET nullable simple types and ProtoBuf nullable wrappers:

.NET types	ProtoBuf types
`double?`	`google.protobuf.DoubleValue`
`float?`	`google.protobuf.FloatValue`
`string?`	`google.protobuf.StringValue`
`bool?`	`google.protobuf.BoolValue`
`ByteString?`	`google.protobuf.BytesValue`
`int?`	`google.protobuf.Int32Value`
`uint?`	`google.protobuf.UInt32Value`
`long?`	`google.protobuf.Int64Value`
`ulong?`	`google.protobuf.UInt64Value`

Table 14.2

`DateTime`, `DateTimeOffset`, and `TimeSpan` have no direct equivalent in ProtoBuf, but the `Google.Protobuf.WellKnownTypes` namespace contained in the `Google.Protobuf` NuGet package contains the `Timestamp` type, which maps from/to `DateTime` and `DateTimeOffset`, and the `Duration` type, which maps from/to `TimeSpan`. The mapping is completely analogous to that of `ByteString`. Thus, for instance, a `Duration` is obtained from a `TimeSpan` with the `Duration.FromTimeSpan` static method, while a `Duration` is transformed into a `TimeSpan` by calling its `.ToTimeSpan` instance method.

The usage of `Duration` and `Timestamp` in `.proto` files is shown in the following:

```
syntax = "proto3"
import "google/protobuf/duration.proto";
import "google/protobuf/timestamp.proto";
message PurchaseMessage {
  string id = 1;
  google.protobuf.Timestamp time = 2;
  string location = 3;
  int32 cost =4;
  google.protobuf.Timestamp purchaseTime = 5;
  google.protobuf.Duration travelDuration = 6;
}
```

Please notice that usage needs the import of predefined `.proto` files.

At the moment, there is no equivalent to the .NET `decimal` type, but it will probably be introduced in the next version. However, you can encode decimals with two integers, one for the integer part and the other for the decimal part, with a message like the one in the following:

```
message ProtoDecimal {
    // Whole units part of the decimal
    int64 units = 1;
    // Nano units of the decimal (10^-9)
    // Must be same sign as units
    sfixed32 nanos = 2;
}
```

We can add implicit conversion to the .NET `decimal`, with a partial class that combines with another partial class, which is automatically generated from the `.proto` file:

```
public partial class DecimalValue
{
    private const decimal nanoFactor = 1000000000m;

    public static implicit operator decimal(ProtoDecimal pDecimal)
    {
        return pDecimal.Units + pDecimal.Nanos / nanoFactor;
    }
    public static implicit operator ProtoDecimal (decimal value)
    {
        return new ProtoDecimal
          {
             Units = decimal.ToInt32(value),
             Nanos= decimal.ToInt32((value - Units) * nanoFactor),
          };
    }
}
```

We have described almost completely the ProtoBuf data description language. The only missing subject is the representation of variable/unknown types, which are rarely used. However, the *Further reading* section contains a link to the official documentation. The next section explains how to serialize and de-serialize messages.

ProtoBuf serialization

An object tree can be serialized as shown in the following:

```
using Google.Protobuf;
...
PurchaseMessage purchase = ....
byte[]? body = null;
using (var stream = new MemoryStream())
{
```

```
        purchase.WriteTo(stream);
        stream.Flush();
        body = stream.ToArray();
    }
```

The `WriteTo` method needs a stream so create an in-memory stream. After, we create a byte array from the stream with `ToArray`, which ensures that the stream buffer is actually written into the stream before attempting the extraction of the byte array:

```
Byte[] body = ...
PurchaseMessage? message = null;
using (var stream = new MemoryStream(body))
{
    message = PurchaseMessage.Parser.ParseFrom(stream);
}
```

Here, since `ParseFrom` also needs a stream, we generate a stream from the message bytes.

The next subsection describes the usage of RPC in microservices.

Efficient and flexible RPC

The RPC approach can be adopted in some application microservices with good results if the following conditions are met:

- The chain of recursive calls is very short, usually just one call without recursive calls.
- Low communication latency and high channel bandwidth. This condition is met by intranet communications that take place on high-speed Ethernet within the same data center.
- Data is serialized quickly and in a very size-efficient format. This condition is met by any efficient binary serializer.

Long chains of recursive calls are avoided whenever RPC is used just to queue a request and to receive confirmation that the request has been correctly queued, without waiting for any processing result. In this case, RPC is used to simulate an asynchronous communication with reception confirmation. If this is the case, all of these conditions are easily met whenever all communicating microservices are part of the same **local area network** (**LAN**) where all computers are connected with high-speed physical connections.

On the contrary, when the communicating microservices are geographically distributed and are part of a WAN instead of a LAN, waiting for confirmation of the reception of an RPC message might be unacceptable for high-traffic microservices. In this case, it is better to rely on message brokers that support completely asynchronous communications.

The gRPC protocol brings all the advantages of ProtoBuf to RPC since, by default, it is based on ProtoBuf. gRPC/ProtoBuf is a binary protocol that works over an HTTP/2 connection. It is worth pointing out that gRPC can't work with HTTP versions less than 2. In the remainder of the chapter, we will always assume that gRPC uses ProtoBuf.

gRPC uses .proto files, but together with data, gRPC .proto files also define services with their RPC methods. Here is a service definition:

```
service Counter {
  // Accepts a counting request
  rpc Count (CountingRequest) returns (CountingReply);
 //Get current count for a given time slot
  rpc GetCount (TimeSlotRequest) returns (TimeSlotDataReply);
}
```

Each service is introduced by the `service` keyword, while each method is introduced by the `rpc` keyword. Each service specifies an input message and an output message. If either of these two messages is empty, we can use the predefined `google.protobuf.Empty` message, as shown in the following:

```
...
import "google/protobuf/empty.proto";
...
service Counter {
  ...
  rpc AllSlots(google.protobuf.Empty) return (AllDataReply);
}
```

`.proto` files can be used to generate both server code and client code. In client code, each service is translated into a proxy class with the same methods declared in the service. Each of the proxy methods automatically invokes the remote service method and returns its result.

The server code, instead, translates each service into an abstract class, whose virtual methods correspond to methods declared in the service. The developer is responsible for inheriting from this abstract class and providing implementations for all service methods.

Below is an example of how to inherit from a similar class:

```
public class CounterService: Counter.CounterBase
{
    ...
    public override async  Task<CountingReply> Count(
         CountingRequest request, ServerCallContext context)
    {
        CountingReply reply =...
          return reply;
    }
}
```

Each method receives both the input message and a context object. Since gRPC services use ASP.NET Core infrastructure, the context object furnishes access to the request `HttpContext` through `context.GetHttpContext()`.

An ASP.NET Core application is enabled to gRPC with `builder.Services.AddGrpc()` and by declaring each service with something like `app.MapGrpcService<CounterService>();`.

More details on both gRPC servers and clients will be given while discussing the example in the *A worker microservice with ASP.NET core* section of *Chapter 21, Case Study*.

Services can receive as input and return continuous streams of data, where a long-term connection between the client and server is established. However, the usage of streams in microservices is not common since microservices are ephemeral processes that are frequently shut down and moved from one processing node to another by orchestrators, so long-term connections are not easy to maintain.

Here is a service that accepts and returns a stream:

```
service StreamExample {
  rpc Echo (stream MyMessage) returns (stream MyMessage);
}
```

Each input stream is passed as an argument to the .NET implementation of the method. If the method returns a stream, the .NET implementation of the method must return a `Task`, and also the output stream is passed as an argument to the method:

```
public override async Task Echo(
     IAsyncStreamReader<MyMessage> requestStream
      IServerStreamWriter<MyMessage> responseStream,
      ServerCallContext context){
     ...
         While(...)
         {
            bool inputFinished =  !await requestStream.MoveNext();
            var current = requestStream.Current;
            ...
            await responseStream.WriteAsync(result);
         }
}
```

On the client side, both input and output streams are available in the `call` object that is returned when the proxy method is called without awaiting it, as shown in the following:

```
var call = client.Echo();
...
await call.RequestStream.WriteAsync(...);
...
bool inputFinished =  ! await call.ResponseStream.MoveNext();
var current = call.ResponseS.Current;
...
call.RequestStream.CompleteAsync();
```

The `CompleteAsync()` method closes the request stream, declaring that the input is finished.

More practical details on the client usage are given in the example in the *A worker microservice with ASP.NET core* section of *Chapter 21, Case Study*, while the *Further reading* section contains a link to the .NET gRPC official documentation.

The next subsection describes how to implement data-driven asynchronous communication.

Reliable data-driven asynchronous communication

Non-blocking communication must necessarily rely on non-volatile queues to decouple the sender thread from the receiving thread. Decoupling can be achieved with just one queue on each communication path, but sometimes additional queues improve performance and increase CPU usage. Queues, can be placed in three places: within the microservice that sends the message, within the microservice that receives the message, or outside both microservices using dedicated services known as message brokers. by using dedicated queuing services called **message brokers**.

Azure Service Bus, which we described in the *.NET communication facilities* subsection of *Chapter 11, Applying a Microservice Architecture to Your Enterprise Application*, is a message broker that, like most message brokers, offers queuing services and publisher/subscriber communication. In this chapter, we will also describe **RabbitMQ**, which offers queuing services and publisher/subscriber communication that is broadly similar to **Azure Service Bus topics**. Since it is easier to debug code that uses a local instance of RabbitMQ, often it is convenient to use RabbitMQ during development and then move to Azure Service Bus.

Queues decouple the sender and receiver but do not ensure that messages are not lost. In the *Resilient task execution* section of *Chapter 11,* we have already discussed strategies for achieving reliable communication. Here we give more practical details for preventing message losses with confirmations and timeouts:

- Queues must be stored on permanent storage; otherwise, their content can be lost if the processes controlling them either crash or are shut down.
- If a confirmation that the message was successfully inserted in the queue doesn't arrive within a timeout time, the source assumes that the message was lost and retries the operation.
- When a message is extracted from a queue, it remains blocked and inaccessible to other consumers. If a confirmation that the message has been successfully processed arrives within a timeout time, the message is removed from the queue; otherwise, it is unblocked and becomes available again to other consumers.

All confirmations can be handled asynchronously with the exception of the insertion in the first queue of a communication path. In fact, if the sending code doesn't remain blocked waiting for the confirmation but moves to further processing and the message is lost, there is no way to resend the message, since the message cannot be taken from any other queue.

For this reason, sometimes microservices that use a message broker also have an internal queue. More specifically, the main microservice thread produces all messages and stores them in a local queue that can be implemented with a database table. Another thread takes care of extracting messages from this queue and sending them to the message broker.

Messages that are removed from the local queue are blocked and removed only when an asynchronous confirmation arrives from the message broker. This technique is used in the example of *Chapter 18, Implementing Frontend Microservices with ASP.NET Core*. The main advantage of the local queue is that confirmation from a local queue usually arrives faster because there is less concurrency with other threads/processes (don't forget that each microservice should have a private database/permanent storage), so the blocking time is more acceptable.

Using a queue inside each receiver is a viable alternative to message brokers. The main advantage of private queues is that the process that handles the queue is not shared among several microservices, so all queue operations are faster. In particular, the confirmation of each insertion is immediate, so the sender can use a blocking RPC call to send the message. However, this simple solution has the following disadvantages:

- There is no way to implement the publisher/subscriber pattern.
- Just one microservice instance can extract messages from the queue. Therefore, microservices can't be scaled horizontally. Limited vertical scaling can be achieved by increasing the number of processor cores and by processing queue messages with parallel threads.

A similar approach can be efficiently implemented with gRPC and ASP.NET Core as follows:

1. The sender sends the message to a gRPC method.
2. The gRPC method just enqueues the message and immediately returns a confirmation to the sender.
3. An ASP.NET Core hosted process takes care of extracting the messages from the queue and passing them to several parallel threads.
4. When a message is passed to a thread, it remains blocked and inaccessible. It is removed only after the thread confirms that the message has been successfully processed. If, instead, a thread reports a failure, the corresponding message is unblocked so it can be passed to another thread.

ASP.NET Core threads take care of the necessary input parallelism. Some horizontal parallelism can be achieved by using load balancers and several web servers. However, in this case, either all the web servers use the same database, thus increasing the concurrency on the queue, or we use several sharded databases.

This approach is described in more detail in the example in the *Implementing worker microservices with ASP.NET core* section. As we will see, it is simple to implement and ensures good response time, but due to its limited scalability, it is adequate just for small or medium-sized applications with low to medium traffic.

If, for some reason, either an insertion in a queue or the processing of a message extracted by a queue requires more time than the timeout time, the operation is repeated so that the same message is processed twice. Therefore, messages must be idempotent, meaning processing them once or several times must have the same effect. Record updates and deletions are intrinsically idempotent since repeating an update or a deletion several times doesn't change the result, but record additions are not.

Idempotency can always be forced by assigning a unique identifier to messages and then storing the identifiers of the already processed messages. This way, each incoming message can be discarded when its identifier is found among the identifiers of the already processed messages. We will use this technique in all examples in this chapter.

Queues, confirmations, and message resends ensure that requests to a single microservice are safely processed, but how can we handle requests that involve several cooperating microservices? We will discover that in the next subsection. There, we will explain how distributed microservices can coordinate and reach agreements to yield coherent behavior with only the help of asynchronous communication.

Distributed transactions

Everyone knows what a database transaction is: several records are modified one after the other, but if a single action fails, all previous modifications are also undone before aborting the transaction. That is, either all operations succeed or they fail simultaneously.

A distributed transaction does the same job, but in this case, the records are not part of a single database but are distributed among the databases associated with several cooperating microservices.

The reliable data-driven communication techniques described so far are the building blocks for solving more complex cooperation problems.

Let's suppose that a user operation triggers processing and storage in several related microservices. The user operation can be considered successfully completed only if all involved processing/storage operations succeed.

Moreover, if a single processing/storage operation also fails for some fundamental reason, retrying the failed operation doesn't help. Think, for instance, of a purchase that fails because the user has not got enough funds to complete the payment: the only way out is to undo all the operations that have already been performed.

In general, similar situations must be handled in a transactional way; either all operations are performed, or no operation is performed. Transactions that span several microservices are known as **distributed transactions**. In theory, **distributed transactions** can be handled with the following two-stage protocol:

1. In the first stage, all operations are executed, each one in the scope of a local transaction (for instance, within the scope of each microservice database transaction). The success or failure of each operation is then returned to a transaction coordinator.
2. In the second stage, the transaction coordinator informs all microservices of the success or failure of the overall operation. In the case of failure, all local transactions are rolled back; otherwise, they are committed.

When using asynchronous messages, confirmations may arrive after quite a large amount of time and may interleave with other transactions performed on the same resources. Therefore, having all local resources blocked by a local transaction during a possibly time-consuming distributed transaction is not acceptable.

For this reason, microservices transactions use the **saga** pattern: all local operations are performed without opening a local transaction, and in the case of failure, they are compensated by other operations that undo the initial operations.

Undoing a database insertion is quite easy since it is enough to remove the added item, but undoing modifications and deletes is quite difficult and requires the storage of additional information. The general solution to this problem is storing records that represent all database changes in a table. These records can be used to compute a compensation operation or to restore the previous database state starting from a reference database state. We already discussed this storage technique, which is called **event sourcing**, in the *Event sourcing* section of *Chapter 7, Understanding the Different Domains in Software Solutions*. Just to recap, and in a few words, each database stores not only the actual state but also the history of all changes up to a certain previous time.

When a saga transaction is undone, if other saga transactions depend on the undone changes, we must also undo them. For instance, suppose that an accepted purchase order depends on the funds uploaded by a user on an e-commerce platform. Then, if the funds upload transaction is undone, the purchase must also be undone.

In order to avoid similar chain reactions when a saga transaction is undone, often new transactions are accepted only if they depend on changes that took place before a certain safety interval. Thus, for instance, uploaded funds are made available only after, say, 5-10 minutes, because it is very unlikely that a transaction will be undone after more than 5-10 minutes.

Saga transactions may use two fundamental techniques:

- **Orchestration**: When the transaction starts, an orchestrator component is created that takes care of sending the necessary messages to all involved microservices and receiving their success/failure messages. This technique is easy to implement but creates dependencies between the software lifetimes of the involved microservices since the orchestrator must depend on the details of all microservices involved in the saga. Moreover, this technique may have poor performance since the orchestrator becomes a bottleneck.
- **Choreography**: There is no centralized control of the transaction but each microservice is invoked by a different sending microservice and forwards the success/failure messages it receives to other communication neighbors. Choreography overcomes the disadvantages of orchestration but it is more difficult to implement and test.

The following table summarizes the pros and cons of the two techniques.

	Code maintainability	**Difficulties in designing and debugging**
Choreography	Good	Quite high
Orchestration	Low	No particular difficulty

Table 14.3: Pros and cons of choreography and orchestration

Implementing worker microservices with ASP.NET Core

In order to avoid blocking the caller's synchronous request for too much time, an ASP.NET Core-based solution requires the implementation of an internal queue where it can store all received messages. This way, when a message is received, it is immediately enqueued without processing it, so that a "received" response can be immediately returned.

Therefore, the application level needs a repository interface that handles the queue. Here is a possible definition of this interface:

```
public interface IMessageQueue
{
    public Task<IList<QueueItem>> Top(int n);
    public Task Dequeue(IEnumerable<QueueItem> items);
    public Task Enqueue(QueueItem item);
}
```

Where:

- `QueueItem` is a class that contains all request information
- `Enqueue` adds a new message to the queue
- `Top` returns the first `n` queue items without removing them from the queue
- `Dequeue` removes the first `n` messages from the queue

The actual implementation of the preceding interface can be based on a database table, or any other storage media.

The application level can be implemented with an ASP.NET Core gRPC project that organizes all the gRPC stuff for you:

gRPC **ASP.NET Core gRPC Service**

A project template for creating a gRPC service using ASP.NET Core, with optional support for publishing as native AOT.

C# **Linux** **macOS** **Windows** **Cloud** **Service** **Web**

Figure 14.3: Creating a gRPC Server project

The actual request processing is performed by a worker-hosted service that runs in parallel with the ASP.NET Core pipeline. It is implemented with the hosted services we discussed in the *Using generic hosts* section of *Chapter 11, Applying a Microservice Architecture to Your Enterprise Application*. It is worth recalling that hosted services are implementations of the `IHostedService` interface defined in the dependency injection engine as follows:

```
builder.Services.AddHostedService<MyHostedService>();
```

Being defined in the dependency injection engine, they are automatically injected services in their constructors. Hosted services are used to execute parallel threads that run independently of the remainder of the application. Usually, they are not defined by directly implementing the `IHostedService` interface, but by inheriting from the abstract `BackgroundService` class and overriding its `Task ExecuteAsync(CancellationToken token)` abstract method.

The `ExecuteAsync` method usually contains an endless loop that exits only when the application is shut down. This endless loop defines the behavior of a worker-hosted service that repeats a certain task. In our case, the task to repeat is the continuous extraction and processing of `N` items from the queue.

Here is a possible implementation of our hosted service:

```
public class ProcessPurchases : BackgroundService
{
    IServiceProvider services;
    public ProcessPurchases(IServiceProvider services)
    {
        this.services = services;
    }
    protected override async Task ExecuteAsync(CancellationToken stoppingToken)
    {
        bool queueEmpty = false;
        while (!stoppingToken.IsCancellationRequested)
        {
            while (!queueEmpty && !stoppingToken.IsCancellationRequested)
            {
              ...
            }
             await Task.Delay(100, stoppingToken);
             queueEmpty = false;
        }
    }
}
```

The class constructor is not injected with the specific services it needs but instead has the `IServiceProvider` that can be used to get any service defined in the dependency injection engine. The reason for this choice is that it will launch several threads (one for each of the `N` messages extracted from the queue), and, in general, different threads can't share the same service instance.

The problem is caused by services with a session scope. Usually, these services are not designed to be thread-safe since the single session-scoped instance used throughout a whole ASP.NET Core request is never shared among parallel threads. However, we are not going to use our services from within the usual ASP.NET Core pipeline but from within parallel threads launched by our hosted service. Therefore, we need a different session scope for each parallel thread.

Thus, the right way to process is to use `IServiceProvider` to create each necessary scope and then use each scope to get a different instance for each parallel thread.

The inner `while` loop runs until the queue is empty, then the worker thread sleeps for 100 milliseconds and then tries the inner loop again to see if in the meantime some new message reached the queue.

When the application is shut down, the `stoppingToken` `CancellationToken` is signaled and both loops exit, so that the whole `ExecuteAsync` method exits and the worker thread dies.

Here is the content of the inner loop:

```
using (var scope = services.CreateScope())
{
    IMessageQueue queue = scope.ServiceProvider.
GetRequiredService<IMessageQueue>();

    var toProcess = await queue.Top(10);
    if (toProcess.Count > 0)
    {
        Task<QueueItem?>[] tasks = new Task<QueueItem?>[toProcess.Count];
        for (int i = 0; i < tasks.Length; i++)
        {
            tasks[i] = toExecute();
        }
        await Task.WhenAll(tasks);
        await queue.Dequeue(tasks.Select(m => m.Result)
            .Where(m => m != null).OfType<QueueItem>());
    }
    else queueEmpty = true;
}
```

A session scope surrounds the whole code since we need a unique instance of `IMessageQueue` to manipulate the queue.

The code tries to extract `N` messages from the queue. If no message is found, `queueEmpty` is set to `true`, so that the inner loop exits; otherwise, a `for` loop creates a separate task for each extracted request and inserts it in the `tasks` array.

Then, `Task.WhenAll` awaits all tasks. Finally, `queue.Dequeue` removes from the queue all not-null requests returned from the tasks. Since a not-null request is returned only in the case of successful processing, `queue.Dequeue` removes just the successfully processed requests.

The `toExecute` method performs the actual request processing that depends on the specific application.

A complete example containing all details and a step-by-step guide to its practical implementation is described in the *A worker microservice with ASP.NET Core* section of *Chapter 21, Case Study*. The complete source code of the example is contained in the folder associated with this chapter in the book's GitHub repository.

The next section shows you how to modify the code of this example to use queued communication based on the **RabbitMQ** message broker.

Implementing microservices with .NET worker services and message brokers

This section explains the modifications needed to use a message broker instead of gRPC communication with an internal queue. This kind of solution is usually more difficult to test and design but allows for better horizontal scaling.

The message broker used in the code is **RabbitMQ**. However, we could also replace it with **Azure Service Bus** using the code available in the GitHub repository associated with the book. The next subsection explains how to install RabbitMQ on your development machine. We used RabbitMQ to give the reader the opportunity to install and study it, since Azure Service Bus needs less configuration and is immediately ready to use. In an actual production system, one might choose RabbitMQ, just so you are not tied to a specific cloud provider, because while Azure Service Bus is available just on Azure, RabbitMQ can be installed in any cloud or on-premises environment.

Installing RabbitMQ

Before installing **RabbitMQ**, you need to install **Erlang** from the link given in the *Technical requirements* section. Just download and execute the installer from an administrative account. After that, you can download and install RabbitMQ from the link in the *Technical requirements* section.

If installation is successful, you should find a service called **RabbitMQ** among your machine's Windows services. If either you don't find it or it is not running, restart your computer.

Administrative commands can be issued to RabbitMQ from the command prompt, which you can find in the **RabbitMQ Server** Windows menu folder.

You can also enable a web-based administrative UI. Let's open the RabbitMQ command prompt and issue the following command:

```
rabbitmq-plugins enable rabbitmq_management
```

Then, go to `http://localhost:15672`. You will be prompted for a username and password. Initially, they are both set to **guest**. From there, you may inspect all active connections and channels and all communication queues that have been created. The queues page contains all queues that have been defined. By clicking on each of them, you move to a queue-specific page where you can inspect the queue content and perform various operations on the specific queue.

The next subsection contains a short survey of RabbitMQ features.

RabbitMQ basics

Natively, RabbitMQ supports the AMQP asynchronous message protocol, which is one of the most used asynchronous protocols, the other being MQTT, which has a specific syntax for the publisher/subscriber pattern.

Support for MQTT can be added with a plugin, but RabbitMQ has facilities for implementing easily a publisher/subscriber pattern on top of AMQP. Moreover, RabbitMQ offers several tools to support scalability, disaster recovery, and redundancy, so it fulfills all requirements to be a first-class actor in cloud and microservices environments. More specifically, it supports data replication like most SQL and NoSQL databases and also supports cooperation among several servers based on sophisticated and flexible techniques. For lack of space, in this section, we will describe just RabbitMQ's basic operations, but the reader can find more details in the tutorials and documentation of RabbitMQ's official website: `https://www.rabbitmq.com/`.

RabbitMQ messages must be prepared in binary format since RabbitMQ messages must be just an array of bytes. Therefore, we need to serialize .NET objects with a binary formatter before sending them. In the example in this section, we will test both the ProtoBuf serializer and a fast .NET-specific serializer called *Binaron*. It might also be possible to use a JSON serializer to ensure better compatibility if there are compatibility issues among microservices implemented with different frameworks by different teams, and/or if there are legacy microservices. It is worth recalling that JSON is usually more compatible but less efficient, while binary formats are less compatible. ProtoBuf tries to solve the binary compatibility issue by defining a universal binary language, but it is not an official standard but a de facto standard.

Messages are not sent directly to queues, but to other entities called **exchanges** that route them to queues. Exchanges are AMQP-specific concepts, and are RabbitMQ's way of configuring complex communication protocols like the publisher/subscriber protocol.

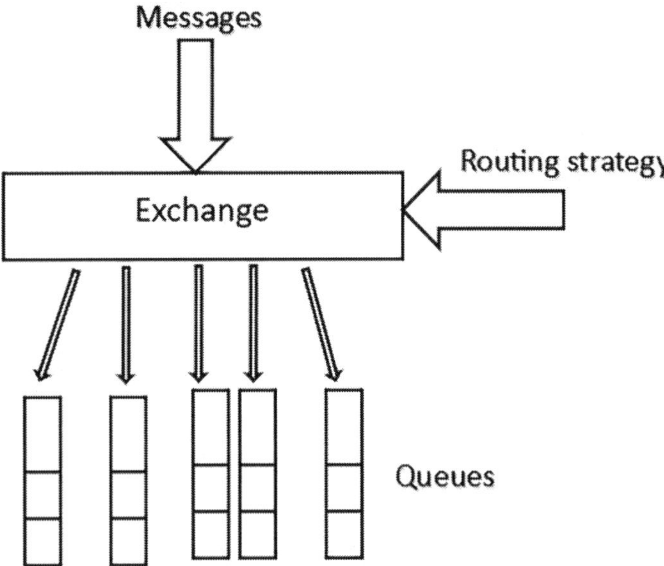

Figure 14.4: RabbitMQ exchanges

To adequately define the exchange routing strategy, we can implement several patterns. More specifically:

- When we use a default exchange, the message is sent to a single queue and we can implement asynchronous direct calls.
- When we use a `fanout` exchange, the exchange will send the message to all queues that subscribe to that exchange. This way, we can implement the publisher/subscriber pattern.
- There is also a `topic` exchange that enhances the publisher/subscriber pattern by enabling the matching of several events with wildcard chars. However, it is not usually needed in microservices for enterprise applications.

Our examples will describe just direct calls, but the *Further reading* section contains a link to RabbitMQ tutorials that show examples of publisher/subscriber implementations.

The next section explains how to modify the code in the previous section to use RabbitMQ-based direct communication.

Replacing internal queues with RabbitMQ

As previously discussed, in high-traffic WAN networks also receiving a synchronous received-message acknowledgment has an unacceptable performance impact, so no RPC protocol can be used. Moreover, often microservices use the publisher/subscriber pattern to achieve the best decoupling. In these cases, using a message broker is a MUST. Finally, having all queues handled by a unique scalable broker enables the independent and easy scaling of the communication resources. This capability is fundamental for optimizing the performance of applications made of hundreds or thousands of microservices.

Summing up, there are cases where message brokers are a MUST or are at least the best choice. Therefore, in this section, we will show how to use them by transforming the previous project so that it uses RabbitMQ instead of gRPC and internal queues.

Unluckily this transformation requires a complete restructuration of the microservice project. We can save business and data layers but we need to move from an ASP.NET Core project to a different project template called **Worker Service**.

Therefore, let's replace the ASP.NET Core project with a **Worker Service** project:

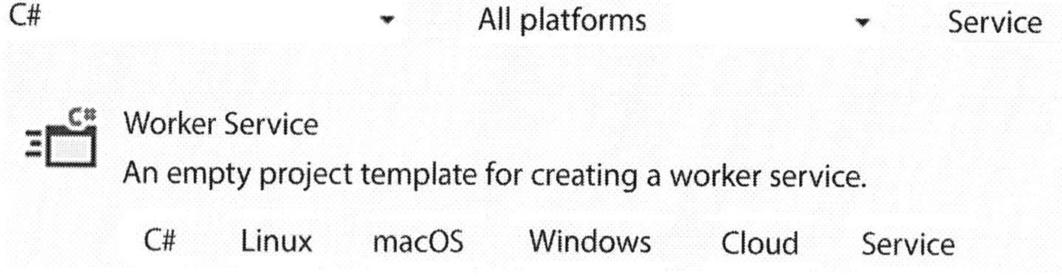

Figure 14.5: Setup Process for a gRPC Server Project in ASP.NET Core

We don't need the gRPC services anymore, but we need ProtoBuf because RabbitMQ works with binary messages.

The Worker Service project automatically scaffolds a hosted service (hosted services were discussed in detail in the *Using generic hosts* section of *Chapter 11, Applying a Microservice Architecture to Your Enterprise Application*). However, the `ExecuteAsync` method of this hosted service must be a little bit different:

```
protected override async Task ExecuteAsync(CancellationToken stoppingToken)
{
    while (!stoppingToken.IsCancellationRequested)
    {
        try
        {
            var factory = new ConnectionFactory() { HostName = "localhost" };
            using (var connection = factory.CreateConnection())
            using (var channel = connection.CreateModel())
            {
                channel.QueueDeclare(queue: "purchase_queue",
                                     durable: true,
                                     exclusive: false,
                                     autoDelete: false,
                                     arguments: null);
                channel.BasicQos(prefetchSize: 0, prefetchCount: 1, global:
                                false);
                var consumer = new EventingBasicConsumer(channel);
                consumer.Received += async (sender, ea) =>
                {
                    // Message received even handler
                    ...
                };
                channel.BasicConsume(queue: "purchase_queue",
                            autoAck: false,
                            consumer: consumer);
                 await Task.Delay(1000, stoppingToken);
            }
        }
        catch { }
    }
}
```

Inside the main loop, if an exception is thrown, it is intercepted by the empty `catch`. Since the two `using` statements are left, both the connection and channel are disposed of. Therefore, after the exception, a new loop is executed that creates a new fresh connection and a new channel.

Intercepting exceptions is fundamental for several reasons:

- First of all, it avoids the microservice crash.
- It enables a complete reset of all client objects involved in the communication with the RabbitMQ server that might be damaged by the error.
- It allows an error logging that, in the actual production environment, is the basic monitoring tool. For simplicity, error logging is not shown in the code snippets.

In the `using` statement body, we ensure that our queue exists, and then set `prefetch` to `1`.

Ensuring queues exist and creating them if they don't exist is better than relying on a single microservice for creating them since this approach avoids introducing complex dependencies and maintenance challenges related to the sequence in which microservices will run.

Setting `prefetch` to `1` causes each server to extract just one message at a time, which ensures a fair distribution of the load among all servers. However, setting `prefetch` to `1` might not be convenient when each server runs several equal parallel threads to process the incoming messages since it sacrifices thread usage optimization in favor of fair distribution of messages among servers. As a consequence, threads that could successfully process further messages (after the first) might remain idle, thus possibly wasting processor cores available on each server machine.

Then, we define a `message received` event handler. `BasicConsume` starts the actual message reception. With `autoAck` set to `false`, when a message is read from the queue, it is not removed but just blocked, so it is not available to other servers that read from the same queue. The message is actually removed when a confirmation that it has been successfully processed is sent to RabbitMQ. We can also send a failure confirmation, in which case the message is unblocked and becomes available for processing again.

If no confirmation is received, the message remains blocked till the connection and channel are disposed of.

Since `BasicConsume` is non-blocking, the `Task.Delay` after it blocks until the cancellation token is signaled. In any case, after 1 second `Task.Delay` unblocks and both the connection and the channel are replaced with fresh ones. This prevents non-confirmed messages from remaining blocked forever.

Making instructions like `BasicConsume` non-blocking prevents a thread from wasting processor cores by remaining blocked while waiting for an event. Instead, the thread is put in sleeping mode by instructions like `Task.Delay`, thus freeing up all its resources and its assigned processor core, which, this way, can be assigned to another parallel thread that was waiting for a free core for its execution.

Let's move on to the code inside the "message received" event. This is the place where the actual message processing takes place.

As a first step, the code verifies if the application is being shut down, in which case it disposes of the channel and connection and returns without performing any further operations:

```
if (stoppingToken.IsCancellationRequested)
{
    channel.Close();
    connection.Close();
    return;
}
```

Then, a session scope is created to access all session-scoped dependency injection services:

```
using (var scope = services.CreateScope())
{
  try
  {
  // actual application dependent message processing
  ...
  }
  catch {
    ((EventingBasicConsumer)sender).Model.BasicNack(ea.DeliveryTag, false,
true);
  }
}
```

In the case that an exception is thrown during the message processing, a `Nack` message is sent to RabbitMQ to inform it that the message processing failed. `ea.DeliveryTag` is a tag that uniquely identifies the message. The second argument set to `false` informs RabbitMQ that the `Nack` is just for the message identified by `ea.DeliveryTag` that doesn't also involve all other messages waiting for confirmation from this server. Finally, the last argument set to `true` asks RabbitMQ to requeue the message whose processing failed.

Inside the `try` block, there is the actual message processing. Its first step is the message deserialization:

```
var body = ea.Body.ToArray();
MyMessageClass? message = null;
using (var stream = new MemoryStream(body))
{
    message = PurchaseMessage.Parser.ParseFrom(stream);
}
```

After that, there is the actual application-dependent message processing. If this processing fails, we must send a `Nack`; otherwise, we must send an `Ack`:

```
if(success)
    ((EventingBasicConsumer)sender).Model
        .BasicAck(ea.DeliveryTag, false);
else
```

```
    ((EventingBasicConsumer)sender).Model
        .BasicNack(ea.DeliveryTag, false, true);
```

The full code of a complete example is in the `GrpcMicroServiceRabbitProto` subfolder of the `ch15` folder in the GitHub repository of this book. A detailed description of this example is in the *A worker microservice based on RabbitMQ* section of *Chapter 21, Case Study*.

The next chapter describes service-oriented architecture and how to implement it with ASP.NET Core.

Summary

In this chapter, we analyzed various options for efficient internal microservices communication. We explained the importance of a binary serialization that is interoperable and that ensures compatibility with previous message versions, and we described ProtoBuf in detail.

We analyzed the limits of RPC communication and why data-driven communication must be preferred. Then, we focused on how to achieve reliable asynchronous communication and efficient distributed transactions.

After having described the conceptual problems and techniques of reliable asynchronous communication, we looked at two architectures. The first one was based on gRPC, ASP.NET Core, and internal queues, and the second one was based on message brokers like RabbitMQ and .NET worker services.

The chapter explained, using practical examples, how to implement all the communication protocols that have been discussed and the architectural options for implementing worker microservices that are available in .NET.

Questions

1. Why are queues so important in microservices communication?
2. How do we recall another `.proto` file?
3. How can we represent a `TimeSpan` in the ProtoBuf language?
4. What are the advantages of ProtoBuf and gRPC over other binary options?
5. What are the advantages of using message brokers instead of internal queues?
6. Why is it acceptable to use a blocking gRPC call to enqueue a message in a recipient queue?
7. How do we enable `.proto` file code generation in a .NET project file?
8. How do I send a message on a RabbitMQ channel with the official .NET client?
9. How do you ensure that a message sent on a RabbitMQ channel is safely saved on disk using the official .NET client?

Further reading

- The official .NET documentation on ProtoBuf can be found here: `https://docs.microsoft.com/it-it/aspnet/core/grpc/protobuf?view=aspnetcore-6.0`.
- The .NET documentation on gRPC is here: `https://docs.microsoft.com/it-it/aspnet/core/grpc/?view=aspnetcore-6.0`.

- The official Google documentation on the whole ProtoBuf language is here: `https://developers.google.com/protocol-buffers/docs/proto3`.
- Complete tutorials on RabbitMQ can be found here: `https://www.rabbitmq.com/tutorials/tutorial-two-dotnet.html`.
- The complete documentation for RabbitMQ is here: `https://www.rabbitmq.com/`.

Learn more on Discord

To join the Discord community for this book – where you can share feedback, ask questions to the authors, and learn about new releases – follow the QR code below:

`https://packt.link/SoftwareArchitectureCSharp12Dotnet8`

15

Applying Service-Oriented Architectures with .NET

The term **Service-Oriented Architecture** (**SOA**) refers to a modular architecture where interaction between system components is achieved through communication. This approach has evolved for years and is now the basis of all communication between systems over the Internet. SOA allows applications from different organizations to exchange data and transactions automatically. Besides that, it allows organizations to offer services on the Internet. For instance, in a banking application, SOA can allow separate services for account management, transaction processing, and customer support to communicate seamlessly. More than that, it can enable suppliers to access customer support directly.

Moreover, as we discussed in *Chapter 11, Applying a Microservice Architecture to Your Enterprise Application,* communication-based interaction solves the binary compatibility and version mismatch problems that inevitably appear in complex systems made up of modules that share the same address space. Moreover, with SOA and its pattern of communication, you do not need to deploy different copies of the same component in the various systems/subsystems that use it – each component only needs to be deployed in one place, even if they are written in different programming languages, simplifying the overall cycle of **Continuous Integration/Continuous Delivery** (**CI/CD**).

If a newer version conforms to the communication interface that is declared to the clients, no incompatibilities can occur. For instance, if you have a backend service that calculates tax based on a specific rule and the entry of selling data, if the specific rule changes, but the selling data doesn't, you will be able to update the service without changing the application in the clients. On the other hand, with DLLs/packages, when the same interface is maintained, incompatibilities may arise because of possible version mismatches in terms of the dependencies of other DLLs/packages that the library module might have in common with its clients.

Organizing clusters/networks of cooperating services was discussed in *Chapter 11, Applying a Microservice Architecture to Your Enterprise Application*. In this chapter, we will focus on the two main communication interfaces used all over the world. More specifically, we will discuss the following topics:

- Understanding the principles of the SOA approach

- SOAP and REST web services
- How does .NET 8 deal with SOA?

By the end of this chapter, you will know how to publicly expose data from an application through an ASP.NET Core service.

Technical requirements

This chapter requires the Visual Studio 2022 free Community edition or better with all the database tools installed.

All the concepts in this chapter will be clarified with practical examples based on the WWTravelClub book use case, located in *Chapter 21, Case Study*. You will find the code for this chapter at `https://github.com/PacktPublishing/Software-Architecture-with-C-Sharp-12-and-.NET-8-4E`.

Understanding the principles of the SOA approach

Like classes in an object-oriented architecture, services are implementations of interfaces that, in turn, come from a system's functional specifications. Therefore, the first step in *service* design is the definition of its *abstract interface*. During this initial stage, you might have two approaches:

- Define all the service operations as interface methods that operate on the types of your favorite language (C#, Java, C++, JavaScript, and so on) and decide which operations to implement with synchronous communication and which ones to implement with asynchronous communication.
- Create the contract first in an interoperable format. In this approach, you can use definition files using patterns like OpenAPI, Protobuf, WSDL, and AsyncAPI without touching the programming language with which the services will be developed, using some tools to help.

The interfaces that are defined in this initial stage will not necessarily be used in the actual service implementation and are just useful design tools. Once we have decided on the architecture of the services, these interfaces are usually redefined so that we can adapt them to the peculiarity of the architecture.

It is worth pointing out that SOA messages must keep the same kind of semantics as method calls/answers. Besides, SOA follows stateless development; that is, the reaction to a message must not depend on any previously received messages because the server does not save information from prior requests, which means the messages must be independent of each other.

For instance, if the purpose of messages is to create a new database entry, this semantic must not change with the context of other messages, and the way the database entry is created must depend on the content of the current message and not on other previously received messages. Consequently, a client cannot create sessions and cannot log in to a service, perform some operations, and then log out. An authentication token must be repeated in each message.

The reasons for this constraint are modularity, testability, and maintainability. In fact, a session-based service would be very hard to test and modify due to the interactions that are *hidden* in the session data.

Once you have decided on the interface that is going to be implemented by a service, you must decide which communication stack/SOA to adopt. The communication stack must be part of some official or *de facto* standard to ensure the interoperability of the service.

Interoperability is the main constraint prescribed by SOA: services must offer a communication interface that does not depend on a specific library used, implementation language, or deployment platform.

Considering you have decided on the communication stack/architecture, you need to adapt your previous interfaces to the peculiarities of the architecture (see the *REST web services* subsection of this chapter for more details). Then, you must translate these interfaces into the chosen communication language. This means that you must map all the programming language types into types that are available in the chosen communication language.

The actual translation of data is usually performed automatically by the SOA libraries that are used by your development environment. However, some configuration might be needed, and, in any case, we must be aware of how our programming language types are transformed before each communication. For instance, some numeric types might be transformed into types with less precision or with different ranges of values. In .NET 8, for instance, you should be aware that floating-point numeric types vary between **float** (~6-9 digits), **double** (~15-17 digits), and **decimal** (~28-29 digits). You may consider the alternative of using string variables to reduce the risk of imprecision while transferring numeric types.

The interoperability constraint can be interpreted in a lighter form in the case of microservices that are not accessible outside of their clusters since they need to communicate with other microservices that belong to the same cluster. In this case, this means that the communication stack might be platform-specific so that it can increase performance, but it must be standard to avoid compatibility problems with other microservices that might be added to the cluster as the application evolves.

We have spoken of the *communication stack* and not of the *communication protocol* because SOA communication standards usually define the format of the message's content and provide different possibilities for the specific protocol that is used to embed those messages. For instance, REST services usually run over HTTP/HTTPS based on JSON messages, while the SOAP protocol just defines an XML-based format for the various kinds of messages, but SOAP messages can be conveyed by various protocols. Usually, the most common protocol that is used for SOAP is also HTTP, but you may decide to jump to the HTTP level and send SOAP messages directly over TCP/IP for better performance.

The choice of communication stack you should adopt depends on several factors, as described below. When it comes to accessing data, maybe the communication stack will be mandatory and decided by the provider, but you should also be concerned about these factors when providing a service:

- **Compatibility constraints**: If your service must be publicly available on the Internet to business clients, then you must conform to the most common choices, which means using SOAP over either HTTP or REST services. The most common choices are different if your clients are not business clients but **Internet of Things** (**IoT**) clients. Also, within IoT, the protocols that are used in different application areas can be different. For instance, marine vehicle status data is typically exchanged with *Signal K*. Although this protocol is too specific and is presented here just as an example, as a software architect, you must understand that you may face this kind of standard in a specific area.

- **Development/deployment platform:** Not all communication stacks are available on all development frameworks and on all deployment platforms, but luckily, all the most common communication stacks that are used in public business services, such as SOAP- and JSON-based REST communication, are available on all the main development/deployment platforms.
- **Performance:** If your system is not exposed to the outside world and is a private part of your microservice cluster, performance considerations have a higher priority. In this scenario, gRPC, which we will discuss soon in this chapter, can be noted as a good option.
- **Availability of tools and knowledge in your team:** Knowing about the availability of tools in your team/organization is important when it comes to choosing between acceptable communication stacks.

However, this kind of constraint always has less priority than compatibility constraints since it makes no sense to conceive a system that is easy to implement for your team but that almost nobody can use.

- **Flexibility versus available features:** Some communication solutions, while less complete, offer a higher degree of flexibility, while other solutions, though more complete, offer less flexibility. The need for flexibility started a movement from SOAP-based services to more flexible REST services in the last few years. This point will be discussed in more detail when we describe SOAP and REST services in the remainder of this section.
- **Service description:** When services must be exposed on the Internet, client applications need a publicly available description of the service specifications to design their communication clients. Some communication stacks include languages and conventions to describe service specifications. Formal service specifications that are exposed this way can be processed so that they automatically create communication clients. SOAP goes further and allows service discoverability by means of a public XML-based directory containing information about the tasks each web service can carry out.

Once you have chosen the communication stack you wish to use, you must use the tools that are available in your development environment to implement the service in a way that conforms to the chosen communication stack. Sometimes, communication stack compliance is automatically ensured by the development tools, but sometimes, it may require some development effort. For instance, in the .NET world, the compliance of SOAP services is automatically ensured by development tools if you use WCF, while the compliance of REST services falls under the developer's responsibility, although you have, since .NET 5, automatic support for the OpenAPI standard using Swagger. Some of the fundamental features of SOA solutions are as follows:

- **Authentication:** Allows the client to authenticate to access service operations.
- **Authorization:** Handles the client's permissions.
- **Security:** This is how communication is kept safe, that is, how to prevent unauthorized systems from reading and/or modifying the content of the communication. Typically, encryption prevents both unauthorized modifications and reading, while electronic signature algorithms prevent just modifications.
- **Exceptions:** Returns exceptions to the client.
- **Message reliability:** Ensures that messages reliably reach their destination in case of possible infrastructure faults.

Though sometimes desirable, the following features are not always necessary:

- **Distributed transactions**: The capability to handle distributed transactions, thus undoing all the changes you have made whenever the distributed transactions fail or are aborted.
- **Support for the Publisher/Subscriber pattern**: If and how events and notifications are supported.
- **Addressing**: If and how references to other services and/or methods are supported.
- **Routing**: If and how messages can be routed through a network of services.

The remainder of this section will describe SOAP services a bit. However, the focus will be REST services since today they are the *de facto* standard for business services that are exposed outside of their clusters/servers. For performance reasons, microservices use other protocols, discussed in *Chapter 11, Applying a Microservice Architecture to Your Enterprise Application*, *Chapter 14, Implementing Microservices with .NET*. For inter-cluster communication, **Advanced Message Queuing Protocol** (**AMQP**) is used, and links are given in the *Further reading* section.

SOAP web services

The **Simple Object Access Protocol** (**SOAP**) allows both one-way messages and request/reply messages. Communication can be both synchronous and asynchronous, as explained in *Chapter 1, Understanding the Importance of Software Architecture*, and *Chapter 2, Non-Functional Requirements*, but if the underlying protocol is synchronous, such as in the case of HTTP, the sender receives an acknowledgment saying that the message was received (but not necessarily processed). When asynchronous communication is used, the sender must listen for incoming communications. Often, asynchronous communication is implemented with the Publisher/Subscriber pattern, which we described in *Chapter 6, Design Patterns and .NET 8 Implementation*.

Messages are represented as XML documents called **envelopes**. Each envelope contains `header`, `body`, and `fault` elements. The `body` is where the actual content of the message is placed. The `fault` element contains possible errors, so it is the way exceptions are exchanged when communication occurs. Finally, the `header` contains any auxiliary information that enriches the protocol but does not contain domain data. For example, the `header` may contain an authentication token and/or a signature if the message is signed.

You can find the default namespace for the SOAP envelope at `https://www.w3.org/2003/05/soap-envelope/`.

The underlying protocol that is used to send the XML envelopes is usually HTTP, since this is the protocol of the Internet, but the SOAP specification allows any protocol, so we can use TCP/IP or SMTP directly. As a matter of fact, the more diffused underlying protocol is HTTP, so if you do not have a good reason to choose another protocol, you should use HTTP to maximize the interoperability of the service.

SOAP specifications

SOAP specifications contain the basics of message exchange, while other auxiliary features are described in separate specification documents called `WS- *` and are usually handled by adding extra information in the SOAP header. `WS-*` specifications handle all the fundamental and desirable features of SOA we listed previously. We have some of them below:

WS-*	Main objective
`WS-Security`	Takes care of security, including authentication, authorization, and encryption/signatures
`WS-Eventing` / `WS-Notification`	Two alternative ways of implementing the Publisher/Subscriber pattern
`WS-ReliableMessaging`	Concerned with the reliable delivery of messages in case of possible faults
`WS-Transaction`	Concerned with distributed transactions

Table 15.1: Summary of Key WS- Specifications and Their Main Objectives in SOAP-Based SOA*

The preceding `WS- *` specifications are in no way exhaustive but are the more relevant and supported features. In fact, actual implementations in various environments (such as Java and .NET) furnish the more relevant `WS- *` services, but no implementation supports all the `WS- *` specifications.

All the XML documents/document parts involved in the SOAP protocol are formally defined in XSD documents, like in the example below, which are special XML documents whose content provides a description of XML structures.

```
<?xml version="1.0"?>
<xs:schema id="sample" targetNamespace="http://tempuri.org/sample.xsd"
elementFormDefault="qualified" xmlns="http://tempuri.org/sample.xsd"
xmlns:xs="http://www.w3.org/2001/XMLSchema">
    <xs:element name='mySample'>
        <xs:complexType>
            <xs:simpleContent>
                <xs:extension base='xs:decimal'>
                    <xs:attribute name='sizing' type='xs:string' />
                </xs:extension>
            </xs:simpleContent>
        </xs:complexType>
    </xs:element>
</xs:schema>
```

Also, all your custom data structures (classes and interfaces in an object-oriented language) must be translated into XSD if they are going to be part of a SOAP envelope.

Each XSD specification has an associated `namespace` that identifies the specification and a physical location where it can be found. Both the namespace and the physical location are URIs. The location URI does not need to be publicly accessible if the web service is accessible just from within an intranet.

The whole definition of a service is an XSD specification that may contain references to other namespaces, that is, to other XSD documents. Simply put, all the messages via SOAP communication must be defined in an XSD specification. Then, a server and a client can communicate if they refer to the same XSD specifications. This means, for instance, that you need to create a new XSD specification each time you add another field to a message. After that, you need to update all the XSD files that reference the old message definition to the new message definition by creating a new version of them. In turn, these modifications require the creation of other versions for other XSD files, and so on. Therefore, simple modifications that maintain compatibility with the previous behavior (clients could simply ignore the field that was added) may cause an exponential chain of version changes.

Difficulties associated with the standard

In the last few years, the difficulty in handling modifications, along with the complexity of handling the configuration of all the `WS- *` specifications and performance problems, caused a gradual move toward the simpler REST services that we will describe in the upcoming sections. This move started with services that were called from JavaScript due to the difficulty of implementing complete SOAP clients that were able to run efficiently in a web browser. Moreover, the complex SOAP machinery was oversized for the simple needs of the typical clients running in a browser and may have caused a complete waste of development time.

For this reason, services aimed at non-JavaScript clients started a massive move toward REST services, and nowadays, the preferred choice is REST services, with SOAP being used either for compatibility with legacy systems or when features that are not supported by REST services are needed.

Today, we can consider REST services that transfer data with JSON, the most-used approach all over the world. Security aspects, design patterns for enabling transactional support, performance, and even documentation have improved all over the years, so this is certainly the best alternative for applying SOAs nowadays. Let's have a look at REST web services in the next topic.

REST web services

REST services were initially conceived to avoid the complex machinery of SOAP in simple cases, such as calls to a service from the JavaScript code of a web page. Then, they gradually became the preferred choice for complex systems. REST services use HTTP to exchange data in JSON or, less commonly, in XML format. Simply put, they replace the SOAP body with the HTTP body, the SOAP header with the HTTP header, and the HTTP response code replaces the fault element and furnishes further auxiliary information on the operation that was performed.

The main reason for the success of REST services is that HTTP already offers most of the SOAP features natively, which means we can avoid building a SOAP level on top of HTTP. Moreover, the whole HTTP machinery is simpler than SOAP: simpler to program, simpler to configure, and simpler to implement efficiently.

Moreover, REST services impose fewer constraints on the clients. Type compatibility between servers and clients conforms to the more flexible JavaScript type compatibility model because JSON is a subset of JavaScript. Moreover, when XML is used in place of JSON, it maintains the same JavaScript type compatibility rules. No XML namespaces need to be specified.

When using JSON and XML, if the server adds some more fields to the response while keeping the same semantics of all the other fields compatible with the previous client, they can simply ignore the new fields. Accordingly, changes that are made to a REST service definition only need to be propagated to previous clients in the case of breaking changes that cause actual incompatible behavior in the server.

Moreover, it is likely that changes will be self-limited and won't result in an exponential chain of changes because type compatibility does not require the reference to a specific type to be defined in a unique shared place and simply requires that the shape of types is compatible.

Service type compatibility rules

Let's clarify the REST service type compatibility rules with an example. Imagine that several services use a `Person` object that contains `Name`, `Surname`, and `Address` string fields. This object is served by **S1**:

```
{
    Name: string,
    Surname: string,
    Address: string
}
```

Type compatibility is ensured if the service and client refer to different copies of the preceding definition. It is also acceptable for the client to use a definition with fewer fields since it can simply ignore all the other fields:

```
{
    Name: string,
    Surname: string,
}
```

You can only use a definition with fewer fields within your "own" code. Attempting to send information back to the server without the expected fields may cause problems.

Now, imagine the scenario where you have an **S2** service that takes `Person` objects from **S1** and adds them to the responses it returns on some of its methods. Suppose the **S1** service that handles the `Person` object replaces the `Address` string with a complex object:

```
{
    Name: string,
    Surname: string,
    Address:
        {
```

```
            Country: string,
            Town: string,
            Location: string
        }
}
```

After the breaking change, the **S2** service will have to adapt its communication client that calls the **S1** service to the new format. Then, it can convert the new `Person` format into the older one before using `Person` objects in its responses. This way, the **S2** service avoids propagating the breaking change of **S1**.

In general, basing type compatibility on the object shape (tree of nested properties) instead of a reference to the same formal type definition increases flexibility and modifiability. The price we pay for this increased flexibility is that type compatibility cannot be computed automatically by comparing the formal definition of server and client interfaces. In fact, in the absence of a univocal specification, each time a new version of the service is released, the developer must verify that the semantics of all the fields that the client and server have in common remain unchanged from the previous version.

The basic idea behind REST services is to give up the severity checks and complex protocols for greater flexibility and simplicity, while SOAP does exactly the opposite.

REST and native HTTP features

The REST services manifesto states that REST uses native HTTP features to implement all the required service features. So, for instance, authentication will be performed directly with the HTTP `Authorization` field, encryption will be achieved with HTTPS, exceptions will be handled with an HTTP error status code, and routing and reliable messaging will be handled by the machinery the HTTP protocol relies on. Addressing is achieved by using URLs to refer to services, their methods, and other resources.

There is no native support for asynchronous communication since HTTP is a synchronous protocol. There is also no native support for the Publisher/Subscriber pattern, but two services can interact with the Publisher/Subscriber pattern by each exposing an endpoint to the other. More specifically, the first service exposes a subscription endpoint, while the second one exposes an endpoint where it receives its notifications, which are authorized through a common secret that is exchanged during the subscription. This pattern is quite common. GitHub also allows us to send repository events to our REST services.

REST services offer no easy options when it comes to implementing distributed transactions, since HTTP is stateless. However, approaches like the SAGA pattern, described in *Chapter 14, Implementing Microservices with .NET*, and event sourcing, described in *Chapter 7, Understanding the Different Domains in Software Solutions*, helped a lot in the last years to solve this difficulty. Besides, luckily, most application areas do not need the strong form of consistency that is ensured by distributed transactions. For them, lighter forms of consistency, such as *eventual consistency*, are enough and are preferred for performance reasons. Please refer to *Chapter 12, Choosing Your Data Storage in the Cloud*, for a discussion on the various types of consistencies.

The REST manifesto not only prescribes the usage of the predefined solutions that are already available in HTTP but also the usage of a web-like semantic. In general, service operations can be conceived as CRUD operations, but not limited to them on resources that are identified by URLs (the same resource may be identified by several URLs). In fact, REST is an acronym for **Representational State Transfer**, meaning that each URL is the representation of some sort of entity. As a best practice, each kind of service request needs to adopt the appropriate HTTP verb and return the status code as follows:

- `GET` (read operation): The URL represents the resource that is returned by the read operation. Thus, `GET` operations mimic pointer dereferencing. In the case of a successful operation, a 200 (OK) status code is returned.
- `POST` (creation operation): The JSON/XML object that is contained in the request body is added as a new resource to the object represented by the operation URL. If the new resource is successfully created immediately, a 201 (created) status code is returned, along with a response object that depends on the operation and an indication as to where the created resource can be retrieved from. The response object should contain the most specific URL that identifies the created resource. If creation is deferred to a later time, a 202 (accepted) status code is returned.
- `PUT` (edit operation): The JSON/XML object contained in the request body replaces the object referenced by the request URL. In the case of a successful operation, a 200 (OK) status code is returned. This operation is idempotent, meaning that repeating the same request twice causes the same modification. 204 (No Content) is also a possible return value.
- `PATCH`: The JSON/XML object contained in the request body contains instructions on how to modify the object referenced by the request URL. This operation is not idempotent since the modification may be an increment of a numeric field. In the case of a successful operation, a 200 (OK) status code is returned.
- `DELETE`: The resource referenced by the request URL is removed. In the case of a successful operation, a 200 (OK) status code is returned.

If the resource has been moved from the request URL to another URL, a redirect code is returned:

- `301` (moved permanently), plus the new URL where we can find the resource
- `307` (moved temporarily), plus the new URL where we can find the resource

If the operation fails, a status code that depends on the kind of failure is returned. Some examples of failure codes are as follows:

- `400` (bad request): The request that was sent to the server is ill formed.
- `404` (not found): When the request URL does not refer to any known object.
- `405` (method not allowed): When the request verb is not supported by the resource referenced by the URL.
- `401` (unauthorized): The operation requires authentication, but the client has not furnished any valid authorization header.
- `403` (forbidden): The client is correctly authenticated but has no right to perform the operation.
- `409` (conflict): The operation failed due to some conflict with the current state of the server.
- `412` (precondition failed): The operation failed due to some precondition desired.

- `422` (unprocessable content): The request was well formatted, but there are semantic errors in it.

The preceding list of status codes is not exhaustive. A reference to an exhaustive list will be provided in the *Further reading* section.

It is fundamental to point out that `POST`/`PUT`/`PATCH`/`DELETE` operations may have – and usually have – side effects on other resources. Otherwise, it would be impossible to code operations that act simultaneously on several resources.

In other words, the HTTP verb must conform with the operation that is performed on the resource and referenced by the request URL, but the operation might affect other resources. The same operation might be performed with a different HTTP verb on one of the other involved resources. It is the developer's responsibility to choose which way to perform the same operation to implement it in the service interface.

Thanks to the side effects of HTTP verbs, REST services can encode all these operations as CRUD operations on resources represented by URLs.

Often, moving an existing service to REST requires us to split the various inputs between the request URL and the request body. More specifically, we extract the input fields that univocally define one of the objects involved in the method's execution and use them to create a URL that univocally identifies that object. Then, we decide on which HTTP verb to use based on the operation that is performed on the selected object. Finally, we place the remainder of the input in the request body.

If our services were designed with an object-oriented architecture focused on the business domain objects (such as DDD, as described in *Chapter 7, Understanding the Different Domains in Software Solutions*), the REST translation of all the service methods should be quite immediate since services should already be organized around domain resources. Otherwise, moving to REST might require some service interface redefinitions.

The adoption of full REST semantics has the advantage that services can be extended with or without small modifications being made to the preexisting operation definitions. In fact, extensions should mainly manifest as additional properties of some objects and as additional resource URLs with some associated operations. Therefore, preexisting clients can simply ignore them.

Example of methods in the REST language

Now, let us learn how methods can be expressed in the REST language with a simple example of an intra-bank money transfer. We will present here two approaches.

In the first one, a bank account can be represented by a URL as follows:

```
https://mybank.com/accounts/{bank account number}
```

If we imagine a bank transfer we may represent it as a `PATCH` request, whose body contains an object with properties representing the amount of money, time of transfer, description, and the account receiving the money.

The operation modifies the account mentioned in the URL but also the receiving account as a *side effect*. If the account doesn't have enough money, a `409` (conflict) status code is returned, along with an object with all the error details (an error description, the available funds, and so on).

However, since all the bank operations are recorded in the account statement, the creation and addition of a new transfer object for a *bank account operations* collection associated with the bank account is a better way to represent the transfer. In this second approach, the URL might be something like the following:

```
https://mybank.com/accounts/{bank account number}/transactions
```

Here, the HTTP verb is `POST` since we are creating a new object. The body content is the same, and a `422` status code is returned if there is a lack of funds.

Both representations of the transfer cause the same changes in the database. Moreover, once the inputs are extracted from the different URLs and from the possibly different request bodies, the subsequent processing is the same. In both cases, we have the same inputs and the same processing – it is just the exterior appearance of the two requests that are different.

However, the introduction of the virtual *transactions* collection allows us to extend the service with several more *transaction* collection-specific methods. It is worth pointing out that the *transaction* collection does not need to relate to a database table or any physical object: it lives in the world of URLs and creates a convenient way for us to model the transfer.

The increased usage of REST services leads to a description of REST service interfaces to be created like the ones developed for SOAP. This standard is called **OpenAPI**. We will talk about this in the following subsection.

The OpenAPI standard

OpenAPI is a specification that is used worldwide for describing the REST APIs. The OpenAPI Initiative was founded in November 2015, as an open-source project under the Linux Foundation, with the help of companies like SmartBear, Google, IBM, and Microsoft. The specification is currently versioned as 3.1. The whole service is described by a JSON or YAML endpoint, that is, an endpoint that describes the service with a JSON object. This JSON object has a general section that applies to the whole service and contains the general features of the service, such as its version and description, as well as shared definitions.

You can find OpenAPI Specification examples at `https://github.com/OAI/OpenAPI-Specification/`.

Then, each service endpoint has a specific section that describes the endpoint URL or URL format (in case some inputs are included in the URL), all its inputs, all the possible output types and status codes, and all the authorization protocols. Each endpoint-specific section can reference the definitions contained in the general section.

A complete description of the OpenAPI syntax is out of the scope of this book, but you will find visual editors on the Internet that can help you clarify the specification mentioned before. A great example is provided by SmartBear, one of the companies that founded the initiative, and it is called Swagger Editor. In the beta version of the online tool, you can load an example using OpenAPI version 3.1.0. This helps companies to create API contracts even before deciding the programming language of the API.

Various development frameworks automatically generate OpenAPI documentation by processing the REST API code, and further information is provided by the developer, so your team does not need to have in-depth knowledge of OpenAPI syntax. An example of this is the `Swashbuckle.AspNetCore` NuGet package that we will present in this chapter.

The *How does .NET 8 deal with SOA?* section explains how we can automatically generate OpenAPI documentation in ASP.NET Core REST API projects, while the use case presented in *Chapter 21, Case Study,* will provide a practical example of its usage.

We will end this subsection by talking about how to handle authentication and authorization in REST services.

REST service authorization and authentication

Since REST services are stateless, when authentication is required, the client must send an authentication token in every single request. That token is usually placed in the HTTP authorization header, but this depends on the type of authentication protocol you are using. The simplest way to authenticate is through the explicit transmission of a shared secret. This can be done with the following code:

```
Authorization: Api-Key <string known by both server and client>
```

The shared secret is called an API key. Since, at the time of writing, there is no standard on how to send it, API keys can also be sent in other headers, as shown in the following code:

```
X-API-Key: <string known by both server and client>
```

It is worth mentioning that API-key-based authentication needs HTTPS to stop shared secrets from being stolen. API keys are very simple to use, but they do not convey information about user authorizations, so they can be adopted when the operations allowed by the client are quite standard, and there are no complex authorization patterns. Moreover, when exchanged in requests, API keys are susceptible to being attacked on the server or client side. A common pattern to mitigate this is to create a "service account" user and restrict their authorizations to just those needed and use the API keys from that specific account when interacting with the API.

If you need a more sophisticated authentication service, you may consider using the OAuth 2.0 protocol. For instance, when you implement "Sign in with [Some specific social media]," you are probably using this protocol. Of course, to use it, you have to define an authentication service provider.

Safer techniques use shared secrets that are valid for a long period of time, just by the user logging in. Then, the login returns a short-life token that is used as a shared secret in all the subsequent requests. When the short-lived secret is going to expire, it can be renewed with a call to a renew endpoint.

The whole logic is completely decoupled from the short-life token-based authorization logic. The login is usually based on login endpoints that receive long-term credentials and return short-life tokens. Login credentials are either usual username-password pairs that are passed as input to the login method or other kinds of authorization tokens that are converted into short-life tokens that are served by the login endpoint. Login can also be achieved with various authentication protocols based on X.509 certificates.

The most widespread short-life token type is the so-called bearer token. Each bearer token encodes information about how long it lasts and a list of assertions, called claims, that can be used for authorization purposes. Bearer tokens are returned by either login operations or renewal operations. Their characteristic feature is that they are not tied to the client that receives them or to any other specific client, but they identify the client, which can simply use them in its invocations.

No matter how a client gets a bearer token, this is all a client needs to be granted, including all the rights implied by its claims. It is enough to transfer a bearer token to another client to empower that client with all the rights implied by all the bearer token claims since no proof of identity is required by bearer-token-based authorization.

Therefore, once a client gets a bearer token, it can delegate some operations to third parties by transferring its bearer token to them. Typically, when a bearer token must be used for delegation, during the login phase, the client specifies the claims to include to restrict what operations can be authorized by the token.

Compared to API key authentication, bearer-token-based authentication is disciplined by standards. They must use the following `Authorization` header:

```
Authorization: Bearer <bearer token string>
```

Bearer tokens can be implemented in several ways. REST services typically use JWTs that are strings with a Base64 URL encoding of JSON objects. More specifically, JWT creation starts with a JSON header, as well as a JSON payload. The JSON header specifies the kind of token and how it is signed, while the payload consists of a JSON object that contains all the claims as property/value pairs. The following is an example header:

```
{
  "alg": "RS256",
  "typ": "JWT"
}
```

The following is an example payload:

```
{
  "iss": "wwtravelclub.com"
  "sub": "example",
  "aud": ["S1", "S2"],
  "roles": [
    "ADMIN",
```

```
    "USER"
  ],
  "exp": 1512975450,
  "iat": 1512968250230
}
```

Then, the header and payload are Base64 URL-encoded, and the corresponding string is concatenated as follows:

```
<header BASE64 string>.<payload base64 string>
```

The preceding string is then signed with the algorithm specified in the header, which, in our example, is `RSA +SHA256`, and the signature string is concatenated with the original string as follows:

```
<header BASE64 string>.<payload base64 string>.<signature string>
```

The preceding code is the final bearer token string. A symmetric signature can be used instead of RSA, but, in this case, both the JWT issuer and all the services using it for authorization must share a common secret, while, with RSA, the private key of the JWT issuer does not need to be shared with anyone, since the signature can be verified with just the issuer public key.

Some payload properties are standard, such as the following:

- `iss`: Issuer of the JWT.
- `aud`: The audience, that is, the services and/or operations that can use the token for authorization. If a service does not see its identifier within this list, it should reject the token.
- `sub`: A string that identifies the *principal* (that is, the user) to which the JWT was issued.
- `iat`, `exp`, and `nbf`: These are for the time the JWT was issued, its expiration time, and, if set, the time after which the token is valid, respectively. All the times are expressed as seconds from midnight UTC on January 1, 1970. Here, all the days are considered as having exactly 86,400 seconds in them.

Other claims may be defined as public if we represent them with a unique URI; otherwise, they are considered private to the issuer and to the services known to the issuer.

API versioning

Considering a natural scenario where the number of APIs will increase in your application, and, more than that, the business logic will obviously evolve, as a software architect, you must decide how you are going to version the APIs, guaranteeing the compatibility between your services and the clients that consume these services.

It is important to mention that there are several versioning options for doing so:

- **URI:** It consists of defining the version of the API in its URI, for example, `https://wwtravelclub.com/v1/trips`.
- **Parameter:** You can define a parameter in the request that defines the version, for instance, `https://wwtravelclub.com/trips?version=2`.

- **Media type**: In this case, the desired version of the API will be presented in the HTTP `Accept` header.
- **Custom request header**: Like the media type versioning technique, but in this case the HTTP header will be customized by you.

The first two alternatives are the most commonly used, but the important point here is that you must consider crucial the implementation of a versioning technique.

How does .NET 8 deal with SOA?

WCF technology has not been ported to .NET 5+ and there are no plans to perform a complete port of it. Part of the source code was donated, and an open-source project started out of it. You can find information about this project at `https://github.com/CoreWCF/CoreWCF`. Instead, Microsoft is investing in gRPC, Google's open-source technology. Besides, .NET 8 has excellent support for REST services through ASP.NET Core.

There is a tool developed by Microsoft to help you with the migration of WCF applications to the latest .NET. You can find it at `https://devblogs.microsoft.com/dotnet/migration-wcf-to-corewcf-upgrade-assistant/`.

The main reasons behind the decision to abandon WCF are as follows:

- As we have already discussed, SOAP technology has been overtaken by REST technology in most application areas.
- WCF technology is strictly tied to Windows, so it would be very expensive to reimplement all its features from scratch in .NET 5+. Since support for full .NET will continue, users who need WCF can still rely on it.
- As a general strategy, with .NET 5+, Microsoft prefers investing in open-source technologies that can be shared with other competitors. That is why, instead of investing in WCF, Microsoft provided a gRPC implementation starting from .NET Core 3.0.

The next subsections will cover the support provided inside Visual Studio for each technology we have mentioned.

SOAP client support

In WCF, service specifications are defined through .NET interfaces, and the actual service code is supplied in classes that implement those interfaces. Endpoints, underlying protocols (HTTP and TCP/IP), and any other features are defined in a configuration file. In turn, the configuration file can be edited with an easy-to-use configuration tool. Therefore, the developer is responsible for providing just the service behavior as a standard .NET class and for configuring all the service features in a declarative way. This way, the service configuration is completely decoupled from the actual service behavior, and each service can be reconfigured so that it can be adapted to a different environment without the need to modify its code.

While .NET 8 does not support SOAP technology for creating new services, it does support the usage of SOAP clients when there are many SOAP services as legacy. More specifically, it is quite easy to create a SOAP service proxy for an existing SOAP service in Visual Studio (please refer to *Chapter 6, Design Patterns and .NET 8 Implementation*, for a discussion of what a proxy is and of the Proxy pattern).

In the case of services, a proxy is a class that implements the service interface and whose methods perform their jobs by calling the analogous methods of the remote service.

To create a service proxy, right-click **Dependencies** in your project in **Solution Explorer**, and then select **Add connected service**. Then, in the form that appears, select **Microsoft WCF Service Reference Provider**. There, you can specify the URL of the service (where the WSDL service description is contained), the namespace where you wish to add the proxy class, and much more. At the end of the wizard, Visual Studio automatically adds all the necessary NuGet packages and scaffolds the proxy class. This is enough to create an instance of this class and to call its methods so that we can interact with the remote SOAP service.

There are also third parties, such as NuGet packages, that provide limited support for SOAP services, but currently, they aren't very useful since such limited support does not include features that aren't available in REST services.

gRPC support

The .NET SDK supports the gRPC project template, which scaffolds both a gRPC server and a gRPC client. gRPC implements a remote procedure call pattern that offers both synchronous and asynchronous calls, reducing the traffic of messages between the client and server.

Using gRPC is super easy since Visual Studio's gRPC project template scaffolds everything so that the gRPC service and its clients are working. The developer just needs to define the application-specific C# service interface and a class that implements it.

For configuring it, services are defined through interfaces written in a Protobuf file, and their code is provided in C# classes that implement those interfaces, while clients interact with those services through proxies that implement the same service interfaces.

gRPC is a good option for internal communications within a microservices cluster. Since there are gRPC libraries for all the main languages and development frameworks, it can be used in Kubernetes-based clusters. Besides, gRPC is more efficient than the REST services protocol due to its more compact representation of data and its being easier to use since everything to do with the protocol is taken care of by the development framework.

For this reason, we have added a brand-new chapter dedicated to discussing this implementation, *Chapter 14, Implementing Microservices with .NET*, and you can check details about the technology at `https://docs.microsoft.com/en-us/aspnet/core/tutorials/grpc/grpc-start?view=aspnetcore-8.0`.

The remainder of the section is dedicated to .NET support for REST services from both the server and client sides.

A short introduction to ASP.NET Core

ASP.NET Core applications are .NET applications based on the *Host* concept we described in the *Using generic hosts* subsection of *Chapter 11, Applying a Microservice Architecture to Your Enterprise Application.*

Using C# 12 and .NET 8, the template for creating ASP.NET Core apps has changed a bit. The main purpose is to simplify how we set it up. The `Program.cs` file of each ASP.NET application now creates a host, builds it, and runs it without needing the `Startup` class anymore, as we can see in the following code:

```
var builder = WebApplication.CreateBuilder(args);

// Add services to the container.

builder.Services.AddControllers();
// Learn more about configuring Swagger/OpenAPI at https://aka.ms/aspnetcore/
swashbuckle
builder.Services.AddEndpointsApiExplorer();
builder.Services.AddSwaggerGen();

var app = builder.Build();

// Configure the HTTP request pipeline.
if (app.Environment.IsDevelopment())
{
    app.UseSwagger();
    app.UseSwaggerUI();
}

app.UseHttpsRedirection();

app.UseAuthorization();

app.MapControllers();

app.Run();
```

`Environment` is taken from the `ASPNETCORE_ENVIRONMENT` environment variable. In turn, it is defined in the `Properties\launchSettings.json` file when the application runs in Visual Studio over **Solution Explorer**. In this file, you can define several environments that can be selected with the dropdown next to Visual Studio's run button, **IIS Express**. By default, the **IIS Express** setting sets `ASPNETCORE_ENVIRONMENT` to `Development`. The following is a typical `launchSettings.json` file:

```
{
  "iisSettings": {
```

```
    "windowsAuthentication": false,
    "anonymousAuthentication": true,
    "iisExpress": {
      "applicationUrl": "http://localhost:48638",
      "sslPort": 44367
    }
  },
  "profiles": {
    "http": {
      "commandName": "Project",
      "dotnetRunMessages": true,
      "launchBrowser": true,
      "launchUrl": "swagger",
      "applicationUrl": "http://localhost:5085",
      "environmentVariables": {
        "ASPNETCORE_ENVIRONMENT": "Development"
      }
    },
    "https": {
      "commandName": "Project",
      "dotnetRunMessages": true,
      "launchBrowser": true,
      "launchUrl": "swagger",
      "applicationUrl": "https://localhost:7214;http://localhost:5085",
      "environmentVariables": {
        "ASPNETCORE_ENVIRONMENT": "Development"
      }
    },
    "IIS Express": {
      "commandName": "IISExpress",
      "launchBrowser": true,
      "launchUrl": "swagger",
      "environmentVariables": {
        "ASPNETCORE_ENVIRONMENT": "Development"
      }
    }
  }
}
```

The value to use for `ASPNETCORE_ENVIRONMENT` when the application is published can be added to the published XML file after it has been created by Visual Studio. This value is `<EnvironmentName>Staging</EnvironmentName>`. It can also be specified in your Visual Studio ASP.NET Core project file (`.csproj`):

```
<PropertyGroup>
<EnvironmentName>Staging</EnvironmentName>
</PropertyGroup>
```

Each middleware in the pipeline is defined by an `app.Use<something>` method, which often accepts some options. Each of them processes the requests and then either forwards the modified request to the next one in the pipeline or returns an HTTP response. When an HTTP response is returned, it is processed by all the previous ones in reverse order.

Modules are inserted in the pipeline in the order they are defined by the `app.Use<something>` method calls. The preceding code adds an error page if `ASPNETCORE_ENVIRONMENT` is `Development`. A complete description of the ASP.NET Core pipeline will be given in the *Understanding the presentation layers of web applications* section of *Chapter 17, Presenting ASP.NET Core*.

In the next subsection, we will explain how the MVC framework lets you implement REST services.

Implementing REST services with ASP.NET Core

Today, we can guarantee that the use of MVC and a web API is consolidated. In the MVC framework, HTTP requests are processed by classes called controllers. Each request is mapped to the call of a controller public method. The selected controller and controller methods depend on the shape of the request path, and they are defined by routing rules, which, for the REST API, are usually provided through attributes associated with both the `Controller` class and its methods.

ASP.NET Core 6 has introduced minimal APIs to simplify the mechanism of implementing APIs with C#. You can find a good explanation of it at `https://docs.microsoft.com/en-us/aspnet/core/fundamentals/minimal-apis`.

`Controller` methods that process HTTP requests are called action methods. When the controller and action methods are selected, the MVC framework creates a controller instance to serve the request. All the parameters of the controller constructors are resolved with dependency injection.

Please refer to the *Using generic hosts* subsection of *Chapter 11, Applying a Microservice Architecture to Your Enterprise Application*, for a description of how to use dependency injection with a .NET host and to the *Dependency injection pattern* subsection of *Chapter 6, Design Patterns and .NET 8 Implementation*, for a general discussion of dependency injection.

The following is a typical REST API controller and its controller method definitions:

```
[Route("api/[controller]")]
[ApiController]
```

```
public class ValuesController : ControllerBase
{
    // GET api/values/5
    [HttpGet("{id}")]
    public ActionResult<string> Get(int id)
    {
        ...
```

The `[ApiController]` attribute declares that the controller is a REST API controller. `[Route("api/[controller]")]` declares that the controller must be selected on paths that start with `api/<controller name>`. The controller's name is the name of the controller class without the `Controller` postfix. This is preferred over hardcoding a controller name to save time on refactoring. Thus, in this case, we have `api/values`.

`[HttpGet("{id}")]` declares that the method must be invoked on GET requests of the `api/values/<id>` type, where `id` must be a number that's passed as an argument to the method invocation. This can be done with `Get(int id)`. There is also an `Http<verb>` attribute for each HTTP verb: `HttpPost` and `HttpPatch`.

We may also have another method defined like so:

```
[HttpGet]
public ... Get()
```

This method is invoked on `GET` requests of the `api/values` type, that is, on `GET` requests without `id` after the controller's name.

Several action methods can have the same name, but only one should be compatible with each request path; otherwise, an exception is thrown. In other words, routing rules and `Http<verb>` attributes must univocally define which controller and which of its action methods to select for each request.

By default, parameters are passed to the action methods of API controllers according to the following rules.

Simple types (`integers`, `floats`, and `DateTimes`) are taken from the request path if routing rules specify them as parameters, as in the case of the previous example's `[HttpGet("{id}")]` attribute. If they are not found in the routing rules, the ASP.NET Core framework looks for query string parameters with the same name. Thus, for instance, if we replace `[HttpGet("{id}")]` with `[HttpGet]`, the ASP.NET Core framework will look for something like `api/values?id=<id type>` or `api/values/{id}`.

Complex types are extracted from the request body by formatters. The right formatter is chosen according to the value of the request's `Content-Type` header. If no `Content-Type` header is specified, the JSON formatter is taken. The JSON formatter tries to parse the request body as a JSON object and then tries to transform this JSON object into an instance of the .NET complex type. If either the JSON extraction or the subsequent conversion fails, an exception is thrown. As described in *Chapter 2, Non-Functional Requirements,* be careful with exceptions since their computational costs are much higher than a normal code flow.

If an exception is inevitable, consider using the recommendations for logging described in *Chapter 4, Best Practices in Coding C# 12*. By default, just the JSON input formatter is supported, but you can also add an XML formatter that can be used when `Content-Type` specifies XML content.

You can customize the source that is used to fill an action method parameter by prefixing the parameter with an adequate attribute. The following code shows some examples of this:

```
...MyActionMethod(....[FromHeader] string myHeader....)
// x is taken from a request header named myHeader
...MyActionMethod(....[FromServices] MyType x....)
// x is filled with an instance of MyType through dependency injection
```

The return type of an action method can be an `IActionResult` interface, a type that implements that interface, or a DTO directly. In turn, `IActionResult` has just the following method:

```
Task ExecuteResultAsync(ActionContext context);
```

This method is called by the MVC framework at the right time to create the actual response and response headers. The `ActionContext` object, when passed to the method, contains the whole context of the HTTP request, which includes a request object with all the necessary information about the original HTTP requests (headers, body, and cookies), as well as a response object that collects all the pieces of the response that is being built.

You do not have to create an implementation of `IActionResult` manually since `ControllerBase` already has methods to create `IActionResult` implementations so that all the necessary HTTP responses are generated. Some of these methods are as follows:

- `OK`: This returns a 200 status code, as well as an optional result object. It is used as either `return OK()` or `return OK(myResult)`.
- `BadRequest`: This returns a 400 status code, as well as an optional response object.
- `Created(string uri, object o)`: This returns a 201 status code, as well as a result object and the URI of the created resource.
- `Accepted`: This returns a 202 status result, as well as an optional result object and resource URI.
- `Unauthorized`: This returns a 401 status result, as well as an optional result object.
- `Forbid`: This returns a 403 status result, as well as an optional list of failed permissions.
- `StatusCode(int statusCode, object o = null)`: This returns a custom status code, as well as an optional result object.

An action method can return a result object directly with `return myObject`. This is equivalent to returning `OK(myObject)`.

When all the result paths return a result object of the same type, say, `MyType`, the action method can be declared as returning `ActionResult<MyType>`. You may also return responses like `NotFound`, but for sure, you will get a better type of check with this approach.

By default, result objects are serialized in JSON in the response body. However, if an XML formatter has been added to the ASP.NET Core framework processing pipeline, as shown previously, the way the result is serialized depends on the `Accept` header of the HTTP request. More specifically, if the client explicitly requires XML format with the `Accept` header, the object will be serialized in XML; otherwise, it will be serialized in JSON.

Complex objects that are passed as input to action methods can be validated with validation attributes as follows:

```
public record MyType
{
   [Required]
    public string Name{get; set;}
    ...
    [MaxLength(64)]
    public string Description{get; set;}
}
```

If the controller has been decorated with the `[ApiController]` attribute and if validation fails, the ASP.NET Core framework automatically creates a `BadRequest` response containing a dictionary with all the validation errors detected, without executing the action method. Therefore, you do not need to add further code to handle validation errors.

Action methods can also be declared as `async` methods, as follows:

```
public async Task<IActionResult>MyMethod(......)
{
    await MyBusinessObject.MyBusinessMethod();
    ...
}
public async Task<ActionResult<MyType>>MyMethod(......)
{
    ...
```

Practical examples of controllers/action methods will be shown in *Use case – exposing WWTravelClub packages*, presented in *Chapter 21, Case Study*. In the next subsection, we will explain how to handle authorization and authentication with JWTs.

ASP.NET Core service authorization

When using a JWT, authorizations are based on the claims contained in the JWT. All the token claims in any action method can be accessed through the `User.Claims` controller property. Since `User.Claims` is an `IEnumerable<Claim>`, it can be processed with LINQ to verify complex conditions on claims.

If authorization is based on *role* claims, you can simply use the `User.IsInRole` function, as shown in the following code:

```
If(User.IsInRole("Administrators") || User.IsInRole("SuperUsers"))
{
    ...
}
else return Forbid();
```

However, permissions are not usually checked from within action methods and are automatically checked by the MVC framework according to authorization attributes that decorate either the whole controller or a single action method. If an action method or the whole controller is decorated with `[Authorize]`, then access to the action method is possible only if the request has a valid authentication token, which means we don't have to perform a check on the token claims. It is also possible to check whether the token contains a set of roles using the following code:

```
[Authorize(Roles = "Administrators,SuperUsers")]
```

More complex conditions on claims require that authorization policies be defined while building the app in `Program.cs`, as shown in the following code:

```
var builder = WebApplication.CreateBuilder(args);
// Add services to the container.
builder.Services.AddControllers();
...
builder.Services.AddAuthorization(options =>
{
    options.AddPolicy("CanDrive", policy =>
        policy.RequireAssertion(context =>
        context.User.HasClaim(c => c.Type == "HasDrivingLicense")));
});
```

After that, you can decorate the action methods or controllers with `[Authorize(Policy = "Father")]`.

Before using JWT-based authorization, you must configure it in `Program.cs`. First, you must add the middleware that processes authentication tokens in ASP.NET Core, as shown here:

```
var app = builder.Build();
...
app.UseAuthorization();
app.MapControllers();
app.Run();
```

Then, you must configure the authentication services. There, you define the authentication options that will be injected through dependency injection into the authentication middleware:

```
var builder = WebApplication.CreateBuilder(args);

// Add services to the container.
builder.Services.AddControllers();
...
builder.Services.AddAuthentication(JwtBearerDefaults.AuthenticationScheme)
    .AddJwtBearer(options => {
        options.TokenValidationParameters =
          new TokenValidationParameters
          {
              ValidateIssuer = true,
              ValidateAudience = true,
              ValidateLifetime = true,
              ValidateIssuerSigningKey = true,
              ValidIssuer = "My.Issuer",
              ValidAudience = "This.Website.Audience",
              IssuerSigningKey = new
                  SymmetricSecurityKey(Encoding.ASCII.GetBytes("MySecret"))
          };
    });
```

The preceding code provides a name to the authentication scheme, that is, a default name. Then, it specifies JWT authentication options. Usually, we require that the authentication middleware verifies that the JWT is not expired (`ValidateLifetime = true`), that it has the right issuer and audience (see the *REST service authorization and authentication* section of this chapter), and that its signature is valid.

The preceding example uses a symmetric signing key generated from a string. This means that the same key is used to sign and verify the signature. This is an acceptable choice if JWTs are created by the same website that uses them, but it is not an acceptable choice if there is a unique JWT issuer that controls access to several web API sites.

Here, we should use an asymmetric key (typically, an `RsaSecurityKey`), so JWT verification requires just the knowledge of the public key associated with the actual private signing key. IdentityServer 4 can be used to quickly create a website that works as an authentication server. It emits a JWT with the usual username/password credentials or converts other authentication tokens. If you use an authentication server such as IdentityServer 4, you do not need to specify the `IssuerSigningKey` option since the authorization middleware is able to retrieve the required public key from the authorization server automatically.

It is enough to provide the authentication server URL, as shown here:

```
.AddJwtBearer(options => {
options.Authority = "https://www.MyAuthorizationserver.com";
options.TokenValidationParameters =...
      ...
```

On the other hand, if you decide to emit a JWT in your web API's site, you can define a `Login` action method that accepts an object with a username and password and that, while relying on database information, builds the JWT with code similar to the following:

```
var claims = new List<Claim>
{
   new Claim(...),
   new Claim(...) ,
   ...
};
var token = new JwtSecurityToken(
          issuer: "MyIssuer",
          audience: ...,
          claims: claims,
          expires: DateTime.UtcNow.AddMinutes(expiryInMinutes),
          signingCredentials:
          new SymmetricSecurityKey(Encoding.ASCII.GetBytes("MySecret"));
          return OK(new JwtSecurityTokenHandler().WriteToken(token));
```

Here, `JwtSecurityTokenHandler().WriteToken(token)` generates the actual token string from the token properties contained in the `JwtSecurityToken` instance.

In the next subsection, we will learn how to empower our web API with an OpenAPI documentation endpoint so that proxy classes for communicating with our services can be generated automatically.

ASP.NET Core support for OpenAPI

Most of the information that is needed to fill in an OpenAPI JSON document can be extracted from web API controllers through reflection, that is, input types and sources (path, request body, and header) and endpoint paths (these can be extracted from routing rules). Returned output types and status codes, in general, cannot be easily computed since they can be generated dynamically.

Therefore, the MVC framework provides the `ProducesResponseType` attribute so that we can declare a possible return type – a status code pair. It is enough to decorate each action method with as many `ProducesResponseType` attributes as there are possible types, that is, possible status code pairs, as shown in the following code:

```
[HttpGet("{id}")]
[ProducesResponseType(typeof(MyReturnType), StatusCodes.Status200OK)]
```

```
[ProducesResponseType(typeof(MyErrorReturnType), StatusCodes.
Status404NotFound)]
public IActionResult GetById(int id)...
```

If no object is returned along a path, we can just declare the status code as follows:

```
[ProducesResponseType(StatusCodes.Status403Forbidden)]
```

We can also specify just the status code when all the paths return the same type and when that type is specified in the action method return type as `ActionResult<CommonReturnType>`.

Once all the action methods have been documented, to generate any actual documentation for the JSON endpoints, we must install the `Swashbuckle.AspNetCore` NuGet package and place some code in the `Program.cs` file:

In .NET 5+, you can automatically include it by leaving **OpenAPI support** checked when creating a project.

```
var builder = WebApplication.CreateBuilder(args);
...
//open api middleware
builder.Services.AddSwaggerGen(c =>
{
    c.SwaggerDoc("v1", new() { Title = "WWTravelClubREST60", Version = "v1" });
});
var app = builder.Build();
...
app.UseSwagger();
app.UseSwaggerUI(c => c.SwaggerEndpoint("/swagger/v1/swagger.json",
"WWTravelClubREST60 v1"));
...
app.Run();
```

The first argument of the `SwaggerDoc` method is the documentation endpoint name. By default, the documentation endpoint is accessible through the `<webroot>//swagger/<endpoint name>/swagger.json` path, but this can be changed in several ways. The rest of the information contained in the `Info` class is self-explanatory.

We can add several `SwaggerDoc` calls to define several documentation endpoints. However, by default, all the documentation endpoints will contain the same documentation, which includes a description of all the REST services included in the project. This default can be changed by calling the `c.DocInclusionPredicate(Func<string, ApiDescription> predicate)` method from within `services.AddSwaggerGen(c => {...})`.

`DocInclusionPredicate` must be passed a function that receives a JSON document name and an action method description and must return `true` if the documentation of the action must be included in that JSON document.

To declare that your REST APIs need a JWT, you must add the following code within `services.AddSwaggerGen(c => {...})`:

```
var security = new Dictionary<string, IEnumerable<string>>
{
    {"Bearer", new string[] { }},
};
c.AddSecurityDefinition("Bearer", new ApiKeyScheme
{
    Description = "JWT Authorization header using the Bearer scheme.
    Example: \"Authorization: Bearer {token}\"",
    Name = "Authorization",
    In = "header",
    Type = "apiKey"
});
c.AddSecurityRequirement(security);
```

You can enrich the JSON documentation endpoint with information that has been extracted from triple-slash comments, which are usually added to generate automatic code documentation. The following code shows some examples of this. The following snippet shows how we can add a method description and parameter information:

```
/// <summary>
/// Deletes a specific TodoItem.
/// </summary>
/// <param name="id">id to delete</param>
[HttpDelete("{id}")]
public IActionResultDelete(long id)
```

The following snippet shows how we can add an example of usage:

```
/// <summary>
/// Creates an item.
/// </summary>
/// <remarks>
/// Sample request:
///
/// POST /MyItem
/// {
/// "id": 1,
/// "name": "Item1"
```

```
/// }
///
/// </remarks>
```

The following snippet shows how we can add parameter descriptions and return type descriptions for each HTTP status code:

```
/// <param name="item">item to be created</param>
/// <returns>A newly created TodoItem</returns>
/// <response code="201">Returns the newly created item</response>
/// <response code="400">If the item is null</response>
```

To enable extraction from triple-slash comments, we must enable code documentation creation by adding the following code to our project file (`.csproj`):

```
<PropertyGroup>
<GenerateDocumentationFile>true</GenerateDocumentationFile>
<NoWarn>$(NoWarn);1591</NoWarn>
</PropertyGroup>
```

Then, we must enable code documentation processing from within `services.AddSwaggerGen(c => {...})` by adding the following code:

```
var xmlFile = $"{Assembly.GetExecutingAssembly().GetName().Name}.xml";
var xmlPath = Path.Combine(AppContext.BaseDirectory, xmlFile);
c.IncludeXmlComments(xmlPath);
```

Once our documentation endpoints are ready, we can add some more middleware that is contained in the same `Swashbuckle.AspNetCore` NuGet package to generate a friendly user interface that we can test our REST API on:

```
app.UseSwaggerUI(c =>
{
    c.SwaggerEndpoint("/swagger/<documentation name>/swagger.json", "
    <api name that appears in dropdown>");
});
```

If you have several documentation endpoints, you need to add a `SwaggerEndpoint` call for each of them. We will use this interface to test the REST API defined in the book use case, presented in *Chapter 21, Case Study*. There you will also find out how to use Postman, an API platform for building and using APIs.

Once you have a working JSON documentation endpoint, you can automatically generate the C# or TypeScript code of a proxy class, presented in *Chapter 6, Design Patterns and .NET 8 Implementation*, with one of the following methods:

- The NSwagStudio Windows program, which is available at `https://github.com/RicoSuter/NSwag/wiki/NSwagStudio`.

- The `NSwag.CodeGeneration.CSharp` or `NSwag.CodeGeneration.TypeScriptNuGet` packages if you want to customize code generation.
- The `NSwag.MSBuild` NuGet package if you want to tie code generation to Visual Studio build operations. The documentation for this can be found at `https://github.com/RicoSuter/NSwag/wiki/NSwag.MSBuild`.

In the next subsection, you will learn how to invoke a REST API from another REST API or from a .NET client.

.NET HTTP clients

The `HttpClient` class in the `System.Net.Http` namespace is a .NET Standard 2.0 built-in HTTP client class. While it could be used directly whenever we need to interact with a REST service, there are some problems in creating and releasing `HttpClient` instances repeatedly, as follows:

- Their creation is expensive.
- When an `HttpClient` is released, for instance, in a using statement, the underlying connection is not closed immediately but at the first garbage collection session. Therefore, repeated creation and release operations quickly exhaust the maximum number of connections the operating system can handle.

Therefore, either a single `HttpClient` instance is reused, such as a Singleton, or `HttpClient` instances are somehow pooled. Starting from the 2.1 version of .NET Core, the `HttpClientFactory` class was introduced to pool HTTP clients. More specifically, whenever a new `HttpClient` instance is required for an `HttpClientFactory` object, a new `HttpClient` is created. However, the underlying `HttpClientMessageHandler` instances, which are expensive to create, are pooled until their maximum lifetime expires.

`HttpClientMessageHandler` instances must have a finite duration since they cache DNS resolution information that may change over time. The default lifetime of `HttpClientMessageHandler` is 2 minutes, but it can be redefined by the developer.

Using `HttpClientFactory` allows us to automatically pipeline all the HTTP operations with other operations. For instance, we can add a Polly retry strategy to handle all the failures of all our HTTP operations automatically. For an introduction to Polly, please refer to the *Resilient task execution* subsection of *Chapter 5, Implementing Code Reusability in C# 12*.

The simplest way to exploit the advantages offered by the `HttpClientFactory` class is to add the `Microsoft.Extensions.Http` NuGet package and then follow these steps:

1. Define a proxy class, say, `MyProxy`, to interact with the desired REST service.
2. Let `MyProxy` accept an `HttpClient` instance in its constructor.
3. Use the `HttpClient` that was injected into the constructor to implement all the necessary operations.
4. Declare your proxy in the services configuration method of your host, which, in the case of an ASP.NET Core application, is in the `Program.cs` class. In the simplest case, the declaration is something similar to `builder.Services.AddHttpClient<MyProxy>()`.

This will automatically add `MyProxy` to the services that are available for dependency injection, so you can easily inject it, for instance, in your controller's constructors. Moreover, each time an instance of `MyProxy` is created, an `HttpClient` is returned by an `HttpClientFactory` and is automatically injected into its constructor.

In the constructors of the classes that need to interact with a REST service, we may also need an interface instead of a specific proxy implementation with a declaration of the type:

```
builder.Services.AddHttpClient<IMyProxy, MyProxy>()
```

This way, each client that is passed to the proxy is preconfigured so that it requires a JSON response and must work with a specific service. Once the base address has been defined, each HTTP request needs to specify the relative path of the service method to call.

The following code shows how to perform a `POST` to a service. This requires an extra package, `System.Net.Http.Json`, because of the usage of `PostAsJsonAsync`. Here, we are stating that the `HttpClient` that was injected into the proxy constructor has been stored in the `webClient` private field:

```
//Add a bearer token to authenticate the call
webClient.DefaultRequestHeaders.Add("Authorization", "Bearer " + token);
...
//Call service method with a POST verb and get response
var response = await webClient.PostAsJsonAsync<MyPostModel>("my/method/
relative/path",
    new MyPostModel
    {
        //fill model here
        ...
    });
//extract response status code
var status = response.StatusCode;
...
//extract body content from response
string stringResult = await response.Content.ReadAsStringAsync();
```

If you use Polly, you do not need to intercept and handle communication errors since this job is performed by Polly. First, you need to verify the status code to decide what to do next. Then, you can parse the JSON string contained in the response body to get a .NET instance of a type that, in general, depends on the status code. The code to perform the parsing is based on the `System.Text.Json` NuGet package's `JsonSerializer` class and is as follows:

```
var result =
  JsonSerializer.Deserialize<MyResultClass>(stringResult);
```

Performing a `GET` request is similar, but instead of calling `PostAsJsonAsync`, you need to call `GetAsync`, as shown here. The use of other HTTP verbs is completely analogous:

```
var response =
   await webClient.GetAsync("my/getmethod/relative/path");
```

As you can see from this section, accessing HTTP APIs is quite simple and requires the implementation of some .NET 6 libraries. Since the beginning of .NET Core, Microsoft has been working a lot on improving the performance and simplicity of this part of the framework. It is up to you to keep yourself updated on the documentation and facilities they keep implementing.

Summary

In this chapter, we introduced SOA, its design principles, and its constraints. Among them, interoperability is worth remembering.

Then, we focused on well-established standards for business applications that achieve the interoperability that is needed for publicly exposed services. Therefore, SOAP and REST services were discussed in detail, along with the transition from SOAP services to REST services that has taken place in most application areas in the last few years. Then, REST service principles, authentication/authorization, and documentation were described in greater detail.

Finally, we looked at the tools that are available in .NET 8 that we can use to implement and interact with services. We looked at a variety of frameworks for intra-cluster communication, such as .NET remoting and gRPC, and tools for SOAP- and REST-based public services.

Here, we mainly focused on REST services. Their ASP.NET Core implementations were described in detail, along with the techniques we can use to authenticate/authorize them and their documentation. We also focused on how to implement efficient .NET proxies so that we can interact with REST services.

In the next chapter, we will learn how to use .NET 8 to implement microservices with ASP.NET Core.

Questions

1. Can services use cookie-based sessions?
2. Is it good practice to implement a service with a custom communication protocol? Why or why not?
3. Can a `POST` request to a REST service cause a deletion?
4. How many dot-separated parts are contained in a JWT bearer token?
5. By default, where are the complex type parameters of a REST service's action methods taken from?
6. How is a controller declared as a REST service?
7. What are the main documentation attributes of ASP.NET Core services?
8. How are ASP.NET Core REST service routing rules declared?
9. How should a proxy be declared so that we can take advantage of .NET `HttpClientFactory` class features?

Further reading

- This chapter mainly focused on the more commonly used REST service. If you are interested in SOAP services, a good place to start is the Wikipedia page regarding SOAP specifications: `https://en.wikipedia.org/wiki/List_of_web_service_specifications`. On the other hand, if you are interested in the Microsoft .NET WCF technology for implementing SOAP services, you can refer to WCF's official documentation here: `https://docs.microsoft.com/en-us/dotnet/framework/wcf/`.
- This chapter mentioned the AMQP protocol as an option for intra-cluster communication without describing it. Detailed information on this protocol is available on AMQP's official site: `https://www.amqp.org/`.
- More information on gRPC is available on Google gRPC's official site: `https://grpc.io/`. More information on the Visual Studio gRPC project template can be found here: `https://docs.microsoft.com/en-US/aspnet/core/grpc/`. You may also want to check out gRPC-Web at `https://devblogs.microsoft.com/aspnet/grpc-web-for-net-now-available/`.
- More details on ASP.NET Core services are available in the official documentation: `https://docs.microsoft.com/en-US/aspnet/core/web-api/`. More information on the .NET HTTP client is available here: `https://docs.microsoft.com/en-US/aspnet/core/fundamentals/http-requests`.
- Minimal APIs are described at `https://docs.microsoft.com/en-us/aspnet/core/fundamentals/minimal-apis`.
- More information on JWT authentication is available here: `https://jwt.io/`. If you would like to generate JWTs with IdentityServer, you may refer to its official documentation page: `https://docs.duendesoftware.com/identityserver/v7`.
- More information on OpenAPI is available at `https://swagger.io/docs/specification/about/`, while more information on Swashbuckle can be found on its GitHub repository page: `https://github.com/domaindrivendev/Swashbuckle`.

16

Working with Serverless – Azure Functions

In *Chapter 10, Deciding on the Best Cloud-Based Solution*, we explored the fundamentals and strategic advantages of different cloud architectures and serverless can be considered one of the newest ways to provide flexible cloud-based solutions. We delved into how serverless systems offer scalability, cost-efficiency, and agility – key factors that drive today's software architecture decisions.

Building on that foundation, this chapter delves deeper into a pivotal component of serverless architecture: Azure Functions.

Azure Functions stands out as the component that Microsoft delivers as a prime example of serverless architecture in action. It offers a versatile, event-driven approach that integrates seamlessly with the .NET ecosystem, making it the for architects and developers aiming to build efficient, scalable, and responsive applications.

We will navigate through the intricacies of Azure Functions, emphasizing their application in complex enterprise environments. This chapter will arm you with practical insights into leveraging Azure Functions for robust application architecture, discussing best practices, design patterns, and advanced features specific to the .NET stack.

This chapter provides a comprehensive understanding of Azure Functions, focusing on enhancing your technical mastery of this platform. We delve into the specifics of Azure Functions, covering its setup, programming using C#, and various hosting plans like the Consumption, Premium, and App Service plans. By the end of this chapter, you will have a thorough understanding of Azure Functions, equipped with the knowledge to deploy, maintain, and optimize its functions effectively in your projects.

In this chapter, we will cover the following topics:

- Understanding the Azure Functions app
- Programming Azure Functions using C#
- Maintaining Azure Functions

By the end of this chapter, you will understand how to use Azure Functions in C# to speed up your development cycle.

Technical requirements

This chapter requires that you have the following:

- The free Visual Studio 2022 Community Edition or, even better, with all the Azure tools installed.
- A free Azure account. The *Creating an Azure account* section of *Chapter 1, Understanding the Importance of Software Architecture*, explains how to create one.

Understanding the Azure Functions app

The Azure Functions app is an Azure **PaaS** (**platform as a service**) where you can build pieces of code (functions), connect them to your application, and use triggers to start them. The concept is quite simple – you build a function in the language you prefer and decide on the trigger that will start it. You can write as many functions as you want in your system. There are cases where the system is written entirely with functions.

The steps to create the necessary environment are as simple as the ones we need to follow to create the function itself. The following screenshot shows the parameters that you must decide on when you create the environment. After you select **Create a resource** in Azure and filter by **Function App**, upon clicking the **Create** button, you will see the following screen:

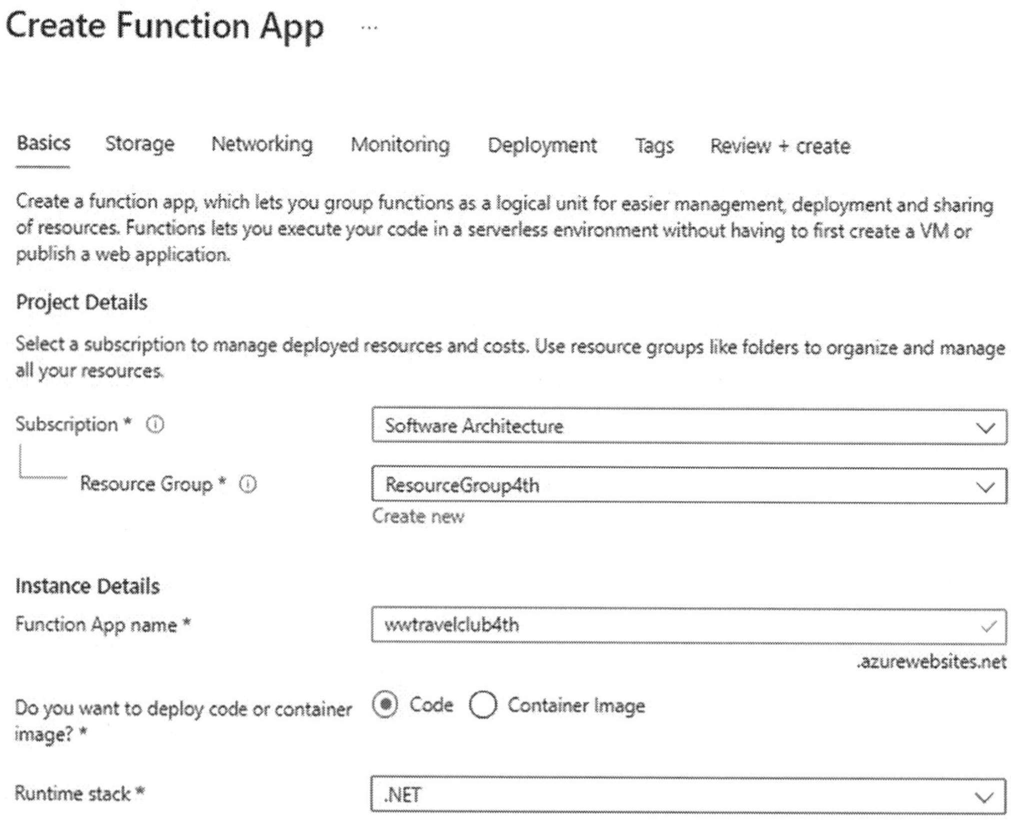

Create Function App ...

Basics Storage Networking Monitoring Deployment Tags Review + create

Create a function app, which lets you group functions as a logical unit for easier management, deployment and sharing of resources. Functions lets you execute your code in a serverless environment without having to first create a VM or publish a web application.

Project Details

Select a subscription to manage deployed resources and costs. Use resource groups like folders to organize and manage all your resources.

Subscription * Software Architecture

Resource Group * ResourceGroup4th

Create new

Instance Details

Function App name * wwtravelclub4th

.azurewebsites.net

Do you want to deploy code or container image? * Code Container Image

Runtime stack * .NET

Figure 16.1: Creating an Azure function app

There are a couple of key points that you should consider while creating your Azure Functions environment. The possibilities given for running functions increase from time to time, as do the programming language options and publishing styles. One of the most important configurations we have is the hosting plan, which is where you will run your functions. There are three options for the hosting plan: a Consumption (Serverless), Premium, and App Service plan. Let's talk about them.

Consumption plan

If you choose a Consumption plan, your functions will only consume resources when they are executed. This means that you will only be charged while your functions are running. Scalability and memory resources will be automatically managed by Azure. This is truly what we call serverless.

Something we need to take note of while writing functions in this plan is the timeout. By default, after 5 minutes, the function will time out. You can change the timeout value using the `functionTimeout` parameter in the `host.json` file. The maximum value is 10 minutes.

When you choose the Consumption plan, how you will be charged will depend on what you are executing, the execution time, and memory usage. More information on this can be found at `https://azure.microsoft.com/en-us/pricing/details/functions/`.

Note that this can be a good option when you do not have app services in your environment, and you are running functions with low periodicity. On the other hand, if you need continuous processing, you may want to consider using a Premium plan or an App Service plan. Let's have a look at them below.

Premium plan

Depending on what you use your functions for, especially if they need to run continuously or almost continuously, or if some function executions take longer than 10 minutes, you may want to consider a Premium plan. Besides, you may need to connect your function to a VNET/VPN environment, and in this case, you will be forced to run in this plan.

You may also need more CPU or memory options than what is provided with the Consumption plan. The Premium plan gives you one-core, two-core, and four-core instance options.

It is worth mentioning that even with unlimited time to run your function if you decide to use an HTTP trigger function, 230 seconds is the maximum allowed for responding to a request. The reason this is a limit is related to the default idle timeout value of Azure Load Balancer.

You may have to redesign your solution in such situations to adhere to the best practices set by Microsoft (`https://docs.microsoft.com/en-us/azure/azure-functions/functions-best-practices`).

Although the Premium plan is a great alternative, if you want to optimize the usage of your App Services instances, the best option is the App Service plan. Let's have a look at it.

The App Service plan

The App Service plan is one of the options you can choose when you want to create an Azure Functions app. Here are a couple of reasons (suggested by Microsoft) why you should use the App Service plan instead of the Consumption plan to maintain your functions:

- You can use underutilized existing App Service instances.
- You can run your function app on a custom image if you want to.

In the App Service plan scenario, the `functionTimeout` value varies according to the Azure Functions runtime version. However, the value needs to be at least 30 minutes.

You can find a tabled comparison between the timeouts in each Consumption plan at `https://docs.microsoft.com/en-us/azure/azure-functions/functions-scale#timeout`.

Now that we have a foundational understanding of the Azure Functions app and its role in serverless architecture, let's explore how to bring these concepts into action. In the following section, we'll dive into programming Azure Functions using C#, turning theoretical knowledge into practical application.

Programming Azure Functions using C#

In this section, you will learn how to create Azure Functions. It is worth mentioning that there are several ways to create them using C#. The first one is by creating the functions and developing them in the Azure portal itself. To do this, let us assume that you have created an Azure Functions app with similar configurations to the ones in the screenshot at the beginning of the chapter.

By selecting the resource created and navigating to the **Functions** menu, you will be able to add new functions to this environment, as you can see in the following screenshot:

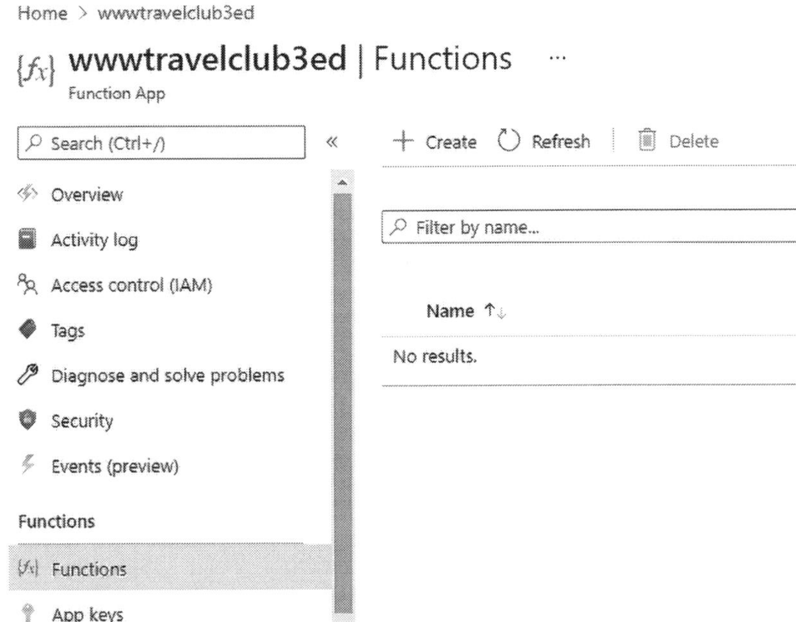

Figure 16.2: Adding a function

Here, you will need to decide the kind of trigger that you want to use to start the execution. The most frequently used ones are the **HTTP trigger** and the **Timer trigger**. The first enables the creation of an HTTP API that will trigger the function. The second means functions will be triggered by a timer you set.

When you decide on the trigger you want to use, you must name the function. Depending on the trigger you decide on, you will have to set up some parameters. For instance, an **HTTP trigger** requires that you set up an authorization level. Three options are available: **Function**, **Anonymous**, and **Admin**. The **Function** option requires a specific key to access each HTTP trigger, while **Anonymous** does not require anything. For the **Admin** option, the key used is the master one, which is created together with the function app.

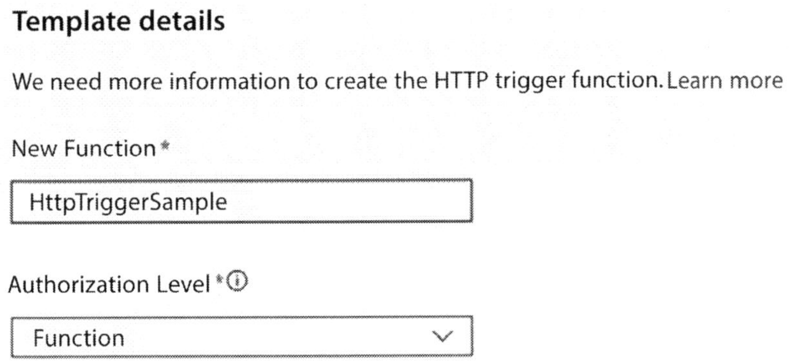

Template details

We need more information to create the HTTP trigger function. Learn more

New Function *

HttpTriggerSample

Authorization Level *

Function

Figure 16.3: Configuring an HTTP function

It is important to note that this book does not cover all the options that are available when it comes to building functions. As a software architect, you should understand that Azure provides a good service for serverless architectures in terms of functions. This can be useful in several situations. This was discussed in more detail in *Chapter 10, Deciding on the Best Cloud-Based Solution.*

The result of this is as follows. Notice that Azure provides an editor that allows us to run the code, check logs, and test the function that we have created. This is a good interface for testing and coding basic functions:

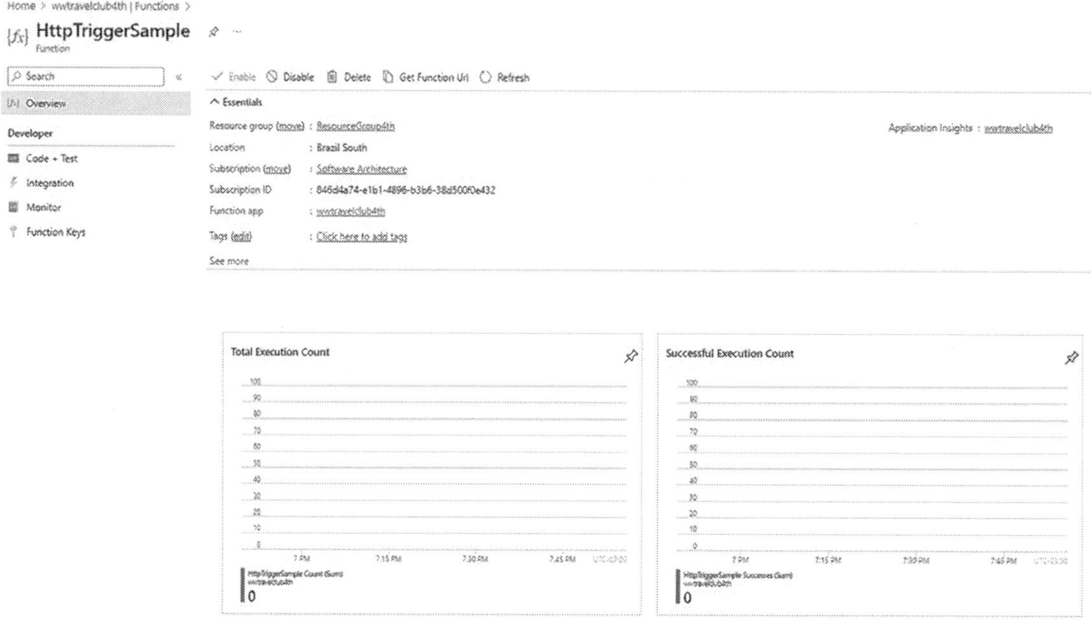

Figure 16.4: HTTP function environment

However, if you want to create more sophisticated functions, you may need a more sophisticated environment so that you can code and debug them more efficaciously. This is where the Visual Studio Azure Functions project can help you. Besides, using Visual Studio to execute the development of the function moves you in the direction of using source control and CI/CD for your functions.

In Visual Studio, you can create a project dedicated to Azure Functions by going to **Create a new project**:

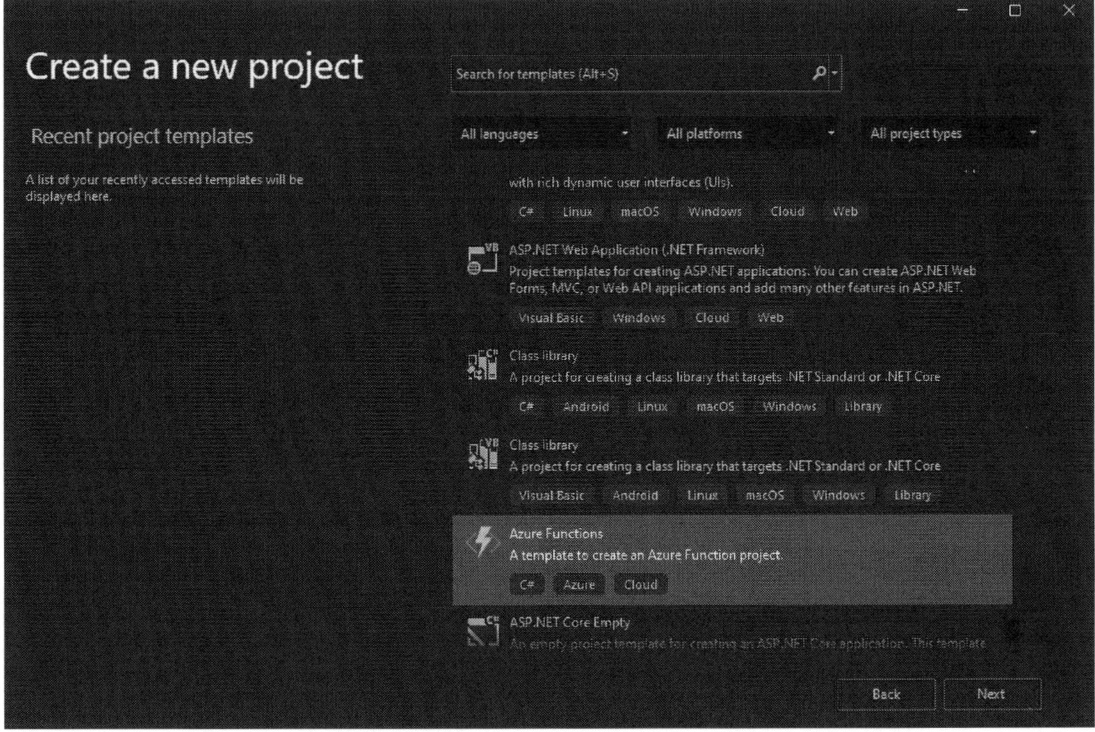

Figure 16.5: Creating an Azure Functions project in Visual Studio 2022

Once you have created your project, Visual Studio will ask you for the type of triggers you are using and for the Azure version that your function will run on. It is worth mentioning that, for some scenarios, a storage account is required while creating the function app, such as managing triggers and logging executions.

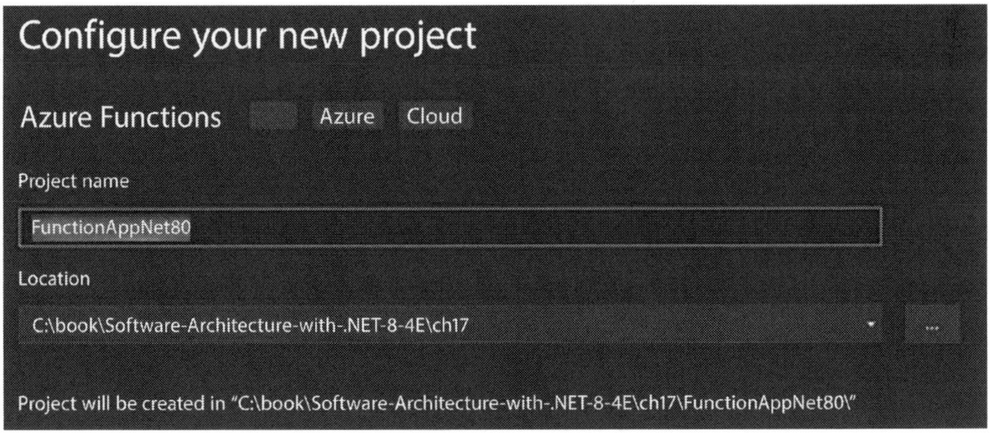

Figure 16.6: Creating a new Azure Functions application

It is worth mentioning that Azure Functions supports different platforms and programming languages. At the time of writing, there are two available runtime versions of Azure Functions with support provided. The first version (v1) is compatible with .NET Framework 4.8. The v2 and v3 versions are not supported anymore, so for .NET 8, you shall use version 4 (v4).

You can always check for up-to-date information about it at `https://learn.microsoft.com/en-us/azure/azure-functions/functions-versions`.

As a software architect, you must keep code reusability in mind. In this case, you should pay attention to which version of Azure Functions you decide to build your functions in. However, it is always recommended that you use the latest version of the runtime as soon as it acquires general availability status.

By default, the code that is generated is similar to that generated when you create Azure Functions in the Azure portal:

```
using System.Net;
using Google.Protobuf.WellKnownTypes;
using Microsoft.AspNetCore.WebUtilities;
using Microsoft.Azure.Functions.Worker;
using Microsoft.Azure.Functions.Worker.Http;
using Microsoft.Extensions.Logging;

namespace FunctionAppSampleIsolated
{
    public class AzureFunctionHttpSampleNet8
    {
        private readonly ILogger _logger;

        public AzureFunctionHttpSampleNet8(ILoggerFactory loggerFactory)
        {
            _logger = loggerFactory.CreateLogger<AzureFunctionHttpSampleNet8>();
        }

        [Function("AzureFunctionHttpSampleNet8")]
        public HttpResponseData Run([HttpTrigger(AuthorizationLevel.Function,
"get", "post")] HttpRequestData req)
        {
            _logger.LogInformation("C# HTTP trigger function processed a
request.");
```

```
            string responseMessage = "This HTTP triggered function executed
successfully. Pass a name in the query string or in the request body for a
personalized response.";

            var queryDictionary = QueryHelpers.ParseQuery(req.Url.Query);

            if (queryDictionary.ContainsKey("name"))
                responseMessage = $"Hello, {queryDictionary["name"]}. This HTTP
triggered function executed successfully.";


            var response = req.CreateResponse(HttpStatusCode.OK);
            response.Headers.Add("Content-Type", "text/plain; charset=utf-8");

            response.WriteString(responseMessage);

            return response;
        }
    }
}
```

Since you have understood the basis for creating Azure Functions using C#, it is also important to understand the number of triggers that are available as templates for Azure Functions. Let's have a look at that.

Listing Azure Functions templates

There are several templates in the Azure portal that you can use to create Azure Functions. The number of templates that you can choose from is updated continuously. The following are just a few of them:

- **Blob Trigger**: You may want to process something for a file as soon as the file is uploaded to your blob storage. This can be a good use case for Azure Functions.
- **Cosmos DB Trigger**: You may want to synchronize data that arrives in a Cosmos DB database with a processing method. Cosmos DB was discussed in detail in *Chapter 12, Choosing Your Data Storage in the Cloud*.
- **Event Grid Trigger**: This is a good way to manage Azure events. Functions can be triggered so that they manage each event.
- **Event Hub Trigger**: With this trigger, you can build functions that are linked to any system that sends data to Azure Event Hubs.
- **HTTP Trigger**: This trigger is useful for building serverless APIs and web app events.

- **IoT Hub Trigger**: When your application is connected to devices using IoT Hub, you can use this trigger whenever a new event is received by one of the devices.
- **Queue Trigger**: You can handle queue processing using a function-as-a-service solution.
- **Service Bus Queue Trigger**: This is another messaging service that can be a trigger for functions. Azure Service Bus was covered in more detail in *Chapter 11, Applying a Microservice Architecture to Your Enterprise Application.*
- **Timer Trigger**: This is commonly used with functions and is where you specify time triggers so that you can continuously process data from your system.

You can find the complete list of triggers and bindings available for Azure Functions at `https://docs.microsoft.com/en-us/azure/azure-functions/functions-triggers-bindings`.

With a solid understanding of how to program Azure Functions in C#, let's now ensure their longevity and performance. In the upcoming section, we will uncover the best practices and tools necessary for the effective management and monitoring of your serverless architecture.

Maintaining Azure Functions

Once you have created and programmed your function, you need to monitor and maintain it. To do this, you can use a variety of tools, all of which you can find in the Azure portal. These tools will help you solve problems due to the amount of information you will be able to collect with them.

The first option when it comes to monitoring your function is using the **Monitor** menu inside the Azure Functions interface in the Azure portal. There, you will be able to check all your function executions, including successful results and failures:

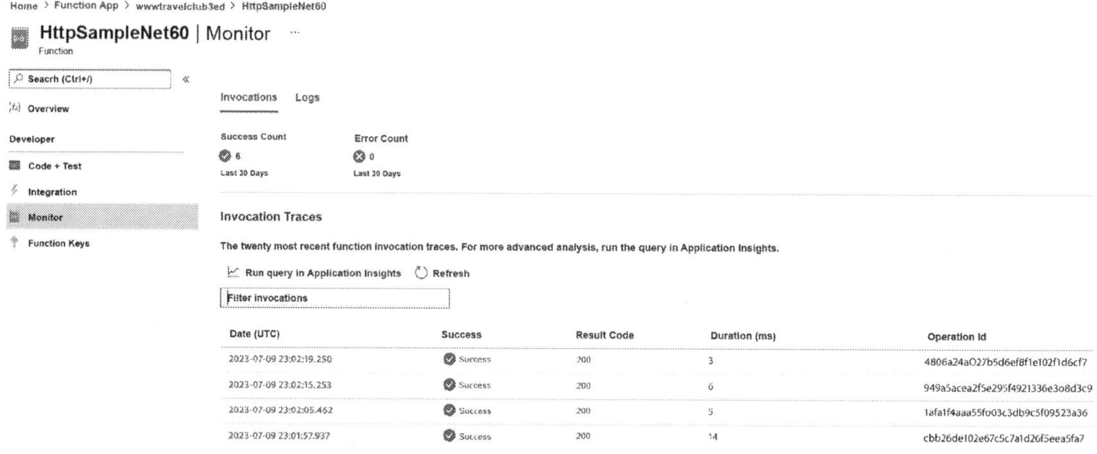

Figure 16.7: Monitoring a function

It will take about 5 minutes for any results to be available. The date shown in the grid is in UTC time.

By clicking on **Run query in Application Insights**, the same interface allows you to connect to this tool. This will take you to a world of almost infinite options that you can use to analyze your function data. Application Insights is an excellent option for **Application Performance Management** (**APM**):

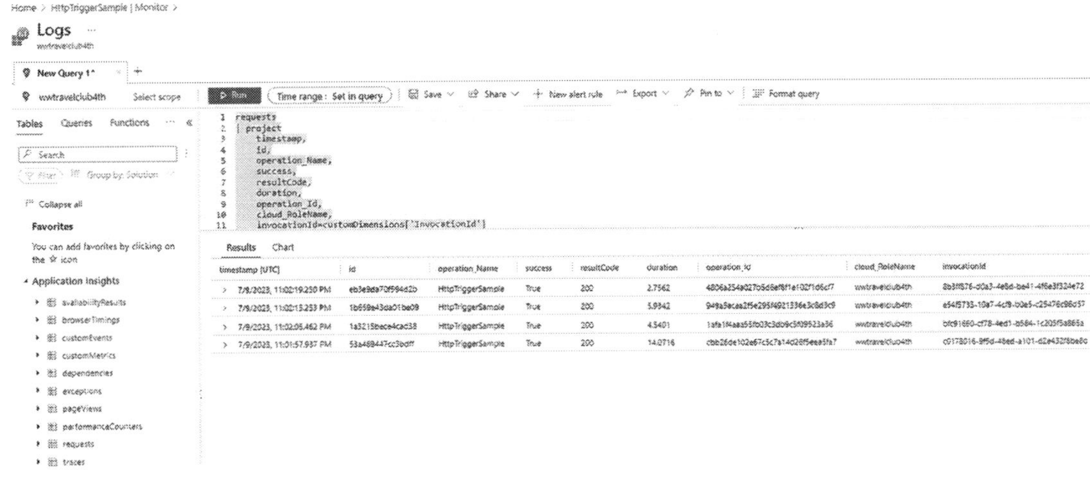

Figure 16.8: Monitoring using Application Insights

Beyond the query interface, you can also check all the performance issues of your function using the Application Insights interface in the Azure portal. There, you can analyze and filter all the requests that have been received by your solution and check their performance and dependencies. You can also trigger alerts when something abnormal happens to one of your endpoints.

You can find this resource in the Azure portal by selecting your function resource and searching for **Application Insights**.

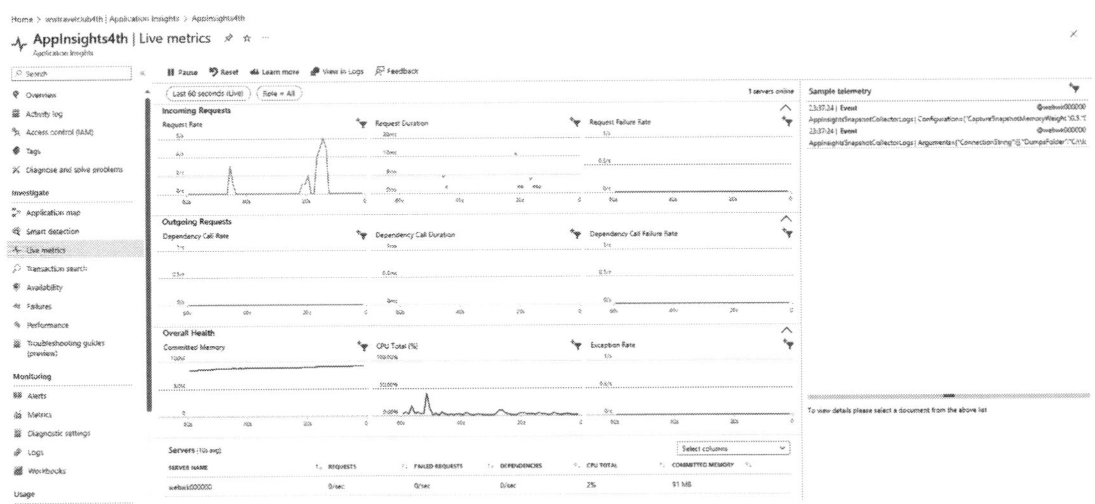

Figure 16.9: Monitoring using Application Insights live metrics

As a software architect, you will find a good daily helper for your projects in this tool. Please remember that Application Insights works on several other Azure services, such as Web Apps and Virtual Machines. This means that you can monitor the health of your system and maintain it using the wonderful features provided by Azure.

Azure Durable Functions

If you decide to delve deeper into the usage of serverless, you may consider Azure Durable Functions as a good option for designing orchestration scenarios. Azure Durable Functions let us write stateful workflows, managing the state behind the scenes. To do so, you will have to write an **orchestrator function**, which is basically a procedure that defines the workflow that you want to run. You may also need some **entity functions** to enable the reading of small pieces of state.

The following are some application patterns where this solution can be used; however, it is important to remember that it is not suitable for all applications:

- **Function chaining:** When you need to execute a sequence of functions in a particular order.
- **Async HTTP APIs:** A good way to solve long-running operations with external clients, where you will have the opportunity to get a status API because of the orchestrator function. There is a sample code of this pattern as soon as you create an orchestrator function in Visual Studio.
- **Fan-out/fan-in:** The ability to run multiple functions in parallel and wait for them to finish to conclude work in an aggregate function.
- **Monitors:** A way to monitor a process without using a timer trigger, enabling configured intervals to monitor many instances of a process.
- **Human interaction:** A way to automate a process even when you need human interaction, but you need to monitor the response after a period.
- **Aggregator:** A way to address event data over a period into a single entity.

When it comes to pricing, we should keep in mind that Azure Durable Functions are billed the same way common Azure Functions are. The only concern you must consider is that orchestrator functions might replay several times throughout the lifetime of an orchestration, and you will be billed for each replay.

Once we have covered the possibilities presented by Azure Durable Functions, it is also important to evaluate the roadmap of Azure Functions. The reason why we keep writing about this arises from the changes Azure Functions has suffered since its creation. Considering that a serverless application based on Azure Functions can be the kernel of your solution, this is a very important topic that needs to be discussed. Let's check it out now.

Azure Functions roadmap

The structure of Azure Functions has changed since it was rolled out in 2016. The number of people using the tool and the changes related to .NET caused some compatibility problems that saw Microsoft come up with a new way of delivering the deployment of functions. This new way is called the isolated process model, and it has been available since .NET 5. It is also important to mention that the currently supported available runtime versions for Azure Functions are v1 and v4.

According to the current roadmap, using the isolated process model is the only way to run Azure Functions in .NET 8 and future versions. There is a plan to have the in-process model for .NET 8, but no date has been confirmed yet.

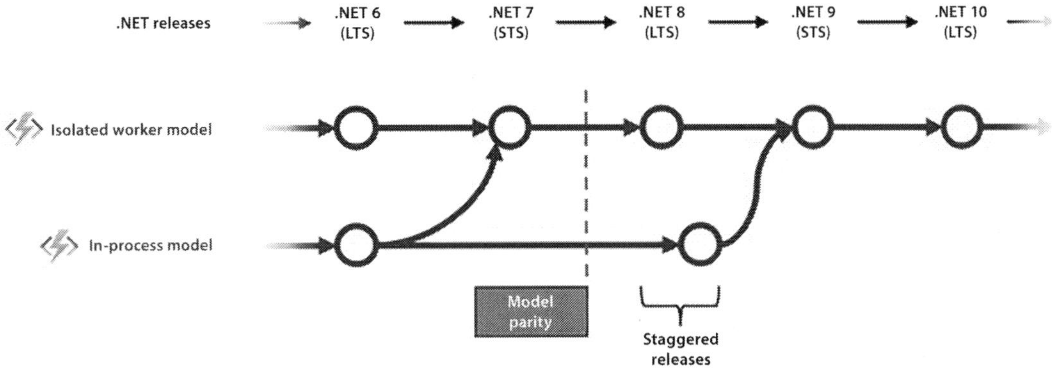
The isolated worker model is reaching parity. We intend for .NET 8 to be the last LTS release to receive in-process model support in Azure Functions.
The in-process option for .NET 8 will trail slightly behind the .NET 8 release.
.NET releases
.NET 6 (LTS)
.NET 7 (STS)
.NET 8 (LTS)
.NET 9 (STS)
.NET 10 (LTS)
Isolated worker model
In-process model
Model parity
Staggered releases

Figure 16.10: Azure Functions roadmap

As a software architect, you must keep an eye on the roadmaps provided so that you can decide on the best implementation for your solution.

When implementing an Azure function using the isolated process model, you will have access to the startup of the function in a `Program.cs` file. This means that you will have to configure and create the instance of your function:

```
var host = new HostBuilder()
.ConfigureFunctionsWorkerDefaults()
.ConfigureServices(services =>
{
    services.AddApplicationInsightsTelemetryWorkerService();
    services.ConfigureFunctionsApplicationInsights();
})
.Build();
```

It is worth mentioning that to do so, you will need `Microsoft.Azure.Functions.Worker.Extensions` packages. You can find a very good guide to doing this at `https://docs.microsoft.com/en-us/azure/azure-functions/dotnet-isolated-process-guide`.

The decision to use serverless and Azure Functions

Even with the benefits presented during this chapter, there is always a question about why one would use a serverless function over having it as part of a bigger web application.

If you think exclusively about HTTP Trigger functions, this question is more difficult to answer because you can create a Web API application that generally solves the problems in this scenario.

However, there are some use cases where an Azure Function is truly the best option. Let's list them to help you with this decision in your scenario:

- **When you need to execute a periodic task:** Azure Functions with *Timer Trigger* is, for sure, a great option. Using Cron expressions, you will be able to set different periods to have your function running. You can check out more details at `https://learn.microsoft.com/en-us/azure/azure-functions/functions-bindings-timer`.
- **When you want to execute a task after some data changes**: By using triggers like *Blob Trigger*, *Queue Trigger*, or *CosmosDB Trigger*, you can monitor data changes and subsequently execute a specific task in response to these changes, which may be useful in some scenarios. There is a great example of how to use it at `https://learn.microsoft.com/en-us/azure/azure-functions/functions-create-cosmos-db-triggered-function`.
- **When you want to execute a task after some event happens on devices or another system:** Again, without needing to pool data, you can use *Event Grid Trigger*, *Event Hub Trigger*, *IoT Hub Trigger*, or *Service Bus Queue Trigger* to track an event and start a task with the information provided by it. You can check out more information about it at `https://learn.microsoft.com/en-us/azure/azure-functions/functions-bindings-event-hubs-trigger`.

To make this decision easier, in *Chapter 21*, *Case Study*, you will find the complete tutorial to implement the architecture presented below.

To give users a great experience, all the emails that are sent by the application will be queued asynchronously, thereby preventing significant delays in the system's responses.

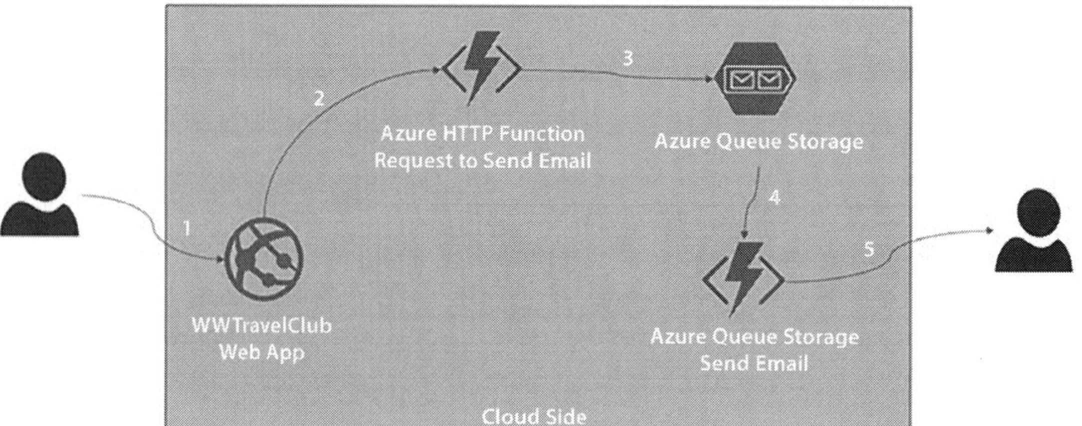

Figure 16.11: Architectural design for sending emails

The great thing about this design is that although you have a solution with different components, you cannot recognize some computational characteristics, like the amount of memory used, the number of CPUs designed for this process, or even the storage needed to guarantee the solution quality. This is what we call serverless in its essential meaning – a solution where the focus is not on where the code runs.

Summary

In this chapter, we looked at some of the advantages of developing functionality with serverless Azure Functions. You can use it as a guideline to check the different types of triggers that are available in Azure Functions and to plan how to monitor them. We also saw how to program and maintain Azure Functions.

In the next chapter, we will discuss the current news related to ASP.NET Core MVC.

Questions

1. What are Azure Functions?
2. What are the programming options for Azure Functions?
3. What are the plans that can be used with Azure Functions?
4. How can you deploy Azure Functions with Visual Studio?
5. What triggers can you use to develop Azure Functions?
6. What is the difference between Azure Functions v1, v2, v3, and v4?
7. How does Application Insights help us to maintain and monitor Azure Functions?
8. What are Azure Durable Functions?

Further reading

If you want to learn more about creating Azure functions, check out the following links:

- Azure Functions scale and hosting: `https://docs.microsoft.com/en-us/azure/azure-functions/functions-scale`
- *Microsoft Azure For .NET Developers [Video], by Trevoir Williams:* `https://www.packtpub.com/product/microsoft-azure-for-net-developers-video/9781835465059`
- *Azure Serverless Computing Cookbook - Third Edition, by Praveen Kumar Sreeram:* `https://www.packtpub.com/product/azure-serverless-computing-cookbook-third-edition/9781800206601`
- Azure Functions runtime overview: `https://docs.microsoft.com/en-us/azure/azure-functions/functions-versions`
- An overview of Azure Event Grid: `https://docs.microsoft.com/en-us/azure/event-grid/`
- Timer trigger for Azure Functions: `https://docs.microsoft.com/en-us/azure/azure-functions/functions-bindings-timer`

- The *Application Insights* section of the book *Azure for Architects*, by Ritesh Modi: `https://subscription.packtpub.com/book/virtualization_and_cloud/9781788397391/12/ch12lvl1sec95/application-insights`
- The *Monitoring Azure Functions using the Application Insights* section of the book *Azure Serverless Computing Cookbook*, by Praveen Kumar Sreeram: `https://subscription.packtpub.com/book/virtualization_and_cloud/9781788390828/6/06lvl1sec34/monitoring-azure-functions-using-application-insights`
- Get started with Azure Queue storage using .NET: `https://docs.microsoft.com/en-us/azure/storage/queues/storage-dotnet-how-to-use-queues`
- Azure Functions triggers and bindings concepts: `https://docs.microsoft.com/en-us/azure/azure-functions/functions-triggers-bindings`
- Azure Queue Storage bindings for Azure Functions: `https://docs.microsoft.com/en-us/azure/azure-functions/functions-bindings-storage-queue`
- Azure emulator for local Azure Storage Development: `https://docs.microsoft.com/en-us/azure/storage/common/storage-use-azurite`
- Azure Durable Functions: `https://docs.microsoft.com/en-us/azure/azure-functions/durable/`

Learn more on Discord

To join the Discord community for this book – where you can share feedback, ask questions to the authors, and learn about new releases – follow the QR code below:

`https://packt.link/SoftwareArchitectureCSharp12Dotnet8`

17

Presenting ASP.NET Core

In this chapter, you will learn how to implement a web application and a web-based presentation layer. More specifically, you will learn about ASP.NET Core and how to implement a web application presentation layer based on ASP.NET Core MVC.

ASP.NET Core is a .NET framework for implementing web applications. The ASP.NET Core Web API was partially described in previous chapters, so this chapter will focus mainly on ASP.NET Core in general and on ASP.NET Core MVC. More specifically, this chapter will cover the following topics:

- Understanding the presentation layers of web applications
- Understanding the basics of ASP.NET Core
- Understanding how ASP.NET Core MVC creates the response HTML
- Understanding the connection between ASP.NET Core MVC and design principles

We will review and provide further details on the structure of the ASP.NET Core framework, which we discussed in part in earlier chapters. Here, the main focus is on how to implement web-based presentation layers based on the so-called **Model View Controller** (**MVC**) architectural pattern.

We will also analyze how server-side HTML is created with ASP.NET Core MVC's **Razor** template language.

Each concept is explained using code examples, and *Chapter 18, Implementing Frontend Microservices with ASP.NET Core*, is dedicated to the description of a frontend microservice implemented with ASP.NET Core MVC. For a complete practical example of how to put into practice the general principles discussed in this and the next chapter, please refer to the *A frontend microservice* section in *Chapter 21, Case Study*.

Technical requirements

This chapter requires the free Visual Studio 2022 Community edition, ideally with all the database tools installed.

Understanding the presentation layers of web applications

This chapter discusses an architecture for implementing the presentation layers of web applications based on the ASP.NET Core framework. The presentation layers of web applications are based on three techniques:

- **Mobile or desktop native applications that exchange data with servers through REST or SOAP services:** We will discuss desktop applications in *Chapter 19, Client Frameworks: Blazor*.
- **Single-Page Applications** (**SPAs**): These are HTML-based applications whose dynamic HTML is created on the client, either in JavaScript or with the help of WebAssembly (a kind of cross-browser assembly that can be used as a high-performance alternative to JavaScript). Like native applications, SPAs exchange data with the server through HTTP-based APIs, but they have the advantage of being independent of the device and its operating system, since they run in a browser. *Chapter 19, Client Frameworks: Blazor*, describes the Blazor SPA framework, which is based on WebAssembly, since it is based itself on a .NET runtime compiled in WebAssembly.
- **HTML pages created by the server whose content depends on the data to be shown to the user:** The ASP.NET Core MVC framework, which will be discussed in this chapter, is a framework for creating such dynamic HTML pages.

The remainder of this chapter focuses on how to create HTML pages on the server side and, more specifically, on ASP.NET Core MVC.

Understanding the basics of ASP.NET Core

ASP.NET Core is based on the concept of the generic host, as explained in the *Using generic hosts* subsection of *Chapter 11, Applying a Microservice Architecture to Your Enterprise Application*. The basic architecture of ASP.NET Core was outlined in the *A short introduction to ASP.NET Core* subsection of *Chapter 15, Applying Service-Oriented Architectures with .NET*.

It is worth remembering that the host configuration consists mainly of adding services to the **Dependency Injection** (**DI**) engine through the `Services` property of a host builder instance, whose type implements the `IServiceCollection` interface:

```
var builder = WebApplication.CreateBuilder(args);
// Add services to the container.
builder.Services.AddTransient<IMyService, MyService>();
...
// Add services to the container through extension methods.
builder.Services.AddControllersWithViews();
builder.Services.AddAllQueries(typeof(ManagePackagesController).Assembly);
...
...
var app = builder.Build();
```

The `IServiceCollection` interface implemented by `builder.Services` defines all the services that can be injected into object constructors through DI.

Services can be defined either by calling the various overloads of `AddTransient` and `AddSingleton` directly in `Program.cs`, or by grouping these calls in some `IServiceCollection` extension methods, which are then called in `Program.cs`. The way services are handled in .NET is explained in detail in the *Using generic hosts* section of *Chapter 11*. Here, it is worth pointing out that, together with singleton and transient services, ASP.NET Core also supports another kind of service lifetime, session lifetime, which is the lifetime of a single web request served by the ASP.NET Core application. Session-scoped services are declared with `AddScoped` overloads that are completely analogous to the overloads of `AddTransient` and `AddSingleton`.

Session-scoped services are useful for storing data that are specific to a single request that must be used throughout the whole request by several application components. A typical example of a .NET session-scoped service is the Entity Framework Core `DBContexts`. In fact, all operations performed on the various aggregates involved in the request must use the same request-specific `DBContext` so that all changes can be saved to the database in a single transaction, with a unique `SaveChanges` operation.

Practical applications of session-scoped `DBContexts` and other services are described in more detail in *Chapter 18, Implementing Frontend Microservices with ASP.NET Core.*

Usually, all applications define most of the application configuration through the host builder so that after the host is built with `var app = builder.Build()`, you need to call `app.Run()` or `await app.RunAsync()` to launch the application.

The ASP.NET Core host instead performs another configuration step after it has been built; it defines the so-called ASP.NET Core HTTP request processing pipeline, which will be described in more detail in the next subsection.

ASP.NET Core middleware

ASP.NET Core contains an internal web server called Kestrel that has just the basic web server functionalities. So in simple applications such as IoT applications, or worker microservices, we can avoid the overhead of a fully optional complex web server like IIS, Apache, or NGINX.

If ASP.NET Core is used to implement the application layer of a frontend microservice/application or a classic website, Kestrel can be interfaced with all major web servers that proxy their request to Kestrel.

In version 8, by default, Kestrel supports all protocols up to and including version HTTP/3.

In turn, Kestrel passes all requests to a set of configurable modules that you can assemble according to your needs. Each module takes care of a functionality that you may or may not need. Examples of such functionalities include authorization, authentication, static file processing, protocol negotiation, and CORS handling. Since most of the modules apply transformations to the incoming request and the final response, these modules are usually referred to as **middleware**.

You can put together all the **middleware** modules you need by inserting them into a common processing framework called the **ASP.NET Core pipeline.**

More specifically, ASP.NET Core requests are processed by pushing a context object through a pipeline of ASP.NET Core modules, as shown in the following diagram:

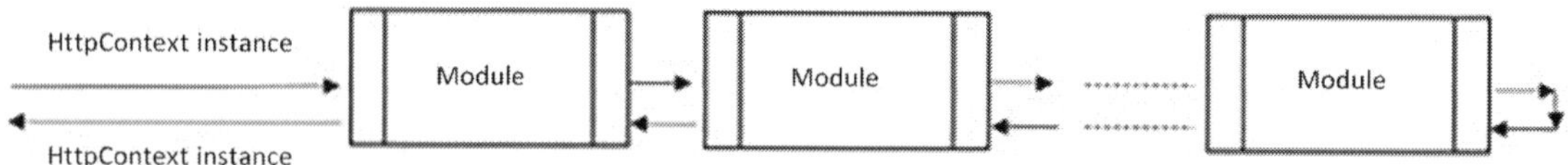

Figure 17.1: ASP.NET Core pipeline

The object that is inserted into the pipeline is an `HttpContext` instance that contains the data of the incoming request. More specifically, the `Request` property of `HttpContext` contains an `HttpRequest` object whose properties represent the incoming request in a structured way. There are properties for headers, cookies, the request path, parameters, form fields, and the request body.

The various modules can contribute to the construction of the final response that is written in an `HttpResponse` object, contained in the `Response` property of the `HttpContext` instance. The `HttpResponse` class is similar to the `HttpRequest` class, but its properties refer to the response being built.

Some modules can build an intermediate data structure that is then used by other modules in the pipeline. In general, such intermediary data can be stored in custom entries of the `IDictionary<object, object>`, which is contained in the `Items` property of the `HttpContext` object. However, there is a predefined property, `User`, that contains information about the currently logged-in user. The logged-in user is not computed automatically, so it must be computed by an authentication module. The *ASP.NET Core service authorization* subsection of *Chapter 15, Applying Service-Oriented Architectures with .NET*, explained how to add the standard module that performs JWT-based authentication into the ASP.NET Core pipeline.

`HttpContext` also has a `Connection` property that contains information on the underlying connection established with the client, as well as a `WebSockets` property that contains information on possible WebSocket-based connections established with the clients.

`HttpContext` also has a `Features` property that contains `IDictionary<Type, object>`, which specifies the features supported by the web server that hosts the web application and by the pipeline. Features can be set using the `.Set<TFeature>(TFeature o)` method and retrieved using the `.Get<TFeature>()` method.

Web server features are automatically added by the framework, while all other features are added by pipeline modules when they process `HttpContext`.

`HttpContext` also gives us access to the DI engine through its `RequestServices` property. You can get an instance of a type managed by the dependency engine by calling the `.RequestServices.GetService(Type t)` method or, even better, the `.GetRequiredService<TService>()` extension method that is built on top of it.

However, as we will see in the remainder of this chapter, all types managed by the DI engine are usually automatically injected into constructors, so these methods are only used when we're building custom **middleware** or other customizations of the ASP.NET Core engine.

The `HttpContext` instance that is created for processing a web request is not only available to modules but also to the application code, through DI. It is sufficient to insert an `IHttpContextAccessor` parameter into the constructor of a class that is automatically dependency injected, and then access its `HttpContext` property. All controllers that inherit from `Controller` or `ControllerBase` (see later in this section) expose an `HttpContext` property that contains the request `HttpContext`.

A middleware module is any class with the following structure:

```
public class CoreMiddleware
{
    private readonly RequestDelegate _next;
    public CoreMiddleware(RequestDelegate next, ILoggerFactory
    loggerFactory)
    {
        ...
        _next = next;
        ...
    }
    public async Task InvokeAsync(HttpContext context)
    {
        /*
            Insert here the module specific code that processes the
            HttpContext instance before it is passed to the next
            module.

        */

        await _next.Invoke(context);
        /*
            Insert here other module specific code that processes the
            HttpContext instance, after all modules that follow this
            module finished their processing.
        */
    }
}
```

It is also possible to pass InvokeAsync directly as a lambda to app.Use, as shown here:

```
app.Use(async (context, next) =>
{
    ...
    await next(context);
});
```

In general, each piece of middleware processes the HttpContext instance that was passed by the previous module in the pipeline, and then it calls await _next.Invoke(context) to invoke the modules in the remainder of the pipeline. When the other modules have finished their processing and the response for the client has been prepared, each module can perform further post-processing of the response in the code that follows the _next.Invoke(context) call.

Modules are registered in the ASP.NET Core pipeline by calling the UseMiddleware<T> method of the built host, as shown here:

```
   var app = builder.Build();
...
    app.UseMiddleware<MyCustomModule>
    ...
    app.Run();
```

Middleware modules are inserted into the pipeline in the same order when UseMiddleware is called. Since each functionality that's added to an application might require several modules and operations other than adding modules, you usually define an IApplicationBuilder extension such as UseMyFunctionality, as shown in the following code:

```
public static class MyMiddlewareExtensions
{
    public static IApplicationBuilder UseMyFunctionality(this
    IApplicationBuilder builder,...)
    {
        //other code
        ...
        builder.UseMiddleware<MyModule1>();
        builder.UseMiddleware<MyModule2>();
        ...
        //Other code
        ...
        return builder;
    }
}
```

After that, the whole functionality can be added to the application by calling `app.UseMyFunctionality(...)`. For instance, the ASP.NET Core MVC functionality can be added to the ASP.NET Core pipeline by calling `app.UseEndpoints(....)`.

Often, functionalities that are added with each `app.Use...` require that some .NET types are added to the application DI engine. In these cases, we also define an `IServiceCollection` extension named `AddMyFunctionality`, which must be called by `builder.Services` in `Program.cs`.

For instance, ASP.NET Core MVC requires a call such as the following:

```
builder.Services.AddControllersWithViews(o =>
{
    //set here MVC options by modifying the o option parameter
}
```

If you don't need to change the default MVC options, you can simply call `builder.Services.AddControllersWithViews()`.

The next subsection describes another important feature of the ASP.NET Core framework – namely, how to handle application configuration data.

Loading configuration data and using it with the options framework

Understanding how ASP.NET Core applications handle configuration is crucial for effective application setup. In the default .NET template where an ASP.NET Core application starts, it reads configuration information (such as a database connection string) from the `appsettings.json` and `appsettings.[EnvironmentName].json` files, where `EnvironmentName` is a string value that depends on where the application is deployed.

Typical values for the `EnvironmentName` string are as follows:

- `Production` is used for production deployment
- `Development` is used during development
- `Staging` is used when the application is tested in staging

The two JSON trees that were extracted from the `appsettings.json` and `appsettings.[EnvironmentName].json` files are merged into a unique tree, where the values contained in `[EnvironmentName].json` override the values contained in the corresponding paths of `appsettings.json`. This way, the application can be run with different configurations in different deployment environments. In particular, you can use a different database connection string and, hence, a different database instance in each different environment.

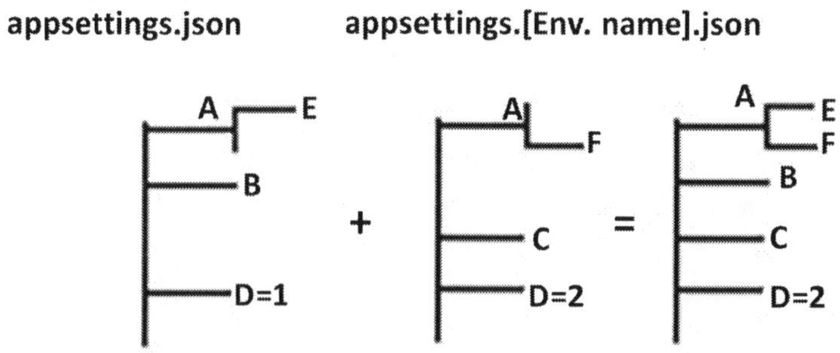

Figure 17.2: Configuration files merging

Configuration information can also be passed from other sources. Given a lack of space, we list here all the other possibilities without discussing them:

- XML files
- `.ini` files
- Operating system environment variables. The variable name is the name of the setting prefixed by the `ASPNETCORE_` string, while the variable value is the setting value.
- Command-line arguments of a `dotnet` command that invokes the application.
- An in-memory collection of key-value pairs

The JSON format is, in my opinion, the most practical and readable, but JSON, XML, and `.ini` are substantially equivalent, and choosing among them is just a matter of preference.

In memory, collections of key-value pairs offer the possibility of taking data from a database, so they are useful options for those parameters that need to be changed by an administrator while the application is running.

Finally, command-line arguments and environment variables are good options when the application can't easily access disk storage – for instance, in the case of deployments running in a Kubernetes cluster. In fact, environment variables can be passed as parameters in the Kubernetes `.yaml` files (see the *ReplicaSets and Deployments* section of *Chapter 20, Kubernetes*). They are also an acceptable choice for passing sensitive data that it is not adequate to store in files in a plain format.

From version 8 onward, ASP.NET Core allows you to set Kestrel HTTP and HTTPS listening ports as configuration variables. More specifically, `HTTP_PORTS` contains a semicolon-separated list of all Kestrel HTTP listening ports, while `HTTPS_PORTS` contains a semicolon-separated list of all HTTPs listening ports whose defaults are the usual HTTP and HTTPs ports, that is, `80` and `443`, respectively.

The `[EnvironmentName]` string itself is taken from the `ENVIRONMENT` configuration setting. Clearly, since it is needed to decide which configuration files to use, it cannot be contained in a configuration file, so it must be taken from the `ASPNETCORE_ENVIRONMENT` operating system environment variable, or from the arguments of the `dotnet` command used to launch the application.

> When the application is deployed to IIS instead of being launched as a standalone program, ASPNETCORE_ENVIRONMENT can't be passed on the dotnet command line.

In this case, it can be set in the IIS application settings. This can be done after the applications have been deployed, by clicking on the Configuration Editor and then selecting the system.webServer/aspNetCore section. In the window that opens, select environmentVariables, and then add the ASPNETCORE_ENVIRONMENT variable with its value.

Collection Editor - system.webServer/aspNetCore/environmentVariables/

Items:

	name	value	Entry Path
environmentVariable	ASPNETCORE_ENVIRONMENT	Staging	

Figure 17.3: Changing ASPNETCORE_ENVIRONMENT in IIS

However, when the application is modified and deployed again, the setting is reset to its default value, which is Production, and it must be set again.

A better choice is to modify the publish profile in Visual Studio, as follows:

1. During Visual Studio deployment, Visual Studio's **Publish** wizard creates an XML publish profile. Once the preferred deployment type (Azure, Web Deploy, folder, and so on) has been chosen, and before publishing, you can edit the publish settings by choosing **Edit** from the **More actions** dropdown in the window that appears.
2. Once you have your publish file properly set, in Visual Studio **Solution Explorer**, open the profile that you just prepared with the Visual Studio wizard. Profiles are saved in the Properties/PublishProfiles/<profile name>.pubxml path of the project folder.
3. Then, edit the profile with a text editor, and add an XML property such as <EnvironmentName>Staging</EnvironmentName>. Since all the already defined publish profiles can be selected during the application's publication, you can define a different publish profile for each of your environments, and then, you can select the one you need during each publication.

The value you must set ASPNETCORE_ENVIRONMENT to during deployment can also be specified in the Visual Studio ASP.NET Core project file (.csproj) of your application, by adding the following code:

```
<PropertyGroup>
    <EnvironmentName>Staging</EnvironmentName>
</PropertyGroup>
```

This is the simplest way to do ASPNETCORE_ENVIRONMENT, but not the most modular, since we are forced to change the application code before publishing to a different environment.

Specifying the environment either in the publish profile or the project file works only for deployment types based on direct communication between Visual Studio and the web server, as in other deployment types, Visual Studio cannot inform the web server on how to set ASPNETCORE_ENVIRONMENT or on how to pass the environment when the application is launched. At the time of writing, the techniques described work just for Web Deploy or when publishing on Azure.

During development in Visual Studio, the value to give to ASPNETCORE_ENVIRONMENT when the application is run can be specified in the Properties\launchSettings.json file of the ASP.NET Core project. The launchSettings.json file contains several named groups of settings. These settings configure how to launch the web application when it is run from Visual Studio. You can choose to apply all the settings of a group by selecting the group name with the drop-down list next to Visual Studio's run button:

Figure 17.4: Choice of launch settings group

Your selection from this drop-down list will be visible on the run button, with the default selection being **IIS Express**.

Consider a development environment setup, as illustrated in this typical launchSettings.json file:

```
{
  "iisSettings": {
    "windowsAuthentication": false,
    "anonymousAuthentication": true,
    "iisExpress": {
      "applicationUrl": "http://localhost:2575",
      "sslPort": 44393
    }
  },
  "profiles": {
    "IIS Express": {
      "commandName": "IISExpress",
      "launchBrowser": true,
      "environmentVariables": {
```

```
            "ASPNETCORE_ENVIRONMENT": "Development"
          }
        },
        ...
        ...
        }
    }
}
```

The named groups of settings are under the `profiles` properties. There, you can choose where to host the application (`IIS Express`), where to launch the browser, and the values of some environment variables.

The current environment that's been loaded from the `ASPNETCORE_ENVIRONMENT` operating system environment variable is available in the `app.Environment` property during the ASP.NET Core pipeline definition.

`app.Environment.IsEnvironment(string environmentName)` checks whether the current value of `ASPNETCORE_ENVIRONMENT` is `environmentName`. There are also specific shortcuts for testing development (`.IsDevelopment()`), production (`.IsProduction()`), and staging (`.IsStaging()`). The `app.Environment` property also contains the current root directory of the ASP.NET Core application (`.WebRootPath`) and the directory reserved for the static files (`.ContentRootPath`) that are served as is by the web server (CSS, JavaScript, images, and so on).

Both `launchSettings.json` and all publish profiles can be accessed as children of the **Properties** node in Visual Studio Explorer, as shown in the following screenshot:

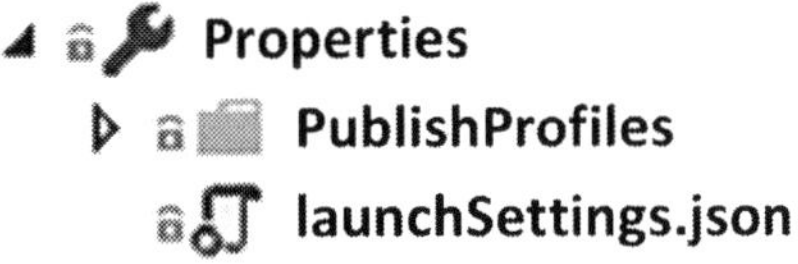

Figure 17.5: Launch settings file

Understanding how to map the merged configuration settings to .NET objects is key for effective data management in ASP.NET Core applications.

Once `appsettings.json` and `appsettings.[EnvironmentName].json` have been loaded, the configuration tree resulting from their merge can be mapped to the properties of .NET objects. For example, let's suppose we have an `Email` section of the `appsettings` file that contains all of the information needed to connect to an email server, as shown here:

```
{
    "ConnectionStrings": {
        "DefaultConnection": "...."
    },
    "Logging": {
```

```
        "LogLevel": {
            "Default": "Warning"
        }
    },
    "Email": {
        "FromName": "MyName",
        "FromAddress": "info@MyDomain.com",
        "LocalDomain": "smtps.MyDomain.com",
        "MailServerAddress": "smtps.MyDomain.com",
        "MailServerPort": "465",
        "UserId": "info@MyDomain.com",
        "UserPassword": "mypassword"
    }
```

Then, the whole `Email` section can be mapped to an instance of the following class:

```
    public class EmailConfig
    {
        public String FromName { get; set; }
        public String FromAddress { get; set; }
        public String LocalDomain { get; set; }
        public String MailServerAddress { get; set; }
        public String MailServerPort { get; set; }
        public String UserId { get; set; }
        public String UserPassword { get; set; }
    }
```

The code that performs the mapping must be inserted in the host building stage, since the `EmailConfig` instance will be available through DI. The code we need is shown here:

```
Var builder = WebApplication.CreateBuilder(args);
....
builder.Services.Configure<EmailConfig>(Configuration.GetSection("Email"));
    ..
```

Once we've configured the preceding settings, classes that need `EmailConfig` data must declare an `IOptions<EmailConfig> options` constructor parameter that will be provided by the DI engine. An `EmailConfig` instance is contained in `options.Value`.

It is worth mentioning that the option classes' properties can be applied to the same validation attributes we will use for ViewModels (see the *Server-side and client-side validation* subsection).

The next subsection describes the basic ASP.NET Core pipeline modules needed by an ASP.NET Core MVC application.

Defining the ASP.NET Core pipeline

Understanding the ASP.NET Core pipeline is key to customizing application behavior. When you create a new ASP.NET Core MVC project in Visual Studio, a standard pipeline is created in the `Program.cs` file. There, if needed, you can add further middleware or change the configuration of the existing middleware.

The initial pipeline definition code handles errors and performs basic HTTPS configuration:

```
if (app.Environment.IsDevelopment())
{




}
else //this is not part of the project template, but it is worth adding it
{
    app.UseDeveloperExceptionPage();
}
app.UseHttpsRedirection();
```

If there are errors, and if the application is in a development environment, the module installed by `UseDeveloperExceptionPage` adds a detailed error report to the response. This module is a valuable debugging tool.

If an error occurs when the application is not in development mode, `UseExceptionHandler` restores the request processing from the path it receives as an argument, that is, from `/Home/Error`. In other words, it simulates a new request with the `/Home/Error` path. This request is pushed into the standard MVC processing until it reaches the endpoint associated with the `/Home/Error` path, where the developer is expected to place the custom code that handles the error.

When the application is not in development, `UseHsts` adds the `Strict-Transport-Security` header to the response, which informs the browser that the application must only be accessed with HTTPS. After this declaration, compliant browsers should automatically convert any HTTP request of the application into an HTTPS request for the time specified in the `Strict-Transport-Security` header. By default, `UseHsts` specifies 30 days as the time in the header, but you can specify a different time and other header parameters by passing `UseHsts` a lambda that configures an `options` object:

```
builder.Services.AddHsts(options =>    {
    ...
    options.MaxAge = TimeSpan.FromDays(60);
    ...
});
```

`UseHttpsRedirection` causes an automatic redirection to an HTTPS URL when an HTTP URL is received, in a way that forces a secure connection. Once the first HTTPS secure connection is established, the `Strict-Transport-Security` header prevents future redirections that might be used to perform man-in-the-middle attacks.

The following code shows the remainder of the default pipeline:

```
app.UseStaticFiles();
// not in the default template but needed in all countries of the European
Union
app.UseCookiePolicy();
app.UseRouting();
app.UseAuthentication();
app.UseAuthorization();
...
```

`UseStaticFiles` makes all files contained in the `wwwroot` folder of the project (typically CSS, JavaScript, images, and font files) accessible from the web through their actual path.

`UseCookiePolicy` has been removed in the .NET 5-8 templates, but you can still add it manually. It ensures that cookies are processed by the ASP.NET Core pipeline, but only if the user has given consent for cookie usage. Consent to cookie usage is given through a consent cookie; that is, cookie processing is enabled only if this consent cookie is found among the request cookies. This cookie must be created by JavaScript when the user clicks a consent button. The whole string that contains both the consent cookie's name and its contents can be retrieved from `HttpContext.Features`, as shown in the following snippet:

```
var consentFeature = context.Features.Get<ITrackingConsentFeature>();
var showBanner = !consentFeature?.CanTrack ?? false;
var cookieString = consentFeature?.CreateConsentCookie();
```

`CanTrack` is `true` only if consent is required and has not been given yet. When the consent cookie is detected, `CanTrack` is set to `false`. This way, `showBanner` is `true` only if consent is required and has not been given yet. Therefore, it tells us whether to ask the user for consent.

The options for the consent module are contained in a `CookiePolicyOptions` instance that must be configured manually with the options framework. The following code snippet shows the default configuration code scaffolded by Visual Studio that configures `CookiePolicyOptions` in the code, instead of using the configuration file:

```
builder.Services.Configure<CookiePolicyOptions>(options =>
{
    options.CheckConsentNeeded = context => true;
});
```

`UseAuthentication` enables authentication schemes and only appears if you select an authentication scheme when the project is created. More specifically, this middleware decodes the authorization tokens (authorization cookies, bearer tokens, etc.), and it uses the information it contains to build a `ClaimsPrincipal` object that is placed in the `HttpContext.User` property.

Specific authentication schemes can be enabled by configuring the options objects in the host building stage, as shown here:

```
builder.Services.AddAuthentication(o =>
{
    o.DefaultScheme =
    CookieAuthenticationDefaults.AuthenticationScheme;
})
.AddCookie(o =>
{
    o.Cookie.Name = "my_cookie";
})
.AddJwtBearer(o =>
{
    ...
});
```

The preceding code specifies a custom authentication cookie name and adds JWT-based authentication for the REST services contained in the application. Both `AddCookie` and `AddJwtBearer` have overloads that accept the name of the authentication scheme before the action, which is where you can define the authentication scheme options. Since the authentication scheme name is necessary for referring to a specific authentication scheme, when it is not specified, a default name is used:

- The standard name contained in `CookieAuthenticationDefaults.AuthenticationScheme` for cookie authentication
- The standard name contained in `JwtBearerDefaults.AuthenticationScheme` for JWT authentication

The name that's passed into `o.DefaultScheme` selects the authentication scheme, used to fill the `User` property of `HttpContext`. Together with `DefaultScheme`, other properties also allow more advanced customizations.

For more information about JWT authentication, please refer to the *ASP.NET Core service authorization* subsection of *Chapter 15, Applying Service-Oriented Architectures with .NET*.

If you just specify `builder.Services.AddAuthentication()`, a cookie-based authentication with default parameters is assumed.

`UseAuthorization` enables authorization based on the `Authorize` attribute. Options can be configured by adding `builder.Services.AddAuthorization` to the host building stage. These options allow you to define the policies for claims-based authorization.

UseRouting and UseEndpoints handle the so-called ASP.NET Core endpoints. An endpoint is an abstraction of a handler that serves specific classes of URLs. These URLs are transformed into an Endpoint instance with patterns. When a pattern matches a URL, an Endpoint instance is created and filled with both the pattern's name and the data that was extracted from the URL. This is a consequence of matching URL parts with named parts of the pattern. This can be seen in the following code snippet:

```
Request path: /UnitedStates/NewYork
Pattern: Name="location", match="/{Country}/{Town}"
Endpoint: DisplayName="Location", Country="UnitedStates", Town="NewYork"
```

UseRouting adds a module that processes the request path to get the request Endpoint instance and adds it to the HttpContext.Features dictionary under the IEndpointFeature type. The actual Endpoint instance is contained in the Endpoint property of IEndpointFeature.

Each pattern also contains the handler that should process all the requests that match the pattern. This handler is passed to Endpoint when it is created.

On the other hand, UseEndpoints adds the middleware that executes the route determined by the UseRouting logic. It is placed at the end of the pipeline, since its middleware produces the final response. Splitting the routing logic into two separate middleware modules enables authorization middleware to sit in between them and, based on the matched endpoint, to decide whether to pass the request to the UseEndpoints middleware for its normal execution, or whether to return a 401 (Unauthorized)/403 (Forbidden) response immediately.

UseAuthorization must always be placed after both UseAuthentication and UseRouting because it needs both the HttpContext.User that is filled by UseAuthentication and the handler selected by UseRouting, in order to verify whether a user is authorized to access the selected request handler.

As the following code snippet shows, patterns are processed in the UseRouting middleware, but they are listed in the UseEndpoints method. While it might appear strange that URL patterns are not defined directly in the middleware that uses them, this was done mainly for coherence with the previous ASP.NET Core versions. In fact, previous versions contained no method analogous to UseRouting and, instead, some unique middleware at the end of the pipeline. In the new version, patterns are still defined at the end of the pipeline for coherence with previous versions, but now, UseEndpoints just creates a data structure containing all patterns when the application starts. Then, this data structure is processed by the UseRouting middleware, as shown in the following code:

```
app.UseRouting();
app.UseAuthentication();
app.UseAuthorization();
app.MapControllerRoute(
    name: "default",
    pattern: "{controller=Home}/{action=Index}/{id?}");
```

Where `app.MapControllerRoute` is a shortcut for:

```
app.UseEndpoints(endpoints =>
{
    endpoints.MapControllerRoute(
        name: "default",
        pattern: "{controller=Home}/{action=Index}/{id?}");


});
```

This shortcut was introduced with the 6.0 version of .NET.

`MapControllerRoute` defines the patterns associated with the MVC engine, which will be described in the next subsection. Other methods define other types of patterns. A call such as `.MapHub<MyHub>("/chat")` maps paths to hubs that handle **SignalR**, an abstraction built on top of `WebSocket`, whereas `.MapHealthChecks("/health")` maps paths to ASP.NET Core components that return application health data.

You can also directly map a pattern to a custom handler with `.MapGet`, which intercepts GET requests, and `.MapPost`, which intercepts POST requests. This is called **route to code**. The following is an example of `MapGet`:

```
MapGet("hello/{country}", context =>
    context.Response.WriteAsync(
    $"Selected country is {context.GetRouteValue("country")}"));
```

We can also write `app.MapGet(...)` directly, since there are shortcuts for `MapGet`, `MapPost`, and so on.

All these shortcuts, together with the new features, have been named **Minimal API**. They offer a lean approach for simpler applications, which is relevant for architects considering performance optimization and API design, particularly in IoT and microservices scenarios.

Moreover, `MapGet`, `MapPost`, and suchlike have been enhanced, and now they have overloads whose lambda returns the result directly to add to the response with no need to call `context.Response.WriteAsync`. If the result isn't a string, it is automatically converted into JSON, and the response `Content-Type` is set to `application/json`. For more complex needs, Minimal APIs can use the static methods of the `Results` class that supports all return types supported by ASP.NET Core controllers. The following is an example of `Results` class usage:

```
app.MapGet("/web-site-conditions", () =>
    Results.File("Contracts/WebSiteConditions.pdf"));
```

Patterns are processed in the order in which they are defined until a matching pattern is found. Since the authentication/authorization middleware is placed after the routing middleware, it can process the `Endpoint` request to verify whether the current user has the required authorizations to execute the `Endpoint` handler.

Otherwise, a 401 (`Unauthorized`) or 403 (`Forbidden`) response is immediately returned. Only requests that survive authentication and authorization have their handlers executed by the `UseEndpoints` middleware.

The Minimal API supports the automatic generation of the OpenAPI metadata we described in *Chapter 15, Applying Service-Oriented Architectures with .NET*. They also support **Ahead-of-Time** (**AOT**) compilation during the application publication. This way, applications are immediately compiled in the target CPU language, saving the time needed by a just-in-time compilation.

Moreover, since AOT runs at publication time, it can perform better code optimizations, and in particular, it can trim DLL unused code. In general, AOT is not supported by controller-based applications since they make greater use of reflection.

Therefore, Minimal APIs are targeted to simple and fast applications, running on small devices such as IoT applications, where, on one hand, speed and reduced application size are fundamental, and on the other hand, the benefit of structuring code through controllers is negligible. We will not describe Minimal APIs in great detail, since this book targets mainly business and enterprise applications.

It is worth mentioning that in the last .NET version, a new **ASP.NET Core API** project was added that scaffolds an application based on the Minimal API.

Like the ASP.NET Core RESTful API described in *Chapter 15*, ASP.NET Core MVC also uses attributes placed on controllers or controller methods to specify authorization rules. However, an instance of `AuthorizeAttribute` can also be added to a pattern to apply its authorization constraints to all the URLs matching that pattern, as shown in the following example:

```
endpoints
  .MapHealthChecks("/health")
  .RequireAuthorization(new AuthorizeAttribute(){ Roles = "admin", });
```

The previous code makes the health check path available only to administrative users.

It is also worth mentioning the `.UseCors()` middleware, which enables the application to handle CORS policies. We will discuss it in the *Communication with the server* section in *Chapter 19, Client Frameworks: Blazor*.

Having described the basic structure of the ASP.NET Core framework, we can now move on to more MVC-specific features. The next subsection describes controllers and explains how they interact with the UI components, known as Views, through ViewModels.

Defining controllers and ViewModels

In ASP.NET Core MVC, controllers and ViewModels are central to handling requests, presenting data, and handling the whole user-application interactions. Let's start by understanding how requests issued at specific paths are passed to controllers.

The various `.MapControllerRoute` calls associate URL patterns with controllers and their methods, where controllers are classes that inherit from the `Microsoft.AspNetCore.Mvc.Controller` class. Controllers are discovered by inspecting all of the application's `.dll` files and are added to the DI engine. This job is performed by the call to `builder.Services.AddControllersWithViews` in the `Program.cs` file.

The pipeline module that's added by `UseEndpoints` takes the controller's name from the `controller` pattern variable, and the name of the controller method to invoke from the `action` pattern variable. Since, by convention, all controller names are expected to end with the `Controller` suffix, the actual controller type name is obtained from the name found in the `controller` variable by adding this suffix. Hence, for instance, if the name found in `controller` is `Home`, then the `UseEndpoints` module tries to get an instance of the `HomeController` type from the DI engine. All of the controller public methods can be selected by the routing rules. The use of a controller public method can be prevented by decorating it with the `[NonAction]` attribute. All controller methods available to the routing rules are called action methods.

MVC controllers work like the API controllers that we described in the *Implementing REST services with ASP.NET Core* subsection in *Chapter 15, Applying Service-Oriented Architectures with .NET*. The only difference is that API controllers are expected to produce JSON or XML, while MVC controllers are expected to produce HTML. For this reason, while API controllers inherit from the `ControllerBase` class, MVC controllers inherit from the `Controller` class, which, in turn, inherits from the `ControllerBase` class and adds its methods, which are useful for HTML generation, such as invoking views, as described in the next subsection, and creating a redirect response.

MVC controllers can also use a routing technique similar to one of the API controllers, that is, routing based on controllers and controller method attributes. This behavior is enabled by calling the `app.MapControllers()` method in the pipeline definition code in `Program.cs`. If this call is placed before all other `app.MapControllerRoute` calls, then the controller routes have priority over `MapControllerRoute` patterns; otherwise, the opposite is true.

`MapControllerRoute` has the advantage of deciding in a single place the whole paths used by the whole application. This way, you can optimize all application paths for a search engine, or simply for better user navigation, by changing a few lines of code in a single place. For these reasons, `MapControllerRoute` is almost always used in MVC applications. However, `MapControllerRoute` is rarely used with the REST API because the priority of the REST API is to avoid changes in the associations between paths and controllers, since they might prevent existing clients from working properly.

All the attributes we have seen for API controllers can also be used with MVC controllers and action methods (`HttpGet`, `HttpPost`, ..., `Authorize`, and so on). Developers can write their own custom attributes by inheriting from the `ActionFilter` class or other derived classes. I will not give details on this right now, but these details can be found in the official documentation, which is referred to in the *Further reading* section.

When the `UseEndpoints` module invokes a controller, all of its constructor parameters are filled by the DI engine, since the controller instance itself is returned by the DI engine, and since DI automatically fills constructor parameters with DI in a recursive fashion.

Action methods take both their input and services from their parameters, so it is crucial to understand how these parameters are filled by ASP.NET Core. They are taken from the following sources:

- Request headers
- Variables in the pattern matched by the current request
- Query string parameters
- Form parameters (in the case of POST requests)
- The request body
- **Dependency injection** (DI), in case of services needed to process the request

While the parameters filled with DI are matched by type, all other parameters are matched by *name* while ignoring the letter casing. That is, the action method parameter name must match the header, query string, form, or pattern variable. In turn, pattern variables are filled by matching the pattern with the request path.

When the parameter is a complex type, the behavior depends on the source.

If the source is the request body, a **formatter** adequate for the request `Content-Type` is selected. **Formatters** are software modules capable of building complex entities, starting from a text representation of them. As a default, the request body is taken as a source for selected `Content-Types`, such as `application/json` and binary MIME types, because each such MIME type requires a different deserialization algorithm that is specific to it.

If the source is not the request body, an algorithm called model binding is used to fill all complex object public properties instead.

The model binding algorithm searches for a match in each property (remember that just properties are mapped; fields are not), using the property name for the match. In the case of nested complex types, a match is searched for each nested property's path, and the name associated with the path is obtained by chaining all the property names in the path and separating them with dots. For instance, a parameter whose name is `Property1.Property2.Property3...Propertyn` is mapped with the `Propertyn` property that is in the following path of nested object properties: `Property1`, `Property2`, ..., `Propertyn`.

The name that's obtained this way must match a header name, pattern variable name, query string parameter name, and so on. For instance, an `OfficeAddress` property containing a complex `Address` object would generate names like `OfficeAddress.Country` and `OfficeAddress.Town`.

The model binding algorithm can also fill collections and dictionaries, but due to a lack of space, we can't describe these cases. However, the *Further reading* section contains a link to an excellent Phil Haack post that explains them in detail.

By default, simple type parameters are matched with pattern variables and query string variables, while complex type parameters are matched with form parameters or the request body (depending on their MIME types). However, the preceding defaults can be changed by prefixing the parameters with attributes, as detailed here:

- `[FromForm]` forces a match with form parameters
- `[FromBody]` forces the extraction of data from the request body

- `[FromHeader]` forces a match with a request header
- `[FromRoute]` forces a match with pattern variables
- `[FromQuery]` forces a match with a query string variable
- `[FromServices]` forces the use of DI

It is worth pointing out that versions 7 and 8 of ASP.NET Core have an enhanced Minimal API to support basically the same parameter bindings of a controller's action methods, as well as all the above parameter attributes.

During the match, the string that was extracted from the selected source is converted into the type of the action method parameter, using the current thread culture. If either a conversion fails or no match is found for an obligatory action method parameter, then the whole action method invocation process fails, and a 404 response is automatically returned. For instance, in the following example, the `id` parameter is matched with query string parameters or pattern variables, since it is a simple type, while `myclass` properties and nested properties are matched with form parameters, since `MyClass` is a complex type. Finally, `myservice` is taken from DI, since it is prefixed with the `[FromServices]` attribute:

```
public class HomeController : Controller
{
    public IActionResult MyMethod(
        int id,
        MyClass myclass,
        [FromServices] MyService myservice)
    {
        ...
```

If no match is found for the `id` parameter, and if the `id` parameter is declared as obligatory in the `MapControllerRoute` pattern, a 404 response is automatically returned, since pattern matching fails. It is common to declare parameters as not optional when they must match not-nullable single types. If, instead, no `MyService` instance is found in the DI container, an exception is thrown because, in this case, the failure doesn't depend on a wrong request but on a design error.

MVC controllers return an `IActionResult` interface or a `Task<IActionResult>` result if they are declared as `async`. `IActionResult` defines the unique method with the `ExecuteResultAsync(ActionContext)` signature, which, when invoked by the framework, produces the actual response.

For each different `IActionResult`, MVC controllers have methods that return them. The most commonly used `IActionResult` is `ViewResult`, which is returned by a `View` method:

```
public IActionResult MyMethod(...)
{
   ...
   return View("myviewName", MyViewModel)
}
```

`ViewResult` is a very common way for a controller to create an HTML response. More specifically, the controller interacts with business/data layers to produce an abstraction of the data that will be shown on the HTML page. This abstraction is an object called a **ViewModel**. The ViewModel is passed as a second argument to the `View` method, while the first argument is the name of an HTML template, called `View`, that is instantiated with the data contained in the ViewModel.

Summing this up, the MVC controllers' processing sequence is as follows:

1. The controllers perform some processing to create the ViewModel, which is an abstraction of the data to show on the HTML page.
2. Then, the controllers create `ViewResult` by passing a View name and ViewModel to the `View` method.
3. The MVC framework invokes `ViewResult` and causes the template contained in the View to be instantiated with the data contained in the ViewModel.
4. The result of the template's instantiation is written in the response with adequate headers.

This way, the controller performs the conceptual job of HTML generation by building a ViewModel, while the View – that is, the template – takes care of all the presentation details.

Views will be described in greater detail in the next subsection, while the Model (ViewModel) View Controller pattern will be discussed in more detail in the *Understanding the connection between ASP.NET Core MVC and design principles* section in this chapter. Finally, a practical example will be provided in *Chapter 18, Implementing Frontend Microservices with ASP.NET Core.*

Another common `IActionResult` is `RedirectResult`, which creates a redirect response, hence forcing the browser to move to a specific URL. Redirects are often used once the user has successfully submitted a form that completes a previous operation. In this case, it is common to redirect the user to a page where they can select another operation.

The simplest way to return `RedirectResult` is by passing a URL to the `Redirect` method. This is the advised way to perform a redirect to a URL that is outside the web application. On the other hand, when the URL is within the web application, it is advisable to use the `RedirectToAction` method, which accepts the controller's name, the action method name, and the desired parameters for the target action method. This method has several overloads, where each overload omits some of the above parameters. In particular, the controller name can be omitted if the URL we define is handled by the same controller.

The framework uses this data to compute a URL that causes the desired action method to be invoked with the parameters provided. This way, if the routing rules are changed during the application's development or maintenance, the new URL is automatically updated by the framework, with no need to modify all occurrences of the old URL in the code.

The following code shows how to call `RedirectToAction`:

```
return RedirectToAction("MyActionName", "MyControllerName",
        new {par1Name=par1Value,..parNName=parNValue});
```

Another useful `IActionResult` is `ContentResult`, which can be created by calling the `Content` method. `ContentResult` allows you to write any string to the response and specify its MIME type, as shown in the following example:

```
return Content("this is plain text", "text/plain");
```

Finally, the `File` method returns `FileResult`, which writes binary data in the response. There are several overloads of this method that allow the specification of a byte array, a stream, or the path of a file, plus the MIME type of the binary data.

Now, let's move on to describing how actual HTML is generated in Views.

Understanding how ASP.NET Core MVC creates the response HTML

Razor Views

ASP.NET Core MVC uses a language called Razor to define the HTML templates contained in the Views. Razor views are files that are compiled into .NET classes when they're first used, when the application has been built, or when the application has been published. By default, both pre compilation on each build and on publish are enabled, but you can also enable runtime compilation so that the Views can be modified once they have been deployed. This option can be enabled by checking the **Enable Razor runtime compilation** checkbox when the project is created in Visual Studio. You can also disable compilation on each build and on publish by adding the following code to the web application project file:

```
<PropertyGroup>
  <TargetFramework> net8.0 </TargetFramework>
  <!-- add code below -->
  <RazorCompileOnBuild>false</RazorCompileOnBuild>
  <RazorCompileOnPublish>false</RazorCompileOnPublish>
  <!-- end of code to add -->
    ...
</PropertyGroup>
```

Views can also be precompiled into Views libraries if you choose a Razor view library project in the window, which appears once you have chosen an ASP.NET Core project.

Also, following the compilation, Views remain associated with their paths, which become their full names. Each controller has an associated folder under the **Views** folder with the same name as the controller, which is expected to contain all the Views used by that controller.

The following screenshot shows the folder associated with a possible `HomeController` and its Views:

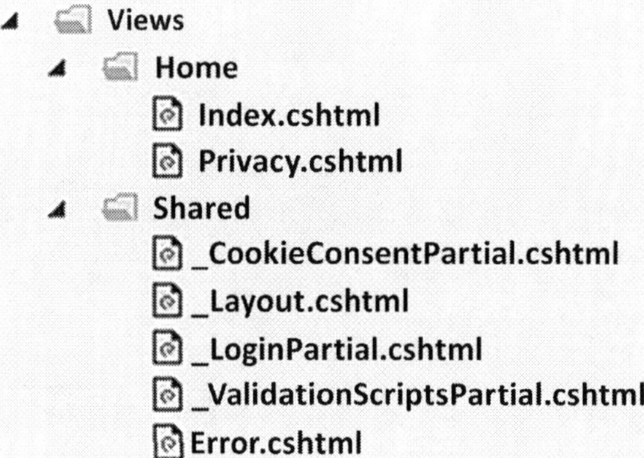

Figure 17.6: View folders associated with controllers and the shared folder

The preceding screenshot also shows the **Shared** folder, which is expected to contain all the Views or partial views used by several controllers. The controller refers to views in the `View` method through their paths without the `.cshtml` extension. If the path starts with `/`, the path is interpreted as relative to the application root. Otherwise, as a first attempt, the path is interpreted as relative to the folder associated with the controller. If no View is found there, the View is searched for in the **Shared** folder.

Hence, for instance, the `Privacy.cshtml` View file in the preceding screenshot can be referred to from within `HomeController` as `View("Privacy", MyViewModel)`. If the name of the View is the same as the name of the action method, we can simply write `View(MyViewModel)`.

Razor views are a mix of HTML code with C# code, plus some Razor-specific statements. They usually begin with a header that contains the type of ViewModel that the View is expected to receive:

```
@model MyViewModel
```

This declaration may be omitted, but in this case, the view will not be specific to a specific type, and we will not be able to use the model property names in the Razor code.

Each view may also contain some `using` statements, whose effect is the same as the `using` statements of standard code files:

```
@model MyViewModel
@using MyApplication.Models
```

`@using` statements declared in the special `_ViewImports.cshtml` file – that is, in the root of the `Views` folder – are automatically applied to all views.

Each view can also require instances of types from the DI engine in its header, with the syntax shown here:

```
@model MyViewModel
@using MyApplication.Models
@inject IViewLocalizer Localizer
```

The preceding code requires an instance of the `IViewLocalizer` interface and places it in the `Localizer` variable. The remainder of the View is a mix of C# code, HTML, and Razor control flow statements. Each area of a view can be either in HTML mode or C# mode. The code in a View area that is in HTML mode is interpreted as HTML, while the code in a View area that is in C# mode is interpreted as C#.

The topic that follows explains the Razor flow of control statements.

Learning the Razor flow of control statements

If you want to write some C# code in an HTML area, you can create a C# area with the `@{..}` Razor flow of a control statement, as shown here:

```
@{
    //place C# code here
    var myVar = 5;
    ...
    <div>
        <!-- here you are in HTML mode again -->
        ...
    </div>
    //after the HTML block you are still in C# mode
    var x = "my string";
}
```

The preceding example shows that it is enough to write an HTML tag to create an HTML area inside the C# area and so on recursively. As soon as the HTML tag closes, you are in C# mode again.

If we need to create an HTML area but don't want to enclose it in an HTML tag, we can use the fake `<text>` tag provided by Razor syntax:

```
<text>
<!-- here you entered HTML mode without adding an enclosing
    HTML tag -->
       ...
</text>
```

C# code produces no HTML, while HTML code is added to the response in the same order in which it appears. You can add text computed with C# code while in HTML mode by prefixing any C# expression with `@`. If the expression is complex, in that it is composed of a chain of properties and method calls, it must be enclosed by parentheses. The following code shows some examples:

```
<span>Current date is: </span>
<span>@DateTime.Today.ToString("d")</span>
...
<p>
  User name is: @($"{myName} {mySurname}")
```

```
</p>
...
<input type="submit" value="@myUserMessage" />
```

The @ itself can be escaped by entering it twice – @@.

Types are converted into strings using the current culture settings (see the *Understanding the connection between ASP.NET Core MVC and design principles* section for details on how to set the culture of each request). Moreover, strings are automatically HTML-encoded to avoid the < and > symbols, which might interfere with the view HTML.

HTML encoding can be prevented with the `@HTML.Raw` function, as shown here:

```
@HTML.Raw(myDynamicHtml)
```

In an HTML area, alternative HTML can be selected with the `@if` Razor statement:

```
@if(myUser.IsRegistered)
{
    //this is a C# code area
    var x=5;
    ...
    <p>
     <!-- This is an HTML area -->
    </p>
    //this is a C# code area again
}
else if(myUser.IsNew)
{
    ...
}
else
{
  ..
}
```

As shown in the preceding code, the beginning of each block of a Razor control flow statement is in C# mode and remains so until the first HTML open tag is encountered, and then, HTML mode starts. C# mode is resumed after the corresponding HTML close tag.

An HTML template can be instantiated several times with the `for`, `foreach`, `while`, and `do` Razor statements, as shown in the following examples:

```
@for(int i=0; i< 10; i++)
{
}
```

```
@foreach(var x in myIEnumerable)
{
}
@while(true)
{


}
@do
{


}
while(true)
```

Razor views can contain comments that do not generate any code. Any text included within `@*...*@` is considered a comment and removed when the page is compiled. With a good understanding of controllers and their operational mechanics, let's now turn to how ASP.NET Core MVC generates HTML responses using Razor views.

Understanding Razor view properties

Some standard variables are predefined in each view. The most important variable is `Model`, which contains the ViewModel that was passed to the view. For instance, if we pass a `Person` model to a view, then `<span>@Model.Name</span>` displays the name of the `Person` model that was passed to the view.

The `ViewData` variable contains `IDictionary<string, object>`, which is shared with the controller that invoked the view; that is, all controllers also have a `ViewData` property containing `IDictionary<string, object>`, and every entry that is set in the controller is also available in the `ViewData` variable of the invoked view. `ViewData` is an alternative to the ViewModel for a controller, allowing the passing of information to its invoked view. It is worth mentioning that the `ViewData` dictionary can also be accessed as a dynamic object through the `ViewBag` property. This means that dynamic `ViewBag` properties are mapped to `ViewData` string indices and that their values are mapped to the `ViewData` entries corresponding to those indices. Using `ViewData` or `ViewBag` is just a matter of preference; neither one has an advantage over the other.

Often, `ViewData` is used to store collateral data such as the value-string pairs used to populate an HTML Select. For instance, let's suppose the ViewModel model contains `TownId` and `TownName` properties that the user can change, by selecting a different town from an HTML Select. In this case, the action method might fill the `"AllTowns"` entry of `ViewData` with all possible town ID and town name pairs:

```
ViewData[=["AllTowns"]= await townsRepo.GetAll();
...
return View(new AddressViewModel{...});
```

Both controllers and Views also contain a `TempData` dictionary, whose entries are remembered between two successive requests. Due to a lack of space, we can't discuss its properties and its usage, but the interested among you can refer to the official Microsoft documentation:

`https://learn.microsoft.com/en-us/aspnet/core/fundamentals/app-state?view=aspnetcore-8.0#tempdata`

The `User` view variable contains the currently logged-in user, that is, the same instance contained in the current request's `Http.Context.User` property. The `Url` variable contains an instance of the `IUrlHelper` interface, whose methods are utilities for computing the URLs of application pages. For instance, `Url.Action("action", "controller", new {par1=valueOfPar1,...})` computes the URL that causes the action method, `action`, of `controller` to be invoked, with all the parameters specified in the anonymous object passed as its parameters.

The `Context` variable contains the whole request's `HttpContext`. The `ViewContext` variable contains data about the context of the view invocation, including metadata about the action method that invoked the view.

The next topic describes how Razor views enhance HTML tag syntax.

Using Razor tag helpers

Tag helpers in ASP.NET Core MVC are powerful tools for enhancing HTML tags with additional functionalities. More specifically, a tag helper either enhances existing HTML tags with new tag attributes or defines completely new tags.

While Razor views are compiled, any tag is matched against existing tag helpers. When a match is found, the source tag is replaced with HTML created by the tag helpers. Several tag helpers may be defined for the same tag. They are all executed in an order that can be configured with a priority attribute associated with each tag helper.

All tag helpers defined for the same tag may cooperate while each tag instance is being processed. This is because they are passed a shared data structure where each of them may apply a contribution. Usually, the final tag helper that is invoked processes this shared data structure to produce the output HTML.

Tag helpers are classes that inherit from the `TagHelper` class. This topic doesn't discuss how to create new tag helpers, but it does introduce the main predefined tag helpers that come with ASP.NET Core MVC. A complete guide on how to define tag helpers is available in the official documentation, which is referenced in the *Further reading* section.

To use a tag helper, you must declare the `.dll` file that contains the tag helper with a declaration like the following:

```
@addTagHelper *, Dll.Complete.Name
```

If you would like to use just one of the tag helpers defined in the `.dll` file, you must replace * with the tag name.

The preceding declaration can be placed either in each view that uses the tag helpers defined in the library or, ultimately, in the `_ViewImports.cshtml` file in the root of the `Views` folder. By default, `_ViewImports.cshtml` adds all predefined ASP.NET Core MVC tag helpers with the following declaration:

```
@addTagHelper *, Microsoft.AspNetCore.Mvc.TagHelpers
```

The anchor tag is enhanced with attributes that automatically compute the URL and invoke a specific action method with given parameters, as shown here:

```
<a asp-controller="{controller name}"
asp-action="{action method name}"
asp-route-{action method parameter1}="value1"
...
asp-route-{action method parametern}="valuen">
    put anchor text here
</a>
```

Below is an example of its usage:

```
<a asp-controller="Home" asp-action="Index">
  Back Home
</a>
```

The HTML created is:

```
<a href="Home/Index">
  Back Home
</a>
```

It might appear that there is almost no advantage in using the tag helper. However, this isn't true! The advantage is that whenever the routing rules change, the tag helper automatically updates the `href` that it generates to conform to the new routing rules.

A similar syntax is added to the `form` tags:

```
<form asp-controller="{controller name}"
asp-action="{action method name}"
asp-route-{action method parameter1}="value1"
...
asp-route-{action method parametern}="valuen"
...
>
...
```

The `script` tag is enhanced with attributes that allow us to fall back to a different source if the download fails. Typical usage is to download scripts from some cloud service to optimize the browser cache and to fall back to a local copy of the script if there is a failure. The following code uses the fallback technique to download the `bootstrap` JavaScript file:

```
<script src="https://stackpath.bootstrapcdn.com/
 bootstrap/4.3.1/js/bootstrap.bundle.min.js"
 asp-fallback-src="~/lib/bootstrap/dist/js/bootstrap.bundle.min.js"
 asp-fallback-test="window.jQuery && window.jQuery.fn && window.jQuery.
fn.modal"
 crossorigin="anonymous"
 integrity="sha384-xrRywqdh3PHs8keKZN+8zzc5TX0GRTLCcmivcbNJWm2rs5C8PRhcEn3czEjh
AO9o">
</script>
```

`asp-fallback-test` contains a JavaScript test that verifies whether the download succeeded. In the preceding example, the test verifies whether a JavaScript object has been created.

All HTML tags that admit an `src` attribute, that is, the `img` and the script tags, can be added as an `asp-append-version` attribute set to `true`. The `asp-append-version` attribute set to `true` doesn't change the syntax of the `img` and `script` tags; it just adds a hash to the `src` query string to prevent cashing each time the image or `script` file changes. Here is an example:

```
<img src="~/images/myImage.png" asp-append-version="true">
```

Which is rendered as:

```
<img src="/images/myImage.png?v=kM_dqr9NVtnMdsM2MUgdskVVFD">
```

The hash passed in the v query parameter is computed from the content of the image file, so it changes whenever the image changes, thereby preventing the browser from rendering an old cached copy of the image.

The ~/ symbol is not a feature specific to the `img` tag helper and, instead, a Razor native feature you can use in all links contained in any tag of a Razor file. It stands for the application root. It is not equivalent to the HTML / symbol that stands for the root of the domain, because ASP.NET Core applications can also be placed in subfolders of the domain. So ~/ translates as / only when the application is placed in the domain root; otherwise, it translates as `/{application subfolder name}/`.

The `environment` tag can be used to select different HTML for different environments (development, staging, and production). Its typical usage is selecting the debug versions of JavaScript files during development, as shown in this example:

```
<environment include="Development">
        @*development version of JavaScript files*@
</environment>
<environment exclude="Development">
```

```
        @*development version of JavaScript files *@
</environment>
```

There is also a cache tag, which caches its content in memory to optimize rendering speed:

```
<cache>
    @* heavy to compute content to cache *@
</cache>
```

By default, content is cached for 20 minutes, but the tag has attributes that must be defined when the cache expires, such as `expires-on="{datetime}"`, `expires-after="{timespan}"`, and `expires-sliding="{timespan}"`. Here, the difference between `expires-sliding` and `expires-after` is that, in the second attribute, the expiration time count is reset each time the content is requested. The `vary-by` attribute causes the creation of a different cache entry for each different value passed to `vary-by`. There are also attributes such as `vary-by-header`, which creates a different entry for each different value assumed by the request header specified in the `vary-by-cookie` attribute, and so on.

All `input` tags – that is, `textarea`, `input`, and `select` – have an `asp-for` attribute that accepts a properties path rooted in the view's ViewModel as their value. For instance, if the view has a `Person` ViewModel, we may have something like this:

```
<input type="text" asp-for"Address.Town"/>
```

The first thing the preceding code does is assign the value of the `Town` nested property to the `value` attribute of the `input` tag. In general, if the value is not a string, it is converted into a string using the current request culture.

However, it also sets the name of the input field to `Address.Town` and the `id` of the input field to `Address_Town`. This is because dots are not allowed in tag `ids`.

A prefix can be added to these standard names by specifying it in `ViewData.TemplateInfo.HtmlFieldPrefix`. For instance, if the previous property is set to `MyPerson`, the name becomes `MyPerson.Address.Town`.

If the form is submitted to an action method that has the same `Person` class as one of its parameters, the name of `Address.Town` that's given to the `input` field will cause the `Town` property of this parameter to be filled with the `input` field. In general, the string contained in the `input` field is converted into the type of property it has been matched with, using the current request culture. Summing this up, the names of `input` fields are created in such a way that a complete `Person` model can be recovered in the action method when the HTML page is posted.

The same `asp-for` attribute can be used in a `label` tag to cause the label to refer to the input field with the same `asp-for` value.

The following code is an example of an `input/label` pair:

```
<label asp-for="Address.Town"></label
<input type="text" asp-for="Address.Town"/>
```

When no text is inserted into the label, the text shown in the label is taken from a `Display` attribute that decorates the property (`Town`, in this example), if any; otherwise, the name of the property is used.

If `span` or `div` contains an `asp-validation-for="Address.Town"` error attribute, then validation messages concerning the `Address.Town` input will be inserted automatically inside that tag. The validation framework will be described in the *Understanding the connection between ASP.NET Core MVC and design principles* section.

It is also possible to automatically create a validation error summary by adding the attribute that follows a `div` or a `span`:

```
asp-validation-summary="ValidationSummary.{All, ModelOnly}"
```

If the attribute is set to `ValidationSummary.ModelOnly`, only messages that are not associated with specific `input` fields will be shown in the summary, while if the value is `ValidationSummary.All`, all error messages will be shown.

The `asp-items` attribute can be applied to any `select` tag to automatically generate all the `select` options. It must be passed an `IEnumerable<SelectListItem>`, where each `SelectListItem` contains both the text and value of an option. `SelectListItem` also contains an optional `Group` property that you can use to organize the options shown in `select` into groups.

Here is an example of how to use `asp-items`:

```
...
@{
  var choices = new List<SelectListItem>
  {
    new SelectListItem {Value="value1", Text="text1", Group="group1"},
    new SelectListItem {Value="value2", Text="text2", Group="group1"}
    ...
    new SelectListItem {..., Group="group2"}
    ...
  }
}
<select asp-for="MyProperty"  asp-items="choices">
  <option value="">Select a value</option>
</select>
...
```

When added, option tags are placed before the ones generated by `asp-items`.

The next topic shows how to reuse view code.

Reusing view code

ASP.NET Core MVC includes several techniques for reusing view code, with the most important being the layout page.

In each web application, several pages share the same structure, for instance, the same main menu or the same left or right bar. In ASP.NET Core, this common structure is factored out in views called layout pages/views.

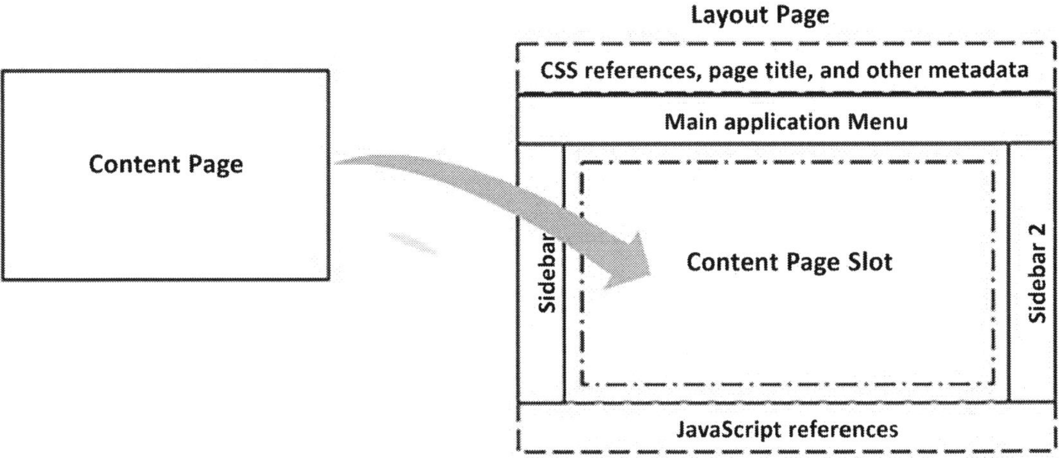

Figure 17.7: Using layout pages

Each view can specify the view to be used as its layout page with the following code:

```
@{
    Layout = "_MyLayout";
}
```

If no layout page is specified, a default layout page, defined in a `_ViewStart.cshtml` file located in the `Views` folder, is used. The default content of `_ViewStart.cshtml` is as follows:

```
@{
    Layout = "_Layout";
}
```

Therefore, the default layout page in the files scaffolded by Visual Studio is `_Layout.cshtml`, which is contained in the `Shared` folder.

The layout page contains the HTML that's shared with all of its children pages, the HTML page headers, and the page references to CSS and JavaScript files. The HTML produced by each view is placed inside its layout page, where the layout page calls the `@RenderBody()` method, as shown in the following example:

```
...
<main role="main" class="pb-3">
    ...
    @RenderBody()
    ...
</main>
...
```

ViewData of each View is copied into ViewData of its layout page, so ViewData can be used to pass information to the view layout page. Typically, it is used to pass the view title to the layout page, which then uses it to compose the page's title header, as shown here:

```
@*In the view *@
@{
    ViewData["Title"] = "Home Page";
}
@*In the layout view*@
<head>
    <meta charset="utf-8" />
    ...
    <title>@ViewData["Title"] - My web application</title>
    ...
```

While the main content produced by each view is placed in a single area of its layout page, each layout page can also define several sections placed in different areas, where each view can place further secondary content.

For instance, suppose a layout page defines a Scripts section, as shown here:

```
...
<script src="~/js/site.js" asp-append-version="true"></script>
@RenderSection("Scripts", required: false)
...
```

Then, the view can use the previously defined section to pass some view-specific JavaScript references, as shown here:

```
.....
@section scripts{
    <script src="~/js/pages/pageSpecificJavaScript.min.js"></script>
}
.....
```

If an action method is expected to return HTML to an AJAX call, it must produce an HTML fragment instead of a whole HTML page. Therefore, in this case, no layout page must be used. This is achieved by calling the PartialView method instead of the View method in the controller action method. PartialView and View have exactly the same overloads and parameters.

Another way to reuse view code is to factor out a view fragment that's common to several views into another view that is called by all previous views. A view can call another view with the partial tag, as shown here:

```
<partial name="_viewname" for="ModelProperty.NestedProperty"/>
```

The preceding code invokes `_viewname` and passes it to the object contained in `Model.ModelProperty.NestedProperty` as its `ViewModel`. When a view is invoked by the `partial` tag, no layout page is used, since the called view is expected to return an HTML fragment.

The `ViewData.TemplateInfo.HtmlFieldPrefix` property of the called view is set to the `ModelProperty.NestedProperty` string. This way, possible input fields rendered in `_viewname.cshtml` will have the same name as if they had been rendered directly by the calling view.

Instead of specifying the ViewModel of `_viewname` through a property of the caller view (ViewModel), you can also directly pass an object that is contained in a variable or returned by a C# expression by replacing `for` with `model`, as shown in this example:

```
<partial name="_viewname" model="new MyModel{...})" />
```

In this case, the `ViewData.TemplateInfo.HtmlFieldPrefix` property of the called view keeps its default value, that is, the empty string.

A view can also call something more complex than another view, that is, another controller method that, in turn, renders a view. Controllers that are designed to be invoked by views are called **view components**. The following code is an example of component invocation:

```
<vc:[view-component-name] par1="par1 value" par2="parameter2 value"> </
vc:[view-component-name]>
```

Parameter names must match the ones used in the view component method. However, both the component's name and parameter names must be translated into kebab case; that is, all the characters must be transformed into lowercase if all the characters in the original name were in uppercase, although the first letter of the name must be preceded by a `-`. For instance, `MyParam` must be transformed into `my-param`.

Actually, view components are either classes that derive from the `ViewComponent` class, classes decorated with the `[ViewComponent]` attribute, or classes whose names end with the `ViewComponent` suffix. When a component is invoked, the framework looks for either an `Invoke` method or an `InvokeAsync` method and passes it all the parameters that were defined in the component's invocation. `InvokeAsync` must be used if the method is defined as `async`; otherwise, we must use `Invoke`.

The following code is an example of a view component definition:

```
public class MyTestViewComponent : ViewComponent
    {

        public async Task<IViewComponentResult> InvokeAsync(
        int par1, bool par2)
        {
            var model= ....
            return View("ViewName", model);
        }

    }
```

The previously defined component must be invoked with a call such as the following:

```
<vc:my-test par1="10" par2="true"></vc:y-test>
```

If the component is invoked by a view of a controller called `MyController`, `ViewName` is searched for in the following paths:

- `/Views/MyController/Components/MyTest/ViewName`
- `/Views/Shared/Components/MyTest/ViewName`

Understanding the connection between ASP.NET Core MVC and design principles

The whole ASP.NET Core framework is built on top of the design principles and patterns that we analyzed in *Chapter 11, Applying a Microservice Architecture to Your Enterprise Application, Chapter 13, Interacting with Data in C# – Entity Framework Core, Chapter 6, Design Patterns and .NET 8 Implementation, Chapter 7, Understanding the Different Domains in Software Solutions*, and *Chapter 5, Implementing Code Reusability in C# 12*.

Moreover, all framework functionalities are provided through DI so that each of them can be replaced by a customized counterpart, without it affecting the remainder of the code. Moreover, these providers are not added individually to the DI engine; instead, they are grouped into collection properties of option objects (see the *Loading configuration data and using it with the options framework* subsection) for improved maintainability, and to conform to the Separation of Concerns principle, which is a generalization of the Single Responsibility principle. In fact, the order in which providers are added to their collection does matter, since they are processed in the same order as they are in the collection. Moreover, the effect of a provider also depends on the other providers that belong to the same collection, so sometimes, it is not enough to replace a provider or add a new provider, but it is necessary to also remove/replace other providers to remove their side effects.

Examples of providers grouped in collections include all model binders, validation providers, and data annotation providers.

Moreover, configuration data, instead of being available from a unique dictionary created from a configuration file, is organized into option objects thanks to the options framework we described in the first section of this chapter. This is also an application of the SOLID Interface Segregation principle.

However, ASP.NET Core also applies other patterns that are specific instances of the general Separation of Concerns principle, which (as mentioned earlier) is a generalization of the Single Responsibility principle. They are as follows:

- The middleware modules architecture (the ASP.NET Core pipeline)
- Factoring out validation and globalization from the application code
- The MVC pattern itself

We will analyze each of these in the various subsections that follow.

Advantages of the ASP.NET Core pipeline

The ASP.NET Core pipeline architecture has two important advantages:

- All the different operations that are performed on the initial request are factored out into different modules, according to the Single Responsibility principle.
- The modules that perform these different operations don't need to call each other because each module is invoked once and for all by the ASP.NET Core framework. This way, the code for each module is not required to perform any action that is connected to responsibilities that have been assigned to other modules.

This ensures maximum independence of functionalities and simpler code. For instance, once the authorization and authentication modules are active, no other module needs to worry about authorization anymore. Each piece controller code can focus on application-specific business stuff.

Server-side and client-side validation

Validation logic has been completely factored out from the application code and has been confined to the definition of validation attributes. The developer just needs to specify the validation rule to apply to each model property, by decorating the property with an adequate validation attribute.

Validation rules are checked automatically when action method parameters are instantiated. Both errors and paths in the model (where they occurred) are then recorded in a dictionary that is contained in the `ModelState` controller property. The developer has the responsibility for verifying whether there are errors by checking `ModelState.IsValid`, in which case the developer must return the same ViewModel to the same view so that the user can correct any errors.

Error messages are automatically shown in the view, with no action required from the developer. The developer is only required to do the following:

- Add `span` or `div` with an `asp-validation-for` attribute next to each input field, which will be automatically filled with the possible error.
- Add `div` with an `asp-validation-summary` attribute that will be automatically filled with the validation error summary. See the *Using Razor tag helpers* section for more details.

It is sufficient to add some JavaScript references by invoking the `_ValidationScriptsPartial.cshtml` view with the `partial` tag, enabling the same validation rules on the client side so that errors are shown to the user before the form is posted to the server. Some predefined validation attributes are contained in the `S stem.ComponentModel.DataAnnotations` and `Microsoft.AspNetCore.Mvc` namespaces and include the following attributes:

- The `Required` attribute requires the user to specify a value for the property that it decorates. An implicit `Required` attribute is automatically applied to all non-nullable properties, such as all floats, integers, and decimals, since they can't have a `null` value.
- The `Range` attribute constrains numeric quantities within a range.
- They also include attributes that constrain string lengths.

Custom error messages can be inserted directly into the attributes, or attributes can refer to the property of the resource types containing them.

The developer can define their custom attributes by providing the validation code, both in C# and in JavaScript for client-side validation. The definition of custom validation attributes is discussed in this article: `https://blogs.msdn.microsoft.com/mvpawardprogram/2017/01/03/asp-net-core-mvc/`.

Attribute-based validation can be replaced by other validation providers, such as the **FluentValidation** library that defines validation rules for each type using a fluent interface. It is enough to change a provider in a collection contained in the MVC options object. This can be configured through an action passed to the `builder.Services.AddControllersWithViews` method.

MVC options can be configured as follows:

```
builder.Services.AddControllersWithViews(o => {
    ...
    // code that modifies o properties
});
```

The validation framework automatically checks whether numeric and date inputs are well formatted according to the selected culture.

ASP.NET Core globalization

In multicultural applications, pages must be served according to the language and cultural preferences of each user. Typically, multicultural applications can serve their content in a few languages, and they can handle dates and numeric formats in several more languages. In fact, while the content in all supported languages must be produced manually, .NET has the native capability of formatting and parsing dates and numbers in all cultures.

For instance, a web application might not support unique content for all English-based cultures (en), but it might support all known English-based cultures regarding number and date formats (en-US, en-GB, en-CA, and so on).

The culture used for numbers and dates in a .NET thread is contained in the `Thread.CurrentThread.CurrentCulture` property. Hence, by setting this property to `new CultureInfo("en-CA")`, numbers and dates will be formatted/parsed according to the Canadian format. `Thread.CurrentThread.CurrentUICulture`, instead, decides on the culture of the resource files; that is, it selects a culture-specific version of each resource file or view. Accordingly, a multicultural application is required to set the two cultures associated with the request thread and organize multilingual content into language-dependent resource files and/or views.

According to the Separation of Concerns principle, the whole logic used to set the request culture according to the user's preferences is factored out into a specific module of the ASP.NET Core pipeline. To configure this module, as a first step, we set the supported date/number cultures, as shown in the following example:

```
var supportedCultures = new[]
{
    new CultureInfo("en-AU"),
    new CultureInfo("en-GB"),
    new CultureInfo("en"),
    new CultureInfo("es-MX"),
    new CultureInfo("es"),
    new CultureInfo("fr-CA"),
    new CultureInfo("fr"),
    new CultureInfo("it-CH"),
    new CultureInfo("it")
};
```

Then, we set the languages supported for the content. Usually, a version of the language that is not specific to any country is selected to keep the number of translations small enough, as shown here:

```
var supportedUICultures = new[]
{
     new CultureInfo("en"),
     new CultureInfo("es"),
     new CultureInfo("fr"),
     new CultureInfo("it")
};
```

Then, we add the culture middleware to the pipeline, as shown here:

```
app.UseRequestLocalization(new RequestLocalizationOptions
{
      DefaultRequestCulture = new RequestCulture("en", "en"),
      // Formatting numbers, dates, etc.
      SupportedCultures = supportedCultures,
      // UI strings that we have localized.
      SupportedUICultures = supportedUICultures,
      FallBackToParentCultures = true,
      FallBackToParentUICultures = true
});
```

If the culture requested by the user is explicitly found among the ones listed in `supportedCultures` or `supportedUICultures`, it is used without modifications. Otherwise, since `FallBackToParentCultures` and `FallBackToParentUICultures` are `true`, the parent culture is tried; that is, for instance, if the required `fr-FR` culture is not found among those listed, then the framework searches for its generic version, `fr`. If this attempt also fails, the framework uses the cultures specified in `DefaultRequestCulture`.

By default, the culture middleware searches the culture selected for the current user, with three providers that are tried in the order shown here:

1. The middleware looks for the culture and ui-culture query string parameters.
2. If the previous step fails, the middleware looks for a cookie named .AspNetCore.Culture, the value of which is expected to be as in this example: c=en-US|uic=en.
3. If both previous steps fail, the middleware looks for the Accept-Language request header sent by the browser, which can be changed in the browser settings, and which is initially set to the operating system culture.

With the preceding strategy, the first time a user requests an application page, the browser culture is taken (the provider listed in *step 3*). Then, if the user clicks a language-change link with the right query string parameters, a new culture is selected by provider 1. Usually, once a language link has been clicked, the server also generates a language cookie to remember the user's choice through provider 2.

The simplest way to provide content localization is to provide a different view for each language. Hence, if we would like to localize the Home.cshtml view for different languages, we must provide views named Home.en.cshtml, Home.es.cshtml, and so on. If no view specific to the ui-culture thread is found, the non-localized Home.cshtml version of the view is chosen.

View localization must be enabled by calling the AddViewLocalization method, as shown here:

```
builder.Services.AddControllersWithViews()
    .AddViewLocalization(LanguageViewLocationExpanderFormat.Suffix)
```

Another option is to store simple strings or HTML fragments in resource files specific to all supported languages. The usage of resource files must be enabled by calling the AddLocalization method in the configure services section, as shown here:

```
builder.Services.AddLocalization(options =>
    options.ResourcesPath = "Resources");
```

ResourcesPath is the root folder where all resource files will be placed. If it is not specified, an empty string is assumed, and the resource files will be placed in the web application root. Resource files for a specific view (say, the /Views/Home/Index.cshtml view) must have a path like this:

```
<ResourcesPath >/Views/Home/Index.<culture name>.resx
```

Hence, if ResourcesPath is empty, resources must have the /Views/Home/Index.<culture name>.resx path; that is, they must be placed in the same folder as the view.

Once the key-value pairs for all the resource files associated with a view have been added, localized HTML fragments can be added to the view, as follows:

- Inject IViewLocalizer into the view with @inject IViewLocalizer Localizer
- Where needed, replace the text in the View with access to the Localizer dictionary, such as Localizer["myKey"], where "myKey" is a key used in the resource files.

The following code shows an example of the `IViewLocalizer` dictionary:

```
@{
    ViewData["Title"] = Localizer["HomePageTitle"];
}
<h2>@ViewData["MyTitle"]</h2>
```

If localization fails because the key is not found in the resource file, the key itself is returned. Strings used in data annotation, such as validation attributes, are used as keys in resource files if data annotation localization is enabled, as shown here:

```
builder.Services.AddControllersWithViews()
    .AddViewLocalization(LanguageViewLocationExpanderFormat.Suffix)
    .AddDataAnnotationsLocalization();
```

Resource files for data annotations applied to a class whose full name is, say, `MyWebApplication.ViewModels.Account.RegisterViewModel` must have the following path:

```
{ResourcesPath}/ViewModels/Account/RegisterViewModel.{culture name}.resx
```

It is worth pointing out that the first segment of the namespace that corresponds to the `.dll` application name is replaced with `ResourcesPath`. If `ResourcesPath` is empty and you use the default namespaces created by Visual Studio, then the resource files must be placed in the same folder that contains the classes they are associated with.

It is possible to localize strings and HTML fragments in controllers, or wherever dependencies can be injected, by associating each group of resource files with a type, such as `MyType`, and then injecting either `IHtmlLocalizer<MyType>` for HTML fragments or `IStringLocalizer<MyType>` for strings that need to be HTML-encoded.

Their usage is identical to the usage of `IViewLocalizer`. The path of the resource files associated with `MyType` is computed, as in the case of data annotations. If you would like to use a unique group of resource files for the whole application, a common choice is to use the `Startup` class as the reference type (`IStringLocalizer<Startup>` and `IHtmlLocalizer<Startup>`). Another common choice is to create various empty classes to use as reference types for various groups of resource files.

Now that we've learned how to manage globalization in our ASP.NET Core projects, in the next subsection, we will describe the more important pattern used by ASP.NET Core MVC to enforce a *separation of concerns*: the MVC pattern itself.

The MVC pattern

MVC is a pattern used to implement the presentation layers of a web application. The basic idea is to apply a *Separation of Concerns* between the logic of the presentation layer and its graphics. Logic is taken care of by controllers, while graphics are factored out into views. Controllers and views communicate through the model, which is often called the ViewModel to distinguish it from the models of the business and data layers.

It is worth pointing out that the original definition of the MVC pattern proposes directly the use of domain models instead of ViewModels, but then, most of the MVC web frameworks started using the concept of ViewModel because specifying the information to render in a view requires just a projection of the original domain model (just some model data possibly organized in a different way) and often additional data, such as, for instance, the items per page of a pager, and the items required by the type input selected.

However, what is the logic of a presentation layer? In *Chapter 1, Understanding the Importance of Software Architecture*, we saw that software requirements can be documented with use cases that describe the interaction between the user and the system.

Roughly speaking, the logic of the presentation layer consists of the management of use cases; hence, roughly, use cases are mapped to controllers, and every single operation of a use case is mapped to an action method of those controllers. Hence, controllers take care of managing the protocol of interaction with the user and rely on the business layer for any business processing involved during each operation.

Each action method receives data from the user, performs some business processing, and, depending on the results of this processing, decides what to show to the user and encodes it in the ViewModel. Views receive ViewModels that describe what to show to the user and decide the graphics to use, that is, the HTML to use.

What are the advantages of separating the logic and user interface into two different components? The main advantages are listed here:

- Changes in graphics do not affect the remainder of the code, so you can experiment with various user interface elements to optimize the interaction with the user, without putting the reliability of the remainder of the code at risk.
- The application can be tested by instantiating controllers and passing the parameters, with no need to use testing tools that operate on the browser pages. In this way, tests are easier to implement. Moreover, they do not depend on the way graphics are implemented, so they do not need to be updated each time the graphics change.
- It is easier to split the job between developers who implement controllers and graphic designers who implement views. Often, graphic designers have difficulties with Razor, so they might just furnish an example HTML page that developers transform into Razor views that operate on the actual data.

For an example of how to put into practice the general principles discussed above, please refer to the *A frontend microservice* section in *Chapter 21, Case Study*, but it is better to read *Chapter 18, Implementing Frontend Microservices with ASP.NET Core*, beforehand. There, we'll look at how to create a frontend microservice with ASP.NET Core MVC.

Summary

In this chapter, we analyzed the ASP.NET Core pipeline and various modules that comprise an ASP.NET Core MVC application in detail, such as authentication/authorization, the options framework, and routing. Then, we described how controllers and Views map requests to the response HTML. We also analyzed all the improvements introduced in the latest versions.

Finally, we analyzed all the design patterns implemented in the ASP.NET Core MVC framework and, in particular, the importance of the Separation of Concerns principle and how ASP.NET Core MVC implements it in the ASP.NET Core pipeline, as well as in its validation and globalization modules. We focused in more detail on the importance of a Separation of Concerns between the presentation layer logic and graphics, as well as how the MVC pattern ensures it.

You can find a full example of how to use ASP.NET Core MVC in the next chapter, which deals with frontend microservices and describes a complete frontend microservice, whose presentation layer uses ASP.NET Core MVC.

Questions

1. Can you list all the middleware modules scaffolded by Visual Studio in an ASP.NET Core project?
2. Does the ASP.NET Core pipeline module need to inherit from a base class or implement some interface?
3. Is it true that a tag must have just one tag helper defined for it, as, otherwise, an exception is thrown?
4. Do you remember how to test if validation errors have occurred in a controller?
5. What is the instruction in a layout view for including the output of the main view?
6. How are secondary sections of the main view invoked in a layout view?
7. How does a controller invoke a view?
8. By default, how many providers are installed in the globalization module?
9. Are ViewModels the only way for controllers to communicate with their invoked views?

Further reading

- More details on the ASP.NET Core and ASP.NET Core MVC framework are available in its official documentation at `https://docs.microsoft.com/en-US/aspnet/core/`.
- More details on the Razor syntax can be found at `https://docs.microsoft.com/en-us/aspnet/core/razor-pages/?tabs=visual-studio`.
- How to model bind collections and dictionaries is explained in this excellent Phil Haack post: `http://haacked.com/archive/2008/10/23/model-binding-to-a-list.aspx`.
- Documentation on the creation of custom tag helpers that were not discussed in this chapter can be found at `https://docs.microsoft.com/en-US/aspnet/core/mvc/views/tag-helpers/authoring`.

- Documentation on the creation of custom controller attributes can be found at `https://docs.microsoft.com/en-US/aspnet/core/mvc/controllers/filters`.
- The definition of custom validation attributes is discussed in this article: `https://blogs.msdn.microsoft.com/mvpawardprogram/2017/01/03/asp-net-core-mvc/`

Learn more on Discord

To join the Discord community for this book – where you can share feedback, ask questions to the authors, and learn about new releases – follow the QR code below:

`https://packt.link/SoftwareArchitectureCSharp12Dotnet8`

18

Implementing Frontend Microservices with ASP.NET Core

Chapter 14, Implementing Microservices with .NET, described general techniques for implementing microservices in .NET but focused mainly on worker microservices, that is, on microservices that perform background jobs without communicating with anything outside of the application.

Microservices that communicate with the world outside of the application bring with them other problems and need further techniques.

More specifically, microservices that communicate with a human user must implement a presentation layer, while microservices that expose APIs must conform to well-established standards and should preferably have documentation. Moreover, web APIs that target **single-page applications (SPAs)** must conform with browser policies; that is, either they are exposed on a single domain that is the same domain the SPA was downloaded from, or they must configure CORS policies. We will see how to address both CORS and issues due to browser policies in *Chapter 19, Client Frameworks: Blazor*.

Worth mentioning also are all the challenges brought by any presentation layer, that is, ensuring a fast and effective interaction with the user and managing the state of the interaction with the user with maintainable code without falling into spaghetti code. General usability problems and solutions were discussed in *Chapter 2, Non-Functional Requirements*. We will discuss more technology-specific usability and status management problems in this chapter and in *Chapter 19, Client Frameworks: Blazor*.

Finally, all front end microservices must put solid security policies in place to defend the application from hackers. Some techniques are common to both front-ends and web APIs and are automatically handled by all major web servers, such as countermeasures against path-transversal attacks and denial of service. Others, instead, are specific to HTML pages, such as forgery. ASP.NET Core MVC defenses against forgery are discussed in the *Chapter 21, Case study*.

Techniques for implementing public self-documented web APIs were described in *Chapter 15, Applying Service-Oriented Architectures with .NET*, while techniques for implementing server-based presentation layers were covered in *Chapter 17, Presenting ASP.NET Core*, and techniques for implementing client-based presentation layers will be covered in *Chapter 19, Client Frameworks: Blazor*. Moreover, general techniques for implementing microservices were covered in *Chapter 11, Applying a Microservice Architecture to Your Enterprise Application, Chapter 7, Understanding the Different Domains in Software Solutions*, and *Chapter 14, Implementing Microservices with .NET*.

Therefore, in this chapter, after a short section about concepts and techniques specific to front-end microservices, we will show you how to put all these concepts and techniques together in the practical implementation of a front-end microservice. More specifically, we will discuss various implementation options and how to architect the whole layer structure of a front-end microservice. A complete example that shows how all layers of a front-end microservice work together, in practice, is described in the *A frontend microservice* section of *Chapter 21, Case Study*.

More specifically, this chapter covers the following topics:

- Front-ends and micro-frontends
- Defining the domain layer interface
- Defining the domain layer implementation
- Defining the application layer
- Defining controllers

We will use the onion architecture and the patterns described in *Chapter 7, Understanding the Different Domains in Software Solutions*.

Technical requirements

This chapter requires the free Visual Studio 2022 Community edition or better with all database tools installed.

The code samples necessary to clarify the concepts in this chapter will be taken from a practical example application based on the `WWTravelClub` book use case. The full example application is described in detail in the *A front end microservice* section of *Chapter 21, Case Study*. Its code is available at `https://github.com/PacktPublishing/Software-Architecture-with-C-Sharp-12-and-.NET-8-4E`.

Front-ends and micro-frontends

The main peculiarity of front-end microservices is that they need a robust web server that is able to optimize all the request/response handling and ensure the needed level of security. Moreover, high-traffic applications also need a load balancer.

Examples of services offered by robust web servers like IIS, Apache, and NGINX are:

- Limiting access to just some file types and directories to prevent access to private files and to prevent remote file execution; that is, execution of server commands/scripts through web requests.
- Blocking dangerous requests that might cause access to unwanted files or directories (path-traversal attacks).
- Blocking requests that exceed a customizable length since they might cause a denial of service.
- Logging and IP address blocking to discover and contrast hacker attacks.
- Redirecting requests to the application associated with each URL.
- Queueing requests and assigning them to available threads. This capability is fundamental for performance optimization since executing too many requests compared to the available processor cores might cause unacceptable performance.
- Ensuring the isolation of applications running on the same process but in different threads and more.

If the front-end service is hosted on a Kubernetes cluster, both an adequate web server and load balancing can be provided through an **Ingress**.

Otherwise, **Azure App Service** (see the *Further reading* section) might be a good option since it offers a scalable level of load balancing, excellent security, monitoring services, and so on.

A front-end microservice doesn't need to interface directly with anything outside of an application. In fact, in micro-frontend architectures, there is no unique front-end, but the role of the front-end is split among several microservices. In these architectures, typically, the role of directing traffic toward the right front-end and/or of combining several responses into a unique response is taken by an interface front-end that is load-balanced and carries the burden of ensuring the right level of security.

The reasons for using micro-frontends are the same as the ones for using other microservices. We discussed them in detail in *Chapter 11, Applying a Microservice Architecture to Your Enterprise Application*, but it is worth repeating the more important ones here:

- Optimizing the usage of hardware resources by scaling just the microservices that need more resources
- Having independent software lifecycles for each microservice, so each microservice can evolve independently from the others to match the user needs and so that each microservices developer team can work independently from the others

Micro-frontend architectures use quite different techniques for HTML websites, like ASP.NET Core MVC websites, and for web APIs. Actually, the word "micro-frontend" is used just with HTML websites/SPAs, while web APIs exposed to the outside world are referred to as public web APIs. We will describe public web APIs and HTML micro-frontends and the techniques they use in two dedicated subsections, starting with public web APIs.

Public web APIs

In the case of web APIs, all microservices are accessible through a unique load-balanced piece of software called an **API gateway** that sits in between the clients and the various API services. The basic role of an API gateway is to make the whole API accessible from a unique domain to both avoid problems with the browser's unique domain policy and make the usage of all API services simpler.

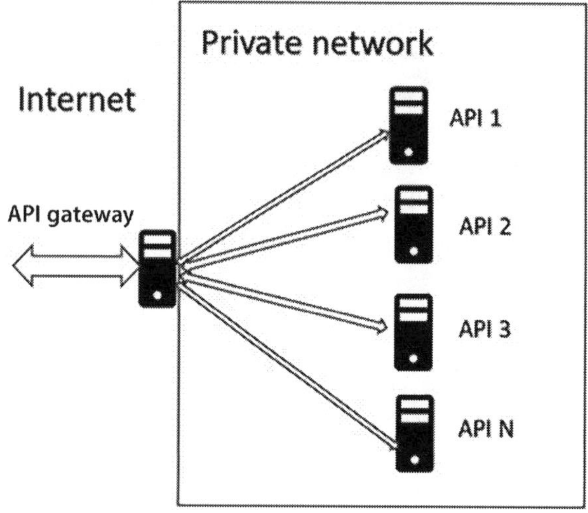

Figure 18.1: API gateway

However, the API gateway offers the opportunity to centralize other functions that are common to all API services, such as:

- **Authentication**, that is, validating and decoding the authentication token that comes with each request (please do not confuse authentication with login).
- **Caching**, that is, caching responses according to configurable caching policies.
- **Translation**, that is, adapting the interface, as seen by the client, to the actual signature of the various API methods. This way, each API can change its interface without affecting existing clients.
- **Versioning**, that is, directing each request toward a compatible version of each API service.
- **Documentation**, that is, offering a unique documentation endpoint.

API gateways have continued to evolve, absorbing and offering more and more functions, giving rise to the so-called **API management systems** that now automate and take care of most of the burden of handling public web APIs.

Azure, like all clouds, offers a good API management service. You can find more information about it here: `https://azure.microsoft.com/en-us/services/api-management/#overview`.

It is also worth mentioning **Ocelot** (`https://docs.microsoft.com/en-us/dotnet/architecture/microservices/multi-container-microservice-net-applications/implement-api-gateways-ith-ocelot"`), a library for easily creating custom API gateways. You can either use it to fill in configuration files or as a base for a completely custom API gateway.

Now, we are ready to discuss HTML micro-frontends, which also add the challenge of combining several HTML fragments into a unique HTML page.

HTML micro-frontends

Several HTML micro-frontends can cooperate on the same application by furnishing each with a different set of web pages. In this case, coordinating them requires nothing more than links pointing to the other micro-frontends and a common sign-in so that users don't need to log in each time they move to a different micro-frontend.

However, very often, several micro-frontends cooperate in the construction of the same page by supplying various page areas. In this case, a software component must take the burden of assembling the various parts into a unique page.

The main difficulty of combining several HTML fragments into a single HTML page is offering a coherent experience to the user, thus avoiding assembling all page areas in a way that is hard to understand for the user. Another problem is avoiding the continuous page flipping and reorganization each time new content reaches the browser. In what follows, we will discuss how these problems are solved by different technologies.

In the case of classic web applications that build the HTML on the server side, an interface application furnishes the page layout and then calls the various micro-frontends to fill the various layout areas.

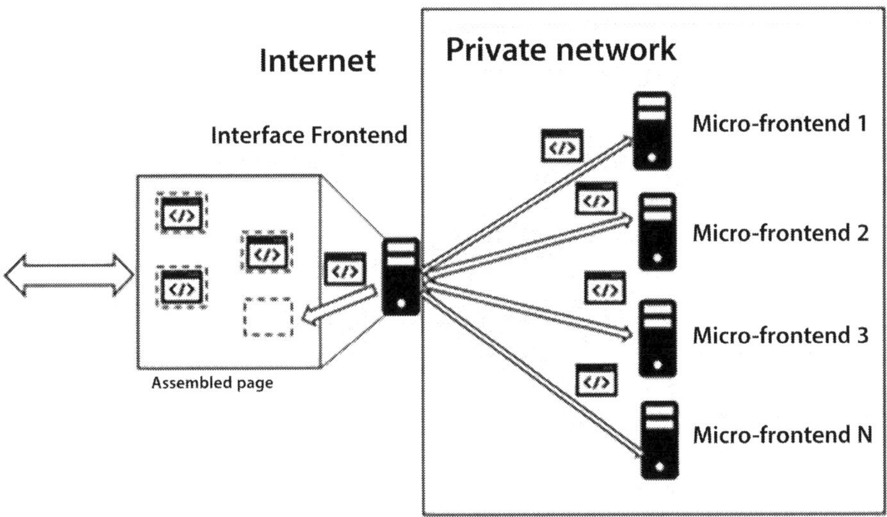

Figure 18.2: Server-side micro-frontend

In this case, there is no browser page flipping and reorganization issue since the whole HTML page is assembled on the server side and sent to the browser only when it is ready. However, we pay for this advantage with the memory consumption for the whole time needed to assemble the whole page before sending it to the browser.

Both the layout to use and which calls to make to the involved micro-frontends are obtained by processing the request URL according to rules that are either hardwired in the code or, better, stored in one or more configuration sources (in the simplest case, a unique configuration file). Using predefined page patterns ensures coherence and a good user experience, but we pay the cost in maintainability because we need to update and test the interface application at each non-trivial change of any single micro-frontend that furnishes page areas.

In the case of SPAs, the assembly process takes place on the client, that is, in the browser:

1. A kernel application furnishes the initial HTML page.
2. The kernel application downloads a JavaScript file from each micro-frontend. Each of these JavaScript files is a micro-SPA that creates page areas.
3. The kernel application, based on the current URL, decides which URL to pass to each micro-SPA and then puts the HTML produced by each micro-SPA in the right place.

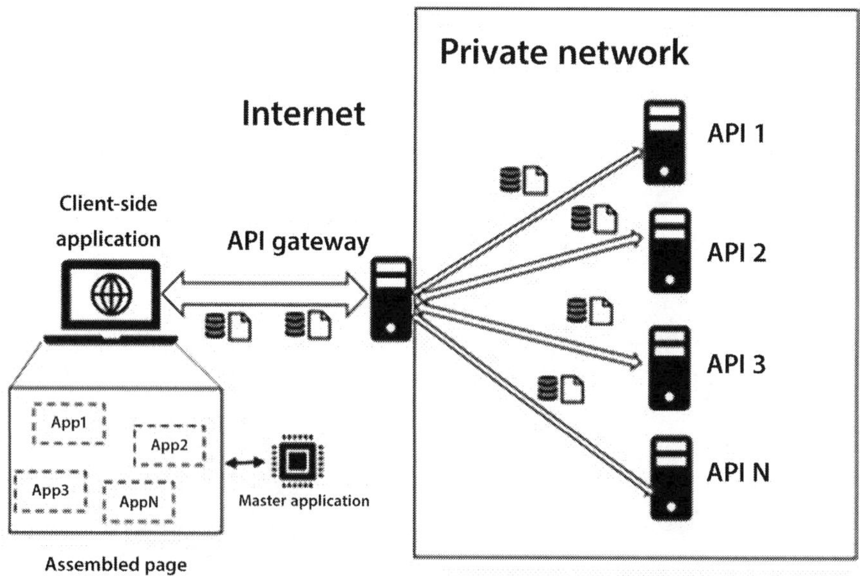

Figure 18.3: Client-side micro-frontend

The various micro-SPAs do not interfere with each other because each of them runs in a separate JavaScript scope. Therefore, for instance, we can mix micro-SPAs implemented with different and incompatible versions of Angular and/or React.

Micro-frontends can also be implemented using WebAssembly frameworks like Blazor (see *Chapter 19, Client Frameworks: Blazor*) that run .NET code. However, in this case, the various micro-SPAs do not run in separate environments, so they must be based on compatible .NET versions.

SPA micro-frontends have the same maintainability costs as server-based micro-frontends and have browser page flipping and reorganization issues since the page is created dynamically as new content and/or data reach the browser. This problem can be solved by pre-allocating each content area of the browser page with fixed-size HTML tags. Thus, for instance, we may pre-allocate a 300 px X 300 px area to show weather forecasts and some pictures or animation while the actual content is loading.

In the next section, we will introduce the architectural schema for building a front-end microservice based on ASP.NET Core MVC.

Defining the application architecture

The application will be implemented with the **Domain-Driven Design** (**DDD**) approach and associated patterns described in *Chapter 7, Understanding the Different Domains in Software Solutions*, and *Chapter 13, Interacting with Data in C# – Entity Framework Core*, so having a good understanding of the content covered in those chapters is a fundamental prerequisite to reading this chapter.

The application is organized based on a DDD approach and uses SOLID principles to map your domain sections. That is, the application is organized into three layers, each implemented as a different project:

- There's a domain layer, which contains the repository's implementation and the classes describing database entities. It is a .NET library project. However, since it needs some interfaces, like `IServiceCollection`, which are defined in `Microsoft.NET.Sdk.web`, and since the `DBContext` layer must inherit from the identity framework in order to also handle the application authentication and authorization database tables, we must add a reference not only to the .NET SDK but also to the ASP.NET Core SDK. However, it is also common to implement custom user management.
- There's also a domain layer abstraction, which contains repository specifications; that is, interfaces that describe repository implementations and DDD aggregates. In our implementation, we decided to implement aggregates by hiding the forbidden operations/properties of root data entities behind interfaces, as discussed in the *How data and domain layers communicate with other layers* section of *Chapter 13, Interacting with Data in C# – Entity Framework Core*. Hence, for instance, the `Package` data layer class, which is an aggregate root, has a corresponding `IPackage` interface in the domain layer abstraction that hides all the property setters of the `Package` entity. The domain layer abstraction also contains the definitions of all the domain events, while the event handlers that will subscribe to these events are defined in the application layer.
- Finally, there's the application layer – that is, the ASP.NET Core MVC application (ASP.NET Core MVC is discussed in *Chapter 17, Presenting ASP.NET Core*) – where we define DDD queries, commands, command handlers, and event handlers. Controllers fill query objects and execute them to get ViewModels they can pass to Views. They update storage by filling command objects and executing their associated command handlers. In turn, command handlers use `IRepository` interfaces and `IUnitOfWork` instances coming from the domain layer to manage and coordinate transactions.

The application uses the **Command Query Responsibility Segregation** (**CQRS**) pattern; therefore, it uses command objects to modify the storage and the query object to query it. CQRS was described in the *Command Query Responsibility Segregation (CQRS) pattern* subsection of *Chapter 7, Understanding the Different Domains in Software Solutions.*

The query is simple to use and implement: controllers fill their parameters and then call their execution methods. In turn, query objects have direct LINQ implementations that project results directly onto the ViewModels used by the controller Views with `Select` LINQ methods. You may also decide to hide the LINQ implementation behind the same repository classes used for the storage update operations, but this would turn the definition and modification of simple queries into very time-consuming tasks.

In any case, it could be beneficial to encapsulate query objects behind interfaces so that their implementations can be replaced by fake implementations when you test controllers.

However, the chain of objects and calls involved in the execution of commands is more complex. This is because it requires the construction and modification of aggregates, as well as a definition of the interaction between several aggregates and between aggregates and other applications through domain events to be provided.

The following diagram is a sketch of how storage update operations are performed. The circles are data being exchanged between the various layers, while the rectangles are the procedures that process them. Moreover, dotted arrows connect interfaces with the types that implement them:

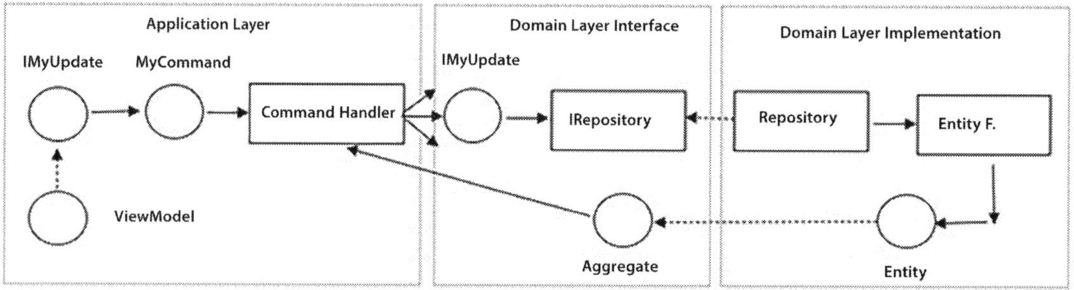

Figure 18.4: Diagram of command execution

Here's the flow of action through *Figure 18.4* as a list of steps:

1. A controller's action method receives one or more ViewModels and performs validation.
2. One or more ViewModels containing changes to apply are hidden behind interfaces (`IMyUpdate`) defined in the domain layer. They are used to fill the properties of a command object. These interfaces must be defined in the domain layer since they will be used as arguments of the repository aggregate methods defined there.
3. A command handler matching the previous command is retrieved via **Dependency Injection** (**DI**) in the controller action method. Then, the handler is executed. During its execution, the handler interacts with various repository interface methods and with the aggregates they return.

4. When creating the command handler discussed in *step 3*, the ASP.NET Core DI engine automatically injects all parameters declared in its constructor. In particular, it injects all `IRepository` implementations needed to perform all command handler transactions. The command handler performs its job by calling the methods of these `IRepository` implementations received in its constructor to build aggregates and modify the built aggregates. Aggregates either represent already-existing entities or newly created ones. Handlers use the `IUnitOfWork` interface contained in each `IRepository`, as well as the concurrency exceptions returned by the data layer, to organize their operations as transactions. It is worth pointing out that each aggregate has its own `IRepository` and that the whole logic for updating each aggregate is defined in the aggregate itself, not in its associated `IRepository`, to keep the code more modular.
5. Behind the scenes, in the data layer, `IRepository` implementations use Entity Framework to perform their job. Aggregates are implemented by root data entities hidden behind interfaces defined in the domain layer, while `IUnitOfWork` methods, which handle transactions and pass changes to the database, are implemented with `DbContext` methods. In other words, `IUnitOfWork` is implemented with the application's `DbContext`.
6. Domain events are generated during each aggregate processing and are added to the aggregates themselves by calling their `AddDomainEvent` methods. However, they are not triggered immediately. Usually, they are triggered at the end of all the aggregates' processing and before changes are passed to the database; however, this is not a general rule.
7. The application handles errors by throwing exceptions. A more efficient approach would be to define a request-scoped object in the dependency engine, where each application subpart may add its errors as domain events. However, while this approach is more efficient, it increases the complexity of the code and the application development time.

The Visual Studio solution is composed of three projects:

- There's a project containing the domain layer abstraction, which is a .NET Standard 2.1 library. When a library doesn't use features or NuGet packages that are specific to a .NET version, it is a good practice to implement it as a .NET Standard library because this way, it doesn't need modifications when the application is moved to a newer .NET version.
- There's a project containing the whole data layer, which is a .NET 8.0 library based on Entity Framework.
- Finally, there's an ASP.NET Core MVC 8.0 project that contains both the application and presentation layers. When you define this project, select **No Authentication**; otherwise, the user database will be added directly to the ASP.NET Core MVC project instead of to the database layer. We will add the user database manually in the data layer.

In the remaining sections, we will describe the implementation of each layer that composes the architecture described so far, starting with domain layer abstraction.

Defining the domain layer interface

Once the `PackagesManagementDomain` Standard 2.1 library project has been added to the solution, we'll add a `Tools` folder to the project root. Then, we'll place all the `DomainLayer` tools contained in the code associated with `ch7`. Since the code contained in this folder uses data annotations and defines DI extension methods, we must also add references to the `System.ComponentModel.Annotations` and `Microsoft.Extensions.DependencyInjection.Abstration` NuGet packages.

Then, we need an `Aggregates` folder containing all the aggregate definitions (which, as already said, we will implement as interfaces).

Below is an example of an aggregate definition:

```
public interface IPackage : IEntity<int>
{
    void FullUpdate(IPackageFullEditDTO packageDTO);
    string Name { get; set; }
    string Description { get;}
    decimal Price { get; set; }
    int DurationInDays { get; }
    DateTime? StartValidityDate { get;}
    DateTime? EndValidityDate { get; }
    int DestinationId { get; }

}
```

It contains the same properties as the `Package` entity, which we saw in *Chapter 13, Interacting with Data in C# – Entity Framework Core*. The only differences are the following:

- It inherits from `IEntity<int>`, which furnishes all basic functionalities of aggregates
- It has no `Id` property since it is inherited from `IEntity<int>`
- All properties are read-only, and it has a `FullUpdate` method since all aggregates can only be modified through update operations defined in the user domain (in our case, the `FullUpdate` method)

Now, let's also add a `DTOs` folder. Here, we place all interfaces used to pass updates to the aggregates. Such interfaces are implemented by the application layer ViewModels used to define such updates. In our case, it contains `IPackageFullEditDTO`, which we can use to update existing packages.

An `IRepositories` folder contains all repository specifications; the following is an example repository interface:

```
public interface IPackageRepository:
        IRepository<IPackage>
{
```

```
    Task<IPackage> Get(int id);
    IPackage New();
    Task<IPackage> Delete(int id);
}
```

Repositories always contain just a few methods since all business logic should be represented as aggregate methods – in our case, just the methods to create a new package, retrieve an existing package, and delete an existing package. The logic to modify an existing package is included in the `FullUpdate` method of `IPackage`.

Finally, we also have an event folder containing all domain event definitions. We can name this folder `Events`. Events are triggered whenever a change to an aggregate has consequences either on other aggregates or on other microservices. They are a way to implement weak interactions between aggregates and microservices while keeping the code of aggregates independent of each other.

By using events, we may keep the code of each aggregate substantially independent of the code of other aggregates that are involved in the same database transactions: each aggregate generates events that might interest other aggregates, such as a price change in a touristic package aggregate, and all other aggregates that depend on this price subscribe to that event, so they can update their data coherently. This way, when a new aggregate that depends on the tourist package price is added during system maintenance, we don't need to modify the tourist package aggregate.

When the event might also interest other microservices, the event is also passed to a message broker, which makes the event also available for subscription to code in other microservices. Message brokers were discussed in *Chapter 14, Implementing Microservices with .NET*.

Below is an example event definition:

```
public class PackagePriceChangedEvent: IEventNotification
{
    public PackagePriceChangedEvent(int id, decimal price,
        long oldVersion, long newVersion)
    {
            PackageId = id;
            NewPrice = price;
            OldVersion = oldVersion;
            NewVersion = newVersion;
     }
    public int PackageId { get; }
    public decimal NewPrice { get; }
    public long OldVersion { get; }
    public long NewVersion { get; }
}
```

When an aggregate sends all its changes to another microservice, it should have a version property. The microservice that receives the changes uses this version property to apply all changes in the right order. An explicit version number is necessary because changes are sent asynchronously, so the order in which they are received may differ from the order in which they were sent. For this purpose, events that are used to publish changes outside of the application have both `OldVersion` (the version before the change) and `NewVersion` (the version after the change) properties. Events associated with delete events have no `NewVersion` since, after being deleted, an entity can't store any versions.

The next subsection explains how all interfaces defined in the domain layer are implemented in the data layer.

Defining the domain layer implementation

The domain layer implementation contains the implementation of all repository interfaces and aggregate interfaces defined in the domain layer interface. In the case of .NET 8, it uses Entity Framework Core entities to implement aggregates. Adding a domain layer interface in between the domain layer's actual implementation and the application layer decouples the application layer from EF and entity-specific details. Moreover, it conforms with the onion architecture, which, in turn, is an advised way to architect microservices.

The domain layer implementation project should contain references to `Microsoft.AspNetCore.Identity.EntityFrameworkCore` and `Microsoft.EntityFrameworkCore.SqlServer` NuGet packages, since we are using Entity Framework Core with SQL Server. It references `Microsoft.EntityFrameworkCore.Tools` and `Microsoft.EntityFrameworkCore.Design`, which is needed to generate database migrations, as explained in the *Entity Framework Core migrations* section of *Chapter 13, Interacting with Data in C# – Entity Framework Core.*

We should have a `Models` folder that contains all database entities. They are similar to the ones in *Chapter 13*. The only differences are as follows:

- They inherit from `Entity<T>`, which contains all the basic features of aggregates. Please note that inheriting from `Entity<T>` is only needed for aggregate roots; all other entities must be defined as explained in *Chapter 13*.
- They have no `Id` since it is inherited from `Entity<T>`.
- Some of them might have an `EntityVersion` property decorated with the `[ConcurrencyCheck]` attribute. It contains the entity version that is needed to send changes to other microservices. The `ConcurrencyCheck` attribute is needed to prevent concurrency errors while updating the entity version. This prevents suffering the performance penalty implied by a transaction.

More specifically, when saving entity changes, if the value of a field marked with the `ConcurrencyCheck` attribute is different from the one that was read when the entity was loaded in memory, a concurrency exception is thrown to inform the calling method that someone else modified this value after the entity was read, but before we attempted to save its changes. This way, the calling method can repeat the whole operation with the hope that this time, no one will write the same entity in the database during its execution.

It is worth analyzing an example entity:

```
public class Package: Entity<int>, IPackage
{
    public void FullUpdate(IPackageFullEditDTO o)
    {
        if (IsTransient())
        {
            Id = o.Id;
            DestinationId = o.DestinationId;
        }
        else
        {
            if (o.Price != this.Price)
                this.AddDomainEvent(new PackagePriceChangedEvent(
                        Id, o.Price, EntityVersion, EntityVersion+1));
        }
        Name = o.Name;
        Description = o.Description;
        Price = o.Price;
        DurationInDays = o.DurationInDays;
        StartValidityDate = o.StartValidityDate;
        EndValidityDate = o.EndValidityDate;
    }
    [MaxLength(128)]
    public string Name { get; set; }
    [MaxLength(128)]
    public string? Description { get; set; }
    public decimal Price { get; set; }
    public int DurationInDays { get; set; }
    public DateTime? StartValidityDate { get; set; }
    public DateTime? EndValidityDate { get; set; }
    public Destination MyDestination { get; set; }
    [ConcurrencyCheck]
    public long EntityVersion{ get; set; }
    public int DestinationId { get; set; }
}
```

The `FullUpdate` method is the only way to update the `IPackage` aggregate. When the price changes, it adds a `PackagePriceChangedEvent` to the entity list of events.

`MainDBContext` implements `IUnitOfWork`. The following code shows the implementation of all methods that start, rollback, and commit a transaction:

```
public async Task StartAsync()
{
    await Database.BeginTransactionAsync();
}
public Task CommitAsync()
{
    Database.CommitTransaction();
    return Task.CompletedTask;
}
public Task RollbackAsync()
{
    Database.RollbackTransaction();
    return Task.CompletedTask;
}
```

However, they are rarely used by command classes in a distributed environment. In fact, like distributed transactions, local database-blocking transactions are also avoided because they might block database resources for too much time, which is incompatible with the maximization of traffic typical of microservices-based applications.

Likely, as already mentioned, all databases support tagging some row fields as **concurrency checks**. In Entity Framework Core, this is done by decorating the entity property corresponding to the field with the `ConcurrencyCheck` attribute.

Concurrency checks detect interferences of another transaction, B, on a record while performing transaction A. This way, we can perform transaction A without blocking any database record or table, and if we detect interference, we abort transaction A and retry it till it succeeds without interference. This technique works well if transactions are very quick and, consequently, interferences are rare.

More specifically, if during transaction A, the value of the concurrency checks specified by an update operation differs from the one stored in the record being updated, the update is aborted, and a concurrency exception is thrown. The rationale is that another transaction, B, modified the concurrency check, thus interfering with the operation being performed by A.

Accordingly, the method that passes all changes applied to `DbContext` to the database performs a check for concurrency exceptions:

```
public async Task<bool> SaveEntitiesAsync()
{
    try
    {
        return await SaveChangesAsync() > 0;
    }
```

```
    catch (DbUpdateConcurrencyException ex)
    {
        foreach (var entry in ex.Entries)
        {
            entry.State = EntityState.Detached;

        }
        throw;
    }
}
```

The preceding implementation just calls the `SaveChangesAsync` `DbContext` context method, which saves all changes to the database, but then it intercepts all concurrency exceptions and detaches all the entities involved in the concurrency error from the context. This way, the next time a command retries the whole failed operation, their updated versions will be reloaded from the database.

In other words, when the update fails because of the interference of transaction B, we allow the interfering transaction B to complete its process. Then, EF automatically reloads all entities modified by B that contain the value of the concurrency check modified by B. This way, when the operation is retried, if no other transaction interferes, there will be no conflict on the concurrency check.

The practical usage of concurrency checks is detailed in the *A frontend microservice* example of *Chapter 21, Case Study*.

All repository implementations are defined in a `Repositories` folder to ensure better maintainability.

Finally, all repositories are automatically discovered and added to the application DI engine, calling the `AddAllRepositories` method, which is defined in the DDD tools we added to the domain layer project. More details on how to ensure this method is called when the application starts are given in the example detailed description in the *A frontend microservice* section of *Chapter 21, Case Study*.

Defining the application layer

The application layer contains the definition of all business operations. These business operations use data provided by the user to modify domain layer abstraction aggregates, such as touristic packages. When all business operations involved in the current user request have been performed, an `IUnitOfWork.SaveEntitiesAsync()` operation is performed to save all changes to the database.

As a first step, for simplicity, let's freeze the application culture to `en-US` by adding the following code to the ASP.NET Core pipeline:

```
app.UseAuthorization();
// Code to add: configure the Localization middleware
var ci = new CultureInfo("en-US");
app.UseRequestLocalization(new RequestLocalizationOptions
{
    DefaultRequestCulture = new RequestCulture(ci),
```

```
    SupportedCultures = new List<CultureInfo>
    {
        ci,
    },
     SupportedUICultures = new List<CultureInfo>
    {
        ci,
    }
});
```

As a second step, we can create a `Tools` folder to place the `ApplicationLayer` code, which you can find in the `ch7` code of the GitHub repository associated with this book. With these tools in place, in `Program.cs`, we can add the code that automatically discovers and adds all queries, command handlers, and event handlers to the DI engine, as shown here:

```
...
...
builder.Services.AddAllQueries(this.GetType().Assembly);
builder.Services.AddAllCommandHandlers(this.GetType().Assembly);
builder.Services.AddAllEventHandlers(this.GetType().Assembly);
```

Then, we must add a `Queries` folder to place all queries and their associated interfaces. As an example, let's have a look at the query that lists all packages:

```
public class PackagesListQuery:IPackagesListQuery
{
    private readonly MainDbContext ctx;
    public PackagesListQuery(MainDbContext ctx)
    {
        this.ctx = ctx;
    }
    public async Task<IReadOnlyCollection<PackageInfosViewModel>>
GetAllPackages()
    {
        return await ctx.Packages.Select(m => new PackageInfosViewModel
        {
            StartValidityDate = m.StartValidityDate,
            ...
        })
            .OrderByDescending(m=> m.EndValidityDate)
            .ToListAsync();
    }
}
```

The query object is automatically injected into the application DB context. The `GetAllPackages` method uses LINQ to project all of the required information into `PackageInfosViewModel` and sorts all results in descending order on the `EndValidityDate` property.

The `Commands` folder contains all commands. As an example, let's have a look at the command used to modify packages:

```
public class UpdatePackageCommand: ICommand
{
    public UpdatePackageCommand(IPackageFullEditDTO updates)
    {
        Updates = updates;
    }
    public IPackageFullEditDTO Updates { get; private set; }
}
```

Command handlers can be placed in the `Handlers` folder. It is worth analyzing the command that updates packages:

```
private readonly IPackageRepository repo;
private readonly IEventMediator mediator;
public UpdatePackageCommandHandler(IPackageRepository repo, IEventMediator
mediator)
{
    this.repo = repo;
    this.mediator = mediator;
}
```

Its constructor has automatically injected the `IPackageRepository` repository and an `IEventMediator` instance needed to trigger event handlers. The following code also shows the implementation of the standard `HandleAsync` command handler method:

```
public async Task HandleAsync(UpdatePackageCommand command)
{
    bool done = false;
    IPackage model;
    while (!done)
    {
        try
        {
            model = await repo.Get(command.Updates.Id);
            if (model == null) return;
            model.FullUpdate(command.Updates);
            await mediator.TriggerEvents(model.DomainEvents);
            await repo.UnitOfWork.SaveEntitiesAsync();
```

```
                done = true;
            }
            catch (DbUpdateConcurrencyException)
            {
              // add some Logging here
            }
        }
    }
```

Command operations are repeated until no concurrency exception is returned. `HandleAsync` uses the repository to get an instance of the entity to modify. If the entity is not found (it has been deleted), the commands stop its execution. Otherwise, all changes are passed to the retrieved aggregate. Immediately after the update, all events contained in the aggregate are triggered. In particular, if the price has changed, the event handler associated with the price change is executed. The concurrency check declared with the `[ConcurrencyCheck]` attribute on the `EntityVersion` property of the `Package` entity ensures that the package version is updated properly (by incrementing its previous version number by 1), as well as that the price-changed event is passed the right version numbers.

Also, event handlers are placed in the `Handlers` folder. As an example, let's have a look at the price-changed event handler:

```
public class PackagePriceChangedEventHandler :
    IEventHandler<PackagePriceChangedEvent>
{
    private readonly IPackageEventRepository repo;
    public PackagePriceChangedEventHandler(IPackageEventRepository repo)
    {
        this.repo = repo;
    }
    public Task HandleAsync(PackagePriceChangedEvent ev)
    {
        repo.New(PackageEventType.CostChanged, ev.PackageId,
            ev.OldVersion, ev.NewVersion, ev.NewPrice);
      return Task.CompletedTask;
    }
}
```

The constructor has automatically injected the `IPackageEventRepository` repository, which handles the database table and all the events to send to other applications. The `HandleAsync` implementation simply calls the repository method that adds a new record to this table.

All records in the table are handled by `IPackageEventRepository`, which can be retrieved and sent to all interested microservices by a parallel task defined in the DI engine with a call such as `builder.Services.AddHostedService<MyHostedService>();`, as detailed in the *Using generic hosts* subsection of *Chapter 11, Applying a Microservice Architecture to Your Enterprise Application*. However, this parallel task is not implemented in the GitHub code associated with this chapter.

It is worth recalling that the usage of events promotes code decoupling, and when events cross the microservice boundary, they implement efficient asynchronous communication between microservices, which improves performance and maximizes hardware resource usage.

The next subsection describes how to define controllers.

Defining controllers

Each controller interacts with a use case that emerged in the analysis stage with its action methods. Action methods do their job by requiring command handlers and query interfaces from the dependency injection engine.

Below is an example of how query objects are required and used:

```
[HttpGet]
public async Task<IActionResult> Index(
    [FromServices] IPackagesListQuery query)
{
    var results = await query.GetAllPackages();
    var vm = new PackagesListViewModel { Items = results };
    return View(vm);
}
```

Below, instead, is an example of the usage of command handlers:

```
public async Task<IActionResult> Edit(
    PackageFullEditViewModel vm,
    [FromServices] ICommandHandler<UpdatePackageCommand> command)
{
    if (ModelState.IsValid)
    {
        await command.HandleAsync(new UpdatePackageCommand(vm));
        return RedirectToAction(
            nameof(ManagePackagesController.Index));
    }
    else
        return View(vm);
}
```

`ICommandHandler<UpdatePackageCommand>` retrieves the command handler associated with the `UpdatePackageCommand` command from DI.

If `ModelState` is valid, `UpdatePackageCommand` is created, and its associated handler is invoked; otherwise, the View is displayed again to the user to enable them to correct all the errors.

Summary

In this chapter, we analyzed the peculiarities of front-end microservices and the techniques used to implement them.

Then, we put together the techniques learned in this chapter and in previous chapters in the complete implementation of a front-end microservice.

We used an onion architecture with a data layer and a domain layer abstraction, and we implemented each as a separate project. The application layer and the presentation layer were implemented together in the same ASP.NET Core MVC project.

The microservice used the CQRS pattern and used a queue implemented with a database table to store the events to send to other microservices.

The next chapter explains how to implement a presentation layer with client-based techniques. We will use Blazor as an example client framework.

Questions

1. What is the difference between a front-end and an API gateway?
2. Why should all front-ends and API gateways use a robust web server?
3. Why should complex blocking database transactions be avoided?
4. When does the concurrency technique ensure a better performance?
5. What is the advantage of using domain events to implement interactions between different aggregates?

Further reading

Since this chapter just put into practice concepts explained in other chapters (mainly *Chapter 7, Understanding the Different Domains in Software Solutions*, *Chapter 11, Applying a Microservice Architecture to Your Enterprise Application*, and *Chapter 13, Interacting with Data in C# – Entity Framework Core*), here we will include just a few links on how to use API gateways and further information on the MediatR library, which was mentioned in the example:

- Ocelot GitHub repository: `https://github.com/ThreeMammals/Ocelot`
- How to implement your API gateway with Ocelot: `https://docs.microsoft.com/en-us/dotnet/architecture/microservices/multi-container-microservice-net-applications/implement-api-gateways-with-ocelot`
- Azure API Management: `https://azure.microsoft.com/en-us/services/api-management/#overview`

- Azure App Service: `https://azure.microsoft.com/en-us/services/app-service/`
- More information on MediatR can be found on MediatR's GitHub repository: `https://github.com/jbogard/MediatR`

Leave a review!

Enjoying this book? Help readers like you by leaving an Amazon review. Scan the QR code below for a 20% discount code.

**Limited Offer*

19

Client Frameworks: Blazor

In this chapter, you will learn how to implement presentation layers based on client technologies. Applications based on server technologies, like ASP.NET Core MVC, run all application layers on the server, thus also creating on the server the HTML that encodes the whole UI. Applications based on client technologies, instead, run the whole presentation layer on the client machine (mobile device, desktop computer, laptop, etc.) thus interacting with a server just to exchange data with the web API.

In other words, in an application based on client technology, the whole UI is created by code that runs on the user device, which also controls the whole user-application interaction. Both the business layer and the domain layer, instead, run on server machines to prevent users from violating business rules and authorization policies by hacking the code that runs on their devices.

In turn, applications based on client technologies can be classified as single-page applications, which benefit from web standards, or as native applications, which are tied to specific operating systems and the advantages of specific device peculiarities.

Single-page applications are based on JavaScript or WebAssembly and run in any browser. As an example of a single-page application, we will analyze the Blazor WebAssembly framework

Blazor WebAssembly applications are developed in C# and use many technologies we already analyzed in *Chapter 17, Presenting ASP.NET Core*, such as dependency injection and Razor. Therefore, we strongly recommend studying *Chapter 17, Presenting ASP.NET Core*, and *Chapter 18, Implementing Frontend Microservices with ASP.NET Core*, before reading this chapter.

As an example of native technologies, we will analyze native .NET MAUI Blazor, which is completely analogous to Blazor WebAssembly but instead of using browser WebAssembly, it uses .NET, which is compiled just in time into the assembly of the target device. Not being limited by browser restrictions, .NET MAUI Blazor can access all device features through adequate .NET libraries.

More specifically, in this chapter, you will learn about the following subjects:

- Comparison of the various types of client technologies
- Blazor WebAssembly architecture
- Blazor pages and components

- Blazor forms and validation
- Blazor advanced features, such as JavaScript interoperability, globalization, authentication, and more
- Third-party tools for Blazor WebAssembly
- .NET MAUI Blazor

While there is also server-side Blazor, which runs on the server like ASP.NET Core MVC, this chapter discusses just Blazor WebAssembly and .NET MAUI Blazor, since the main focus of the chapter is client-side technology. Moreover, server-side Blazor can't provide a performance that is comparable with other server-side technologies, like ASP.NET Core MVC, which we analyzed in *Chapter 17, Presenting ASP.NET Core*.

The first section summarizes and compares the various kinds of client technologies, while the remainder of the chapter discusses in detail Blazor WebAssembly and .NET MAUI Blazor.

Technical requirements

This chapter requires the free Visual Studio 2022 Community edition or better with all the database tools installed.

All concepts are clarified with simple example applications based on the WWTravelClub book use case you can find in the *Using client technologies* section of *Chapter 21, Case Study*.

The code for this chapter is available at `https://github.com/PacktPublishing/Software-Architecture-with-C-Sharp-12-and-.NET-8-4E`.

Comparison of the various types of client technologies

This section discusses the various types of client technologies:

- Single-page applications, which run in the browser with all browser restrictions
- Progressive applications, which run in the browser but can be installed like usual applications and can overcome some browser restrictions (after user permission is granted)
- Native applications, which are tied to a specific device/operating system but can take full advantage of all device/operating system features
- Cross-platform technologies, which, like native applications, can take full advantage of all device features but are compatible with several devices/operating systems

Single-page applications

There are many reasons why web development has increased in recent decades, but the most basic one is the ability to deploy any new version of the application to many users at the same time. Moreover, the security policies that are automatically enforced by all browsers encourage the usage and diffusion of web applications.

So, a good question here would be, why is web development not used today? The best answer would be a lack of connectivity. As a software architect, you need to be alert to this, as we discussed in *Chapter 2, Non-Functional Requirements*.

Sometimes, it is not only a matter of having connectivity or not. Sometimes, a big problem is instability, and don't forget the difficulties you will encounter from unexpected scenarios that web apps will generate once they're out in the world.

For instance, in the WWTravelClub case, there is a first user story that says: *"As a common user, I want to view promotional packages on the home page, so that I can easily find my next vacation."* At first sight, you may determine that a web app is the only option, especially because there is also a system requirement that says: *"The system will run on the Windows, Linux, iOS, and Android platforms."*

However, imagine that a user browsed a lot of destinations and packages to find their perfect vacation, and they are going to reserve it when suddenly, the web application crashes because of a lack of web connectivity. In this situation, the user would lose all their browsing effort and would be forced to start searching for the package from scratch once web connectivity is restored. The issue can be overcome just with an application that is able to save its state instead of crashing when there are web connectivity issues. This way, the user can complete their task as soon as web connectivity is restored, without wasting whatever effort they had already put in before the web connectivity issue.

So maybe, for some parts of the solution, a native application with some data already downloaded would be a better option. However, the issue can also be solved with a particular kind of modern web application, progressive applications, which we will analyze in the next subsection.

Progressive applications

Progressive web applications are single-page applications that run in the browser but can be installed like native applications. Moreover, they can run offline.

Progressive applications are a new web standard that is supported by all mainstream browsers. If you require all the advantages of web applications, but you also need the ability to work offline like a native application, progressive web applications are the right choice for you.

However, keep in mind that progressive web applications can't ensure the same performance and flexibility as native applications.

Blazor WebAssembly, as we will describe in the next sections of this chapter, supports progressive web applications. Check the **Progressive Web Application** checkbox that appears when you create a Blazor WebAssembly project. This is all you need to do to create a Blazor progressive web application.

If you ship your Blazor application as a progressive application, you overcome the problem of the initial download time (4-8 seconds), which is the main disadvantage of Blazor.

While progressive web applications are installed applications, they automatically update to the last available version, because each time they are launched, they verify if a more recent version is available, and if there is one, they automatically download it before running. That is, they have the advantage of automatically running the most recent available version that characterizes all classical web applications.

The option to install the Blazor progressive web application is not available during development because this would interfere with the usual modification test cycle. Therefore, you need to publish your application to test its progressive application peculiarities.

It is worth pointing out that progressive applications must be organized to take full advantage of their ability to work offline. Therefore, following repeated communication errors, the application should save all the data to be sent to the server in the browser's local storage while waiting for a connection to be established successfully.

It is also possible to maintain the whole application state in a centralized service so that the user can serialize and save it to local storage before quitting the application. This way, when the application is offline, data to be sent to the server is not lost because it remains in the application state that is saved to disk.

When a progressive web application doesn't fulfill your requirements because it is not able to use the specific device features you need, but you must support several different devices, you should consider cross-platform native applications, which have full access to all device features but can still support several hardware/software platforms. We will discuss them in the next subsection.

Native applications

Native development can be considered the beginning of UI development. There was no concept of sharing code between machines with diverse hardware when the idea of assigning software production to another person/company originally emerged.

This is the first good answer as to why we have good performance on native applications. We cannot forget that native apps run better just because they are near the hardware, most of the time connected to the OS directly or by using a framework, such as .NET. Be careful; we are not only talking about native mobile apps, but we are also discussing apps delivered in Windows, Linux, Mac, Android, or any other OS that can run apps.

Considering this scenario, the big question is – when do I have to use a native app? There are some cases where this would be a good idea:

- There is no need to deploy on different platforms.
- There is a huge connection to the hardware.
- The performance provided by a web client is not acceptable.
- The application needs device resources that can't be accessed through a browser because of a browser's security policies.
- The place where the application will run has connectivity problems.
- The worst case is the one where you need two things at the same time: better performance than a web client and different platforms. In this scenario, you will probably have to deliver two applications, and the way you have designed the backend of this solution will be extremely important for reducing maintenance and costs as regards development.

The decision between developing native or not can be difficult to take without a **proof of concept** (**POC**). As a software architect, you should be the one to recommend this kind of POC.

Examples of native applications that you can develop with C# are the classical Windows Forms and Windows Presentation Foundation, which are specific to the Windows operating system. Also, there is Xamarin, a platform that allows for the development of applications that can be published on both Android and iOS.

Cross-platform applications

Although performance can be a difficult requirement to achieve, in many scenarios, due to the simplicity of the solution, this is not the Achilles' heel of the application. Considering WWTravelClub, although it would be useful to have the offline experience mentioned before, the performance itself is not the most difficult one to achieve.

In these scenarios, cross-platform technologies make total sense. Among them, it is worth mentioning Xamarin.Forms and the new .NET MAUI, which can be published on Android, iOS, and Windows.

The advised choice of cross-platform application is .NET MAUI. However, at the moment, MAUI supports Windows and all main mobile platforms but not Linux. Uno Platform (`https://platform.uno/`) also supports Linux together with all main mobile platforms but is not a Microsoft product maintained by Microsoft. Anyway, it can be downloaded as a Visual Studio extension.

In this chapter, we will not analyze Uno or all the options offered by .NET MAUI but just .NET MAUI Blazor since it is very similar to Blazor WebAssembly. So, learning Blazor enables us to develop single-page applications, progressive applications, and cross-platform applications.

.NET MAUI Blazor is described in the *.NET MAUI Blazor* section of this chapter, while the next section describes the basics of Blazor WebAssembly architecture.

Blazor WebAssembly architecture

Blazor WebAssembly uses the new WebAssembly browser feature to execute the .NET runtime in the browser. This way, it enables all developers to use the whole .NET code base and ecosystem in the implementation of applications capable of running in any WebAssembly-compliant browser. WebAssembly was conceived as a high-performance alternative to JavaScript. It is an assembly capable of running in a browser and obeying the same limitations as JavaScript code. This means that WebAssembly code, like JavaScript code, runs in an isolated execution environment that has very limited access to all machine resources.

WebAssembly differs from similar options from the past, like Flash and Silverlight, since it is an official W3C standard. More specifically, it became an official standard on December 5, 2019, so it is expected to have a long life. As a matter of fact, all mainstream browsers already support it.

However, WebAssembly doesn't bring just performance with it; it also creates the opportunity to run whole code bases associated with modern and advanced object-oriented languages such as C++ (direct compilation), Java (bytecode), and C# (.NET) in browsers.

At the moment, Microsoft offers two frameworks that run .NET on top of WebAssembly, Blazor WebAssembly and Unity WebAssembly, which is the WebAssembly port of the Unity 3D graphic framework. Unity WebAssembly's main purpose is the implementation of online video games that run in the browser, while Blazor WebAssembly is a **single-page application** framework that uses .NET instead of JavaScript or TypeScript.

Before WebAssembly, presentation layers running in a browser could only be implemented in JavaScript, with all the problems associated with the maintenance of big code bases implemented in a language that is not strictly typed. However, we must consider that on one hand, the usage of TypeScript in part solves JavaScript's lack of strict typing, and on the other hand, .NET brings with it the problem of the binary compatibility of modules implemented with different .NET versions.

Anyway, with Blazor C#, developers can now implement complex applications in their favorite language, with all the comforts offered to this language by the C# compiler and Visual Studio.

Moreover, with Blazor, all .NET developers can use the full power of the .NET framework, with the only limitations imposed by the browser security policies, for the implementation of presentation layers that run in the browser and that share libraries and classes with all other layers that run on the server side.

The subsections that follow describe all the Blazor architectures. The first subsection explores the general concept of a single-page application, describing Blazor's peculiarities.

What is a single-page application?

A **single-page application** (**SPA**) is an HTML-based application, where the HTML is changed by code that runs in the browser instead of issuing a new request to the server and rendering a new HTML page from scratch. SPAs can simulate a multi-page experience by replacing complete page areas with new HTML.

SPA frameworks are frameworks explicitly designed for implementing SPAs. Before WebAssembly, all SPA frameworks were based on JavaScript. The most famous JavaScript-based SPA frameworks are Angular, React.js, and Vue.js.

All SPA frameworks provide ways to transform data into HTML to show to the user and rely on a module called *router* to simulate page changes. Typically, data fills in the placeholders of HTML templates and selects which parts of a template to render (`if-like` constructs) and how many times to render it (`for-like` constructs).

The Blazor template language is Razor, which we described in *Chapter 17, Presenting ASP.NET Core*.

In order to increase modularity, code is organized into components, which are a kind of virtual HTML tag that, once rendered, generates actual HTML markup. Like HTML tags, components have attributes, which are usually called parameters, and custom events. It is up to the developer to ensure that each component uses its parameters to create proper HTML and to ensure that it generates adequate events. Components can be used inside other components in a hierarchical fashion.

Components can be associated with URLs in the application web domain, in which case they are called pages. These URLs can be used in the usual HTML links and following them leads to the upload of the page into an application area thanks to framework services called routers.

Some SPA frameworks also provide a predefined dependency injection engine in order to ensure better separation between components on one side and general-purpose services plus business code that runs in the browser on the other. Among the frameworks listed in this subsection, only Blazor and Angular have an out-of-the-box dependency injection engine.

In order to reduce the overall application file size, SPA frameworks based on JavaScript usually compile all JavaScript code in a few JavaScript files and then perform so-called tree-shaking, that is, the removal of all unused code. This technique sensibly reduces the application load time.

At the moment, instead, Blazor keeps all DLLs referenced by the main application separate and performs tree-shaking on each of them separately.

The next subsection describes the Blazor architecture. We challenge you to create a Blazor WebAssembly project called `BlazorReview`, so you can inspect the code and the constructs explained throughout the chapter. To do this, select the **Blazor WebAssembly Standalone Application** option when creating a new project. Make sure to select **Individual Accounts** as the authentication type and ensure that the **Include sample pages** checkbox is checked, as shown in the picture below.

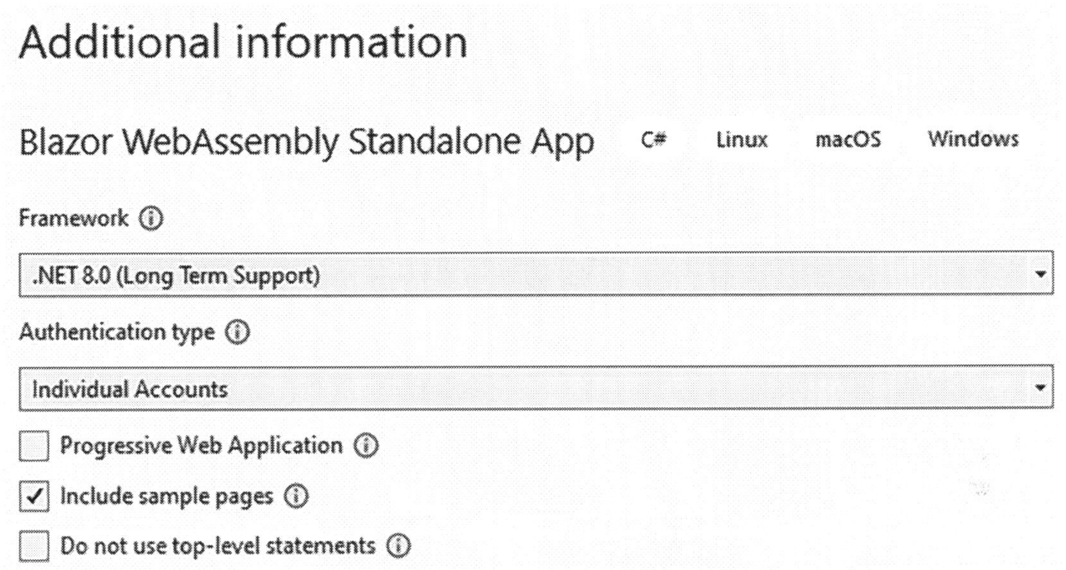

Figure 19.1: Creating the BlazorReview application

If you start the application, the application works properly, but if you try to log in, the following error message will appear: "There was an error trying to log you in: 'Network Error'." This is because you need to configure an identity-provider-authenticated user. As the default, the application is configured to use an OAuth-based identity provider web application. You need to just add the provider configuration data in a configuration file. We will look at this in more detail in the *Authentication and authorization* section.

Loading and starting the application

The folder structure of a Blazor WebAssembly application always includes an `index.html` static HTML page. In our `BlazorReview` project, `index.html` is in `BlazorReview->wwwroot->index.html`. This page is the container where the Blazor application will create its HTML. It contains an HTML header with a `viewport meta` declaration, the title, and CSS for the application's overall styling. The Visual Studio default project template adds an application-specific CSS file and Bootstrap CSS, with a neutral style. You can replace the default Bootstrap CSS either with a customized style or a completely different CSS framework.

The body contains the code that follows:

```
<body>
  <div id="app">
     <svg class="loading-progress">
            <circle r="40%" cx="50%" cy="50%" />
            <circle r="40%" cx="50%" cy="50%" />
     </svg>
     <div id="loading-progress-text"></div>
  </div>
  <div id="blazor-error-ui">
        An unhandled error has occurred.
    <a href="" class="reload">Reload</a>
    <a class="dismiss"> / </a>
  </div>
<script
src="_content/Microsoft.AspNetCore.Components.WebAssembly.Authentication/
AuthenticationService.js">
</script>
<script src="_framework/blazor.webassembly.js"></script>
</body>
```

The initial `div` with the `app id` is where the application will place the code it generates. Any markup placed inside this `div` will appear just while the Blazor application is loading and starting, then it will be replaced by the application-generated HTML. As the default, it contains an `svg` image and text that shows the loading progress, which are both controlled by the JavaScript code that takes care of loading the framework. The loading animation is based on a CSS animation contained in the `css/app.css` main application CSS file. However, you can replace both the default content and the CSS animation.

The second `div` is normally invisible and appears only when Blazor intercepts an unhandled exception.

`blazor.webassembly.js` contains the JavaScript part of the Blazor framework. Among other things, it takes care of downloading the .NET runtime, together with all application DLLs. More specifically, `blazor.webassembly.js` downloads the `blazor.boot.json` file, which lists all application files with their hashes.

Then, `blazor.webassembly.js` downloads all resources listed in this file and verifies their hashes. All resources downloaded by `blazor.webassembly.js` are created when the application is built or published. Loading `blazor.webassembly.js` periodically updates the `--blazor-load-percentage` and `--blazor-load-percentage-text` CSS variables with the loading percentage in numeric format and as text, respectively.

`AuthenticationService.js` is added only when the project enables authentication and takes care of the `OpenID Connect` protocol used by Blazor to exploit other identity providers, to get bearer tokens, which are the preferred authentication credentials for clients that interact with a server through web APIs.

Authentication is discussed in more detail in the *Authentication and authorization* subsection later on in this chapter, while bearer tokens are discussed in the *REST service authorization and authentication* section of *Chapter 15, Applying Service-Oriented Architectures with .NET*.

The Blazor application entry point is in the `BlazorReview->Program.cs` file. This file doesn't contain a class but just the code that must be executed when the application is launched:

```
var builder = WebAssemblyHostBuilder.CreateDefault(args);
builder.RootComponents.Add<App>("#app");
builder.RootComponents.Add< HeadOutlet>("head::after");

// Services added to the application
// Dependency Injection engine declared with statements like:
// builder.Services.Add...
await builder.Build().RunAsync();
```

In fact, the new Blazor WebAssembly project template takes advantage of this new way to define the application entry point that was introduced starting from .NET 7.

`WebAssemblyHostBuilder` is a builder for creating a `WebAssemblyHost`, which is a WebAssembly-specific implementation of the generic host discussed in the *Using generic hosts* subsection of *Chapter 11, Applying a Microservice Architecture to Your Enterprise Application* (you are encouraged to review that subsection). The first builder configuration instruction declares the Blazor root component (`App`), which will contain the whole component tree, and specifies in which HTML tag of the `index.html` page to place it (`#app`). More specifically, `RootComponents.Add` adds a hosted service that takes care of handling the whole Blazor component tree. We can run several Blazor WebAssembly user interfaces on the same HTML page by calling `RootComponents.Add` several times, each time with a different HTML tag reference.

As the default, just another root component is added, `HeadOutlet`, and is placed immediately after the `HTML Head` tag. It is used to dynamically change the `index.html` title (the text shown in the browser tab). For more information on the `HeadOutlet` component, see the *Modifying HTML <head> content from Blazor components* subsection.

builder.Services contains all the usual methods and extension methods to add services to the Blazor application dependency engine: AddScoped, AddTransient, AddSingleton, and so on. Like in ASP.NET Core MVC applications (*Chapter 17, Presenting ASP.NET Core*, and *Chapter 18, Implementing Frontend Microservices with ASP.NET Core*), services are the preferred places to implement business logic and store shared state. While in ASP.NET Core MVC services were usually passed to controllers, in Blazor WebAssembly, they are injected into components.

The default project scaffolded by Visual Studio contains just two services, one for communicating with the server and the other for handling OAuth-based authentication. We will discuss both of them later on in this chapter.

The next subsection explains how the root App component simulates page changes.

Routing

The root App class referenced by the host-building code is defined in the BlazorReview ->App.razor file. App is a Blazor component, and like all Blazor components, it is defined in a file with a .razor extension and uses Razor syntax enriched with component notation, that is, with HTML-like tags that represent other Blazor components. It contains the whole logic for handling application pages:

```
<CascadingAuthenticationState>
  <Router AppAssembly="@typeof(App).Assembly">
    <Found Context="routeData">
      <AuthorizeRouteView RouteData="@routeData"
                   DefaultLayout="@typeof(MainLayout)">
        <NotAuthorized>
         @*Template that specifies what to show
           when user is not authorized *@
        </NotAuthorized>
      </AuthorizeRouteView>
     <FocusOnNavigate RouteData="@routeData" Selector="h1">
    </Found>
    <NotFound Layout="@typeof(MainLayout)">
     <PageTitle>Not found<PageTitle>
      <LayoutView Layout="@typeof(MainLayout)">
        <p>Sorry, there's nothing at this address.</p>
      </LayoutView>
    </NotFound>
  </Router>
</CascadingAuthenticationState>
```

All tags in the preceding code represent either components or particular component parameters, called templates. Components will be discussed in detail throughout the chapter. For the moment, imagine them as a kind of custom HTML tags that we can somehow define with C# and Razor code. Templates, instead, are parameters that accept Razor markup as values. Templates are discussed in the *Templates and cascading parameters* subsection later on in this section.

The `CascadingAuthenticationState` component only has the function of passing authentication and authorization information to all components of the component tree that is inside of it. The Blazor project template generates it only if one chooses to add authorization during project creation.

The `Router` component is the actual application router. It scans the assembly passed in the `AppAssembly` parameter looking for components containing routing information, that is, for components that can work as pages. In the Blazor project template, the `Router` component is passed the assembly that contains the class of the `App` component, that is, the main application. Pages contained in other assemblies can be added through the `AdditionalAssemblies` parameter, which accepts an `IEnumerable` of assemblies.

After that, the router intercepts all page changes performed either by code or through the usual `<a>` HTML tags that point to an address inside of the application base address. Navigation can be handled by code by requiring a `NavigationManager` instance from dependency injection.

The `Router` component has two templates, one for the case where a page for the requested URI is found (`Found`), and the other for the case where it is not found (`NotFound`). When the application uses authorization, the `Found` template consists of the `AuthorizeRouteView` components, which further distinguish whether the user is authorized to access the selected page or not. When the application doesn't use authorization, the `Found` template consists of the `RouteView` component:

```
<RouteView RouteData="@routeData" DefaultLayout="@typeof(MainLayout)" />
```

`RouteView` takes the selected page and renders it inside the layout page specified by the `DefaultLayout` parameter. This specification acts as a default since each page can override it by specifying a different layout page. In the Blazor project template, the default layout page is in the `BlazorReview->Layout->MainLayout.razor` file.

Blazor layout pages work similarly to ASP.NET Core MVC layout pages, described in the *Reusing view code* subsection of *Chapter 17, Presenting ASP.NET Core*, the only difference being that the place to add the page markup is specified with `@Body`:

```
<article class="content px-4">
      @Body
</article>
```

If the application uses authorization, `AuthorizeRouteView` works like `RouteView`, but it also allows the specification of a template for a case where the user is not authorized:

```
<NotAuthorized>
@if (!context.User.Identity.IsAuthenticated)
{
  <RedirectToLogin />
}
else
{
  <p role ="alert">You are not authorized to access this resource.</p>
}
</NotAuthorized>
```

If the user is not authenticated, the `RedirectToLogin` component uses a `NavigationManager` instance to move to the login logic page; otherwise, it informs the users that they haven't got enough privileges to access the selected page.

Blazor WebAssembly also allows the lazy loading of assemblies to reduce the initial application loading time, but we will not discuss it here for lack of space. The *Further reading* section contains references to the official Blazor documentation.

As we will discuss in more detail later on in this chapter, the `PageTitle` component enables the developer to set the page title that appears in the browser tabs. The `FocusOnNavigate` component, instead, sets the HTML focus on the first HTML element that satisfies the CSS selector passed in its `Selector` parameter, immediately after a page is navigated.

Blazor pages and components

In this section, you will learn the fundamentals of Blazor components, including how to construct a component, the structure of components, how to attach events to HTML tags, how to specify the components' characteristics, and how to use other components within your components. We have divided the content into several subsections:

- Component structure
- Templates and cascading parameters
- Error handling
- Events
- Bindings
- How Blazor updates HTML
- Component lifecycle

Component structure

Components are the core of all main client frameworks. They are the key ingredient to building modular UI, whose parts are easily modifiable and reusable. In a few words, they are the graphical counterpart of classes. In fact, just like classes, they allow encapsulation and code organization. Moreover, the component architecture allows the formal definition of efficacious UI update algorithms, as we will see in the *How Blazor updates HTML* section of this chapter.

Components are defined in files with a `.razor` extension. Once compiled, they become classes that inherit from `ComponentBase`. Like all other Visual Studio project elements, Blazor components are available through the **Add New Item** menu. Usually, components to be used as pages are defined in the `Pages` folder, or in its subfolders, while other components are organized in different folders. Default Blazor projects add all their non-page components inside the `Shared` folder, but you can organize them differently.

By default, pages are assigned a namespace that corresponds to the path of the folder they are in. Thus, for instance, in our example project, all pages that are in the `BlazorReview->Pages` path are assigned to the `BlazorReview.Pages` namespace.

However, you can change this default namespace with an @namespace declaration placed in the declaration area that is at the top of the file. This area may also contain other important declarations. The following is an example that shows all declarations:

```
@page "/counter"
@layout MyCustomLayout
@namespace BlazorReview.Pages
@using Microsoft.AspNetCore.Authorization
@implements MyInterface
@inherits MyParentComponent
@typeparam T
@attribute [Authorize]
@inject NavigationManager navigation
```

The first two directives make sense only for components that must work as pages, while all others may appear in any component. Below is a detailed explanation of each declaration:

- The `@layout` directive, when specified, overrides the default layout page with another component.
- The `@page` directive defines the path of the page (**route**) within the application base URL. Thus, for instance, if our application runs at `https://localhost:5001`, then the URL of this page will be `https://localhost:5001/counter`. Page routes can also contain parameters, like in this example: `/orderitem/{customer}/{order}`. Parameter names must match public properties defined as parameters by the components. The match is case-insensitive. Parameters will be explained later on in this subsection.
- The string that instantiates each parameter is converted into the parameter type, and if this conversion fails, an exception is thrown. This behavior can be prevented by associating a type with each parameter, in which case, if the conversion to the specified type fails, the match with the page URL fails. Only elementary types are supported: `/orderitem/{customer:int}/{order:int}`. As a default, parameters are obligatory; that is, if they are not found, the match fails and the router tries other pages. However, you can make parameters optional by post-fixing them with a question mark: `/orderitem/{customer?:int}/{order?:int}`. If an optional parameter is not specified, the default for its type is used.
- From version 6, parameters can also be extracted from the query string: `/orderitem/{customer:int}?order=123`.
- `@namespace` overrides the default namespace of the component, while `@using` is equivalent to the usual C# `using`. The `@using` declared in the special `{project folder}->_Imports.razor` folder is automatically applied to all components.
- `@inherits` declares that the component is a subclass of another component, while `@implements` declares that it implements an interface.
- `@typeparam` is used if the component is a generic class and declares the name of the generic parameter. `@typeparam` also allows the specification of generic constraints with the same syntax used in classes: `@typeparam T where T: class`.

- `@attribute` declares any attribute applied to the component class. Property-level attributes are applied directly to properties defined in the code area, so they don't need special notation. The `[Authorize]` attribute, applied to a component class used as a page, prevents unauthorized users from accessing the page. It works exactly in the same way as when it is applied to a controller or to an action method in ASP.NET Core MVC.
- Finally, the `@inject` directive requires a type instance to the dependency injection engine and inserts it in the field declared after the type name; in the previous example, in the `navigation` parameter.

The middle part of the component file contains the HTML that will be rendered by the component with Razor markup, enriched with the possible invocation of child components.

The bottom part of the file is enclosed by an `@code` construct and contains fields, properties, and methods of the class that implements the component:

```
@code{
  ...
  private string myField="0";
  [Parameter]
  public int Quantity {get; set;}=0;
  private void IncrementQuantity ()
  {
          Quantity++;
  }
  private void DecrementQuantity ()
  {
         Quantity--;
         if (Quantity<0) Quantity=0;
  }
  ...
}
```

Public properties decorated with the `[Parameter]` attribute work as component parameters; that is, when the component is instantiated into another component, they are used to pass values to the decorated properties, and those values are passed to HTML elements in HTML markup:

```
<OrderItem Quantity ="2" Id="123"/>
```

Values can also be passed to component parameters by page route parameters, or query string parameters that match the property name in a case-invariant match:

```
OrderItem/{id}/{quantity}
OrderItem/{id}?quantity = 123
```

However, the match with query string parameters is enabled only if the property is also decorated with the `SupplyParameterFromQuery` attribute:

```
[Parameter]
[SupplyParameterFromQuery]
public int Quantity {get; set;}=0;
```

Component parameters can also accept complex types and functions:

```
<modal title='() => "Test title" ' ...../>
```

If components are generic, they must be passed type values for each generic parameter declared with `typeparam`:

```
<myGeneric T= "string"...../>
```

However, often, the compiler is able to infer generic types from the types of other parameters.

Finally, the code enclosed in the `@code` directive can also be declared in a partial class with the same name and namespace as the component:

```
public partial class Counter
{
  [Parameter]
  public int CurrentCounter {get; set;}=0;
  ...
  ...
}
```

Usually, these partial classes are declared in the same folder as the component and with a filename equal to the component's filename with a `.cs` postfix added. Thus, for instance, the partial class associated with the `counter.razor` component will be `counter.razor.cs`.

Each component may also have an associated CSS file, whose name must be the name of the component file plus the `.css` postfix. Thus, for instance, the CSS file associated with the `counter.razor` component will be `counter.razor.css`. The CSS contained in this file is applied only to the component and has no effect on the remainder of the page. This is called CSS isolation, and at the moment, it is implemented by adding a unique attribute to all component HTML roots. Then, all selectors of the component CSS file are scoped to this attribute so that they can't affect other HTML.

Of course, we can also use global application CSS, and in fact, the Blazor template creates the `wwwroot/css/app.css` file for this purpose.

When the Blazor application is packaged, either during a build or during its publication, all isolated CSS is processed and placed in a unique CSS file called `<assembly name>.Client.styles.css`. That's why the `index.html` page of our `BlazorReview` application contains the following CSS reference:

```
<head>
    ...
    <link href="BlazorReview.Client.styles.css" rel="stylesheet" />
</head>
```

It is worth mentioning that isolated CSS can also be obtained with pure CSS techniques, or using the **Sass** language, which compiles with CSS.

Whenever a component decorates an `IDictionary<string, object>` parameter with `[Parameter(CaptureUnmatchedValues = true)]`, then all unmatched parameters inserted into the tag, that is, all parameters without a matching component property, are added to the `IDictionary` as key-value pairs.

This feature provides an easy way to forward parameters to HTML elements or other child components contained in the component markup. For instance, if we have a `Detail` component that displays a detail view of the object passed in its `Value` parameter, we can use this feature to forward all usual HTML attributes to the root HTML tag of the component, as shown in the following example:

```
<div  @attributes="AdditionalAttributes">
...
</div>
@code{
 [Parameter(CaptureUnmatchedValues = true)]
 public Dictionary<string, object>
 AdditionalAttributes { get; set; }
 [Parameter]
 Public T Value {get; set;}
}
```

This way, usual HTML attributes added to the component tag, for instance, `class`, are forwarded to the root `div` of the components and used to style the component:

```
<Detail Value="myObject" class="my-css-class"/>
```

The next subsection explains how to pass markup-generating functions to components.

Templates and cascading parameters

Blazor works by building a data structure called a **render tree**, which is updated as the UI changes. At each change, Blazor locates the part of the HTML that must be rendered and uses the information contained in the **render tree** to update it.

The `RenderFragment` delegate defines a function that is able to add further markup to a specific position of the **render tree**. There is also `RenderFragment<T>`, which accepts a further argument you can use to drive the markup generation. For instance, you can pass a `Customer` object to `RenderFragment<T>` so that it can render all the data for that specific customer.

You can define `RenderFragment` or `RenderFragment<T>` with C# code, but the simplest way is to define it in your components with Razor markup. The Razor compiler will take care of generating the proper C# code for you:

```
RenderFragment myRenderFragment = @<p>The time is @DateTime.Now.</p>;
RenderFragment<Customer> customerRenderFragment =
(item) => @<p>Customer name is @item.Name.</p>;
```

The information on the location to add the markup is passed in the `RenderTreeBuilder` argument it receives as an argument. You can use `RenderFragment` in your component Razor markup by simply invoking it as shown in the following example:

```
RenderFragment myRenderFragment = ...
  ...
<div>
  ...
  @myRenderFragment
  ...
</div>
  ...
```

The position where you invoke `RenderFragment` defines the location where it will add its markup, since the component compiler is able to generate the right `RenderTreeBuilder` argument to pass to it. `RenderFragment<T>` delegates are invoked as shown here:

```
Customer myCustomer = ...
  ...
<div>
  ...
  @myRenderFragment(myCustomer)
  ...
</div>
  ...
```

Being functions, render fragments can be passed to component parameters like all other types. However, Blazor has a specific syntax to make it easier to simultaneously define and pass render fragments to components: the **template** syntax. First, you define the parameters in your component:

```
[Parameter]
Public RenderFragment<Customer>CustomerTemplate {get; set;}
[Parameter]
Public RenderFragment Title {get; set;}
```

Then, when you call the customer, you can do the following:

```
<Detail>
  <Title>
    <h5>This is a title</h5>
  </Title>
  <CustomerTemplate Context=customer>
    <p>Customer name is @customer.Name.</p>
  </CustomerTemplate>
</Detail>
```

Each RenderFragment parameter is represented by a tag with the same name as the parameter. You can place the markup that defines RenderFragment inside of it. For the CustomerTemplate that has a parameter, the Context keyword defines the parameter name inside the markup. In our example, the chosen parameter name is customer.

When a component has just one render fragment parameter, if it is named ChildContent, the template markup can be enclosed directly between the opening and closing tags of the component:

```
[Parameter]
Public RenderFragment<Customer> ChildContent {get; set;}
..............
..............
<IHaveJustOneRenderFragment Context=customer>
  <p>Customer name is @customer.Name.</p>
</IHaveJustOneRenderFragment>
```

In order to familiarize ourselves with component templates, let's modify the Pages->Weather.razor page so that, instead of using foreach, it uses a Repeater component.

Let's right-click on the Layout folder, select **Add** and then **Razor Component**, and add a new Repeater.razor component. Then, replace the existing code with this:

```
@typeparam T
@foreach(var item in Values)
{
  @ChildContent(item)
}
@code {
    [Parameter]
    public RenderFragment<T> ChildContent { get; set; }
    [Parameter]
    public IEnumerable<T> Values { get; set; }
}
```

The component is defined with a generic parameter so that it can be used with any IEnumerable. Now let's replace the markup in the tbody of the Weather.razor component with this:

```
<Repeater Values="forecasts" Context="forecast">
  <tr>
    <td>@forecast.Date.ToShortDateString()</td>
    <td>@forecast.TemperatureC</td>
    <td>@forecast.TemperatureF</td>
    <td>@forecast.Summary</td>
  </tr>
</Repeater>
```

Since the `Repeater` component has just one template, and since we named it `ChildContent`, we can place our template markup directly within the component open and close tags. Run it and verify that the page works properly. You have learned how to use templates and that markup placed inside a component defines a template.

An important predefined templated Blazor component is the `CascadingValue` component. It renders the content placed inside of it with no changes, but passes a type instance to all its descendant components:

```
<CascadingValue  Value="new MyOptionsInstance{...}">
......
</CascadingValue>
```

All components placed inside of the `CascadingValue` tag and all their descendant components can now capture the instance of `MyOptionsInstance` passed in the `CascadingValue` parameter. It is enough that the component declares a public or private property with a type that is compatible with `MyOptionsInstance` and that decorates it with the `CascadingParameter` attribute:

```
[CascadingParameter]
private MyOptionsInstance options {get; set;}
```

Matching is performed by type compatibility. If there's ambiguity with other cascaded parameters with a compatible type, we can specify the `Name` optional parameter of the `CascadingValue` component and pass the same name to the `CascadingParameter` attribute: `[CascadingParameter("myUnique name")]`.

The `CascadingValue` tag also has an `IsFixed` parameter that should be set to `true` whenever possible for performance reasons. In fact, propagating cascading values is very useful for passing options and settings, but it has a very high computational cost.

When `IsFixed` is set to `true`, propagation is performed just once, the first time that each piece of content involved is rendered, and then no attempt is made to update the cascaded value during the content's lifetime. Thus, `IsFixed` can be used whenever the pointer of the cascaded object is not changed during the content's lifetime.

An example of a cascading value is the `CascadingAuthenticationState` component we encountered in the *Routing* subsection, which cascades authentication and authorization information to all rendered components.

Error handling

As the default, when an error in a component occurs, the exception is intercepted by the .NET runtime, which automatically makes visible the error code contained in `index.html`:

```
<div id="blazor-error-ui">
        An unhandled error has occurred.
    <a href="" class="reload">Reload</a>
    <a class="dismiss"> / </a>
</div>
```

However, component errors can be intercepted and handled locally by enclosing the component inside an `ErrorBoundary` component. Below, the code of the `Repeater` example in the previous subsection has been modified to locally handle errors that might occur in each row:

```
<Repeater Values="forecasts" Context="forecast">
  <tr>
   <ErrorBoundary>
    <ChildContent>
    <td>@forecast.Date.ToShortDateString()</td>
    <td>@forecast.TemperatureC</td>
    <td>@forecast.TemperatureF</td>
    <td>@forecast.Summary</td>
    </ChildContent>
    <ErrorContent>
     <td colspan="4" class="my-error">Nothing to see here. Sorry!</td>
    </ErrorContent>
   </ErrorBoundary>
  </tr>
</Repeater>
```

The standard code is placed in the `ChildContent` template, while the `ErrorContent` template is shown if there's an error.

Events

Both HTML tags and Blazor components use attributes/parameters to get input. HTML tags provide output to the remainder of the page through events, and Blazor allows C# functions to be attached to HTML `on{event name}` attributes. The syntax is shown in the `Pages->Counter.razor` component:

```
<p role="status">Current count: @currentCount</p>
<button class="btn btn-primary" @onclick="IncrementCount">Click me</button>
@code {
private int currentCount = 0;
private void IncrementCount()
    {
        currentCount++;
    }
}
```

The function can also be passed inline as a lambda. Moreover, it accepts the C# equivalent of the usual `event` argument. The *Further reading* section contains a link to the Blazor official documentation page that lists all supported events and their arguments.

Since Blazor components are designed as enhanced versions of HTML elements—with added capabilities—they can also have events. However, unlike standard HTML elements, both the features and implementations of these events in Blazor components are defined by the developer.

Blazor events enable components to return output, too. Component events are defined as parameters whose type is either `EventCallBack` or `EventCallBack<T>`. `EventCallBack` is the type of component event with no arguments while `EventCallBack<T>` is the type of component event with an argument of type `T`. In order to trigger an event, say `MyEvent`, the component calls:

```
await MyEvent.InvokeAsync()
```

or

```
await MyIntEvent.InvokeAsync(arg)
```

These calls execute the handlers bound to the events or do nothing if no handler has been bound.

Once defined, component events can be used exactly in the same way as HTML element events, the only difference being that there is no need to prefix the event name with an `@`, since `@` in HTML events is needed to distinguish between the HTML attribute and the Blazor-added parameter with the same name:

```
[Parameter]
publicEventCallback MyEvent {get; set;}
[Parameter]
publicEventCallback<int> MyIntEvent {get; set;}
...
...
<ExampleComponent
MyEvent="() => ..."
MyIntEvent = "(i) =>..." />
```

Actually, HTML element events are also `EventCallBack<T>` events. That is why both event types behave in exactly the same way. `EventCallBack` and `EventCallBack<T>` are structs, not delegates, since they contain a delegate, together with a pointer to the entity that must be notified that the event has been triggered. Formally, this entity is represented by a `Microsoft.AspNetCore.Components.IHandleEvent` interface. Needless to say, all components implement this interface. The notification informs `IHandleEvent` that a state change took place. State changes play a fundamental role in the way Blazor updates the page HTML. We will analyze them in detail in the next subsection.

For HTML elements, Blazor also provides the possibility to stop the event's default action and the event bubbling by adding the `:preventDefault` and `:stopPropagation` directives to the attribute that specifies the event, like in these examples:

```
@onkeypress="KeyHandler" @onkeypress:preventDefault="true"
@onkeypress:stopPropagation  ="true"
```

Bindings

Often, a component parameter value must be kept synchronized with an external variable, property, or field. The typical application of this kind of synchronization is an object property being edited in an input component or HTML tag. Whenever the user changes the input value, the object property must be updated coherently, and vice versa. The object property value must be copied into the component as soon as the component is rendered so that the user can edit it.

Similar scenarios are handled by parameter-event pairs. More specifically, from one side, the property is copied in the input component parameter. From the other side, each time the input changes value, a component event that updates the property is triggered. This way, property and input values are kept synchronized.

This scenario is so common and useful that Blazor has a specific syntax for simultaneously defining the event and copying the property value into the parameter. This simplified syntax requires that the event has the same name as the parameter involved in the interaction but with a `Changed` postfix.

Suppose, for instance, that a component has a `Value` parameter. Then, the corresponding event must be `ValueChanged`. Moreover, each time the user changes the component value, the component must invoke the `ValueChanged` event by calling `await ValueChanged.InvokeAsync(arg)`. With this in place, a property called `MyObject.MyProperty` can be synchronized with the `Value` property with the syntax shown here:

```
<MyComponent @bind-Value="MyObject.MyProperty"/>
```

The preceding syntax is called `binding`. Blazor takes care of automatically attaching an event handler that updates the `MyObject.MyProperty` property to the `ValueChanged` event.

Bindings of HTML elements work in a similar way, but since the developer can't decide the names of parameters and events, a slightly different convention must be used. First of all, there is no need to specify the parameter name in the binding, since it is always the HTML input `value` attribute. Therefore, the binding is written simply as `@bind="object.MyProperty"`. By default, the object property is updated on the `change` event, but you can specify a different event by adding the `@bind-event: @bind-event="oninput"` attribute.

Moreover, bindings of HTML inputs try to automatically convert the input string into the target type. If the conversion fails, the input reverts to its initial value. This behavior is quite primitive since, in the event of errors, no error message is provided to the user, and the culture settings are not taken into account properly (HTML5 inputs use invariant culture but text input must use the current culture). We advise binding inputs only to string target types. Blazor has specific components for handling dates and numbers that should be used whenever the target type is not a string. We will describe these components in the *Blazor forms and validation* section.

In order to familiarize ourselves with events, let's write a component that synchronizes the content of an input-type text when the user clicks a confirmation button. Let's right-click on the `Layout` folder and add a new `ConfirmedText.razor` component. Then replace its code with this:

```
<input type="text" @bind="Value" @attributes="AdditionalAttributes"/>
<button class="btn btn-secondary" @onclick="Confirmed">@ButtonText</button>
@code {
    [Parameter(CaptureUnmatchedValues = true)]
    public Dictionary<string, object> AdditionalAttributes { get; set; }
    [Parameter]
    public string Value {get; set;}
    [Parameter]
    public EventCallback<string> ValueChanged { get; set; }
    [Parameter]
    public string ButtonText { get; set; }
    async Task Confirmed()
    {
        await ValueChanged.InvokeAsync(Value);
    }
}
```

The `ConfirmedText` component exploits the button-click event to trigger the `ValueChanged` event. Moreover, the component uses `@bind` to synchronize its `Value` parameter with the HTML input. It is worth pointing out that the component uses `CaptureUnmatchedValues` to forward all HTML attributes applied to its tag to the HTML input. This way, users of the `ConfirmedText` component can style the input field by simply adding `class` and/or `style` attributes to the component tag.

Now, let's use this component in the `Pages->Index.razor` page by placing the following code at the end of `Home.razor`:

```
<ConfirmedText @bind-Value="textValue" ButtonText="Confirm" />
<p>
    Confirmed value is: @textValue
</p>
@code{
private string textValue = null;
}
```

If you run the project and play with the input and its **Confirm** button, you will see that each time the **Confirm** button is clicked, not only are the input values copied in the `textValue` page property but also the content of the paragraph that is behind the component is coherently updated.

We explicitly synchronized `textValue` with the component with `@bind-Value`, but what takes care of keeping `textValue` synchronized with the content of the paragraph? The answer can be found in the next subsection.

How Blazor updates HTML

When we write the content of a variable, property, or field in Razor markup with something like `@model.property`, Blazor not only renders the actual value of the variable, property, or field when the component is rendered but tries also to update the HTML each time that this value changes, with a process called **change detection**. Change detection is a feature of all the main SPA frameworks, but the way Blazor implements it is very simple and elegant.

The basic idea is that once all HTML has been rendered, changes may occur only because of code executed inside of events. That is why `EventCallBack` and `EventCallBack<T>` contain a reference to an `IHandleEvent`. When a component binds a handler to an event, the Razor compiler creates an `EventCallBack` or `EventCallBack<T>`, passing its struct constructor the function bound to the event, and the component where the function was defined (`IHandleEvent`).

Once the code of the handler has been executed, the Blazor runtime is notified that the `IHandleEvent` might have changed. In fact, the handler code can only change the values of variables, properties, or fields of the component where the handler was defined. In turn, this triggers a change detection process rooted in the component. Blazor verifies which variables, properties, or fields used in the component Razor markup changed and updates the associated HTML.

If a changed variable, property, or field is an input parameter of another component, then the HTML generated by that component might also need updates. Accordingly, another change detection process rooted in that component is recursively triggered.

The algorithm sketched previously discovers all relevant changes only if the following conditions are met:

- No component references data structures belonging to other components in an event handler.
- All inputs to a component arrive through its parameters and not through method calls or other public members.

When there is a change that is not detected because of the failure of one of the preceding conditions, the developer must manually declare the possible change of the component. This can be done by calling the `StateHasChanged()` component method. Since this call might result in changes to the page's HTML, its execution cannot take place asynchronously but must be queued in the HTML page's UI thread. This is done by passing the function to be executed to the `InvokeAsync` component method.

Summing up, the instruction to execute is `await InvokeAsync(StateHasChanged)`.

The next subsection concludes the description of components with an analysis of their lifecycle and the associated lifecycle methods.

Component lifecycle

Each component lifecycle event has an associated method. Some methods have both synchronous and asynchronous versions, some have just an asynchronous version, and some others have just a synchronous version.

The component lifecycle starts with parameters passed to the component being copied in the associated component properties. You can customize this step by overriding the following method:

```
public override async Task SetParametersAsync(ParameterView parameters)
{
  await ...
  await base.SetParametersAsync(parameters);
}
```

Typically, customization consists of the modification of additional data structures, so the base method is called to also perform the default action of copying parameters in the associated properties.

After that, there is the component initialization that is associated with the two methods:

```
protected override void OnInitialized()
{
    ...
}
protected override async Task OnInitializedAsync()
{
  await ...
}
```

They are called once in the component lifetime, immediately after the component has been created and added to the render tree. Please place any initialization code there, and not in the component constructor, as this will improve component testability. This is because there, you have all parameters set and future Blazor versions might pool and reuse component instances.

If the initialization code subscribes to some events or performs actions that need a cleanup when the component is destroyed, implement `IDisposable`, and place all the cleanup code in its `Dispose` method. Whenever a component implements `IDisposable`, Blazor calls its `Dispose` method before destroying it.

After the component has been initialized, and each time a component parameter changes, the following two methods are called:

```
protected override async Task OnParametersSetAsync()
{
  await ...
}
protected override void OnParametersSet()
{
    ...
}
```

They are the right place to update data structures that depend on the values of the component parameters.

After that, the component is rendered or re-rendered. You can prevent component re-rendering after an update by overriding the `ShouldRender` method:

```
protected override bool ShouldRender()
{
...
}
```

Letting a component re-render only if you are sure its HTML code will change is an advanced optimization technique used in the implementation of component libraries.

The component rendering stage also involves the invocation of its children components. Therefore, component rendering is considered complete only after all its descendant components have completed their rendering too. When rendering is complete, the following methods are called:

```
protected override void OnAfterRender(bool firstRender)
{
    if (firstRender)
    {
    }
...
}
protected override async Task OnAfterRenderAsync(bool firstRender)
{
    if (firstRender)
    {
        await...
        ...
    }
    await ...
}
```

Since when the preceding methods are called, all component HTML has been updated and all children components have executed all their lifetime methods, the preceding methods are the right places for performing the following operations:

- Calling JavaScript functions that manipulate the generated HTML. JavaScript calls are described in the JavaScript interoperability subsection.
- Processing information attached to parameters or cascaded parameters by descendant components. In fact, tab-like components and other components might need to register some of their subparts in the root component, so the root component typically cascades a data structure where some children components can register. Code written in `AfterRender` and `AfterRenderAsync` can rely on the fact that all the parts have completed their registration.

The next section describes Blazor tools for collecting user input.

Blazor forms and validation

Similar to all major SPA frameworks, Blazor offers specific tools for processing user input while providing valid feedback to the user with error messages and immediate visual clues.

In classic HTML websites, HTML forms are used to collect input, validate it, and send it to the server. In client frameworks, data is not sent to the server by submitting forms, but forms retain their validation purpose. More specifically, they act as validation units, that is, as a container for inputs that must be validated together because they belong to a unique task. Accordingly, when a submit button is clicked, an overall validation is performed, and the system notifies of the result via events. This way, the developer can define what to do in case of errors and what actions to take when the user has successfully completed their input.

It is worth pointing out that validation performed on the client side doesn't ensure data integrity because a malicious user could easily hack all client validation rules because they have full access to the client-side code in their browser. The purpose of client-side validation is just to provide immediate feedback to the user.

Accordingly, the validation step must be repeated on the server side to enforce data integrity.

Both server-side and client-side validation can be performed with the same code shared between the Blazor client and the server. In fact, both the ASP.NET Core REST API and Blazor support validation based on validation attributes, so it is enough to share the same ViewModels equipped with validation attributes between the Blazor and server projects by putting them in a library that is referenced by both projects. ASP.NET Core validation is discussed in the *Server-side and client-side validation* section of *Chapter 17, Presenting ASP.NET Core*.

The whole toolset is known as **Blazor Forms** and consists of a form component called `EditForm`, various input components, a data annotation validator, a validation error summary, and validation error labels.

`EditForm` takes care of orchestrating the state of all input components through an instance of the `EditContext` class that is cascaded inside of the form. The orchestration comes from the interaction of both input components and the data annotation validator with this `EditContext` instance. A validation summary and error message labels don't take part in the orchestration but register to some `EditContext` events to be informed about errors.

`EditForm` must be passed the object whose properties must be rendered in its `Model` parameter. It is worth pointing out that input components bound to nested properties are not validated, so `EditForm` must be passed a flattened ViewModel. `EditForm` creates a new `EditContext` instance, passes the object received in its `Model` parameter in its constructor, and cascades it so it can interact with the form content.

You can also directly pass an `EditContext` custom instance in the `EditContext` parameter of `EditForm` instead of passing the object in its `Model` parameter, in which case `EditForm` will use your custom copy instead of creating a new instance. Typically, you do this when you need to subscribe to the `EditContext` `OnValidationStateChanged` and `OnFieldChanged` events.

When EditForm is submitted with a **Submit** button and there are no errors, the form invokes its OnValidSubmit callback, where you can place the code that uses and processes the user input. If instead there are validation errors, they are displayed, and the form invokes its OnInvalidSubmit callback.

The state of each input is reflected in some CSS classes that are automatically added to them, namely valid, invalid, and modified. You can use these classes to provide adequate visual feedback to the user. The default Blazor template already provides some CSS for them.

Here is a typical form:

```
<EditForm Model="FixedInteger"OnValidSubmit="@HandleValidSubmit" >
  <DataAnnotationsValidator />
  <ValidationSummary />
  <div class="form-group">
    <label for="integerfixed">Integer value</label>
    <InputNumber @bind-Value="FixedInteger.Value"
         id="integerfixed" class="form-control" />
    <ValidationMessage For="@(() => FixedInteger.Value)" />
  </div>
  <button type="submit" class="btn btn-primary"> Submit</button>
</EditForm>
```

The label is a standard HTML label, while InputNumber is a Blazor-specific component for number properties. ValidationMessage is the error label that appears only in the event of a validation error. By default, it is rendered with a validation-message CSS class. The property associated with the error message is passed in the for parameter with a parameterless lambda, as shown in the example.

The DataAnnotationsValidator component adds a validation based on the usual .NET validation attributes, such as RangeAttribute, RequiredAttribute, and so on. You can also write your custom validation attributes by inheriting from the ValidationAttribute class.

You can provide custom error messages in the validation attributes. If they contain a {0} placeholder, this will be filled with the property display name declared in a DisplayAttribute, if one is found, otherwise with the property name.

Together with the InputNumber component, Blazor also supports an InputText component for string properties, an InputTextArea component for string properties to be edited in an HTML textarea, an InputCheckbox component for bool properties, and an InputDate component that renders DateTime and DateTimeOffset as dates. They all work in exactly the same way as the InputNumber component. No component is available for other HTML5 input types. In particular, no component is available for rendering time or date and time, or for rendering numbers with a range widget.

If you need HTML5 inputs that are not available as Blazor input form components, you are left with the option of implementing them yourself or of using a third-party library that supports them.

You can implement rendering time or date and time by inheriting from the `InputBase<TValue>` class and overriding the `BuildRenderTree`, `FormatValueAsString`, and `TryParseValueFromString` methods. The sources of the `InputNumber` component show how to do this: `https://github.com/dotnet/aspnetcore/blob/main/src/Components/Web/src/Forms/InputNumber.cs`. You can also use the third-party libraries described in the *Third-party tools for Blazor WebAssembly* section.

Blazor also has a specific component for rendering a `select`, which works as in the following example:

```
<InputSelect @bind-Value="order.ProductColor">
  <option value="">Select a color ...</option>
  <option value="Red">Red</option>
  <option value="Blue">Blue</option>
  <option value="White">White</option>
</InputSelect>
```

Starting from .NET 6, `InputSelect` can also be bound to `IEnnumerable<T>` properties, in which case it is rendered as a multi-select.

One can also render enumerations with a radio group thanks to the `InputRadioGroup` and `InputRadio` components, as shown in the following example:

```
<InputRadioGroup Name="color" @bind-Value="order.Color">
  <InputRadio Name="color" Value="AllColors.Red" /> Red<br>
  <InputRadio Name="color" Value="AllColors.Blue" /> Blue<br>
  <InputRadio Name="color" Value="AllColors.White" /> White<br>
</InputRadioGroup>
```

Finally, Blazor also offers an `InputFile` component together with all the tools for processing and uploading the file. We will not cover this here, but the *Further reading* section contains links to the official documentation.

The next section describes Blazor tools for modifying the host page `<head>` tag.

Modifying HTML <head> content from Blazor components

Since the whole component tree is placed inside the body of the `index.html` host page, the components markup has no direct access to the `index.html` host page `<head>` tag. Modifying the content of the `<head>` tag is necessary when the developer would like to adapt the title shown in the browser tab to the actual Blazor page that is being displayed. In fact, this title is contained within the `<head>` tag:

```
<head>
    <title>This is the title shown in the browser tab</title>
    ...
</head>
```

For this reason, the .NET 6 version of Blazor introduced specific constructs for modifying the host page `<head>` tag from inside Blazor components.

First of all, we must inform the Blazor application about how to reach the `<head>` tag content. This is done in `Program.cs` with the same technique used to specify the Blazor application root:

```
var builder = WebAssemblyHostBuilder.CreateDefault(args);
builder.RootComponents.Add<App>("#app");
// The line below adds support for modifying
// the <head> tag content
builder.RootComponents.Add<HeadOutlet>("head::after");
...
```

After that, each component can replace the HTML title by specifying the new string inside a `PageTitle` component instance:

```
<PageTitle>This string replaces the page title</PageTitle>
```

Moreover, each component can append other HTML content to the `<head>` tag by placing it inside a `HeadContent` instance:

```
<HeadContent>
    <meta name="description" content="This is a page description">
</HeadContent>
```

In this section, you learned all that is needed to write a simple Blazor application that doesn't exchange data with a server. The next section analyzes some advanced features and will enable you to interact with a server to handle authentication, authorization, and more.

Blazor advanced features

This section provides short descriptions of various Blazor advanced features organized into subsections:

- References to components and HTML elements
- JavaScript interoperability
- Globalization and localization
- Authentication and authorization
- Communication with the server
- AOT compilation

Because of a lack of space, we can't give all the details of each feature, but the details are covered by links in the *Further reading* section. We start with how to reference components and HTML elements defined in Razor markup.

References to components and HTML elements

Sometimes, we might need a reference to a component in order to call some of its methods. This is the case, for instance, for a component that implements a modal window:

```
<Modal @ref="myModal">
...
</Modal>
...
<button type="button" class="btn btn-primary"
   @onclick="() => myModal.Show()">
   Open modal
</button>
...
@code{
private Modal  myModal {get; set;}
 ...
}
```

As the preceding example shows, references are captured with the `@ref` directive. The same `@ref` directive can also be used to capture references to HTML elements. HTML references have an `ElementReference` type and are typically used to call JavaScript functions on HTML elements, as explained in the next subsection.

JavaScript interoperability

Since Blazor doesn't expose all JavaScript features to C# code, and since it is convenient to take advantage of the huge JavaScript code base, sometimes it is necessary to invoke JavaScript functions. Blazor allows this through the `IJSRuntime` interface that can be injected into a component via dependency injection.

Once we have an `IJSRuntime` instance, a JavaScript function that returns a value can be called as shown here:

```
T result = await jsRuntime.InvokeAsync<T>(
   "<name of JavaScript function or method>", arg1, arg2....);
```

Functions that do not return any argument can be invoked as shown here:

```
await jsRuntime.InvokeAsync(
   "<name of JavaScript function or method>", arg1, arg2....);
```

Arguments can be either basic types or objects that can be serialized in JSON, while the name of the JavaScript function is a string that can contain dots that represent access to properties, sub-properties, and method names, such as the `"myJavaScriptObject.myProperty.myMethod"` string.

Thus, for instance, we can save a string in the browser's local storage with the following code:

```
await jsRuntime
    .InvokeVoidAsync("window.localStorage.setItem",
myLocalStorageKey, myStringToSave);
```

Arguments can also be ElementReference instances captured with the @ref directive, in which case they are received as HTML elements on the JavaScript side.

The JavaScript functions invoked must be defined either in the Index.html file or in JavaScript files referenced in Index.html.

If you are writing a component library with a Razor library project, JavaScript files can be embedded together with CSS files as resources in the DLL library. You just need to add a wwwroot folder in the project root and place the needed CSS and JavaScript files in that folder or some subfolder of it. After that, these files can be referenced as follows:

```
_content/<dll name>/<file path relative to wwwroot>
```

Accordingly, if the filename is myJsFile.js, the DLL name is MyCompany.MyLibrary, and the file is placed in the js folder inside wwwroot, then its reference will be:

```
_content/MyCompany.MyLibrary/js/myJsFile.js
```

It is worth pointing out that all CSS files added to components (CSS isolation) we mentioned earlier in this chapter are compiled into a unique CSS file that is added as a DLL resource. This file must be referenced in the index.html page as:

```
<assembly name>.Client.styles.css
```

If your JavaScript files are organized as ES6 modules, you can avoid referencing them in Index.html and can load the modules directly, as shown here:

```
// _content/MyCompany.MyLibrary/js/myJsFile.js  JavaScript file
export function myFunction ()
{
...
}
...
//C# code
var module = await jsRuntime.InvokeAsync<JSObjectReference>(
    "import", "./_content/MyCompany.MyLibrary/js/myJsFile.js");
...
T res= await module.InvokeAsync<T>("myFunction")
```

In addition, instance methods of C# objects can be called from JavaScript code, by taking the following steps:

1. Say the C# method is called MyMethod. Decorate the MyMethod method with the [JSInvokable] attribute.
2. Enclose the C# object in a DotNetObjectReference instance and pass it to JavaScript with a JavaScript call:

```
var objRef = DotNetObjectReference.Create(myObjectInstance);
//pass objRef to JavaScript
....
//dispose the DotNetObjectReference
objRef.Dispose()
```

3. On the JavaScript side, say the C# object is in a variable called `dotnetObject`. Then, we just need to invoke:

```
dotnetObject.invokeMethodAsync("<dll name>", "MyMethod", arg1, ...).
then(result => {...})
```

The **Awesome Blazor** project (`https://github.com/AdrienTorris/awesome-blazor`) lists a lot of open-source projects that use JavaScript's interoperability to build .NET wrappers for well-known JavaScript libraries. There, you can find wrappers for 3D graphics JavaScript libraries, plot JavaScript libraries, and so on.

The next section explains how to handle contents and number/date localization.

Globalization and localization

As soon as the Blazor application starts, both the application culture and the application UI culture are set to the browser culture. However, the developer can change both of them by assigning the chosen cultures to `CultureInfo.DefaultThreadCurrentCulture` and `CultureInfo.DefaultThreadCurrentUICulture`. Typically, the application lets the user choose one of its supported cultures, or it accepts the browser culture only if it is supported; otherwise, it falls back to a supported culture. In fact, it is possible to support just a reasonable number of cultures because all application strings must be translated into all supported cultures.

If the application must support a single culture, this culture can be set once and for all in `program.cs` after the host has been built but before the host is run.

This can be done by replacing await `builder.Build().RunAsync()` with:

```
var host = builder.Build();
…
CultureInfo.DefaultThreadCurrentCulture = new CultureInfo(…);
CultureInfo.DefaultThreadCurrentUICulture = new CultureInfo(…);
…
await host.RunAsync();
```

If the application must support several languages, the code is similar, but the culture information must be taken from the browser's local storage, where the user must be given the option to store it in some applications option page.

Once the `CurrentCulture` is set, dates and numbers are automatically formatted according to the conventions of the chosen culture. For the UI culture, the developer must manually provide resource files with the translations of all application strings in all supported cultures. Blazor uses the same localization/globalization techniques, so please refer to the *ASP.NET Core globalization* section of *Chapter 17, Presenting ASP.NET Core*, for more details.

There are two ways to use resource files. With the first option, you create a resource file, say, `myResource.resx`, and then add all language-specific files: `myResource.it.resx`, `myResource.pt.resx`, and so on. In this case, Visual Studio creates a static class named `myResource` whose static properties are the keys of each resource file. These properties will automatically contain the localized strings corresponding to the current UI culture. You can use these static properties wherever you like, and you can use pairs composed of a resource type and a resource name to set the `ErrorMessageResourceType` and `ErrorMessageResourceName` properties of validation attributes or similar properties of other attributes. This way, the attributes will use an automatically localized string.

With the second option, you add only language-specific resource files (`myResource.it.resx`, `myResource.pt.resx`, and so on). In this case, Visual Studio doesn't create any class associated with the resource file, and you can use resource files together with `IStringLocalizer` and `IStringLocalizer<T>` injected in components as you use them in ASP.NET Core MVC views (see the *ASP.NET Core globalization* section of *Chapter 17, Presenting ASP.NET Core*).

Authentication and authorization

In the *Routing* subsection, we discussed how the `CascadingAuthenticationState` and `AuthorizeRouteView` components prevent unauthorized users from accessing pages protected with an `[Authorize]` attribute. Let's go deeper into the details of how page authorization works.

In .NET applications, authentication and authorization information is usually contained in a `ClaimsPrincipal` instance. In server applications, this instance is built when the user logs in, taking the required information from a database. In Blazor WebAssembly, such information must be provided by some remote server that takes care of SPA authentication too. Since there are several ways to provide authentication and authorization to a Blazor WebAssembly application, Blazor defines the `AuthenticationStateProvider` abstraction.

Authentication and authorization providers inherit from the `AuthenticationStateProvider` abstract class and override its `GetAuthenticationStateAsync` method, which returns `Task<AuthenticationState>`, where `AuthenticationState` contains the authentication and authorization information. Actually, `AuthenticationState` contains just a `User` property with a `ClaimsPrincipal`.

Once we've defined a concrete implementation of `AuthenticationStateProvider`, we must register it in the dependency engine container in the application's `Program.cs` file:

```
builder.services.AddScoped<AuthenticationStateProvider,
    MyAuthStateProvider>();
```

We will return to the predefined implementations of `AuthenticationStateProvider` offered by Blazor after having described how Blazor uses authentication and authorization information provided by a registered `AuthenticationStateProvider`.

The `CascadingAuthenticationState` component calls the `GetAuthenticationStateAsync` method of the registered `AuthenticationStateProvider` and cascades the returned `Task<AuthenticationState>`. You can intercept this cascading value with a `[CascadingParameter]` defined as follows in your components:

```
[CascadingParameter]
private Task<AuthenticationState> myAuthenticationStateTask { get; set; }
......
ClaimsPrincipal user = (await myAuthenticationStateTask).User;
```

However, Blazor applications typically use `AuthorizeRouteView` and `AuthorizeView` components to control user access to content.

`AuthorizeRouteView` prevents access to pages if the user doesn't satisfy the prescriptions of the page's `[Authorize]` attribute; otherwise, the content in the `NotAuthorized` template is rendered. `AuthorizeRouteView` also has an `Authorizing` template that is shown while user information is being retrieved.

`AuthorizeView` can be used within components to show the markup it encloses only to authorized users. It contains the same `Roles` and `Policy` parameters of the `[Authorize]` attribute that you can use to specify the constraints the user must satisfy to access the content:

```
<AuthorizeView Roles="Admin,SuperUser">
//authorized content
</AuthorizeView>
```

`AuthorizeView` can also specify `NotAuthorized` and an `Authorizing` template:

```
<AuthorizeView>
  <Authorized>
    ...
  </Authorized>
  <Authorizing>
    ...
  </Authorizing>
  <NotAuthorized>
    ...
  </NotAuthorized>
</AuthorizeView>
```

If one adds authorization while creating a Blazor WebAssembly project, the following method call is added to the application dependency engine:

```
builder.Services.AddOidcAuthentication(options =>
{
    // Configure your authentication provider options here.
    // For more information, see https://aka.ms/blazor-standalone-auth
    builder.Configuration.Bind("Local", options.ProviderOptions);
});
```

This method adds an `AuthenticationStateProvider` that extracts the user information from the authentication cookie of an OAuth provider. The OAuth protocol with the OAuth provider is performed with the help of the `AuthenticationService.js` JavaScript file we saw in the *Loading and starting the application* subsection of this chapter. The OAuth provider endpoint returns user information in the form of a bearer token that can, then, also be used to authenticate communications with the server's web API. Bearer tokens are described in detail in the *REST service authorization and authentication* and *ASP.NET Core service authorization* sections of *Chapter 15, Applying Service-Oriented Architectures with .NET*. Blazor WebAssembly communication is described in the next subsection.

The previous code takes the OAuth parameters from a configuration file you must add as `wwwroot/appsettings.json`:

```
{
  "Local": {
    "Authority": "{AUTHORITY}",
    "ClientId": "{CLIENT ID}"
  }
}
```

If you use Google as the authentication provider, `AUTHORITY` is `https://accounts.google.com/`, while `CLIENT ID` is the client ID you receive when you register your Blazor application with the Google Developers program.

Google needs some more parameters, namely the return URL to return once the authentication process is completed and the page to return to after a logout:

```
{
  "Local": {
    "Authority": "https://accounts.google.com/",
    "ClientId": "2...7-e...q.apps.googleusercontent.com",
    "PostLogoutRedirectUri": "https://localhost:5001/authentication/logout-
callback",
    "RedirectUri": "https://localhost:5001/authentication/login-callback",
    "ResponseType": "id_token"
  }
}
```

Where `https://localhost:5001` must be replaced with the actual domain of the Blazor application.

Before any authentication or if the authentication fails, an unauthenticated `ClaimsPrincipal` is created. This way, when the user tries to access a page that is protected by an `[Authorize]` attribute, the `AuthorizeRouteView` component invokes the `RedirectToLogin` component, which, in turn, navigates to the `Authentication.razor` page, passing it a login request in its `action` route parameter:

```
@page "/authentication/{action}"
@using Microsoft.AspNetCore.Components.WebAssembly.Authentication
<RemoteAuthenticatorView Action="@Action"  />
@code{
    [Parameter] public string Action { get; set; }
}
```

The `RemoteAuthenticatorView` acts as an interface with the usual ASP.NET Core user login/registration system, and whenever it receives an "action" to perform, it redirects the user from the Blazor application to the proper ASP.NET Core server page (login, registration, logout, and user profile).

Once the user logs in, they are redirected to the Blazor application page that caused the login request. The redirect URL is computed by the `BlazorReview.Layout->RedirectToLogin.razor` component, which extracts it from the `NavigationManager` and passes it to the `RemoteAuthenticatorView` component. This time, the `AuthenticationStateProvider` is able to get the user information from the authentication cookie that has been created by the login operation.

It is possible both to design a custom OAuth provider for your Blazor application or to design a completely custom way to get a bearer token with an internal login Blazor page without leaving the Blazor application. In this last case, you must provide a custom implementation of the `AuthenticationStateProvider`. More details on these advanced custom scenarios are available in the official documentation reference in the *Further reading* section.

Having learned how to authenticate with an external OAuth provider and how to handle authorization within the Blazor application, we are ready to learn how to exchange data and how to authenticate with a REST API.

The next subsection describes a Blazor WebAssembly-specific implementation of the `HttpClient` class and related types.

Communication with the server

Blazor WebAssembly supports the same .NET `HttpClient` and `HttpClientFactory` classes described in the *.NET HTTP clients* section of *Chapter 15, Applying Service-Oriented Architectures with .NET*. However, due to the communication limitations of browsers, their implementations are different and rely on the browser's **fetch API**.

In fact, for security reasons, all browsers, do not allow direct opening of generic **TCP/IP** connections but force all server communications to pass either through **Ajax** or through the **fetch API**.

This way, when you attempt a communication toward a URL that differs from the domain where the browser downloaded the SPA, the browser automatically switches to the CORS protocol, thus informing the server that the communication was started by a browser application that was downloaded by a different domain and that might potentially be a phishing website.

In turn, the server accepts CORS communications just from well-known domains that are pre-listed in its code. This way, the server is sure that the request can't come from a phishing website.

In *Chapter 15, Applying Service-Oriented Architectures with .NET*, we analyzed how to take advantage of `HttpClientFactory` to define typed clients. You can also define typed clients in Blazor with exactly the same syntax.

However, since an authenticated Blazor application needs to send the bearer token created during the authentication process in each request to the application server, it is common to define a named client as shown here:

```
builder.Services.AddHttpClient("BlazorReview.ServerAPI", client =>
         client.BaseAddress = new Uri("https://<web api URL>"))
.AddHttpMessageHandler<BaseAddressAuthorizationMessageHandler>();
```

`AddHttpMessageHandler` adds a `DelegatingHandler`, that is, a subclass of the `DelegatingHandler` abstract class. Implementations of `DelegatingHandler` override its `SendAsync` method in order to process each request and each relative response:

```
protected override async Task<HttpResponseMessage> SendAsync(
        HttpRequestMessage request,
        CancellationToken cancellationToken)
{
//modify request
   ...
HttpResponseMessage= response = await base.SendAsync(
   request, cancellationToken);
//modify response
   ...
return response;
}
```

If this bearer token is expired or is not found at all, it tries to get a new bearer token by using the authentication cookie received when the user manually logged in with the OAuth provider. This way, it can obtain a fresh bearer token without requesting a new manual login. If this attempt also fails, an `AccessTokenNotAvailableException` is thrown. Typically, this exception is captured and used to trigger a redirection to the login page by calling its `Redirect` method, as shown below:

```
try
{
       //server call here
```

```
}
catch (AccessTokenNotAvailableException exception)
{
        exception.Redirect();
}
```

If both the Blazor application and the Web API are deployed in different subfolders of the same domain, Blazor requests are issued without the CORS protocol, so they are automatically accepted by the server. Otherwise, the ASP.NET Core server must enable CORS requests, and must list the Blazor application URL among the allowed CORS domains with something like:

```
builder.Services.AddCors(o => {
    o.AddDefaultPolicy(pbuilder =>
    {
        pbuilder.AllowAnyMethod();
        pbuilder.WithHeaders(HeaderNames.ContentType, HeaderNames.
Authorization);
        pbuilder.WithOrigins(https://<Blazor client url>, …, https://<Another
client url>);
    });
 });
```

Then, you must also place the `app.UseCors()` middleware in the ASP.NET Core pipeline.

The example data shown on the `Weather` page of the `ReviewBlazor` application are downloaded from a static file located in the `wwwroot/sample-data` folder of the same Blazor application, so a normal, not-CORS request is issued and no bearer token is needed to request. Accordingly, the `Weatherpage` uses a default `HttpClient` defined in `Program.cs` as:

```
builder.Services.AddScoped(sp => new HttpClient { BaseAddress = new
Uri(builder.HostEnvironment.BaseAddress) });
```

The next subsection explains how to improve the performance of computation-intensive applications with Blazor AOT compilation.

AOT compilation

Once uploaded in the browser, .NET assemblies are not compiled **Just in Time** (**JIT**) at their first execution as is the case for other platforms. Instead, they are interpreted by a very fast interpreter. Just the .NET runtime is pre-compiled and uploaded in the browser directly in WebAssembly.

JIT compilation is avoided since it would considerably increase the application start time, which is already quite high because of the high application download size (about 10 MB). In turn, the download size is high due to the .NET libraries that any Blazor application needs to work properly.

In order to reduce download size, during the compilation in release mode, Blazor .NET assemblies are tree-shaken to remove all unused types and methods. However, notwithstanding this tree-shaking, the typical download size remains quite high. A good download improvement is achieved with the default caching of the .NET runtime, which reduces the download size to 2-4 MB. However, the download size still remains high the first time a Blazor application is visited.

Starting from .NET 6, Blazor offers an alternative to JIT compilation: **Ahead-of-Time** (**AOT**) compilation. With AOT, all application assemblies are compiled into a unique WebAssembly file during the application publication.

AOT compilation is very slow and may last something like 10-30 minutes, even in the case of small applications. On the other hand, it must be executed only once when the application is published, so the compilation time doesn't impact the application start time.

Unfortunately, AOT compilation more than doubles the download size, since the compiled code is more verbose than the source .NET code. Therefore, AOT should be adopted only in performance-critical applications that can trade a higher start time for better performance.

.NET WebAssembly AOT compilation requires an additional build tool that must be installed as an optional .NET SDK workload in order to use it. The first time, you can install it with the following shell command:

```
dotnet workload install wasm-tools
```

Instead, when a new .NET version is installed, we just need to launch the following command to update all previously installed workloads:

```
dotnet workload update
```

Once the AOT workload has been installed, AOT compilation can be enabled on a per-project basis by adding the `<RunAOTCompilation>true</RunAOTCompilation>` declaration to the Blazor project file, as shown here:

```
<Project Sdk="Microsoft.NET.Sdk.BlazorWebAssembly">
  <PropertyGroup>
    <TargetFramework>net8.0</TargetFramework>
    <RunAOTCompilation>true</RunAOTCompilation>
  </PropertyGroup>
  ...
```

The next section briefly discusses some of the most relevant third-party tools and libraries that complete Blazor's official features and help increase productivity in Blazor projects.

Third-party tools for Blazor WebAssembly

Notwithstanding Blazor being a young product, its third-party tool and product ecosystem is already quite rich. Among the open source, free products, it is worth mentioning the **Blazorise** project (`https://github.com/stsrki/Blazorise`), which contains various free basic Blazor components (inputs, tabs, modals, and so on) that can be styled with various CSS frameworks, such as Bootstrap and Material. It also contains a simple editable grid and a simple tree view.

Also worth mentioning is **BlazorStrap** (`https://github.com/chanan/BlazorStrap`), which contains pure Blazor implementations of all Bootstrap 4 components and widgets.

Among all the commercial products, it is worth mentioning **Blazor Controls Toolkit** (`https://blazorct.azurewebsites.net/`), which is a complete toolset for implementing commercial applications. It contains all input types with their fallbacks in case they are not supported by the browser; all Bootstrap components; other basic components; a complete, advanced drag-and-drop framework; and advanced customizable and editable components, like detail views, detail lists, grids, and a tree-repeater (a generalization of the tree view). All components are based on a sophisticated metadata representation system that enables the user to design the markup in a declarative way using data annotations and inline Razor declarations.

Moreover, it contains additional sophisticated validation attributes, tools for undoing user input, tools for computing changes to send to the server, sophisticated client-side and server-side query tools based on the OData protocol, and tools to maintain and save the whole application state.

It is also worth mentioning the **bUnit** open-source project (`https://github.com/egil/bUnit`), which provides all the tools for testing Blazor components.

The **Awesome Blazor** project (`https://github.com/AdrienTorris/awesome-blazor`) lists thousands of open-source and commercial Blazor resources, such as tutorials, posts, libraries, and example projects.

A complete example of a Blazor WebAssembly application based on the WWTravelClub book use case can be found in the *Using client technologies* section of *Chapter 21, Case Study*. The next section explains how to use Blazor to implement cross-platform applications. The actual code is contained in the folder associated with this chapter in the GitHub repository of the book.

.NET MAUI Blazor

.NET MAUI is Microsoft's advised choice to implement cross-platform applications. In fact, .NET MAUI applications can be just-in-time compiled for all Windows, Android, iOS, and other Linux-based devices. .NET MAUI contains a common abstraction of all target devices, and at the same time takes advantage of each device's peculiarities by offering platform-specific libraries each containing platform-specific features of a target platform.

We will not describe .NET MAUI in detail, but after a short introduction to .NET MAUI, we will focus just on .NET MAUI Blazor. This way, by learning just Blazor, you will be able to develop single-page applications, progressive applications, and cross-platform applications.

What is .NET MAUI?

.NET MAUI extends Xamarin.Forms' cross-platform capabilities from Android and iOS to also include Windows and macOS. Thus, .NET MAUI is a cross-platform framework for creating both native mobile and desktop apps with C#.

The basis of .NET MAUI is Xamarin.Forms. In fact, Microsoft has provided a guide for migrating original Xamarin.Forms apps to .NET MAUI, as can be seen at the following link: `https://docs.microsoft.com/en-us/dotnet/maui/get-started/migrate`. However, .NET MAUI has been conceived to be the new-generation framework for any native/desktop app development in C#:

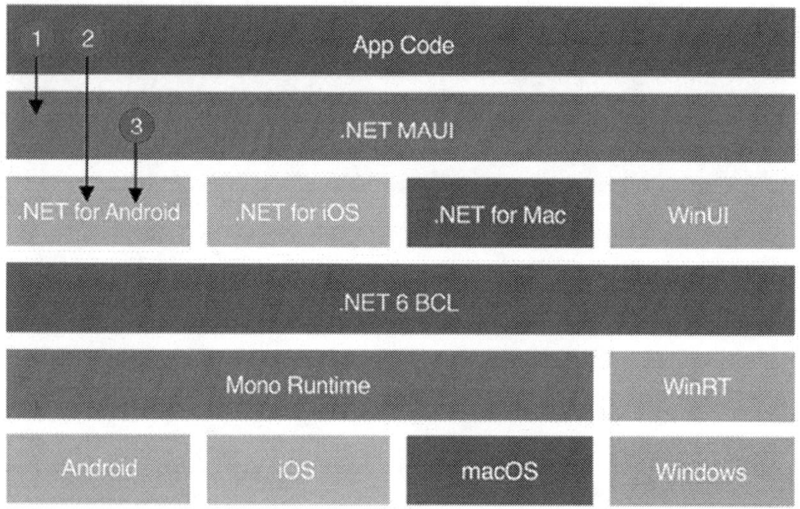

Figure 19.2: .NET MAUI high-level architecture

There is a specific difference between Xamarin.Forms and .NET MAUI. In Xamarin.Forms, there is a specific native project for any kind of device we would like to publish to on the app, while in .NET MAUI, this approach is based on as single project targeting multiple platforms.

The next section explains how to use .NET MAUI to run a Blazor application as a native application.

Developing native applications with Blazor

.NET MAUI is not installed by default when you install Visual Studio 2022, but you need to select the .NET MAUI workload in the Visual Studio installer. Therefore, if you don't see MAUI projects when you start a new project in your Visual Studio installation, you need to run the Visual Studio installer and modify your existing installation with the addition of the .NET MAUI workload.

Once you have the MAUI workload installed, in the project creation wizard, you should be able to select **C#/All platforms/MAUI**, and then select **.NET MAUI Blazor Hybrid App**, as shown here:

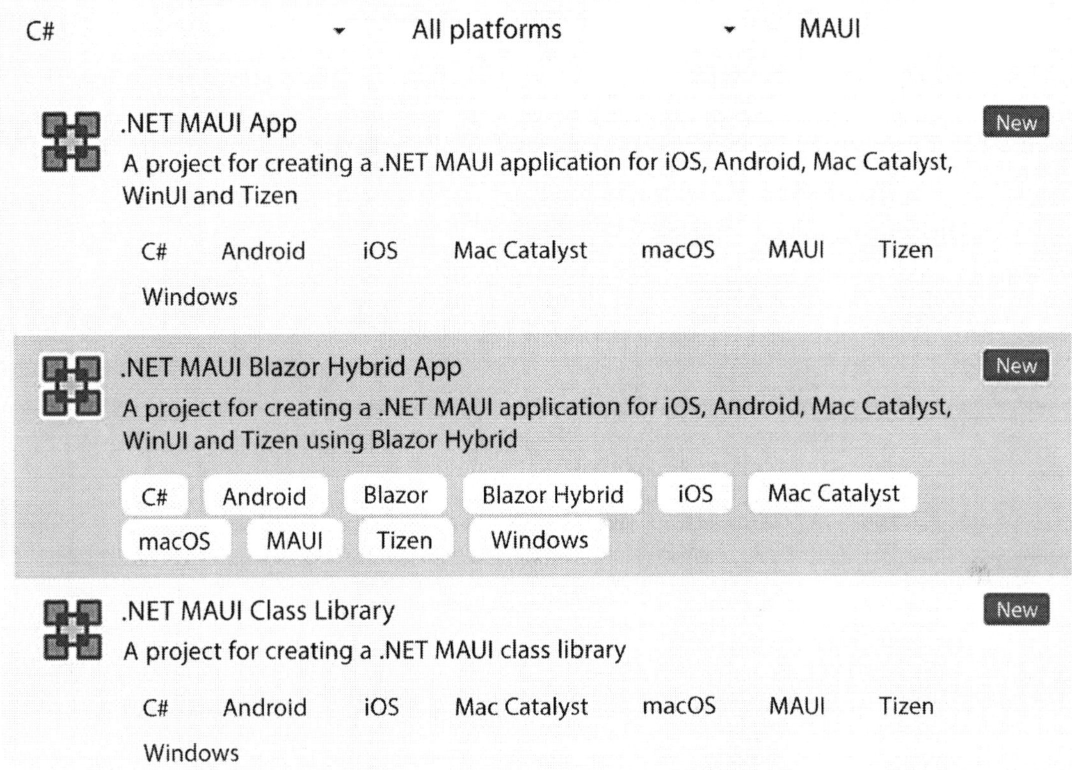

Figure 19.3: Creating a .NET MAUI Blazor application

Create a MAUI Blazor project and call it `MAUIBlazorReview`. The MAUI Blazor application contains the usual `Layout` and `Pages` folders where you can place your Blazor components and pages, but they are placed inside a `Components` folder. It also contains a `wwwroot` folder containing the usual `index.html` page and all the CSS and JavaScript you might need. Finally, it also contains the usual `_Imports.razor` page where you can place all your default `using` statements.

A MAUI Blazor application also uses layout pages that you can place in the `Shared` folder and may reference Razor libraries containing CSS components and JavaScript files.

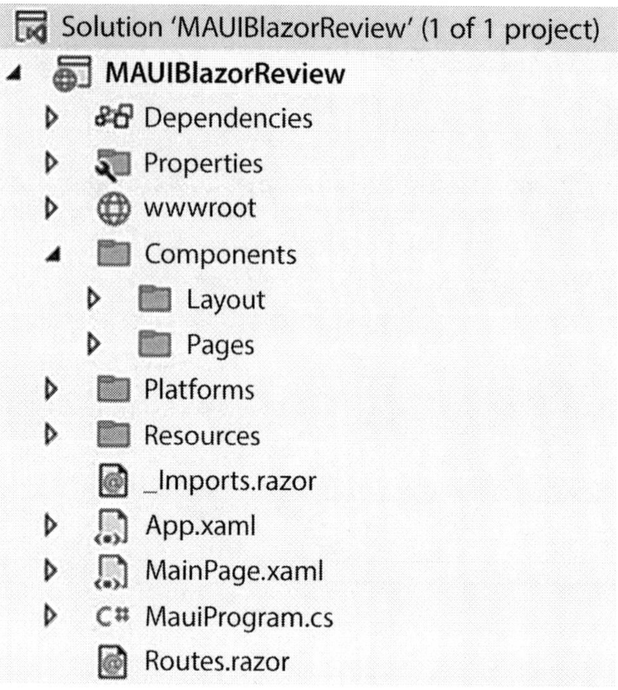

Figure 19.4: .NET MAUI Blazor project

The only difference is that services, instead of being declared in `Program.cs` files, are declared in `MauiProgram.cs` together with MAUI-specific code:

```
public static class MauiProgram
{
    public static MauiApp CreateMauiApp()
    {
        var builder = MauiApp.CreateBuilder();
        builder
            .UseMauiApp<App>()
            .ConfigureFonts(fonts =>
            {
                fonts.AddFont("OpenSans-Regular.ttf", "OpenSansRegular");
            });

        builder.Services.AddMauiBlazorWebView();

        #if DEBUG
        builder.Services.AddBlazorWebViewDeveloperTools();
```

```
            builder.Logging.AddDebug();
            #endif

             //this is a service
builder.Services.AddSingleton<WeatherForecastService>();

            return builder.Build();
        }
    }
```

Attention must be paid when using an `HttpClient` class to communicate with a server. Blazor web applications may use URLs relative to the domain where they were downloaded, while MAUI Blazor applications must use absolute URLs since they are not associated with any default URL. Therefore, an `HttpClient` definition is added to the services with something like this:

```
builder.Services.AddScoped(sp => new HttpClient
{ BaseAddress = new Uri("https://localhost:7215") });
```

The `Platforms` folder contains a subfolder for each platform supported by the application, where each subfolder contains platform-specific code.

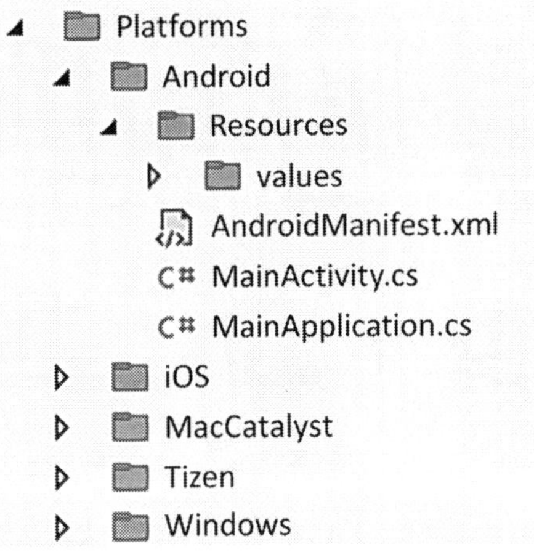

Figure 19.5: Platforms folder

Supported folders can be changed by editing the `TargetFrameworks` element of the `MAUIBlazorReview.csproj` file:

```
<TargetFrameworks>net8.0-android;net8.0-ios;net8.0-maccatalyst</
TargetFrameworks>
```

You can select the platform to run the application from using the dropdown next to the green Visual Studio run button. On a Windows machine, you can select just Windows and Android. If you select Android, an Android device simulator is launched.

In order to debug for iOS/Mac platforms on a Windows machine, you need to connect an iOS/Mac device to your computer.

When you build the project, the build may ask you to install an Android SDK version. If this is the case, please follow the simple instructions in the error message.

Summary

In this chapter, you learned about client-side technologies. In particular, you learned what an SPA is and how to build one based on the Blazor WebAssembly framework. The chapter first described the Blazor WebAssembly architecture, and then explained how to exchange input/output with Blazor components and the concept of binding.

After having explained Blazor's general principles, the chapter focused on how to get user input while providing the user with adequate feedback and visual clues in the event of errors. Then, the chapter provided a short description of advanced features, such as JavaScript interoperability, globalization, authentication with authorization, and client-server communication.

Finally, the last section explained how to use Blazor to implement cross-platform applications based on Microsoft MAUI and how to transform a Blazor WebAssembly project into a .NET MAUI Blazor project.

Complete examples of Blazor applications based on the WWTravelClub book use case can be found in the *Using client technologies* section of *Chapter 21*, *Case Study*.

Questions

1. What is WebAssembly?
2. What is an SPA?
3. What is the purpose of the Blazor `router` component?
4. What is a Blazor page?
5. What is the purpose of the `@namespace` directive?
6. What is an `EditContext`?
7. What is the right place to initialize a component?
8. What is the right place to process the user input?
9. What is the `IJSRuntime` interface?
10. What is the purpose of `@ref`?

Further reading

- The Blazor official documentation is available at `https://docs.microsoft.com/en-us/aspnet/core/blazor`.
- Lazy loading assemblies is described at `https://docs.microsoft.com/en-US/aspnet/core/blazor/webassembly-lazy-load-assemblies`.
- All HTML events supported by Blazor together with their event arguments are listed at `https://docs.microsoft.com/en-us/aspnet/core/blazor/components/event-handling#event-arguments-1`.

- Blazor supports the same validation attributes as ASP.NET MVC, with the exception of `RemoteAttribute`: `https://docs.microsoft.com/en-us/aspnet/core/mvc/models/validation#built-in-attributes`.
- A description of the `InputFile` component, and how to use it, can be found here: `https://docs.microsoft.com/en-US/aspnet/core/blazor/file-uploads`.
- More details on Blazor localization and globalization are available here: `https://docs.microsoft.com/en-US/aspnet/core/blazor/globalization-localization`.
- More details on Blazor authentication and all its related URLs are available here: `https://docs.microsoft.com/en-US/aspnet/core/blazor/security/webassembly/`.
- The Blazorise project: `https://github.com/stsrki/Blazorise`.
- BlazorStrap: `https://github.com/chanan/BlazorStrap`.
- Blazor Controls Toolkit: `https://blazorct.azurewebsites.net/`.
- bUnit: `https://github.com/egil/bUnit`.
- The Awesome Blazor project: `https://github.com/AdrienTorris/awesome-blazor`.

Learn more on Discord

To join the Discord community for this book – where you can share feedback, ask questions to the authors, and learn about new releases – follow the QR code below:

`https://packt.link/SoftwareArchitectureCSharp12Dotnet8`

20

Kubernetes

This chapter is dedicated to describing the Kubernetes container orchestrator and its implementation in Azure, called **Azure Kubernetes Service** (**AKS**). We discussed the importance and the tasks handled by orchestrators in the *Which tools are needed to manage microservices?* section of *Chapter 11, Applying a Microservice Architecture to Your Enterprise Application*. Here, it is worth recalling just that Kubernetes is the de facto standard for orchestrators.

We will show also how to install and use minikube on your local machine, which is a one-node Kubernetes simulator you can use to try out all of the examples in this chapter, and also to test your own applications. Simulators are useful both to avoid wasting too much money on an actual cloud-based Kubernetes cluster, and to provide a different Kubernetes cluster to each developer.

This chapter explains the fundamental Kubernetes concepts and then focuses on how to interact with a Kubernetes cluster and how to deploy a Kubernetes application. All concepts are put into practice with simple examples. We recommend reading *Chapter 11, Applying a Microservice Architecture to Your Enterprise Application*, before reading this chapter, since we will use concepts explained in previous chapters.

More specifically, in this chapter, we will cover the following topics:

- Kubernetes basics
- Interacting with Azure Kubernetes clusters
- Advanced Kubernetes concepts

By the end of this chapter, you will have learned how to implement and deploy a complete solution using Azure Kubernetes Service.

Technical requirements

In this chapter, you will require the following:

- Visual Studio 2022 free Community Edition or better, with all the database tools installed, or any other `.yaml` file editor, such as Visual Studio Code.

- A free Azure account. The *Creating an Azure account* section in *Chapter 1, Understanding the Importance of Software Architecture*, explains how to create one.
- An optional minikube installation. Installation instructions will be given in the *Using minikube* section of this chapter.

The code for this chapter is available at `https://github.com/PacktPublishing/Software-Architecture-with-C-Sharp-12-and-.NET-8-4E`.

Kubernetes basics

Kubernetes is an advanced open source software for managing distributed applications running on a computer network. Kubernetes can be used on your private machine's cluster, or you can use hardware-scalable Kubernetes offerings from all main cloud providers. This kind of software is called an **orchestrator** since it dynamically allocates microservices to the available hardware resources in order to maximize performance. Moreover, orchestrators like Kubernetes provide stable virtual addresses to microservices that they move around from one machine to another, thus changing their physical addresses. At the time of writing, Kubernetes is the most widespread orchestrator and the *de facto* standard for cluster orchestration that can be used with a wide ecosystem of tools and applications. While not being tied to specific languages or frameworks, Kubernetes is a fundamental tool for managing hardware resources and communications in .NET distributed applications based on microservices. This section introduces the basic Kubernetes concepts and entities.

A Kubernetes cluster is a cluster of virtual machines running the Kubernetes orchestrator.

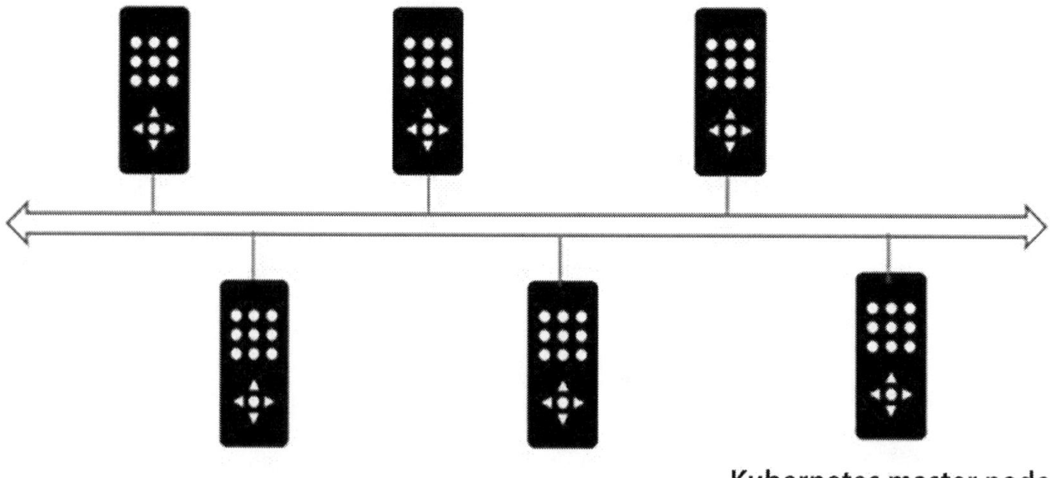

Figure 20.1: Computer network equipped with Kubernetes

Generally, Kubernetes is installed on specific machines referred to as **master nodes**, while all other computers simply run an interface software that connects with the software running on the master nodes.

The virtual machines composing the cluster are called **nodes**. The smallest software unit we can deploy on Kubernetes is not a single application, but an aggregate of containerized applications called **Pod**. While Kubernetes supports various types of containers, the most commonly used container type is Docker, which we analyzed in *Chapter 11, Applying a Microservice Architecture to Your Enterprise Application*, so we will confine our discussion here to Docker. Pods are aggregates of Docker images, each containing one of your .NET microservices or microservices implemented with other technologies.

More specifically, Pods are sets of Docker images constrained to be placed together on the same node during the overall life of the application. They can be moved to other nodes, but they must be moved together. This means that they can easily communicate through localhost ports. Communication between different Pods, however, is more complex since the IP addresses of Pods are ephemeral resources because Pods have no fixed node where they run, but rather are moved from one node to another by the orchestrator. Moreover, Pods may be replicated to increase performance, so, in general, it makes no sense to address a message to a specific Pod; instead, we address it to any of the identical replicas of the same Pod.

Cluster nodes and Pods are managed by master nodes that communicate with cluster administrators through an API server, as shown in the following diagram:

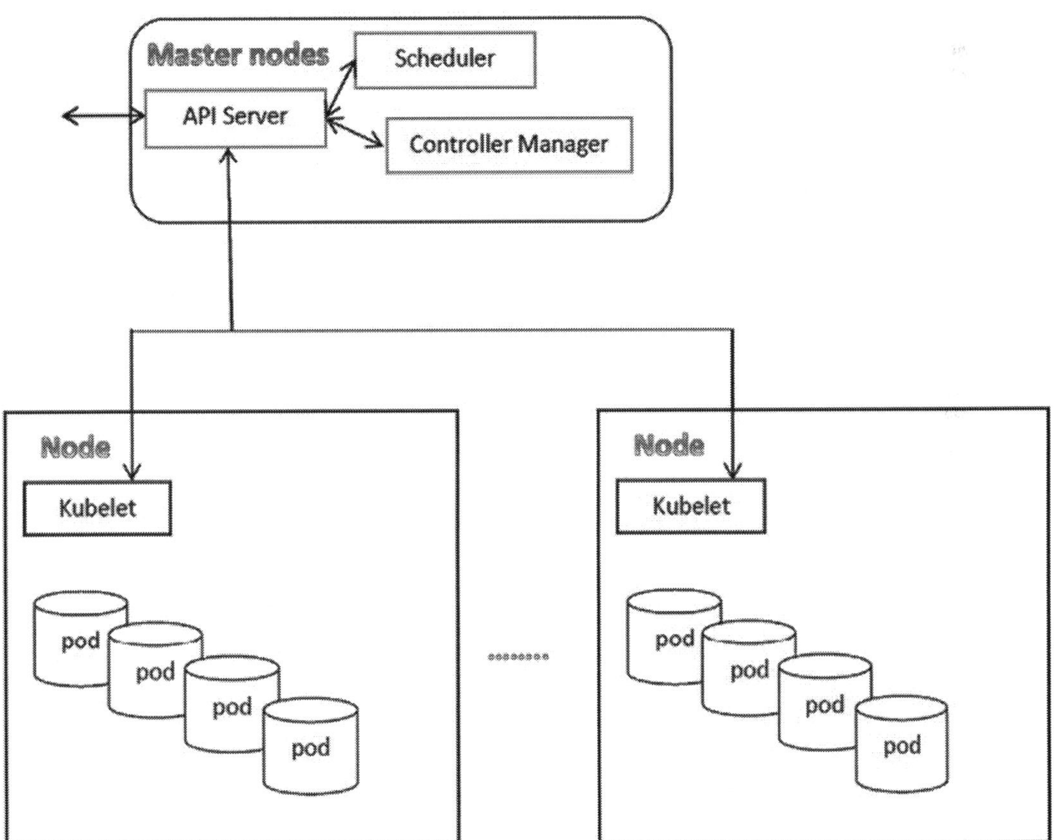

Figure 20.2: Kubernetes cluster

The scheduler allocates Pods to nodes according to the administrator constraints, while the controller manager groups several daemons that monitor the cluster's actual state and try to move it toward the desired state declared through the API server. There are controllers for several Kubernetes resources, from Pod replicas to communication facilities. In fact, each resource has some target objectives to be maintained while the application runs, and the controller verifies these objectives are actually achieved, possibly triggering corrective actions if not, such as moving some Pods running too slowly to less crowded nodes.

The kubelet manages the interaction of each non-master node with the master nodes.

In Kubernetes, communication between Pods is handled by resources called **Services** that are assigned virtual addresses by the Kubernetes infrastructure and that forward their communications to sets of identical Pods. In short, Services are Kubernetes' way of assigning consistent virtual addresses to sets of Pod replicas.

All Kubernetes entities may be assigned name-value pairs called **labels** that are used to reference them through a pattern-matching mechanism. More specifically, Selectors select Kubernetes entities by listing labels they must have.

Thus, for instance, all Pods that receive traffic from the same Service are selected by specifying labels that they must have in the Service definition.

The way a Service routes its traffic to all connected Pods depends on the way Pods are organized. Stateless Pods are organized in so-called `ReplicaSets`. `ReplicaSets` have a unique virtual address assigned to the whole group and traffic is split equally among all Pods of the group.

Stateful Kubernetes Pod replicas are organized into so-called `StatefulSets`. `StatefulSets` use sharding to split the traffic between all their Pods. For this reason, Kubernetes Services assign a different name to each Pod of the `StatefulSet` they are connected to. These names look like the following: `basename-0.<base URL>`, `basename-1.<base URL>`, ..., `basename-n.<base URL>`. This way, message sharding is easily accomplished as follows:

1. Each time a message must be sent to a `StatefulSet` composed of *N* replicas, you compute a hash between `0` and `N-1`, say `X`.
2. Add the postfix `X` to a base name to get a cluster address, such as `basename-x.<base URL>`.
3. Send the message to the `basename-x.<base URL> cluster address`.

Kubernetes has no predefined storing facilities, and you can't use node disk storage since Pods are moved between the available nodes, so long-term storage must be provided with sharded cloud databases or with other kinds of cloud storage. While each Pod in a StatefulSet can access a sharded cloud database with the usual connection string technique, Kubernetes offers a technique to abstract disk-like cloud storage provided by the external Kubernetes cluster environment. We will describe this storage in the *Advanced Kubernetes concepts* section.

All Kubernetes entities mentioned in this short introduction can be defined in a `.yaml` file, which, once deployed to a Kubernetes cluster, causes the creation of all entities defined in the file. The subsection that follows describes `.yaml` files, while the other subsections thereafter describe in detail all the basic Kubernetes objects mentioned so far, and explain how to define them in a `.yaml` file. Other Kubernetes objects will be described throughout the chapter.

.yaml files

The desired configuration of a cluster and the structure of Kubernetes objects are described by the developer with a language called YAML, and are packaged in files with a `.yaml` extension.

`.yaml` files, like JSON files, can be used to describe nested objects and collections in a human-readable way, but they do it with a different syntax. You have objects and lists, but object properties are not surrounded by `{}`, and lists are not surrounded by `[]`. Instead, nested objects are declared by simply indenting their content with spaces. The number of spaces can be freely chosen, but once they've been chosen, they must be used consistently.

List items can be distinguished from object properties by preceding them with a hyphen (`-`).

Here is an example involving nested objects and collections:

```
Name: John
Surname: Smith
Spouse:
  Name: Mary
  Surname: Smith
Addresses:
- Type: home
  Country: England
  Town: London
  Street: My home street
- Type: office
  Country: England
  Town: London
  Street: My home street
```

The preceding `Person` object has a `Spouse` nested object and a nested collection of addresses.

The same example in JSON would be:

```
{
Name: John
Surname: Smith
Spouse:
{
  Name: Mary
  Surname: Smith
}
Addresses:
[
 {
  Type: home
```

```
    Country: England
    Town: London
    Street: My home street
  },
  {
    Type: office
    Country: England
    Town: London
    Street: My home street
  }
 ]
}
```

As you can see, the syntax is more readable, since it avoids the overhead of parentheses.

`.yaml` files can contain several sections, each defining a different entity, that are separated by a line containing the `---` string. Comments are preceded by a # symbol, which must be repeated on each comment line.

Each section starts with the declaration of the Kubernetes API group and version. In fact, not all objects belong to the same API group. For objects that belong to the `core` API group, we can specify just the API version, as in the following example:

```
apiVersion: v1
```

While objects belonging to different API groups must also specify the API name, as in the following example:

```
apiVersion: apps/v1
```

In the next subsection, we analyze ReplicaSets and the Deployments that are built on top of them.

ReplicaSets and Deployments

The most important building block of Kubernetes applications is the ReplicaSet, that is, a Pod replicated *N* times. Usually, however, you use a more complex object that is built on top of the ReplicaSet – the Deployment. Deployments not only create a ReplicaSet, but also monitor them to ensure that the number of replicas is kept constant regardless of hardware faults and other events that might involve the ReplicaSets. In other words, they are a declarative way of defining ReplicaSets and Pods.

Replicating the same functionalities, and thus the same Pods, is the simplest operation to optimize for performance: the more replicas we create of the same Pod, the more hardware resources and threads must be made available for the functionality encoded by that Pod. Thus, when we discover that a functionality becomes a bottleneck in the system, we may just increase the number of replicas of the Pod that encodes that functionality.

Each Deployment has a name (`metadata->name`), an attribute that specifies the desired number of replicas (`spec->replicas`), a key-value pair (`spec -> selector-> matchLabels`) that selects the Pods to monitor, and a template (`spec->template`) that specifies how to build the Pod replicas:

```
apiVersion: apps/v1
kind: Deployment
metadata:
  name: my-deployment-name
  namespace: my-namespace #this is optional
spec:
   replicas: 3
   selector:
     matchLabels:
       my-pod-label-name: my-pod-label-value
         ...
   template:
      ...
```

`namespace` is optional and, if not provided, a namespace called `default` is assumed. Namespaces are a way of keeping separate the objects of a Kubernetes cluster. For instance, a cluster can host the objects of two completely independent applications, each placed in a separate `namespace` in order to prevent possible name collisions. In a few words, Kubernetes namespaces have the same purpose as .NET namespaces: preventing name collisions.

Indented inside the template is the definition of the Pod to replicate. Complex objects such as Deployments can also contain other kinds of templates, for instance, a template of disk-like memory required by the external environment. We will discuss this in more detail in the *Advanced Kubernetes concepts* section.

In turn, the Pod template contains a `metadata` section with the labels used to select the Pods, and a `spec` section with a list of all of the containers:

```
metadata:
  labels:
    my-pod-label-name: my-pod-label-value
      ...
spec:
  containers:
  ...
  - name: my-container-name
    image: <Docker imagename>
    resources:
      requests:
        cpu: 100m
```

```
          memory: 128Mi
        limits:
          cpu: 250m
          memory: 256Mi
      ports:
      - containerPort: 6379
      env:
      - name: env-name
        value: env-value
         ...
```

Each container has a name and must specify the name of the Docker image to use to create the containers. If the Docker image is not contained in the public Docker registry, the name must be a URI that also includes the repository's location.

Then, containers must specify the memory and CPU resources that they need to be created in the `resources->requests` object. A Pod replica is created only if these resources are currently available. The `resources->limits` object, instead, specifies the maximum resources a container replica can use. If, during the container execution, these limits are exceeded, action is taken to limit them. More specifically, if the CPU limit is exceeded, the container is throttled (its execution is stopped to restore its CPU consumption), while, if the memory limits are exceeded, the container is restarted. `containerPort` must be the port exposed by the container. Here, we can also specify further information, such as the protocol used.

CPU time is expressed in millicores; `1,000` millicores means `100%` of the CPU time, while memory is expressed in mebibytes (`1Mi = 1,024*1,024 bytes`), or other units. `env` lists all the operating system environment variables to pass to the containers with their values.

Both containers and Pod templates can contain other fields, such as properties that define virtual files, and properties that define commands that return the readiness and the health state of the container. We will analyze these fields in the *Advanced Kubernetes concepts* section.

The following subsection describes Pod sets conceived to store state information.

StatefulSets

StatefulSets are very similar to ReplicaSets, but while the Pods of a ReplicaSet are indistinguishable processors that contribute in parallel to the same workload through load-balancing strategies, Pods in a StatefulSet have a unique identity and can contribute to the same workload only through sharding. This is because StatefulSets were conceived to store information, and information cannot be stored in parallel, merely split among several stores through sharding.

For the same reason, each Pod instance is always kept tied to any virtual disk space it requires (see the *Advanced Kubernetes concepts* section) so that each Pod instance is responsible for writing to a specific store.

Moreover, StatefulSets' Pod instances have ordinal numbers attached to them. They are started in sequence according to these numbers, and they are stopped in reverse order. If the StatefulSet contains *N* replicas, these numbers go from `0` to `N-1`. Moreover, a unique name for each instance is obtained by chaining the Pod name specified in the template with the instance ordinal, in the following way – `<pod name>-<instance ordinal>`. Thus, instance names will be something like `mypodname-0`, `mypodname-1`, and so on. As we will see in the *Services* subsection, instance names are used to build unique cluster network URIs for all instances, so that other Pods can communicate with a specific instance of a StateFulSet Pod.

Since Pods in a StateFulSet have memory, each of them can only serve the requests that can be processed with the data contained in them. Therefore, in order to take advantage of several Pods in a StatefulSets, we must share the whole data space in easy-to-compute subsets. This technique is called sharding. For instance, Pods of a StatefulSet that handle customers could each be assigned a different set of customer names according to their first letters. One could handle all customers whose names start with letters in the interval A-C, another the names in the interval D-F, and so on.

Here is a typical StatefulSet definition:

```
apiVersion: apps/v1
kind: StatefulSet
metadata:
  name: my-stateful-set-name
spec:
  selector:
    matchLabels:
      my-pod-label-name: my-pod-label-value
...
  serviceName: "my-service-name"
  replicas: 3
  template:
    ...
```

The template part is the same as that of Deployments. The main difference between StatefulSets and Deployments is the `serviceName` field. This specifies the name of a service that must be connected with the StatefulSet to provide unique network addresses for all Pod instances. We will discuss this subject in more detail in the *Services* subsection. Moreover, usually, StatefulSets use some form of storage. We will discuss this in detail in the *Advanced Kubernetes concepts* section.

It is also worth pointing out that the default order of the creation and stop strategy of StatefulSets can be changed by specifying an explicit `Parallel` value for the `spec->podManagementPolicy` property (the default value is `OrderedReady`).

The following table summarizes the differences between StatefulSets and ReplicaSets:

Features	StatefulSets	ReplicaSets
Unique address for the whole set	No. Each Pod in the set has a different address and takes care of a different kind of requests.	Yes. Pods in ReplicaSets are indistinguishable so each request can be served by any of them.
Number of replicas can be increased during application lifetime	No. Since each Pod is in charge of a specific kind of requests and has a unique address, we can't add more Pods.	Yes. Since Pods are indistinguishable, more Pods can't cause problems, but just improve the performance of the whole set.
Pods can store permanent data inside of them	Yes, they are designed for this. Requests are issued to Pods with the sharding technique.	No, because they are designed to be undistinguishable, and storing a specific datum in a specific Pod would make a Pod different from the others in the set.

Table 20.1: StataefulSets versus ReplicaSets

The following subsection describes how to provide stable network addresses to both ReplicaSets and StatefulSets.

Services

Since Pod instances can be moved between nodes, they have no stable IP address attached to them. Services take care of assigning a unique and stable virtual address to a whole ReplicaSet and of load balancing the traffic to all its instances. Services are not software objects created in the cluster, but just an abstraction of the various settings and activities needed to implement their functionalities.

Services work at level 4 of the protocol stack, so they understand protocols such as TCP, but they aren't able to perform, for instance, HTTP-specific actions/transformations, such as ensuring a secure HTTPS connection. Therefore, if you need to install HTTPS certificates on the Kubernetes cluster, you need a more complex object that is capable of interacting at level 7 of the protocol stack. The `Ingress` object was conceived for this. We will discuss this in the next subsection.

Services also handle assigning a unique virtual address to each instance of a StatefulSet. In fact, there are various kinds of Services; some were conceived for ReplicaSets and others for StatefulSets.

A `ClusterIP` service type is assigned a unique cluster internal IP address. It specifies the ReplicaSets or Deployments it is connected to through label pattern matching. It uses tables maintained by the Kubernetes infrastructure to load balance the traffic it receives between all the Pod instances to which it is connected.

Therefore, other Pods can communicate with the Pods connected to a Service by interacting with this Service that is assigned the stable network name `<service name>.<service namespace>.svc.cluster.local`. Since they are just assigned local IP addresses, a `ClusterIP` service can't be accessed from outside the Kubernetes cluster.

A ClusterIP is the usual communication choice for Deployments and ReplicaSets that do not communicate with anything outside of their Kubernetes cluster.

Here is the definition of a typical `ClusterIP` service:

```
apiVersion: v1
kind: Service
metadata:
  name: my-service
  namespace: my-namespace
spec:
  selector:
    my-selector-label: my-selector-value
    ...
  ports:
    - name: http
      protocol: TCP
      port: 80
      targetPort: 9376
    - name: https
      protocol: TCP
      port: 443
      targetPort: 9377
```

Each Service can work on several ports and can route any port (`port`) to the ports exposed by the containers (`targetPort`). However, it is very often the case that `port = targetPort`. Ports can be given names, but these names are optional. Also, the specification of the protocol is optional; when not explicitly specified, all supported level 4 protocols are allowed. The `spec->selector` property specifies all the name/value pairs that select the Pods for the Service to which to route the communications it receives.

Since a `ClusterIP` service can't be accessed from outside the Kubernetes cluster, we need other Service types to expose a Kubernetes application on a public IP address.

`NodePort`-type Services are the simplest way to expose Pods to the outside world. In order to implement a `NodePort` service, the same port `x` is opened on all nodes of the Kubernetes cluster and each node routes the traffic it receives on this port to a newly created `ClusterIP` service.

In turn, the `ClusterIP` service routes its traffic to all Pods selected by the service:

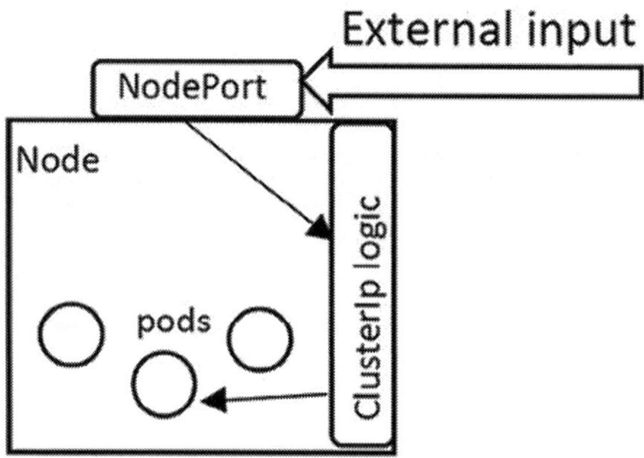

Figure 20.3: NodePort service

Therefore, you can simply communicate with port `x` through a public IP of any cluster node in order to access the Pods connected to the `NodePort` service. Of course, the whole process is completely automatic and hidden from the developer, whose only preoccupation is getting the port number `x` so they know where to forward the external traffic.

The definition of a `NodePort` service is similar to the definition of a `ClusterIP` service, the only difference being that they specify a value of `NodePort` for the `spec->type` property:

```
...
spec:
  type: NodePort
  selector:
  ...
```

As a default, a node port `x` in the range 30000-32767 is automatically chosen for each `targetPort` specified by the `Service`. The `port` property associated with each `targetPort` is meaningless for `NodePort` Services since all traffic passes through the selected node port `x`, and, by convention, is set to the same value as the `targetPort`.

The developer can also set the NodePort `x` directly through a `nodePort` property:

```
...
ports:
    - name: http
      protocol: TCP
      port: 80
      targetPort: 80
      nodePort: 30007
    - name: https
```

```
      protocol: TCP
      port: 443
      targetPort: 443
      nodePort: 30020
...
```

When the Kubernetes cluster is hosted on a cloud, the more convenient way to expose some Pods to the outside world is through a `LoadBalancer` service, in which case the Kubernetes cluster is exposed to the outside world through a level 4 load balancer of the selected cloud provider.

A LoadBalancer is the usual communication choice for Deployments and ReplicaSets that do communicate outside of their Kubernetes cluster but don't need advanced HTTP features.

The definition of a `LoadBalancer` service is similar to that of a `ClusterIp` service, the only difference being that the `spec->type` property must be set to `LoadBalancer`:

```
...
spec:
  type: LoadBalancer
  selector:
  ...
```

If no further specification is added, a dynamic public IP is randomly assigned. However, if a specific public IP address is required, it can be set as a public IP address for the cluster load balancer by specifying it in the `spec->loadBalancerIP` property:

```
...
spec:
  type: LoadBalancer
  loadBalancerIP: <your public ip>
  selector:
  ...
```

In **Azure Kubernetes Service** (**AKS**), you must also specify the resource group where the IP address was allocated in an annotation:

```
apiVersion: v1
kind: Service
metadata:
  annotations:
    service.beta.kubernetes.io/azure-load-balancer-resource-group: <IP resource
group name>
  name: my-service-name
...
```

In AKS, you can remain with a dynamic IP address, but you can get a public static domain name of the type `<my-service-label>.<location>.cloudapp.azure.com`, where `<location>` is the geographic label you have chosen for your resources. `<my-service-label>` is a label that you have verified that makes the previous domain name unique. The chosen label must be declared in an annotation of your service, as shown here:

```
apiVersion: v1
kind: Service
metadata:
  annotations:
service.beta.kubernetes.io/azure-dns-label-name: <my-service-label>
  name: my-service-name
...
```

StatefulSets don't need any load balancing since each Pod instance has its own identity, but do require a unique URL address for each Pod instance. This unique URL is provided by the so-called **headless Services**. Headless Services are defined like `ClusterIP` services, the only difference being that they have their `spec->clusterIP` property set to none:

```
...
spec:
  clusterIP: none
  selector:
...
```

All StatefulSets handled by a headless Service must place the Service name in their `spec-> serviceName` property, as already stated in the *StatefulSets* subsection.

The unique name provided by a headless Service to all `StatefulSets` Pod instances it handles is `<unique pod name>.<service name>.<namespace>.svc.cluster.local`.

Services only understand low-level protocols, such as TCP/IP, but most web applications are situated on the more sophisticated HTTP protocol. That's why Kubernetes offers higher-level entities called **Ingresses** that are built on top of services.

Ingresses are fundamental in the implementation of all web-based applications that need support for HTTP. Moreover, since at the moment, a substantial amount of applications are web applications, ingresses are a **must** for all microservices applications. In particular, they are needed by all microservices based on ASP.NET Core, which we will discuss in the remainder of the book.

The following subsection describes these and explains how to expose a set of Pods through a level 7 protocol load balancer, which can be used to get access to typical HTTP services, instead of through a `LoadBalancer` Service.

Ingresses

Ingresses were conceived to enable each application running in a Kubernetes cluster to expose an HTTP-based interface. This is a fundamental requirement for any orchestrator, since nowadays all microservices applications are web applications that interact with their clients through HTTP-based protocols. Moreover, Ingresses must be very efficient since all communications with the Kubernetes cluster will pass through them.

Accordingly, ingresses offer all of the typical services offered by an advanced and efficient web server. They provide the following services:

- HTTPS termination. They accept HTTPS connections and route them in HTTP format to any service in the cluster.
- Name-based virtual hosting. They associate several domain names with the same IP address and route each domain, or `<domain>/<path prefix>`, to a different cluster Service.
- Load balancing.

An ingress is the usual communication choice for Deployments and ReplicaSets that do communicate outside of their Kubernetes cluster and need advanced HTTP features.

Since rewriting all functionalities of an advanced web server from scratch would be substantially impossible, Ingresses rely on existing web servers to offer their services. More specifically, Kubernetes offers the possibility to add an interface module called Ingress Controllers to connect each Kubernetes cluster with an existing web server, such as NGINX and Apache.

Ingress Controllers are custom Kubernetes objects that must be installed in the cluster. They handle the interface between Kubernetes and the pre-existing web server software, which can be either an external web server or a web server that is part of the Ingress Controller installation.

We will describe the installation of an Ingress Controller based on the NGINX web server software in the *Advanced Kubernetes concepts* section, as an example of the use of Helm. However, there are Ingress Controllers for all main web servers. The *Further reading* section contains information on how to install also an Ingress Controller that interfaces an external Azure Application Gateway.

HTTPS termination and name-based virtual hosting (see the explanation of these terms at the beginning of this subsection) can be configured in the Ingress definition in a way that is independent of the chosen Ingress Controller, while the way load balancing is achieved depends on the specific Ingress Controller chosen and on its configuration. Some Ingress Controller configuration data can be passed in the `metadata-> annotations` field of the Ingress definition.

Name-based virtual hosting is defined in the `spec-> rules` section of the Ingress definition:

```
...
spec:
...
  rules:
  - host: *.mydomain.com
    http:
      paths:
      - path: /
        pathType: Prefix
        backend:
          service:
            name: my-service-name
            port:
              number: 80
  - host: my-subdomain.anotherdomain.com
...
```

Each rule specifies an optional hostname that can contain the * wildcard. If no hostname is provided, the rule matches all hostnames. For each rule, we can specify several paths, each redirected to a different service/port pair, where the service is referenced through its name. The way the match with each `path` is carried out depends on the value of `pathType`; if this value is `Prefix`, the specified `path` must be a prefix of any matching path. Otherwise, if this value is `Exact`, the match must be exact. Matches are case-sensitive.

HTTPS termination on a specific hostname is specified by associating it with a certificate encoded in a Kubernetes secret:

```
...
spec:
...
  tls:
  - hosts:
      - www.mydomain.com
      secretName: my-certificate1
      - my-subdomain.anotherdomain.com
      secretName: my-certificate2
...
```

HTTPS certificates can be obtained free of charge at `https://letsencrypt.org/`. The procedure is explained on the website, but basically, as with all certificate authorities, you provide a key and they return the certificate based on that key. It is also possible to install a **certificate manager** that takes care of automatically installing and renewing the certificate. The way a key/certificate pair is encoded in a Kubernetes secret string is detailed in the *Advanced Kubernetes concepts* section.

The whole Ingress definition is as follows:

```
apiVersion: networking.k8s.io/v1
kind: Ingress
metadata:
  name: my-example-ingress
  namespace: my-namespace
spec:
  tls:
  ...
  rules:
...
```

Here, the `namespace` is optional, and if not specified, is assumed to be `default`.

In the next section, we will put into practice some of the concepts explained here by defining an Azure Kubernetes cluster and deploying a simple application.

Interacting with Kubernetes clusters

In this section, we will explain both how to create an Azure Kubernetes cluster, and how to install minikube, a Kubernetes simulator, on your local machine. All examples can be run on both Azure Kubernetes and your local minikube instance.

Creating an Azure Kubernetes cluster

To create an AKS cluster, do the following:

1. Type `AKS` into the Azure search box.
2. Select **Kubernetes services**.
3. Then click the **Create** button.

After that, the following form will appear:

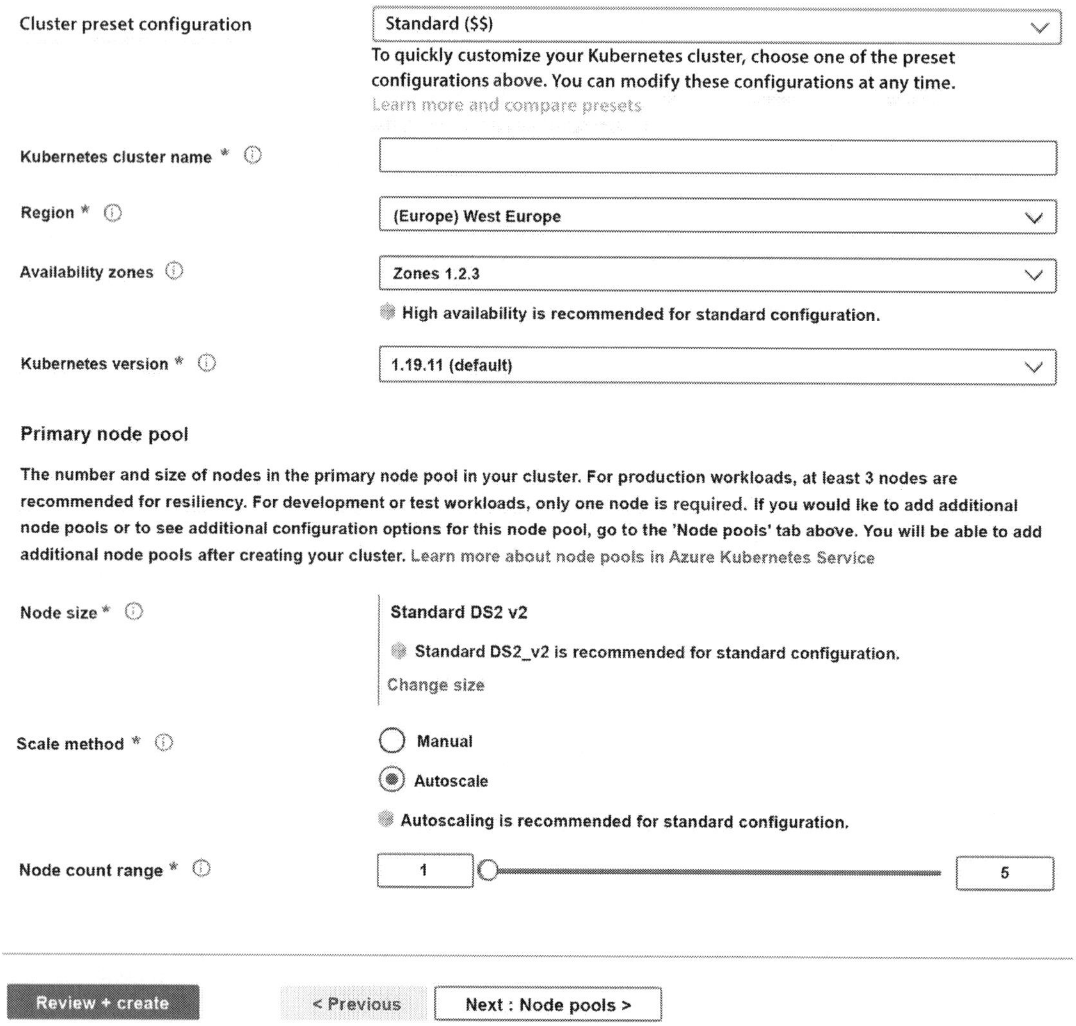

Cluster preset configuration: Standard ($$)

To quickly customize your Kubernetes cluster, choose one of the preset configurations above. You can modify these configurations at any time. Learn more and compare presets

Kubernetes cluster name *

Region *: (Europe) West Europe

Availability zones: Zones 1,2,3

High availability is recommended for standard configuration.

Kubernetes version *: 1.19.11 (default)

Primary node pool

The number and size of nodes in the primary node pool in your cluster. For production workloads, at least 3 nodes are recommended for resiliency. For development or test workloads, only one node is required. If you would lke to add additional node pools or to see additional configuration options for this node pool, go to the 'Node pools' tab above. You will be able to add additional node pools after creating your cluster. Learn more about node pools in Azure Kubernetes Service

Node size *: Standard DS2 v2

Standard DS2_v2 is recommended for standard configuration.

Change size

Scale method *: Manual / Autoscale

Autoscaling is recommended for standard configuration.

Node count range *: 1 – 5

Review + create | < Previous | Next : Node pools >

Figure 20.4: Creating a Kubernetes cluster

It is worth mentioning that you can get help simply by hovering over any ⓘ with the mouse.

As usual, you are required to specify a subscription, resource group, and region. Then, you can choose a unique name (**Kubernetes cluster name**) and the version of Kubernetes you would like to use. For computational power, you are asked to select a machine template for each node (**Node size**) and the number of nodes. While for an actual application, it is recommended to select at least three nodes, let's select just two nodes for our exercise in order to save our free Azure credit.

Moreover, the default virtual machine should also be set to a cheap one, so click **Change size** and select **DS2 v2**. Finally, set **Scale method** to **Manual** to prevent the number of nodes from being automatically changed, which might quickly burn through your free Azure credit.

The **Availability zones** setting allows you to spread your nodes across several geographic zones for better fault tolerance. The default is three zones. Please change it to two zones since we have just two nodes.

After implementing the preceding changes, you should see the following settings:

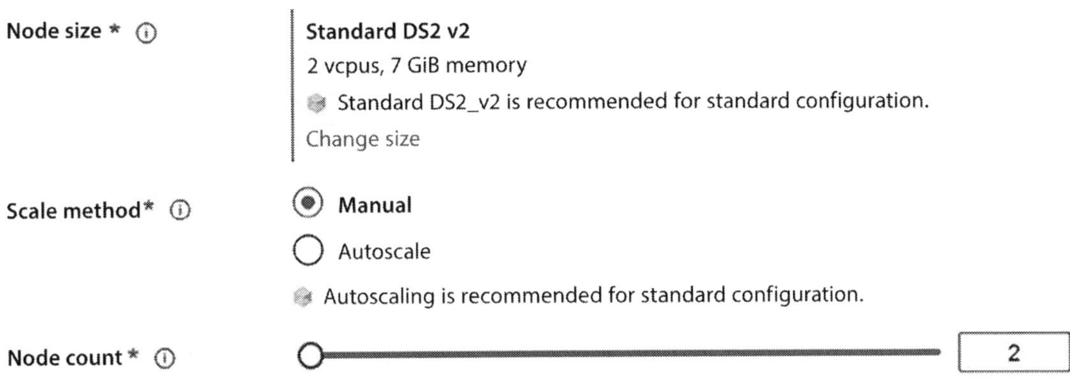

Figure 20.5: Chosen settings

Now you can create your cluster by clicking the **Review + create** button. A review page should appear. Confirm and create the cluster.

If you click **Next** instead of **Review + create**, you can also define other node types, and then you can provide security information, namely, a *service principal*, and specify whether you wish to enable role-based access control. In Azure, service principals are accounts that are associated with services you may use to define resource access policies. You may also change the default network settings and other settings.

Deployment may take a little while (10-20 minutes). After that time, you will have your first Kubernetes cluster! At the end of the chapter, when the cluster is no longer required, please don't forget to delete it in order to avoid wasting your free Azure credit.

In the next subsection, you will learn how to install and use minikube, a single-node Kubernetes simulator, on your local machine.

Using minikube

The easiest way to install minikube is the usage of the Windows installer you can find in the official installation page: `https://minikube.sigs.k8s.io/docs/start/`.

During the installation you will be prompted on the kind of virtualization tool to use. If you already installed Docker Desktop and WSL, please specify Docker.

If you have a different operating system, please follow the default choices, instead.

The installation of Docker Desktop is explained in the technical requirements of *Chapter 11, Applying a Microservice Architecture to Your Enterprise Application*. Please note that both WSL and Docker Desktop must be installed and Docker must be configured to use Linux containers by default.

Once you have minikube installed, you must add its binary to your computer `PATH`. The easiest way to do it is to open a PowerShell console and run the following command:

```
$oldPath=[Environment]::GetEnvironmentVariable('Path',
[EnvironmentVariableTarget]::Machine)
if ($oldPath.Split(';') -inotcontains 'C:\minikube'){ '
 [Environment]::SetEnvironmentVariable('Path', $('{0};C:\minikube' -f
$oldPath), [EnvironmentVariableTarget]::Machine) '
}
```

Once installed, your cluster can be run with:

```
minikube start
```

When you have finished working with the cluster, it can be stopped with:

```
minikube stop
```

In the next subsection, you will learn how to interact with your minikube instance or Azure cluster through Kubernetes' official client, kubectl.

Using kubectl

Once you have created your Azure Kubernetes cluster, you can interact with it via the Azure Cloud Shell. Click on the console icon in the top right of your Azure portal page. The following screenshot shows the Azure Shell icon:

Figure 20.6: Azure Shell icon

When prompted, select the **Bash Shell**. Then you will be prompted to create a storage account, so confirm and create it.

We will use this shell to interact with our cluster. At the top of the shell there is a file icon that we will use to upload our `.yaml` files:

Figure 20.7: How to upload files in Azure Cloud Shell

It is also possible to download a client called Azure CLI and to install it on your local machine (see `https://docs.microsoft.com/en-US/cli/azure/install-azure-cli`), but, in this case, you also need to install all the tools needed to interact with the Kubernetes cluster (kubectl and Helm) that are pre-installed in Azure Cloud Shell.

Once you've created a Kubernetes cluster, you can interact with it through the `kubectl` command-line tool. `kubectl` is integrated into Azure Cloud Shell, so you just need to activate your cluster credentials to use it. You can do this with the following Azure Cloud Shell command:

```
az aks get-credentials --resource-group <resource group> --name <cluster name>
```

The preceding command stores the credentials that were automatically created to enable your interaction with the cluster in a `/.kube/config` configuration file. From now on, you can issue your `kubectl` commands with no further authentication.

If, instead, you need to interact with your local minikube cluster, you need a local installation of `kubectl`, but minikube installs it automatically for you.

In order to use the automatically-installed `kubectl`, all `kubectl` commands must be preceded by the `minikube` command and `kubectl` must be followed by --. Thus, for instance, if you wanted to run the following command:

```
kubectl get all
```

Then you would have to write the following:

```
minkube kubectl -- get all
```

In the remainder of the chapter, we will write commands that work on actual Kubernetes clusters such as Azure Kubernetes. Therefore, when using minikube, remember to replace `kubectl` with `minikube kubectl` -- in your commands.

If you issue the `kubectl get nodes` command, you get a list of all your Kubernetes nodes. In general, `kubectl get <object type>` lists all objects of a given type. You can use it with `nodes`, `pods`, `statefulset`, and so on. `kubectl get all` shows a list of all the objects created in your cluster. If you also add the name of a specific object, you will get information on just that specific object, as shown here:

```
kubectl get <object type><object name>
```

If you add the `--watch` option, the object list will be continuously updated, so you can see the state of all the selected objects changing over time. You can leave this watch state by hitting *Ctrl* + *C*.

The following command shows a detailed report on a specific object:

```
kubectl describe <object name>
```

All objects described in a `.yaml` file, say `myClusterConfiguration.yaml`, can be created with the following command:

```
kubectl create -f myClusterConfiguration.yaml
```

Then, if you modify the `.yaml` file, you can reflect all the modifications in your cluster with the `apply` command, as shown here:

```
kubectl apply -f myClusterConfiguration.yaml
```

`apply` does the same job as `create` but, if the resource already exists, `apply` overrides it, while `create` exits with an error message.

You can destroy all objects that were created with a `.yaml` file by passing the same file to the `delete` command, as shown here:

```
kubectl delete -f myClusterConfiguration.yaml
```

The `delete` command can also be passed an object type and a list of names of objects of that type to destroy, as shown in the following example:

```
kubectl delete deployment deployment1 deployment2...
```

The preceding `kubectl` commands should suffice for most of your practical needs. For more details, the *Further reading* section contains a link to the official documentation.

In the next subsection, we will use `kubectl create` to install a simple demo application.

Deploying the demo Guestbook application

The Guestbook application is a demo application used in the examples in the official Kubernetes documentation. We will use it as an example of a Kubernetes application since its Docker images are available in the public Docker repository, so we don't need to write software.

The Guestbook application stores the opinions of customers who visit a hotel or a restaurant.

It is composed of a UI, and an in-memory database, based on Redis. Moreover, updates are sent to the master copy of the Redis database, which is automatically replicated in *N* read-only Redis replicas.

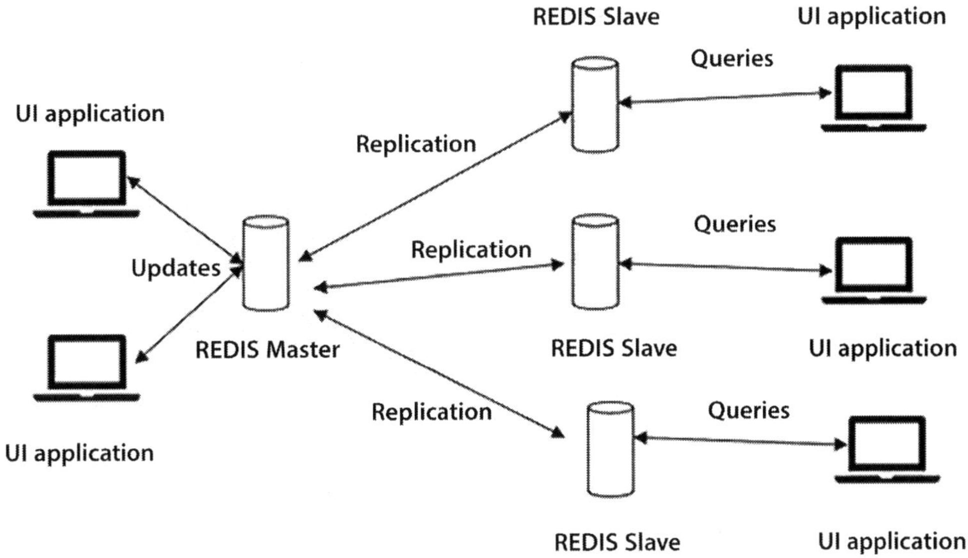

Figure 20.8: Architecture of the Guestbook application

The UI application can be deployed in Kubernetes as a Deployment, since it is memoryless.

The Redis master store is deployed as a single pod `Deployment`. We can't implement it with an *N*-pods `Deployment` since we need sharding for parallelizing updates. However, we might have used a `StatefulSet` assigning a different data shard to each different master Pod. However, since this is your first Kubernetes exercise and since write operations should not be predominant, a single master database should suffice in the practical case of a single restaurant/hotel.

Since all slave copies contain the same data and consequently are undistinguishable, they can be implemented with a `Deployment`, too.

The whole application is composed of three `.yaml` files that you can find in the GitHub repository associated with this book (`https://github.com/PacktPublishing/Software-Architecture-with-C-Sharp-12-and-.NET-8-4E`).

Here is the code for the master storage based on Redis that is contained in the `redis-master.yaml` file:

```
apiVersion: apps/v1
kind: Deployment
metadata:
  name: redis-master
  labels:
    app: redis
spec:
  selector:
    matchLabels:
      app: redis
      role: master
      tier: backend
  replicas: 1
  template:
    metadata:
      labels:
        app: redis
        role: master
        tier: backend
    spec:
      containers:
      - name: master
        image: docker.io/redis:6.0.5
        resources:
          requests:
            cpu: 100m
            memory: 100Mi
        ports:
        - containerPort: 6379
---
apiVersion: v1
kind: Service
metadata:
  name: redis-leader
  labels:
    app: redis
    role: master
    tier: backend
spec:
```

```
  ports:
  - port: 6379
    targetPort: 6379
  selector:
    app: redis
    role: master
    tier: backend
```

The file is composed of two object definitions separated by a line containing just `---`, that is, the object definition separator of `.yaml` files. It is common to group related objects, such as a Deployment with its associated Service, in the same file separated by the `---` objects separator symbol in order to increase code readability.

The first object is a `Deployment` with a single replica, and the second object is a `ClusterIP` Service that exposes the `Deployment` on the `6379` port at the internal `redis-leader.default.svc.cluster.local` network address. The Deployment pod template defines the three `app`, `role`, and `tier` labels with values that are used in the `selector` definition of the Service to connect the Service with the unique Pod defined in the `Deployment`.

Let's upload the `redis-master.yaml` file to Azure Cloud Shell, and then deploy it in the cluster with the following command:

```
kubectl create -f redis-master.yaml
```

Once the operation is complete, you can inspect the contents of the cluster with `kubectl get all`.

The slave storage is defined in the `redis-slave.yaml` file and is created in the same way, the only difference being that this time we have two replicas, and a different Docker image. The full code is in the GitHub repository associated with this book.

Let's upload this file as well and deploy it with the following command:

```
kubectl create -f redis-slave.yaml
```

The code for the UI tier is contained in the `frontend.yaml` file. `Deployment` has three replicas and a different Service type. Let's upload and deploy this file with the following command:

```
kubectl create -f frontend.yaml
```

It is worthwhile analyzing the Service code in the `frontend.yaml` file:

```
apiVersion: v1
kind: Service
metadata:
  name: frontend
  labels:
    app: guestbook
    tier: frontend
```

```
spec:
  type: LoadBalancer
  ports:
  - port: 80
  selector:
    app: guestbook
    tier: frontend
```

Again, the full code is in the GitHub repository associated with the book.

This Service is of the `LoadBalancer` type. Since this Pod is the application interface with the world outside of the Kubernetes cluster, its service must have a fixed IP and must be load balanced. Therefore, we must use a `LoadBalancer` service since this is the unique service type that satisfies those requirements. (See the *Services* section of this chapter for more information.)

If you are in Azure Kubernetes or any other cloud Kubernetes service, in order to get the public IP address assigned to the service, and then to the application, use the following command:

```
kubectl get service
```

The preceding command should display information on all the installed services. You should find the public IP in the `EXTERNAL-IP` column of the list. If you see only `<none>` values, please repeat the command until the public IP address is assigned to the load balancer.

If no IP is assigned after a few minutes, please verify whether there is some error or warning in any of the service descriptions. If not, please check whether all deployments are actually running using the following command:

```
kubectl get deployments
```

If, instead, you are on minikube, `LoadBalancer` services can be accessed by issuing this command:

```
minikube service <service name>
```

Thus, in our case:

```
minikube service frontend
```

The command should automatically open the browser.

Once you get the IP address, navigate with the browser to this address. The application's home page should now appear!

If the page doesn't appear, verify whether any service has an error by issuing the following command:

```
kubectl get service
```

If not, also verify that all deployments are in the running state with the following:

```
kubectl get deployments
```

If you find problems, please look for errors in the `.yaml` files, correct them, and then update the object defined in the file with:

```
kubectl update -f <file name>
```

Once you have finished experimenting with the application, make sure to remove the application from the cluster to avoid wasting your free Azure credit (public IP addresses cost money) with the following commands:

```
kubectl delete deployment frontend redis-master redis-slave
```

```
kubectl delete service frontend redis-leader redis-follower
```

In the next section, we will analyze other important Kubernetes features.

Advanced Kubernetes concepts

In this section, we will discuss other important Kubernetes features, including how to assign permanent storage to StatefulSets; how to store secrets such as passwords, connection strings, or certificates; how a container can inform Kubernetes about its health state; and how to handle complex Kubernetes packages with Helm. All of these subjects are organized into dedicated subsections. We will start with the problem of permanent storage.

Requiring permanent storage

Since Pods are moved between nodes, they can't store data on the disk storage offered by the current node where they are running, or they would lose that storage as soon as they are moved to a different node. This leaves us with two options:

- **Using external databases**: With the help of databases, ReplicaSets can also store information. However, if we need better performance in terms of write/update operations, we should use distributed sharded databases based on non-SQL engines such as Cosmos DB or MongoDB (see *Chapter 12, Choosing Your Data Storage in the Cloud*). In this case, in order to take maximum advantage of table sharding, we need StatefulSets, where each Pod instance takes care of a different table shard.
- **Using cloud storage:** Not being tied to a physical cluster node, cloud storage can be associated permanently with specific Pod instances of StatefulSets. Cloud storage is discussed in the *Redis* and *Azure storage accounts* sections of *Chapter 12*.

Since access to external databases doesn't require any Kubernetes-specific techniques but can be done with the usual connection strings, we will concentrate on cloud storage.

Kubernetes offers an abstraction of storage called **PersistentVolumeClaim** (**PVC**) that is independent of the underlying storage provider. More specifically, PVCs are allocation requests that are either matched to predefined resources or allocated dynamically. When the Kubernetes cluster is in the cloud, typically, you use dynamic allocation carried out by dynamic providers installed by the cloud provider. For more information on cloud storage, please refer to *Chapter 12*.

Cloud providers such as Azure offer different storage classes with different performance and different costs. Moreover, the PVC can also specify the `accessMode`, which can be:

- `ReadWriteOnce`: The volume can be mounted as read-write by a single Pod.
- `ReadOnlyMany`: The volume can be mounted as read-only by many Pods.
- `ReadWriteMany`: The volume can be mounted as read-write by many Pods.

Volume claims can be added to StatefulSets in a specific `spec->volumeClaimTemplates` object:

```
volumeClaimTemplates:
-  metadata:
     name: my-claim-template-name
   spec:
     resources:
       request:
         storage: 5Gi
     volumeMode: Filesystem
     accessModes:
      - ReadWriteOnce
     storageClassName: my-optional-storage-class
```

The `storage` property contains the storage requirements. `volumeMode` set to `Filesystem` is a standard setting that means the storage will be available as a file path. The other possible value is `Block`, which allocates the memory as `unformatted`. `storageClassName` must be set to an existing storage class offered by the cloud provider. If it's omitted, the default storage class will be assumed.

All available storage classes can be listed with the following command:

```
kubectl get storageclass
```

Once `volumeClaimTemplates` has defined how to create permanent storage, then each container must specify which file path to attach that permanent storage to in the `spec->containers->volumeMounts` property:

```
...
volumeMounts
- name: my-claim-template-name
  mountPath: /my/requested/storage
  readOnly: false
...
```

Here, `name` must correspond to the name given to the PVC.

The following subsection shows how to use Kubernetes secrets.

Kubernetes secrets

Some data, such as passwords and connection strings, cannot be exposed but need to be protected by some kind of encryption. Kubernetes handles private sensitive data that need encryption through specific objects called **secrets. Secrets** are sets of key-value pairs that are encrypted to protect them. They can be created by putting each value in a file, and then invoking the following `kubectl` command:

```
kubectl create secret generic my-secret-name \
  --from-file=./secret1.bin \
  --from-file=./secret2.bin
```

In this case, the filenames become the keys and the files' contents are the values.

When the values are strings, they can be specified directly in the `kubectl` command, as shown here:

```
kubectl create secret generic dev-db-secret \
  --from-literal=username=devuser \
  --from-literal=password='$dsd_weew1'
```

In this case, keys and values are listed one after the other, separated by the = character. In the previous example, the actual password is enclosed between single quotes to escape special characters like $ that are usually required to build strong passwords.

Once defined, secrets can be referred to in the `spec->volume` property of a Pod (Deployment or StatefulSet template), as shown here:

```
...
volumes:
  - name: my-volume-with-secrets
    secret:
      secretName: my-secret-name
...
```

After that, each container can specify on which path to mount them in the `spec->containers->volumeMounts` property:

```
...
volumeMounts:
    - name: my-volume-with-secrets
      mountPath: "/my/secrets"
      readOnly: true
...
```

In the preceding example, each key is seen as a file with the same name as the key. The content of the file is the secret value, base64-encoded. Therefore, the code that reads each file must decode its content (in .NET, `Convert.FromBase64` will do the job).

When secrets contain strings, they can also be passed as environment variables in the `spec->containers->env` object:

```
env:
      - name: SECRET_USERNAME
        valueFrom:
          secretKeyRef:
            name: dev-db-secret
            key: username
      - name: SECRET_PASSWORD
        valueFrom:
          secretKeyRef:
            name: dev-db-secret
            key: password
```

Here, the `name` property must match the secret's name. Passing secrets as environment variables is very convenient when containers host ASP.NET Core applications, since, in this case, environment variables are all immediately available in the configuration object (see the *Loading configuration data and using it with the options framework* section of *Chapter 17, Presenting ASP.NET Core*).

Secrets can also encode the key/certificate pair of an HTTPS certificate with the following `kubectl` command:

```
kubectl create secret tls test-tls --key="tls.key" --cert="tls.crt"
```

Secrets defined in this way can be used to enable HTTPS termination in Ingresses. You can do this by placing the secret names in the `spec->tls->hosts->secretName` properties of an Ingress.

Liveness and readiness checks

Kubernetes automatically monitors all containers to ensure they are still alive and that they keep their resource consumption within the limits declared in the `spec->containers->resources->limits` object. When some conditions are violated, the container is either throttled, or restarted, or the whole Pod instance is restarted on a different node. How does Kubernetes know that a container is in a healthy state? While it can use the operating system to check the healthy state of nodes, it has no universal check that works with all containers.

Therefore, the containers themselves must inform Kubernetes of their health, otherwise Kubernetes cannot verify them. Containers can inform Kubernetes of their health in two ways: either by declaring a console command that returns their health, or by declaring an endpoint that provides the same information.

Both declarations are provided in the `spec-> containers-> livenessProb` object. The console command check is declared as shown here:

```
...
  livenessProbe:
    exec:
```

```
      command:
      - cat
      - /tmp/healthy
    initialDelaySeconds: 10
    periodSeconds: 5
...
```

If `command` returns `0`, the container is considered healthy. In the preceding example, the software running in the container records its state of health in the `/tmp/healthy` file, so the `cat/tmp/healthy` command returns it. `PeriodSeconds` is the time between checks, while `initialDelaySeconds` is the initial delay before performing the first check. An initial delay is always necessary so as to give the container time to start.

The endpoint check is quite similar:

```
...
  livenessProbe:
    exec:
      httpGet:
        path: /healthz
        port: 8080
        httpHeaders:
          - name: Custom-Health-Header
          value: container-is-ok
    initialDelaySeconds: 10
    periodSeconds: 5
...
```

The test is successful if the HTTP response contains the declared header with the declared value. You may also use a pure TCP check, as shown here:

```
...
  livenessProbe:
    exec:
      tcpSocket:
        port: 8080
    initialDelaySeconds: 10
    periodSeconds: 5
...
```

In this case, the check succeeds if Kubernetes is able to open a TCP socket to the container on the declared port.

Similarly, the readiness of containers once they are installed is monitored with a readiness check. The readiness check is defined in a similar way as the liveness check, the only difference being that `livenessProbe` is replaced with `readinessProbe`.

The following subsection explains how to autoscale Deployments.

Autoscaling

Instead of manually modifying the number of replicas in a Deployment to adapt it to a decrease or increase in load, we can let Kubernetes decide for itself the number of replicas needed to keep a declared resource's consumption constant. Thus, for instance, if we declare a target of 10% CPU consumption, then when the average resource consumption of each replica exceeds this limit, a new replica will be created. If the average CPU consumption falls below this limit, a replica is destroyed. The typical resource used to monitor replicas is CPU consumption, but we can also use memory consumption.

In actual high-traffic production systems, autoscaling is a **must**, because it is the only way to adapt quickly the system to changes in the load.

Autoscaling is achieved by defining a `HorizontalPodAutoscaler` object. Here is an example of the `HorizontalPodAutoscaler` definition:

```
apiVersion: autoscaling/v2beta1
kind: HorizontalPodAutoscaler
metadata:
  name: my-autoscaler
spec:
  scaleTargetRef:
    apiVersion: extensions/v1beta1
    kind: Deployment
    name: my-deployment-name
  minReplicas: 1
  maxReplicas: 10
  metrics:
  - type: Resource
    resource:
      name: cpu
      targetAverageUtilization: 25
```

`spec-> scaleTargetRef->name` specifies the name of the Deployment to autoscale, while `targetAverageUtilization` specifies the target resource (in our case, `cpu`) percentage usage (in our case, 25%).

The following subsection gives a short introduction to the Helm package manager and Helm charts and explains how to install Helm charts on a Kubernetes cluster. An example of how to install an Ingress Controller is given as well.

Helm – installing an Ingress Controller

Helm charts are a way to organize the installation of complex Kubernetes applications that contain several .yaml files. A Helm chart is a set of .yaml files organized into folders and subfolders. Here is a typical folder structure of a Helm chart taken from the official documentation:

```
Chart.yaml          # A YAML file containing information about the chart
LICENSE             # OPTIONAL: A plain text file containing the license for the chart
README.md           # OPTIONAL: A human-readable README file
values.yaml         # The default configuration values for this chart
values.schema.json  # OPTIONAL: A JSON Schema for imposing a structure on the values.yaml file
charts/             # A directory containing any charts upon which this chart depends.
crds/               # Custom Resource Definitions
templates/          # A directory of templates that, when combined with values,
                    # will generate valid Kubernetes manifest files.
templates/NOTES.txt # A plain text file containing short usage notes
```

Figure 20.9: Folder structure of a Helm chart

The .yaml files specific to the application are placed in the top templates directory, while the charts directory may contain other Helm charts used as helper libraries. The top-level Chart.yaml file contains general information on the package (name and description), together with both the application version and the Helm chart version. The following is a typical example:

```
apiVersion: v2
name: myhelmdemo
description: My Helm chart
type: application
version: 1.3.0
appVersion: 1.2.0
```

Here, type can be either application or library. Only application charts can be deployed, while library charts are utilities for developing other charts. library charts are placed in the charts folder of other Helm charts.

In order to configure each specific application installation, Helm chart .yaml files contain variables that are specified when Helm charts are installed. Moreover, Helm charts also provide a simple templating language that allows some declarations to be included only if some conditions depending on the input variables are satisfied. The top-level values.yaml file declares default values for the input variables, meaning that the developer needs to specify just the few variables for which they require values different from the defaults. We will not describe the Helm chart template language because it would be too extensive, but you can find it in the official Helm documentation referred to in the *Further reading* section.

Helm charts are usually organized in public or private repositories in a way that is similar to Docker images. There is a Helm client that you can use to download packages from a remote repository and to install charts in Kubernetes clusters. The Helm client is immediately available in Azure Cloud Shell, so you can start using Helm for your Azure Kubernetes cluster without needing to install it.

A remote repository must be added before using its packages, as shown in the following example:

```
helm repo add <my-repo-local-name> https://charts.helm.sh/stable
```

The preceding command makes the packages of a remote repository available and gives a local name to that remote repository. After that, any package from the remote repository can be installed with a command such as the following:

```
helm install <instance name><my-repo-local-name>/<package name> -n <namespace>
```

Here, `<namespace>` is the namespace in which to install the application. As usual, if it's not provided, the `default` namespace is assumed. `<instance name>` is the name that you give to the installed application. You need this name to get information about the installed application with the following command:

```
helm status <instance name>
```

You can get also information about all applications installed with Helm with the help of the following command:

```
helm ls
```

The application name is also needed to delete the application from the cluster by means of the following command:

```
helm delete <instance name>
```

When we install an application, we may also provide a `.yaml` file with all the variable values we want to override. We can also specify a specific version of the Helm chart, otherwise the most recent version is used. Here is an example with both the version and values overridden:

```
helm install <instance name><my-repo-local-name>/<package name> -f  values.yaml
--version <version>
```

Finally, value overrides can also be provided in-line with the `--set` option, as shown here:

```
...--set <variable1>=<value1>,<variable2>=<value2>...
```

We can also upgrade an existing installation with the `upgrade` command, as shown here:

```
helm upgrade <instance name><my-repo-local-name>/<package name>...
```

The `upgrade` command may be used to specify new value overrides with the `-f` option or with the `--set` option, and a new version with `--version`.

Let's use Helm to provide an Ingress for the Guestbook demo application. More specifically, we will use Helm to install an Ingress Controller based on Nginx. The detailed procedure to be observed is as follows:

1. Add the remote repository:

```
helm repo add gcharts https://charts.helm.sh/stable
```

2. Install the Ingress Controller:

```
helm install ingress gcharts/nginx-ingress
```

3. When the installation is complete, you should see an entry for the installed Ingress Controller among the installed services if you type `kubectl get service`. The entry should contain a public IP. Please make a note of this IP since it will be the public IP of the application.
4. Open the `frontend.yaml` file and remove the `type: LoadBalancer` line. Save and upload this to Azure Cloud Shell. We changed the service type of the frontend application from `LoadBalancer` to `ClusterIP` (the default). This service will be connected to the new Ingress you are going to define.
5. Deploy `redis-master.yaml`, `redis-slave.yaml`, and `frontend.yaml` with `kubectl`, as detailed in the *Deploying the demo Guestbook application* subsection. Create a `frontend-ingress.yaml` file and place the following code in it:

```
apiVersion: extensions/v1beta1
kind: Ingress
metadata:
  name: simple-frontend-ingress
spec:
  rules:
  - http:
      paths:
      - path:/
        backend:
          serviceName: frontend
          servicePort: 80
```

6. Upload `frontend-ingress.yaml` to Azure Cloud Shell and deploy it with the following command:

```
kubectl apply -f frontend-ingress.yaml
```

7. Open the browser and navigate to the public IP you made a note of in *step 3*. There, you should see the application running.

The public IP allocated to the `Ingress-Controller` at *Step 3* is listed also in the **Azure Public IP Addresses** section of Azure. You can find it by searching for this section in the Azure search box. Once in this section, you should see this IP address listed. There you can also assign it a hostname of the type `<a name you can choose>.<your Azure region>.cloudeapp.com`.

We recommend studying the `https://letsencrypt.org/` documentation on how to require a certificate, assign a hostname to the application's public IP, and then use this hostname to get a free HTTPS certificate from `https://letsencrypt.org/`. Unfortunately, we can't give more details since the procedure to require a certificate is too extensive. Once you get a certificate, you can generate a secret from it with the following command:

```
kubectl create secret tls guestbook-tls --key="tls.key" --cert="tls.crt"
```

Then you can add the preceding secret to your `frontend-ingress.yaml Ingress` by adding the following `spec->tls` section to it:

```
...
spec:
...
  tls:
  - hosts:
      - <chosen name>.<your Azure region>.cloudeapp.com
      secretName: guestbook-tls
```

Following the correction, upload the file to your Azure Cloud Shell instance and update the previous Ingress definition with the following:

```
kubectl apply -f frontend-ingress.yaml
```

At this point, you should be able to access the Guestbook application with HTTPS.

When you are done experimenting, please don't forget to delete everything from your cluster to avoid wasting your free Azure credit. You can do this by means of the following commands:

```
kubectl delete -f frontend-ingress.yaml
kubectl delete -f frontend.yaml
kubectl delete -f redis-slave.yaml
kubectl delete -f redis-master.yaml
helm delete ingress
```

Summary

In this chapter, we described Kubernetes' basic concepts and objects, and then we explained how to create an AKS cluster. We also showed how to deploy applications and how to monitor and inspect the state of your cluster with a simple demo application.

The chapter also described more advanced Kubernetes features that have fundamental roles in practical applications, including how to provide persistent storage to the containers running on Kubernetes, how to inform Kubernetes of the health state of your containers, and how to offer advanced HTTP services, such as HTTPS and name-based virtual hosting.

Finally, we reviewed how to install complex applications with Helm, and gave a short description of Helm and Helm commands.

Up next, we have the book's case study.

Questions

1. Why are Services needed?
2. Why is an Ingress needed?
3. Why is Helm needed?
4. Is it possible to define several Kubernetes objects in the same `.yaml` file? If yes, how?
5. How does Kubernetes detect container faults?
6. Why are persistent volume claims needed?
7. What is the difference between a ReplicaSet and a StatefulSet?

Further reading

- A good book for extending the knowledge acquired in this chapter is the following: `https://www.packtpub.com/product/hands-on-kubernetes-on-azure-second-edition/9781800209671`.
- The official documentation for Kubernetes and `.yaml` files can be found here: `https://kubernetes.io/docs/home/`.
- More information on Helm and Helm charts can be found in the official documentation. This is extremely well written and contains some good tutorials: `https://helm.sh/`.
- The official documentation for Azure Kubernetes can be found here: `https://docs.microsoft.com/en-US/azure/aks/`.
- The official documentation on the Azure Application Gateway-based Ingress Controller is available here: `https://github.com/Azure/application-gateway-kubernetes-ingress`.
- Ingress certificate release and renewal can be automated as explained here: `https://docs.microsoft.com/azure/application-gateway/ingress-controller-letsencrypt-certificate-application-gateway`. While the procedure specifies an Azure Application Gateway-based ingress controller, it is adequate for any Ingress Controller.

Leave a review!

Enjoying this book? Help readers like you by leaving an Amazon review. Scan the QR code below for a 20% discount code.

**Limited Offer*

21

Case Study

As mentioned during the previous chapters, for this new edition, we reformulated the way we present the case study of the book – **World Wild Travel Club** (**WWTravelClub**). This case study will take you through the process of creating the software architecture for a travel agency.

The purpose of this case study is not to furnish a production-ready application, but just to help you understand the theory explained in each chapter and to provide an example of how to develop an enterprise application with Azure, Azure DevOps, C# 12, .NET 8, ASP.NET Core, and all other technologies introduced in this book.

Let's start with a description of what our case study application is. Then, we will gradually move to formal specifications.

Introducing World Wild Travel Club

WWTravelClub is a travel agency that was created to revolutionize vacation planning and travel experiences globally. To do so, they are developing an online service, where each aspect of a trip is meticulously curated and supported by a dedicated team of destination-specific experts.

The concept of this platform is that you can be both a visitor and a destination expert at the same time. The more you participate as an expert in a destination, the more points you score. These points can then be redeemed for tickets that people buy online using the platform.

The responsible for the WWTravelClub project came with the following requirements list for the platform:

- Common user view:
    - Promotional packages on the home page
    - Get a recommendation
    - Search for packages
    - Details for each package:
        - Buy a package

    - Buy a package with a club of experts included
    - Comment on your experience
    - Ask an expert
    - Evaluate an expert
    - Register as a common user
- Destination expert view:
    - The same view as the common user view
    - Answer questions asking for your destination expertise
    - Manage the points you scored by answering questions
    - Exchange points for tickets
- Administrator view:
    - Manage packages
    - Manage common users
    - Manage destination experts

Besides the functionalities asked for on the platform, it is important to note that WWTravelClub intends to have more than 100 destination experts per package and will offer around 1,000 different packages all over the world.

It is important to know that, in general, customers do not bring the requirements ready for development. That is why the process of gathering requirements is so important, as described in *Chapter 1, Understanding the Importance of Software Architecture*. This process will transform the list presented above into user needs and system requirements. Let's check how this will work in the next section.

User needs and system requirements

As presented in *Chapter 1, Understanding the Importance of Software Architecture*, to summarize the user needs, you may use the User Story pattern. We have used this approach here so that you can read the following user stories for WWTravelClub:

- `US_001`: As a common user, I want to view promotional packages on the home page so that I can easily find my next vacation.
- `US_002`: As a common user, I want to search for packages I cannot find on the home page so that I can explore other trip opportunities.
- `US_003`: As a common user, I want to see the details of a package so that I can decide which package to buy.
- `US_004`: As a common user, I want to register myself so that I can start buying the package.
- `US_005`: As a registered user, I want to process the payment so that I can buy a package.
- `US_006`: As a registered user, I want to buy a package with an expert recommendation included so that I can have an exclusive trip experience.

- `US_007`: As a registered user, I want to ask for an expert so that I can find out the best things to do on my trip.
- `US_008`: As a registered user, I want to comment on my experience so that I can give feedback on my trip.
- `US_009`: As a registered user, I want to review an expert who has helped me so that I can share with others how fantastic they were.
- `US_010`: As a registered user, I want to register as a destination expert view so that I can help people who travel to my city.
- `US_011`: As an expert user, I want to answer questions about my city so that I can score points to be exchanged in the future.
- `US_012`: As an expert user, I want to exchange points for tickets so that I can travel around the world more.
- `US_013`: As an administrator user, I want to manage packages so that users can have fantastic opportunities to travel.
- `US_014`: As an administrator user, I want to manage registered users so that WWTravelClub can guarantee good service quality.
- `US_015`: As an administrator user, I want to manage expert users so that all the questions regarding our destinations are answered.
- `US_016`: As an administrator user, I want to offer more than 1,000 packages around the world so that different countries can experience the WWTravelClub service.
- `US_017`: As the CEO, I want to have more than 1,000 users simultaneously accessing the website so that the business can scale effectively.
- `US_018`: As a user, I want to access WWTravelClub in my native language so that I can easily understand the package offered.
- `US_019`: As a user, I want to access WWTravelClub in the Chrome, Firefox, and Edge web browsers so that I can use the web browser of my preference.
- `US_020`: As a user, I want to know that my credit card information is stored securely, so I can buy packages safely.
- `US_021`: As a user, I want to get a recommendation of a good place to visit according to other people from my city, so I can find out about new places that fit my style.

Notice that while writing the stories, information related to non-functional requirements such as security, environment, performance, and scalability can be included.

However, some system requirements may be omitted when you write user stories and need to be included in the software specification. These requirements can be related to legal aspects, hardware, and software prerequisites, or even points of attention for the correct system delivery. We discussed them in *Chapter 2, Non-Functional Requirements*. So non-functional requirements need to be mapped and listed, as well as the user stories. The WWTravelClub system requirements are presented in the following list. Note that requirements are written in the future tense because the system does not exist yet:

- `SR_001`: The system shall use cloud computing components to deliver the scalability required.
- `SR_002`: The system shall respect **General Data Protection Regulation** (**GDPR**) requirements.
- `SR_003`: Any web page of this system shall respond within at least 2 seconds of 1,000 users accessing it concurrently.

The idea of having this list of user stories and system requirements is to help you understand how complex the development of a platform might be if you think about it from an architectural perspective.

Now that we have the list of user stories for the platform, it is time to start selecting the .NET project types that will be used at WWTravelClub. Let's check them in the next topic.

Main types of .NET projects used at WWTravelClub

The development of this book's use case will be based on various kinds of .NET Core Visual Studio projects. This section describes all of them. Let us select **New project** in the Visual Studio **File** menu.

For instance, you can filter **.NET Core** project types by typing them into the search engine as follows:

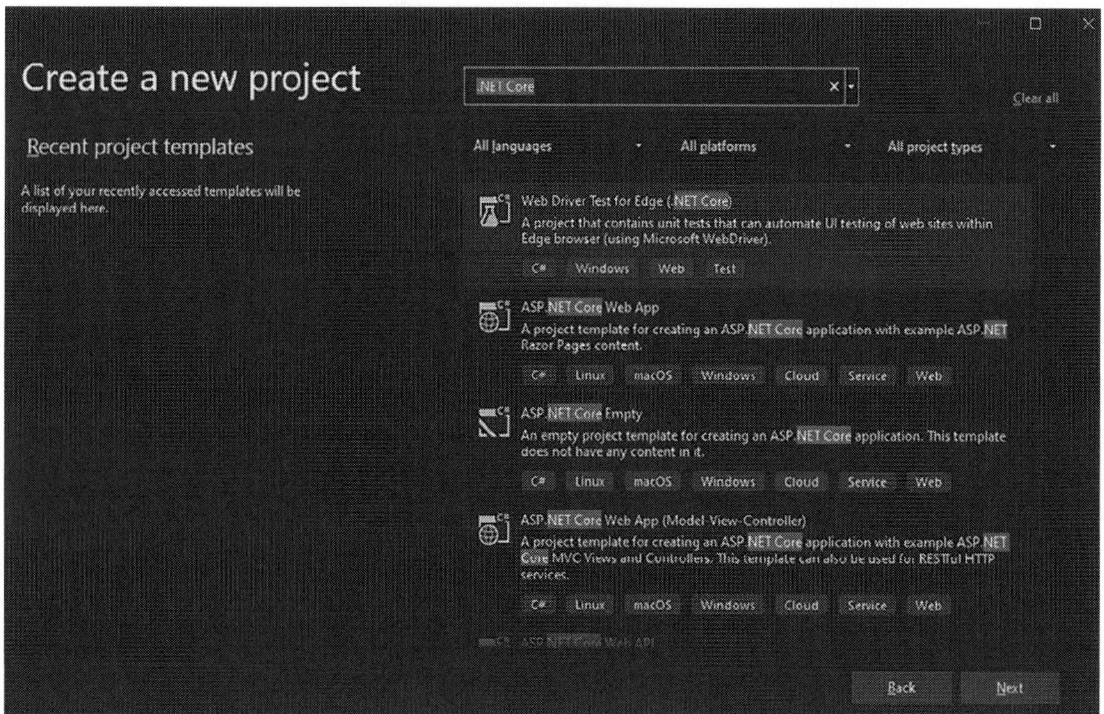

Figure 21.1: Searching types of .NET Core projects in Visual Studio

There, you will find common C# projects (console, a class library, Windows Forms, and WPF), and various types of test projects, each based on a different test framework: xUnit, NUnit, and MSTest. Choosing among the various testing frameworks is just a matter of preference since they all offer comparable features. Adding tests to each piece of software that composes a solution is a common practice and allows the software to be modified frequently without jeopardizing its reliability.

You may also want to define your class library projects under **.NET Standard**, which was discussed in *Chapter 5, Implementing Code Reusability in C# 12*. These class libraries are based on standards that make them compatible with several .NET versions. For instance, libraries based on 2.0 standards are compatible with all .NET Core versions greater than or equal to 2.0, with all .NET versions greater than 5, and with all .NET Framework versions greater than 4.6. This compatibility advantage comes at the price of having fewer available features.

Besides filtering **project types** to the **cloud**, we have several more project types. Some of them will enable us to define microservices. Microservice-based architectures allow an application to be split into several independent microservices. Several instances of the same microservice can be created and distributed across several machines to fine-tune the performance of each application part. If you want to learn about microservices, we have talked about them in the following chapters:

- *Chapter 11, Applying a Microservice Architecture to Your Enterprise Application*
- *Chapter 14, Implementing Microservices with .NET*
- *Chapter 20, Kubernetes*

In *Chapter 2, Non-Functional Requirements,* we described an ASP.NET Core application project in the subsection *Creating a scalable web app with .NET 8*. There, we defined an ASP.NET Core application, but Visual Studio also contains project templates for projects based on RESTful APIs and the most important single-page application frameworks, such as Angular, React, Vue.js, and the Blazor framework based on WebAssembly, which was discussed in *Chapter 19, Client Frameworks: Blazor*. Some of them are available with the standard Visual Studio installation, while others require the installation of an SPA package, called **ASP.NET and web development** workload.

To finish, testing projects were discussed in detail in *Chapter 9, Testing Your Enterprise Application*. We suggest you, as a software architect, try all the templates available at Visual Studio by creating proofs of concept that may help you define the best project types for your solution.

Now that we have checked these different project types, let's have a look at Azure DevOps and how it can be helpful in managing WWTravelClub is requirements.

Managing WWTravelClub's requirements using Azure DevOps

As discussed in *Chapter 3, Managing Requirements,* an important step for a software development project is where and how the team will organize the user stories mapped from the user needs. There, as described in the *Managing system requirements in Azure DevOps* section, Azure DevOps enables you to document system requirements using work items, which are mainly tasks or actions that need to be completed to deliver a product or service.

It is also important to remember that the work items available depend on the *work item process* you select while creating the Azure DevOps project.

Considering the scenario described for WWTravelClub, we decided to use the Agile process and have defined three Epic work items as follows:

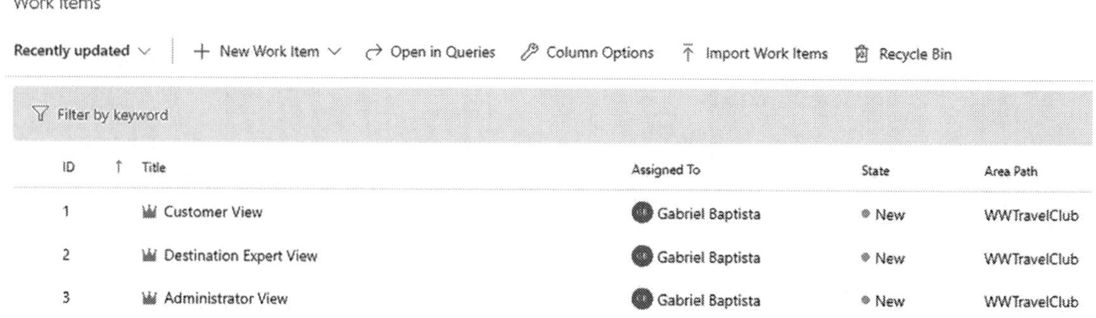

Figure 21.2: User case Epics

The creation of these work items is quite simple:

1. Inside each work item, we link the different types of work items, as you can see in *Figure 21.3*.
2. It is important to determine that the connections between work items are useful during software development. Hence, as a software architect, you must provide this knowledge to your team, and, more than that, you must incentivize them to make these connections:

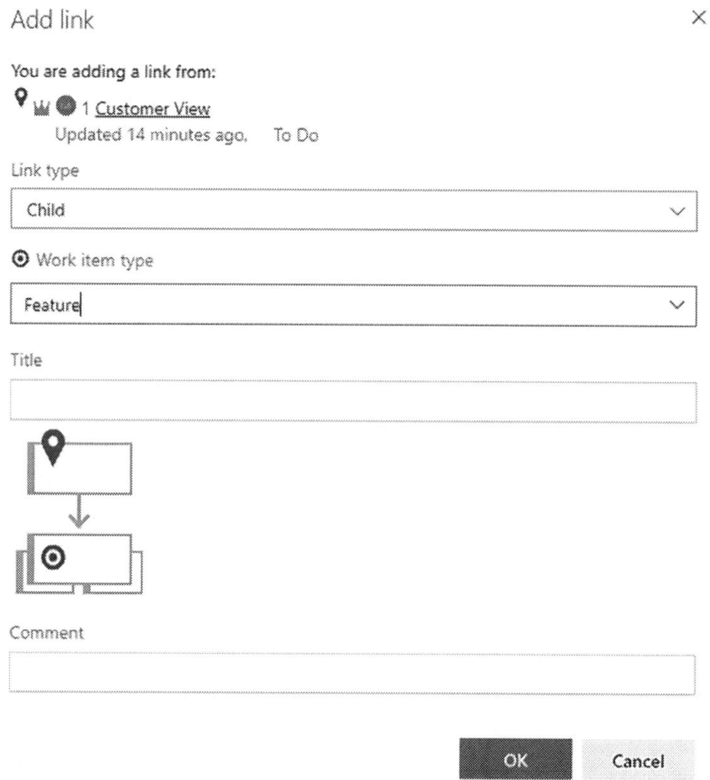

Figure 21.3: Defining a Feature link to the Epic selected

3. As soon as you create a **Feature** work item, you will be able to connect it to several User Story work items that detail its specifications. The following screenshot shows the details:

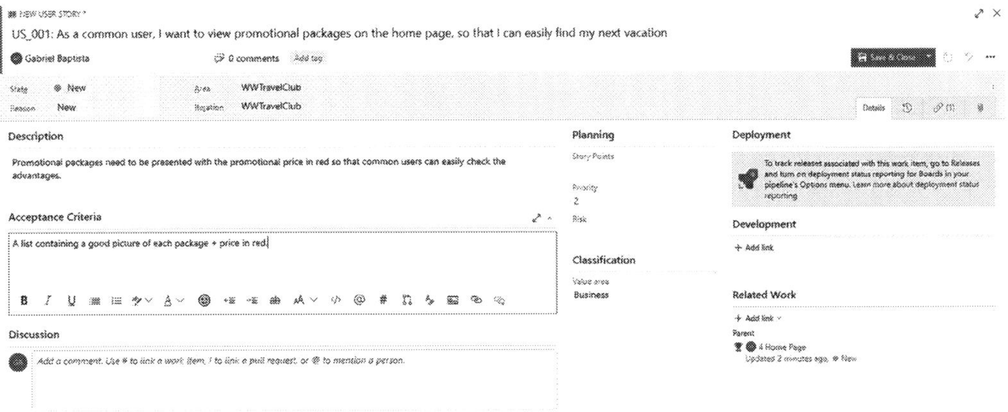

Figure 21.4: Product Backlog work item

4. After that, Task and Test Case work items can be created for each User Story work item. The user interface provided by Azure DevOps is efficacious because it enables you to track the chain of functionalities and the relationships between them.

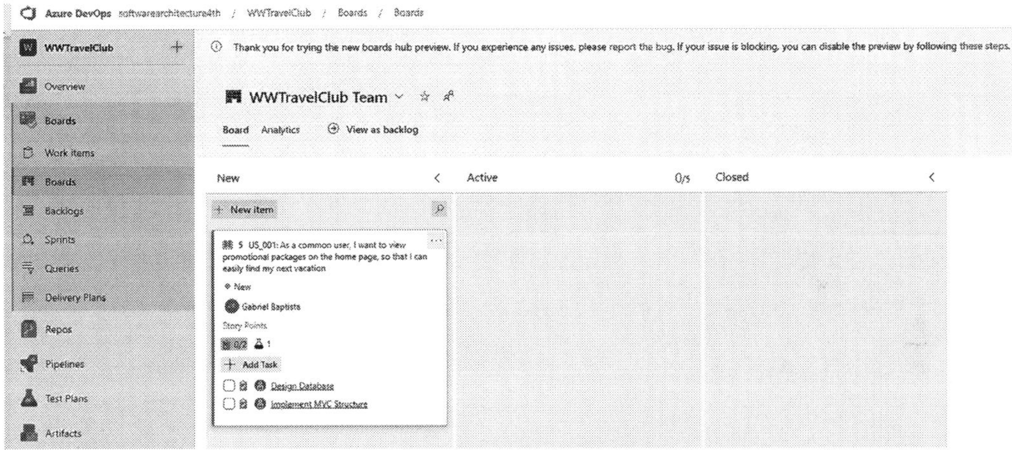

Figure 21.5: Board view

5. Considering we are using Scrum as the basis for the Agile process, as soon as you complete the input for the User Story and Task work items, you will be able to plan the project sprints together with your team. The plan view enables you to drag and drop User Story work items to each planned sprint/iteration:

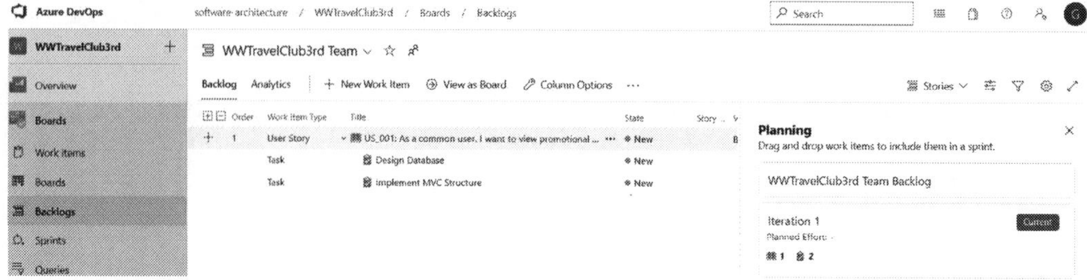

Figure 21.6: Backlogs view

6. By clicking on a specific sprint on the right, you will see just the work items assigned to that sprint. Each sprint page is quite like the backlog page but contains more tabs, where you can define **Sprint Period** and **Team Capacity**, for instance.

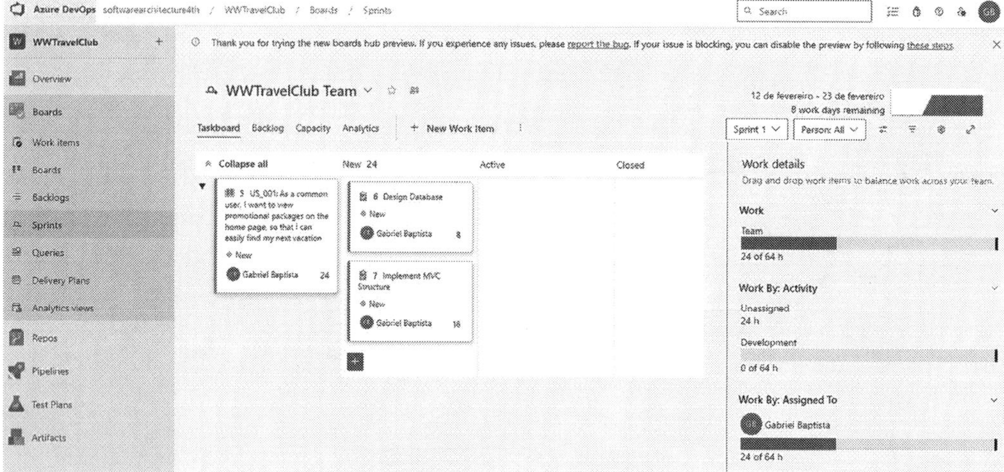

Figure 21.7: Planning view

Also useful is the **Sprints** menu on the left, which enables each user to jump immediately to the current sprints of all the projects they are engaged in.

This is how these work items are created. Once you understand this mechanism, you will be able to create and plan any software project. It is worth mentioning that the tool itself will not solve problems related to team management. However, the tool is a great way to incentivize the team to update the project status, so you can maintain a clear perspective of how the project is evolving.

Now that we have defined how we will manage WWTravelClub requirements, it is time to start thinking about the code standard that will be followed by the developers. Let's check this out in the next section.

Code standard for WWTravelClub – Dos and don'ts when writing code

In *Chapter 4, Best Practices in Coding C# 12,* we learned that, as a software architect, you must define a code standard that matches the needs of the company you are working for.

In the sample project of this book, this is no different. The way we decided to present the standard for it is by describing a list of dos and don'ts. We have followed this list while writing the samples we produced. It is worth mentioning that the list is a good way to start your standard and, as a software architect, you should discuss this list with the developers you have in the team so that you can develop it in a practical and good manner.

It is also important to remember that, in the *Understanding and applying tools that can evaluate C# code* section of *Chapter 4, Best Practices in Coding C#12,* we have discussed some good tools that can help you define a *coding style* for your team.

In addition, the statements below are designed to clarify the communication between team members and improve the performance and maintenance of the software you are developing.

You may consider the list below a waste of space in the book since we have great C# community coding standards without the need to enforce a standard. However, how can you guarantee maintainability without it? If defining coding standards was not necessary, we wouldn't have so many projects with maintenance issues. So, let's check the list of dos and don'ts defined for the WWTravelClub project:

- DO write your code in English.
- DO use PascalCasing for all public member, type, and namespace names consisting of multiple words.
- DO use camelCasing for parameter names.
- DO write classes, methods, and variables with understandable names.
- DO comment public classes, methods, and properties.
- DO use the `using` statement whenever possible.
- DO use `async` implementation whenever possible.
- DON'T write empty `try-catch` statements.
- DON'T write methods with a cyclomatic complexity score of more than 10.
- DON'T use `break` and `continue` inside `for/while/do-while/foreach` statements.

These dos and don'ts are simple to follow and, better than that, will yield great results for the code your team produces. It is worth mentioning that these DOs and DON'Ts are a guide, not a set of hard-and-fast rules to be followed by every team. They can be adapted as needed for the specific needs of a team before they are sent out to the team members. As a software architect, it is essential that all team members follow the same DOs and DON'Ts.

Considering we now have a coding standard defined, let's learn how to apply SonarCloud as a tool for helping us in code analysis.

Applying SonarCloud to WWTravelClub APIs

Now that we have already created the WWTravelClub repository, we can Improve the code quality, as discussed in *Chapter 4, Best Practices in Coding C# 12*. As we saw in that chapter, Azure DevOps enables continuous integration, and this can be useful. In this section, we will discuss more reasons why the DevOps concept and the Azure DevOps platform are so useful.

For now, the only thing we would like to introduce is the possibility of analyzing code after it is committed by the developers but before it has been published. Nowadays, in a SaaS world for application life cycle tools, this is only possible because of some of the SaaS code analysis platforms that we have. This use case will use SonarCloud.

SonarCloud is the SaaS version provided by Sonar. Also, it might be worth noting that SonarCloud is exceptionally easy to self-host; this way, sensitive security information may be kept within an enterprise. It is free for open-source code and can analyze code stored in GitHub, Bitbucket, and Azure DevOps. The user needs a registration for these platforms. As soon as you log in, assuming your code is stored in Azure DevOps, you can follow the steps described in the following article to create a connection between your Azure DevOps and SonarCloud: `https://docs.sonarcloud.io/`.

Sonar also provides a self-managed edition that can be useful for scenarios where SonarCloud cannot be used. Please check `https://www.sonarsource.com/` for more details.

After setting up the connection between your project in Azure DevOps and SonarCloud, you will have a build pipeline like the one that follows:

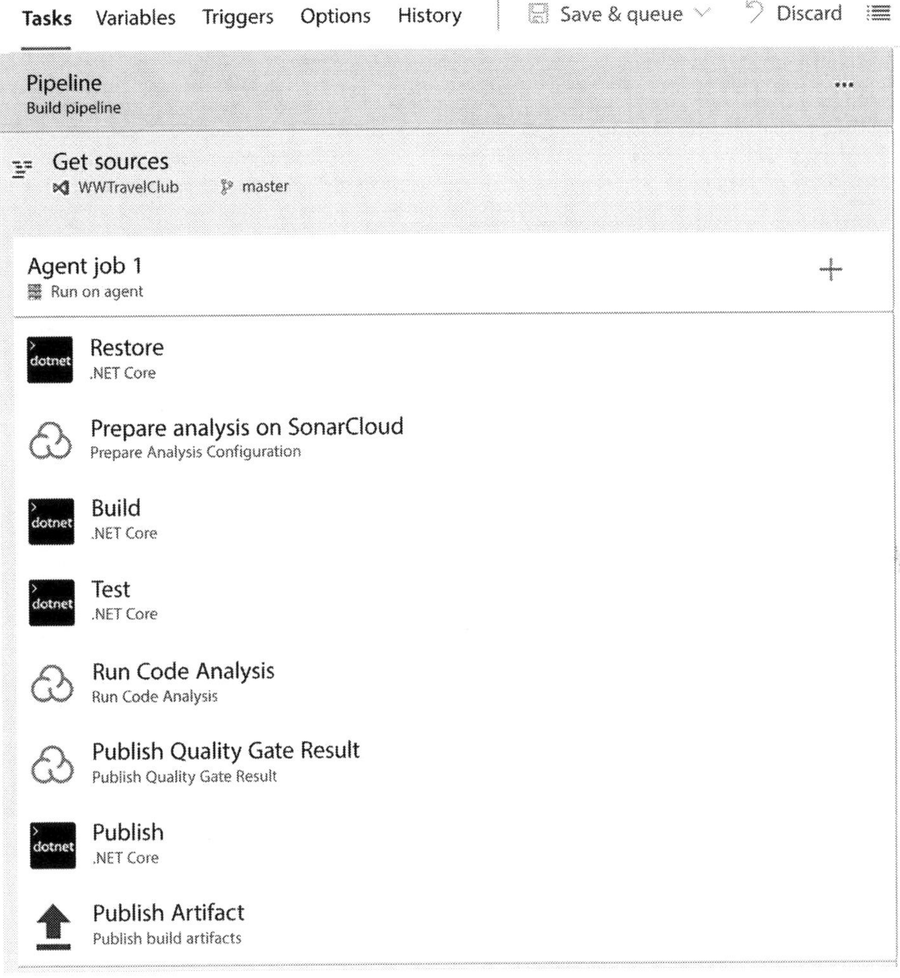

Figure 21.8: SonarCloud configuration in the Azure build pipeline

It is worth mentioning that C# projects do not have a GUID number, and this is required by SonarCloud. You can easily generate one using this link: `https://www.guidgenerator.com/`, or using the **Create GUID** tool in Visual Studio (**Tools** -> **Create GUID**). The GUID will need to be placed as in the following screenshot:

```
<Project Sdk="Microsoft.NET.Sdk.Web">

  <PropertyGroup>
    <TargetFramework>net8.0</TargetFramework>
    <Nullable>enable</Nullable>
    <ImplicitUsings>enable</ImplicitUsings>
    <ProjectGuid>a68647ba-8adf-47ae-8878-2fea9cba7154</ProjectGuid>
  </PropertyGroup>

  <ItemGroup>
    <PackageReference Include="Microsoft.AspNetCore.OpenApi" Version="8.0.0-preview.1.23112.2" />
    <PackageReference Include="Swashbuckle.AspNetCore" Version="6.4.0" />
  </ItemGroup>
</Project>
```

Figure 21.9: SonarCloud project GUID

As soon as you finish the build, the result of the code analysis will be presented in SonarCloud, as can be seen in the following screenshot. If you want to navigate to this project, you can visit `https://sonarcloud.io/summary/overall?id=gabrielbaptista_wwtravelclub-4th`:

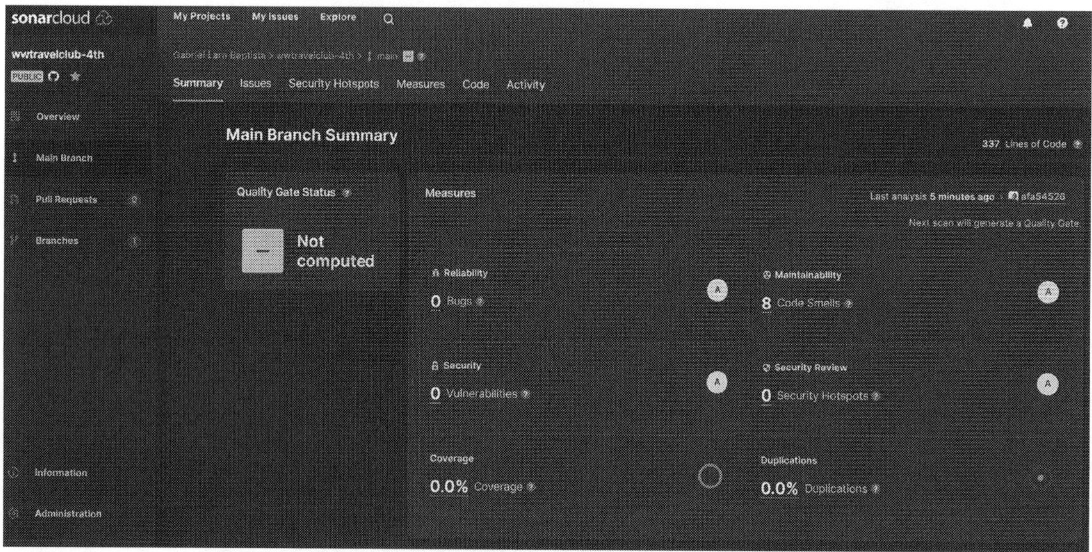

Figure 21.10: SonarCloud results

Also, by this time, the code analyzed is not yet in the release, so this can be useful for getting the next step of quality before releasing your system. You can use this approach as a reference for automating code analysis during committal.

Considering we have implemented a way to continuously evaluate code quality, it is time to design reusable software. Let's look at this in the next section.

Reusing code as a fast way to deliver good and safe software

As we checked in *Chapter 5, Implementing Code Reusability in C# 12*, a good approach for accelerating the delivery of good software is creating reusable components. The final design of the solution for evaluating content for WWTravelClub can be checked in the diagram below. This approach consists of using many topics that were discussed in that chapter. First, all the code is placed in a .NET 8 class library. This means that you can add this code to different types of solutions, such as ASP.NET Core web apps and Xamarin apps for the Android and iOS platforms:

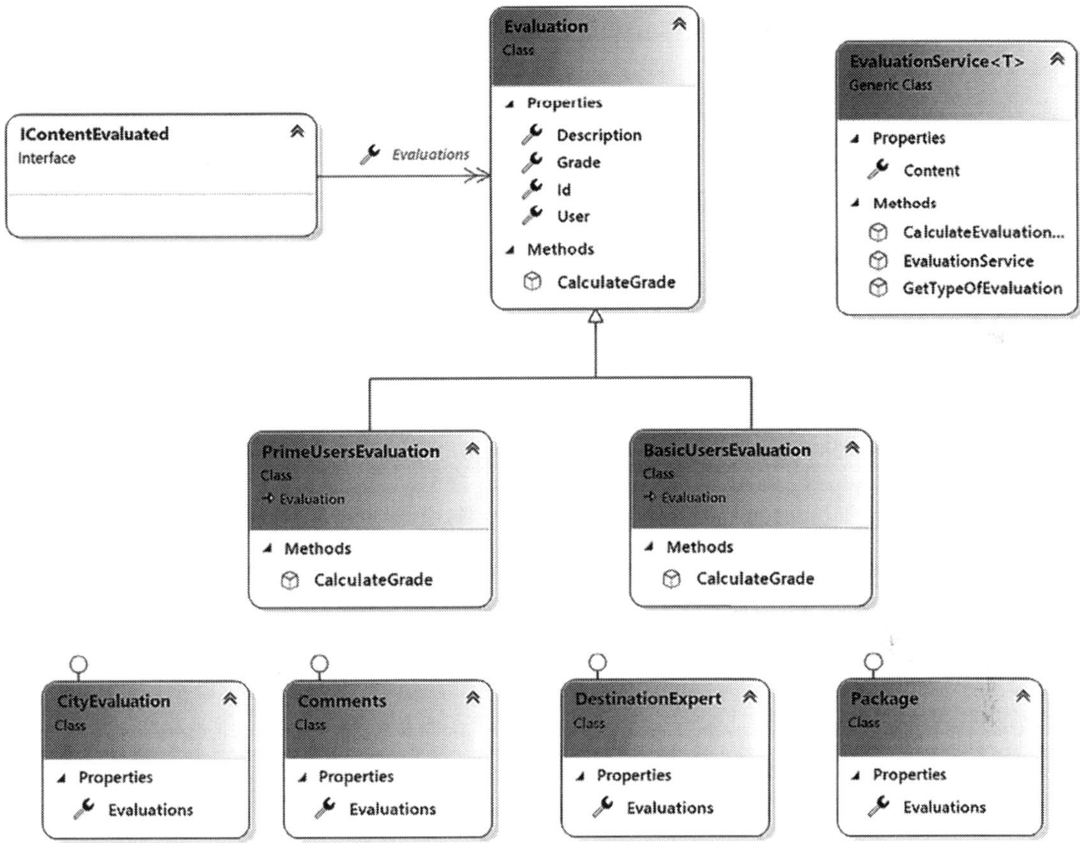

Figure 21.11: WWTravelClub reuse approach

This design makes use of object-oriented principles such as inheritance, so you do not need to write properties and methods more than once that can be used in many classes. The design also makes use of the polymorphism principle so that you can change the behavior of the code without changing the name of the method.

To finish, the design abstracts the idea of the content by introducing generics as a tool that can facilitate the manipulation of similar classes, such as the ones we have in WWTravelClub, to evaluate content regarding cities, comments, destination experts, and travel packages.

The big difference between a team that incentivizes code reuse and one that does not is the velocity of delivering good software to end users. Of course, beginning this approach is not easy, but rest assured that you will get good results after some time working with it.

Since we have covered the possibilities of code reuse using object-oriented principles, what about organizing the application using domains created by **domain-driven design** (**DDD**)? We will check it in the next section.

Understanding the domains of the WWTravelClub application

In this section we will perform the DDD analysis of the WWTravelClub system, trying to identify all its domains (also called **bounded contexts**), that is, the subsystems characterized by different languages used by the experts. Once identified, each domain might be assigned to a different development team and will give rise to a different microservice.

From the requirements listed in the *Introducing World Wild Travel Club* and *User needs and system requirements* sections, we know that the WWTravelClub system is composed of the following parts:

- Information about the available destinations and packages.
- Reservation/purchase orders subsystem.
- Communication with the experts/review subsystem.
- Payment subsystem. We briefly analyzed the features of this subsystem and its relationship with the reservation purchase subsystem at the beginning of *Chapter 7*, in the *Understanding DDD* section.
- User accounts subsystem.
- Statistics reporting subsystem.

Do the preceding subsystems represent different bounded contexts? Can some subsystems be split into different bounded contexts? The answers to these questions are given by the languages that are spoken in each subsystem:

- The language that's spoken in subsystem 1 is the language of **travel agencies**. There is no concept of a customer, just of locations, packages, and their features.
- The language that's spoken in subsystem 2 is common to all service purchases, such as the available resources, reservations, and purchase orders. This is a separate bounded context.

- The language that's spoken in subsystem 3 has a lot in common with subsystem 1's language. However, there are also typical **social media** concepts, such as ratings, chats, post sharing, media sharing, and so on. This subsystem can be split into two parts: a social media subsystem that has a new Bounded Context and an available information subsystem that is part of the Bounded Context of subsystem 1.
- As we pointed out in the *Understanding DDD* section in *Chapter 7*, in subsystem 4, we speak the language of **banking**. This subsystem communicates with the reservation purchase subsystem and executes tasks that are needed to carry out a purchase. From these observations, we can see that it is a different Bounded Context and has a customer/supplier relationship with the purchase/reservation system.
- Subsystem 5 is a separate Bounded Context (as in almost all web applications). It has a relationship with all the bounded contexts that have either the concept of a user or the concept of a customer because the concept of user accounts always maps to these concepts. You must be wondering how. Well, it's quite simple—the currently logged-in user is assumed to be the social media user of the social media bounded context, the customer of the reservation/purchase bounded context, and the payer of the payment Bounded Context.
- The query-only subsystem (that is, 6) speaks the language of analytics and statistics and differs a lot from the languages that are spoken in the other subsystems. However, it has a connection with almost all the bounded contexts since it takes all its input from them. The preceding constraints force us to adopt CQRS in its strong form, thereby considering it a query-only separated Bounded Context.

In conclusion, each of the listed subsystems defines a different Bounded Context, but part of the communication with the experts/review subsystem must be included in the information about the available destinations, and the package's Bounded Context.

As the analysis continues and a prototype is implemented, some bounded contexts may split and some others may be added, but it is fundamental to immediately start modeling the system and to immediately start analyzing the relationships among the bounded contexts with the partial information we have since this will drive further investigations and will help us define the communication protocols and ubiquitous languages that are needed so that we can interact with the domain experts.

The following is a basic first sketch of the domain map:

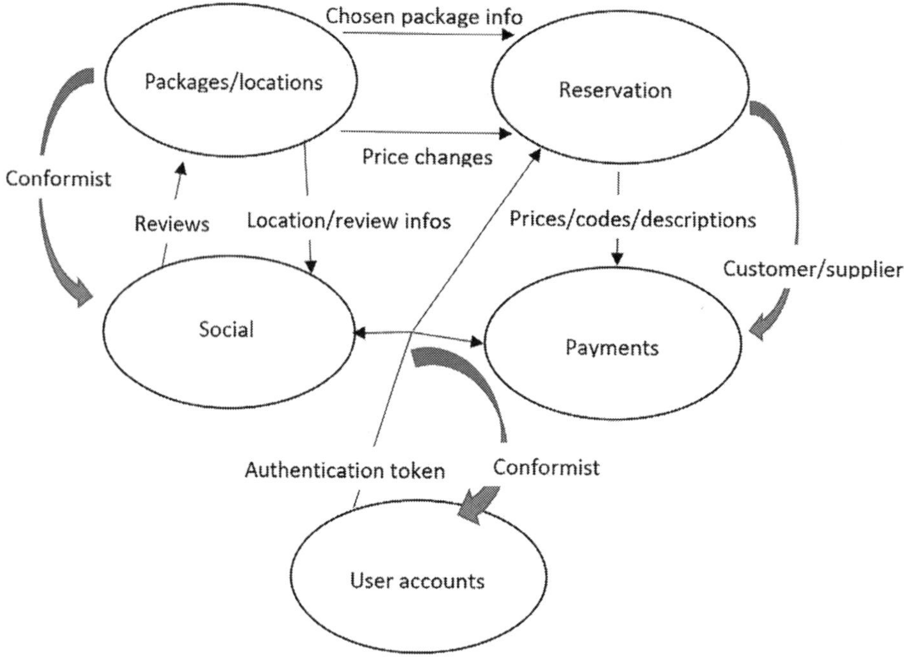

Figure 21.12: WWTravelClub domain map. Thin black arrows represent data exchanged between bounded contexts, while thick blue arrows represent the relationships between bounded contexts (conformist, customer/supplier, and so on)

For simplicity, we've omitted the **Statistics reporting** bounded context. We say just that it collects statistics on the daily purchases of each package.

Here, we're assuming that the **User accounts** and **Social** bounded contexts have a **conformist** relationship with all the other counded contexts that communicate with them because they are implemented with already existing software, so all the other components must adapt to them.

As we mentioned previously, the relationship between **Reservation** and **Payments** is **customer/supplier** because **Payments** provides services that are used to execute the tasks of **Reservation.** All the other relationships are classified as **partners.** The various concepts of customer/user that most bounded contexts have are coordinated by the **User accounts Authorization token** arrow, which indirectly takes care of mapping these concepts between all the counded contexts.

The **Packages/locations** subsystem communicates the following information to **Reservation:**

- **Chosen package info**, which contains the package information that's needed to carry out a reservation/purchase
- **Price changes**, which takes care of informing pending purchase orders of possible price changes

Social interactions are started from an existing review provided by users (the **Reviews** arrow between **Packages/locations** and **Social**) and are supported by **Location/review info** communications from **Packages/locations** to **Social**.

Finally, **Reservation** communicates purchase codes, descriptions, and prices to **Payments** through the **Prices/codes/descriptions** arrow.

Having identified our application's bounded contexts, we are in a position to organize the application DevOps cycle.

The WWTravelClub DevOps approach

During *Chapter 8, Understanding DevOps Principles and CI/CD*, screenshots from the WWTravelClub project showed the steps needed to implement a good DevOps cycle. The WWTravelClub team has decided to use Azure DevOps because they understand that the tool is essential for getting the best DevOps experience for the whole cycle. In fact, it appears the most complete of the tools offered by GitHub, since it covers the whole CI/CD cycle from requirements collection to deployment in staging and production. Moreover, all team members already know it very well.

The requirements were written using user stories, which can be found in the **Work items** section of Azure DevOps. The code is placed in the repository of the Azure DevOps project. Both concepts were explained in *Chapter 3, Managing Requirements*.

The management life cycle used for getting things done is Scrum, presented in *Chapter 1, Understanding the Importance of Software Architecture*. This approach divides the implementation into sprints, which forces value to be delivered by the end of each cycle. Using the CI facilities we learned in this chapter, code will be compiled each time the team merges new code into the master branch of the repository.

Once the code is compiled and tested, the first stage of the deployment is done. The first stage is normally named development/test because you enable it for internal tests. Both Application Insights and Test and Feedback can be used to get the first feedback on the new release.

If the tests and the feedback of the new release pass, it is time to go to the second stage, quality assurance. Application Insights and Test and Feedback can be used again, but now in a more stable environment.

The cycle ends with the authorization to deploy in the production stage. This certainly is a tough decision, but DevOps indicates that you must do it continuously so you can get better feedback from customers. Application Insights keeps being a useful tool since you can monitor the evolution of the new release in production, even comparing it to past releases.

The WWTravelClub project approach described here can be used in many other modern application development life cycles. As a software architect, you must oversee the process. The tools are ready to go, and it depends on you to make things right!

For this reason, even considering WWTravelClub as a hypothetical scenario, some concerns were considered while building it:

- CI is enabled, but a multi-stage scenario is enabled too.
- Even with a multi-stage scenario, the **PR** (**Pull Request**) is a way to guarantee that only good-quality code will be presented in the first stage.
- To do a good job in the PR, peer reviews are undertaken.
- The peer reviews check, for instance, the presence of a feature flag while creating a new feature.
- The peer reviews check both unit and functional tests developed during the creation of the new feature.

The preceding steps are not exclusively for WWTravelClub. You, as a software architect, will need to define the approach to guarantee a safe CI/CD scenario. You may use this as a starting point. It is worth pointing out that both in Azure DevOps and GitHub, we can completely disable pushing on the master branch, thus forcing the usage of PR for merging modifications on the master branch.

In the next section, we will start with the actual code, by showing how to choose among various data storage options.

How to choose your data storage in the cloud

In *Chapter 12, Choosing Your Data Storage in the Cloud,* we learned how to use NoSQL. Now we must decide whether NoSQL databases are adequate for our book use case WWTravelClub application. We need to store the following families of data:

- **Information about available destinations and packages:** Relevant operations for these data are reads since packages and destinations do not change very often. However, they must be accessed as fast as possible from all over the world to ensure a pleasant user experience when users browse the available options. Therefore, a distributed relational database with geographically distributed replicas is possible but not necessary since packages can be stored inside their destinations in a cheaper NoSQL database.
- **Destination reviews:** In this case, distributed write operations have a non-negligible impact. Moreover, most writes are additions since reviews are not usually updated. Additions benefit a lot from sharding and do not cause consistency issues like updates do. Accordingly, the best option for this data is a NoSQL collection.
- **Reservations:** In this case, consistency errors are not acceptable because they may cause overbooking. Reads and writes have a comparable impact, but we need reliable transactions and good consistency checks. Luckily, data can be organized in a multi-tenant database where tenants are destinations since reservation information belonging to different destinations is completely unrelated. Accordingly, we may use sharded Azure SQL Database instances.

In conclusion, the best option for data in the first and second bullet points is Cosmos DB, while the best option for the third point is Azure SQL Server. Actual applications may require a more detailed analysis of all data operations and their frequencies. In some cases, it is worth implementing prototypes for various possible options and executing performance tests with typical workloads on all of them.

In the remainder of this section, we will migrate the destinations/packages data layer we looked at in *Chapter 13, Interacting with Data in C# – Entity Framework Core*, to Cosmos DB.

Implementing the destinations/packages database with Cosmos DB

Let's move on to the database example we built in *Chapter 13, Interacting with Data in C# – Entity Framework Core*, and implement this database with Cosmos DB by following these steps:

1. First, we need to make a copy of the WWTravelClubDB project and rename its root folder as `WWTravelClubDBCosmo`.
2. Open the project and delete the `Migrations` folder since migrations are not required anymore.
3. We need to replace the SQL Server Entity Framework provider with the Cosmos DB provider. To do this, go to **Manage NuGet Packages** and uninstall the `Microsoft.EntityFrameworkCore.SqlServer` NuGet package. Then, install the `Microsoft.EntityFrameworkCore.Cosmos` NuGet package.
4. Then, do the following on the `Destination` and `Package` entities:
    - Remove all data annotations.
    - Add the `[Key]` attribute to their `Id` properties since this is obligatory for Cosmos DB providers.
    - Transform the type of the `Id` properties of both `Package` and `Destination` and the `PackagesListDTO` classes from `int` to `string`. We also need to turn the `DestinationId` external references in `Package` and in the `PackagesListDTO` classes into `string`. In fact, the best option for keys in distributed databases is a string generated from a GUID, because it is hard to maintain an identity counter when table data is distributed among several servers.
5. In the `MainDBContext` file, we need to specify that packages related to a destination must be stored inside the destination document itself. This can be achieved by replacing the **Destination-Package** relation configuration in the `OnModelCreating` method with the following code:

```
builder.Entity<Destination>()
    .OwnsMany(m =>m.Packages);
```

6. Here, we must replace `HasMany` with `OwnsMany`. There is no equivalent to `WithOne` since once an entity is owned, it must have just one owner, and the fact that the `MyDestination` property contains a pointer to the father entity is evident from its type. Cosmos DB also allows the use of `HasMany`, but in this case, the two entities are not nested one in the other. There is also an `OwnOne` configuration method for nesting single entities inside other entities.
7. Both `OwnsMany` and `OwnsOne` are available for relational databases, but in this case, the difference between `HasMany` and `HasOne` is that children entities are automatically included in all queries that return their father entities, with no need to specify an `Include` LINQ clause. However, child entities are still stored in separate tables.

8. `LibraryDesignTimeDbContextFactory` must be modified to use Cosmos DB connection data, as shown in the following code:

```
using Microsoft.EntityFrameworkCore;
using Microsoft.EntityFrameworkCore.Design;
namespace WWTravelClubDB
{
    public class LibraryDesignTimeDbContextFactory
        : IDesignTimeDbContextFactory<MainDBContext>
    {
        private const string endpoint = "<your account endpoint>";
        private const string key = "<your account key>";
        private const string databaseName = "packagesdb";
        public MainDBContext CreateDbContext(params string[] args)
        {
            var builder = new DbContextOptionsBuilder<MainDBContext>();
            builder.UseCosmos(endpoint, key, databaseName);
            return new MainDBContext(builder.Options);
        }
    }
}
```

9. Finally, in our test console, we must explicitly create all entity principal keys using GUIDs:

```
var context = new LibraryDesignTimeDbContextFactory()
    .CreateDbContext();
context.Database.EnsureCreated();
var firstDestination = new Destination
{
    Id = Guid.NewGuid().ToString(),
    Name = "Florence",
    Country = "Italy",
    Packages = new List<Package>()
    {
    new Package
    {
        Id=Guid.NewGuid().ToString(),
        Name = "Summer in Florence",
        StartValidityDate = new DateTime(2019, 6, 1),
        EndValidityDate = new DateTime(2019, 10, 1),
        DurationInDays=7,
        Price=1000
    },
```

```
        new Package
        {
            Id=Guid.NewGuid().ToString(),
            Name = "Winter in Florence",
            StartValidityDate = new DateTime(2019, 12, 1),
            EndValidityDate = new DateTime(2020, 2, 1),
            DurationInDays=7,
            Price=500
        }
    }
};
```

10. Here, we call `context.Database.EnsureCreated()` instead of applying migrations since we only need to create the database. Once the database and collections have been created, we can fine-tune their settings from the Azure portal. Hopefully, future versions of the Cosmos DB Entity Framework Core provider will allow us to specify all collection options.
11. Finally, the final query (which starts with `context.Packages.Where...`) must be modified since queries can't start with entities that are nested in other documents (in our case, `Packages` entities). Therefore, we must start our query from the unique root `DbSet<T>` property we have in our `DBContext`, that is, `Destinations`. We can move from listing the external collection to listing all the internal collections with the help of the `SelectMany` method, which performs a logical merge of all nested `Packages` collections. However, since Cosmos DB SQL doesn't support `SelectMany`, we must force `SelectMany` to be simulated on the client with `AsEnumerable()`, as shown in the following code:

```
var list = context.Destinations
    .AsEnumerable() // move computation on the client side
    .SelectMany(m =>m.Packages)
    .Where(m => period >= m.StartValidityDate....)
    ...
```

12. The remainder of the query remains unchanged. If you run the project now, you should see the same outputs that were received in the case of SQL Server (except for the primary key values).

After executing the program, go to your Cosmos DB account. You should see something like the following:

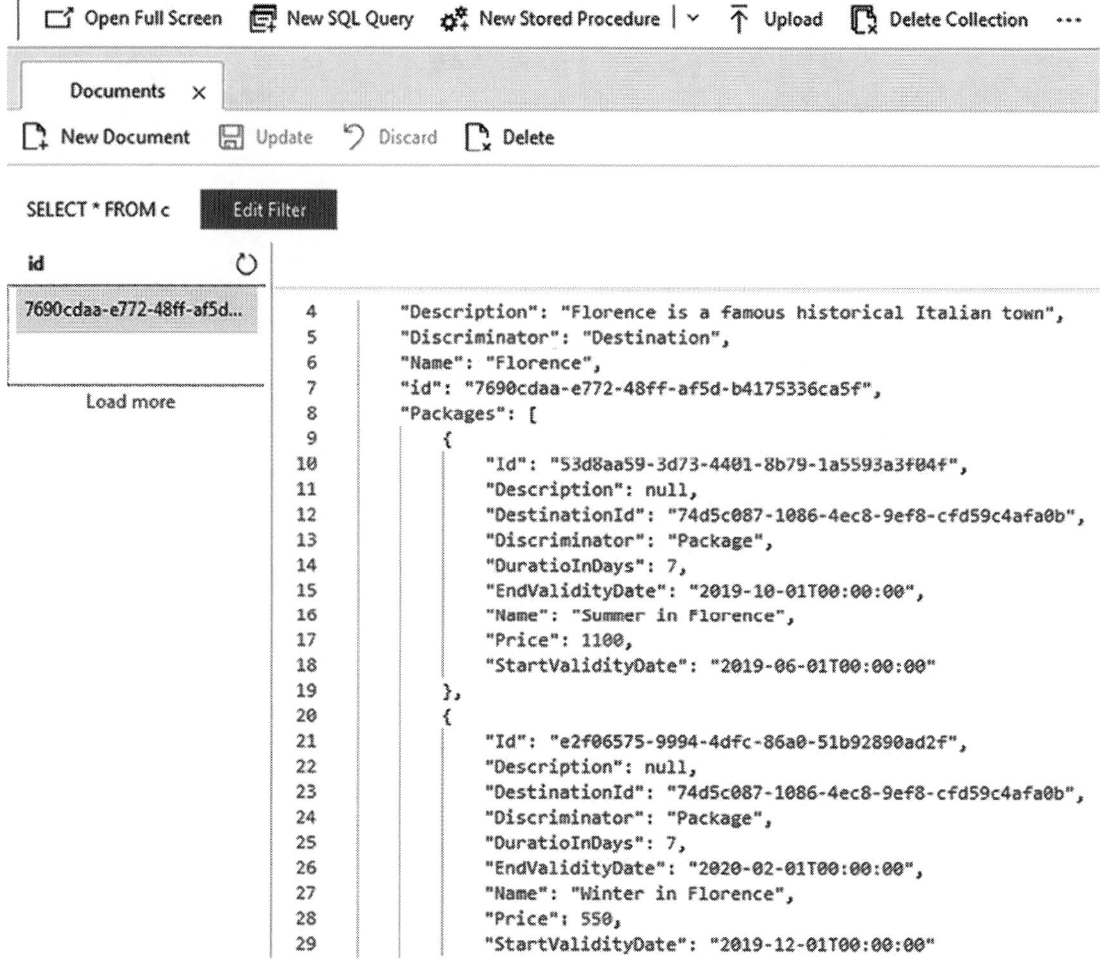

Figure 21.13: Execution results

The packages have been nested inside their destinations as required and Entity Framework Core creates a unique collection that has the same name as the `DBContext` class.

If you would like to continue experimenting with Cosmos DB development without wasting all your free Azure portal credit, you can install the Cosmos DB emulator, available at this link: `https://aka.ms/cosmosdb-emulator`.

Having learned how to choose the best options for data storage, we are in a position to start coding our first microservice.

A worker microservice with ASP.NET Core

In this section, we will show you how to implement a microservice that receives communications through gRPC and an internal queue based on a database table. The first subsection briefly describes the microservice specifications and the overall architecture. You are encouraged to review *Chapter 14, Implementing Microservices with .NET,* which contains all the theory behind this example.

The specifications and architecture

Our example microservice is required to compute the daily sums of all purchases. According to the data-driven approach, we suppose that all daily sums are pre-computed by receiving messages that are sent as soon as a new purchase is finalized. The purpose of the microservice is to maintain a database of all purchases and all daily sums that can be queried by an administrative user. We will implement just the functionalities needed to fill the two database tables.

The implementation described in this section is based on an ASP.NET Core application that hosts a gRPC service. The gRPC service simply fills a messages queue and immediately returns to avoid the sender remaining blocked for the whole time of the computation.

The actual processing is performed by an ASP.NET Core-hosted service declared in the dependency injection engine associated with the application host. The worker-hosted service executes an endless loop where it extracts `N` messages from the queue and passes them to `N` parallel threads that process them.

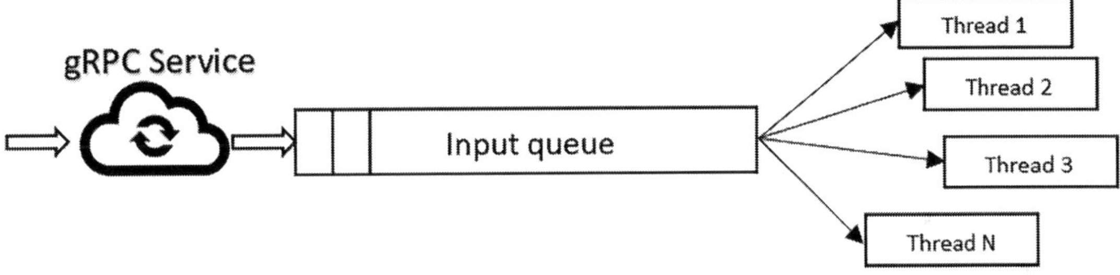

Figure 21.14: gRPC microservice architecture

When the `N` messages are taken from the queue, they are not immediately removed but are simply marked with the extraction time. Since messages can only be extracted from the queue if their last extraction time is far enough ahead (say, a time `T`), no other worker thread can extract them again while they are being processed. When message processing is successfully completed, the message is removed from the queue. If the processing fails, no action is taken on the message, so the message remains blocked in the queue till the `T` interval expires, and then it can be picked up again by the worker thread.

The microservice can be scaled vertically by increasing the processor cores and the number `N` of threads. It can be scaled horizontally, too, by using a load balancer that splits the loads into several identical copies of the ASP.NET Core application. This kind of horizontal scaling increases the number of threads that can receive messages and the number of worker threads, but since all ASP.NET Core applications share the same database, it is limited by database performance.

The database layer is implemented in a separate **DLL** (**Dynamic Link Library**) and all functionalities are abstracted in two interfaces, one for interacting with the queue and another for adding a new purchase to the database.

The next subsection briefly describes the database layer. We will not give all the details since the main focus of the example is the microservice architecture and the communication technique. However, the full code is available in the `ch15/GrpcMicroService` folder of the GitHub repository associated with the book.

Having defined the overall architecture, let's start with the storage layer code.

The storage layer

The storage layer is based on a database. It uses Entity Framework Core and is based on three entities with their associated tables:

- A `QueueItem` entity that represents a queue item
- A `Purchase` entity that represents a single purchase
- A `DayTotal` entity that represents the total of all purchases performed in a given day

Below is a definition of the interface that manipulates the queue:

```
public interface IMessageQueue
{
    public Task<IList<QueueItem>> Top(int n);
    public Task Dequeue(IEnumerable<QueueItem> items);
    public Task Enqueue(QueueItem item);
}
```

`Top` extracts the `N` messages to pass to a maximum of `N` different threads. `Enqueue` adds a new message to the queue. Finally, `Dequeue` removes the items that have been successfully processed from the queue.

The interface that updates the purchase data is defined as shown below:

```
public interface IDayStatistics
{
    Task<decimal> DayTotal(DateTimeOffset day);
    Task<QueueItem?> Add(QueueItem model);
}
```

`Add` adds a new purchase to the database. It returns the input queue item if the addition is successful, and `null` otherwise. `DayTotal` is a query method that returns a single day total.

The application layer communicates with the database layer through these two interfaces, through the three database entities, through the `IUnitOfWork` interface (which, as explained in the *How data and domain layers communicate with other layers* section of *Chapter 13, Interacting with Data in C# – Entity Framework Core* abstracts the `DbContext`), and through a dependency injection extension method like the one below:

```
public static class StorageExtensions
{
    public static IServiceCollection AddStorage(this IServiceCollection
services,
        string connectionString)
    {
        services.AddDbContext<IUnitOfWork,MainDbContext>(options =>
            options.UseSqlServer(connectionString, b =>
b.MigrationsAssembly("GrpcMicroServiceStore")));
        services.AddScoped<IMessageQueue, MessageQueue>();
        services.AddScoped<IDayStatistics, DayStatistics>();
        return services;
    }
}
```

This method, which will be called in the application layer dependency injection definition, receives as input the database connection string and adds the `DbContext` abstracted with `IUnitOfWork`, with the two interfaces we defined before.

The database project, called `GrpcMicroServiceStore`, is contained in the `ch15/GrpcMicroService` folder of the GitHub repository associated with the book. It already contains all the necessary database migrations, so you can create the needed database with the steps below:

1. In the Visual Studio **Package Manager Console**, select the **GrpcMicroServiceStore** project.
2. In Visual Studio **Solution Explorer**, right-click on the **GrpcMicroServiceStore** project and set it as the startup project.
3. In the Visual Studio **Package Manager Console**, issue the `Update-Database` command.

Having a working storage layer, we can proceed with the microservices application layer.

The application layer

The application layer is an **ASP.NET Core gRPC service** project called `GrpcMicroService`. When the project is scaffolded by Visual Studio, it contains a `.proto` file in its `Protos` folder. This file needs to be deleted and replaced by a file called `counting.proto`, whose content must be as follows:

```
syntax = "proto3";
option csharp_namespace = "GrpcMicroService";
import "google/protobuf/timestamp.proto";
package counting;
```

```
service Counter {
  // Accepts a counting request
  rpc Count (CountingRequest) returns (CountingReply);
}
message CountingRequest {
  string id = 1;
  google.protobuf.Timestamp time = 2;
  string location = 3;
  sint32 cost =4;
  google.protobuf.Timestamp purchaseTime = 5;
}.
message CountingReply {}
```

The above code defines the gRPC service with its input and output messages and the .NET namespace where you place them. We import the `google/protobuf/timestamp.proto` predefined `.proto` file because we need the `TimeStamp` type. The request contains purchase data, the `time` when the request message was created, and a unique message `id` that is used to force message idempotency.

In the database layer, the implementation of the `IDayStatistics.Add` method uses this `id` to verify if a purchase with the same `id` has already been processed, in which case it returns immediately:

```
bool processed = await ctx.Purchases.AnyAsync(m => m.Id == model.MessageId);
if (processed) return model;
```

Automatic code generation for this file is enabled by replacing the existing `protobuf` XML tag with:

```
<Protobuf Include="Protos\counting.proto" GrpcServices="Server" />
```

The `Grpc` attribute set to `"Server"` enables server-side code generation.

In the `Services` project folder, the predefined gRPC service scaffolded by Visual Studio must be replaced with a file named `CounterService.cs` with the content below:

```
using Grpc.Core;
using GrpcMicroServiceStore;
namespace GrpcMicroService.Services;
public class CounterService: Counter.CounterBase
{
    private readonly IMessageQueue queue;
    public CounterService(IMessageQueue queue)
    {
      If (queue == null) throw new
ArgumentNullException(nameof(queue));
        this.queue = queue;
    }
    public override async  Task<CountingReply> Count(CountingRequest request,
```

```
        ServerCallContext context)
    {
        await queue.Enqueue(new GrpcMicroServiceStore.Models.QueueItem
        {
            Cost = request.Cost,
            MessageId = Guid.Parse(request.Id),
            Location = request.Location,
            PurchaseTime = request.PurchaseTime.ToDateTimeOffset(),
            Time = request.Time.ToDateTimeOffset()
        });
        return new CountingReply {  };
    }
}
```

The actual service that receives the purchase messages inherits from the `Counter.CounterBase` abstract class created by the code generator from the `counting.proto` file. It receives the database layer interface `IMessageQueue` using dependency injection and overrides the abstract `Count` method inherited from `Counter.CounterBase`. Then, `Count` uses `IMessageQueue` to enqueue each received message.

Before compiling, a few other steps are necessary:

1. We must add a reference to the database-layer `GrpcMicroServiceStore` project.
2. We must add the database connection string to the `appsettings.json` setting file:

```
"ConnectionStrings": {
        "DefaultConnection": "Server=(localdb)\\
mssqllocaldb;Database=grpcmicroservice;Trusted_
Connection=True;MultipleActiveResultSets=true"
}
```

3. We must add all the necessary database-layer interfaces to the dependency injection by calling the `AddStorage` database layer extension method:

```
builder.Services.AddStorage(
builder.Configuration.GetConnectionString("DefaultConnection"));
```

4. In `Program.cs`, we must remove the declaration of the gRPC service scaffolded by Visual Studio, and we must replace it with:

```
app.MapGrpcService<CounterService>();
```

At this point, compilation should succeed. Having completed the application-layer infrastructure, we can move to the hosted service that performs the actual queue processing.

Processing the queued requests

The actual request processing is performed by a worker-hosted service that runs in parallel with the ASP.NET Core pipeline. It is implemented with the hosted services we discussed in the *Using generic hosts* section of *Chapter 11, Applying a Microservice Architecture to Your Enterprise Application*. It is worth recalling that hosted services are implementations of the `IHostedService` interface defined in the dependency injection engine as follows:

```
builder.Services.AddHostedService<MyHostedService>();
```

We already described how to implement hosted services for the implementation of ASP.NET Core-based worker microservices in the *Implementing worker microservices with ASP.NET Core* section of *Chapter 14, Implementing Microservices with .NET*.

Below, we repeat the whole code with all details that are specific to our example. The hosted service is defined in the `ProcessPurchases.cs` file placed in the `HostedServices` folder:

```
using GrpcMicroServiceStore;
using GrpcMicroServiceStore.Models;
namespace GrpcMicroService.HostedServices;
public class ProcessPurchases : BackgroundService
{
    IServiceProvider services;
    public ProcessPurchases(IServiceProvider services)
    {
        this.services = services;
    }
    protected override async Task ExecuteAsync(CancellationToken stoppingToken)
    {
        bool queueEmpty = false;
        while (!stoppingToken.IsCancellationRequested)
        {
           while (!queueEmpty && !stoppingToken.IsCancellationRequested)
           {
             ...
           }
            await Task.Delay(100, stoppingToken);
            queueEmpty = false;
        }
    }
}
```

Below is the content of the inner loop:

```
using (var scope = services.CreateScope())
{
    IMessageQueue queue = scope.ServiceProvider.
GetRequiredService<IMessageQueue>();

    var toProcess = await queue.Top(10);
    if (toProcess.Count > 0)
    {
        Task<QueueItem?>[] tasks = new Task<QueueItem?>[toProcess.Count];
        for (int i = 0; i < tasks.Length; i++)
        {
            var toExecute = ...
            tasks[i] = toExecute();
        }
        await Task.WhenAll(tasks);
        await queue.Dequeue(tasks.Select(m => m.Result)
            .Where(m => m != null).OfType<QueueItem>());
    }
    else queueEmpty = true;
}
```

The above code was already explained in the *Implementing worker microservices with ASP.NET Core* section of *Chapter 14, Implementing Microservices with .NET*. Therefore, here, we will analyze just the `toExecute` lambda that is specific to our example:

```
var toExecute = async () =>
{
    using (var sc = services.CreateScope())
    {
        IDayStatistics statistics = sc.ServiceProvider.
GetRequiredService<IDayStatistics>();
        return await statistics.Add(toProcess[i]);
    }
};
```

Each task creates a different session scope so it can have a private copy of `IDayStatistics`, and then processes its request with `statistics.Add`.

That's all! Now we need a source of purchase data to test our code. In the next subsection, we will create a fake microservice that randomly creates purchase data and passes it to the `Counter` gRPC service.

Testing the GrpcMicroservice project with a fake purchase requests generator

Let's implement another microservice that feeds the previous microservice with randomly generated requests. The right project for a worker service that is not based on ASP.NET Core is the **Worker Service** project template. This project template automatically scaffolds a host containing a unique hosted service called `Worker`. We called this project `FakeSource`. In order to enable gRPC client usage, we must add the following NuGet packages: `Google.Protobuf`, `Grpc.NET.Client`, and `Grpc.Tools`.

Then, we must add the same `counting.proto` file as was added to the previous project. However, this time, we must require client code generation by placing the code below in the `FakeSource` project file:

```
<ItemGroup>
    <Protobuf Include="..\GrpcMicroService\Protos\counting.proto"
GrpcServices="Client">
      <Link>Protos\counting.proto</Link>
    </Protobuf>
 </ItemGroup>
```

The `GrpcServices` attribute set to `Client` is what enables client code generation instead of server code generation. The `link` tag appears since we added the same `counting.proto` file of the `GrpcMicroService` project as a link instead of copying it into the new project.

The hosted service is defined with the usual endless loop:

```
using Grpc.Net.Client;
using GrpcMicroService;
using Google.Protobuf.WellKnownTypes;
namespace FakeSource;
public class Worker : BackgroundService
{
    private readonly string[] locations = new string[]
           { "Florence", "London", "New York", "Paris" };
    protected override async Task ExecuteAsync(CancellationToken stoppingToken)
    {
        Random random = new Random();
        while (!stoppingToken.IsCancellationRequested)
        {
          try
          {
             ...
             await Task.Delay(2000, stoppingToken);
          }
          catch (OperationCanceledException)
          {
```

```
                return;
            }
            catch { }
        }
    }
}
```

The `locations` array contains locations that will be randomly selected. As soon as the `ExecuteAsync` method starts, it creates the `Random` instance that will be used in all random generations.

Each loop is enclosed in a `try/catch`; if an `OperationCanceledException` is generated, the method exits, since a similar exception is created when the application is being shut down and the thread is killed. In the case of other exceptions, the code tries to recover by simply moving to the next loop. In an actual production application, the final `catch` should contain instructions to log the intercepted exception and/or instructions for a better recovery strategy. In the next example, we will see more sophisticated exception handling that is adequate for actual production applications.

Inside the `try`, the code creates a purchase message, sends it to the `Counter` service, and then sleeps for 2 seconds.

Below is the code that sends the requests:

```
var purchaseDay = new DateTimeOffset(DateTime.UtcNow.Date, TimeSpan.Zero);
//randomize a little bit purchase day
purchaseDay = purchaseDay.AddDays(random.Next(0, 3) - 1);
//message time
var now = DateTimeOffset.UtcNow;
//add random location
var location = locations[random.Next(0, locations.Length)];
var messageId = Guid.NewGuid().ToString();
//add random cost
int cost = 200 * random.Next(1, 4);
//send message
using var channel = GrpcChannel.ForAddress("http://localhost:5000");
var client = new Counter.CounterClient(channel);
//since this is a fake random source
//in case of errors we simply do nothing.
//An actual client should use Polly
//to define retry policies
try
{
    await client.CountAsync(new CountingRequest
    {
        Id = messageId,
```

```
            Location = location,
            PurchaseTime = Timestamp.FromDateTimeOffset(purchaseDay),
            Time = Timestamp.FromDateTimeOffset(now),
            Cost = cost
        });

}
catch {}
```

The code just prepares the message with random data; then, it creates a communication channel for the gRPC server address and passes it to the constructor of the `Counter` service proxy. Finally, the `Count` method is called on the proxy. The call is enclosed in a `try/catch`, and in the case of an error, the error is simply ignored, since we are just sending random data. Instead, an actual production application should use **Polly** to retry the communication with predefined strategies. **Polly** was described in the *Resilient task execution* section of *Chapter 11, Applying a Microservice Architecture to Your Enterprise Application*. We will show you how to use **Polly** in the example in the next section.

And there you have it! Now it is time to test everything. Right-click on the solution and select **Set Startup Projects**, then set both `FakeSource` and `GrpcMicroService` to start. This way, both projects will be launched simultaneously when the solution is run.

Launch Visual Studio and then let both processes run for a couple of minutes, then go to **SQL Server Object Explorer** and look for a database called `grpcmicroservice`. If the **SQL Server Object Explorer** window is not available in the left menu of Visual Studio, go to the top **Window** menu and select it.

Once you have located the database, show the content of the `DayTotals` and `Purchases` tables. You should see all computed daily sums and all processed purchases.

You can also inspect what happens in the server project by opening the `HostedServices/ProcessPurchases.cs` file and placing breakpoints on the `queue.Top(10)` and `await queue.Dequeue(...)` instructions.

You can also move `FakeSource` into a different Visual Studio solution so that you can simultaneously run several copies of `FakeSource` each in a different Visual Studio instance. It is also possible to double-click on the `FakeSource` project, which gives the option to save a new Visual Studio solution containing just a reference to the `FakeSource` project.

The full code is in the `GrpcMicroService` subfolder of the `ch15` folder of the book's GitHub repository. The next section shows you how to solve the same problem with queued communication using the RabbitMQ message broker.

A worker microservice based on RabbitMQ

This section explains the modifications needed to use a message broker instead of gRPC communication with an internal queue. This kind of solution is usually more difficult to test and design but allows for better horizontal scaling, and also enables extra features at almost no cost since they are offered by the message broker itself.

We assume that RabbitMQ has already been installed and adequately prepared, as explained in the *Installing RabbitMQ core* subsection of *Chapter 14, Implementing Microservices with .NET*.

First, the ASP.NET Core project must be replaced by another **Worker Service** project. Also, this project must add the connection string to its configuration file and must call the `AddStorage` extension method to add all the database services to the dependency injection engine. Below is the full content of the `Program.cs` file:

```
using GrpcMicroService.HostedServices;
using GrpcMicroServiceStore;
IHost host = Host.CreateDefaultBuilder(args)
    .ConfigureServices((hostContext, services) =>
    {
        services.AddStorage(hostContext.Configuration
            .GetConnectionString("DefaultConnection"));
        services.AddHostedService<ProcessPurchases>();
    })
    .Build();
await host.RunAsync();
```

We don't need the gRPC services and service proxies anymore, just ProtoBuf for the binary messages, so both the `FakeSource` process and the `GrpcMicroService` projects must add just the `Google.Protobuf` and `Grpc.Tools` NuGet packages. Both projects need the following `messages.proto` file, which defines just the purchase message:

```
syntax = "proto3";
option csharp_namespace = "GrpcMicroService";
import "google/protobuf/timestamp.proto";
package purchase;
message PurchaseMessage {
  string id = 1;
  google.protobuf.Timestamp time = 2;
  string location = 3;
  int32 cost =4;
  google.protobuf.Timestamp purchaseTime = 5;
}
```

The automatic generation of the message classes is enabled in both projects with the same XML declaration in their project files:

```
<ItemGroup>
    <Protobuf Include="Protos\messages.proto" GrpcServices="Client" />
</ItemGroup>
```

Both projects need to specify `Client` code generation since no service needs to be created.

To communicate with the RabbitMQ server, both projects must add the `RabbitMQ.Client` NuGet package.

Finally, `FakeSource` also adds the `Polly NuGet` package because we will use Polly to define reliable communication strategies.

The `ExecuteAsync` method of the client project is a little bit different:

```
protected override async Task ExecuteAsync(CancellationToken stoppingToken)
{
    Random random = new Random();
    var factory = new ConnectionFactory{ HostName = "localhost" };
    IConnection? connection =null;
    IModel? channel = null;
    try
    {
        while (!stoppingToken.IsCancellationRequested)
        {
        ...
        }
    }
    finally
    {
        if (connection != null)
        {
            channel.Dispose();
            connection.Dispose();
            channel = null;
            connection = null;
        }
    }
}
```

Communication requires the creation of a connection factory, then the creation factory generates a connection, and the connection generates a channel. The connection factory is created outside of the main loop since it can be reused several times, and it is not invalidated by communication errors.

For the connection and channel, outside of the main loop, we just define the variables and where to place them since they are invalidated in the case of communication exceptions, so we must dispose of them and recreate them from scratch after each exception.

The main loop is enclosed in `try/finally` to ensure that any channel/connection pair is disposed of before leaving the method.

Inside the main loop, as a first step, we create the purchase message:

```
var purchaseDay = DateTime.UtcNow.Date;
//randomize a little bit purchase day
purchaseDay = purchaseDay.AddDays(random.Next(0, 3) - 1);
var purchase = new PurchaseMessage
{
    //message time
    PurchaseTime = Timestamp.FromDateTime(purchaseDay),
    Time = Timestamp.FromDateTime(DateTime.UtcNow),
    Id = Guid.NewGuid().ToString(),
    //add random location
    Location = locations[random.Next(0, locations.Length)],
    //add random cost
    Cost = 200 * random.Next(1, 4)
};
```

Then, the message is serialized:

```
byte[]? body = null;
using (var stream = new MemoryStream())
{
    purchase.WriteTo(stream);
    stream.Flush();
    body = stream.ToArray();
}
```

Before executing the communication, we define a Polly policy:

```
var policy = Policy
    .Handle<Exception>()
    .WaitAndRetry(6,
        retryAttempt => TimeSpan.FromSeconds(Math.Pow(2,
        retryAttempt)));
```

The above policy is an exponential retry, which, in the case of an exception, waits for an exponentially growing amount of time. So, if six attempts are made, then the second attempt is made after 2 seconds, the third after 4 seconds, the fourth after 8 seconds, and so on. If all attempts fail, the exception is rethrown and causes the message to be lost. If it's important that messages can't be lost, we can combine this strategy with a circuit break strategy (see *Resilient task execution* in *Chapter 11, Applying a Microservice Architecture to Your Enterprise Application*).

Once we have defined the retry policy, we can execute all the communication steps in the context of this policy:

```
policy.Execute(() =>
{
try
{
    if(connection == null || channel == null)
    {
        connection = factory.CreateConnection();
        channel = connection.CreateModel();
        channel.ConfirmSelect();
    }
    //actual communication here
    ...
    ...
}
catch
{
    channel.Dispose();
    connection.Dispose();
    channel = null;
    connection = null;
    throw;
}
```

If there are no valid connections or channels, they are created. `channel.ConfirmSelect()` declares that we need confirmation that the message was safely received and stored on disk. In the case that an exception is thrown, both the channel and the connection are disposed of, since they might have been corrupted by the exception. This way, the next communication attempt will use fresh communication and a new channel. After the disposal, the exception is rethrown so it can be handled by the Polly policy.

Finally, here are the actual communication steps:

1. First of all, if the queue doesn't already exist, it is created. The queue is created as `durable`; that is, it must be stored on disk and not be `exclusive` so that several servers can extract messages from the queue in parallel:

   ```
   channel.QueueDeclare(queue: "purchase_queue",
       durable: true,
       exclusive: false,
       autoDelete: false,
     arguments: null);
   ```

2. Then, each message is declared as persistent; that is, it must be stored on disk:

```
var properties = channel.CreateBasicProperties();
properties.Persistent = true;
```

3. Finally, the message is sent through the default exchange, which sends it to a specific named queue:

```
channel.BasicPublish(exchange: "",
        routingKey: "purchase_queue",
        basicProperties: properties,
        body: body);
```

4. As a final step, we wait until the message is safely stored on disk:

```
channel.WaitForConfirmsOrDie(new TimeSpan(0, 0, 5));
```

If a confirmation doesn't arrive within the specified timeout, an exception is thrown that triggers the Polly retry policy. When messages are taken from a local database queue, we can also use a non-blocking confirmation that triggers the removal of the message from the local queue.

The `ExecuteAsync` method of the server-hosted process is defined in the `HostedServices/ProcessPurchase.cs` file:

```
protected override async Task ExecuteAsync(CancellationToken stoppingToken)
{
    while (!stoppingToken.IsCancellationRequested)
    {
        try
        {
            var factory = new ConnectionFactory() { HostName = "localhost" };
            using (var connection = factory.CreateConnection())
            using (var channel = connection.CreateModel())
            {
                channel.QueueDeclare(queue: "purchase_queue",
                                     durable: true,
                                     exclusive: false,
                                     autoDelete: false,
                                     arguments: null);
                channel.BasicQos(prefetchSize: 0, prefetchCount: 1, global:
false);
                var consumer = new EventingBasicConsumer(channel);
                consumer.Received += async (sender, ea) =>
                {
                    // Message received even handler
                    ...
                };
```

```
                channel.BasicConsume(queue: "purchase_queue",
                                     autoAck: false,
                                     consumer: consumer);
                await Task.Delay(1000, stoppingToken);
            }
        }
        catch { }
    }
}
```

Inside the main loop, if an exception is thrown, it is intercepted by the empty `catch`. Since the two `using` statements are left, both the connection and channel are disposed of. Therefore, after the exception, a new loop is executed that creates a new fresh connection and a new channel.

In the `using` statement body, we ensure that our queue exists, and then set `prefetch` to `1`. This means that each server must extract just one message at a time, which ensures a fair distribution of the load among all servers. However, setting `prefetch` to `1` might not be convenient when servers are based on several parallel threads since it sacrifices thread usage optimization in favor of fair distribution among servers. As a consequence, threads that could successfully process further messages (after the first) might remain idle.

Then, we define a `message received` event handler. `BasicConsume` starts the actual message reception. With `autoAck` set to `false`, when a message is read from the queue, it is not removed but just blocked so it is not available to other servers that read from the same queue. The message is actually removed when a confirmation that it has been successfully processed is sent to RabbitMQ. We can also send a failure confirmation, in which case, the message is unblocked and becomes available for processing again.

If no confirmation is received, the message remains blocked till the connection and channel are disposed of.

`BasicConsume` is non-blocking, so the `Task.Delay` after it blocks till the cancelation token is signaled. In any case, after 1 second, `Task.Delay` unblocks and both the connection and the channel are replaced with fresh ones. This prevents non-confirmed messages from remaining blocked forever.

Let's move on to the code inside the *message received* event. This is the place where the actual message processing takes place.

As a first step, the code verifies if the application is being shut down, in which case it disposes of the channel and connection and returns without performing any further operations:

```
if (stoppingToken.IsCancellationRequested)
{
    channel.Close();
    connection.Close();
    return;
}
```

Then, a session scope is created to access all session-scoped dependency injection services:

```
using (var scope = services.CreateScope())
{
  try
  {
  // actual message processing
  ...
  }
  catch {
    ((EventingBasicConsumer)sender).Model.BasicNack(ea.DeliveryTag, false,
true);
  }
}
```

When an exception is thrown during the message processing, a `Nack` message is sent to RabbitMQ to inform it that the message processing failed. `ea.DeliveryTag` is a tag that uniquely identifies the message. The second argument set to `false` informs RabbitMQ that the `Nack` is just for the message identified by `ea.DeliveryTag` that doesn't also involve all other messages waiting for confirmation from this server. Finally, the last argument set to `true` asks RabbitMQ to requeue the message whose processing failed.

Inside the `try` block, we get an instance of `IDayStatistics`:

```
IDayStatistics statistics = scope.ServiceProvider
    .GetRequiredService<IDayStatistics>();
```

Then, we deserialize the message body to get a `PurchaseMessage` instance and add it to the database:

```
var body = ea.Body.ToArray();
PurchaseMessage? message = null;
using (var stream = new MemoryStream(body))
{
    message = PurchaseMessage.Parser.ParseFrom(stream);
}
var res = await statistics.Add(new Purchase {
    Cost= message.Cost,
    Id= Guid.Parse(message.Id),
    Location = message.Location,
    Time = new DateTimeOffset(message.Time.ToDateTime(), TimeSpan.Zero),
    PurchaseTime = new DateTimeOffset(message.PurchaseTime.ToDateTime(),
TimeSpan.Zero)
});
```

If the operation fails, the `Add` operation returns `null`, so we must send a `Nack`; otherwise, we must send an `Ack`:

```
if(res != null)
    ((EventingBasicConsumer)sender).Model
        .BasicAck(ea.DeliveryTag, false);
else
    ((EventingBasicConsumer)sender).Model
        .BasicNack(ea.DeliveryTag, false, true);
```

That's all! The full code is in the `GrpcMicroServiceRabbitProto` subfolder of the `ch15` folder in the GitHub repository of this book. You can test the code by setting both the client and server projects as the start project and running the solution. After 1–2 minutes, the database should be populated with new purchases and new daily totals. In a staging/production environment, you can run several copies of both the client and server.

The `GrpcMicroServiceRabbit` subfolder in the `ch15` folder of the GitHub repository contains another version of the same application that uses the *Binaron* NuGet package for serialization. It is faster than ProtoBuf, but being .NET-specific, it is not interoperable. Moreover, it has no features to facilitate message versioning. It is useful when performance is critical and versioning and interoperability are not a priority.

The *Binaron* version differs in that it has no `.proto` files or other ProtoBuf stuff, but it explicitly defines a `PurchaseMessage` .NET class. Moreover, ProtoBuf serialization and deserialization instructions are replaced by the following:

```
byte[]? body = null;
using (var stream = new MemoryStream())
{
    BinaronConvert.Serialize(purchase, stream);
    stream.Flush();
    body = stream.ToArray();
}
```

Together with:

```
PurchaseMessage? message = null;
using (var stream = new MemoryStream(body))
{
    message = BinaronConvert.Deserialize<PurchaseMessage>(stream);
}.
```

Now that we have created a microservice connected to a message broker, it is also important to learn how to expose packages from WWTravelClub using web APIs. Let's see this in the next section.

Exposing WWTravelClub packages using Web APIs

In this section, we will implement an ASP.NET REST service that lists all the packages that are available for a given vacation's start and end dates. For didactic purposes, we will not structure the application according to the best practices we have described previously; instead, we will simply generate the results with a LINQ query that will be directly placed in the controller action method. A well-structured ASP.NET Core application has been presented in *Chapter 18, Implementing Frontend Microservices with ASP.NET Core.*

Let us make a copy of the `WWTravelClubDB` solution folder and rename the new folder `WWTravelClubWebAPI80`. The WWTravelClubDB project was built step by step in the various sections of *Chapter 13, Interacting with Data in C# – Entity Framework Core*. Let us open the new solution and add a new ASP.NET Core API project to it named `WWTravelClubWebAPI80` (the same name as the new solution folder). For simplicity, select **No Authentication**. Right-click on the newly created project and select **Set as StartUp project** to make it the default project that is launched when the solution is run.

Finally, we need to add a reference to the WWTravelClubDB project.

ASP.NET Core projects store configuration constants in the `appsettings.json` file. Let's open this file and add the database connection string for the database we created in the WWTravelClubDB project to it, as shown here:

```
{
    "ConnectionStrings": {
        "DefaultConnection": "Server=
   (localdb)\\mssqllocaldb;Database=wwtravelclub;
Trusted_Connection=True;MultipleActiveResultSets=true"
    },
    ...
    ...
}
```

Now, we must add the WWTravelClubDB entity framework database context to `Program.cs`, as shown here:

```
builder.Services.AddDbContext<WWTravelClubDB.MainDBContext>(options =>
options.UseSqlServer(
builder.Configuration.GetConnectionString("DefaultConnection"),
            b =>b.MigrationsAssembly("WWTravelClubDB")))
```

The option object settings that are passed to `AddDbContext` specify the usage of SQL Server with a connection string that is extracted from the `ConnectionStrings` section of the `appsettings.json` configuration file with the `Configuration.GetConnectionString("DefaultConnection")` method. The `b =>b.MigrationsAssembly("WWTravelClubDB")` lambda function declares the name of the assembly that contains the database migrations (see *Chapter 13, Interacting with Data in C# – Entity Framework Core*), which, in our case, is the DLL that was generated by the WWTravelClubDB project.

For the preceding code to compile, you should add the `Microsoft.EntityFrameworkCore` namespace.

Since we want to enrich our REST service with OpenAPI documentation, let's add a reference to the `Swashbuckle.AspNetCore` NuGet package. Now, we can add the following very basic configuration to `Program.cs`:

```
var builder = WebApplication.CreateBuilder(args);
...
builder.Services.AddSwaggerGen(c =>
{
    c.SwaggerDoc("v2", new() { Title = "WWTravelClub REST API - .NET 8",
Version = "v2" });
});
var app = builder.Build();
...
app.UseSwagger();
app.UseSwaggerUI(c => c.SwaggerEndpoint("/swagger/v2/swagger.json",
"WWTravelClub REST API - .NET 8"));
...
app.Run();
```

Now, we are ready to encode our service. Let's delete `WeatherForecastController`, which is automatically scaffolded by Visual Studio. Then, right-click on the `Controllers` folder and select **Add | Controller**. Now, choose an empty API controller called `PackagesController`. First, let's modify the code as follows:

```
[Route("api/packages")]
[ApiController]
public class PackagesController : ControllerBase
{
    [HttpGet("bydate/{start}/{stop}")]
    [ProducesResponseType(typeof(IEnumerable<PackagesListDTO>), 200)]
    [ProducesResponseType(400)]
    [ProducesResponseType(500)]
    public async Task<IActionResult> GetPackagesByDate(
        [FromServices] WWTravelClubDB.MainDBContext ctx,
        DateTime start, DateTime stop)
    {
    }
}
```

The `Route` attribute declares that the basic path for our service will be `api/packages`. The unique action method that we implement is `GetPackagesByDate`, which is invoked on `HttpGet` requests on paths of the `bydate/{start}/{stop}` type, where `start` and `stop` are the `DateTime` parameters that are passed as input to `GetPackagesByDate`. The `ProduceResponseType` attributes declare the following:

- When a request is successful, a 200 code is returned, and the body contains an `IEnumerable` of the `PackagesListDTO` type (which we will soon define) containing the required package information.
- When the request is ill formed, a 400 code is returned. We don't specify the type returned since bad requests are automatically handled by the ASP.NET Core framework through the `ApiController` attribute.
- In the case of unexpected errors, a 500 code is returned with the exception error message.

Now, let's define the `PackagesListDTO` class in a new `DTOs` folder:

```
namespace WWTravelClubWebAPI80.DTOs;
public record PackagesListDTO
{
    public int Id { get; set; }
    public string Name { get; set; }
    public decimal Price { get; set; }
    public int DurationInDays { get; set; }
    public DateTime? StartValidityDate { get; set; }
    public DateTime? EndValidityDate { get; set; }
    public string DestinationName { get; set; }
    public int DestinationId { get; set; }
}
```

Finally, let's add the following `using` clauses to our controller code so that we can easily refer to our DTO and Entity Framework LINQ methods:

```
using Microsoft.EntityFrameworkCore;
using WWTravelClubWebAPI80.DTOs;
```

Now, we are ready to fill the body of the `GetPackagesByDate` method with the following code.

```
try
{
    var res = await ctx.Packages
        .Where(m => start >= m.StartValidityDate
        && stop <= m.EndValidityDate)
        .Select(m => new PackagesListDTO
        {
            StartValidityDate = m.StartValidityDate,
            EndValidityDate = m.EndValidityDate,
            Name = m.Name,
            DurationInDays = m.DurationInDays,
            Id = m.Id,
            Price = m.Price,
```

```
                DestinationName = m.MyDestination.Name,
                DestinationId = m.DestinationId
            })
            .ToListAsync();
        return Ok(res);
}
catch (Exception err)
{
        return StatusCode(500, err.ToString());
}
```

It is important to remember that we are focusing only on presenting the results of an API exposed using the `Swashbuckle.AspNetCore` NuGet package. It is not a good practice to make use of the `DbContext` in a `Controller` class, and as a software architect, you may define the best architectural design for your application (multi-tier, hexagonal, onion, clean, DDD, and so on).

The LINQ query is like the one contained in the `WWTravelClubDBTest` project we tested in *Chapter 13, Interacting with Data in C# – Entity Framework Core*. Once the result has been computed, it is returned with an `OK` call. The method's code handles internal server errors by catching exceptions and returning a 500 status code since bad requests are automatically handled before the `Controller` method is called by the `ApiController` attribute.

Let's run the solution. When the browser opens, it is unable to receive any result from our ASP.NET Core website. Let's modify the browser URL so that it is `https://localhost:<previous port>/swagger`. It is worth mentioning that you can also configure your local settings file to either launch and go to the Swagger URL automatically, or have Swagger live under the root.

The user interface of the OpenAPI documentation will look as follows:

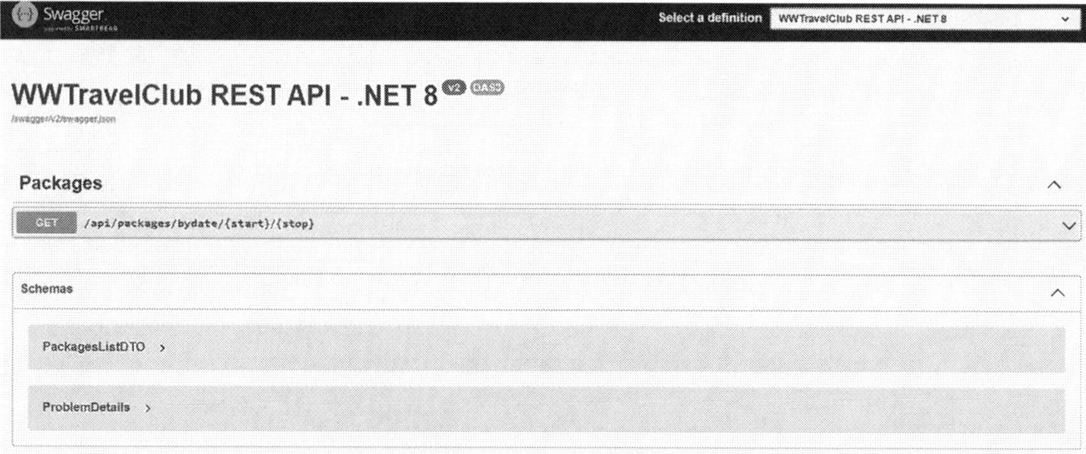

Figure 21.15: Swagger output

PackagesListDTO is the model we defined to list the packages, while **ProblemDetails** is the model that is used to report errors in the event of bad requests. By clicking the **GET** button, we can get more details about our `GET` method and we can also test it, as shown in the following screenshot:

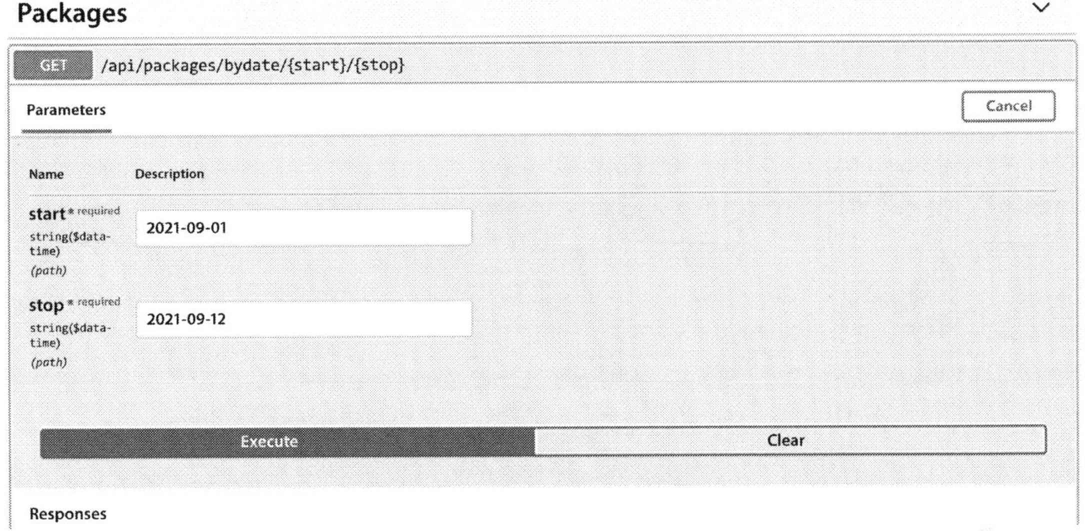

Figure 21.16: GET method details

Pay attention when it comes to inserting dates that are covered by packages in the database; otherwise, an empty list will be returned. The ones shown in the preceding screenshot should work.

Dates must be entered in a correct JSON format; otherwise, a 400 Bad Request error is returned, like the one shown in the following code:

```
{
  "errors": {
    "start": [
      "The value '2019' is not valid."
    ]
  },
  "title": "One or more validation errors occurred.",
  "status": 400,
  "traceId": "80000008-0000-f900-b63f-84710c7967bb"
}
```

If you insert the correct input parameters, the Swagger UI returns the packages that satisfy the query in JSON format.

That is all! You have implemented your first API with OpenAPI documentation! Now let's check how easy it can be to implement a serverless solution using Azure Functions.

Implementing Azure Functions to send emails

Here, we will use a subset of the Azure components. The use case from WWTravelClub proposes a worldwide implementation of the service, and there is a chance that this service will need different architecture designs to achieve all the key performance points that we described in *Chapter 1, Understanding the Importance of Software Architecture*.

If you go back to the user stories that were described in this chapter, you will find that many needs are related to communication. Because of this, it is common to have some alerts provided by emails in the solution. This implementation will focus on how to send emails. The architecture will be totally serverless. The benefits of using an architecture like that are explained below.

The following diagram shows the basic structure of the architecture. To give users a great experience, all the emails that are sent by the application will be queued asynchronously, thereby preventing significant delays in the system's responses:

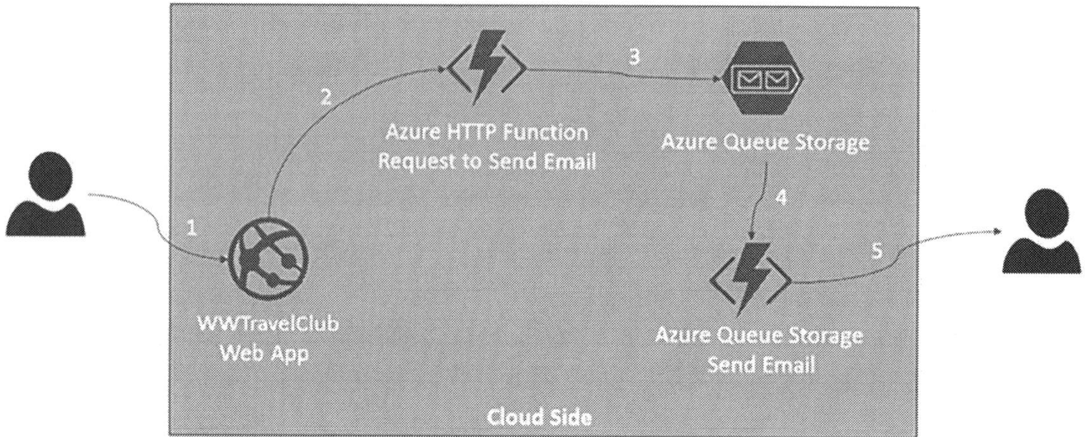

Figure 21.17: Architectural design for sending emails

Basically, when a user does any action that requires sending an alert (1), the alert is posted in a **send email request function** (2), which stores the request in Azure Queue Storage (3). So, for the user, the alert is already performed at this moment, and they can keep working. However, since we have a queue, no matter the number of alerts sent, they will be processed by the **send email function** that is triggered (4) as soon as a request is made, respecting the time needed to process the requests, but guaranteeing that the receiver will get the alert (5). Note that there are no dedicated servers that manage Azure Functions for enqueuing or dequeuing messages from Azure Queue Storage. This is exactly what we call serverless, as described in *Chapter 16, Working with Serverless - Azure Functions*. It is worth mentioning that this architecture is not restricted to only sending emails – it can also be used to process any HTTP `POST` request.

Now, we will learn, in three steps, how to set up security in the API so that only authorized applications can use the given solution.

First step — creating an Azure queue storage

It is quite simple to create storage in the Azure portal. Let us learn how. First, you will need to create a storage account by clicking on **Create a resource** on the main page of the Azure portal and searching for **Storage account**. Then, you will be able to set up its basic information, such as **Storage account name** and **Location**. Information about **Networking** and **Data protection**, as shown in the following screenshot, can be checked in this wizard, too. There are default values for these settings that we will cover the demo:

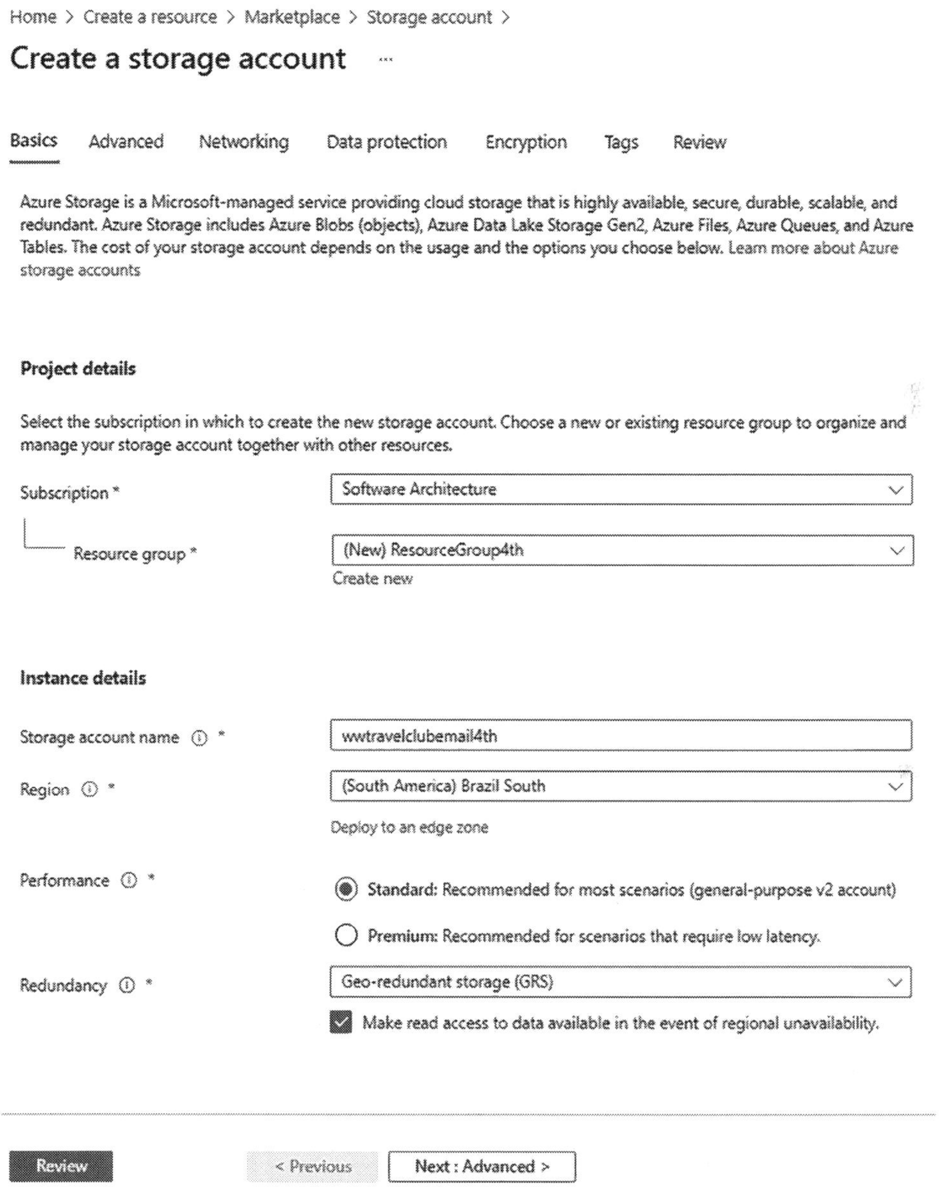

Home > Create a resource > Marketplace > Storage account >

Create a storage account ...

Basics Advanced Networking Data protection Encryption Tags Review

Azure Storage is a Microsoft-managed service providing cloud storage that is highly available, secure, durable, scalable, and redundant. Azure Storage includes Azure Blobs (objects), Azure Data Lake Storage Gen2, Azure Files, Azure Queues, and Azure Tables. The cost of your storage account depends on the usage and the options you choose below. Learn more about Azure storage accounts

Project details

Select the subscription in which to create the new storage account. Choose a new or existing resource group to organize and manage your storage account together with other resources.

Subscription * Software Architecture

Resource group * (New) ResourceGroup4th

Create new

Instance details

Storage account name * wwtravelclubemail4th

Region * (South America) Brazil South

Deploy to an edge zone

Performance * **Standard:** Recommended for most scenarios (general-purpose v2 account)

Premium: Recommended for scenarios that require low latency.

Redundancy * Geo-redundant storage (GRS)

Make read access to data available in the event of regional unavailability.

Review < Previous Next : Advanced >

Figure 21.18: Creating an Azure storage account

Once you have the storage account in place, you will be able to set up a queue. You will find this option by clicking on the **Overview** link in the storage account and selecting the **Queue service** option or by selecting **Queues** via the **Storage account** menu. Then, you will find an option to add the queue (**+ Queue**), where you just need to provide its name:

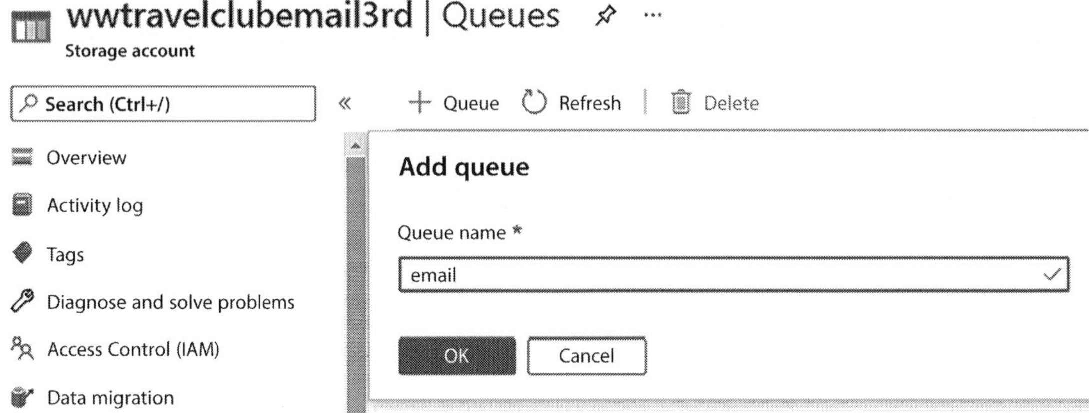

Figure 21.19: Defining a queue to monitor emails

The created queue will give you an overview of the Azure portal. There, you will find your queue's URL and be able to use Storage Explorer:

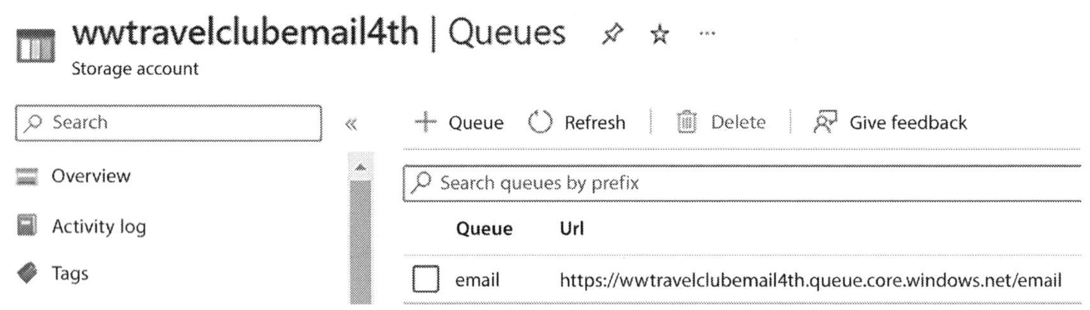

Figure 21.20: Queue created

Note that you will also be able to connect to this storage using Microsoft Azure Storage Explorer (`https://azure.microsoft.com/en-us/features/storage-explorer/`):

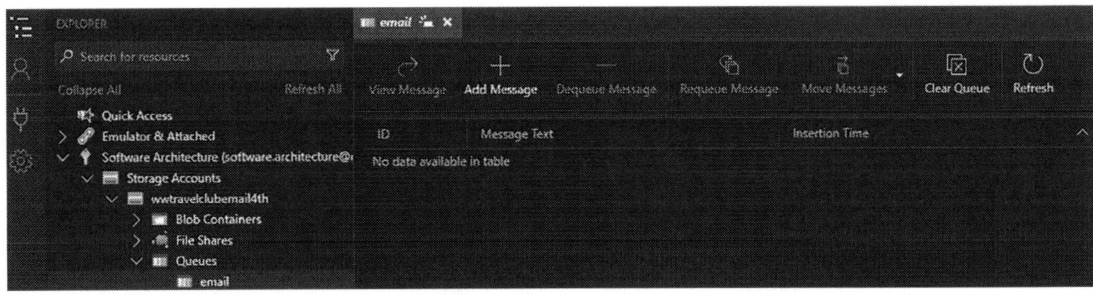

Figure 21.21: Monitoring the queue using Microsoft Azure Storage Explorer

This tool is especially useful if you are not connected to the Azure portal. Let's move to the second step, where we will create the function that receives the requests to send emails.

Second step — creating the function to send emails

Now, you can start programming in earnest, informing the queue that an email is waiting to be sent. Here, we need to use an HTTP trigger. Note that the function is a static class that runs asynchronously. The following code, written in Visual Studio, gathers the request data coming from the HTTP trigger and inserts the data into a queue that will be processed later. It is worth mentioning that the environment variable `EmailQueueConnectionString` is set in the function app settings, and it contains the information provided by the Azure Queue Storage connection string.

We have below a code snippet from the function available in the GitHub repository of the book:

```
public static class SendEmail
{
    [FunctionName(nameof(SendEmail))]
    public static async Task<HttpResponseMessage>RunAsync(
[HttpTrigger(AuthorizationLevel.Function, "post")] HttpRequestMessage req,
ILogger log)
    {
        var requestData = await req.Content.ReadAsStringAsync();
        var connectionString = Environment.
GetEnvironmentVariable("EmailQueueConnectionString");
        var storageAccount = CloudStorageAccount.Parse(connectionString);
        var queueClient = storageAccount.CreateCloudQueueClient();
        var messageQueue = queueClient.GetQueueReference("email");
        var message = new CloudQueueMessage(requestData);
        await messageQueue.AddMessageAsync(message);
        log.LogInformation("HTTP trigger from SendEmail function processed a
request.");
        var responseObj = new { success = true };
        return new HttpResponseMessage(HttpStatusCode.OK)
        {
```

```
            Content = new StringContent(JsonConvert.
SerializeObject(responseObj), Encoding.UTF8, "application/json"),
        };
    }
}
```

In some scenarios, you may try to avoid the queue setup indicated in the preceding code by using a queue output binding. Check out the details at `https://docs.microsoft.com/en-us/azure/azure-functions/functions-bindings-storage-queue-output?tabs=csharp`.

You can use a tool such as Postman to test your function. Before that, you just need to run the app in Visual Studio, which will launch Azure Functions Core Tools and its emulator:

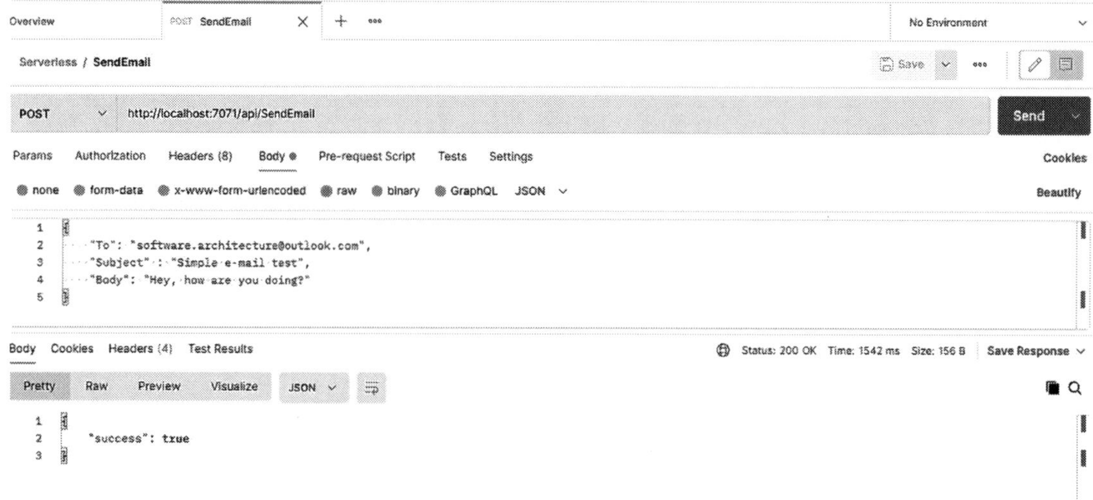

Figure 21.22: Postman function test

The result will appear in Microsoft Azure Storage Explorer and the Azure portal. In the Azure portal, you can manage each message and dequeue each of them or even clear the queue storage:

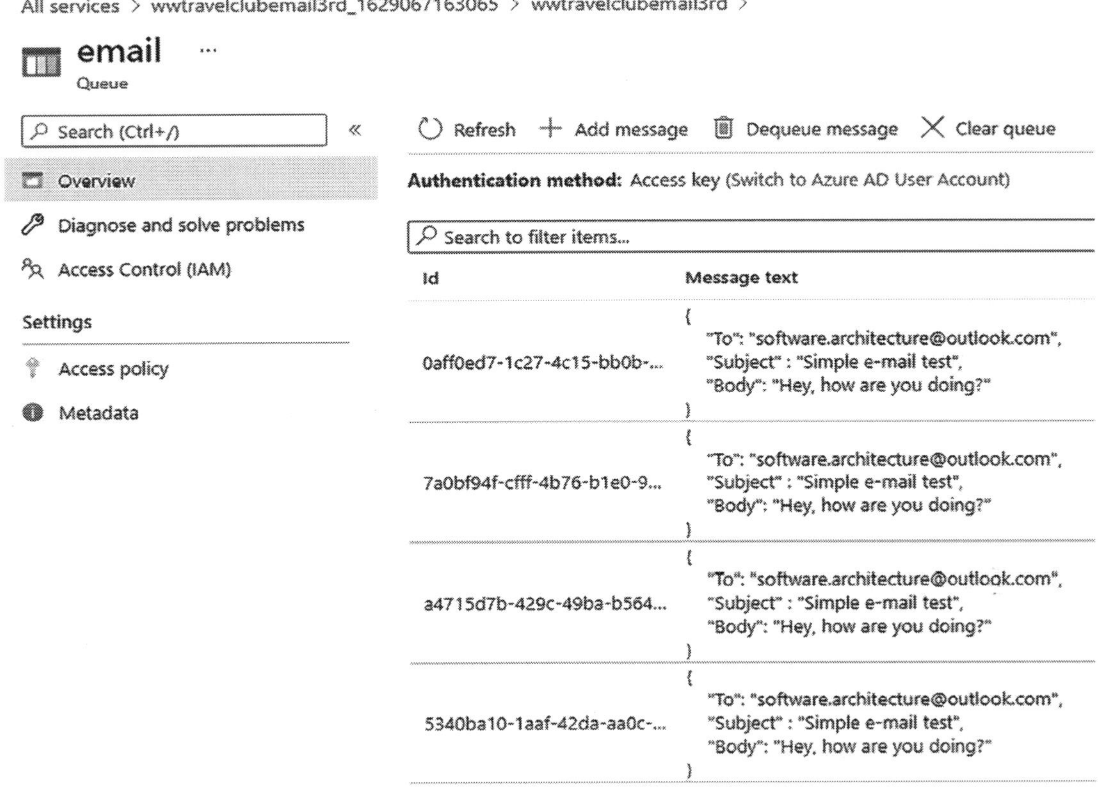

Figure 21.23: HTTP trigger and queue storage test

To finish this topic, let's move on to the final third step, where we will create the function that will process the requests for sending emails.

Third step — creating the queue trigger function

After this, you can create a second function by right-clicking the project and selecting **Add -> New Azure Function**. This one will be triggered by data entering your queue. It is worth mentioning that, for Azure Functions v4, you will have the `Microsoft.Azure.WebJobs.Extensions.Storage` library added as a NuGet reference automatically:

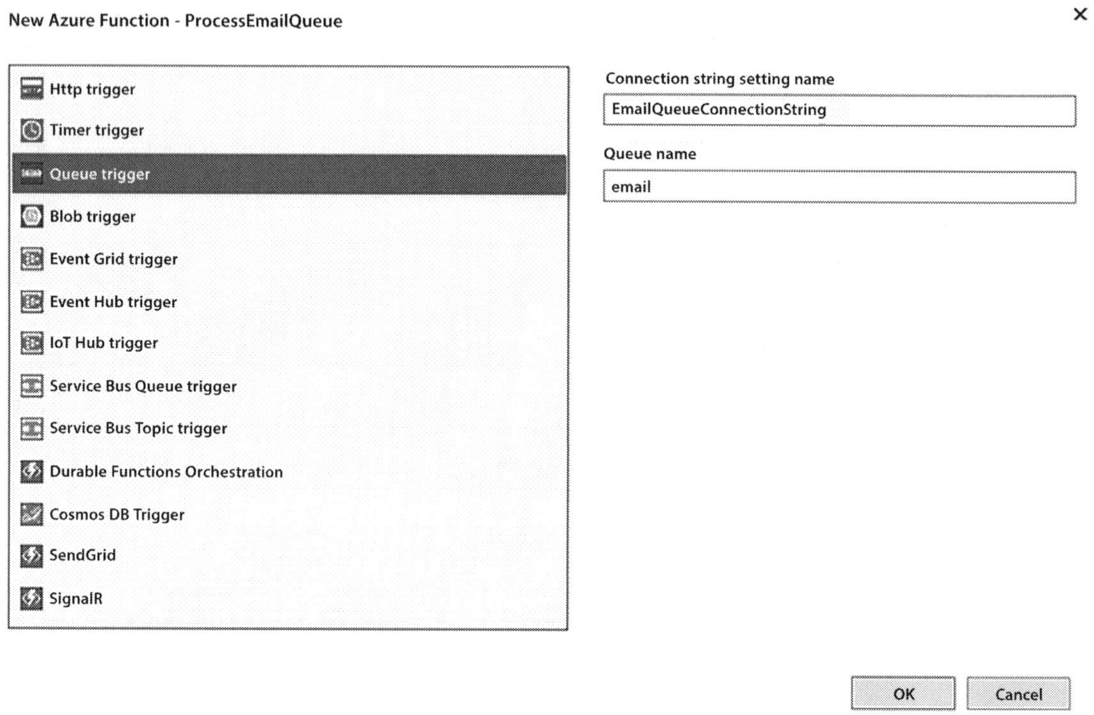

Figure 21.24: Creating a queue trigger

Once you have set the connection string inside `local.settings.json`, you will be able to run both functions and test them with Postman. The difference is that, with the second function running, if you set a breakpoint at the start of it, you will be able to check whether the message has been sent:

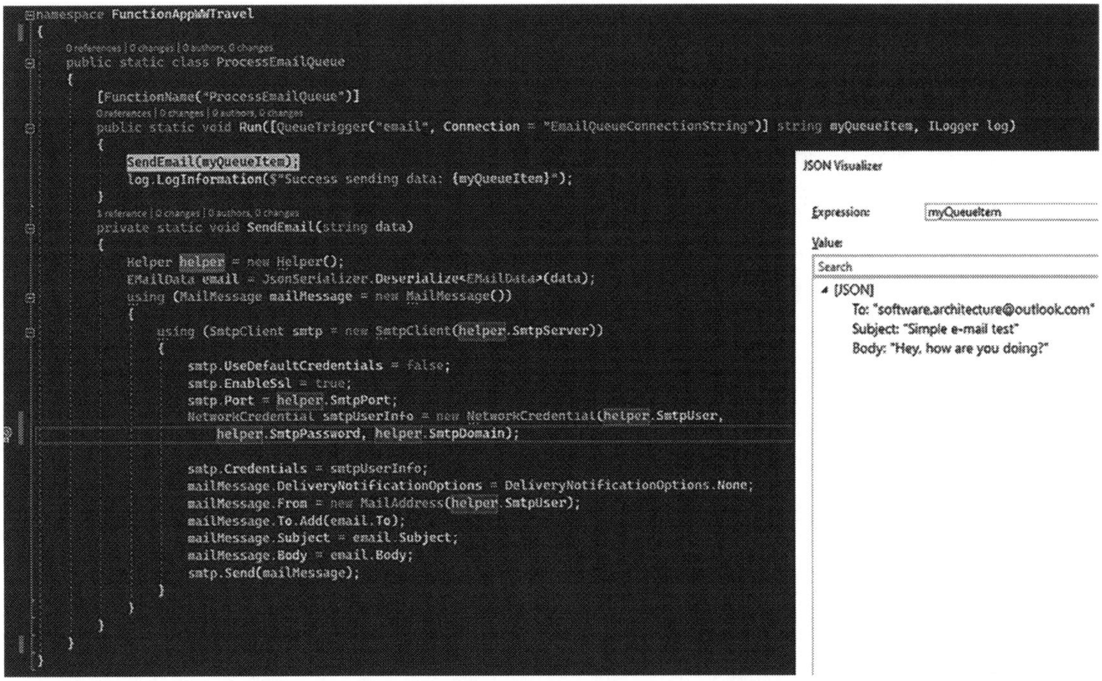

Figure 21.25: Queue triggered in Visual Studio 2022

From this point, the way to send emails will depend on the email options you have. You may decide to use a proxy or connect directly to your email server.

There are several advantages to creating an email service this way:

- Once your service has been coded and tested, you can use it to send emails from any of your applications. This means that your code can always be reused.
- Apps that use this service will not be stopped from sending emails due to the asynchronous advantages of posting in an HTTP service.
- You do not need to pool the queue to check whether data is ready for processing.

Finally, the queue process runs concurrently, which delivers a better experience in most cases. It is possible to turn it off by setting some properties in `host.json`. All the options for this can be found in the *Further reading* section at the end of this chapter.

In this part of the case study, we checked an example of an architecture where you connect multiple functions to avoid pooling data and enable concurrent processing. We have seen with this demo how great the fit between serverless and event-driven architecture is.

Now, let's change the subject a bit, and discuss how to implement a frontend microservice.

A frontend microservice

In this section, as an example of an ASP.NET Core MVC frontend microservice described in *Chapter 18, Implementing Frontend Microservices with ASP.NET Core*, we will implement the administrative panel for managing the destinations and packages of the `WWTravelClub` book use case. The application will be implemented with the DDD approach and associated patterns described in *Chapter 7, Understanding the Different Domains in Software Solutions*. So, having a good understanding of that chapter is a fundamental prerequisite to reading this chapter. The subsections that follow describe the overall application specifications and organization. The full code of the example can be found in the `ch19` folder of the GitHub repository associated with the book.

As usual, let's start by stating clearly our frontend microservice specifications.

Defining application specifications

The destinations and packages were described in *Chapter 13, Interacting with Data in C# – Entity Framework Core*. Here, we will use the same data model, with the necessary modifications to adapt it to the DDD approach. The administrative panel must allow packages, a destination listing, and CRUD operations on it. To simplify the application, the two listings will be quite simple: the application will show all destinations sorted according to their names, while all packages will be sorted starting from the ones with a later validity date.

Furthermore, we make the following assumptions:

- The application that shows destinations and packages to the user shares the same database used by the administrative panel. Since only the administrative panel application needs to modify data, there will be just one write copy of the database with several read-only replicas.
- Price modifications and package deletions are immediately used to update the user's shopping carts. For this reason, the administrative application must send asynchronous communications about price changes and package removals. We will not implement all the communication logic here, but we will just add all such events to an event table, which should be used as input to a parallel thread that's in charge of sending these events to all relevant microservices.

Here, we will give the full code for just package management; most of the code for destination management is designed as an exercise for you. The full code is available in the `ch16` folder of the GitHub repository associated with this book. In the remainder of this section, we will describe the application's overall organization and discuss some relevant samples of code. We start with an overall description of the application architecture.

Defining the application architecture

The application is organized based on the guidelines described in *Chapter 7, Understanding the Different Domains in Software Solutions*, while considering the DDD approach and related patterns. That is, the application is organized into three layers, each implemented as a different project:

- There's a domain implementation layer, which contains the repository's implementation and the classes describing database entities. It is a .NET library project. However, since it needs some interfaces, like `IServiceCollection`, which are defined in `Microsoft.NET.Sdk.web`, and since the layer `DBContext` must inherit from the identity framework in order to also handle the application authentication and authorization database tables, we must add a reference not only to the .NET SDK but also to the ASP.NET Core SDK. This can be done as follows:
    1. Right-click on the project icon in Solution Explorer and select **Edit project file**, or just double-click the project name.
    2. In the **Edit** window, add:

    ```
    <ItemGroup>
        <FrameworkReference
                  Include="Microsoft.AspNetCore.App" />
    </ItemGroup>
    ```

There's also a domain layer abstraction, which contains repository specifications – that is, interfaces that describe repository implementations and DDD aggregates. In our implementation, we decided to implement aggregates by hiding the forbidden operations/properties of root data entities behind interfaces. Hence, for instance, the `Package` entity class, which is an aggregate root, has a corresponding `IPackage` interface in the domain layer abstraction that hides all the property setters of the `Package` entity. The domain layer abstraction also contains the definitions of all the domain events, while the event handlers that will subscribe to these events are defined in the application layer. `IPackage` has also the associated `IPackageRepository` repository interface.

All repository interfaces inherit from the empty `IRepository` interface.

This way, they declare it as a repository interface, and all repository interfaces can be automatically discovered with reflection and added to the dependency injection engine together with their implementations.

Finally, there's the application layer – that is, the ASP.NET Core MVC application – where we define DDD queries, commands, command handlers, and event handlers. Controllers fill query objects and execute them to get ViewModels they can pass to Views. They update storage by filling command objects and executing their associated command handlers. In turn, command handlers use `IRepository` interfaces (that is, interfaces that inherit from the empty `IRepository` interface) and `IUnitOfWork` instances coming from the domain layer to manage and coordinate transactions.

It is worth pointing out that, in more complex microservices, the application layer may be implemented as a separate library project and would contain just DDD queries, commands, command handlers, and event handlers. While, the MVC project would contain just controllers, UIs, and dependency injection.

The application uses the **Command Query Responsibility Segregation** (**CQRS**) pattern; therefore, it uses command objects to modify the storage and the query object to query it.

The query is simple to use and implement: controllers fill their parameters and then call their execution methods. In turn, query objects have direct LINQ implementations that project results directly onto the ViewModels used by the controller Views with `Select` LINQ methods. You may also decide to hide the LINQ implementation behind the same repository classes used for the storage update operations, but this would turn the definition and modification of simple queries into very time-consuming tasks.

In any case, it can be beneficial to encapsulate query objects behind interfaces so that their implementations can be replaced by fake implementations when you test controllers.

However, the chain of objects and calls involved in the execution of commands is more complex. This is because it requires the construction and modification of aggregates (as well as a definition of the interaction between several aggregates and between aggregates and other applications through domain events) to be provided.

The following diagram is a sketch of how storage update operations are performed. The circles are data being exchanged between the various layers, while rectangles are the procedures that process them. Moreover, dotted arrows connect interfaces with types that implement them:

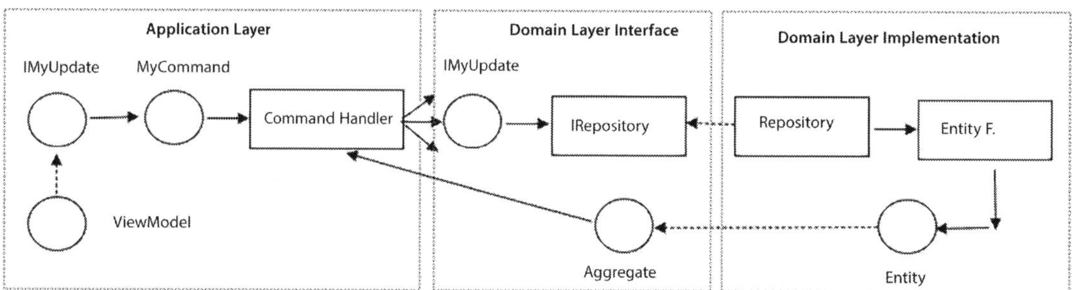

Figure 21.26: Diagram of command execution

Here's the flow of action through *Figure 21.26* as a list of steps:

1. A controller's action method receives one or more ViewModels and performs validation.
2. One or more ViewModels containing changes to apply are hidden behind interfaces (`IMyUpdate`) defined in the domain layer. They are used to fill the properties of a command object. These interfaces must be defined in the domain layer since they will be used as arguments of the repository aggregate methods defined there.
3. A command handler matching the previous command is retrieved via **Dependency Injection** (**DI**) in the controller action method (through the `[FromServices]` parameter attribute we described in the *Defining controllers and views* subsection). Then, the handler is executed. During its execution, the handler interacts with various repository interface methods and with the aggregates they return.

4. When creating the command handler discussed in *step 3*, the ASP.NET Core DI engine automatically injects all parameters declared in its constructor. In particular, it injects all repository implementations needed to perform all command handler transactions. The command handler performs its job by calling the methods of these `IRepository` implementations received in its constructor to build aggregates and modify the built aggregates. Aggregates either represent already-existing entities or newly created ones. Handlers use the `IUnitOfWork` interface contained in each repository interface, as well as the concurrency exceptions returned by the data layer, to organize their operations as transactions. It is worth pointing out that each aggregate has its own repository implementation, and that the whole logic for updating each aggregate is defined in the aggregate itself, not in its associated repository implementation, to keep the code more modular.
5. Behind the scenes, in the domain layer implementation, repository implementations use Entity Framework to perform their job. Aggregates are implemented by root data entities hidden behind interfaces defined in the domain layer, while `IUnitOfWork` methods, which handle transactions and pass changes to the database, are implemented with `DbContext` methods. In other words, `IUnitOfWork` is implemented with the application's `DbContext`.
6. Domain events are generated during each aggregate process and are added to the aggregates themselves by calling their `AddDomainEvent` methods. However, they are not triggered immediately. Usually, they are triggered at the end of all the aggregates' processing and before changes are passed to the database; however, this is not a general rule.
7. The application handles errors by throwing exceptions.

A more efficient approach would be to define a request-scoped object in the dependency engine, where each application subpart may add its errors as domain events. However, while this approach is more efficient, it increases the complexity of the code and the application development time.

The Visual Studio solution is composed of three projects:

- There's a project containing the domain layer abstraction called `PackagesManagementDomain`, which is a .NET Standard 2.1 library. When a library doesn't use features or NuGet packages that are specific to a .NET version, it is a good practice to implement it as a .NET Standard library because, this way, it doesn't need modifications when the application is moved to a newer .NET version.
- There's a project containing the whole domain layer implementation called `PackagesManagementDB`, which is a .NET 8.0 library.
- Finally, there's an ASP.NET Core MVC 8.0 project called `PackagesManagement` that contains both the application and presentation layers. When you define this project, select **No Authentication**; otherwise, the user database will be added directly to the ASP.NET Core MVC project instead of to the database layer. We will add the user database manually in the data layer.

Let's start by creating the `PackagesManagement` ASP.NET Core MVC project so that the whole solution has the same name as the ASP.NET Core MVC project. Then, we'll add the other two library projects to the same solution.

Finally, let the ASP.NET Core MVC project reference both projects, while `PackagesManagementDB` references `PackagesManagementDomain`. We suggest you define your own projects and then copy the code of this book's GitHub repository into them as you read this section.

The next subsection describes the code of the `PackagesManagementDomain` domain layer abstraction project.

Defining the domain layer abstraction

Once the `PackagesManagementDomain` Standard 2.1 library project has been added to the solution, we'll add a `Tools` folder to the project root. Then, we'll place all the `DomainLayer` tools contained in the code associated with `ch11`. Since the code contained in this folder uses data annotations and defines DI extension methods, we must also add references to the `System.ComponentModel.Annotations` and `Microsoft.Extensions.DependencyInjection.Abstration` NuGet packages.

Then, we need an `Aggregates` folder containing all the aggregate definitions (remember, we implemented aggregates as interfaces) – namely, `IDestination`, `IPackage`, and `IPackageEvent`. Here, `IPackageEvent` is the aggregate associated with the table where we will place events to be propagated to other applications.

As an example, let's analyze `IPackage`:

```
public interface IPackage : IEntity<int>
{
    void FullUpdate(IPackageFullEditDTO packageDTO);
    string Name { get; set; } = null!;
    string Description { get;} = null!;
    decimal Price { get; set; }
    int DurationInDays { get; }
    DateTime? StartValidityDate { get;}
    DateTime? EndValidityDate { get; }
    int DestinationId { get; }

}
```

It contains the same properties as the `Package` entity, which we saw in *Chapter 13, Interacting with Data in C# – Entity Framework Core*. The only differences are the following:

- It inherits from `IEntity<int>`, which furnishes all basic functionalities of aggregates
- It has no `Id` property since it is inherited from `IEntity<int>`
- All properties are read-only, and it has a `FullUpdate` method since all aggregates can only be modified through update operations defined in the user domain (in our case, the `FullUpdate` method)

Now, let's also add a `DTOs` folder. Here, we place all interfaces used to pass updates to the aggregates. Such interfaces are implemented by the application layer ViewModels used to define such updates.

In our case, it contains `IPackageFullEditDTO`, which we can use to update existing packages. If you would like to add the logic to manage destinations, you must define an analogous interface for the `IDestination` aggregate.

An `IRepositories` folder contains all repository specifications – namely, `IDestinationRepository`, `IPackageRepository`, and `IPackageEventRepository`. Here, `IPackageEventRepository` is the repository associated with the `IPackageEvent` aggregate. As an example, let's have a look at the `IPackageRepository` repository:

```
public interface IPackageRepository:
        IRepository<IPackage>
{
    Task<IPackage?> GetAsync(int id);
    IPackage New();
    Task<IPackage?> Delete(int id);
}
```

Repositories always contain just a few methods since all business logic should be represented as aggregate methods – in our case, just the methods to create a new package, to retrieve an existing package, and to delete an existing package. The logic to modify an existing package is included in the `FullUpdate` method of `IPackage`.

Finally, as with all domain layer projects, `PackagesManagementDomain` contains an `Events` folder containing all domain event definitions. In our case, the folder is named `Events` and contains the package-deleted event and the price-changed event:

```
public class PackageDeleteEvent: IEventNotification
{
    public PackageDeleteEvent(int id, long oldVersion)
    {
        PackageId = id;
        OldVersion = oldVersion;
    }
    public int PackageId { get; }
    public long OldVersion { get; }

}
public class PackagePriceChangedEvent: IEventNotification
{
    public PackagePriceChangedEvent(int id, decimal price,
        long oldVersion, long newVersion)
    {
            PackageId = id;
            NewPrice = price;
```

```
            OldVersion = oldVersion;
            NewVersion = newVersion;
        }
        public int PackageId { get; }
        public decimal NewPrice { get; }
        public long OldVersion { get; }
        public long NewVersion { get; }
    }
```

When an aggregate sends all its changes to another application, it should have a version property. The application that receives the changes uses this version property to apply all changes in the right order. An explicit version number is necessary because changes are sent asynchronously, so the order in which they are received may differ from the order in which they were sent. For this purpose, events that are used to publish changes outside of the application have both `OldVersion` (the version before the change) and `NewVersion` (the version after the change) properties. Events associated with delete events have no `NewVersion` since, after being deleted, an entity can't store any versions.

For more details on how to use and process version information to restore the right order of incoming messages, please refer to the *A worker microservice with ASP.NET Core* section of this chapter.

The next subsection explains how all interfaces defined in the domain layer abstraction are implemented in the domain layer implementation.

Defining the domain layer implementation

The data layer project contains references to the `Microsoft.AspNetCore.Identity.EntityFrameworkCore` and `Microsoft.EntityFrameworkCore.SqlServer` NuGet packages, since we are using Entity Framework Core with SQL Server. It references `Microsoft.EntityFrameworkCore.Tools` and `Microsoft.EntityFrameworkCore.Design`, which are needed to generate database migrations, as explained in the *Entity Framework Core migrations* section of *Chapter 13, Interacting with Data in C# – Entity Framework Core*.

We have a `Models` folder that contains all database entities. They are similar to the ones in *Chapter 13, Interacting with Data in C# – Entity Framework Core*. The only differences are as follows:

- They inherit from `Entity<T>`, which contains all the basic features of aggregates. Please note that inheriting from `Entity<T>` is only needed for aggregate roots; all other entities must be defined as explained in *Chapter 7, Understanding the Different Domains in Software Solutions*. In our example, all entities are aggregate roots.
- They have no `Id` since it is inherited from `Entity<T>`.
- Some of them have an `EntityVersion` property that is decorated with the `[ConcurrencyCheck]` attribute. It contains the entity version, which is essential for propagating all entity changes to other applications. The `ConcurrencyCheck` attribute is needed to prevent concurrency errors while updating the entity version. This prevents suffering the performance penalty implied by a transaction.

More specifically, when saving entity changes, if the value of a field marked with the ConcurrencyCheck attribute is different from the one that was read when the entity was loaded in memory, a concurrency exception is thrown to inform the calling method that someone else modified this value after the entity was read but before we attempted to save its changes. This way, the calling method can repeat the whole operation with the hope that this time, no one will write the same entity in the database during its execution.

The only alternative to the ConcurrencyCheck attribute would be:

1. Start a transaction.
2. Read the interested aggregate.
3. Increment its EntityVersion property.
4. Update the aggregate.
5. Save all changes.
6. Close the transaction.

The transaction duration would be unacceptably long since the transaction should be maintained for the time of various database commands – namely, from the initial read to the final update – thus, preventing other requests from accessing the involved tables/records for too long a time.

On the contrary, by using the ConcurrencyCheck attribute, we open just a very short single-command transaction when the aggregate is saved to the database:

1. Read the interested aggregate.
2. Increment the value of the EntityVersion property.
3. Update the aggregate.
4. Save all changes with a fast single-command transaction.

It is worth analyzing the code of the Package entity:

```
public class Package: Entity<int>, IPackage
{
    public void FullUpdate(IPackageFullEditDTO o)
    {
        if (IsTransient())
        {
            Id = o.Id;
            DestinationId = o.DestinationId;
        }
        else
        {
            if (o.Price != this.Price)
                this.AddDomainEvent(new PackagePriceChangedEvent(
                        Id, o.Price, EntityVersion, EntityVersion+1));
        }
```

```
        Name = o.Name;
        Description = o.Description;
        Price = o.Price;
        DurationInDays = o.DurationInDays;
        StartValidityDate = o.StartValidityDate;
        EndValidityDate = o.EndValidityDate;
    }
    [MaxLength(128)]
    public string Name { get; set; }= null!;
    [MaxLength(128)]
    public string? Description { get; set; }
    public decimal Price { get; set; }
    public int DurationInDays { get; set; }
    public DateTime? StartValidityDate { get; set; }
    public DateTime? EndValidityDate { get; set; }
    public Destination MyDestination { get; set; }= null!;
    [ConcurrencyCheck]
    public long EntityVersion{ get; set; }
    public int DestinationId { get; set; }
}
```

The `FullUpdate` method is the only way to update the `IPackage` aggregate. When the price changes, add `PackagePriceChangedEvent` to the entity list of events.

The `MainDBContext.cs` file contains the database context definition. It doesn't inherit from `DbContext` but from the following predefined context class:

```
IdentityDbContext<IdentityUser<int>, IdentityRole<int>, int>
```

This context defines the user's tables needed for the authentication. In our case, we opted for the `IdentityUser<T>` standard and `IdentityRole<S>` for users and roles, respectively, and used integers for both the `T` and `S` entity keys. However, we may also use classes that inherit from `IdentityUser` and `IdentityRole` and then add further properties.

In the `OnModelCreating` method, we must call `base.OnModelCreating(builder)` in order to apply the configuration defined in `IdentityDbContext`.

`MainDBContext` implements `IUnitOfWork`. The following code shows the implementation of all methods that start, roll back, and commit a transaction:

```
public async Task StartAsync()
{
    await Database.BeginTransactionAsync();
}
public Task CommitAsync()
```

```
{
    Database.CommitTransaction();
    return Task.CompletedTask;
}
public Task RollbackAsync()
{
    Database.RollbackTransaction();
    return Task.CompletedTask;
}
```

However, they are rarely used by command classes in a distributed environment. This is because retrying the same operation until no concurrency exception is returned usually ensures better performance than transactions.

It is worth analyzing the implementation of the method that passes all changes applied to `DbContext` to the database:

```
public async Task<bool> SaveEntitiesAsync()
{
    try
    {
        return await SaveChangesAsync() > 0;
    }
    catch (DbUpdateConcurrencyException ex)
    {
        foreach (var entry in ex.Entries)
        {
            entry.State = EntityState.Detached;

        }
        throw;
    }
}
```

The preceding implementation just calls the `SaveChangesAsync` `DbContext` context method, which saves all changes to the database, but then it intercepts all concurrency exceptions and detaches all the entities involved in the concurrency error from the context. This way, the next time a command retries the whole failed operation, their updated versions will be reloaded from the database.

The `Repositories` folder contains all repository implementations. It is worth analyzing the implementation of the `IPackageRepository.Delete` method:

```
public async Task<IPackage?> Delete(int id)
{
    var model = await GetAsync(id);
```

```
        if (model is not Package package) return null;
        context.Packages.Remove(package);
        model.AddDomainEvent(
            new PackageDeleteEvent(
                model.Id, package.EntityVersion));
        return model;
    }
```

It reads the entity from the database and formally removes it from the `Packages` dataset. This will force the entity to be deleted from the database when changes are saved to the database. Moreover, it adds `PackageDeleteEvent` to the aggregate list of events.

The `Extensions` folder contains the `DBExtensions` static class, which, in turn, defines two extension methods to be added to the application DI engine and the ASP.NET Core pipeline, respectively. Once added to the pipeline, these two methods will connect the database layer to the application layer.

The `IServiceCollection` extension of `AddDbLayer` accepts (as its input parameters) the database connection string and the name of the `.dll` file that contains all migrations. Then, it does the following:

```
services.AddDbContext<MainDbContext>(options =>
                options.UseSqlServer(connectionString,
                b => b.MigrationsAssembly(migrationAssembly)));
```

That is, it adds the database context to the DI engine and defines its options – namely, that it uses SQL Server, the database connection string, and the name of the `.dll` file that contains all migrations.

Then, it does the following:

```
services.AddIdentity<IdentityUser<int>, IdentityRole<int>>()
                .AddEntityFrameworkStores<MainDbContext>()
                .AddDefaultTokenProviders();
```

That is, it adds and configures all the types needed to handle database-based authentication and authorization. It adds `UserManager`, which the application layer can use to manage users. `AddDefaultTokenProviders` adds the provider that creates the authentication tokens using data contained in the database when users log in.

Finally, it discovers and adds to the DI engine all repository implementations by calling the `AddAllRepositories` method, which is defined in the DDD tools we added to the domain layer project.

The `UseDBLayer` extension method ensures migrations are applied to the database by calling `context.Database.Migrate()`, and then it populates the database with some initial objects. In our case, it uses `RoleManager` and `UserManager` to create an administrative role and an initial administrator, respectively. Then, it creates some sample destinations and packages.

`context.Database.Migrate()` is useful to quickly set up and update staging and test environments. When deploying in production, if we don't have the credentials for creating a new database or for modifying its structure, we can also produce an SQL script from the migrations using the migration tools. Then, this script should be examined before being applied by the person in charge of maintaining the database and, finally, applied with their credentials.

To create migrations, we must add the aforementioned extension methods to the ASP.NET Core MVC `Program.cs` file, as shown here:

```
...
builder.Services.AddRazorPages();
builder.Services.AddDbLayer(
    builder.Configuration.GetConnectionString("DefaultConnection"),
    "PackagesManagementDB");
...
app.UseAuthentication();
app.UseAuthorization();
...
```

Please be sure that both the authorization and authentication middleware have been added to the ASP.NET Core pipeline in the right order; otherwise, the authentication/authorization engine will not work.

Then, we must add the connection string to the `appsettings.json` file, as shown here:

```
{
    "ConnectionStrings": {
        "DefaultConnection": "Server=(localdb)\\mssqllocaldb;Database=package-
management;Trusted_Connection=True;MultipleActiveResultSets=true"

    },
    ...
}
```

Finally, let's add `Microsoft.EntityFrameworkCore.Design` to the ASP.NET Core project.

At this point, let's open the Visual Studio Package Manager Console, select `PackageManagementDB` as the default project, and then launch the following command:

```
Add-Migration Initial -Project PackageManagementDB
```

The preceding command will scaffold the first migration. We may apply it to the database with the `Update-Database` command. Please note that if you copy the project from GitHub, you don't need to scaffold migrations since they have already been created, but you still need to update the database.

In the next subsection, we will define the application layer that contains the business logic for manipulating the aggregates.

Defining the application layer

As a first step, for simplicity, let's freeze the application culture to `en-US` by adding the following code to the ASP.NET Core pipeline:

```
app.UseAuthorization();
// Code to add: configure the Localization middleware
var ci = new CultureInfo("en-US");
app.UseRequestLocalization(new RequestLocalizationOptions
{
    DefaultRequestCulture = new RequestCulture(ci),
    SupportedCultures = new List<CultureInfo>
    {
        ci,
    },
     SupportedUICultures = new List<CultureInfo>
    {
        ci,
    }
});
```

Then, let's create a `Tools` folder and place the `ApplicationLayer` code there, which you can find in the `ch11` code of the GitHub repository associated with this book. With these tools in place, we can add the code that automatically discovers and adds all queries, command handlers, and event handlers to the DI engine, as shown here:

```
...
...
builder.Services.AddAllQueries(this.GetType().Assembly);
builder.Services.AddAllCommandHandlers(this.GetType().Assembly);
builder.Services.AddAllEventHandlers(this.GetType().Assembly);
```

Then, we must add a `Queries` folder to place all queries and their associated interfaces. As an example, let's have a look at the query that lists all packages:

```
public class PackagesListQuery(MainDbContext ctx) :IPackagesListQuery
{
    public async Task<IReadOnlyCollection<PackageInfosViewModel>>
GetAllPackages()
    {
        return await ctx.Packages.Select(m => new PackageInfosViewModel
        {
            StartValidityDate = m.StartValidityDate,
            EndValidityDate = m.EndValidityDate,
```

```
            Name = m.Name,
            DurationInDays = m.DurationInDays,
            Id = m.Id,
            Price = m.Price,
            DestinationName = m.MyDestination.Name,
            DestinationId = m.DestinationId
        })
            .OrderByDescending(m=> m.EndValidityDate)
            .ToListAsync();
    }
}
```

The query object is automatically injected into the application DB context. The `GetAllPackages` method uses LINQ to project all of the required information into `PackageInfosViewModel` and sorts all results in descending order on the `EndValidityDate` property.

Projections that involve several properties are time-wasting and error-prone; that's why there are mapping libraries that automatically generate these projections using naming conventions and configuration settings. Mapping libraries helps also in copying data from one object to another, such as, for example, from a ViewModel to a DTO, and vice versa.

Among all mapping software, it is worth at least mentioning AutoMapper (`https://www.nuget.org/packages/AutoMapper`).

`PackageInfosViewModel` is placed in the `Models` folder together with all other ViewModels. It is common practice to organize ViewModels into folders by defining a different folder for each controller. It is worth analyzing the ViewModel used for editing packages:

```
public class PackageFullEditViewModel: IPackageFullEditDTO
    {
        public PackageFullEditViewModel() { }
        public PackageFullEditViewModel(IPackage o)
        {
            Id = o.Id;
            DestinationId = o.DestinationId;
            Name = o.Name;
            Description = o.Description;
            Price = o.Price;
            DurationInDays = o.DurationInDays;
            StartValidityDate = o.StartValidityDate;
            EndValidityDate = o.EndValidityDate;
        }
        ...
        ...
```

It has a constructor that accepts an `IPackage` aggregate. This way, package data is copied into the ViewModel that is used to populate the edit view. It implements the `IPackageFullEditDTO` DTO interface defined in the domain layer. This way, it can be directly used to send `IPackage` updates to the domain layer.

All properties contain validation attributes that are automatically used by client-side and server-side validation engines. Each property contains a `Display` attribute that defines the label to give to the input field that will be used to edit the property. It is better to place the field labels in the ViewModels than it is to place them directly into the views since, this way, the same names are automatically used in all views that use the same ViewModel. The following code block lists all its properties:

```
public int Id { get; set; }
[StringLength(128, MinimumLength = 5), Required]
[Display(Name = "name")]
public string Name { get; set; }= null!;
[Display(Name = "package infos")]
[StringLength(128, MinimumLength = 10), Required]
public string Description { get; set; }= null!;
[Display(Name = "price")]
[Range(0, 100000)]
public decimal Price { get; set; }
[Display(Name = "duration in days")]
[Range(1, 90)]
public int DurationInDays { get; set; }
[Display(Name = "available from"), Required]
public DateTime? StartValidityDate { get; set; }
[Display(Name = "available to"), Required]
public DateTime? EndValidityDate { get; set; }
[Display(Name = "destination")]
public int DestinationId { get; set; }
```

The `Commands` folder contains all commands. As an example, let's have a look at the command used to modify packages:

```
public class UpdatePackageCommand: ICommand
{
    public UpdatePackageCommand(IPackageFullEditDTO updates)
    {
        Updates = updates;
    }
    public IPackageFullEditDTO Updates { get; private set; }
}
```

Its constructor must be invoked with an implementation of the `IPackageFullEditDTO` DTO interface, which, in our case, is the edit ViewModel we described previously. Command handlers are placed in the `Handlers` folder. It is worth analyzing the command that updates packages:

```
public class UpdatePackageCommandHandler(IPackageRepository repo,
IEventMediator mediator)
```

Its principal constructor has automatically injected the `IPackageRepository` repository and an `IEventMediator` instance needed to trigger event handlers. The following code also shows the implementation of the standard `HandleAsync` command handler method:

```
public async Task HandleAsync(UpdatePackageCommand command)
{
    bool done = false;
    IPackage model;
    while (!done)
    {
        try
        {
            model = await repo.GetAsync(command.Updates.Id);
            if (model == null) return;
            model.FullUpdate(command.Updates);
            await mediator.TriggerEvents(model.DomainEvents);
            await repo.UnitOfWork.SaveEntitiesAsync();
            done = true;
        }
        catch (DbUpdateConcurrencyException)
        {
          // add some logging here
        }
    }
}
```

`HandleAsync` uses the repository to get an instance of the entity to modify. If the entity is not found (it has been deleted), the commands stop its execution. Otherwise, all changes are passed to the retrieved aggregate. Immediately after the update, all events contained in the aggregate are triggered. In particular, if the price has changed, the event handler associated with the price change is executed. The concurrency check declared with the `[ConcurrencyCheck]` attribute on the `EntityVersion` property of the `Package` entity ensures that the package version is updated properly (by incrementing its previous version number by 1), as well as that the price-changed event is passed the right version numbers.

Also, event handlers are placed in the `Handlers` folder. As an example, let's have a look at the price-changed event handler:

```
public class PackagePriceChangedEventHandler( IPackageEventRepository repo) :
     IEventHandler<PackagePriceChangedEvent>
{
    public Task HandleAsync(PackagePriceChangedEvent ev)
    {
        repo.New(PackageEventType.CostChanged, ev.PackageId,
            ev.OldVersion, ev.NewVersion, ev.NewPrice);
      return Task.CompletedTask;
    }
}
```

The principal constructor has automatically injected the `IPackageEventRepository` repository, which handles the database table and all the events to send to other applications. The `HandleAsync` implementation simply calls the repository method, which adds a new `IPackageEvent` to a queue of events to be sent to other microservices.

The `IPackageEvent` records should be extracted by the above queue and sent to all interested microservices by a parallel task, which is not implemented in the GitHub code associated with this section. It can be implemented as a hosted service (thus inheriting from the `BackgroundService` class) and then added to the DI engine with a call such as `builder.Services.AddHostedService<MyHostedService>()`, as detailed in the *Using generic hosts* subsection of *Chapter 11, Applying a Microservice Architecture to Your Enterprise Application.*

We are almost finished! Just the presentation layer is missing, which, in the case of an MVC-based application, consists of controllers and views. The next subsection defines both controllers and views needed by our microservice.

Defining controllers and views

We need to add two more controllers to the one automatically scaffolded by Visual Studio – namely, `AccountController`, which takes care of user login/logout and registration, and `ManagePackageController`, which handles all package-related operations. It is enough to right-click on the `Controllers` folder and then select **Add | Controller**. Then, choose the controller name and select the empty MVC controller to avoid the possibility of Visual Studio scaffolding code you don't need.

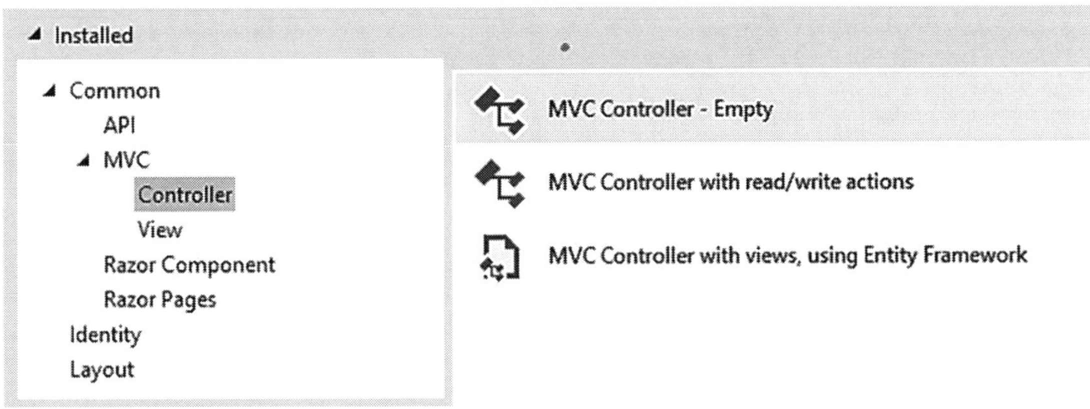

Figure 21.27: Adding AccountController

It is worth pointing out that Visual Studio can automatically scaffold all of the UI for managing users if one selects to automatically add authentication when the MVC project is created. However, scaffolded code doesn't respect any layer or onions architecture: it inserts everything in the MVC project. That's why we decided to proceed manually.

For simplicity, our implementation of `AccountController` just has login and logout methods, so you can log in just with the initial administrator user. However, you can add further action methods that use the `UserManager` class to define, update, and delete users.

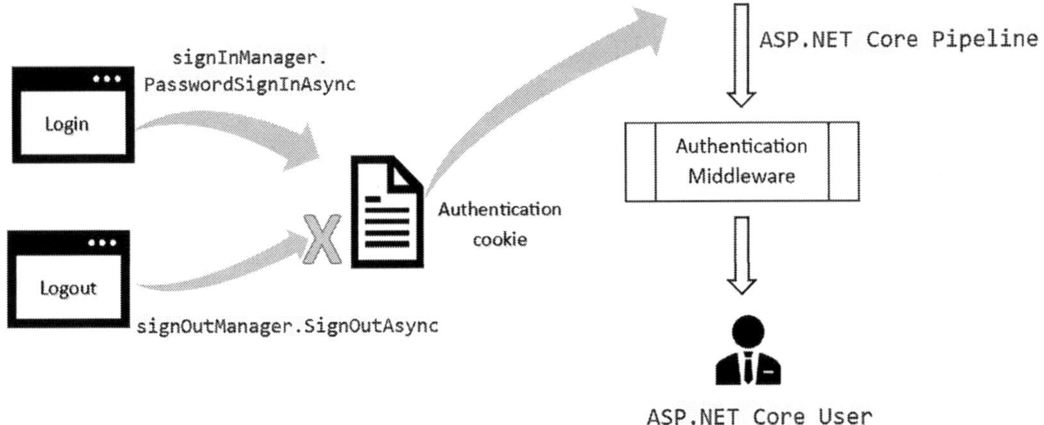

Figure 21.28: Login, logout, and authentication

The `UserManager` class can be provided through DI, as shown here:

```
public AccountController(
  UserManager<IdentityUser<int>> userManager,
  SignInManager<IdentityUser<int>> signInManager) : Controller
```

`SignInManager` takes care of login/logout operations. The `Logout` action method is quite simple and is shown here (for more information on authentication in ASP.NET Core, please refer to the *Defining the ASP.NET Core pipeline* section of *Chapter 17, Presenting ASP.NET Core*):

```
[HttpPost]
public async Task<IActionResult> Logout()
{
    await signInManager.SignOutAsync();
    return RedirectToAction(nameof(HomeController.Index), "Home");
}
```

It just calls the `signInManager.SignOutAsync` method and then redirects the browser to the home page. To avoid it being called by clicking a link, it is decorated with `HttpPost`, so it can only be invoked via a form submit.

All requests that cause modifications must never use a `GET` verb; otherwise, someone might erroneously trigger those actions either by clicking a link or by writing the wrong URL in the browser. An action triggered by GET might also be exploited by a phishing website that might adequately "camouflage" a link that triggers a dangerous GET action. The GET verb should be used just for retrieving information.

Login, on the other hand, requires two action methods. The first one is invoked via `GET` and shows the login form, where the user must place their username and password. It is shown here:

```
[HttpGet]
public async Task<IActionResult> Login(string? returnUrl = null)
{
    // Clear the existing external cookie
    //to ensure a clean login process
    await HttpContext
        .SignOutAsync(IdentityConstants.ExternalScheme);
    ViewData["ReturnUrl"] = returnUrl;
    return View();
}
```

It receives `returnUrl` as its parameter when the browser is automatically redirected to the login page by the authorization module. This happens when an unlogged-in user tries to access a protected page. `returnUrl` is stored in the `ViewState` dictionary that is passed to the login view.

The form in the login view passes it back to the controller, together with the username and password when it is submitted, as shown in this code:

```
<form asp-route-returnurl="@ViewData["ReturnUrl"]" method="post">
...
</form>
```

The form post is intercepted by an action method with the same `Login` name but decorated with the `[HttpPost]` attribute, as shown here:

```
[ValidateAntiForgeryToken]
public async Task<IActionResult> Login(
    LoginViewModel model,
    string? returnUrl = null)
        {
            ...
```

The preceding method receives the `Login` model used by the login view, together with the `returnUrl` query string parameter. The `ValidateAntiForgeryToken` attribute verifies a token (called an anti-forgery token) that MVC forms automatically. This is then added to a hidden field to prevent XSRF/CSRF attacks.

Forgery attacks exploit authentication cookies stored in the victim's browser to submit a legitimate authenticated request to a web application. They do this by inducing the user to click a button on a phishing website that causes a submit to the target web application. The fraudulent request is accepted since, once a form is submitted, the authentication cookies for the target URL are automatically sent by the browser. There are just two defenses against this kind of attack:

- Authentication cookies are defined as same-origin – that is, they are sent from other domains just in case of GET requests. Thus, when a form is submitted from a phishing website to the target application, they are not sent.
- Anti-forgery tokens added to forms. In this case, if authentication cookies are sent together with the submitted form, the application understands that the request comes from a different website and blocks it since it is missing a valid anti-forgery token.

As a first step, the action method logs the user out if they are already logged in:

```
if (User.Identity.IsAuthenticated)
{
     await signInManager.SignOutAsync();

}
```

Otherwise, it verifies whether there are validation errors, in which case, it shows the same view filled with the data of the ViewModel to let the user correct their errors:

```
if (ModelState.IsValid)
{
    ...
}
else
 // If we got this far, something failed, redisplay form
 return View(model);
```

If the model is valid, `signInManager` is used to log the user in:

```
var result = await signInManager.PasswordSignInAsync(
    model.UserName,
    model.Password, model.RememberMe,
    lockoutOnFailure: false);
```

If the result returned by the operation is successful, the action method redirects the browser to `returnUrl` if it's not null; otherwise, it redirects the browser to the home page:

```
if (result.Succeeded)
{
    if (!string.IsNullOrEmpty(returnUrl))
        return LocalRedirect(returnUrl);
    else
        return RedirectToAction(nameof(HomeController.Index), "Home");
}
else
{
    ModelState.AddModelError(string.Empty,
        "wrong username or password");
    return View(model);
}
```

If the login fails, it adds an error to `ModelState` and shows the same form to let the user try again.

`ManagePackagesController` contains an `Index` method that shows all packages in table format (for more details on controllers, views, and the MVC pattern in general, please refer to the *The MVC pattern* section of *Chapter 17, Presenting ASP.NET Core*):

```
[HttpGet]
public async Task<IActionResult> Index(
    [FromServices] IPackagesListQuery query)
{
```

```
    var results = await query.GetAllPackages();
    var vm = new PackagesListViewModel { Items = results };
    return View(vm);
}
```

The query object is injected into the action method by DI. Then, the action method invokes it and inserts the resulting `IEnumerable` into the `Items` property of a `PackagesListViewModel` instance. It is a good practice to include `IEnumerables` in ViewModels instead of passing them directly to the views so that, if necessary, other properties can be added without the need to modify the existing view code.

Moreover, it is good practice to define enumerable properties of ViewModels as `IReadOnlyCollection<T>` if the enumerables are read-only or as `IList<T>` if the enumerables can be modified or if they are involved in model binding. In fact, `ICollection<T>` has a `Count` property, which may be very useful when rendering ViewModels in views, while `IList<T>` also has indexers that are necessary for rendering all items with appropriate names for model binding to succeed (see this Phil Haack post: `http://haacked.com/archive/2008/10/23/model-binding-to-a-list.aspx`). `IEnumerable<T>` should be preferred only in the case that one needs the typical lazy evaluation of `IEnumerable<T>`.

The results are shown in a Bootstrap table since Bootstrap CSS is automatically scaffolded by Visual Studio. Bootstrap is a good choice for a CSS framework, since it is quite simple and extensible, and is not connected to any particular company but is handled by an independent team.

The result is shown here:

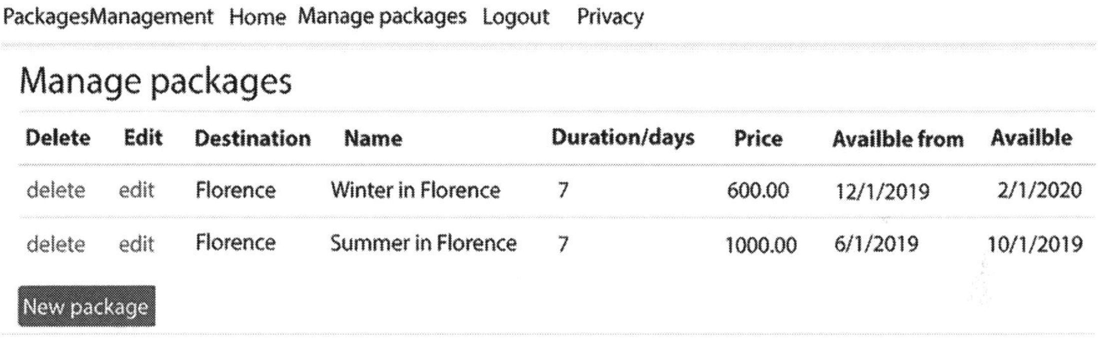

PackagesManagement Home Manage packages Logout Privacy

Manage packages

Delete	Edit	Destination	Name	Duration/days	Price	Availble from	Availble
delete	edit	Florence	Winter in Florence	7	600.00	12/1/2019	2/1/2020
delete	edit	Florence	Summer in Florence	7	1000.00	6/1/2019	10/1/2019

New package

Figure 21.29: Application packages handling page

The **New package** link (it is shaped like a **Bootstrap** button, but it is a link) invokes a controller `Create` action method, while the **delete** and **edit** links in each row invoke a `Delete` and `Edit` action method, respectively, and pass them the ID of the package shown in the row.

Here is the implementation of the two row links:

```
@foreach(var package in Model.Items)
{
<tr>
    <td>
        <a asp-controller="ManagePackages"
```

```
                asp-action="@nameof(ManagePackagesController.Delete)"
                asp-route-id="@package.Id">
                delete
            </a>
        </td>
        <td>
            <a asp-controller="ManagePackages"
                asp-action="@nameof(ManagePackagesController.Edit)"
                asp-route-id="@package.Id">
                edit
            </a>
        </td>
        ...
        ...
```

It is worth describing the code of the `HttpGet` and `HttpPost` `Edit` action methods:

```
[HttpGet]
public async Task<IActionResult> Edit(
    int id,
    [FromServices] IPackageRepository repo)
{
    if (id == 0) return RedirectToAction(
        nameof(ManagePackagesController.Index));
    var aggregate = await repo.Get(id);
    if (aggregate == null) return RedirectToAction(
        nameof(ManagePackagesController.Index));
    var vm = new PackageFullEditViewModel(aggregate);
    return View(vm);
}
```

The `Edit` method of `HttpGet` uses `IPackageRepository` to retrieve the existing package. If the package is not found, that means it has been deleted by some other user, and the browser is redirected again to the list page to show the updated list of packages. Otherwise, the aggregate is passed to the `PackageFullEditViewModel` ViewModel, which is rendered by the `Edit` view.

The view used to render the package must render an HTML `select` with all possible package destinations, so it needs an instance of the `IDestinationListQuery` query that was implemented to assist with the destination selection HTML logic. This query is injected directly into the view since it is the view's responsibility to decide how to enable the user to select a destination. The code that injects the query and uses it is shown here:

```
@inject PackagesManagement.Queries.IDestinationListQuery destinationsQuery
@{
```

```
    ViewData["Title"] = "Edit/Create package";
    var allDestinations =
        await destinationsQuery.AllDestinations();
}
```

The action method that processes the post of the view form is given here:

```
[HttpPost]
public async Task<IActionResult> Edit(
    PackageFullEditViewModel vm,
    [FromServices] ICommandHandler<UpdatePackageCommand> command)
{
    if (ModelState.IsValid)
    {
        await command.HandleAsync(new UpdatePackageCommand(vm));
        return RedirectToAction(
            nameof(ManagePackagesController.Index));
    }
    else
        return View(vm);
}
```

If `ModelState` is valid, `UpdatePackageCommand` is created and its associated handler is invoked; otherwise, the View is displayed again to the user to enable them to correct all the errors.

The new links to the package list page and login page must be added to the main menu, which is in the `_Layout` view, as shown here:

```
@if (User.Identity.IsAuthenticated)
{
     <li class="nav-item">
              <a class="nav-link text-dark"
                     asp-controller="ManagePackages"
                            asp-action="Index">Manage packages</a>
     </li>

     <li class="nav-item">
        <a class="nav-link text-dark"
            href="javascript:document.getElementById('logoutForm').submit()">
            Logout
        </a>
    </li>
}
else
```

```
{
    <li class="nav-item">
        <a class="nav-link text-dark"
            asp-controller="Account" asp-action="Login">Login</a>
    </li>
}
```

logoutForm is an empty form whose only purpose is to send a post to the Logout action method. It has been added to the end of the body, as shown here:

```
@if (User.Identity.IsAuthenticated)
{
    <form asp-area="" asp-controller="Account"
            asp-action="Logout" method="post"
            id="logoutForm" ></form>
}
```

Now, the application is ready! You can run it, log in, and start to manage packages.

After having learned how to implement, in practice, a presentation layer with server-side technologies in this section, we now just need to learn how to implement it also with client-side technologies. We will do this in the next section.

Using client technologies

In this section, we will implement a package search application for the WWTravelClub book use case. The first subsection explains how to set up the solution exploiting the domain layer and data layer of the MVC application we implemented in the previous section of this chapter.

Preparing the solution

We will modify the PackagesManagement project both to save coding time and to show how to transform a solution based on server-side MVC technology into a solution based on the Blazor client-side technology.

First of all, create a copy of the PackagesManagement solution folder we created in the previous section and rename it PackagesManagementBlazor.

To open the solution, right-click on the web project (the one named PackagesManagement) and remove it (the Remove menu item). Then, go to the solution folder and delete the whole web project folder (the one named PackagesManagement).

Now, right-click on the solution and select **Add New Project**. Add a new **Blazor WebAssembly Standalone App** project called PackagesManagementBlazor.Client. Select **None** for the authentication type, **Configure for https**, and **Include Sample Pages**. We don't need authentication since the search-by-location feature we are going to implement must also be available to unregistered users.

Now, add a `PackagesManagementBlazor.Server` **ASP.NET Core Web API** project. Select **None** for the authentication type, **Configure for https**, **Enable OpenAPI Support**, and **Use Controllers**.

Finally, add a `PackagesManagementBlazor.Shared` **Class Library** project, delete the default `Class1` class created by Visual Studio, and add this project to both `PackagesManagementBlazor.Client` and `PackagesManagementBlazor.Server` as reference.

The server project needs to reference both the domain implementation (`PackagesManagementDB`) and the domain abstraction (`PackagesManagementDomain`) projects, so please add them as references.

Both `PackagesManagementBlazor.Client` and `PackagesManagementBlazor.Server` must start simultaneously, so define them as starting projects by right-clicking on the solutions, selecting **Configure Startup Projects**, and choosing them as startup projects.

Now, launch the solution to verify that everything works properly. Two browser windows should open, one for testing the REST API project and the other containing a Blazor application.

Take note of the Blazor application URL (`https://localhost:7027/` in my case) since we will need it.

The Blazor website will exchange data with the REST API website, which runs on a different domain (a domain is identified by both hostname and port number). REST API calls coming from browsers running on different domains are clues of potential phishing attacks; therefore, the receiving server only accepts them if they come from well-known domains (this way, they are sure they don't come from phishing websites).

On the other hand, when a browser application tries to communicate with a different URL, the browser detects it and issues the call with a different protocol called CORS. Therefore, as soon as it detects the CORS protocol, the receiving server understands it is dealing with a request coming from a different website, and serves the request only if the other domain has been registered with a so-called CORS policy.

In ASP.NET Core, CORS policies are registered with the `builder.Services.AddCors` extension method in `Program.cs`.

Therefore, in our case, we need to register a CORS policy for the domain of the `PackagesManagementBlazor.Client` web application in the `PackagesManagementBlazor.Server` web application, since all REST API calls of `PackagesManagementBlazor.Client` will be issued to `PackagesManagementBlazor.Server`.

Accordingly, let's open `Program.cs` of the `PackagesManagementBlazor.Server` project and enable it for CORS by adding this:

```
builder.Services.AddCors(o => {
    o.AddDefaultPolicy(pbuilder =>
    {
        pbuilder.AllowAnyMethod();
        pbuilder.WithHeaders(HeaderNames.ContentType, HeaderNames.
Authorization);
        pbuilder.WithOrigins("https://localhost:7027/");
    });
});
```

Also, add `app.UseCors();` in the ASP.NET Core pipeline, immediately before `app.UseAuthorization();`.

Now, we must enable the Blazor application to communicate with this server. Launch the solution again and take note of the REST API URL (in my case, `https://localhost:7269/`), and then replace the URL in the `HttpClient` configuration in the `Program.cs` file of the Blazor application with this URL:

```
builder.Services.AddScoped(sp => new HttpClient {
 BaseAddress = new Uri("https://localhost:7269/")});
```

Let's also copy the same connection string of the old web project into the `PackagesManagementBlazor.Server` `appsettings.json` file:

```
"ConnectionStrings": {
        "DefaultConnection": "Server=(localdb)\\mssqllocaldb;Database=package-
management;Trusted_Connection=True;MultipleActiveResultSets=true"
 },
```

This way, we can reuse the database we have created. We also need to add the same DDD tools we added to the old web project. Add a folder named `Tools` in the project root and copy the contents of the `ch07` -> `ApplicationLayer` folder of the GitHub repository associated with the book there.

In order to finish the solution setup, we just need to connect `PackagesManagementBlazor.Server` with the domain layer by adding the following code at the end of the services configuration code in the `Program.cs` file:

```
builder.services.AddDbLayer(Configuration
                .GetConnectionString("DefaultConnection"),
                "PackagesManagementDB");
```

It is the same method we added to the old web project. Finally, we can also add the `AddAllQueries` extension method, which discovers all queries in the web project:

```
builder.services.AddAllQueries(this.GetType().Assembly);
```

We don't need other automatic discovery tools since this is a query-only application.

Due to a bug in Entity Framework Core 8, you also need to change a setting in the server project that prevents the usage of .NET culture. You must change the `InvariantGlobalization` project setting to `false`:

```
<InvariantGlobalization>false</InvariantGlobalization>
```

At this point, we have the project completely configured. We just need to implement server-side code and client-side code that implements our package search.

The next subsection explains how to design the server-side REST API.

Implementing the required ASP.NET Core REST APIs

As the first step, let's define the ViewModels used in the communication between the server and the client applications. They must be defined in the `PackagesManagementBlazor.Shared` project that is referenced by both applications.

Let's start with the `PackageInfosViewModel` ViewModel, which will be the data structure used by the Blazor application to exchange package info with the server-side REST API:

```
using System;
namespace PackagesManagementBlazor.Shared
{
    public class PackageInfosViewModel
    {
        public int Id { get; set; }
        public required string Name { get; set; }
        public decimal Price { get; set; }
        public int DurationInDays { get; set; }
        public DateTime? StartValidityDate { get; set; }
        public DateTime? EndValidityDate { get; set; }
        public required string DestinationName { get; set; }
        public int DestinationId { get; set; }
        public override string ToString()
        {
            return $"{Name}. {DurationInDays} days in {DestinationName}, price:
{Price}";
        }
    }
}
```

Then, add the ViewModel that encloses all packages to return to the Blazor application:

```
using System.Collections.Generic;
namespace PackagesManagementBlazor.Shared
{
    public class PackagesListViewModel
    {
        Public required ReadOnlyCollection<PackageInfosViewModel>
            Items { get; set; }
    }
}
```

Now, we can also add our query that searches packages by location. Let's add a `Queries` folder in the root of the `PackagesManagementBlazor.Server` project and then add the interface that defines our query, `IPackagesListByLocationQuery`:

```
using DDD.ApplicationLayer;
using PackagesManagementBlazor.Shared;
using System.Collections.Generic;
using System.Threading.Tasks;
```

```
namespace PackagesManagementBlazor.Server.Queries
{
    public interface IPackagesListByLocationQuery: IQuery
    {
        Task<ReadOnlyCollection<PackageInfosViewModel>>
            GetPackagesOf(string location);
    }
}
```

Finally, let's also add the query implementation:

```
public class PackagesListByLocationQuery(MainDbContext
ctx):IPackagesListByLocationQuery
{

    public async   Task<ReadOnlyCollection<PackageInfosViewModel>>
            GetPackagesOfAsync(string location)
    {
        Return new ReadOnlyCollection<PackageInfosViewModel>
     (await ctx.Packages
            .Where(m => m.MyDestination.Name.StartsWith(location))
            .Select(m => new PackageInfosViewModel
        {
            StartValidityDate = m.StartValidityDate,
            EndValidityDate = m.EndValidityDate,
            Name = m.Name,
            DurationInDays = m.DurationInDays,
            Id = m.Id,
            Price = m.Price,
            DestinationName = m.MyDestination.Name,
            DestinationId = m.DestinationId
        })
            .OrderByDescending(m=> m.EndValidityDate)
            .ToListAsync());
    }
}
```

We are finally ready to define our `PackagesController`:

```
using Microsoft.AspNetCore.Mvc;
using PackagesManagementBlazor.Server.Queries;
using PackagesManagementBlazor.Shared;
using System.Threading.Tasks;
```

```
namespace PackagesManagementBlazor.Server.Controllers
{
    [Route("[controller]")]
    [ApiController]
    public class PackagesController : ControllerBase
    {
        // GET api/<PackagesController>/Flor
        [HttpGet("{location}")]
        public async Task<PackagesListViewModel>
            GetAsync(string location,
            [FromServices] IPackagesListByLocationQuery query )
        {
            return new PackagesListViewModel
            {
                Items = await query.GetPackagesOf(location)
            };
        }
    }
}
```

The server-side code is finished! Let's move on to the definition of the Blazor service that communicates with the server.

Implementing the business logic in a service

Let's add a `ViewModels` and a `Services` folder to the `PackagesManagementBlazor.Client` project. Most of the ViewModels we need were defined in the **PackagesManagementBlazor.Shared** project. We only need a ViewModel for the search form. Let's add it to the `ViewModels` folder:

```
using System.ComponentModel.DataAnnotations;
namespace PackagesManagementBlazor.Client.ViewModels
{
    public class SearchViewModel
    {
        [Required]
        public string? Location { get; set; }
    }
}
```

Let's call our service `PackagesClient`, and let's add it to the `Services` folder:

```
namespace PackagesManagementBlazor.Client.Services
{
    public class PackagesClient
```

```
    {
        private HttpClient client;
        public PackagesClient(HttpClient client)
        {
            this.client = client;
        }
        public async Task<IEnumerable<PackageInfosViewModel>>
            GetByLocationAsync(string location)
        {
            var result =
                await client.GetFromJsonAsync<PackagesListViewModel>
                    ("Packages/" + Uri.EscapeDataString(location));
            return result.Items;
        }
    }
}
```

The code is straightforward! The `Uri.EscapeDataString` method URL-encodes the parameter so it can be safely appended to the URL.

Finally, let's register the service in the dependency injection:

```
builder.Services.AddScoped<PackagesClient>();
```

It is worth pointing out that in a commercial application, we should have registered the service through an `IPackagesClient` interface in order to be able to mock it in the tests (`.AddScoped<IPackagesClient, PackagesClient>()`).

With everything in place, we just need to build the UI.

Implementing the user interface

As the first step, let's delete the application pages we don't need – namely, `Pages->Counter.razor` and `Pages->Weather.razor`. Let's also remove their links from the side menu in `Shared` -> `NavMenu.razor`.

We will put our code in the `Pages` -> `Home.razor` page. Let's replace the code of this page with the following:

```
@using PackagesManagementBlazor.Client.ViewModels
@using PackagesManagementBlazor.Shared
@using PackagesManagementBlazor.Client.Services
@inject PackagesClient client
@page "/"
<h1>Search packages by location</h1>
<EditForm Model="search"
          OnValidSubmit="Search">
```

```
    <DataAnnotationsValidator />
    <div class="form-group">
      <label for="integerfixed">Insert location starting chars</label>
      <InputText @bind-Value="search.Location" />
      <ValidationMessage For="@(() => search.Location)" />
    </div>
    <button type="submit" class="btn btn-primary">
          Search
    </button>
</EditForm>
@code{
    SearchViewModel search { get; set; } = new SearchViewModel();
    async Task Search()
    {
        ...
    }
}
```

The preceding code adds the needed `@using` statements, injects our `PackagesClient` service into the page, and defines the search form. When the form is successfully submitted, it invokes the `Search` callback, where we will place the code that retrieves all the results.

It is time to add the logic to display all the results and to complete the `@code` block. The following code must be placed immediately after the search form:

```
@if (packages != null)
{
...
}
else if (loading)
{
    <p><em>Loading...</em></p>
}
@code{
    SearchViewModel search { get; set; } = new SearchViewModel();
    private IEnumerable<PackageInfosViewModel> packages;
    bool loading;
    async Task Search()
    {
        packages = null;
        loading = true;
        await InvokeAsync(StateHasChanged);
        packages = await client.GetByLocationAsync(search.Location);
```

```
            loading = false;
        }
    }
```

The omitted code in the `if` block is responsible for rendering a table with all the results. We will show it after having commented on the preceding code.

Before retrieving the results with the `PackagesClient` service, we remove all previous results and set the `loading` field so the Razor code selects the `else if` path that replaces the previous table with a loading message. Once we've set these variables, we are forced to call `StateHasChanged` to trigger change detection and refresh the page. After all the results have been retrieved and the callback returns, there is no need to call `StateHasChanged` again because the termination of the callback itself triggers change detection and causes the required page refresh.

Here is the code that renders the table with all the results:

```
<div class="table-responsive">
  <table class="table">
    <thead>
      <tr>
        <th scope="col">Destination</th>
        <th scope="col">Name</th>
        <th scope="col">Duration/days</th>
        <th scope="col">Price</th>
        <th scope="col">Available from</th>
        <th scope="col">Available to</th>
      </tr>
    </thead>
    <tbody>
      @foreach (var package in packages)
      {
        <tr>
          <td>
            @package.DestinationName
          </td>
          <td>
            @package.Name
          </td>
          <td>
            @package.DurationInDays
          </td>
          <td>
            @package.Price
          </td>
```

```
            <td>
              @(package.StartValidityDate.HasValue ?
                package.StartValidityDate.Value.ToString("d")
                :
                String.Empty)
            </td>
            <td>
              @(package.EndValidityDate.HasValue ?
                package.EndValidityDate.Value.ToString("d")
                :
                String.Empty)
            </td>
          </tr>
        }
      </tbody>
    </table>
  </div>
```

Run the project and write the initial characters of Florence. Since we inserted Florence as a location in the same database in previous chapters (see the *Querying and updating data with Entity Framework Core* section of *Chapter 13, Interacting with Data in C# – Entity Framework Core*), some results should appear. If you inserted different data, please try with different starting words.

Usually, together with web-based clients, all applications also furnish mobile-native applications to get a better performance with possibly slow mobile devices. So, let's also design a mobile-native client application!

Adding a Blazor MAUI version

In this section, we explain how to add a Blazor MAUI version to the application of the previous solution.

First of all, right-click on the solution icon in Solution Explorer and add a new project to the solution. Select a MAUI Blazor application and call it `PackagesManagementMAUIBlazor`.

Open the `PackagesManagementMAUIBlazor` project file and remove all the platforms you don't want to support (I removed Android, iOS, and Mac Catalyst, and kept only Windows):

```
<TargetFrameworks> Condition="$([MSBuild]::IsOSPlatform('windows'))">$(TargetFr
ameworks);net8.0-windows10.0.19041.0 </TargetFrameworks>
```

Then, add a reference to the `PackagesManagementBlazor.Shared` project.

Now, right-click on the client WebAssembly project and select **Open Folder in File Explorer**. Then, copy the `ViewModels` and `Services` folders, and paste them in Visual Studio Solution Explorer under the newly created `PackagesManagementMAUIBlazor` node.

Then, change the namespaces of the files contained in these folders to be, respectively, `PackagesManagementMAUIBlazor.ViewModels` and `PackagesManagementMAUIBlazor.Services`.

Now, replace the content of the `Shared` and `Pages` folders of the newly created project with the content of the `Layout` and `Pages` folders of the client Blazor WebAssembly project.

Edit the newly copied `Home.razor` file and replace its header with:

```
@using PackagesManagementMAUIBlazor.Services
@using PackagesManagementBlazor.Shared
@using PackagesManagementMAUIBlazor.ViewModels
@inject PackagesClient client
@page "/"
```

Finally, add the same `HttpClient` and `PackagesClient` configurations of the WebAssembly project to `MAUIProgram.cs`:

```
builder.Services.AddScoped(sp => new HttpClient
    { BaseAddress = new Uri("https://localhost:7269/") });
builder.Services.AddScoped<PackagesClient>();
```

With this, you must add `PackagesManagementMAUIBlazor` to the projects to start. Right-click on the solution and select **Configure Startup Projects**.

In the windows that open, select also the newly created MAUI Blazor project.

Now, you can launch the application. Three windows should open (two browser windows and a Windows window) but both client project windows should show exactly the same application.

After having discussed all the components of our WWTravelClub application, we need just to describe how to test it.

Testing the WWTravelClub application

In this section, we add some unit and functional test projects to the `PackagesManagement` frontend microservice we described in the *A frontend microservice* section of this chapter. If you don't have it, you can download it from the section of the GitHub repository associated with the book in the `ch19` folder. It is worth pointing out that in real-world projects, unit test batteries are enhanced by integration tests, and acceptance tests would include not only functional tests but also various kinds of performance tests.

You are encouraged to review *Chapter 9*, *Testing Your Enterprise Application*, before continuing with this section.

As a first step, let's make a new copy of the solution folder and name it `PackagesManagementWithTests`. Then, open the solution and add it to an xUnit .NET C# test project named `PackagesManagementTest`. Finally, add a reference to the ASP.NET Core project (`PackagesManagement`), since we will test it, and a reference to the latest version of the `Moq NuGet` package, since we require mocking capabilities.

It is worth remembering that Moq is a mocking library and that the purpose of mocking is to decouple dependencies between classes by replacing actual classes with mocked classes whose behavior is under the complete control of the test code. This way, each class can be unit tested independently from the behavior of other classes it references. For more details about Moq, please refer to *Chapter 9, Testing Your Enterprise Application*.

At this point, we are ready to write our tests.

As an example, we will write unit tests for the `Edit` method decorated with `[HttpPost]` of the `ManagePackagesController` controller, which is shown as follows:

```
[HttpPost]
public async Task<IActionResult> Edit(
    PackageFullEditViewModel vm,
    [FromServices] ICommandHandler<UpdatePackageCommand> command)
{
    if (ModelState.IsValid)
    {
        await command.HandleAsync(
            new  UpdatePackageCommand(vm));
        return RedirectToAction(
            nameof(ManagePackagesController.Index));
    }
    else
        return View(vm);
}
```

Before writing our test methods, let's rename the test class that was automatically included in the test project as `ManagePackagesControllerTests`.

The first test verifies that if there are errors in `ModelState`, the action method renders a view with the same model it received as an argument so that the user can correct all errors. We need to test all possibilities. Let's delete the existing test method and write an empty `DeletePostValidationFailedTest` method, as follows:

```
[Fact]
public async Task DeletePostValidationFailedTest()
{
}
```

The method must be async and the return type must be Task since the Edit method that we have to test is async. In this test, we don't need mocked objects since no injected object will be used. Thus, as a preparation for the test, we just need to create a controller instance, and we must add an error to ModelState as follows:

```
var controller = new ManagePackagesController();
controller.ModelState
    .AddModelError("Name", "fake error");
```

Then, we invoke the method, injecting ViewModel and a null command handler as its arguments, since the command handler will not be used:

```
var vm = new PackageFullEditViewModel();
var commandDependency =
                new Mock<ICommandHandler<UpdatePackageCommand>>();
var result = await controller.Edit(vm, commandDependency.Object);
```

In the verification stage, we verify that the result is ViewResult and that it contains the same model that was injected into the controller:

```
var viewResult = Assert.IsType<ViewResult>(result);
Assert.Equal(vm, viewResult.Model);
```

Now, we also need a test to verify that if there are no errors, the command handler is called, and then the browser is redirected to the Index controller action method. We call the DeletePostSuccessTest method:

```
[Fact]
public async Task DeletePostSuccessTest()
{
}
```

This time, the preparation code must include the preparation of a command handler mock, as follows:

```
var controller = new ManagePackagesController();
var commandDependency =
    new Mock<ICommandHandler<UpdatePackageCommand>>();
commandDependency
    .Setup(m =>
     m.HandleAsync(It.IsAny<UpdatePackageCommand>()))
    .Returns(Task.CompletedTask);
var vm = new PackageFullEditViewModel();
```

Since the handler HandleAsync method returns no async value, we can't use ReturnsAsync, but we have to return just a completed Task (Task.Complete) with the Returns method. The method to test is called with both ViewModel and the mocked handler:

```
var result = await controller.Edit(vm,
    commandDependency.Object);
```

In this case, the verification code is as follows:

```
commandDependency.Verify(m => m.HandleAsync(
    It.IsAny<UpdatePackageCommand>()),
    Times.Once);
var redirectResult = Assert.IsType<RedirectToActionResult>(result);
Assert.Equal(nameof(ManagePackagesController.Index),
    redirectResult.ActionName);
Assert.Null(redirectResult.ControllerName);
```

As the first step, we verify that the command handler has actually been invoked once. A better verification should also include a check that it was invoked with a command that includes `ViewModel` passed to the action method. We will take it up as an exercise.

Then we verify that the action method returns `RedirectToActionResult` with the right action method name and with no controller name specified.

Once all the tests are ready, if the test window does not appear on the left bar of Visual Studio, we may simply select the **Run all tests** item from the Visual Studio **Test** menu. Once the test window appears, further invocations can be launched from within this window.

If a test fails, we can add a breakpoint to its code, so we can launch a debug session on it by right-clicking on it in the test window and then selecting **Debug selected tests**. It is worth remembering that failures do not depend necessarily on errors in the code under test but might also depend on errors in the testing code itself.

In the next subsection, we will show how to upload our code to a shared Azure DevOps repository and how to automatize our tests with an Azure DevOps pipeline.

Connecting to an Azure DevOps repository

Tests play a fundamental role in the application CI/CD cycle, specifically in CI. They must be executed at least each time the master branch of the application repository is modified to verify that changes don't introduce bugs.

The following steps show how to connect our solution to an Azure DevOps repository, where we will define an Azure DevOps pipeline that builds the project, and that also launches all the unit tests we defined in the `PackagesManagementTest` project at each build.

However, the functional tests that we defined in the `PackagesManagementFTest` project must be executed only before a sprint is released. Therefore, they must be placed in a different pipeline that takes care of delivering the application.

In this way, every day after all developers have pushed their changes, we can launch the pipeline to verify that the repository code compiles and passes all the unit tests:

1. As a first step, we need a free DevOps subscription. If you don't already have one, please create one by clicking the **Start free** button on this page: `https://azure.microsoft.com/en-us/services/devops/`. Here, let's follow the wizard to define an organization and then a project.
2. On the project page, select the **Files** menu, click on the **Repos** menu item, and then copy the repository URL:

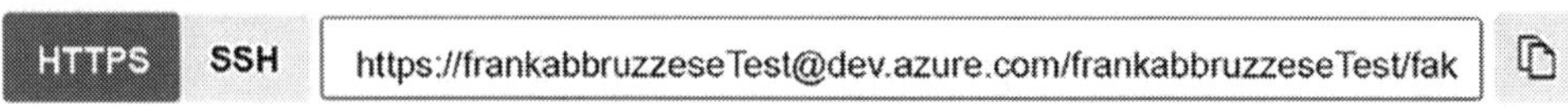

Figure 21.30: Copying the repository URL

3. Ensure you are logged in to Visual Studio with your Azure account (the same one used in the creation of the DevOps account). In the **Git Changes** tab, click the **Create Git Repository...** button:

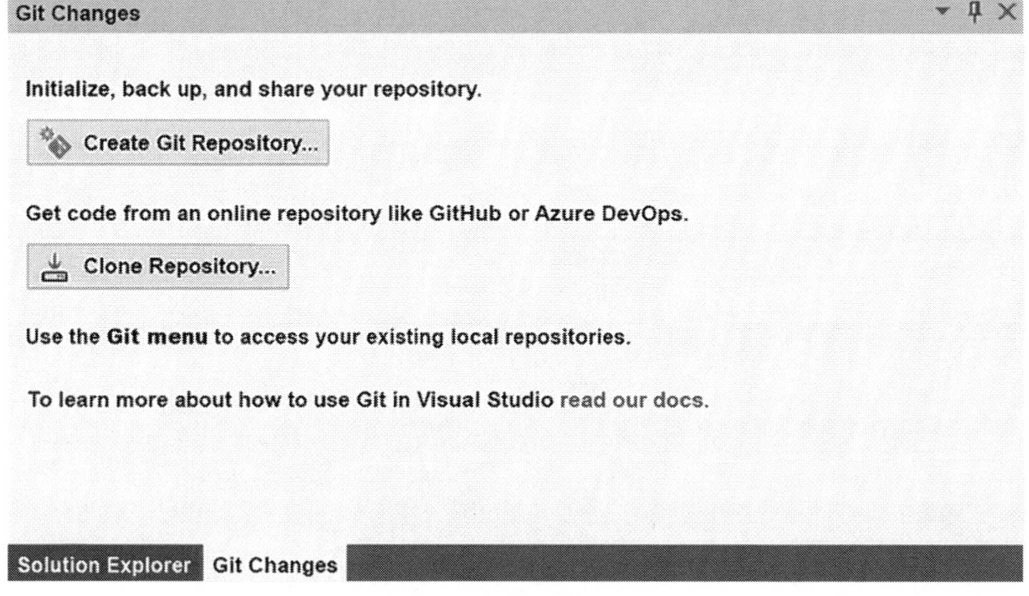

Figure 21.31: Opening the connection window

4. In the window that opens, select **Existing remote** from the left menu and copy and paste the remote repository URL:

Figure 21.32: Connection window

5. Then, click the **Create and Push** button and wait until the ready icon in the bottom-left corner of Visual Studio is checked:

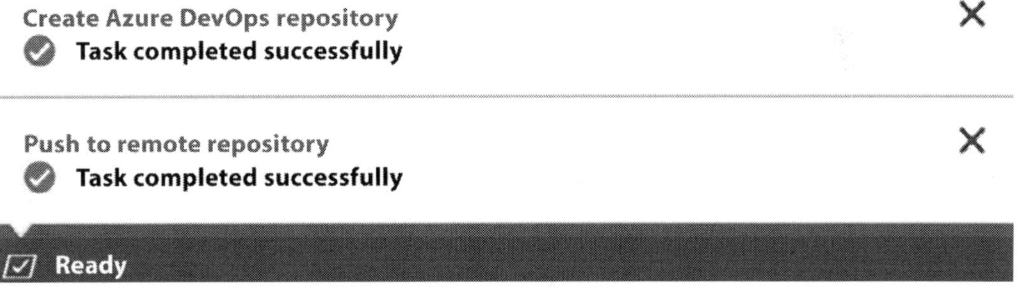

Figure 21.33: Operation completed

6. At this point, the repository has been created locally, connected with the selected remote repository, and all changes have been committed and pushed to the remote repository.

7. Now, click the **Pipelines** menu item to create a DevOps pipeline to build and test your project. In the window that appears, click the button to create a new pipeline:

Create your first Pipeline

Automate your build and release processes using our wizard. and go from code to cloud-hosted within minutes.

Figure 21.34: Pipeline page

8. You will be prompted to select where your repository is located:

New pipeline

Where is your code?

Figure 21.35: Repository selection

9. Select **Azure Repos Git** and then your repository. Then, you will be prompted about the nature of the project:

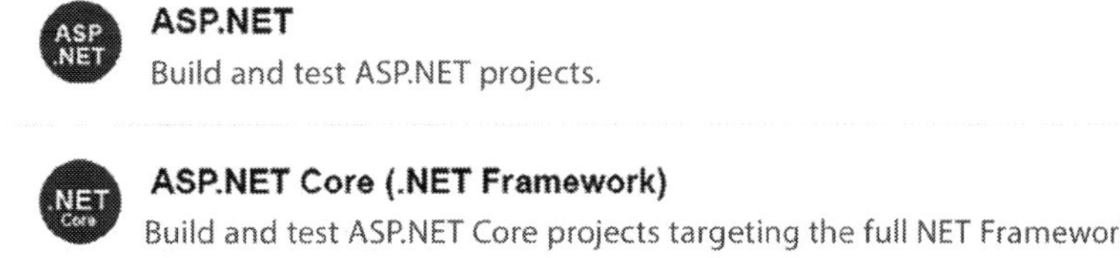

Figure 21.36: Pipeline configuration

10. Select **ASP.NET Core**. A pipeline for building and testing your project will be automatically created for you. Save it by committing the newly created `.yaml` file to your repository:

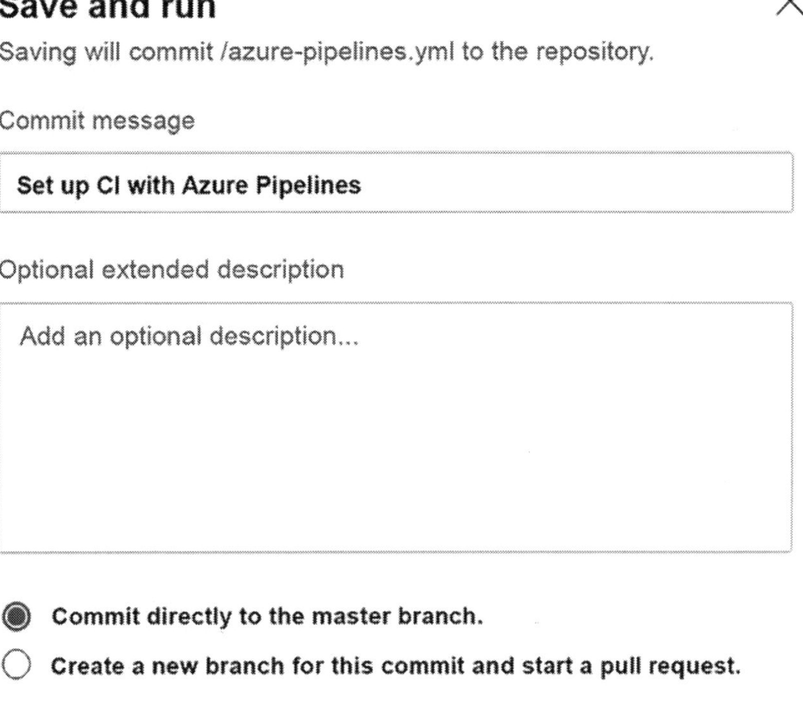

Figure 21.37: Pipeline properties

11. The pipeline can be run by selecting the **Queue** button, but since the standard pipeline scaffolded by DevOps has a trigger on the master branch of the repository, it is automatically launched each time changes to this branch are committed and each time the pipeline is modified. The pipeline can be modified by clicking the **Edit** button:

```
trigger:
- master

pool:
  vmImage: 'windows-latest'

variables:
  solution: '**/*.sln'
  buildPlatform: 'Any CPU'
  buildConfiguration: 'Release'

steps:
Settings
- task: UseDotNet@2
  inputs:
    packageType: 'sdk'
    version: '3.x'
    includePreviewVersions: true

Settings
- task: NuGetToolInstaller@1

Settings
- task: NuGetCommand@2
  inputs:
    command: 'restore'
    restoreSolution: '$(solution)'

Settings
- task: VSBuild@1
  inputs:
    solution: '$(solution)'
    msbuildArgs: '/p:DeployOnBuild=true /p:WebPublishMethod=Package /p:PackageAsSingleFile=true /p:SkipInvalidConfigurations=true
    platform: '$(buildPlatform)'
    configuration: '$(buildConfiguration)'

Settings
- task: VSTest@2
  inputs:
    testSelector: 'testAssemblies'
    testAssemblyVer2: |
      **\PackagesManagementTest.dll
      !**\*TestAdapter.dll
      !**\obj\**
    searchFolder: '$(System.DefaultWorkingDirectory)'
    platform: '$(buildPlatform)'
    configuration: '$(buildConfiguration)'
```

Figure 21.38: Pipeline code

12. Once in edit mode, all pipeline steps can be edited by clicking the **Settings** link that appears above each of them. New pipeline steps can be added as follows:

    a. Write `- task:` where the new step must be added and then accept one of the suggestions that appear while you are typing the task name.

    b. Once you have written a valid task name, a **Settings** link appears above the new step. Click it.

    c. Insert the desired task parameters in the window that appears and then save.

13. To have our test working, we need to specify the criteria to locate all assemblies that contain tests. In our case, since we have to execute just the tests contained in `PackagesManagementTest.dll` and not the ones contained in `PackagesManagementFTest.dll`, we must specify the exact `.ddl` name.

    Click the **Settings** link of the `VSTest@2` test task and replace the content that is automatically suggested for the **Test files** field with the following:

    ```
    **\PackagesManagementTest.dll
    !**\*TestAdapter.dll
    !**\obj\**
    ```

14. Then, click **Add** to modify the actual pipeline content. As soon as you confirm your changes in the **Save and run** dialog, the pipeline is launched and, if there are no errors, test results are computed. The results of tests launched during a specific build can be analyzed by selecting the specific build in the pipeline **Runs** tab and by clicking the **Tests** tab on the page that appears. In our case, we should see something like the following screenshot:

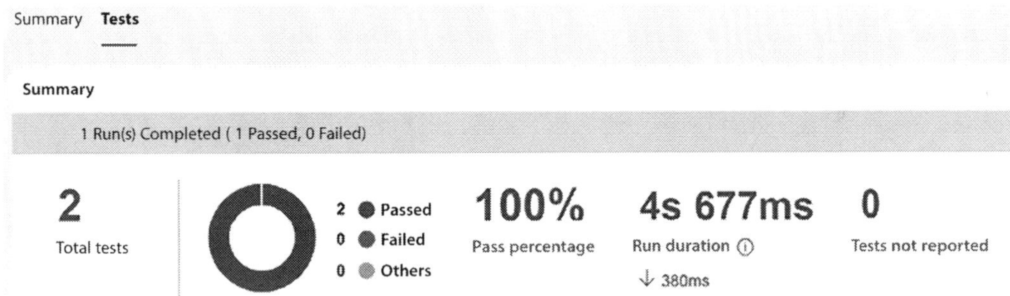

Figure 21.39: Test results

Summing up, we created a new Azure DevOps repository, published the solution to the new repository, and then created a build pipeline that executes our tests after each build. The build pipeline is executed as soon as we save it and will be executed each time someone commits to the master branch.

Summary

The main purpose of this chapter was to deliver pieces of implementations that can be useful to begin the challenge of delivering a software solution for an enterprise. Although we have not shown the complete implemention of the WWTravelClub application, we are confident that the microservices and code provided here can help you in your professional projects; this is in line with what we understand to be the main purpose of a software architect—to help the team in developing software that meets the users' needs exactly as required.

Leave a review!

Enjoyed this book? Help readers like you by leaving an Amazon review. Scan the QR code below for a 20% discount code.

**Limited Offer*

22

Case Study Extension: Developing .NET Microservices for Kubernetes

In this chapter, we bridge the insights from *Chapter 21, Case Study*, where we explored the practical implementation of .NET microservices, with the foundational knowledge of Kubernetes presented in *Chapter 20, Kubernetes*. Our focus here is on preparing .NET code for seamless integration with Kubernetes, encompassing the complete development cycle—from coding to debugging, and even troubleshooting post-deployment challenges.

We will guide you through the process of setting up a development workstation optimized for Kubernetes, learn the intricacies of packaging code with Docker, and understand how to organize your codebase for flawless execution across varied environments, such as Docker Desktop, local minikube installations, and production or staging Kubernetes clusters.

Also, this chapter delves into the nuances of remote debugging, providing you with the necessary skills to efficiently troubleshoot and debug your application. Here, you will learn how to prepare each developer workstation, how to package the code with Docker, and how to organize the code so that it can immediately run both on the developer Docker Desktop, on the developer's local Minikube installation, and on the production/staging Kubernetes clusters, without modifications.

By the end of the chapter, you will have mastered remote debugging techniques for applications in production or staging environments, enabling swift issue resolution and system reliability.

More specifically, you will learn about the following topics:

- The tools needed for .NET Kubernetes development
- Organizing the development process
- Running your application in Minikube
- Remote debugging of a Kubernetes application

All concepts will be explained with the help of a previous example taken from *Chapter 21*, *Case Study*, which we will adapt for Kubernetes execution.

You'll adapt the `GrpcMicroService` microservice from *Chapter 21, Case Study*, seeing firsthand how a real-world application transitions to Kubernetes.

To fully leverage this chapter, fortify your understanding of Docker and Kubernetes as laid out in *Chapter 11, Applying a Microservice Architecture to Your Enterprise Application*, and *Chapter 20, Kubernetes*, which form the foundation for the advanced practices discussed herein.

Technical requirements

This chapter requires Visual Studio 2022 free Community Edition or better, with all the database tools installed.

You will also need these:

- **WSL** (**Windows Subsystem for Linux**) and *Docker Desktop for Windows*. Detailed instructions on how to install both of them are given in the *Technical requirements* section of *Chapter 11, Applying a Microservice Architecture to Your Enterprise Application*.
- A Minikube installation that specifies Docker as a virtualization tool. Minikube installation is described in the *Using Minikube* section of *Chapter 20, Kubernetes*.
- A SQL Server database that allows TCP/IP connections. You can't use *SQL Server Express LocalDB*, which comes with Visual Studio installation, since it doesn't allow TCP/IP connections. So you need either a full SQL Express installation or an Azure SQL Server database. More details on how to fulfill this requirement will be given in the *Tools needed for .NET Kubernetes development* section of this chapter.

All the code of this chapter can be found in the GitHub repository associated with this book: `https://github.com/PacktPublishing/Software-Architecture-with-C-Sharp-12-and-.NET-8-4E`.

The Tools needed for .NET Kubernetes development

Each single microservice can be unit-tested and debugged independently from the remainder of its application, with the technique you learned *Chapter 9, Testing Your Enterprise Application*. You don't need to package it inside a Docker image to do this.

However, debugging and performing integration tests on the whole application or parts of it requires that all involved microservices interact and are packaged as in the final application.

You can use a staging environment to beta-test your application. Prior to staging deployment, ensure your application's stability in the development environment to prevent time-consuming troubleshooting, because the staging environment doesn't have all the facilities that are available in a development environment. Otherwise, troubleshooting all frequent bugs and crashes discovered in the staging environment might imply an unacceptable time cost.

Therefore, it is preferable to reach good application stability before deploying the application in a staging environment. Moreover, for easier and more efficient debug-fix cycles, it is desirable that all microservices run on each single developer machine. That's why each developer workstation must be equipped with both Docker and Minikube.

Furthermore, the developer machine must be able to simulate all communications between microservices and between services and other storage media, like databases.

It is likely that, Minikube can run and simulate all communications that occur in an actual Kubernetes cluster, including when it runs on a single development machine.

We can also let all involved Docker images communicate among them before loading them on Minikube because Docker Desktop allows the creation of virtual networks that are accessible by the local Docker images.

Finally, both Docker and Minikube virtual networks automatically include the development machine that hosts them, so we can place storage services like disk volumes and databases on the development machine itself.

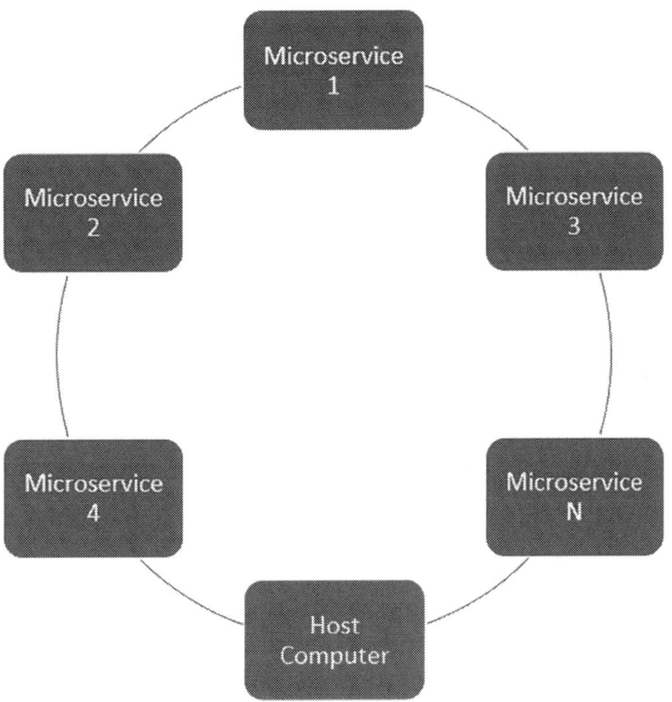

Figure 22.1: Minikube and Docker network structure

However, the sophisticated virtual network facilities of both Docker and Kubernetes are not enough to ensure an efficient development and debugging environment, and further tools are needed.

Below are all the issues we need to fix to configure an efficacious development-debugging environment and how to solve them:

- As a default, Visual Studio installs *SQL Server Express LocalDB* instead of *SQL Server Express*, and SQL Server Express LocalDB is not able to communicate via actual or virtual networks. Therefore, we need either an SQL Server Express installation or an external database.

- Since Kubernetes nodes have just virtual addresses that are handled by the Kubernetes engine itself, a Visual Studio debugger can be attached to a running microservice just through the REST API of the Kubernetes engine. At the time of writing, the best tool available for Visual Studio is *Bridge to Kubernetes,* which, in turn, uses *kubectl* to interact with the API of any Kubernetes cluster, Minikube included. Unluckily, we can't use the Kubectl installation that runs on the virtual machine that hosts Minikube as we did in *Chapter 20, Kubernetes,* but we need an installation that runs directly in the development machine.

We describe how to install and configure all tools mentioned in the above points in two dedicated subsections.

Installing and configuring SQL Server Express

If you have access to an SQL Server instance running in your development machine, you can use that one. Otherwise, you can choose between creating an SQL Server database in Azure following the instructions contained in *Chapter 12, Choosing Your Data Storage in the Cloud,* or installing a local instance of SQL Server Express:

1. Begin by downloading the SQL Server installer from `https://www.microsoft.com/en-US/download/details.aspx?id=104781`.
2. You can freely choose between SQL Server Express and SQL Server Express Advanced, but please select a complete installation that includes both **SQL Server Management Studio** and the **SQL Server Management console.**
3. Select to install SQL Server as the default instance on your machine (the default in the installation procedure).

   Immediately after the installation, you must run SQL Server Management Console (just write this name in the Windows search box) to enable TCP/IP-based connections. In order to configure SQL Server properly, follow all the steps below.

4. Once in the SQL Server Management Console, expand the **SQL Server Network Configuration** node.
5. Select **Protocols for <your instance name>.**
6. On the right detail pane, you should see all the available communication protocols.
7. Right-click on **TCP/IP** and select **Enable.**
8. Now, TCP/IP is enabled but on a dynamic port. In order to impose a fixed port, right-click on the same TCP/IP node and select **Properties.**

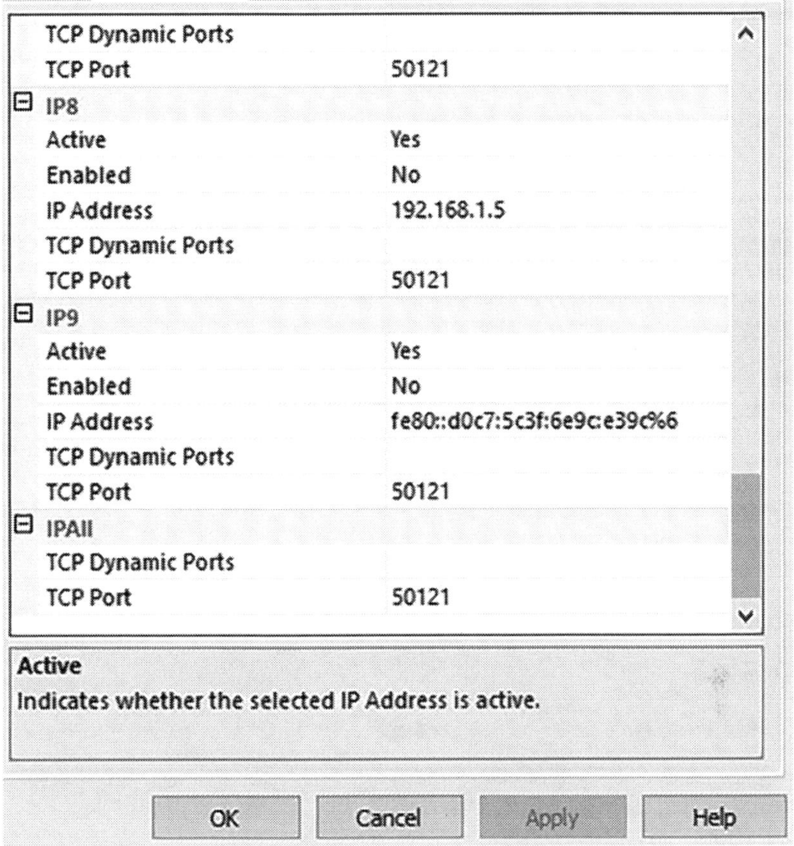

Figure 22.2: Forcing a static IP address

9. Select the **IP Addresses** tab.
10. You should see several IP addresses. These are all IP addresses that are associated with your computer, and each of them executes the next step.
11. Remove the **0** that is in **TCP Dynamic Port** and keep this field empty, and then write `1433` in the **TCP Port** field.
12. Once finished, click on the **OK** button.
13. Now, you need to restart the SQL Server service. Select **SQL Server Services** in the left pane.
14. Finally, in the right detail pane, right-click on **SQL Server <your instance name>** and select **Restart**.

15. Once installed, the SQL Server only has Windows authentication enabled. In order to use the instance on a non-Windows network, you must enable username-based authentication and define at least one administrative user. This is a necessary step because Windows authentication will not work on Docker networks and Kubernetes.
16. You can do this in SQL Server Management Studio. Once SQL Server Management Studio opens, it prompts you for an instance to connect with and for authentication information. The instance name of the database you just installed should be something like `<computer name>\SQLEXPRESS`; select it and also select **Windows Authentication**, as shown below:

Figure 22.3: Connecting with SQL Server Management Studio

Once connected with the database, you can enable username-based authentication as follows:

1. Right-click on your server icon in Object Explorer and choose **Properties**.
2. In the window that opens, select **Security** in the left pane.

3. Select **SQL Server and Windows Authentication mode**, as shown in the screenshot below:

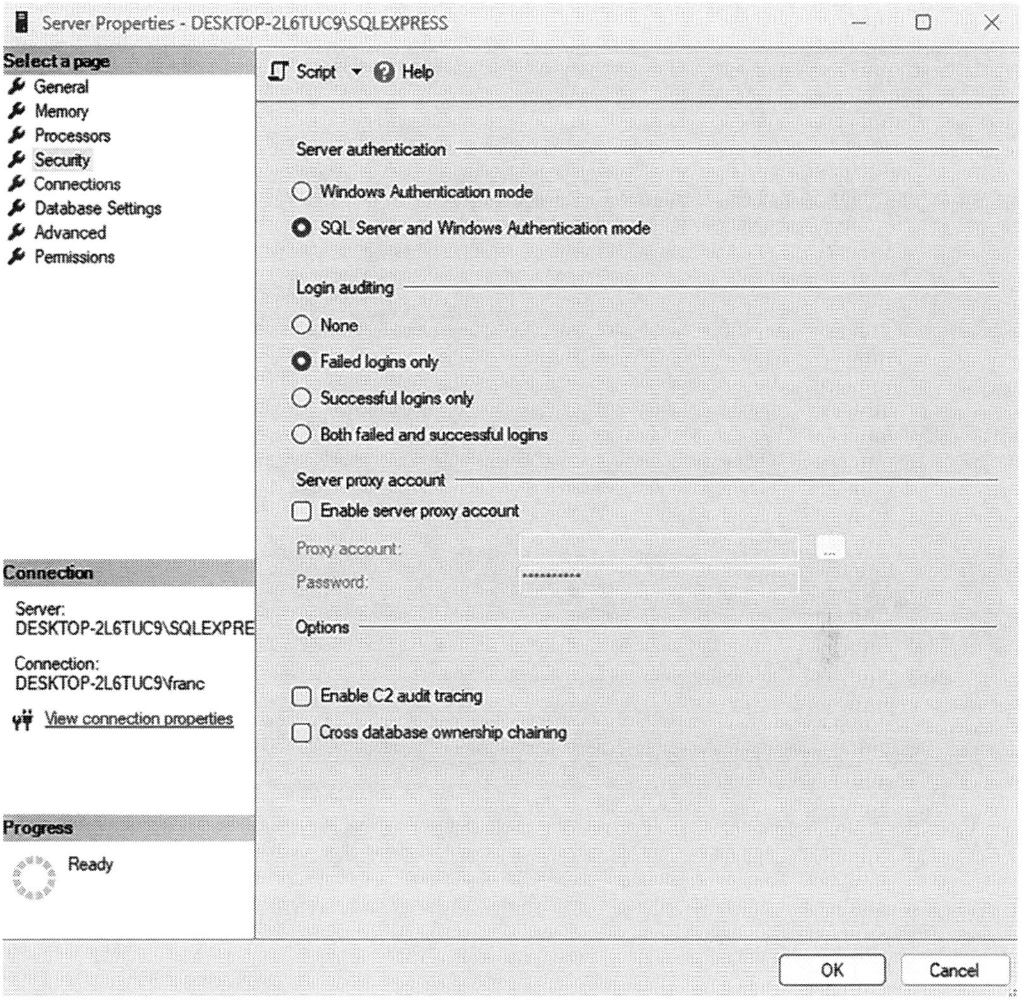

Figure 22.4: Enabling SQL Server authentication

In order to make your changes effective, you must restart SQL Server. You can do it by right-clicking on your server icon in Object Explorer and by selecting **Restart**.

Now, you need to define at least one user by following the steps below:

1. Expand the `Security` folder under your server icon in Object Explorer.
2. Right-click on the **Logins** folder and select **New Login**.
3. In the window that opens, insert a username.

4. Select **SQL Server authentication**, insert a password, and confirm it by retyping the same password in the **Confirm password** field, as shown in the screenshot below:

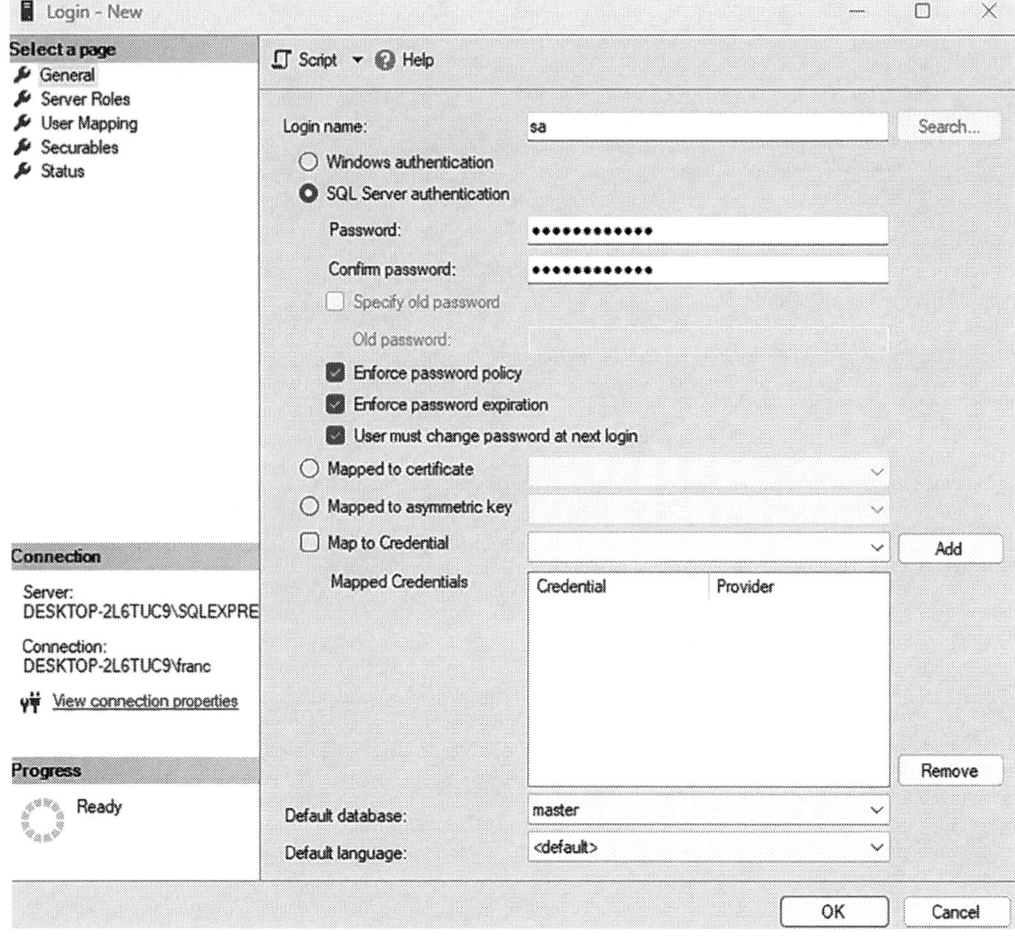

Figure 22.5: Defining user name and password

5. Finally, right-click on **Server Roles** and enable the **sysadmin** role to give all rights to the new user.

And there you have it! Now, your SQL Server instance can be used by both Docker and Minikube.

The next subsection explains how to configure Visual Studio for debugging applications running on Minikube or any other Kubernetes cluster.

Enabling Kubernetes application debugging with Bridge to Kubernetes

Since microservices running on Kubernetes have no fixed IP address and ports attached to them, only virtual addresses that are solved at runtime by Kubernetes, we can't attach the Visual Studio debugger directly to any running microservice. That's why we need software like Bridge to Kubernetes, which interacts with the Kubernetes API to enable debugging.

Bridge to Kubernetes is a Visual Studio extension that's easy to install, but it requires Kubectl to be installed on your development machine, which presents a challenge, as there is no direct Windows installer for Kubectl. In this subsection, we'll guide you through the process of installing both Bridge to Kubernetes and Kubectl, overcoming the lack of a direct Windows installer for the latter.

Bridge to Kubernetes enables Kubernetes application debugging by interacting with the Kubernetes API via Kubectl. However, it is not a debugger driver or a debugger extension. It does a completely different job; it asks you to select a service running in a Kubernetes cluster and reroute all communication with this service to a locally running Visual Studio POD replica instead of the actual cluster POD.

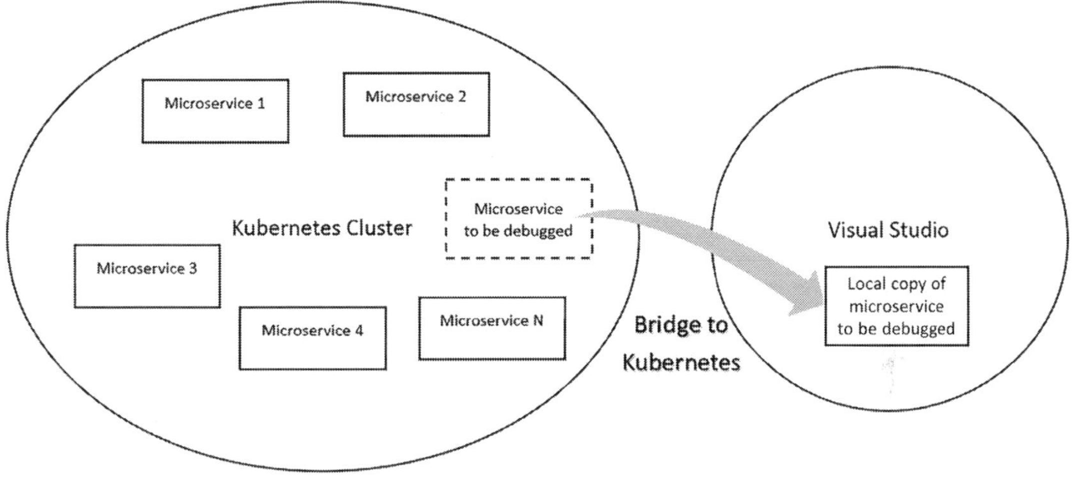

Figure 22.6: How Bridge to Kubernetes works

Therefore, the developer debugs a local copy of the POD code but in exactly the same dynamic Kubernetes environment as the original POD. This way, you have all the facilities offered by a usual local debugging session, but while you are debugging it, your code interacts with the actual Kubernetes cluster you need to fix.

Bridge to Kubernetes doesn't work just with Minikube; it works with any Kubernetes cluster. Thus, you can use it for debugging the whole application on your development machine, and also for debugging the staging application or the production application.

Since you debug just the local code and not the deployed code, you are not forced to compile an application in debug mode in order to debug it. You can deploy the application with all compilation optimizations you want without caring about possible debugging needs; it is enough to have local copies of the PODs you would like to debug compiled in debug mode.

You will learn how to use Bridge to Kubernetes in practice in the *Remote debugging of a Kubernetes application* section. The remainder of this section will explain all the steps needed to install Bridge to Kubernetes on a development machine.

First of all, you need to install Kubectl. The simplest way to do it is by using the Chocolatey package manager.

Chocolatey is a package manager like NuGet. Similarly, it consists of a public repository containing all packages and a client you must install on your machine, in order to interact with the public repository.

If you don't have Chocolatey already installed, you can install it from a PowerShell prompt, as follows:

1. Search **PowerShell** in the Windows search box.
2. Right-click on the PowerShell link and select to execute it as an administrator.
3. Finally, execute the PowerShell command suggested on the official Chocolatey page: `https://chocolatey.org/install#individual`.

The PowerShell command to execute is repeated below for your convenience:

```
Set-ExecutionPolicy Bypass -Scope Process -Force; [System.
Net.ServicePointManager]::SecurityProtocol = [System.Net.
ServicePointManager]::SecurityProtocol -bor 3072; iex ((New-Object System.Net.
WebClient).DownloadString('https://community.chocolatey.org/install.ps1'))
```

Once installation is complete, run `choco -?` to verify that the installation was successful and that the Chocolatey user interface works properly.

With Chocolatey installed, installing Kubectl is super easy; just open a Windows Command Prompt as an administrator and type this:

```
choco install kubernetes-cli
```

You can check whether everything works properly by typing `kubectl version -client`.

Kubectl should be configured to access a specific cluster, but when you start Minikube with `minikube start`, Minikube automatically configures it to access the local Minikube cluster, so you don't need to worry about Kubectl configuration.

Now, you are ready to install Bridge to Kubernetes, as follows:

1. Open Visual Studio and select **Extensions -> Manage Extensions**.
2. Search `Bridge to Kubernetes`.
3. Select it and install it.

And there you have it! Now, your development machine is ready for .NET Kubernetes development. The next section details the development process and explains how to modify an existing project to run with both the local Docker installation and any Kubernetes cluster.

Organizing the development process

Since Visual Studio and other IDEs offer good support for Docker and a good integration with Docker Desktop, the best option for most of the development time is working with just Dockerized images without running them inside of Minicube.

In fact, as we will see shortly, once we have added Docker support to our projects, it is enough to click the Run Visual Studio button to start all our Dockerized microservices and to enable them to communicate through a Docker network. Conversely, running our application in Minikube requires several manual steps, and it takes some time to load the Docker images on Minikube and to create all the necessary Kubernetes objects.

Doing this in Visual Studio is super easy. It is enough to add Docker support for all microservice projects in your solution and to select the option of launching several projects simultaneously when the solution is run. Then, Visual Studio will automatically perform all the necessary tasks when your solution is run, namely:

1. Compile and link all code.
2. Build all microservice Docker images.
3. Insert the Docker images into the Docker Desktop local repository.
4. Launch all Docker images simultaneously.
5. Attach the debugger to all launched Docker images.

You just need to take care of microservice communication by defining a virtual network with Docker Desktop.

We will explain all the details of the development process with a simple example in the next subsection.

gRPC worker microservices revisited

In the code associated with *Chapter 14, Implementing Microservices with .NET,* and described in *Chapter 21, Case study,* there is a solution called `GrpcMicroService`. The solution is composed of two microservices. The first microservice simulates purchases by generating random data, while the second one uses this data to compute statistics that it stores in a database. The whole code is available in the `ch15->GrpcMicroService` folder of the GitHub repository associated with the book.

Let's make a copy of the whole `GrpcMicroService` folder and call it `GrpcMicroServiceDocker`.

The steps below describe all the modifications that need to be made to Docker to enable all microservices.

Adding Docker support to GrpcMicroServiceDocker

Open the `GrpcMicroServiceDocker` solution in Visual Studio. The solution contains two microservices, called `FakeSource` and `GrpcMicroservice`. The last project is just the data layer of the `GrpcMicroservice` project.

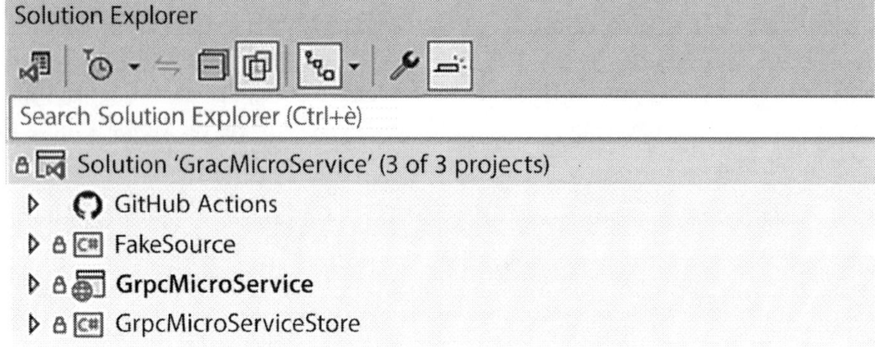

Figure 22.7: GrpcMicroServiceDocker solution

The solution is already configured to launch the two microservices when it is run. In other cases, you might need to configure multiple project launches by right-clicking on the solution node and selecting **Set Startup Projects...**.

Adding Docker support to both microservices is super easy. Right-click on each microservice project within Visual Studio. Navigate to **Add**, and then select **Docker Support**. If prompted, choose the operating system for your Docker environment. If you are using Minikube, you must select **Linux**.

All the necessary Docker files are automatically created and configured by Visual Studio. And that's it!

Now, we need to move the database to the newly installed SQL Server instance.

Moving GrpcMicroServiceDocker to SQL Server Express

You need to change all connection strings and configure the string that will be used at runtime so that it can be used from inside a Docker image.

First of all, let's change the connection string that is inside `GrpcMicroServiceStore-> LibraryDesignTimeDbContextFactory.cs`. The new string should be something like this:

```
@"Server=<your machine name>\<your instance
name>;Database=grpcmicroservice;Trusted_Connection=True;Trust Server
Certificate=True;MultipleActiveResultSets=true"
```

where the instance name should be `SQLEXPRESS`. You can take the above connection string directly from Visual Studio, as follows:

1. Open the **SQL Server Object Explorer** window.
2. Right-click on the **SQL Server** node and select **Add SQL Server**.
3. In the window that opens, Visual Studio should enumerate all available SQL Server instances. Choose the newly installed SQL Server instance.

4. Select **Windows authentication** and connect.
5. A new server icon should appear below the **SQL Server** node. Select it.
6. In the **Visual Studio Properties** tab, you should see all database connection properties. Take the value of **General-> Connection string**.

Now, you have to run all migrations to recreate the database in the new SQL Server instance. As usual, right-click on the library project and define it as a startup project. Then, in the Visual Studio Package Manager Console **Default Project**, select `GrpcMicroServiceStore` and issue the `Update-Database` command.

After the new database has been created, restore the two microservices as simultaneous startup projects.

Finally, update the runtime connection string in `GrpcMicroService -> appsettings.json`. If the newly installed SQL Server instance has been defined as the default instance on your machine, the connection string below should work:

```
Server=host. Docker.internal;Database=grpcmicroservice;User
Id=<your user name>;Password=<your user password>;Trust Server
Certificate=True;MultipleActiveResultSets=true"
```

where `host. Docker.internal` is the URL used by Docker Desktop images to communicate with the host machine. If your SQL Server is not the machine's default instance, you must replace `host.docker.internal` with `host.docker.internal\<your instance name>`.

If, instead, you are using an external database, you can use its standard connection string with no modifications.

Enabling communication among microservices with a Docker virtual network

Creating a Docker virtual network in Docker Desktop is easy; just open a Windows console and run the following command:

```
docker network create test-net,
```

where `test-net` is the virtual network name. Once the network has been defined when we create a container instance from an image, we can specify that the launched container must be connected to our network and its hostname, with something like:

```
docker run --rm --net test-net --name grpcmicroservice <microservice image
name>,
```

Here, the `rm` option specifies that the container must be destroyed when it stops running, `--net test-net` specifies the network where to connect the created container, and `--name grpcmicroservice` is the name of the created container that will also act as its hostname in the network.

We need to add to our `test-net` just the containers that must act as servers—in our case, the `GrpcMicroService` microservice.

Since Visual Studio automatically issues all necessary `run` Docker commands when the solution is launched, we need just to specify the command options to add to Visual Studio's original command. They must be specified in each microservice project file with the `DockerfileRunArguments` parameter. Below is how to modify the `GrpcMicroService` microservice project file, which is the only microservice acting as a server:

```
<PropertyGroup>
<TargetFramework>net8.0</TargetFramework>
     <Nullable>enable</Nullable>
     <UserSecretsId>b4f03ff2-033c-4d5e-a33b-65f26786b052</UserSecretsId>
     <DockerDefaultTargetOS>Linux</DockerDefaultTargetOS>
<DockerfileRunArguments>
--rm --net test-net --name grpcmicroservice
</DockerfileRunArguments>
</PropertyGroup>
```

No modification is required to the `FakeSource` project, since it must not act as a server.

Now, the `grpcmicroservice` hostname must be used by `FakeSource` to communicate with the `GrpcMicroService` microservice.

Therefore, we must replace the URL in the `FakeSource->Worker.cs` file with `http://grpcmicroservice:8080`, as shown in the code snippet below:

```
…
using var channel = GrpcChannel.ForAddress("http://grpcmicroservice:8080");
var client = new Counter.CounterClient(channel);
…
```

where we use the `8080` default Kestrel `http` port to communicate with the microservice. Therefore, we need to the Kestrel options in `GrpcMicroService ->Program.cs` that force Kestrel to listen to the `5000` port by replacing the code below:

```
builder.WebHost.ConfigureKestrel(options =>
{
    options.ListenLocalhost(5000, o =>
        o.Protocols = Microsoft.AspNetCore.Server.Kestrel.Core.HttpProtocols.
Http2);
});
```

Now, we are ready to run our project. To be sure that both microservices are started with Docker, please select each of them as a single startup project, and then select **Docker** in the select box next to the run solution Visual Studio button, as shown in the image below:

Figure 22.8: Selecting Docker execution

After that, you can restore the simultaneous launch of both microservices. Visual Studio will launch both of them with Docker.

Now, we can launch the solution. In order to verify that the server is properly receiving purchase information, place a breakpoint in the `GrpcMicroService->HostedServices-> ProcessPurchases.cs` file inside of the `if` block below:

```
if (toProcess.Count > 0)
{
    ...
}
```

In fact, `GrpcMicroService` enters that block only if it finds something in the input queue.

You can also inspect the content of the `dbo.Purchases` database table to verify that it is filled with statistics on purchases. You can do it from within **SQL Server Object Explorer** by right-clicking on the table and choosing **View Data.**

Having understood how to test our application with a Docker network, we must now understand when and how to test it with Minikube also.

When to test the application with Minikube

Most of the debug-fix cycle involved in the application development can be done with the Docker virtual network.

Docker networks usually work well without creating issues. So, if you experience communication problems, they are probably due to misspelled service URLs. Therefore, please double-check the URLs in all calls to the microservice that does not receive communications.

From time to time, we need to test an application with Minikube for the following reasons:

- Both ReplicaSets and StatefulSets can be tested with Docker and Visual Studio, but we are limited to a single POD for each of them.
- We must also test the `.yaml` Kubernetes configuration file, which might contain more complex objects like ingresses, permanent storage, secrets, and other complex configurations.
- You might need to integrate your microservices with other modules developed by other teams.

Therefore, each developer should spend most of their time testing a few microservices that strongly interact among them with the Docker virtual network, but from time to time, they should try a wider integration with Minikube. This can be done before committing their code at the end of the working day, or just before closing a development iteration of the agile application development process.

Having learned when and how to test the application with Minikube, we must learn how to load and run our application on Minikube.

Running your application in Minikube

When Visual Studio runs your microservices with Docker, it creates special images that also contain information needed by the Visual Studio debugger and have a `dev` version name. These special images can be run just from Visual Studio, and if you try to launch them manually, you will get an error. For the same reason, you can't use them in Minikube.

Therefore, the first step for running your microservice in Minikube is to create different "standard" images. You can do this by right-clicking both the `FakeSource` and `GrpcMicroService` Docker files in Visual Studio Solution Explorer and by selecting **Build Docker Image**.

This way, you will create a `grpcmicroservice` and a `fakesource` image, both with the `latest` version name, as shown in the image below:

NAME ↑	TAG	IMAGE ID	CREATED	SIZE
fakesource	latest	24df27741e7e	less than a minute ago	198.05 MB
fakesource	dev	a942aa0c7536	about 2 hours ago	194.59 MB
gcr.io/k8s-minikube/kicbase	v0.0.28	e2a6c047bedd	about 2 years ago	1.08 GB
grpcmicroservice	latest	59e186ac39c2	about 2 hours ago	234.46 MB
grpcmicroservice	dev	9aa1f7b55b87	about 2 hours ago	217.88 MB
mcr.microsoft.com/dotnet/aspnet	8.0-preview	35144b62062e	about 1 month ago	217.88 MB

Figure 22.9: Creating Minikube-ready Docker images

As a next step, you must start Minikube:

```
minikube start
```

Now, you must load your Docker images inside of the Minikube images cache with the following commands:

```
minikube image load fakesource:latest
minikube image load grpcmicroservice:latest
```

You can verify that your images have been correctly loaded by listing all the images loaded in Minikube:

```
minikube image ls
```

Now, we need to define a `.yaml` Kubernetes configuration file with two deployments and a service that forwards communications to `grpcmicroservice`, which is the only microservice acting as a server. Let's call it `minikubedeploy.yaml`.

The definition of the `grpcmicroservice` deployment is straightforward:

```
apiVersion: apps/v1
kind: Deployment
metadata:
  name: grpcmicroservice
  labels:
```

```
      app: statistics
  spec:
    selector:
      matchLabels:
        app: statistics
        role: worker
    replicas: 1
    template:
      metadata:
        labels:
          app: statistics
          role: worker
      spec:
        containers:
        - name: grpcmicroservice
          image: grpcmicroservice:latest
          imagePullPolicy: Never
          resources:
            requests:
              cpu: 10m
              memory: 10Mi
          env:
          - name: ASPNETCORE_HTTP_PORTS
            value: "8080"
          ports:
          - containerPort: 8080
            name: http
```

The code above requires just one replica, but you can experiment with two or three replicas. The `ASPNETCORE_HTTP_PORTS` environment variable is a standard ASP.NET setting that informs Kestrel on the HTTP port where to listen.

The `imagePullPolicy: Never` setting specifies the image caching policy within the Kubernetes cluster. It prevents Minikube from trying to download a fresher version of the image from the original source into its cache. We need this setting, since there is no "original source" containing our image because we uploaded the image directly to the Minikube cache with the `minikube image load` command.

You must always specify this setting when images are not available in a shared image repository but are uploaded directly to the Minikube cache from the Docker Desktop local repository. Shared images, instead, do not need to be uploaded manually in the Minikube cache but can be simply referenced with their full URL in the Kubernetes `.yaml` file.

All other settings are quite standard.

The definition of the `fakesource` deployment is completely analogous but doesn't contain information about the container ports, since this microservice doesn't act as a server:

```
apiVersion: apps/v1
kind: Deployment
metadata:
  name: fakesource
  labels:
    app: sale
spec:
  selector:
    matchLabels:
      app: sales
      role: source
  replicas: 1
  template:
    metadata:
      labels:
        app: sales
        role: source
    spec:
      containers:
      - name: fakesource
        image: fakesource:latest
        imagePullPolicy: Never
        resources:
          requests:
            cpu: 10m
            memory: 10Mi
```

The definition of the service that forwards communications to `grpcmicroservice` is quite standard:

```
apiVersion: v1
kind: Service
metadata:
  name: grpcmicroservice
  labels:
    app: contract
    role: worker
spec:
  ports:
  - port: 8080
    name: http
    protocol: TCP
    targetPort: 8080
  selector:
    app: statistics
    role: worker
```

You must pay attention only to the port numbers that must be coherent in all settings and to the service name, since they will be used in the URLs of all communication to the `grpcmicroservice`.

If the service names match the hostnames in the Docker virtual network, the URLs will work both in Kubernetes and the Docker virtual network. So, you don't need to modify any code or configuration to adapt the code that runs in the Docker virtual network to Minikube or any other Kubernetes clusters.

The whole `minkubedeploy.yaml` file is available in the `ch22` folder of the GitHub repository associated with the book.

Now, let's open a Windows prompt in the folder that contains the `minkubedeploy.yaml` file, issuing the command below that will load the application configuration in the Minikube cluster:

```
kubectl create -f minkubedeploy.yaml
```

Then, issue the `kubectl get deployment` command to verify that all deployments have been correctly defined and are running.

You can verify that the application is properly running by inspecting the data in the `dbo.Purchases` database table, by right-clicking on the `dbo.Purchases` table in **SQL Server Object Explorer** and choosing **View Data**:

dbo.Purchases [Data]

Max Rows: 1000

Id	Time	PurchaseTime	Location	Cost
e94-0113b8f06981	08/10/2023 18:4...	09/10/2023 00:0...	New York	400,00
14a244c1-3007-...	08/10/2023 18:4...	08/10/2023 00:0...	London	200,00
18b8ab8a-20c4...	08/10/2023 18:4...	09/10/2023 00:0...	London	200,00
971f8e69-1b9c-...	08/10/2023 18:4...	08/10/2023 00:0...	Paris	600,00
8d58b36f-7c13-...	08/10/2023 18:4...	09/10/2023 00:0...	Florence	200,00
152b4c2d-2e75...	08/10/2023 18:5...	07/10/2023 00:0...	Florence	200,00
5571e7cc-f670-...	08/10/2023 18:5...	09/10/2023 00:0...	Paris	600,00
9856fc8a-5372-...	08/10/2023 18:5...	08/10/2023 00:0...	New York	200,00
85ce8ea9-ed18-...	08/10/2023 18:5...	09/10/2023 00:0...	New York	400,00
968a9e40-8e47-...	08/10/2023 18:4...	09/10/2023 00:0...	London	200,00
01949f43-105c-...	08/10/2023 18:4...	09/10/2023 00:0...	Florence	200,00
172ad8ee-6d58...	08/10/2023 18:4...	09/10/2023 00:0...	Paris	200,00

Figure 22.10: dbo.Purchases table

Each time you click the table refresh button, you should see new rows added to the database table. If new rows do not appear after several refreshes, your microservice is probably experiencing some communication problem, or some exception was thrown before data was computed.

You can discover what the problem is just by debugging the application. The next section explains how to verify in detail what is happening in the application, with the help of Bridge to Kubernetes. Please do not delete all Kubernetes objects created with `minkubedeploy.yaml` because we need the running application to attach Bridge to Kubernetes.

Remote debugging a Kubernetes application

As a final step, we will debug `GrpcMicroService` with Bridge to Kubernetes. Let's set `GrpcMicroService` as a starting project and change the project start from **Docker** to **Bridge to Kubernetes**, as shown in the image below:

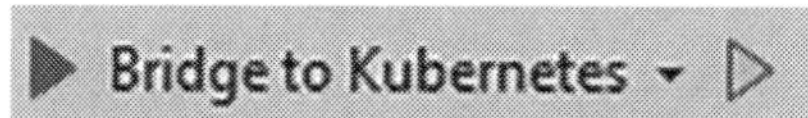

Figure 22.11: Debugging GrpcMicroService with Bridge to Kubernetes

Let's place a breakpoint in the `GrpcMicroService->HostedServices-> ProcessPurchases.cs` file inside of the `if` block, as shown below:

```
if (toProcess.Count > 0)
{
    ...
}
```

Then, start debugging. As soon as you click the **run** button, a window appears that prompts you to configure Bridge to Kubernetes:

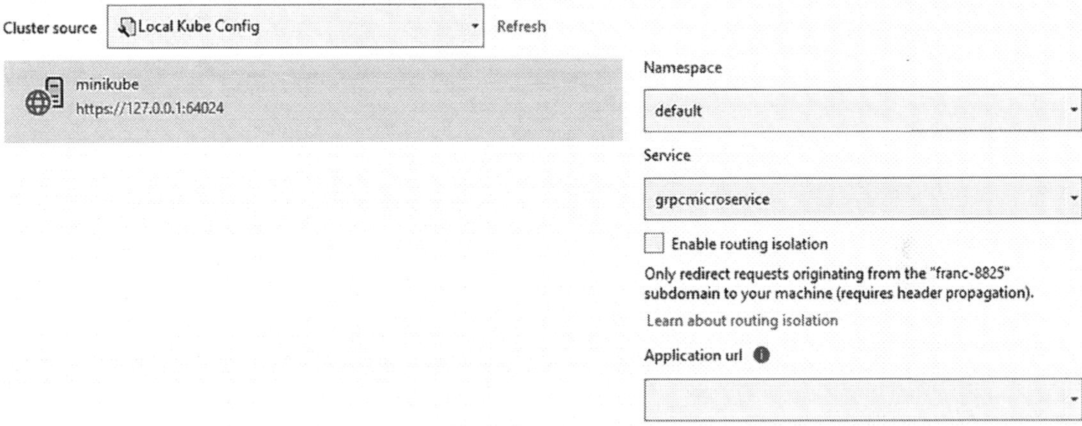

Figure 22.12: Configuring Bridge to Kubernetes

If the window above doesn't open, or you can't see any Minikube node, `Kubectl` is probably not working or configured for Minikube. Try issuing a `Kubectl` command like `kubectl get all`. If you face any issues, try stopping and restarting Minikube with `minikube stop`, followed by `minikube start`.

Bridge to Kubernetes prompts us to select a namespace—in our case, `default`—and then choose a specific service within that namespace—in our case, `grpmicroservice`. All communications to that service will be forwarded to the `GrpcMicroService` code running on our development machine. Let's set up the configuration window, as shown in the screenshot above. As soon as you submit your Bridge to Kubernetes configuration, debugging will automatically start. In a short time, the breakpoint will be hit, and our local copy of the microservice will start interacting with the remainder of the code that is running in Minikube!

After you finish debugging, please restore the project start to **Docker**, and restore the simultaneous start of both microservices so that you can continue working with the Docker virtual network.

After having finished working with Minikube, you need to remove all objects created by `minkubedeploy.yaml` with the command below:

```
kubectl delete -f minkubedeploy.yaml
```

It is important to free up resources as soon as you don't need them anymore; otherwise, they will continue wasting CPU time and memory, and if you constantly add more and more applications, sooner or later, you will experience performance problems on your development machine.

If you want to free up Minikube disk space, you can also remove the microservices images previously loaded in the Minikube cache with the commands below:

```
minikube image rm fakesource:latest
minikube image rm grpcmicroservice:latest
```

Finally, you need to stop Minikube with:

```
minikube stop
```

Summary

In this chapter, we explained how to prepare a developer workstation for .NET Kubernetes development and how to organize code testing and bug-fix cycles.

We also explained how to define a Docker virtual network to ensure microservices communication during development and name conventions for hostnames and Kubernetes services, enabling the same code to run both on the Docker virtual network, Minikube, and any other Kubernetes cluster.

Finally, we explained all the steps needed to run an application in Minikube and how to test it with Bridge to Kubernetes.

We've now reached the end of our journey through this book, and what a journey it has been!

Packed with numerous new and challenging ideas, this book is sure to be your good friend on your journey as a software architect.

These learnings will not only empower you to craft innovative solutions but also support your growth in the dynamic world of software projects. We sincerely hope you've enjoyed the adventure as much as we have creating this latest edition for you.

Questions

1. Why can't the SQL Server installation that comes with Visual Studio be used for Kubernetes development?
2. What is Bridge to Kubernetes?
3. Is it true that Bridge to Kubernetes works just with Minikube?
4. How do you load the Minikube images cache?
5. How do we define Minikube as the Kubectl default cluster?

Further reading

Most of the references in this chapter are the same as those previously listed in *Chapter 11*, *Applying a Microservice Architecture to Your Enterprise Application*, and *Chapter 14*, *Implementing Microservices with .NET*. Here, it is worth adding the link to the official documentation about Bridge to Kubernetes: `https://learn.microsoft.com/en-us/visualstudio/bridge/`

Learn more on Discord

To join the Discord community for this book – where you can share feedback, ask questions to the authors, and learn about new releases – follow the QR code below:

`https://packt.link/SoftwareArchitectureCSharp12Dotnet8`

Answers

Chapter 1

1. A software architect needs to be aware of any technology that can help them solve problems faster and ensure they can create better quality software.
2. Azure helps software architects by providing scalable cloud infrastructure, diverse development tools, and services for building, deploying, and managing enterprise applications efficiently, with strong support for security and compliance.
3. The best software development process model depends on the kind of project, team, and budget you have. As a software architect, you need to consider all these variables and understand different process models so that you can fit the environment's needs.
4. A software architect pays attention to any user or system requirement that can influence performance, security, usability, system architecture, structure, organization, and so on.
5. A software architect should verify both functional and non-functional requirements, with a special focus on system architecture, performance, scalability, security, maintainability, and compatibility in the requirements specification.
6. Design thinking and design sprint help a software architect to understand user needs deeply and rapidly prototyping solutions, ensuring the requirements gathered align closely with user expectations and project goals.
7. User stories are good when we want to define functional requirements. They can be written quickly and commonly deliver not only the feature required but also the acceptance criteria for the solution.
8. Effective techniques for developing high-performance software include optimizing code, using efficient algorithms, leveraging parallel processing, and implementing effective memory management.
9. To check that the implementation is correct, a software architect compares it with models and prototypes that have already been designed and validated.

Chapter 2

1. Vertically and horizontally.
2. Yes, you can deploy automatically to an already-defined web app or create a new one directly using Visual Studio.
3. To take advantage of available hardware resources by minimizing the time they remain idle.
4. Code behavior is deterministic, so it is easy to debug. The execution flow mimics the flow of sequential code, which means it is easier to design and understand.
5. Because the right order minimizes the number of gestures that are needed to fill in a form.

6. Because it allows for the manipulation of path files in a way that is independent of the operating system.
7. It can be used with several .NET Core versions, as well as with several versions of the classic .NET Framework.
8. Console, .NET Core, .NET (5+), and .NET Standard class libraries; ASP.NET Core, test projects, microservices, and much more.

Chapter 3

1. No, it is available for several platforms.
2. Automatic, manual, and load test plans.
3. Yes, they can – through Azure DevOps feeds.
4. To manage requirements and organize the whole development process.
5. Epic work items represent higher-level system subparts that are made up of several features.
6. A parent-child relationship.
7. They can organize projects using the same concept we have in Azure DevOps.
8. Both options are great tools for running agile projects. The best option depends on your team's experience.

Chapter 4

1. Maintainability gives you the opportunity to deliver the software you designed quickly. It also allows you to fix bugs easily.
2. Cyclomatic complexity is a measure of code complexity based on the control flow graph. It detects the number of nodes a method has. The higher the number, the worse the effect.
3. A version control system will guarantee the integrity of your source code, giving you the opportunity to analyze the history of each modification that you've made. It offers the possibility of branching your code development, then merging different branches, and much more.
4. A garbage collector is a system in .NET Core, .NET (5+), and .NET Framework that monitors your application and detects objects that you aren't using anymore. It disposes of these objects to free up memory.
5. The `IDisposable` interface is important firstly because it is a good pattern for deterministic cleanup. Secondly, it is required in classes that instantiate objects that need to be disposed of by the programmer, since the garbage collector cannot dispose of them.
6. .NET 8 encapsulates some key design patterns in some of its libraries, such as dependency injection and the Builder pattern, in a way that can guarantee safer, more reliable code.
7. Well-written code is code that any person skilled in that programming language can handle, modify, and evolve.
8. Roslyn is the .NET compiler that's used for code analysis inside Visual Studio.
9. Code analysis is a practice that considers the way code is written to detect bad practices before compilation.

10. Code analysis can find problems that happen even with apparently good software, such as memory leaks and bad programming practices.
11. Roslyn is an engine that provides an API that enables analyzers to inspect your code for style, quality, maintainability, design, and other issues. This is done during design time, so you can check the mistakes before compiling your code.
12. Visual Studio extensions are tools that have been programmed to run inside Visual Studio. These tools can help you out in some cases where the Visual Studio IDE doesn't have the appropriate feature for you to use.
13. `SonarLint` and the `SonarAnalyzer.CSharp` NuGet package.

Chapter 5

1. Copy-and-paste is an inadequate form of code reuse, since it leads to duplicated code, making maintenance and updates more difficult. In fact, there is no safe way to discover all duplicates, and then it is very difficult to modify all of them.
2. The best approaches for code reuse are creating libraries, using generics, object-oriented inheritance, and more.
3. Yes. You can find components that have already been created in the libraries you've created before, and then you increase these libraries by creating new components that can be reused in the future.
4. .NET Standard is a specification that allows compatibility across different .NET frameworks, from .NET Framework to Unity. .NET Core is one .NET implementation of .NET and is open source.
5. By creating a .NET Standard library, you will be able to use it in different .NET implementations, such as .NET Core, .NET, .NET Framework, and Xamarin.
6. You can enable code reuse using object-oriented principles (e.g., inheritance, encapsulation, abstraction, and polymorphism).
7. Generics is a sophisticated implementation that simplifies how objects with the same characteristics are treated, by defining a placeholder that will be replaced with the specific type at compile time.
8. The answer to this question is well explained by Immo Landwerth on the .NET blog: `https://devblogs.microsoft.com/dotnet/the-future-of-net-standard/`. The basic answer is that .NET versions 5 and above need to be thought of as the foundation for sharing code moving forward.
9. The challenges related to refactoring include ensuring that changes don't introduce bugs, maintaining the functionality and performance of code, and improving readability and maintainability without altering the external behavior of software components.

Chapter 6

1. Design patterns are good solutions to common problems in software development.
2. While design patterns give you code implementation for typical problems we face in development, design principles help you select the best options when it comes to implementing the software architecture.
3. The Builder pattern will help you generate sophisticated objects without the need to define them in the class you are going to use them in.
4. The Factory pattern is useful in situations where you have multiple kinds of objects from the same abstraction, and you don't know which of them needs to be created at compile time.
5. The Singleton pattern is useful when you need a class that has only one instance during the software's execution.
6. The Proxy pattern is used when you need to provide an object that controls access to another object.
7. The Command pattern is used when you need to execute a command that will affect the behavior of an object.
8. The Publisher/Subscriber pattern is useful when you need to provide information about an object to a group of other objects.
9. The DI pattern is useful if you want to implement the Inversion of Control principle. Instead of creating instances of the objects that the component depends on, you just need to define their dependencies, declare their interfaces, and enable the reception of the objects by injection. Typically, you can do this by using the constructor of the class to receive the objects, tagging some class properties to receive the objects, or defining an interface with a method to inject all the necessary components.

Chapter 7

1. Changes in the language used by experts and changes in the meaning of words.
2. Context mapping is the main tool used to coordinate the development of a separate bounded context, helping to define and manage interactions between different contexts.
3. No; the whole communication passes through the entity, that is, the aggregate root.
4. There is a single aggregate root in a part-subpart hierarchy to ensure the consistency of and enforce rules across all elements of the aggregate, acting as the main entry point for external interactions.
5. Just one, since repositories are aggregate-centric.
6. The application layer manipulates repository interfaces. Repository implementations are registered in the dependency injection engine.
7. To coordinate operations on several aggregates in single transactions.
8. The specifications for updates and queries are usually quite different, especially in simple **CRUD** systems. The reason for its strongest form is mainly the optimization of query response times.
9. Dependency injection.

10. No; a serious impact analysis must be performed so that we can adopt it.

Chapter 8

1. DevOps is the approach of delivering value to the end user continuously. To do this with success, continuous integration, continuous delivery, and continuous feedback must be undertaken.
2. **Continuous integration** (**CI**) allows you to check the quality of the software you are delivering every single time you commit a change. You can implement this by turning on this feature in Azure DevOps.
3. **Continuous delivery** (**CD**) allows you to deploy a solution once you are sure that all the quality checks have passed the tests you designed. Azure DevOps helps you with that by providing you with relevant tools.
4. Yes, you can have DevOps separately and then enable **CI** later. You can also have CI enabled without **CD** enabled. Your team and process need to be ready and attentive for this to happen.
5. You might confuse **CI** with a CD process, which could cause damage to your production environment. In the worst-case scenario, for example, a feature that is not ready might be deployed, causing disruptions at inconvenient times for your customers, or you could even suffer a bad collateral effect due to an incorrect fix.
6. A multi-stage environment protects production from bad releases when fully automated build and deployment pipelines are in place.
7. Automated tests anticipate bugs and bad behaviors in preview scenarios.
8. Pull requests allow code reviews before commits are made in the master branch.
9. No; pull requests can help you in any development approach where you have Git as your source control.
10. Continuous feedback is the adoption of tools in the DevOps life cycle that enable fast feedback when it comes to performance, usability, and other aspects of the application you are developing.
11. The build pipeline will let you run tasks to build and test your application, while the release pipeline will give you the opportunity to define how the application will be deployed in each scenario.
12. Application Insights is a helpful tool for monitoring the health of the system you've deployed, which makes it a fantastic continuous feedback tool.
13. Test and Feedback is a tool that allows stakeholders to analyze the software you are developing and enables a connection with Azure DevOps to open tasks and even bugs.
14. The main goal of service design thinking is to enhance user experience and satisfaction by optimizing the service's usability, efficiency, and effectiveness in meeting user needs.
15. Azure DevOps is a tool that can automate the whole application life cycle when it comes to software development. However, many software architects tend to also use GitHub to do so, and Microsoft has developed the platform a lot in the last few years.

Chapter 9

1. Because most of the tests must be repeated after any software change occurs.
2. Because the probability of the same error occurring in a unit test and its associated application code is very low.
3. `[Theory]` is used when the test method defines several tests, while `[Fact]` is used when the test method defines just one test.
4. Assert.
5. `Setup`, `Returns`, and `ReturnsAsync`.
6. Yes, with `ReturnAsync`.
7. No; it depends on the complexity of the user interface and how often it changes.
8. The ASP.NET Core pipeline isn't executed, but inputs are passed directly to controllers.
9. Usage of the `Microsoft.AspNetCore.Mvc.Testing` NuGet package.
10. Usage of the `AngleSharp` NuGet package.

Chapter 10

1. IaaS is a good option when you are migrating from an on-premises solution or if you have an infrastructure team.
2. PaaS is the best option for fast and safe software delivery in systems where the team is focused on software development.
3. If the solution you intend to deliver is provided by a well-known player, such as a SaaS, you should consider using it.
4. Serverless is an option when you are building a new system if you don't have people who specialize in infrastructure and you don't want to worry about it for scaling.
5. Azure SQL Database can be up in minutes, and you will have all the power of Microsoft SQL Server afterward. Moreover, Microsoft will handle the database server infrastructure.
6. Azure provides a set of services called Azure Cognitive Services. These services provide solutions for vision, speech, language, search, and knowledge.
7. In a hybrid scenario, you have the flexibility to decide on the best solution for each part of your system, while respecting the solution's development path in the future.

Chapter 11

1. The modularity of code and deployment modularity.
2. No. Other important advantages include handling the development team and the whole **CI/CD** cycle well, and the possibility of mixing heterogeneous technologies easily and effectively.
3. A library that helps us implement resilient communication.
4. Once you've installed Docker on your development machine, you can develop, debug, and deploy Dockerized .NET applications. You can also add Docker images to Service Fabric applications that are handled with Visual Studio.

5. Orchestrators are software that manages microservices and nodes in microservice clusters. Azure supports two relevant orchestrators: Azure Kubernetes Service and Azure Service Fabric.
6. Because it decouples the actors that take place in a communication.
7. A message broker. It takes care of service-to-service communication and events.
8. The same message can be received several times because the sender doesn't receive confirmation of reception before its time-out period, so the sender resends the message again. Therefore, the effect of receiving a single message once or several times must be the same.

Chapter 12

1. Redis is a distributed in-memory storage based on key-value pairs and supports distributed queuing. Its most well-known usage is for distributed caching, but it can be used as an alternative to relational databases, since it is able to persist data to disk.
2. Yes, they are. Most of this chapter's sections are dedicated to explaining why.
3. Write operations.
4. The main weaknesses of NoSQL databases are their consistency and transactions, while their main advantage is performance, especially when it comes to handling distributed writes.
5. Eventual, Consistency Prefix, Session, Bounded Staleness, and Strong.
6. No, they are not efficient in a distributed environment. GUID-based strings perform better, since their uniqueness is automatic and doesn't require synchronization operations.
7. `OwnsMany` and `OwnsOne`.
8. Yes, they can. Once you use `SelectMany`, indices can be used to search for nested objects.

Chapter 13

1. With the help of database-dependent providers.
2. Either by calling them `Id` or by decorating them with the `Key` attribute. This can also be done with a fluent configuration approach.
3. With the `MaxLength` and `MinLength` attributes, or with their equivalent fluent configuration methods.
4. With something similar to `builder.Entity<Package>().HasIndex(m => m.Name);`.
5. With something similar to the following:

```
builder.Entity<Destination>()
.HasMany(m => m.Packages)
.WithOne(m => m.MyDestination)
.HasForeignKey(m => m.DestinationId)
.OnDelete(DeleteBehavior.Cascade);
```

6. With `Add-Migration` and `Update-Database` in the package-manager console, or with `dotnet ef migrations add` and `dotnet ef database update` in the operating system console.

7. No, but you can forcefully include them with the `Include LINQ` clause or by using the `UseLazyLoadingProxies` option when configuring your `DbContext`. With Include, related entities are loaded together with the main entities, while with `UseLazyLoadingProxies`, related entities are lazy-loaded; that is, they are loaded as soon as they are required.
8. Yes, it is, thanks to the `Select LINQ` clause.
9. By calling `context.Database.Migrate()`.

Chapter 14

1. Because using queues are the only way to avoid time-consuming blocking calls.
2. With the `import` declaration.
3. With the standard `Duration` message.
4. Version compatibility and interoperability while maintaining good performance.
5. Better horizontal scalability, and support for the Publisher/Subscriber pattern.
6. For two reasons. The operation is very fast, and the insertion in the first queue of a communication path must necessarily be a blocking operation. At least one blocking operation is always necessary to store the message in some permanent storage (usually a queue), so it can be recovered if the ongoing processing might fail for some reason.
7. With the following XML code:

```
<ItemGroup>
    <Protobuf Include="Protos\file1.proto" GrpcServices="Server/Client"
/>
   <Protobuf Include="Protos\file2.proto" GrpcServices="Server/Client" />
   ...
</ItemGroup>
```

   Where `Protos\file1.proto` and `Protos\file2.proto` must be replaced with the actual paths to the `ProtoBuf` files within our project. Moreover, the `GrpcServices` attribute must be set to `"Server"` or `"Client"`, depending on whether the `proto` file describes a server or not.

8. With `channel.BasicPublish(…)`.
9. With `channel.WaitForConfirmsOrDie(timeout)`.

Chapter 15

1. No, since this would violate the principle that a service reaction to a request must depend on the request itself, and not on other messages/requests that had previously been exchanged with the client.
2. No, implementing a service with a custom communication protocol is generally not good practice because it compromises interoperability, increases development and maintenance complexity, and isolates the service from widely used standards and tools. Standard protocols such as HTTP/REST, gRPC, and others are preferred for their broad support, ease of integration, and community backing.

3. Yes, it can. The primary action of a POST must be creation, but deletion can be performed as a side effect. The HTTP verb to use is determined by the virtual table named in the URL (in our case, a POST, since the operation is an addition), but other operations can be performed on other virtual tables that are not mentioned in the URL as side effects.
4. Three; they are `Base64` encoding of the header, `Base64` encoding of the body, and the signature.
5. From the request body.
6. The `ApiController` attribute sets up some default behaviors that help in the implementation of REST services.
7. The `ProducesResponseType` attribute.
8. When using API controllers, they are declared with the `Route` and `Http<verb>` attributes. When using a minimal API, they are declared in the first argument of `MapGet`, `MapPost`, ... `Map{Http verb}`.
9. By adding something like `builder.Services.AddHttpClient<MyProxy>()` in the dependency injection part of the host configuration.

Chapter 16

1. Azure Functions is an Azure PaaS component that allows you to implement FaaS solutions.
2. You can program Azure Functions in different languages, such as C#, F#, PHP, Python, and Node.js. You can also create functions using the Azure portal and Visual Studio Code. Additional stacks can be used by using custom handlers: `https://docs.microsoft.com/en-au/azure/azure-functions/functions-custom-handlers`.
3. There are two plan options in Azure Functions. The first plan is the Consumption Plan, where you are charged according to the amount you use. The second plan is the App Service Plan, where you share your App Service resources with the function's needs.
4. The process of deploying functions in Visual Studio is the same as in web app deployment.
5. There are lots of ways we can trigger Azure Functions, such as using Blob Storage, Cosmos DB, Event Grid, Event Hubs, HTTP, Microsoft Graph Events, Queue Storage, Service Bus, Timer, and Webhooks.
6. Azure Functions v1 needs the .NET Framework Engine, whereas v2 needs .NET Core 2.2, and v3 needs .NET Core 3.1 and .NET 5-6. v4 is the current version for .NET 6, 7, and 8.
7. The execution of every Azure function can be monitored by Application Insights. Here, you can check the time it took to process, resource usage, errors, and exceptions that happened in each function call.
8. They are functions that will let us write stateful workflows, managing the state behind the scenes.

Chapter 17

1. Typical middleware modules scaffolded by Visual Studio in an ASP.NET Core project include a developer exception page, request routing, static file serving, HTTPS redirection, authentication, and authorization.
2. No.
3. False. Several tag helpers can be invoked on the same tag.
4. `ModelState.IsValid`.
5. `@RenderBody()`.
6. We can use `@RenderSection("Scripts", required: false)`.
7. We can use `return View("viewname", ViewModel)`.
8. Three providers are included in ASP.NET Core, but they must be configured. If different providers are needed, they must be implemented by the developers and added to the providers list.
9. No, `ViewModels` are not the only way for controllers to communicate with views in ASP.NET Core. Controllers can also use `ViewData`, `ViewData`, and `TempData` to pass data to views.

Chapter 18

1. API gateways work as interfaces for API microservices, while frontends take care of building web pages' HTML.
2. Robust web servers optimize the whole request/response handling and ensure the needed level of security.
3. Because they have an impact on performance that is usually unacceptable for high-traffic microservices.
4. When transactions are quite fast and the probability of collision between transactions is low.
5. A better decoupling of the aggregates and commands methods.

Chapter 19

1. It is a W3C standard: the assembly of a virtual machine running in W3C-compliant browsers.
2. A web UI where dynamic HTML is created in the browser itself.
3. Selecting a page based on the current browser URL.
4. A Blazor component with routes attached to it. For this reason, the Blazor router can select it.
5. Defining the .NET namespace of a Blazor component class.
6. A local service that takes care of storing and handling all form-related information, such as validation errors and changes in HTML inputs.
7. Either `OnInitialized` or `OnInitializedAsync`.
8. Callbacks and services.
9. Blazor's way to interact with JavaScript.
10. Getting a reference to a component or HTML element instance.

Chapter 20

1. Services are needed to dispatch communication to pods, since a pod has no stable IP address.
2. Kubernetes offers higher-level entities called Ingresses that are built on top of services, empowering clusters with all the advanced capabilities offered by a web server, such as routing HTTP/HTTPS URLs from outside the cluster to internal service URLs inside the cluster.
3. Helm charts are a way to organize the templating and installation of complex Kubernetes applications that contain several `.yaml` files.
4. Yes, with the `---` separator.
5. Kubernetes detects container faults through liveness and readiness probes that check the health and availability of containers, ensuring they run as expected.
6. Because Pods, having no stable location, can't rely on the storage of the node where they are currently running.
7. `StatefulSet` is assumed to have state and achieve write/update parallelism through sharding, while `ReplicaSet` has no state, so as it is indistinguishable, it can achieve parallelism by splitting the load.

Chapter 21

1. It is because it doesn't support TCP/IP communications.
2. Visual Studio's recommended tool to debug Kubernetes applications.
3. No, it works with any Kubernetes cluster that has been configured as the default cluster in the local Kubectl installation.
4. With something like `minikube image load grpcmicroservice:latest`.
5. It is enough to start Minikube, and Minikube's start procedure will do it for you.

Learn more on Discord

To join the Discord community for this book – where you can share feedback, ask questions to the authors, and learn about new releases – follow the QR code below:

`https://packt.link/SoftwareArchitectureCSharp12Dotnet8`

packt.com

Subscribe to our online digital library for full access to over 7,000 books and videos, as well as industry leading tools to help you plan your personal development and advance your career. For more information, please visit our website.

Why subscribe?

- Spend less time learning and more time coding with practical eBooks and Videos from over 4,000 industry professionals
- Improve your learning with Skill Plans built especially for you
- Get a free eBook or video every month
- Fully searchable for easy access to vital information
- Copy and paste, print, and bookmark content

At www.packt.com, you can also read a collection of free technical articles, sign up for a range of free newsletters, and receive exclusive discounts and offers on Packt books and eBooks.

Other Books You May Enjoy

If you enjoyed this book, you may be interested in these other books by Packt:

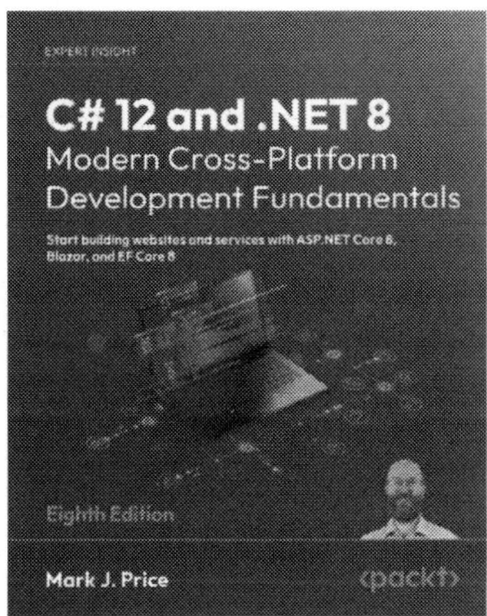

C# 12 and .NET 8 – Modern Cross-Platform Development Fundamentals - Eighth Edition

Mark J. Price

ISBN: 9781837635870

- Discover C# 12's new features, including aliasing any type and primary constructors
- Try out the native AOT publish capability for ASP.NET Core 8 Minimal APIs web services
- Build rich web experiences using Blazor Full Stack, Razor Pages, and other ASP.NET Core features
- Integrate and update databases in your apps using Entity Framework Core models
- Query and manipulate data using LINQ
- Build and consume powerful services using Web API and Minimal API

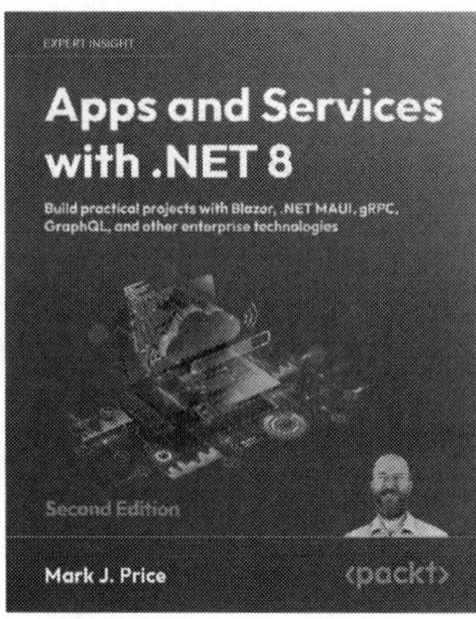

Apps and Services with .NET 8 - Second Edition

Mark J. Price

ISBN: 9781837637133

- Familiarize yourself with a variety of technologies to implement services, such as gRPC and GraphQL
- Store and manage data locally and cloud-natively with SQL Server and Cosmos DB
- Use ADO.NET SqlClient to implement web services with native AOT publish support
- Leverage Dapper for improved performance over EF Core
- Implement popular third-party libraries such as Serilog, FluentValidation, Humanizer, and Noda Time
- Explore the new unified hosting model of Blazor Full Stack

Architecting ASP.NET Core Applications - Third Edition

Carl-Hugo Marcotte

ISBN: 9781805123385

- Apply the SOLID principles for building flexible and maintainable software
- Test your apps effectively with automated tests, including black-box testing
- Enter the path of ASP.NET Core dependency injection mastery
- Work with GoF design patterns such as strategy, decorator, facade, and composite
- Design REST APIs using Minimal APIs and MVC
- Discover layering techniques and the tenets of clean architecture
- Use feature-oriented techniques as an alternative to layering
- Explore microservices, CQRS, REPL, vertical slice architecture, and many more patterns

Packt is searching for authors like you

If you're interested in becoming an author for Packt, please visit `authors.packtpub.com` and apply today. We have worked with thousands of developers and tech professionals, just like you, to help them share their insight with the global tech community. You can make a general application, apply for a specific hot topic that we are recruiting an author for, or submit your own idea.

Share your thoughts

Now you've finished *Software Architecture with C# 12 and .NET 8, Fourth Edition* we'd love to hear your thoughts! Scan the QR code below to go straight to the Amazon review page for this book and share your feedback or leave a review on the site that you purchased it from.

`https://packt.link/r/1805127659`

Your review is important to us and the tech community and will help us make sure we're delivering excellent quality content.

Index

Symbols

A

C

E

F

G

H

N

O

P

R

T

U

V

W

Download a free PDF copy of this book

Thanks for purchasing this book!

Do you like to read on the go but are unable to carry your print books everywhere?

Is your eBook purchase not compatible with the device of your choice?

Don't worry, now with every Packt book you get a DRM-free PDF version of that book at no cost.

Read anywhere, any place, on any device. Search, copy, and paste code from your favorite technical books directly into your application.

The perks don't stop there, you can get exclusive access to discounts, newsletters, and great free content in your inbox daily

Follow these simple steps to get the benefits:

1. Scan the QR code or visit the link below.

`https://packt.link/free-ebook/9781805127659`

2. Submit your proof of purchase.
3. That's it! We'll send your free PDF and other benefits to your email directly.